Play Me My Song
The Music of Genesis

Philip Stichtenoth

Play Me My Song
The Music of Genesis

Philip Stichtenoth

WYMER
PUBLISHING
Bedford, England

First published in 2023
Wymer Publishing
Bedford, England www.wymerpublishing.co.uk Tel: 01234 326691
Wymer Publishing is a trading name of Wymer (UK) Ltd

Copyright © 2023 Philip Stichtenoth / Wymer Publishing.
ISBN: 978-1-915246-31-8

The Author hereby asserts their rights to be identified
as the author of this work in accordance with sections
77 to 78 of the Copyright, Designs & Patents Act 1988.

All rights reserved. No part of this publication may be
reproduced or transmitted in any form or by any means,
electronic or mechanical, including photocopying, or any
information storage and retrieval system, without written
permission from the publisher.

This publication is sold subject to the condition that it shall not,
by way of trade or otherwise, be lent, re-sold, hired out or
otherwise circulated without the publishers' prior consent in any
form of binding or cover other than that in which it is published
and without a similar condition including this condition
being imposed on the subsequent purchaser.

A catalogue record for this book is available from the British Library.

Design by Andy Bishop / 1016 Sarpsborg
Printed by CMP, Dorset, England

For Dad

Contents

INTRODUCTION 7

PART I: THE SONGS 9

PART II: THE ALBUMS 415

PART III: THE BAND 444

INDEX 472

BIBLIOGRAPHY 474

Introduction

Hello, and welcome! What you have in your hands is my book, and though I'm admittedly a little biased, I daresay it's a book quite unlike any other. For one thing, it's a book about the band Genesis, which narrows the competition considerably. Yet even within that very niche realm of "books about the band Genesis," this book is different. If you've ever had cause to look into books about Genesis before, you will have found that they approach the subject from a number of different angles. One book might be a biography, walking you through the band's lengthy career, telling behind-the-scenes stories along the way. Another might be a series of interview transcriptions, the band telling you about their music in their own words. Another might be an attempt to catalogue the details of every studio recording the to form a complete compendium of the music. There are, as you can see, a lot of ways to approach writing a book about the band Genesis. With that in mind, as you begin to read this particular book I think you'll quickly realise that it is very much like all of the above examples, all at once, and therefore is not truly like any of them. This is confusing, I know. Perhaps a brief history of how this book came to be will help make sense of things, yeah?

See, there's this website. It's called Reddit; maybe you've heard of it. It's kind of like the evolution of what the original Internet message boards were. To that end, Reddit has a myriad of smaller communities, appropriately called "subreddits," where users can have specific discussions about whatever subject they want to build a community around. Whatever your interest, there's probably a subreddit out there for it. It should be no surprise, then, that one of these so-called subreddits is a community dedicated to the band Genesis. Being a Genesis fan myself, I decided on a whim to join this community, interested to see just what kinds of discussion a bunch of Genesis fans on a Genesis forum could have. Mind you, this was some months before the band announced their Last Domino? Tour, so there was no actual news to speak of.

I don't know what I really expected, but what I found was predictable: users posting pictures of the band, users posting links to their favourite songs, users wishing Peter Gabriel a happy birthday, that sort of thing. Very typical fan stuff. Then one day, a fan posted a poll to the site, asking users a simple question: if you could eliminate one song from the Genesis album *Trespass*, which would you choose? Users were prompted to discuss, debate, and vote, and immediately the r/Genesis subreddit (as it is officially called) was a far more interesting place. These kinds of polls continued for a couple months before fading away altogether, but during that time I'd discovered that my own taste in Genesis music was a bit out of sync with the community at large. Overlapping in a lot of big ways to be sure, but also diverging significantly at times.

Now, most people might have that realisation and say, "Huh, interesting," and then move on with their day. For better or worse, I am not most people. I felt compelled to see just how deep the rabbit hole went, and spent the next few months listening to every single Genesis song several times over so that I could force-rank the whole lot of them. It was a mammoth exercise, but a fruitful one – I heard a lot of Genesis that I hadn't been exposed to before, and a lot of that was stuff I really liked. Then I made another momentous decision: I was going to share my rankings with the r/Genesis community in a daily countdown format. Of course, just saying "57 is Such and Such Song" isn't particularly substantive, so I knew I wanted to add a little spice to the proceedings to drive engagement.

To that end I figured I'd pepper in a few sentences explaining my general feelings about the song, and then maybe find a quote from one of the band members about the song to share the songwriter's perspective as well. Nothing too involved, mind you – this was only meant to be a fun little diversion in the morning before I scarpered off to work. But sometimes these things have minds of their own. As I got more into the rhythm of what I was doing, I found myself gradually expanding each entry along the way. Which also meant I was spending a little more time researching each song to find more history, details, and band quotes. And then I found myself getting slightly bored of writing in what I had begun to feel was a bog-standard song review format, and began to improvise. You know, trying to find a new angle to make that day's entry a little more interesting, or at times even going into full-on creative writing mode. Anything to keep it fresh.

The community noticed. Engagement steadily increased over the nine-plus month length of the project, as did my own obsession. At one point a user referred to what I was doing as "writing essays about every single Genesis song," and I had never really thought about it in that light before. In my mind I was still just trying to do the bare minimum to keep this thing going, even if somewhere in the back of my mind I realised that the "bare minimum" as I saw it was leagues beyond what it had been at the start. What can I say? That's my nagging perfectionism at work. I was at once aghast at what the project had become and yet immensely proud of the work I was doing, so I continued the ever-expanding nature of the thing all the way to the end, working nights and weekends on writing and research to get it all out, all at a high quality, all while meeting my own self-imposed deadlines.

I've heard it said that creativity is like a faucet. Sometimes it can be really hard to turn on; maybe a rusty knob or some kind of plumbing problem that prevents you from ever getting started. Yet once that faucet is on, it can be equally difficult to stop the flow, in large part because you don't really even want to. So it was that even as I was pouring all my free time into this project to cover every Genesis song, I took on even more. Albums? Yeah, why not? Makes total sense. Solo careers? Eh, that's a *lot* of material to cover, but sure, I'll do an essay for each songwriter in the band, yeah. I just couldn't stop writing about Genesis. I didn't know how. But eventually, it was done. All of it had been created, edited, and posted, and I could rest.

That respite lasted about a month before I decided it was time to turn all of that writing into this book, which ended up meaning well over another year of work. Additional writing, massive amounts of editing, etc. But now that's done, too. Now you've got this book – my book – in your hands. "But what," you may still be asking, "*is* this book?"

This book is not just a straightforward ranking of every song Genesis ever officially recorded, though it is also that.

This book is not just a bunch of opinions about Genesis music held by some random dude, though it is also that.

This book is not just a retelling of both well-known and little-known stories from the band's career, though it is also that.

This book is not just an enormous aggregation of band quotes from many disparate sources, though it is also that.

This book is not just a shameless creative writing exercise across more than two hundred essays, though it is also that.

This book is like every Genesis book you have ever read. It is like no Genesis book you have ever read. It is my sincere hope that you find this book to be informative, entertaining, and surprising in all the right ways. It is also my sincere hope that my personal rankings of the songs don't make you so mad you'll throw this book straight in the bin, but I suppose time will tell.

Bon appétit!

Part I: The Songs

Deep dives into every Genesis song, ranked by personal enjoyment

197 - Who Dunnit?

from *Abacab*, 1981

Many bands, if they're lucky enough to have significantly long careers, hit a kind of musical crossroads over time. It's that place where, for one reason or another, the band's trademark style simply isn't as appealing to the people creating the music anymore. There are a few reasons why that might be. Maybe it's because the style has gone out of public favour and the band is chasing sales by trying to keep up with the times. Maybe it's because the band found some new influence and is really passionate about discovering where that might lead, even if where it leads isn't the band's natural territory, so to speak. Maybe they just get bored with their old material and want to shake it up with something new. Or maybe, just maybe, it could even be all three.

Getting tired of their own output? That sounds shocking, but it does sort of make sense if you look at it from the perspective of someone in the band who has to live and breathe this stuff day in and day out. After all, that's one of the reasons Steve Hackett left the band during the mixing of *Seconds Out*:

> **Steve:** *I think we'd just mixed 'I Know What I Like' and I was thinking, "I can't face listening to this song any more. I've heard this song a thousand times; we're going over old ground here."* [1]

At the time this may have been a cause for scoffing from the rest of the band, but just a few years down the road the rest of them started to feel that same strain as well.

> **Tony:** *As we began to write the material for Abacab, it seemed we might be in danger of repeating ourselves. It seemed a good time for us to change things around, to make our writing and recording process more streamlined and straightforward. So we got rid of the big choruses and the tambourines and the keyboard solos and aimed to hone everything down, something we also tried to reflect in the album's abstract cover design. We underlined this change of direction by bringing in a new producer. We had had a good relationship with [previous producer] Dave Hentschel, but to make any significant kind of change in what we were doing we really needed to change producers too.* [1]

Hugh Padgham was doing exciting things with Peter Gabriel, XTC, and Phil Collins all when he got called up to do work for the band on Abacab. And if there was any doubt among the band that they had the right guy for the job, that likely evaporated as soon as Phil's solo debut *Face Value* started rocketing up the charts.

> **Tony:** *I think [his success] threatened the group in a way; it must have done. I remember when he had the big success with 'In the Air Tonight' we were actually in the process of writing the next album, Abacab. And so it was sort of there. It didn't happen sort of away from us. I think his single came in at 29 on the charts, and it was all, "Oh, well done Phil! Really good! Really good!" Next week it was 2. "Aww shit, here we go." So it was kind of like, you had to take it on board...perhaps in a way [he] was slightly a junior member of the band, even at that stage as a three-piece, just because that's how it was. So the dynamic changed quite a bit, really. I think his own confidence grew a lot, and his own writing ability...gained more of a part within Genesis.* [2]

There's fear of "is this guy going to leave," but once it's clear he's probably not, that fear pretty quickly turns into excitement: "We can get some of that secret sauce too!" So hey, Phil knows music, and Hugh knows music, so what should we be doing this time around, boys?

> **Phil:** *We started to scale down a little bit the keyboard arrangements. We started to scale down, "Do we really need that overdub? Do we really need the sound to be that thick?" I mean, everybody used to be a bit tunnel vision, you know: "This is my sound, I like it, and I'm gonna use it!" Now we were getting a bit better in the studio, a bit more used to what we wanted it to sound like, and also trying to reinvent ourselves. Because punk had left some mark, and we realised that we didn't want to be - though we still were and still are - we didn't really want to be thought of as being "stuck in that thing."* [3]

In a way it's an astonishing admission: even after ten albums of steadily increasing success, Genesis were still sensitive to appearances. Punk was a wild force in the music scene, and one that wouldn't allow itself to go ignored. We like to think of Genesis as these highly accomplished songwriters and musicians, and so maybe let ourselves believe that they might be immune to any kind of criticism or backlash to their music. And yet…

> **Mike:** *Everybody likes to be liked. I don't believe any artist who says he doesn't give a shit.* [4]

> **Phil:** *We felt the hand of punk was shaking the tree. We didn't like most of the bands they didn't like either, so we were all for it, but unfortunately the punk period saw us as one of the things they were trying to shake out of the tree.* [1]

In a very real way then, *Abacab* marked a departure in sound for the band because of all three of the above concepts I laid out. They were getting a little weary of "the Genesis sound," they had a new producer and a surge forward from their third songwriter, and like it or not, yes: they were also chasing relevance lest the music industry leave them behind.

So there they are in the rehearsal room, tossing out ideas and sounds that they all have to like, but that also shouldn't sound too much like Genesis. No problem, right? And along the way, you've got Tony sitting there fiddling with his synthesizer, trying to make strange sounds just for kicks.

> **Tony:** *I had a Prophet-5 synthesizer which I really used to abuse. If you played certain notes and then changed the tones while you held the notes down the keyboard would produce some very strange sounds which I loved. I think I was the only one who did like these sounds, and the others probably thought, "Oh god, Tony…"* [1]

> **Phil:** *Tony Banks had this keyboard…it was like he was just fiddling around with it. You know, he'd have a chord then "Ziyou eck NYEAHZ!" He was just trying to get these different sounds and it was all in rhythm for some reason…It was the most horrible sound…* [3]

This is all fun and games, except apparently Tony would do this basically every single day in the studio. Got a few minutes between takes or a tea break? REEEOOOOOOWWWWW. Phil and Mike eventually hit a breaking point, and it's worth noting in this retrospective that Mike apparently has nothing to say about the music whatsoever, such is his apparent disdain.

> **Tony:** *I really like it, but that's perhaps almost perverse…I would sit there, and I'm doing this all the time. And Mike and Phil were just sort of, "The only way we're going to shut him up is if we record this," so we recorded it. Phil put on this very simple, very slappy sort of drum…* [3]

> **Phil:** *I started playing, and that was it.* [3]

> **Tony:** *We put the track down; Phil added some filthy drums, Mike the bass, and Phil went off to write a silly lyric for it.* [1]

Uh oh. See, this is a problem. In democratic Genesis, the person who writes the lyrics for a song is typically the person who feels closest to that song, or most connected to whatever idea they feel might be coming across. This is how it's always worked. So for Phil to be the one to go off and write a lyric, that must mean that somewhere along the way he got converted.

> **Phil:** *We did our own punk track…which was fantastic…we really liked [it]!* [3]

Oh heavens no.

> **Tony:** *It's a daft track, but it certainly characterises the spontaneity of the sessions…Phil wrote an idiotic lyric to it. I thought it was great.* [5]

Nope, nope, nope.

> **Tony:** *We put it down on tape with this drum music that Phil was playing and we improvised on it for thirty minutes - there is a thirty minute version of the song for people who really like*

the song - and we cut it down and it was a great result. I liked it because it was very extreme, and I am a perverse kind of person, and I like to explore different areas. [6]

Would you rather listen to a 30 minute version of 'Who Dunnit?' or slowly freeze to death in a blizzard? As Phil Connors famously declared in the classic film Groundhog Day, "I'm thinkin'!"

And then, democracy that the band was, there was the matter of deciding whether the song with the working title of 'Weird Synth' should make the album. Here's how I expect the votes went:

Mike: Absolutely not. Are you kidding me? What's wrong with you guys?
Tony: Resounding yes, this is brilliant!
Phil: Sure, it's fun!
Ahmet Ertegun, Head of Atlantic Records (Genesis' US label): I'm afraid you have to put that track on.

Well if the bossman says so, I guess we're doing this. God help us all.

Tony: *'Who Dunnit?' is a notorious track...I've always loved this track and virtually everyone else, it seems to me, hates it. There's something about it that appeals to me, the fact that it managed to provoke such strong emotion in people. It was unlike anything I had ever done, a hypnotic piece, a brave track to include...It gave the album a very definite character...* [1]

You know those monkey statues that represent "Hear No Evil," "See No Evil," and "Speak No Evil?" This Tony quote makes it seem like he's trying to be all three at once. But hey, at least we're just talking about a studio album, so you can skip over the track, right? Not like they're going to play something this awful in concert! So you buy your tickets and head over to the Genesis show, and...oh no. Oh no no no.

Phil: *We did it live, you know. Fantastic. People used to put goggles on, snorkels and stuff. It was a kind of surreal moment.* [3]

Please, no.

Phil: *And actually when we played this Abacab album live, I remember in Holland in this particular place...we were booed. Every time we played an Abacab track they booed us. They didn't like the scaled down thing at all.* [3]

Getting heavily booed by your own fans surely means you're going to stop the madness, right? The people have spoken, right?

Tony: *We used to get booed when we played it! We played Leiden in Holland and we got booed and so we went back there and we played there again.* [6]

WHAT?!

Tony: *[It] became a focus whenever we played it on stage. The crowd would boo and I found the whole thing very funny. The band wore silly hats, I'd put on a little snorkel and play a Prophet-5 keyboard specially tuned just for that one song. It was supposed to be a joke, but I think it also has a certain charm that I like a lot.* [1]

Come on guys, that's so rude! Nobody is on board with this! Especially not the roadies who had to hear it night after night after excruciating night:

Tony: *You know, you mention it around here sometimes, some of the roadies, "Ugggh. Not 'Who Dunnit?'!"* [3]

And not Mike either, who evidently didn't like the song in the first place and now had nothing to do on stage for three and a half minutes thanks to the arrangement:

Tony: *There are only three things on it in fact which are drums, guitar, and the Prophet 5. It sounds like there are a lot of other things going on because the synthesizer is going through a lot of peculiar sounds but it was a fun thing to do.* [7]

See? Tony can play, Phil can sing, Chester's drumming, Daryl's playing guitar...what on earth is Mike supposed to do?

> **Mike:** *I look a bit like Mick Fleetwood if I put a berry on, which I suppose gives me some excuse for playing the drums and I just fancied a thrash on the skins during the show. It's true that I'm loosening up a bit as well...Before I go on stage...I have a couple glasses of wine to get relaxed and get the ol' adrenaline going.* [4]

Oh great. That's just wonderful. Mike's going to get drunk and go play drums because why not at this point? Everyone's going to hate it anyway, so might as well find your liquid coping mechanism and bang on through it.

You know what's *really* telling? On the Three Sides Live DVD chronicling the Abacab Tour, there's a bunch of live footage taken from the various Genesis concerts. You can see how much the audience loves even the other songs from *Abacab* as they're performed. And then you get to the footage of "Who Dunnit?" and...where's the audience? Not a soul in sight outside of that stage, and not a peep to be heard from the masses supposedly on the ground several feet away.

Genesis couldn't include proper concert footage of "Who Dunnit?" in that film because *it would be filled with booing*. So instead they had to toss in a run through from a rehearsal or a sound check. And then they included it in the film anyway!

On the one hand, good for Genesis for shattering some boundaries and doing a piece purely for the fun of it. I can respect the heart of the decision, and the need of the band to push back against themselves and their own comfort zones. It's a really bold choice to create something intentionally horrendous and then stand by it in the face of overwhelming opposition.

But was it the *right* choice?

> **Tony:** *For many people it's kind of the worst track we ever did.* [3]

Yes, Tony, it is.

> **Tony:** *I listened to that album recently and one of my favourite tracks was the one that everybody hates: 'Who Dunnit?'. I thought that's a great track. Why didn't we do more like that?* [6]

Ugh.

196 - Going Out to Get You

Demo, 1969

From Genesis to Revelation was released in March of 1969, while *Trespass* wasn't recorded until the summer of 1970 (and then wasn't released until that October). Because the sounds of those two albums are so different, it begs the question of how the band got from point A to point B.
'Going Out to Get You' is one such transitional song. Indeed, it might be considered *the* transitional song in the band's line-up, given that the period between two albums marked not only a move from one studio album to the next, and not only a move from one record label to the next, but also a move from Genesis being a studio band to a bona-fide live one.

> **Tony:** *There was a massive development between From Genesis to Revelation and Trespass. Having made the decision to play live, we had become a working band and so had been able to get a direct response to the songs. We had two really long, loud tracks, 'The Knife' and 'Going Out to Get You', which at one point were both something like twenty minutes long, and from playing them live we slowly realised that we couldn't do that in front of an audience.* [1]

The only official release of this song is a demo from 1969, so the version we have readily available clocks at just under five minutes. Often something like this might represent a paring down from the grand epic live, but in this case it's a matter of catching a song in its relative infancy before it became the sprawling, uncontrollable live behemoth it would eventually be remembered as.
And indeed, at its core it's as straightforward as anything on the debut album, but if you listen to the demo's ending after the vocals conclude, you can hear just a taste of things to come when they spend over a minute just letting their instruments do all the talking. It might be more jazz-blues oriented than the type of symphonic prog rock we'd later come to expect from the band, but one can easily imagine them taking that jam and running away with it on stage.

> **Tony:** *'Going Out to Get You'...became [a] main strength of our live show... [It] went through hundreds of changes and never made it to an album, which was strange because it was such a key song for us. I think it might have made it onto the album after Trespass, but by that time Ant had left the band and the song part of it was his bit, so it kind of went with him.* [1]

Normally I'd say it's a shame a live staple never got refined and put on an album, but in this case it's probably a blessing in disguise. My dad, who you'll see pop up a number of other times throughout this book, is a near-lifelong Genesis fan. Yet buried as this song was only on the rarities disc of *Genesis Archive 1967-75*, "Going Out to Get You" is a track he'd never actually heard before. When he saw that I had ranked it here as the second worst Genesis song ever put on record, he was a little surprised and felt the need to check it out for himself. Which is when I got this text message from him:

> **My Dad:** "In hearing 'Going Out to Get You' for the first time, they sound like guys who got together so they could be in a band, and had to work with an embarrassingly self-indulgent singer who maybe was tolerated and given the mic solely because his parents worked days, so he was able to furnish a suitable garage for practice. [They sound like they had] no right to ever become anything beyond ne'er-do-wells and never-weres. I endorse your ranking."

I mean, tell us how you *really* feel, Dad. Hard to disagree though. Past the underwhelming intro, Peter Gabriel kicks in with a voice that sounds like it's struggling to hit puberty. Do you remember that episode of the Brady Bunch where Peter Brady is trying to sing but his voice changes and they have to figure out how to make it sound good? This song is kind of like that. One could craft a conspiracy theory that the writers of that episode (which aired in 1972) were really just big Genesis fans recalling the broken voice of another guy named Peter, but I'll leave such tin foil hat stuff to others.

> **Tony:** *We went and did a single version of the song 'Going Out To Get You' which was quite good - Peter was really screaming and squeaking his way through that one!* [6]

Tony puts a friendly spin on it, but let's call a spade a spade: Pete's singing here is pretty rough. It's tough to properly judge a demo track, and given how important this song was to helping the band develop their live following I don't want to dismiss it out of hand, but this is Gabriel sneering and shouting without the benefit of having that style mesh with what's happening musically. And what's happening musically isn't that interesting, either. It's just Tony frantically mashing at the piano while everyone tries to keep up. Not a great effort, and I suppose the band must've realised that too, since they continued to evolve it over time into something more entertaining.

Still though, I've got to work with what I've got, and what I've got is a demo that, yes, sounds like a bad garage band that will never amount to anything. It's a good thing they kept going and became so much more, of course, but I think it's probably also a good thing that this one got left behind.

> **Ant:** *When we started rehearsing for live concerts, there were other songs on the set list. [...] For instance...a very loud song called 'Going Out to Get You', which was not so good.* [8]

Right-O, Anthony.

195 - A Place to Call My Own

from *From Genesis to Revelation*, 1969

The closer to the band's debut album, 'A Place to Call My Own' is a two minute track made up of two distinct halves: the first half is Peter singing over a sober piano, while the second half is a bright, hopeful instrumental. This ties neatly into the lyrics, which appear to be sung from the perspective of a baby on the verge of being born; the first half of the song is the tense calm just before delivery, while the second half is this new child experiencing the world for the first time.

While all that sounds lovely in text, it just doesn't quite get there musically. The first half *almost* works, but Peter's voice is non-committal and the idea never has time to develop into more than a feeling that it could've been more. The second half doesn't work much at all, with some background "la la la" singing that just feels really out of place. It's certainly listenable, but there's not much of quality here to work with. So it's a little surprising that, like 'Going Out to Get You' earlier in this countdown, 'A Place to Call My Own' is actually just a fragment of something much larger.

> **Tony:** *There was also one quite ambitious long piece [on the first album] called 'A Place to Call My Own', mainly written by Ant, which was originally about three times as long as the version that ended up on the album, a first example of us heading towards a longer format. But at that time we decided in the end to use only the final section on the album, and get rid of the other sections, which were probably not as consistent all the way through.* [1]

If you're anything like me, this statement from Tony fills you with a kind of morbid curiosity. This is only a third of the song? The rest was more ambitious? Surely that would be better, right? Even if those other sections are somehow "less consistent" it's hard to imagine them being any less *interesting* than the bit we actually got, you know? Even the ending of the song is caught somewhere between a fade-out and big finish, as though the novice engineer recording the music forgot to actually apply the fade effect to the end and nobody caught the mistake until the record went to press. If that sounds harsh, bear in mind that the bloke filling that role on *From Genesis to Revelation* was a guy named Tom Allom who went on to become a successful producer for bands like Judas Priest, but whose first gig was as an audio engineer for this very album. I'm not making this up.

So at any rate, while I'd certainly like to hear the longer, original form of 'A Place to Call My Own', its giant edit might be a kind of silver lining in itself: at a runtime of just under two minutes, this is the shortest song on *From Genesis to Revelation*. Consider that a mercy, since it's also for my money the worst that album has to offer. It may be the last thing you'll hear from these cheeky baroque pop wannabes, but at least you won't have to hear it for long.

194 - The Mystery of the Flannan Isle Lighthouse

Demo, 1968

The mystery of the lighthouse keepers on the Flannan Isles is actually pretty interesting. Three men went onto the primary island to man the lighthouse, and a week later the lighthouse was dark during a night time storm. The captain of the ship passing by told the mainland that there was some trouble, but because of the weather no help could be sent right away. In fact, it took eleven days for anyone else to actually set foot on the island to begin an investigation. What they found was surprising: evidence of damage to one of the island's landings, but no damage anywhere else. Logs from the three lighthouse keepers indicating they were aware of the damage. One set of rain gear, but not the other two. And strangest of all, no lighthouse keepers. The three men, simply gone without a trace. So what happened? The best guesses are that the storm that damaged the landing was more intense than the keepers realised at the time, and created a huge wave that somehow snagged all three of them and pulled them into the ocean. The idea is that two of the keepers went out to secure some equipment on the damaged landing while the third stayed in the lighthouse, where he saw an oncoming tidal wave and rushed out without his protective gear in order to warn the other two, only for all three of them to be caught in it and swept out to the rocky sea. Yet that doesn't answer every question: the lighthouse gates and doors were closed, and who takes the time to do that when sprinting to warn of impending doom? And if the bodies were swept to the sea, why did they never wash ashore? So you see, it's a compelling unsolved mystery, one that's captured a lot of imaginations over the years.

What's sadly not quite so compelling is the song Genesis penned in their formative years about the same event. For starters, the actual story is discarded in favour of a vague lyrical assertion that Flannan Isle (singular here instead of a set of islands) is haunted. Far less interesting. On top of that, the entire tune is, in a word, *jaunty*. If you're writing a song about a haunted island that sinks ships and steals men's souls, is "jaunty" the mood you'd shoot for? It's a bizarre decision.

From there the piece itself doesn't do itself many other favours. Peter's teenage voice is weak and unsteady. The backing vocals aren't much better. The guitar just strums in sync with the piano. I'm not sure Mike is even playing. It's pretty much just Tony slamming away on a halfway decent piano riff trying desperately to keep the song afloat. Unfortunately, like the giant wave that probably claimed the lives of the three actual lighthouse keepers who inspired these lyrics, the song pulls even Tony's heroic effort down into the depths, from where it would never return.

The mystery of the lighthouse keepers may be a head scratcher worth remembering, but there's no mystery when it comes to this track: it's one story best left forgotten.

Tony: *'Mystery of The Flannan Island Lighthouse'* was another one [that Jonathan King rejected]. [6]

A wise choice.

193 - Me and Virgil

from *3x3*, 1982

An outtake from the *Abacab* sessions that really should have stayed out-took, 'Me and Virgil' found release on the band's *3x3* EP in 1982 before being released worldwide on the non-live side of *Three Sides Live*. It tells the story of a country boy who takes care of his mother after his father walks out on the family; a simple and not particularly engaging story in itself, but one that at least has the potential for success, depending on how it gets presented.

Sad to say, the presentation is downright terrible. It feels like an incomplete idea that somehow made it to a recording anyway. You know how you can sometimes catch behind-the-scenes footage or old demos of songs that you know and love? These work-in-progress tunes always have their warts, and very often they're not completed. Maybe they roll into another verse that isn't there in the final version because the section that *is* there instead hadn't been written yet, so they just kind of rolled on in rehearsal repeating the first bit over again. That's what 'Me & Virgil' feels like, except of course it *is* supposedly a complete idea.

> **Tony:** ...*We decided not to include 'Me & Virgil' [on Abacab], which was a sort of Band type song.* [6]

The Band was pretty influential back in the mid-60s as Bob Dylan's backing band, and into the late 60s/early 70s doing their own thing. They were notable for the way they blended lots of different sounds and influences, creating this sort of weird folk/jazz/country/blues/R&B vibe. And Genesis in 1981 were at the height of their efforts to experiment with sounds and forms outside their comfort zone. So it's no surprise really that they'd seek to emulate The Band while trying to break out of their own trappings.

Yet they weren't up to the task. In the end 'Me & Virgil' is just a bunch of empty vamps and repeated, half-hearted lyrics like "Pa, you broke her heart," except it's stretched out to over six minutes - an inexcusably interminable effort. There is a section in the middle where some different things happen, which is exciting solely because those things actually are different, and not because those things are particularly good.

Reportedly, Collins has called this song "a dog" and sought to bury it, though I can't find a surviving source for that direct interview anywhere. It is telling, though, that the international version of *Three Sides Live* featuring this track was replaced in reprints with the original British version, which effectively turns it into Four Sides Live - Now With 100% Less 'Me & Virgil'.

Furthermore, when *Genesis Archive 2: 1976-1992* was released, 'Me and Virgil' was nowhere to be found, despite the other two tunes from *3x3* making the cut. Tony explains why:

> **Tony:** *'Me and Virgil' I would've been happy with musically but Phil found it lyrically unfortunate...* [9]

So credence lent to the Phil-hate, at any rate. The song only finally resurfaced in the 2007 box set remaster. If Collins truly sought to bury this track for good, I wish he'd have tried a little harder.

192 - In the Beginning

from *From Genesis to Revelation*, 1969

It's not exactly common knowledge even among the Genesis fandom, but the album title of *From Genesis to Revelation* was actually a nod to the fact that the band at that time had to use two different names: one in England, and another in the United States.

> **Tony:** *We needed a name for the band and [producer Jonathan] King suggested Genesis. We thought it was quite nice. When we got to the album we called ourselves Revelation [in North America]; that's why the album is called From Genesis to Revelation. We were Genesis in England and Revelation [in America], 'cause there was another group called Genesis [there] at the time.* [10]

But the title served another, more creative purpose as well. See, when Genesis set about writing material for their first studio album, they had a little bit of trouble coming up with ideas to fill space. Producer Jonathan King suggested that - playing off their dual names - they write a loose concept album, opening with the Book of Genesis, closing with the Book of Revelation, and doing whatever was necessary in between to link the two. Or, you know, not. It wasn't neither a fully-fledged nor fully executed idea, but out of that notion was written 'In the Beginning' to fill the "Book of Genesis" niche.

Dismissing the first twenty-odd seconds of stylistic distortion, which is unpleasant but more a product of the album's concept than of this song itself, 'In the Beginning' is a track with a strong forward drive and great energy. Unfortunately, that's about where the positives end. The melody is pretty poor throughout, and the main guitar riff isn't strong enough to pick up the slack. In Pete's voice you can start to hear signs of the power and tone to come in future albums, but he hasn't fully grown into it yet - he was only 18 when this album was recorded, after all. They didn't fare much better with it live, either.

> **Ant:** *I remember there was one…gig [that] was a nightmare because I had restrung [my guitar] and I shouldn't have done, and I had a loose machine head. We began with 'In The Beginning' and we got to the bit where I had the first break, and two strings had slipped really badly. And I just turned really wildly and I didn't know what I was doing and all these people were looking round - an absolute nightmare.* [11]

All in all, on an album full of songs that the band wasn't particularly passionate about anyway (they would much rather have been writing music like what showed up on *Trespass* and beyond, but were trying to cater to King's tastes), 'In the Beginning' feels as though it were thrown together just to mark something off on a checklist for an album concept that never really worked in the first place. Some people really like it for the energy and passion it brings to the table, but me? I'd just as soon it have never begun.

191 - One Eyed Hound

B-side to 'A Winter's Tale', 1968

Released before *From Genesis to Revelation* was even recorded, one would think a band trying to find material for a full album wouldn't dismiss the two songs that comprised their most recent single. Perhaps it was the single's lack of commercial success, or maybe just that it didn't jive with the concept album lite that they were going for, but either way 'A Winter's Tale' didn't make the initial cut, and neither did its B side, 'One Eyed Hound'.

Musically, 'One Eyed Hound' does a few decent things. Occasionally you can hear Ant Phillips' guitar rise above the mesh of the fuzzy background and play something interesting. And though the main melody of the tune is lacking, the overall feel of the verses is at least pleasant. Surprisingly, given the general lack of vocal talent in the band behind Peter at this point in time, I'm actually a bit of a fan of the call and answer verse structure: "This man committed a sin / this man, he never can win" is a catchier line than it really has a right to be. There's of course also the novelty value of hearing the varied vocals in general, so make no mistake about it: just because I think this is a bottom ten Genesis song doesn't mean I hate everything it's doing.

But the problem is that all the good stuff is juxtaposed against a heavier, harder sound coming after each exclamation that "Night is the time for chasing the one eyed hound!" and the dichotomy doesn't quite work. This is a taste of Genesis being a little more aggressive with their playing, but without any real payoff and in a context where it's not entirely welcome. Maybe you could make an argument that they're trying to show a musical difference between day and night, where the days are gentle but night is a more aggressive time, but I think that's giving a little too much credit. After all, the lyrics don't hold up well to scrutiny, instead coming off like uninspired bits of nothing, and there are frankly too many of them. Each line feels as though it has perhaps one or two too many words. Unfortunately that would also be a sign of things to come from the band, even into their progressive heyday. Doesn't seem like rampant verbosity would be the right thing to double down on from your failed single's B-side, but that's certainly the route the Charterhouse boys took.

Both 'A Winter's Tale' and 'One Eyed Hound' would eventually show up as bonus tracks on reissues of *From Genesis to Revelation*, though neither track was included on *Genesis Archive 1967-1975*, presumably because of rights issues. Nor were they present on the 2007 box set, again because Jonathan King still owns the rights to the FGTR catalogue of which these songs are a part. That's a small shame for those trying to build a comprehensive collection, but not a problem to the casual fan, who would be better off skipping this song entirely.

190 - Try a Little Sadness

Demo, 1967

Genesis sent Jonathan King two different batches of demo tapes when trying to win over his attention and get started in the industry. The first tape was a little more of a straightforward pop affair, generally speaking, while the second was a bit more ambitious. It featured Genesis trying to stretch themselves in ways that would presage the band's work throughout the 70s, and they were really excited by what they produced. That Jonathan King disliked this second batch of demos to the point of nearly dropping the band altogether probably tells you all you need to know about the Genesis music of the 60s. Here's a transcription of a letter Peter Gabriel received from King's publishing business partner Joe Roncoroni:

> Dear Peter,
>
> I must apologise for not writing to you before about the tape you left with me of your songs. The reason I have not written is that it has only been possible for Jonathan to hear these this week and I am sorry to tell you that we were not very impressed - the previous batch you did are, in our opinion, much better. [1]

Talk about oof. Now I can't say for sure which demo tape housed 'Try a Little Sadness'. The track listing on *Genesis Archive 1967-75* lists only the year of 1967, and despite the presence of later demos from 1968 on that album collection, the letter Peter received above was dated November 29th, 1967. So this particular song could well have been on either tape. Regardless, it's something of a pick-your-poison situation: was this song on the demo tape that King liked but cut from *From Genesis to Revelation* because it couldn't measure up to the quality of even that middling material? Or was it on the second tape that wasn't even good enough to get the band back in the studio?

Whatever the case, it's clear that this track is a weak link. Perhaps that's because, even by late 60s Genesis pop standards, it's just a bit too schlocky to get by. The melody isn't the worst of the era, particularly in the verses, but the backing vocals are horrendous. Maybe if they'd properly recorded the song beyond a demo that aspect would get fixed, but I'm not so sure. The voices in the band at this time just didn't quite blend seamlessly, and the vocal arrangement highlights that fact in the worst way. It's a tough listen at every chorus, which is a shame because the verses aren't bad - awkward jazz piano notwithstanding.

Frankly, when I hear this song I don't even think of Genesis. I've got a compilation kitsch album by the name of *Spaced Out: The Best of William Shatner and Leonard Nimoy*. It's nice to spin up for a laugh once in a while, if nothing else, and this track would feel right at home in that Nimoy section. It would also be better for his performing it, if only because then it would be easier to not take so seriously. But alas, here we are.

189 - Ravine

from *The Lamb Lies Down on Broadway*, 1974

As I was going through my rigorous ranking process (actually something more akin to chimpanzees with a typewriter, but who's counting?) during the fall of 2019, I found 'Ravine' to be a really tough one to nail down. So far in this book I've been talking about songs that I truly just don't care for. Songs that, while they may have some redeeming quality that I make an effort to highlight, overall just aren't very good to my ears. Songs that I wouldn't miss if they weren't part of the Genesis discography whatsoever. And now, in the bottom ten of all Genesis songs on this enormous list, we get to 'Ravine', which I don't even mildly dislike.

In fact, given the incredible stature the album has among progressive rock fans and Genesis fans in particular, it's probably something of a shock to see a track from *The Lamb Lies Down on Broadway* this low on the list. And indeed, in the pages to come I expect everyone reading this will have at least one moment of "What in the world is wrong with this guy?" when seeing where I've ranked a particular song or other. Yet 'Ravine' is a different kind of case. You see, it's primarily just a victim of context. It's not down here in the dregs because it's a bad song, but rather because it's hardly a song at all. It's two minutes of pure atmosphere, with only a slight claim to being a "tune" in any meaningful sense.

Within the story and structure of *The Lamb*, 'Ravine' is a moment of hesitation and reflection. Protagonist Rael has just watched a giant raven steal his most precious possession and drop it into the rushing waters at the bottom of a deep gorge. The companion story written in the album's liner notes say that Rael "stands impotent and glowers" in reaction, and that's basically the entire subject matter of 'Ravine'. Rael just standing there in angry silence, feeling powerless to do anything. It's two minutes of broody mood, complete with the sound of harsh winds.

And really, the track *is* entirely successful at conveying the imagery and feelings the story needs it to. You can sense the despairing resignation, and the helplessness that accompanies it. You can almost feel the whipping air rising out of the chasm, stinging Rael's skin and eyes even as he wilts from the sting to his pride. While it's not a strictly critical song for the flow of the album either narratively or musically, it's very effective in its role and works terrifically in that context.

But of course, this countdown isn't about what tracks best serve the overall structure of *The Lamb*. It's about what my personal favourite Genesis songs are overall, and in a vacuum I'm not sure I'd ever find myself saying "You know, I'd really like to sit down and give 'Ravine' a listen, because it's just so good." It can't stand on its own as anything more than inoffensive background radiation. There's nothing inherently wrong with that, and I certainly don't have anything against the track, but ultimately, I didn't feel I could reasonably put it any higher than this. Your mileage may vary.

188 - Ballad of Big

from ...And Then There Were Three..., 1978

While most of ...And Then There Were Three... consisted of individually-written songs that the band members brought with them to the sessions, there were three songs that they wrote as a unit. One of those became their first big hit. Another became a solid album cut. And the third, which was neither of those things, was 'Ballad of Big'.

The track opens with some great atmospheric keyboard playing, commensurate with the sort of style that pervades the rest of the album, and so you naturally think you're in for a real treat. Then, suddenly, the entire mood shifts to something intense, like the feel of riding a horse to a barfight. It doesn't really mesh with the overall album sound, but it does have a groove of its own that you can start to get into after a few measures, once you've adjusted to it. That said, as soon as you finally do get accustomed to that bouncy rhythm, another sudden transition takes you into big, melodic keyboard sounds. It's not as full or powerful a chorus as the other things the album has to offer, but you can tell it's coming from a similar inspirational place.

Now transitions between different sounding sections - even sudden ones - are staples of progressive rock, so I don't have a problem with them in principle. What I do object to is the fact that these particular sections barely even seem to cohere. Instead of feeling like different ideas that were blended, they feel like different ideas that were shoved up against one another without any respect to song flow. The ideas themselves aren't necessarily bad individually, but they just don't work in combination. It's all too abrupt. The music never really has any time to catch its breath until the very end of the song, much less the listener. So the end result is a relatively brief, quirky little instrumental ditty that does some interesting things even if it can't quite hold it all together.

Which brings me to my biggest problem with the track: it's not actually an instrumental. Not only are the lyrics to it, but this haphazard piece is blanketed over with some of the worst lyrics I've ever heard. I hear the name 'Ballad of Big', I'm not thinking of keyboard arrangements or drum patterns or subtle guitar licks. Inevitably all that pops into my mind is this: "HE GOT MAD!" Like, that's the key chorus line. Or it would be, if Genesis had bothered to actually construct the chorus to have any kind of consistent melody. Nevertheless, that's the first thing you hear when the chorus keyboards jump in. "HE GOT MAD!" I'd tell you that context improves that line, but I don't really want to lie to you.

See, the song tells a story about a guy who liked to act tough. One day in a bar, someone calls him a coward, so he runs off to get himself killed. By the end of the song the words change to "HE WAS SCARED! BIG JIM WAS SCARED!" and I have no idea if we're supposed to feel compassion or schadenfreude. There's simply nothing compelling or interesting about the story itself, and the words the band uses to tell it have no impact either. It's like the random scenes they give Marty McFly in the Back to the Future series where someone calls him chicken and he turns into an idiot. Except Genesis made that the entire plot of this song.

To be frank, the whole thing irks me just to think about. And so, I think, I shan't think about it anymore.

187 - The Serpent

from *From Genesis to Revelation*, 1969

When a Genesis that was still in school at Charterhouse wanted to get the attention of Jonathan King, they asked a buddy to take their demo tape and plop it in his car while he was visiting the campus. One imagines this was because it simultaneously allowed the nervous kids to avoid actual human contact in addition to maintaining a level of plausible deniability if King hated the thing, but of course he didn't. Why? Well, there was a little song on that tape called 'She is Beautiful'.

> **Tony:** *I think we always felt this was a song which had an excitement about it we liked.* [1]

This song actually dates back to the very beginnings of the band - the genesis of Genesis, as it were. Anthony Phillips and Mike Rutherford had managed to secure some time in a room with recording equipment (calling it a studio would be vastly overstating the thing), but they needed a little help on keys, and Anthony knew a guy in school named Tony Banks.

> **Ant:** *I got Tony Banks to come and play the keyboards on [the session] and he was going to bring Peter, his vocalist who I hadn't really heard sing, to do one song. The deal was that Banks would come along and play keyboards if we recorded one song of theirs, and of course their song was far better than any of our stuff.* [11]

Defined by a strong piano riff that opens the action, the groove on the track was very strong, especially compared to anything else any of the boys in the band were writing at the time. The melody, by contrast, was pretty poor, with problematic backing vocals. And the lyrics were completely throwaway. But still! There was enough there to catch King's attention.

> **Ant:** *We actually got the publishing deal on the basis of...'She Is Beautiful', which became 'The Serpent', and it was really good.* [11]

See, when the concept of *From Genesis to Revelation* was determined, and the band knew they wanted to include 'She is Beautiful' - the strength of their catalogue - on the album, they decided to give the lyrics a rewrite. Now instead of exclaiming "She's a model!" the words were about the creation and temptation of man. A little bit better, though for me they still don't quite hit the mark.

The album arrangement improves the instrumentation substantially, in addition to being recorded properly instead of on a demo tape made at a friend's house. But for me, the song can't quite escape its bad melody and not-quite-in-tune backup vocals. I do enjoy the ~40 second instrumental interlude on the album that precedes the song, which is encapsulated in the track runtime, though I wouldn't consider it part of 'The Serpent' proper. All in all there's something here, but for my ears, just not enough.

186 - A Winter's Tale

Single, 1968

After the band's debut single 'The Silent Sun' flopped commercially, Jonathan King had them put out a follow-up a few months later with this effort. You know the old adage. "If at first you don't succeed, try, try again." And at first listen, it's easy to see why this is the song that he chose to be the second single. It immediately grabs you with its air of pleasantness, and has a chorus that seems crafted to get stuck in your head. Perhaps this could be the one to break this fledgling band into the mainstream!

But of course, this single didn't go anywhere either. In fact, it's part of what convinced King to suggest to the band that changes were needed. And while the band would later agree by completely altering their approach to the music and mutually parting ways with King himself, at this early stage they hadn't yet identified that the problem was "these songs aren't good enough." So instead, King suggested that Genesis ought to change the personnel in their rhythm section. Since firing band co-founder Mike Rutherford was a complete non-starter, they directed their attention at drummer Chris Stewart, whose playing was merely rudimentary.

Now I have to say, as regards 'A Winter's Tale' I think Stewart's drumming actually comes through pretty nicely. I mean, it's low in the mix, and he's not doing anything mind-boggling. I'm not saying this is a percussive performance for the ages or anything. But it's *fine,* and really, how could this teenage band really ask for anything more than that? In fact, it's Mike's bass that doesn't seem to be having any impact at all on the track. Is he even playing? Does it even matter?

But naturally, the band knew what they did and didn't have in the rehearsal room, and one can't glean everything about the musicians just from listening to a forgotten single, so perhaps in the end firing Chris Stewart was the right move. He certainly thinks so.

> **Chris:** *I was not a natural drummer. I was an appallingly crap drummer ... The others were right to fire me. They had the potential to get somewhere bigger and better and with me banging away badly in the background they probably wouldn't have...* [1]

Focusing back here on 'A Winter's Tale' itself though, while I feel that the verse melody is pleasant and the chorus is relatively catchy, the immaturity in the band's overall sound is inescapable to my ears. And personal preference here, but the chorus just sounds like an ad jingle of some sort to me. Any time they start in with "You're concealing every feeling" I get involuntary mental images of the band putting on big smiles while drinking Folger's coffee in a log cabin somewhere. It just doesn't feel authentic, somehow. It's a very listenable little ditty, but I'm afraid it doesn't do all that much for me.

185 - Hidden in the World of Dawn

Demo, 1968

You know, I was in a band at one point in time. Don't get too excited: it didn't really go anywhere. We tried and failed repeatedly to even fill out a playing line-up, and eventually everyone quit the band except for me. So, you know, that was a confusing day. Even still, somehow along the way we did manage to record an album, and I daresay it's a pretty good one if you're into that kind of music and you allow for the fact that it was made semi-professionally in some guy's basement. I'm proud of it, in any case. But of course, before we could record the album proper, we had to make our initial recordings so we knew where things stood. And that meant huddling around a laptop in someone *else's* basement so we could get all the tracks laid down, synchronised, edited, all that good stuff.

I bring all this up to say that I've made demo tapes before, and so I feel like I've got a better sense than most of what that process looks like. See, not all demos are created equal. Some are practically as good as the final thing. Less production value, obviously, but often a kind of "live room" energy that makes it compelling in a different way. Maybe all the pieces of the puzzle are already there and so you get a complete idea, just in a different form. Meanwhile, other demos are just really rough sketches, like a proof-of-concept of the beginnings of a song idea. These tend to come either very early in the process, or else represent songs that are never going to truly go anywhere.

'Hidden in the World of Dawn' is one of these latter types of demos. In fact, I'd go so far as to say that out of all the demos from this early time period, this one might sound the *most* stereotypically demo-like. You've got a sound mix driven by little more than "who's sitting closest to the microphone?" You've got half-hearted, out of tune backing vocals. You've got bum notes and trouble staying on rhythm, but "eh, keep it in because it's just a rough take and we'll clean it up when it counts." It's got all the hallmarks of a recording that - ironically given its title - was never meant to see the light of day. Yet here it is, and we don't have any other form by which to judge this tune.

So judge it I must! Tony's piano gives a nice, "easy listening of the 1930s" vibe, and Ant's guitar pleasantly strums beside it, but everything else is just muddy. And I think the sound quality is only a very small part of it. It's under-rehearsed, it's not particularly well arranged to begin with...in short, it's an all-around disappointment.

And yet! If you strip away the (many) flaws in execution and look at the song purely as a composition instead of as the mess the boys made of it, it does improve quite a bit.

> **Tony:** *There was [a demo rejected by Jonathan King] called 'Hidden in the World Of Dawn' which was one of mine. It was quite good actually.* [6]

Well, I don't know that I'd go *that* far, but I will say that the piano melody works decently well, though having the vocals double that melody is uninspired. The swells leading into the chorus are pretty strong. There's *something* here, but it doesn't really ever coalesce. A mostly pleasant song, but one that doesn't have any interest in actually going anywhere. Still though, give the boys a studio, a firm talking-to, and a chance to get it right and I think this could've been one of the highlights of *From Genesis to Revelation*. Instead it's forever hidden in the world of "what if?"

184 - Vancouver

B-side of 'Many Too Many', 1978

By late 1977, Phil Collins' first marriage was beginning to fall apart. The band had released two albums during the calendar year of 1976, and toured extensively to support both of them. It was the summer of '77 when the touring finally stopped, only for the band to head straight into the studio to mix, edit, and release their second live album, *Seconds Out*. And then it was right back to record another album, this time without Steve. Which of course meant it would require an even greater commitment from the remaining three members. And of course there would have to be another tour to support both the album and the new line-up.

Collins had been drama school classmates with his first wife, Andy, and they had reconnected when the band had earlier toured in Vancouver, where she was living. To make a long story short, they hit it off again, got hitched, and she moved to England to be with her new husband...only to eventually find that her husband was never really there.

> **Phil:** *We're playing arenas now, and professionally things couldn't be much better. However, home life is diminishing due to my continued absence… With two young children to mother, Andy has endured a lot - a lot - of being alone. On the rare occasions when I'm home for anything like an extended period, the atmosphere is tense.* [12]

According to Phil, it would still be another few months before he would find out that his wife was having an affair (though Andy has since sued him for defamation of character, it's unclear which parts of his account she contests). She would eventually move herself and the kids back to Vancouver. Which makes this song particularly heart wrenching.

The lyrics tell the story of a girl who has had enough and wants to leave, only to reconsider last minute and try to stick it out. In late 1977, even while his marriage was melting due in large part to his absence, he was spending his time in the studio recording lyrics that communicated hope at the prospect that his wife would stick around. In the song the girl is going to leave because of disagreements with her parents, and the lyrics end with the parties all reconciling. Phil yearned for that reconciliation himself, but it wasn't to be. He was recalling the city where he found his wife, but in a several months it would be the city where she had taken his family. Hoping he might still somehow salvage everything, he would move to Vancouver himself. But it was not to be, and before long he was back in England, bored and miserable, and decided to channel that emotion into a series of songs that would come to be called, collectively, *Face Value*.

The song 'Vancouver' works pretty well at communicating all those same emotions. It produces an atmosphere suitable to that blend of hope and worry that Phil was doubtless feeling at the time. However, the mixing on the track simply isn't very good. There's far too much reverb muddying the waters, and the guitars in particular seem overly loud compared to everything else. Or perhaps the vocals are just a bit underbalanced. Either way, you get the mood but not a sense of cohesion.

Add to all that a lacklustre melody, and the fact that the song ends abruptly like they never figured out an actual conclusion, and you get a tune that ultimately is a much better historical footnote than actual song. It's another one in the bin of "listenable but forgettable," regardless of the subject matter.

183 - The Return of the Giant Hogweed

from *Nursery Cryme*, 1971

After the departure of Anthony Phillips and the band's subsequent decision to press on, it was decided that they might as well replace their drummer if they were already replacing the guitarist anyway. Farewell, John Mayhew. Hello, Phil Collins. And as the timing turned out, Phil landed the drumming gig well before Steve Hackett's successful audition, and so for a few months Genesis was a four-piece band with a new drummer but still no primary guitar player.

Yet, critically, during those few months the band didn't stop performing live. This necessitated that Tony learn to play some lead guitar parts through his fuzzbox on the organ instead, which meant he was beginning to develop his now iconic technique of playing one keyboard with one hand while doing something totally different on a different keyboard with the other. Mike also learned to play the bass pedals, necessary for those sections where a rhythm guitar was needed.

They also continued rehearsing and writing, working to integrate Phil into the group. Out of those sessions came a song called 'The Return of the Giant Hogweed', which would be fully completed and enhanced with Steve's input once he came on board, most notably through his novel style of playing that would later come to be known as "tapping," which features prominently at the beginning of the song.

> **Steve:** *I'd come up with this idea of a guitar technique, which was tapping...It meant that you could play like a keyboard player by using the fret board like a keyboard...Tony and I used to twin these things, so on the intro of 'Return of the Giant Hogweed' it was the two of us doing those parts in harmony.* [3]

This is great history, but as for the song itself, well. Thanks to Peter's lyrical work it's an intrinsically silly piece, warning the masses about sentient weeds trying to take over the human race. That's part of the quirky mindset that helped the band really develop their style and sound, so I'm all for it in principle. Charming eccentricity? That's just early Genesis' bread and butter, baby.

> **Steve:** *I think Pete's idea was a little bit like a movie, where...this thing has escaped. So Pete's imagination running riot with this. And I suggested that the title, instead of just being 'Hogweed' was 'The RETURN of the Giant Hogweed', as if it was a series of successful film franchises...Very strange, sort of quintessentially English sounding thing, isn't it? Truly proggy, very much a story.* [13]

If you're with me so far, you may not be for much longer. But chances are you saw the number I put in front of this song title, remembered the general schtick of this book, and haven't been with me for several paragraphs now. See, I've found that this song is regarded by most Genesis and indeed progressive rock fanatics to be among the best the band has ever done. And, well, let me just say it outright: I...don't really care for it. At all. Just doesn't do it for me. I skip it more often than not when I'm playing through *Nursery Cryme*. I am, as some would say, a "Hogweed Hater." Now, before you pitch this book into the nearest lit fireplace, let me just say something in my defence: yes, I'm down on 'The Return of the Giant Hogweed'. But! So is Tony Banks.

> **Tony:** *I don't feel the album was much of an advance...a lot of low points: 'For Absent Friends', 'Harlequin', and 'Giant Hogweed' are all lesser songs to me.* [10]

That's got to get me *some* kind of pass, right? Let me at least explain why it doesn't work for me. In a nutshell, it's Pete.

Gabriel's vocals are extremely aggressive, and while I understand the reason for the choice, they're just not pleasant at all in this context for me to listen to. The song's verses, which are otherwise mostly fine to my ears, are just drowned and largely ruined in this shouty mess for me. Those verses then go into softer sections where the vocal performance doesn't grate anymore, but there the melody quickly falls apart. It's like a balancing scale where trying to improve one aspect of the thing forces the other to get worse to compensate. It's simply not compelling music to me from between the intro section until about five minutes in when Tony takes over with some moody piano work, which is then spelled by Steve's guitar, then a strong rhythm groove. Legitimately, the stretch of music from about 4:55 to 6:30 in the track is some of the strongest stuff from this era of Genesis, and the only reason this wasn't even lower on my list. I can easily see why the song is as highly regarded as it is, and I'm not even trying to argue that it shouldn't be held in high esteem.

But this isn't a list of the best Genesis songs according to Genesis fans. It's a list of my personal favourite songs in their extensive discography, in a force-ranked order, and I can barely stand listening to this track. I just can't reconcile the first half of the song, and the song's ending after the section I previously praised feels similarly bloated. It takes a minute and a half to do what I feel it could more effectively do in about fifteen seconds. For me, this song is a roller coaster. An exciting intro, a long and pretty lousy vocal section, a very strong instrumental bit, and then an overindulgent ending that ultimately leaves the last taste in my mouth a poor one.

> **Mike:** *'The Return of the Giant Hogweed' had something for everybody in the band: fast drumming for Phil, triplet stuff with Tony and Steve playing harmonies together, and a quirky lyric from Pete about a plant that'd escaped from Kew Gardens.* [14]

Something for everybody in the band, sure, but nothing much for me. I'm sorry, dear reader. I really wanted to like this one more than I did, but 'The Return of the Giant Hogweed' is not only my least favourite song on *Nursery Cryme*, but indeed of the "classic" five piece line-up as a whole. And if that makes you so upset that you can't bear to read another page of this book, I understand.

No refunds, though.

182 - Am I Very Wrong?

From *From Genesis to Revelation*, 1969

What a lovely intro/interlude from Tony! It sounds almost like the start of some kind of traditional hymn, very cheerful but also somewhat prim and proper. You know, a "Please open your books to page 37, and let us sing 'He is Holy'" sort of feel to the endeavour. Which then makes it mildly startling when that whole mood abruptly ends, never to return, and we get the rest of the song instead. It's like one of those Monty Python "And now for something completely different" segues. Abrupt and strange, though not necessarily bad in itself. It really all depends on what comes after.

In this case, what comes next is the first verse of the song. That's a good thing, because the verses of this one are actually quite pretty themselves. Though Pete's performance isn't perfect, it *is* adequate enough to bring out the innate grace of the core melody. And it's spelled by some competent rhythm guitar work, as well as a very early instance of flute playing. You'll find as we go on this journey that I'm something of a sucker for those enchanting flute parts, and 'Am I Very Wrong?' is no exception. On top of all that, after a couple lines of singing Tony's piano comes in again and gives the whole effort a sense of power and maturity beyond most of the band's output at the time. On the basis of the verses alone, this would be one of the best tracks from the debut, totally compelling.

So it's with quite a bit of disappointment that I need to inform you that this song also has a chorus. And frustratingly, it's another of those Pythonesque segues into a totally different atmosphere. Considering that the verses worked so well, the notion of "change all of this" ends up being as bad an idea as it sounds like it would be. Gone are the dark, introspective tones of the verse melodies. Gone are the feelings of weight and strength that propel the band forward, ahead of its time. Gone is the instrumentation that did so much heavy lifting in setting the mood. No, these choruses are, by contrast, light and cheery to a confusing degree. One has to assume that such juxtaposition was the intent, but it doesn't work in the least.

And that's to say nothing of the quality, or lack thereof, of virtually every part of the arrangement within the chorus. Perhaps to increase the perceived contrast between the sections, Peter takes the choruses off and we get Ant and Tony singing instead. The results of that experiment are, well, not so good. Ant's performance, which is mixed higher than it has any right to be, teeters precipitously on the balance beam of being in or out of tune, and he's singing drivel like "Happy friend, everything all right." It's grating. Add to that some ill-advised horn playing instead of things like, you know, piano, and what are we even doing here?

Peter does join back in on the final chorus, which you would think on paper might be a positive development. Alas, you would be very wrong indeed. His return to the microphone actually makes things quite a bit worse; rather than covering the deficiencies of everything else happening behind him, he's content to just kind of do his own thing. It's like an ad lib that nobody bothered to talk him down from. There's no regard for harmonies or rhythms. It's a complete mess.

So this song is effectively three sections: intro, verse, and chorus. I like the intro, love the verse, and absolutely hate the chorus. Add to that the fact that these three sections specifically have no business interacting with one another, and the song ultimately falls pretty low for me. In the end I find myself wishing that they had taken that great verse and developed it into, as the Pythons might say, something completely different.

181 - Papa He Said

B-side of 'Congo', 1997

Back in the early 90s, Genesis had a big hit with a little ditty called 'I Can't Dance'. You may have heard of it. It was an unusual track, relying on a bare beat, a distinct guitar sound, and some quirky charm to make its point. And make its point it did, as the song soared all the way to 7 on both the UK and US charts, proving Genesis had staying power going into a third decade. Well, fourth if you count the 60s and *From Genesis to Revelation*, but you probably shouldn't count that. Yes, 'I Can't Dance' was truly a landmark moment in the Genesis discography.

Now this? This is not that song, but nobody tell Genesis that. It's easy for fans of the band to write off the late 90s stuff the band produced. After all, there was a new singer, which also meant a new drummer (two new drummers, as it turned out). A third of the songwriting tandem that produced so many big hits was removed from the equation, and that element Collins brought to the band was not replaced. And so I find that most Genesis fans, referring to this period loosely as "The Wilson Era" - referring to the band's new lead singer, Ray Wilson - simply dismiss the entirety of the band's final new output as something less-than. "Oh, those Wilson years were terrible."

This is a bit unfair to poor Ray, who did the best with what he had to work with. And it's unfair to the material on the whole, because *Calling All Stations* and its array of extra tracks has a lot of really strong stuff on offer. It pains me to see Genesis fans just brush the era off as though it didn't exist at all. I recall seeing a review of the album written by a Genesis fan deciding to listen to it to see what all the negative fuss was about, ostensibly to give it a fair shake. And then the actual review was full of things like "Listened to ten seconds and it sucks. Moved on to the next track." I was so disappointed.

And yet, then we get to 'Papa He Said', which was wisely left off that last Genesis album, and I think to myself, "Well, I can see where the critics are coming from." To me, it sounds as though they were trying to recapture the lightning in a bottle they had with 'I Can't Dance' six years prior, and ended up with a very similar song and sound. The difference is that the quirky charm that made that hit work was absent this time around. And, of course, there's the nagging issue that they'd already been down this road before. Which is a very strange thing, because all throughout their careers Mike and Tony have strenuously tried to avoid re-treading old ground. And Ray Wilson doesn't have a writing credit on this track, so you can't scapegoat him. I don't even have a problem with his vocal performance here; he's decidedly not the problem.

So for me, 'Papa He Said' is a surprising step backwards. It's competent, well produced, and only slightly annoying (mainly due to the repetition of the title line...and the obnoxiously loud cowbell...okay, it's more than slightly annoying). It's a quasi-grunge, quasi-pop, quasi-funk, quasi-reggae sort of thing, and 'I Can't Dance' does all of it better. Not a bad song per se, but for me, a totally redundant one. But please, stick with me with this late era stuff. I promise it gets better.

Well, I think it does, anyway...

180 - Build Me a Mountain

Demo, 1968

Genesis, as we know, started as a school band (more accurately, as three and then eventually two separate school bands) at Charterhouse. Charterhouse, in turn, was a school defined largely by its socioeconomic niche. The families that sent their kids to the school - and therefore, to an extent, the students themselves - were in that upper middle class, stiff upper lip kind of mould. Mike Rutherford's father was a military officer. Peter Gabriel's house had a pool. These aren't the typical roots of rock and roll. Don't get me wrong, though. The kids were still into rock and roll, naturally. Especially in that kind of closed environment, you take any connection to the outside world that you can. But they weren't "born into it," as it were, and perhaps that's part of why they also weren't very good at it. Thus, when 1970 rolled around and we began to hear Genesis moving in a more progressive direction, it kind of fit. You'd hear *Trespass* and think, "Well yeah, that makes sense."

All of this makes the fact that these guys wrote a straight-up hippie anthem a little surprising to me. Now it's important to remember that the Genesis boys saw themselves as songwriters over and above musicians. They knew their playing was mostly rudimentary, and that their image wasn't quite so Top of the Pops. Really, the only reason Genesis played on *From Genesis to Revelation* in the first place is that nobody else would perform their music. So we have to acknowledge that they were recording demos like 'Build Me a Mountain' not for their own sake so much as to try to sell off the songs for others to perform. They wanted to create hit singles, yes, but hit singles for *other* people while they cashed in the royalty checks. With that in mind, it makes a bit more sense that they'd try to stretch themselves as writers and craft a tune that tied into the counterculture movement of the time.

But it's still weird.

The song itself prominently features Ant's lead guitar, more than the other material they were producing at the time. As the band's best musician at the time, this is decidedly a good thing. And Mike's bass pattern gives it a lot of drive as well, though John Silver's drumming isn't audible half the time. Still, half a rhythm section means it's got pretty good momentum and may have actually caught on as a minor hit somewhere had a more established band or artist bought and recorded it in this time period. It's got a lot of those hallmarks of the genre, and it's easy to imagine a throng of drug-addled 20-somethings swaying together while this blares out from an amplifier on some outdoor stage.

Sadly, 60s hippie rock isn't really my thing. I can appreciate this track for what it is, but it's just not for me. There are rough edges all around the playing, though most of that should be forgiven since it's just a demo, and one that Genesis probably never expected or even wanted to perform themselves. I'm terribly glad this song wasn't successful, as it meant the band wasn't tempted to go off in this direction, but I can't say I hate the song. I'm glad it's on their *Genesis Archive 1967-75* compilation...and I'm even more glad it's *only* there.

179 - Let Us Now Make Love

Live recording, 1970

I defy anyone to read the title of this song without wincing. It's so overt and on the nose; it's as though a group of teenagers got together and convinced themselves they were saying something deep. And in fact, if you had told me this was written in 1967 or 1968 I would have accepted it without hesitation, and dismissed the lyrics as a product of kids who hadn't quite figured it out yet.

But then you realise this was created after the release of *From Genesis to Revelation*, while the band already had songs like 'Looking for Someone' and 'Stagnation' in their repertoire, so it becomes a little harder to justify. And then you see the song has a runtime of over six minutes, and it's a "hoo boy, what have I gotten myself into" kind of moment as a listener.

So it's a really good thing that lyrics alone don't make a song, because there's a bit more happening here. For one thing, we get a healthy dose of Peter's flute playing, which to me is an often undervalued aspect of the early Genesis sound. Ant's guitar playing moves beyond simple strumming and provides beautiful texture. His vocals actually complement Peter's pretty well, too. He's no vocal clone like Phil would end up being, but the two actually harmonise pretty decently here.

Ultimately, this track was left off *Trespass*. Why? Well, hard to say why, actually.

> **Tony:** *For some reason we didn't record it for Trespass. I think it had been seen as a possible single and so we left it behind. It wasn't left off because we didn't think it was good. The idea was that we would do it as a single...We wanted to do 'Let Us Now Make Love' but we didn't do it.* [6]

A possible reason is the fact that it seemed to constantly be in flux, better live than in the studio because of it.

> **Tony:** *I used to play a guitar solo in the middle of 'Let Us Now Make Love' as it happens. I think that song went through its best phase in the early version of it when Ant used to play it on piano to us and it sounded great. Later on we changed the chorus at some point and then Ant changed the chorus yet again! And as a result I think it didn't sound half as good. It was a very nice song and it sounded good live.* [6]

As fate would have it, the song happened to be the starting point of Anthony Phillips' stage fright, which eventually led to his leaving the band.

> **Ant:** *We were starting the song called 'Let Us Now Make Love', just twelve-string and voice. And I remember looking down at my guitar and thinking, "What comes next?" It was an awful moment. I was frozen in time. I really didn't know what had happened...I tried to dismiss it, but the next night it started coming on and on and on, and I began anticipating its onset.* [1]

The song left the repertoire along with its guitarist, which is a mild shame. I think musically it's really pleasant, and certainly pretty well performed in the surviving "live" take available on *Genesis Archive: 1967-75* (it's one of three *Trespass* outtakes recorded for BBC Radio 2's overnight Night Ride program in February, 1970). But the lyrics are so terrible that it does hurt the effort overall for me. Ah well.

178 - Hair on the Arms and Legs

Demo, 1968

If you've been listening to the songs alongside this book as we've gone on, you may get a strange sense of déjà vu from the opening notes of 'Hair on the Arms and Legs'. I want you to know that you're not alone in that, and you're not crazy either. It's because you've already heard them in this very countdown, on the 185 tune, 'Hidden in the World of Dawn'. I couldn't reliably tell you which of these two tracks was written first chronologically, as they're both included on the *Genesis Archive 1967-75* set as demos from 1968 without much else to go on. Were they a month apart? Eleven months apart? Were they written simultaneously? Perhaps the band had both songs going in parallel, intending some kind of self-reference or consistent musical motif for an eventual album. Until someone asks Tony Banks, I don't think we'll ever know.

At any rate, other than that common bar of piano, which does occur a few times throughout the piece, the songs are totally different from one another. While 'Hidden in the World of Dawn' is a gentle, pleasant outing (if mostly uninteresting), 'Hair on the Arms and Legs' has a bit more darkness to it. When Peter temporarily discards the "pop" voice he used on their 60s material for the line "I say, what's the use?" he immediately sounds more mature. Especially at the end, it sounds like the song jumps from 1968 straight to 1973. It's striking. And you know what? Good on him for leaning into that and getting more comfortable in his own skin. Can you imagine hearing a song like 'Back in N.Y.C.' where Gabriel exclusively uses his tight little "Bee Gees pastiche" voice? Talk about yikes. So from that perspective, I do think 'Hair on the Arms and Legs' was an important developmental piece.

It's not just Peter who was developing, however. I'd like to direct your attention to the middle of the piece, where Tony Banks features in a brief yet effective piano solo, notable as a sign of things to come for him as well. Tony's a guy who, at least early on, was never quite as confident in his playing as he was in his songwriting. Something like this in 1968 surely helped build some of that belief that he could adequately deliver the notes he was composing.

Beyond the two of them though, I'm not sure there's too much here to highlight. There are backing vocals, yes, but to say they're of middling quality would be a kindness indeed. The composition itself isn't particularly interesting, with a hit-or-miss kind of melody, lyrics that don't hold attention, and of course that awful title. Nonetheless, there's the germ of something really good here, and a somewhat adventurous quality to the song that isn't really found in their other material of the time.

Interestingly enough, this is one of the few early demos that had a life beyond 1968, showing up again in snippet form in 1970 as part of the song that came to be known as 'Frustration', the bulk of which was reused once more in 1974 on *The Lamb Lies Down on Broadway* for 'Anyway'. So in a very small, probably not valid, transitive-property-of-mathematics kind of way, 'Hair on the Arms and Legs' helped breathe life into one of the seminal concept albums of progressive rock.

All in all, this could be a contender for a bottom ten track, and you wouldn't hear much argument from me, though I think the hints of greater ambition it shows cause me to put it a little higher than that...but not by much. I do think this song deserves its place in the Genesis legend as a historical footnote and a sneak preview of improvements to the band's sound that would arrive in the coming years, yet I can't really recommend it as a listening experience in its own right.

177 - Image Blown Out

Demo, 1968 (and 1967)

The most interesting thing about 'Image Blown Out' is that there are actually two different officially published versions of the song floating around out there, recorded in two different years. In 1967, the band had recorded a rough demo of the song and included it for consideration on *From Genesis to Revelation*. Then, in 1968, they rerecorded the song. I'm not sure if they were unsatisfied with the original demo or just felt that the song had developed enough that an updated version was warranted, but either way the 1968 demo represents a sort of "final cut."

And there is indeed a notable difference between the two versions of the song, which immediately becomes apparent just by glancing at their runtimes. The 1967 version runs 2:48 while the 1968 version only runs 2:12. But this isn't a case of two entirely different songs with the same name; either version you choose, you're getting the same light, jaunty tune when it all comes down to it. It's the sort of thing you'd expect to hear as the backing music in a movie where the main character is walking around town with a big smile because his crush just agreed to go on a date with him, or something in that vein. Just all sunshine and rainbows. I don't say that in a derogatory way, either. It's genuinely a happy listen.

The extra 36 seconds on the earlier cut are comprised of a post-verse section that pops up twice in the song, once near the beginning and once near the end. This does something a little different musically, adding a sense of purposeful motion to the whole picture. Total change in melody and feel, and here the band starts finally adding some layers to the straight piano/vocal sound. For the 1968 version, however, they cut these sections out entirely, and listening to both, I get why. I don't dislike the extra section per se, but the song is just better maintaining a consistent mood. It feels like addition by subtraction.

But that's not an entirely fair statement, because what the 1968 version loses in actual length it makes up for in fullness. They didn't simply remove a couple sections, but they took the depth those sections added in and distributed it over the rest of the song. Things like adding backing vocals and flute to the verses, whereas in 1967 the sound there was sparse to create contrast. It adds a bit of richness and interest to the piece that wasn't there on the original demo, and I really respect the growth it shows in the band's songwriting maturity to fatten up the slim bits while simultaneously trimming the fat elsewhere. It's a shrewd move. Add to that the increased playing and production quality of the 1968 version, and for my money it's easily the better one.

> **Tony:** *We felt that 'The Image Blown Out' was good enough to be the second single [from the band], as it was a good song.* [6]

Despite the improvements, the song didn't make the debut album, probably because it didn't fit the whole loose Biblical theme they were going for. And so it faded into obscurity until 1996, when a reissue of *From Genesis to Revelation* included it as a bonus track. But of course, that reissue (which the band didn't control) included the *first* version with the 2:42 runtime. You know, the one the band had decided three decades prior to move on from. Which is probably why when *Genesis Archive 1967-75* came out two years later, the band made a point to include the 1968 version so that they could get their preferred cut out there.

176 - The Battle of Epping Forest

from *Selling England by the Pound*, 1973

Despite its inherent silliness and fanciful lyrics, 'The Battle of Epping Forest' is actually based on a true story.

> **Peter:** *I read a newspaper item about a gang battle that took place in Epping Forest. I like to collect cuttings from newspapers about any odd happenings. In this case I kept the cutting for ages but could not find out anymore about the battle. I even put an ad in The Times and checked in newspaper libraries. But the story had disappeared off the face of the earth.* [15]

Armed with a really interesting snippet of a story and absolutely no details, Peter decided to just fill them in himself. Creating characters like Liquid Len, Bob the Nob, and Harold Demure, he crafted an ambitious lyrical work that transformed the song into, essentially, musical theatre. It wasn't the first or last time a Genesis song would have multiple in-song characters with different voices, but it is the most extreme example of that style. Peter glides between these voices with great fluidity and grace, which gives me the inescapable feeling whenever I hear the track that I'm at a one-man show. It's truly remarkable how much personality he's able to pack into nearly twelve minutes of runtime.

And as a narrative, 'The Battle of Epping Forest' is sufficiently interesting and fairly amusing. Gangs show up to brutally battle it out over territory boundaries for their respective protection rackets, a grisly affair that eventually sees all its participants dead. With the gangs depleted of manpower, the ground littered with corpses, and nothing actually properly settled, the "gentlemen" at the top of the food chain ultimately decide who won by means of a coin flip. It's the absurd cherry on top of a creative masterwork of character, wordplay, and wit.

Regrettably, then, 'The Battle of Epping Forest' is actually *not* a stage show of any sort, but rather a rock and roll song in the progressive mould. Now, virtually everyone enjoys music in some form or another, to some degree or another. I don't think that's a radical, worldview-shaking statement to make. Given the sheer number of people that statement can apply to, and given the huge range of musical forms that exist, I also don't think it's unfair to suggest that most people would tend to consider a song running nearly twelve minutes to be "rather on the long end, don't you think?" I mean, 'Stairway to Heaven' is considered something of a rock epic, and it clocks in at right around eight minutes. 'The Battle of Epping Forest' is 50% longer than that. So it seems incredible to suggest that 'Epping Forest' might somehow be too short.

Yet to do all the things it sets out to do - namely, to be a one-man stage show *and* a quality rock song in tandem - it needed to be about twice as long as it actually is. A twenty-four minute song sounds absurd until you realise that Genesis had essentially just made one an album prior. Yet that song, 'Supper's Ready', was really more like several different songs joined and blended together to make a cohesive whole. 'Epping Forest' as a side-long track? I don't think it could hold my attention nearly so well.

Of course, this is all just hypotheticals and speculation of ways to "fix" the track well after the fact, because the truth is that 'The Battle of Epping Forest' was never really even considered as a big, epic track in the first place. Rather, it was a smaller piece that began to balloon out of control due to a lack of other available material to rehearse.

> **Tony:** *We were slightly dry of ideas. What we found was that we had about three or four pieces we were [rehearsing] all the time because we didn't have that many things to do. One of those songs became 'The Battle of Epping Forest', which probably ended up having too much in it, because we were adding new bits on a daily basis.* [1]

I think that's why the song doesn't work for me at the length it is. As a shorter song with a verse, chorus, middle eight, etc. it would probably be some fanciful fun. As a really long song the band could explore all its musical ideas while still maintaining at least some semblance of breathing room so that all its intricacies could really shine. At twelve minutes it just lands in this really awkward, overstuffed kind of realm.

> **Phil:** *A classic example...where we had [the song] very well-recorded...some really counter polyrhythmic bits kind of happening here...and then Peter took the song and wrote the lyric, and we recorded the track. And he came in to sing the lyric, and we were just like, "It's like 300 words a line!" Like, there's no space. Any air had been sucked out of it. Not to say that he was in the wrong or we were in the wrong, but if we'd only known, we could've thinned it out. And in those days we didn't go back and re-record things, you know. "This is it...we've got to make do."* [3]

> **Peter:** *It's probably too busy. I'd spent a lot of time building up these characters and setting scenes, and was quite reluctant to edit as severely as I should've done. So I think it did end up too wordy.* [3]

Don't get me wrong here. I'm not saying this is a *bad* performance by the band by any means. The musicianship is very high quality, as would be expected by this time in the band's career. And the individual bits themselves are all pretty good - Tony's keyboard lines particularly. I'm also a big fan of the song's intro section, a whimsical little marching flute that sounds like all the toy soldiers heading off to their little toy war. It's a perfect fit and sets the tone for the piece as well as one could hope for. I'll go so far as to say that there's nothing in this song that I hear and think "Oh, don't like that bit."

> **Steve:** *Even at its weakest, Selling England by the Pound has got great moments in it. Great moments, great humour. A very funny bit in the middle of 'Epping Forest', Pete doing the vicar. Just brilliant.* [3]

No, the problem comes from the fact that it's as long as it is yet never particularly *does* anything. It's a rehearsal jam that people kept chucking bits into, and once it was full nearly to bursting, Pete showed up claiming to have lyrics but actually delivering a completed play. With so much happening, the sound all just sort of homogenises into "morning goo," to borrow a line from the end of the song. The only real melody to be found is in the chorus, and while passable, it's frankly not a very strong hook. So you've got this epic tale of characters and fighting, and a lot of decent backing stuff supporting it, but musically it just feels like nothing ever happens. And let me tell you: twelve minutes of music where nothing ever really grabs you? That's a *tedious* listen.

At this point no song yet to be presented in this book is, in my opinion, a truly poor one. But 'The Battle of Epping Forest'? Man. Every time it's about to come on, I have to ask myself. "Is this *really* how I want to spend the next twelve minutes of my life?" More often than not, the answer is "No. No I do not." It's a shame, really. This song could've been so much more. And should've been so much less.

175 - In Limbo

From *From Genesis to Revelation*, 1969

One of the criticisms I've seen some people lay against the Genesis of the early 80s is that bringing in the Earth, Wind and Fire horn section for a song like 'No Reply at All' or 'Paperlate' was just totally against the band's core sound. Genesis with trumpets? Preposterous! How could they deviate so far from their roots? How shameless a sell-out must we as fans tolerate before we say we've had enough?

These people are passionate, sure, but they're also completely misguided. You see, one might hear this complaint and then slyly point out that Genesis has been using horns since 1969. If anything, *Abacab* was less a departure from the band's roots, and more a return to them! It doesn't get much more "rooty" than your debut album, after all. Of course, it bears mentioning that on *From Genesis to Revelation* the band didn't actually *choose* to include horns, much less write the music with them in mind. No, they were added after the fact (and over the band's complaints) by the album's production team. So it is something of a point of contention, I suppose.

So given that the band was against their inclusion from the outset, and given that it would take twelve years before they'd be willing to give brass another try, one might assume that the horn arrangement for 'In Limbo' is its weakest aspect. Instead, strange as it might sound, the horns are actually the best thing the track has going for it. Which isn't to say the rest of the track is just throwaway or anything. There's a pretty solid groove underlying everything, and the piano/guitar riff provides a strong sense of energy and momentum.

Tony: *I remember feeling fairly happy with 'In Limbo'...It is a period piece in many ways.* [6]

The problem is that the vocals come in and do their darndest to counteract all the liveliness the rest of the piece generates. Going against the rhythmic drive, the vocals are just long intonations - "oohs" and "aahs" without any real melody to speak of. One might think from that description that I'm talking about backing vocals specifically, and while it's true that the backing vocals have this same issue, the real gut punch is that I'm describing Peter's lead here. It's like if someone went to open mic night at a jazz club and performed a Gregorian chant. Just sucks the life right out of the room.

And so we're back to the horns. If it weren't for them playing around on top of all that lethargic droning, the song wouldn't work whatsoever. It'd just be this flavourless lump of musical notes. Sadly, at times that's still the case - the horns disappear for stretches of the tune, leaving the whole affair lurching until the next time they arrive. Then the final thirty seconds of the track are a big wailing section that might have had a lot of power if it had been properly built up to, but of course it wasn't, so the song ends with a whimper rather than a bang. It's pretty disappointing, if only because it's easy to see how the end result could've been much better. Still, there are some really strong ideas in here and, particularly in the opening verse, the arrangement is pretty darn good. The production team was right to inject some life into the song where they could, but it wasn't quite enough polish to make the piece truly shine.

I'm sure there's a joke about the song itself being stuck in limbo in there somewhere.

174 - Anything She Does

from *Invisible Touch*, 1986

Of all the rock bands in the world, particularly in the heart of the 80s as the popularity of hair bands was surging, Genesis perhaps seems the least likely bunch to have pinup posters on the walls of their studio. Stodgy, stiff upper lip, wearing sweaters to rehearsal and making progressive music with a dash of synth pop? Gawking at *women*? Why, it's unheard of. But even if that image doesn't sound somehow incongruent to you, look at the individual men within the band at this time. Which of them seems most likely to actually write a set of lyrics around the idea of pining for one of those pinup models? Did you guess Phil Collins? I bet you guessed Phil Collins. More to the point, I bet you *didn't* guess Tony Banks. Why ever would you?

And yet, here we are. How did we get to this point? I have a theory. Take a trip with me down my own brand of Memory Lane, won't you?

The first time I ever had a band type of experience, I went to the "rehearsal" of the basement band a couple friends were in, fittingly named Down the Stairs. They had a regular singer who was ill and apparently at that time only half committed, so I got invited to come jam with them for an afternoon. I think they wanted to see if there was any chemistry so that if their singer bailed they had a tiny bit of security. Which is funny in hindsight, because they only had two songs, couldn't fully remember how either of them went, and my initial impression of the band was that its music would never actually leave that basement.

In any case, I spent most of that rehearsal just standing around awkwardly, not sure what I was supposed to be doing. On the songs they did have, nobody knew how the vocal part went. No words, no melody, nothing. And they also didn't seem to be so invested in the existing material that they couldn't change it. So I was heartily encouraged to just make stuff up on the fly, whatever sounded good, and go for it. I had never in my life sung in this way, much less in front of people. Invent words and melody out of thin air? Over background playing that was constantly shifting in its own right? How is that even possible?

So I froze. They played, and looked at me from time to time, and I just stood there in a panic trying to somehow write a song in my head. Minutes passed, and I was coming up completely empty. And it was probably just my imagination, but I felt like I could sense the disappointment and scorn coming from the others in the room. "This guy's a total fraud. Why is he even here?" I knew I had to produce *something*, *anything* to justify my continued presence in this dude's house. Behind me, the bassist and drummer were going back and forth, solidifying a new groove they really liked. The guitarist joined in, and the groove became a riff, and now there was something there, however faint, that I could anchor to.

I looked around the basement rehearsal space. The walls were lined with old burlap sacks. Coffee beans from around the world. They were using it as rudimentary soundproofing, but I was struck in that moment by the thought that no matter where I turned, I'd be looking at an empty sack of coffee. The riff came back again, and I felt like it was now or never. Terrified, embarrassed, I nevertheless belted out with as much faux bravado as I could muster: "SACK RACE! I'M COMPETING IN A SACK RACE!" The playing behind me stopped, and I thought, "Welp, there it goes. Here's where they ask me to leave."

I looked at the guys. Everyone was laughing. "What the heck, man? Sack race? You're singing about a sack race?" I could only sheepishly nod, and add, "Yeah...just looked around and saw all these sacks, and it just kind of came out." "No, no, man, that's GREAT! That's hilarious! We should run with that! Let's go again."

Well, that was unexpected.

We ended up spending the entire rest of the rehearsal working on 'Sack Race'. It was a very punchy, not-very-melodic song, but since we all understood it was basically a comedy rock tune, that was OK. More lyrics came along. So did a new, contrasting section of music. Everyone was really enthusiastic about how the jam came together. As soon as I got home I set to work on creating proper lyrics, and along the way arranged the sections of the song into what I figured might be their final form. I also wrote an entire new section towards the end where the drummer would rap from the perspective of bystander whose life was changed by witnessing the titular sack race from afar. If I'm being honest, the whole thing was very, very funny. I was incredibly proud. I sent it all to the guys and suggested that we should try to work out this version of the song at the next rehearsal, and maybe we weren't too far away from recording an initial demo. They loved it. I was overwhelmed with excitement - a band at last!

I never played with Down the Stairs again. Their singer got healthy and renewed his commitment to the band. They rehearsed more, got better, locked down some actual songs, and even began getting gigs. They were a proper band, and I wasn't part of it. I was never part of it. I was just the friend there for a single afternoon to help fill the rehearsal void. I made peace with that a few months after the fact. 'Sack Race' never did see the light of day. During my time with my second (first) band, I went back and asked the Down the Stairs crew for permission to use and develop 'Sack Race'. The reaction from most of them was, "What are you talking about?" So I decided to use it. And then that second band folded too.

This was an exceptionally long tangent, but the parallel I'm trying to draw is that 'Anything She Does', like 'Sack Race', is a product of someone generating lyrics about what they see. It's an improvised setting, everyone's jamming, so what is there to say? "Eh, I see a poster on the wall, that'll do!" So don't worry, Tony. I get it.

> **Tony:** *Kind of condensed out of a jam...the original jams might have lasted twenty minutes, you know, but you kind of start selecting the little bits out of it that you think are good. And it kind of crystallises into quite a short song.* [16]

The music itself is surprising in its own way. In an era of drum machines, here's Phil banging out a simple beat on his kit, which helps the song pop a bit more as it goes. You've got some funky guitar lines going through the intro and verses, which are actually played on a synthesizer, with a sort of siren guitar going at the end. You've got a prominent keyboard melody to kick off the song and then, apart from a reprise of that melody halfway through, the keyboards just seem to disappear completely outside some background twinkling in the chorus - but that's because they're disguised as guitar sounds. The ending neither fades out nor has a big finish; it just kind of abruptly decides it's time to be done.

It's easy to listen to this one and be struck by the eighties-ness of the effort, but the reality is that this song is pretty unlike most anything else the band had done before. They thought they had a hit single on their hands when they were writing it, though they never ended up releasing the song that way - maybe because they'd already had hits with five other tracks on the album and were hitting peak saturation. But in one final act of surprise, they decided to make a music video for the song anyway, and stick Benny Hill in it.

At that point, why not?

173 - The Conqueror

from *From Genesis to Revelation*, 1969

Several pages ago I wrote about the innate strangeness of hearing a song like 'Build Me a Mountain', a tune that might be succinctly described as "Genesis does hippie rock." That song was a product of the band's experimental phase in the late 1960s, trying on different styles of music like they were in the fitting room of a department store, eyeing themselves in the metaphorical musical mirror, asking themselves the age-old question: "Does this make me look fat?" And while 'Build Me a Mountain' (perhaps mercifully) never got past the demo stage, Genesis still had many more outfits yet to try on.

Thus, 'The Conqueror': a bluesy, folky, Rolling Stones-esque kind of thing. Or, at least, that's how Jonathan King envisioned it. Here's *From Genesis to Revelation* drummer John Silver with more:

> **John:** *I can remember during one of the recordings, on 'The Conqueror', Jonathan King told me, "Play like (Rolling Stones drummer) Charlie Watts." He wanted it to sound like 'Get Off My Cloud', so I duly did, because if Jonathan said jump or stand backwards or stand on your head, you did it. This was the nature of the relationship: he was completely omniscient in a truly decent way.* [1]

OK, so the last part of that quote didn't age very well given what we now know about Jonathan King's other interests, but that's another discussion entirely. The point is, at this early point of the band's career, they were by their own admission just trying to write hits. That was the be all and end all. That's why they gravitated toward Jonathan King in the first place: besides also being a Charterhouse alumnus, he was a guy who had a hit! Surely he could get us one too, right? And when you're a bunch of teenagers with frankly no idea what you're doing, and your only real goal is to get on Top of the Pops, it seems like a really good idea to just cast as wide a net as possible. Not so much a case of throwing enough darts at a dartboard to hit the bullseye, but throwing darts wildly at a bunch of *different* dartboards with the thought that you'll be multiplying your odds.

That is, of course, really bad maths and also not how the industry works, but gosh dangit, it made sense at the time! But 'The Conqueror' reveals the shortcomings of that philosophy pretty well. When you're so focused on trying to act like musical chameleons, you're almost certainly not making anything you're truly passionate about. And when you're not passionate about the music you're making, that comes through with the end product. 'The Conqueror' doesn't *sound* like a Genesis song because it's so busy *feeling* like a Genesis business decision.

That may be a cynical view of the effort on display with this tune, but if not for Ant wailing on the electric guitar at the end, this song would sound like it came straight out of the soundtrack of Christopher Guest's mockumentary, A Mighty Wind. Add a few vocal harmonies and it would fit right in. As it turns out, though, I actually love that soundtrack. In fact I think I'd much rather hear "'The Conqueror' by The Folksmen" than "'The Conqueror' by Genesis." I mean, the whole thing is built around a five note bass riff that repeats throughout, and truth be told there's not a lot else that happens in the song. But hey, that's folk music! It's a pretty good riff, and the vocals aren't bad (but they're nothing to write home about, either). It's a really straightforward, easily digestible tune that mostly works for what it is. And that's OK! It just...doesn't belong in this *particular* band's catalogue.

172 - Get 'Em Out by Friday

from *Foxtrot*, 1972

Opening with a really good interplay between Steve and Tony, 'Get 'Em Out By Friday' is a song that has fifteen minutes of good ideas, but a runtime of only eight and a half instead. If you think that sounds like a recipe for disaster, well, I'm personally inclined to agree with you. While it seems that the majority of Genesis fans - or at least fans of the era of the band that included Peter Gabriel - think this song is one of their finest efforts, there is also a significant group of fans who find 'Get 'Em Out By Friday' to be a difficult, largely unenjoyable listen. I fall somewhere between these two camps, but admittedly far closer to the latter group than, say, Tony Banks.

> **Tony:** *The second best song...on this album for me.* [3]

Still, I think the song has some strong merits, and I think the very things that drive me away from the song personally are what make it such a landmark of progressive music. Fifteen minutes of good ideas crammed into eight and a half may be a cacophonic mess to my ears, but it's also in itself a bold choice worthy of praise. 'Get 'Em Out By Friday' is a musical casserole that's been stuffed to the point of bursting, and I think that's the artistic vision that the band was going for - Peter more so than anyone else. How did this come about?

Well, during this period of the band's history, the typical modus operandi for the band's group writing sessions was (loosely) as follows:

1. Get together in the rehearsal room and start trading licks, riffs, melodies, chords, rhythms, and other ideas to see what everyone else could make of them.
2. Splice together the various bits and pieces into some kind of coherent combination of parts that could serve as a section of a song.
3. Develop new complementary bits and pieces to go with what's already completed.
4. Stitch all the various different sections of music together into one complete song.
5. Refine and rehearse the song, filling out the arrangement and getting it into a recordable state.
6. OK Peter, time to lay down your vocal track.
7. Wait, you wrote a novel?
8. Uh oh.

See, Genesis would often write the backing instrumentation before any lyrics or vocal melodies were created. The whole five piece (yes, Peter too, usually playing flute or percussion) would be working together, writing, improvising, and even recording as they went. So you'd get a more or less completed piece of songwriting, except with no vocal bits on it whatsoever - just a sense of where those parts would eventually be needed.

> **Phil:** *We'd go, "You go write a lyric for that, and you go write a lyric for that."* [3]

The benefit of this approach is that the band was able to develop their songs freely from a purely musical point of view. They could hone the songs to a point where they weren't reliant on a slick, melodic vocal hook to make the piece work; the music itself was compelling enough.

But, as outlined above, the big pitfall with that approach is that when the band came up with something that sounded great without vocals, their "completed arrangement" didn't leave room for any. Peter, perhaps quite rightly, didn't fancy spending nearly nine minutes off stage or dancing around with a tambourine, and would insist on adding in vocals. As a result. the vocals would come in only at the very end, often with unpredictable results. In a couple significant instances throughout the band's catalogue, this process worked in their favour (and I'll be covering those moments later on in this book), with extremely strong vocal additions that turned "great" songs into "incredible" ones.

However, with 'Get 'Em Out By Friday' the opposite effect occurred. The backing instrumentation on this track is really intricate, and almost demands a close listen to really appreciate. You've got Tony with his fast-paced semi-melodic chord playing in some places, and in others he's interweaving countermelodies over Steve's guitar. Steve for his part has a short guitar solo that really rends the air, in addition to all his other blended contributions. Mike's playing against all of that with a bass riff that doesn't sound like it should work with the rest, but it does, which only adds to the feeling of complexity. And of course there's Phil doing some really snazzy things on drums throughout. Add to this whole shebang the gentler sections, featuring some truly lovely flute courtesy of Peter, and it's fascinating how it all somehow flows together. As an instrumental it's arguably one of the best pieces they've ever done.

But it's not an instrumental, now is it? The vocal Pete laid on top almost subverts all the effort everyone put into the thing, strictly musically speaking. I think he heard all these layers of sound, already so dense they demanded a listener's full attention, and decided for his part to amplify it even further with his vocals. He wrote a really interesting (and pretty amusing, if I'm honest) lyric about overcrowding and the need to shrink people through genetic engineering to have enough room to hold them all. And then delivered that lyric in the most frantic way possible. As a result, *the song itself* feels as overcrowded as the apartment blocks being described. I don't think this is any accident, but rather a very clever artistic idea from Peter, and it's very effective in that artistry.

> **Mike:** *Great lyric, nice idea. An example of where...we had too much "stuff" on the song. I mean, the track was great without any vocals. It sounded good, but in fact when the vocals came on - it was a very clever lyric and a great performance from Peter - it's almost too much in there...This song suffered a bit from just too many good ideas in it.* [3]

> **Phil:** *Because there was nothing to sing at the time, Peter wouldn't necessarily sing [in rehearsals]...so we'd get these great things that actually sounded like instrumental things, and he'd go away and come back with a lyric. And it would be so crowded, so dense. The idea was great...but we did find that the downside to the way we were writing...meant that we would write these things and come back a little busy. A little dense. By which time it was too late.* [3]

I've heard it said that the best art often requires sacrifice, and unfortunately in this case the artistic vision of 'Get 'Em Out By Friday' had to sacrifice the quality of the music to get there. I really just want to listen to the truly impressive stuff the five bandmates are doing behind the vocals, but the vocals make that extremely difficult, because they're just so omnipresent. I think this track is a very important one for the band, a milestone of their growth into true behemoths of the genre. And I think it represents a true artistic triumph, as well. However, as I don't care at all for its overly busy vocals, and as that ultimately became the entire point of the song, it doesn't do a lot for me on a personal level.

171 - In the Wilderness

from *From Genesis to Revelation*, 1969

Ah, strings. The inclusion of string arrangements on *From Genesis to Revelation* was a big point of contention for the band, and no song from the album more exemplifies that argument than 'In the Wilderness'. The addition of the strings weren't necessarily a surprise to the band; they knew Jonathan King was going to add them, they just didn't know how prevalent they would be.

> **Mike:** *Jonathan King had gone away to put some strings on [the] album. We were thinking...we're going to sound great - and when we heard it, it was like, "Oh gawd."* [1]

> **Tony:** *I think a song like 'In the Wilderness' sounded better without the strings, but it wasn't a big thing for me.* [1]

> **Ant:** *Ah, the strings...I was the one who really blew my top about it. To this day, I still don't understand how the others could be so much more mature and sensible about it...I felt really angry because...in those days you couldn't get back to a previous version, it was too late...And I completely freaked out ... I can only quote all my other friends saying, "He's butchered it." So that I can't really forgive him for...* [1]

I've got to say, while the band - and Ant in particular - really hated the way things turned out, I think the arrangement actually works pretty well here. Sure, the strings can overpower the rest of the music at times, so from a balancing perspective I can easily understand the hate, but I'll be darned if they don't add something positive to the texture of the piece. Heck, that's why they're there!

> **Jonathan King:** *I wanted to give them a slightly more progressive, but also professional, feel with a string section adding little bridges between the numbers, but sometimes playing on top of the numbers as well. I think they work terribly well, actually. It gives the songs a sweetness that wasn't there in the original thing and covers up some of the slight amateurishness of the basic tracks.* [1]

Of course it's a perfectly functional song without the extra baggage as well. More so, if you ask the guys actually in the band. Thus, when *Genesis Archive 1967-75* was released, in an act of quiet protest similar to the one they did with the release of 'Image Blown Out' on that same compilation, the very first song included on side 4 was a stringless, rough mix of the tune. It's as though they're saying, "Here. This is the *proper* way to listen to this song." I respect that, though after hearing it in that form, without the strings, I can't help but think, "Yeah, this is OK, but not quite as good as the album version." Oh well!

Strings aside, I actually like the chorus of this one. That's a change from some other songs of this era, where I've felt that the verses are strong (or at least competent), but the choruses are a bit more problematic. Here the verses are decent, and the chorus is pretty good. Interestingly, the lower harmony on those choruses isn't sung by Tony, or Ant, or even anyone in the band. It's a guy named David Thomas (no, not the Dave Thomas of Wendy's fame), a good friend of Tony's who provided him a place to live when he moved to London.

170 - Say It's Alright Joe

from ...And Then There Were Three..., 1978

Obvious from almost the very first sounds you hear, this is the band's attempt at a sort of "Play it, Sam," *Casablanca* vibe. Three notes in and you see it all: the dimly lit bar...the hopeless sap drowning his sorrows...the bartender polishing a glass while wondering whether to cut him off...the sympathetic piano player, playing his song one more time, hoping for an extra dollar in the jar. It's a masterful creation of atmosphere, and the band wisely leaned into it as much as they could. When they performed the song live, Phil would don a hat and a trenchcoat and lean drunkenly, glass in hand, against Tony's keyboard deck. Those keyboards would be adorned with a single, heavy-shaded lamp, and the rest of the lights in the venue would be shut off.

People often think that the theatrics of Genesis' live performances disappeared after Peter Gabriel's departure, but seeing 'Say It's Alright Joe' performed in concert disabuses one of that notion pretty quickly. It's maybe a little grim given what we know about his later struggles with alcoholism, but Phil really goes all in on this role. He plays up the part so much, in fact, that his drunken pauses and deliberate deliveries manage to add three whole minutes to the song's runtime. It's really a sight to behold.

Stripped of that live aspect, however, the song is forced to rely on its inherent musical merits alone. In those terms, I'd describe the song as a kind of ebb and flow. It's got the aforementioned "dimly lit bar" music, of course, but that's spelled intermittently with a pair of really upbeat sections where the keyboards truly come alive. Those sections are among the strongest bits on the entire album for me, vivid and exciting, but they only comprise 26% of the track (68 seconds out of the 261 second total runtime). Now, maybe those sections don't work as well without the rest of the song being what it is, but I'm far more interested in what's happening there than in the other 74% of the song.

Rutherford wrote this one on his own, and wasn't even confident about it. Again, it's easy to see why: rehearsing something that's intentionally lethargic in order to mirror someone wallowing in depression? Sounds like an absolute *blast*, right?

> **Mike:** *I wasn't very excited about it when we started and thought it wasn't going to work, but it came to life in the mixing stages.* [17]

Which also makes sense. In the mixing stages you get to play around with what's already there, so even something slow and plodding gives you ample things to do. Plus you get to work with those lively parts and make sure everything is well integrated. That's got to be much more interesting than playing slow chords while anxiously waiting for Phil to finish a line. So I say good on the band for sticking it out with this one. It was worth it in the end.

That said, while I think the attempt at creating a certain kind of atmosphere with the song was resoundingly successful, the song itself - with the exception of those two ventures into up-tempo bits - is just, well, a little bit boring. Not bad by any means, but not particularly engaging either. But I suppose that's to be expected. After all, it's not me for whom Joe's playing, is it?

169 - One Day

from *From Genesis to Revelation*, 1969

If 'In Limbo' is Exhibit A for Genesis benefiting from horn sections early in their careers, then 'One Day' is the far more effective Exhibit B. But before we get down to brass tacks (see what I did there?), let's back up a minute and talk about that intro. Is there anything more abundantly pleasant than pastoral guitar spelled by gentle violins? One imagines that this was really just Ant and Mike strumming by themselves in the studio, unaware of that blissful top line that would ice the cake in post-production. As will become increasingly clear through this book, I think early Genesis was at their best when pursuing the gentler path, and that makes this intro one of the most enjoyable things on the debut album in my book.

But all good things must come to an end; in this case, after a mere twenty-four seconds. Tony jumps in with some charming piano work, and one might be fooled into believing the good will of the opening section is going to continue indefinitely, but as soon as the rest of the band kicks in it all goes down the drain. See, the verses of 'One Day' are arranged with backing tracks that are every bit as lovely as the song's opening salvo. It's just that the boys regrettably forgot to put any kind of melody on top, and even the added strings can't save it. The instant Peter comes in with his first line, the entire atmosphere dissipates and transforms the effort into accidental comedy. Really, the verses might as well just be William Shatner doing his signature spoken word; at least then you'd know the effect was intentional.

That's the environment into which this horn arrangement is thrust: a stellar introduction spoiled by a throwaway first verse. In a "naked" version of the track like Genesis originally envisioned, the chorus would arrive heralded only by some heavier guitar chords, which then continue to form the backbone of the refrain. Not strong enough to keep a listener engaged at this point, if you ask me. So instead we have these trumpets jumping in, building excitement before the chorus with a fanfare, and flaring out repeatedly, triumphantly over the chorus itself. I can't really overstate how much water this addition to the song carries. The lyrics of "One day I'll capture you..." speak of winning a woman, but they're not really believable in the original context. But now add some pealing horns blasting out victory, and I buy every line of it.

The end result is a fairly effective chorus, again, almost exclusively because the production crew had the good musical sense to slap horns on the track. I mean, the backing vocals that the band thought might give the section enough pizzazz are just underqualified singers going "ahhhhh" on a mostly static note, when you boil it down. Mike and drummer John Silver are laying down a very simple beat on the rhythm end. The vocal melody is still lacking any real substance. But the horns? They're chucking out lines of countermelody like there's no tomorrow. They lift the entire effort.

> **Tony:** 'One Day' is another song which was really nice when we used to play it, but didn't sound good on the album. There were nice things on it, but not exceptional. [10]

'One Day' marks the mid-point of quality on *From Genesis to Revelation* for me. It's a pretty good compromise between the band's innate but immature songwriting talents, and the more trained ears of industry veterans adding bits and pieces to strengthen the songs. I know the band didn't care for the arrangements added to their music, and I know things like strings and horns can be controversial in general, but for me, on this song, they simply work.

168 - In the Rapids

from *The Lamb Lies Down on Broadway*, 1974

By the time you come to 'In the Rapids' on a full album listen of *The Lamb Lies Down on Broadway*, you've already heard nearly eighty-eight minutes of music. You've been accompanying Rael (and, to a lesser extent, his brother John) on a grand, surreal adventure, and you're curious how it's all going to end. Along the way you've met snake women, slippermen, Death himself, and many other strange beings. It's been an endless nightmare dreamscape moving the story's protagonist and, by extension, you as a listener onward toward some kind of epic conclusion that you believe will probably make sense of it all. 'The Light Dies Down on Broadway' spoke of an exit to all the madness, and that felt like it might have been a pretty good conclusion to the story had Rael but gone through the window and found some kind of catharsis afterward, but of course the album just kept on chugging along from there. What gives?

As it turns out, 'The Light Dies Down on Broadway' *was* a kind of conclusion, but not in the way you as a listener would expect. It's a conclusion in that it ends the frantic movement from one scene to another and transitions the story finally into something much more personal and emotional. I'll have more to say about that song later in this book, but I bring it up here because 'In the Rapids' is meant to be the emotional conclusion to the album. It takes what 'The Light Dies Down' starts and tries to drive home that Rael has been developing and growing as a character and person throughout the narrative, and puts all that on display in one brave, selfless act.

That's a lot of burden to place on a song that runs only a couple minutes long. You need the music to really deliver on the emotional stakes here, letting the listener truly feel the weight of what's happening and, more importantly, be satisfied by that delivery. Again, this is the climactic moment of the entire story of *The Lamb Lies Down on Broadway*. One could argue that the entire album hinges on this two minutes and twenty-three seconds. A grand finish, worthy of the journey. Instead?

> **Tony:** *I never think the fourth side [of the album] really delivers, and if you are making a double album, you want the ending to be really strong. I felt that the album petered out.* [1]

Instead you get a lethargic, sombre piece that only begins to swell into something appropriately grand at the very end, at which point it's already over. It sounds like the introductory section to a much longer piece, but instead it's here trying not only to stand on its own, but also to bear the weight of the entire double album that precedes it. It's an impossible task.

That's not to say it's a song without any merit, mind you. The whole thing is one big crescendo (an effect used a few times over the course of *The Lamb*), which is a really strong effect. The mood it does create, while inappropriate for an album's climax, is still effective in itself. Lyrically, Rael is swimming through a rushing river trying to rescue his brother. As the song builds, Rael gets closer and closer to the rescue, and you can feel his growing urgency. It really works on that level, and I do honestly like the song in general, more or less. It's just that this feels like a track that would musically be better suited to the middle of the album rather than the end. There's no sense of resolution at all, whether musically or lyrically. Good musicianship at work, to be sure - Steve in particular provides quite a lot of texture throughout the piece, and Phil's drumming is impeccable - but it feels like such an overall let-down that I can't help but be disappointed anyway.

167 - The Waiting Room

from *The Lamb Lies Down on Broadway*, 1974

Arguably, 'Who Dunnit?' is Genesis at their most experimental, and of course that was a (somewhat intentional) disaster, but this is a band that has always loved trying to do new things and see what happens. No song of the Gabriel period more exemplifies this trait than 'The Waiting Room'. The song, though not the first track on the second vinyl of the double album, nevertheless marks the turning point of *The Lamb*, beginning its dive into darker, weirder fare.

For the first three minutes of the 5+ minute piece, there's not even any "music" in the expected sense of the term. Instead it's a nightmarish soundscape; very avant-garde and strange. There are chimes, distortions, things shattering, whale calls? The world is shifting into something very sinister. And yet, despite all this, it's not quite random. There's still an underlying sense of flow that is in itself something quite...well, musical.

And then, of course, the music that's been lurking under the surface the whole time bursts out and proves that much more effective for having been withheld up until that point. Some of the strange, distorted playing is still present, but now that it's supported by a proper beat and a key signature and all the other trappings of music, it all makes a heck of a lot more sense.

> **Tony:** *Then there was 'The Waiting Room' which was called 'Evil Jam'. We just sat there and tried to frighten ourselves! Some of the early versions of that were just great before we started to record it and began to think about it too much. The first time we ever did it and I went into that sort of melody, it sounded great because it came out of nowhere and suddenly there was this incredible thing going on. By the time we put it down it had all been thought about and it didn't sound half as good.* [6]
>
> **Phil:** *The highlight of that album to me...I remember when we first played the song, it was pissing with rain outside. We were doing this basic bad to good soundscaping and as Tony started to play some chords the sun came out, there was a rainbow, and the rain stopped. It sounds very cosmic, but it actually did happen.* [1]

As a personal anecdote: My first exposure to *The Lamb* as a larger work (I was familiar already with both the title track and 'Carpet Crawlers') was from a friend who insisted that if I was getting into Genesis, I'd love this album. She was picking me up and we were driving to the nearby Taco Bell, and she had just put in the back half of *The Lamb* before getting me, so I was treated to the last thirty seconds or so of 'Lilywhite Lilith' as she extolled the virtues of this grand piece of art. So of course, the first impression I had of the album as a whole was 'The Waiting Room', and I thought "What on earth am I even listening to?" We arrived at our destination before the "nightmare" section of the song ended, so I never even knew there was more to it. Unfortunately I wrote off the album for a long time because of that experience. It took years before I went back and actually listened to *The Lamb* properly, from the beginning, and with that context said, "Oh, I get it now." I made sure to go back and tell this friend, who I'd by then fallen out of touch with, that she was 100% right, even if she chose the worst possible entry point for me that day!

166 - Where the Sour Turns to Sweet

from *From Genesis to Revelation*, 1969

As with most of the other tracks on the band's debut album, 'Where the Sour Turns to Sweet' is a story of a really good section of music spelled by something a bit less stellar. This time around it's the chorus that dwells in the realm of mediocrity. I've alluded more than once so far to the presence of horns on this album, and in both previous cases I've felt them to be very strong additions to their respective tracks. More than that, I've felt that those brass arrangements elevated their companion songs well above what might otherwise be considered their "rightful" stations.

Sadly, this will not be three-for-three. Between the searing strings and blaring horns competing over one another on the chorus, it's darned near impossible to hear anything the actual band is doing. They're totally drowned out under a mountain of excess. These arrangements are supposed to highlight and enhance the track, but instead it feels like Jonathan King and company wanted to replace it altogether. It's too daggone much, is what I'm saying.

> **Tony:** *Peter Gabriel and I wrote this song...It first had a different chorus, which wasn't as good as the one we ended up with. We decided in the end to make a chorus out of the introduction, which made it a much better piece of music.* [18]

If this is the better chorus, I confess to some morbid curiosity about what the initial one was. Because once you sift through the noise of the extra stuff tossed on top of the mix, you come to a chorus melody that I frankly find rather lacking. It's the sort of callout you'd expect to hear in a song about dancing - "Come and join us now!" might as well be "Come on baby, let's do the twist," except of course there is no twist and nobody could dance to this. It's not an intrinsically *bad* chorus, I guess, but it doesn't really work in the song. Which means the intro and outro also don't really work, since they're the same lines done over simple piano and snaps, like Genesis was performing at a jazz poetry club.

> **Tony:** *This was the fourth piece of music we ever wrote together. In those days, it used to be very much me playing along on the piano with Pete singing along on top. Pete would get his hands on the piano whenever he could. When I hear this song, it takes me right back to those early days with Anthony Phillips and everybody else. We were very naïve back then. We'd all come from a very sheltered background and didn't know much about anything, really. So, what we came up with is a rather sweet kind of piece, with a strong chorus. It probably hinted at what we might do later on. We were definitely thinking in different terms during those early days.* [18]

So if all of the above is true, why do I think this is one of the better songs on the album? Simply put, the verses are gorgeous. More so than almost anywhere else on *From Genesis to Revelation*, in the verses of 'Where the Sour Turns to Sweet' everything just works. It's an outstanding melody. The backing vocals are still just "aaaahs," but here they don't pop out of the texture, instead working brilliantly at *creating* the texture themselves. The rhythm guitar is spot on. Even the strings, overbearing on the chorus, help make the verses something really beautiful. It's some of the best stuff on the album; just, you know, surrounded by all the mediocre bits typical of the rest of the *FGTR* package. For that though, it's always worth a listen in my book.

165 - The Day the Light Went Out

B-side of 'Many Too Many', 1978

Well this might just be the most depressing lyric the band ever penned, yeah? The song tells of a supernatural, sentient darkness that descends on a town, devouring its people even as they riot and destroy themselves. Then, when the dark entity is finally satiated and leaves the town to its few remaining survivors, a second darkness shows up to repeat the process and likely eradicate the rest.

So, you know, that's fun.

The musical feel of the piece is very much in line with the other stuff that made it onto *And Then There Were Three*. It's clearly of that era; the instrumentation, the arrangement, the reverb effect on the vocals... you could swap this song in for virtually any track on that 1978 album and it would be just as cohesive, track order considerations aside. So why this one get relegated to B-side status instead of making the album proper?

Well, the simple answer is "the band didn't like it quite as much," but that's no fun. Instead I'd like to point out what I consider to be the differentiating factor for this song: its energy. Now don't get me wrong here. I'm not saying *And Then There Were Three* is a lethargic album. There's plenty of tempo and oomph to be found there. But 'The Day the Light Went Out' feels like it's in another class entirely. It's got a much more urgent, pressing feel to it than really anything else the band put out that year.

That drive works well for the song, but it's also part of its downfall. Earlier in this book I criticised a pair of classic Gabriel-era tunes ('Get 'Em Out by Friday' and 'The Battle of Epping Forest', to be specific) for their avalanche of lyrics, and talked about how that "word density," if I might coin the term, negatively impacted the musical quality of those songs for me. Along the way I documented quotes from the band that indicated their general agreement with my take. Phil in particular seemed pretty annoyed by the lack of space in those tracks. And so one would imagine that a Genesis with Phil in the lead vocal role would be more wary of that sort of situation.

And yet, maths never lies:

- 'Get 'Em Out by Friday' contains 418 words over a period of 8 minutes and 36 seconds, for an average word density of **0.8 words per second**.
- 'The Battle of Epping Forest' contains 779 words over a period of 11 minutes and 44 seconds, for an average word density of **1.1 words per second**.
- 'The Day the Light Went Out' contains 276 words over a period of 3 minutes and 14 seconds, for an average word density of **1.4 words per second**.

This one is the wordiest of the whole bunch! Now, do I think the shorter runtime helps its case a bit? Sure, if only because it never runs out of energy in the delivery, and that means listening to it is like a jolt of lightning to your bones. I can get behind that. But this is still a striking revelation, the numbers helping me put into words what bothers me about this track. It's simply too much. Add in the fact that I don't care much at all for the falsetto bits ("Now I can rest here..."), and in the end I find that this song is just a bit of a mixed bag for me. I think I could take it or leave it, off the album or altogether.

164 - Hey!

Demo, 1968

Let me get something out of the way up front. This song was left off *From Genesis to Revelation* for a reason, and it's not just that it didn't mesh with the Biblical theme of the album. Clearly this is a weaker effort in terms of pure songwriting than what the band was doing even at the time. I say songwriting because, as a demo, it's not entirely fair to judge the track purely on sound quality. But you can generally tell from a demo whether there's the core of a good song in there or not, and let me tell you: 'Hey!' does not have that core.

That's not to say there's nothing going for it, mind you. I mean, after that opening paragraph you might rightly be wondering why in the world would I rank 'Hey!' above the last 25-30 songs in the discography if I'm sitting here telling you it's not a great piece of music. And I'd say that for starters, it *is* at least listenable, which raises it above the absolute worst the band has on record. The songwriting isn't really special, but Tony's piano work is nice, and lines up reasonably well with Ant's guitar.

Moreover, it's a song with an affable, cheery tone about it. The verse and instrumental groove is pleasant, so it's happy feelings all around. Strip the vocals out and I can think of many, many worse ways to spend two and a half minutes. So no, I wouldn't say 'Hey!' is a case of a good song lurking beneath the surface of a bad one, but I wouldn't say it's a total lost cause, either. Relatively inoffensive, but with no substance that would ever make you want to come back for more.

But then. Oh, but then. Then that title line comes in, and the whole colour changes.

No less than **eighteen times** over the course of the song will some combination of Tony and/or Ant jump in and just call out "Hey!" It rips you right out of the pleasant drifting of the tune, and I swear I start to chuckle every. single. Time.

Remember, these were some teenagers trying their darndest to write a hit pop song. They were looking for that undeniable hook, that catchy slice of pepperoni pizzazz that would elevate the song (and therefore the band themselves) to the heights of stardom. Somewhere along the line, one of them must've come up with the idea and presented it to the rest of the band: "Um, you know, what if the hook was just that we keep shouting 'Hey!' over and over?" And at some point the rest of the band must've said "Okay, yeah, let's give it a shot!" Maybe deep down they always knew this wasn't their ticket to fame, but at some point or another they were hoping they'd struck musical gold with this. It makes the entire affair unintentionally hilarious. You can even hear Tony's voice break on one of the shouts, bless his soul.

Near the end, the song breaks down and Mike starts playing a bass solo. You start to think, "Oh man, this is cool, a little musicianship at last!" Literally four seconds later, the bass solo abruptly gets cut off by Ant and Tony: "HEY!" This is usually when my chuckles become full-blown guffaws. I can't handle it anymore. It's too dang funny. The song finally begins to fade out, and you hear Peter sing "You want to apologise" as the song dissipates. But turn that volume up, friends, because there's one more sound at the very end of the track, just before that sweet fade to black: "HEY!"

Judged on song quality alone, this is one of the absolute worst efforts the band put forth. But as entertainment? Hey, it's pure gold.

163 - Open Door

B-side of 'Duchess', 1980

I've listened to an awful lot of Genesis music. I've heard every song in this book (and therefore every song in the band's official discography) many times over. That probably comes as no surprise, given that you're reading a book I wrote about them all. I bring it up not to brag - and honestly, anyone who *would* brag about listening to the same band over and over for a significant portion of their life is probably not anywhere near as cool as he thinks he is - but to make a point about the song 'Open Door'.

I don't know how this song goes. Again, it's not for lack of listening. I get that it's a relatively forgotten B-side in the band's catalogue, but that doesn't mean I haven't heard it repeatedly. I just listened to it again right before I started writing all this out. That was just a few minutes ago, mind you. Then I ate some lunch, sat back down, and realised I've forgotten how it goes again. It's like the "open door" from the song's title is referring to my ears, because this song goes into one and straight out the other. Why is that?

I think it's because - and let me listen to the song again right now so I can claim to have some clue what I'm talking about - I think it's because 'Open Door' doesn't really have any melody. And even as I read that sentence back, I think it sounds really unfair. "What are you talking about, man? Phil's singing notes! In a sequence! What more could you ask for?!" But while I acknowledge the truth of what my internal devil's advocate is arguing, the melody in 'Open Door' is totally ethereal to me. It's this wispy, insubstantial thing that colours the atmosphere and then disappears without a trace. In my case, clearly, leaving no memory of its passing.

That's not all bad, though. It's that very hazy nature of the thing that makes the song what it is. This thing is four minutes of gentle, easy listening. It's melancholy mood music with just enough of a bright tinge to it that it doesn't leave you down in the dumps. It's very pretty, too. I may not be able to recall any of the melody, but I do know that the whole thing feels melod*ic* as it goes. I remember that there's some guitar strumming that could easily veer into "struggling artist in a coffee shop" territory but employs enough tasteful restraint to avoid that fate. I remember that there are keyboards that provide a glimmer, reflecting some light off the piece without ever shining too brightly. These are fond memories, if still a little vague.

Mostly though, I remember one thing whenever I strain my mind to summon up the sounds of 'Open Door'. I remember that there are a couple moments in the track where the sound gets bigger, with Tony finally kicking in with a sizable chord. And I remember that each time that happens, I suddenly think "Gee, this reminds me quite a bit of 'Alone Tonight'."

See, on *Duke* the band wanted to get back to group songwriting, so each band member only got two solo songs apiece (when you exclude Tony's 'Guide Vocal' as being part of the suite of group-written songs). Mike's two were 'Man of Our Times' and 'Alone Tonight', which meant his third piece, 'Open Door', had to settle for being a B-side. But for my money, 'Open Door' could pass for an early prototype of 'Alone Tonight'. It feels as though Rutherford had a musical concept he wanted to explore, and these were the two versions he came up with. Listen to the subdued, voice-over-guitar verses. The big chords announcing the chorus. It's the same basic formula in two different iterations. But I think 'Alone Tonight' does it better, and maybe that's why this song is a blank spot in my brain. It's trying to fill an 'Alone Tonight' sized hole that's already been filled.

162 - Another Record

from *Abacab*, 1981

I've got two words for you: synthesized harmonica. If that phrase gets your blood pumping, then you might be in for a real treat with 'Another Record'. If instead it gets your blood boiling, then you might want to literally put on another record, because you'll find little joy here. Now while I can't say music has ever made my blood boil, I do find myself generally siding with the "no" camp on this one. When I first heard this song and that bit of instrumentation, all I could think of was "Really? That's what you're going with?"

It's made especially disappointing when you hear the track from the beginning, because 'Another Record' opens with a forty-two second intro that is really, really good. It's got a bass line straight out of the 90s alternative scene, though of course this was 1981. Keyboards chords that fade in and out like the swelling tide. A lead guitar line that promises emotion to come. Whatever song that section might develop into, that's the song I want to hear. Easy contender for the strongest track on *Abacab*, that one would be.

Instead the drums come in and we're treated to what might as well be...ahem...another record entirely. The bass and keyboard double up their lines, Phil sings a half-hearted melody under what sounds like a heavy reverb effect, and though the drums are lively, I can only feel let down. It's like a bait and switch of the worst kind.

There are flashes of positives again. The chord sequence going into the line "Put another record on" is very strong. The drums switch there to a driving beat with lots of space, Tony dances over top with a suspense-driven keyboard line, and there's hope once more that the track can be salvaged into something mostly great. My hopes rise again, and do you know what comes out of the mix to greet me?

Synthesized harmonica. This is one of the absolute worst keyboard sounds I've ever heard, certainly out of Genesis. There's no redeeming quality to it. It sounds just barely enough like a real harmonica that I can tell that's what it's supposed to represent, but it falls so woefully short of that ideal that I wonder who Tony thought he was fooling. If it was used just once it would be once too often, but no: that awful, awful sound becomes a recurrence throughout the rest of the track. I hate it.

The song continues into other bits. And you know what? Despite my deflation at the intro being totally abandoned, when Phil's vocals first came in my initial thought was "Well it's not what I wanted, but I suppose I can roll with this melody." But then? After being subjected to that "harmonica" tone and then getting the melody again over subsequent verses and choruses? I started to realise that the melody was far weaker than I charitably thought it was. And then there's some extra bits, too:- "round and round and round and around - oh!" It does absolutely nothing for me. Although I do want to give a special shout-out to the 'Moribund the Burgermeister' style octave-under vocals Phil does to close the song. That's a weird choice but an interesting one, and I think it almost works.

Mainly though, I might like that part because it signals the beginning of the end of the song. 'Another Record' is a song that starts off absolutely stellar, and then gets noticeably worse every 8 bars until it finally ends. And this is the way Genesis decided to close the *Abacab* album.

I'm not mad. I'm just disappointed.

161 - Silent Sun

from *From Genesis to Revelation*, 1969

After the band had made initial contact with Jonathan King while still in Charterhouse school, they sent a batch of demos over to him to try to get started with this whole "music" thing. Luckily, King enjoyed the demos and decided he wanted to work with the band, but none of those demos were going to be hit singles, and they weren't quite strong enough to warrant investing in a full album, so the boys were encouraged to keep working at it. They sent over a second, more adventurous batch of songs, but King didn't care for them and began to lose interest in the Genesis project altogether.

Enter 'Silent Sun' ('*The* Silent Sun' in its single release), a song specifically crafted to tickle King's fancy. His favourite band of the time was the Bee Gees, whose reputation in the modern era is built almost entirely around the Saturday Night Fever soundtrack and the era of the disco craze. That's not quite fair to the Bee Gees, who were actually a very successful pop group well before that, scoring six UK top ten singles - including a pair of 1 hits - in the late 60s alone. '(The) Silent Sun' is essentially Genesis saying "Well, we think we can do that, too." and trying to get a record deal.

> **Peter:** *It was a reaction to Jonathan's disappointment in the second bout of demos - which we thought were wonderful and very exciting - that we then deliberately tried to write a more poppy song...I was trying to imitate Robin Gibb...which was Jonathan's favourite voice at the time. We'd figured that if I could steer things a little bit in that direction we might have a chance of getting back in the studio.* [1]

> **Ant:** *When Jonathan King tried to get us to start writing these very simple things, I wasn't too keen. I didn't really like 'Silent Sun' very much, but Mike and Tony were much more sensible and they realised that this was the way to go.* [1]

What immediately pops into mind when I hear this song is "Man, you can tell why they thought this was going to be their big hit. And you can also tell why it wasn't." It's pleasant enough, and has the right pop sensibilities for the time period to be successful, but there's also nothing about it that particularly stands out. The melody is fine. The backing musicianship is fine. The strings are fine. It lasts for a mere inoffensive two minutes and change. Nothing about this track is bad, but nothing about it is particularly impressive, either. By the time it might start to make a real impression, it's already over. Accordingly, the song never went anywhere on the charts, and after the commercial flops of both its follow-up single 'A Winter's Tale' and the debut album *From Genesis to Revelation* itself, the band mercifully moved on in other, more interesting directions.

> **Tony:** *I think 'Silent Sun' could have been quite a big hit if other factors had been right, but it didn't work out that way. And probably from our point of view it was a great thing the single wasn't a hit because if it had been we would have been very much stuck in a rut as a Bee Gees copy band.* [1]

I find it hard to imagine a baroque pop, Bee Gees lite Genesis having any kind of staying power, and who knows what might've happened to the guys if and when that all fell apart. What a colossal waste of talent that'd have been. Thank goodness for failure, I guess!

160 - Your Own Special Way

from *Wind & Wuthering*, 1976

Wind and Wuthering is, in the band's opinion, one of Genesis' least immediate albums. Full of complex, longer songs - and with three instrumental tracks to boot - it's an album that was never destined to be much of a commercial hit. And that's something that the band was pretty much OK with, content at this point to do their own thing and let the pop scene pass them by. But you wouldn't necessarily know it from 'Your Own Special Way', which did get some radio play in the US, though it never went anywhere on the charts.

> **Mike:** *A nice song...We felt maybe this band could do something that would get play on the radio, apart from the long songs...* [3]

> **Phil:** *It was the most commercial track on the album.* [10]

The song is pretty straightforward in its structure: verse, verse, chorus, verse, chorus, extended bridge/interlude, verse, chorus. Of course, it's not the first "basic structure" song the band ever produced (and would be far from the last), but something about this one compared to its predecessors makes it seem a little less effective. I honestly think it's the vocals. Phil Collins is an immense vocal talent, but I think this track is his weakest performance with the band. And I don't mean "weak" as a synonym for "bad" or "poor," but rather "weak" as in it has no force or strength behind it. Mike has referred to *Wind and Wuthering* as a "feminine" album, and Tony has called it a "romantic" album. Both are euphemistic ways of saying the album lacks raw power, and stuff like this is why - there's just no oomph.

> **Tony:** *It was a song that fell together. It had three of Mike's bits, and we put them together in this particular way. There are three different time signatures. I think it could have been done better in a different way. The first bit's lovely, but I always felt the marriage between verse and chorus wasn't quite right.* [10]

Now, that's not necessarily a bad thing in all cases. Indeed, 'Your Own Special Way' was written to be a tender love song; primal power wouldn't really suit it. This was Mike, after decades of having to keep everything inside, finally trying to let a little vulnerability into his life. He ought to be commended for it!

> **Mike:** *'Your Own Special Way', which was a love song to [my wife] Angie, had a simple, straightforward lyric and was a bit of an emotional breakthrough for me.* [14]

That's part of why I can say that, despite being six minutes of sappy swells and punchless vocals, this track has some positives to it. Steve's guitar goes in and out of the background texture like a wave, and it's a really effective bit of playing for what the song's trying to do. I dig Tony's keyboard arpeggios going into the final verse, too, as an interesting extra touch on what by then is otherwise becoming a boring affair. And the middle interlude, though not amazing by any stretch, is a bit unlike anything else the band's done before or since. It's a really unique sound, and a pleasant one too.

Ultimately, this does end up as my least favourite song on *Wind & Wuthering*, and I can completely respect why a lot of fans can't stand it, even if I classify it as "merely all right."

159 - That's Me

B-side of 'The Silent Sun', 1968

Offering a huge contrast from its A-side, 'That's Me' is a bluesy kind of rock song breaking entirely from the "Bee Gees lite" mode that the band had donned in order to get a record deal in the first place. It's unlike anything else in the band's catalogue, including the entirety of *From Genesis to Revelation*, where it was left off the track listing until later reissues tacked it onto the end as a bonus. And while it's understandable why they'd leave this one by the wayside in favour of songs that better fit the album's "theme," it is something of a shame, because this would've been one of the better tracks on there.

It's no secret that in the early days of the band, they saw themselves as songwriters over and above players. They played their own music in school because it was fun and they liked the attention, but the only reason they continued playing their own stuff after Charterhouse was that they couldn't convince anyone professional to play it instead. Amateurs that they were, the band pretty much unanimously agrees that Anthony Phillips was the best true musician of the bunch in those early days. He was the driving force behind getting them to improve, take the career seriously, and stay committed to their craft. Which is why his departure, more than even Peter's or Steve's later on, nearly split the band apart.

I bring all this up here because 'That's Me' is pretty much the showcase song for "Ant is better than these other schmos," even back in 1968. I can illustrate that notion just by looking at what everyone is doing on the track:

- Mike and Chris Stewart lay down a simple but competent rhythm. It's fine, and works, but it's a rudimentary thing that doesn't showcase any particular skill.
- Pete starts the song off with some reserved vocal work which suits him well, but as soon as he opens things up to a little more intensity, his performance falls apart. On average I don't think the vocals on this song are very good; probably the weakest element of the song, in fact.
- Tony doesn't have much of anything to do until the chorus, where he plunks away at his piano in what you could call a countermelody if you were feeling particularly generous. Certainly a far cry from the musicianship we'd get from him even a year later on the first full album. He also chimes in with some backing vocals: as usual, just simple "aahs" of mild effect.

Again, none of this is *bad* (except perhaps some of Pete's vocal delivery), but neither is it anything like impressive. Just a few teenagers bangin' around, doing the best they can, and it sounds at about that level of quality.

And then there's Ant. His guitar enters subtly with some chords that really start to give the song shape in the latter half of the first verse. He picks it up in the chorus, giving the thing a lot of energy. But then the chorus ends and out of nowhere he starts playing a lead line that's better than it has any right to be for the time. It's Genesis' first guitar solo, and though it be brief, it's a pretty good one. He's able to blend into the texture in the verses but also pop out as needed to play a really solid lead bit - basically the same hallmark that led the band to choose Steve Hackett as his successor. That's unusual talent for someone his age.

So in the end, no, 'That's Me' isn't one of the better songs in the Genesis library. But for the overall groove it provides and getting to hear Ant briefly break out into something really different, it *is* a worthwhile listen.

158 - Resignation

Genesis Plays Jackson, 1970

In early 1970, as the material for *Trespass* was still coming together, Genesis was asked to write the soundtrack to a BBC documentary about a painter named Jackson. His first name is somewhat lost to time, as historical accounts vary, but the idea was for the band to provide around fifteen minutes of music for the network to use throughout the program. Not having any fully completed songs for the project, the band opted to play some works-in-progress for the show. These songs were then assigned to four different Jackson paintings that would be featured, which were called Provocation, Frustration, Manipulation, and Resignation. As the music Genesis was providing consisted merely of untitled, unfinished proto-songs, the pieces essentially just took over the names of their respective paintings. Thus, for the four paintings, four Genesis works: 'Provocation', 'Frustration', 'Manipulation', and 'Resignation'.

This is all after-the-fact nomenclature, however. You see, though the documentary was completed (or at least the parts that involved the band were), the BBC decided to scrap the whole thing. "The Jackson Documentary," or whatever it might have been called, simply never aired. This meant the songs themselves were lost to time along with it, to the chagrin of any collectors of rarities out there. These four pieces would join the likes of fabled early Genesis songs such as 'Wooden Mask' as unobtainable artifacts of a bygone age, and none but the most diehard of fans would have ever even known about them.

But fortune had a different plan in store for these. Decades after the BBC station abandoned their documentary, they did some housecleaning around the office. They had a bunch of old junk: tapes and records and files that nobody would ever miss and they'd never need again, and so off to the garbage bin would go the lot of it. During this exercise, someone - apparently the son of the television producer who worked on the ill-fated documentary - found this so called "Jackson tape" of four never-before-heard Genesis songs among the mess. Realising what a gold mine unreleased Genesis material might be, this fellow had the audacity to try to auction off the tape.

> **Ant:** *What gives [the would-be auction seller] the right to demand money for something that actually isn't his work?! ... I don't believe that if he's come into the possession of unreleased Genesis tapes that they are his. It's unreleased material. I don't see on what level he can maintain that they belong to him. In what way do they belong to him? He didn't pay for the sessions, he didn't own the rights to the music. He simply has something that has come into his possession by coincidence, really, which happens to belong to somebody else. It's a bit like coming across someone's jewellery in the road. It's a finder's keepers attitude, but I don't think he's got a right to auction it.* [19]

Ant wasn't alone in his fury here; the rest of the *Trespass* era line-up caught wind of things as well, and pretty quickly decided they were going to put a stop to things. Tony, Mike, and Peter got the old team back together not to play or write new music, but to swoop in, get an auction pulled down, and ultimately recover the lost tape for themselves. I imagine it played out like an Indiana Jones movie, except with a lot more paperwork and almost no adventure. In any case, the details are a little sketchy. I've seen in some places that they apparently paid the guy for the tape, which sort of undermines the whole justice angle and lets the "bad guy" win, but I've seen elsewhere that they threatened some legal action and recovered it that way. I have no idea which, if either, is true.

Either way, the end result is that Genesis now owned the songs once again, and finally released them officially in the *Genesis 1970-1975* box set on a disc of bonus material, allowing the public to hear the music officially for the first time. But more than just hearing unrefined jams, the "Jackson tapes" are significant in that we can hear the early stages of some of the band's most famous works. Because, as it turns out, these songs went on to do great things:

- 'Provocation' was eventually split in two, with half of it becoming 'Looking for Someone' just a few months later, and the other half becoming 'The Fountain of Salmacis' for use on *Nursery Cryme*.
- 'Manipulation' was, for the most part, a series of bits that would be reorganised and fleshed out to become 'The Musical Box'.
- 'Frustration' used pieces of the then-unreleased demo 'Hair on the Arms and Legs', but was primarily dominated by a very recognisable rendition of *The Lamb Lies Down on Broadway*'s 'Anyway', albeit with different lyrics.

That leaves 'Resignation' as the only song from these sessions that can't be traced to a singular, different, more "complete" Genesis track. Though it's got many smaller bits and pieces that were part of other past and future Genesis tunes (some lost to history), It's the only one of the "Jackson tape" songs that can be said to really stand on its own as a unique entity - and therefore is the sole representative of that set of songs to appear as its own entry in this book (you can find more details about the other proto-pieces in the text for their respective finished songs).

An instrumental piece, 'Resignation' is all about creating a mood consistent with its namesake. Ant's guitar work is the real highlight of the whole thing. It really feels like a featured Ant piece more than anything else, though he doesn't have big lead moments or anything that might "pop" like that. It's just the feel of the thing, you know? Oddly, and perhaps owing to the nature of making a soundtrack for a TV program, the song fades in and out a few times over its three minute duration. You can almost see that camera zooming in for a close-up shot of this painting, panning slowly to the right so the viewer can take in all the details. Or maybe the band's vision for the piece all along was one of coming and going. It's hard to really say, I suppose.

Ant: *Well, I think it was sort of the pre-cursor to some of the longer instrumental pieces.* [19]

My guess? My guess is that Genesis likely didn't have any major vision for this piece whatsoever. There doesn't appear to be a single complete idea on this track, though there are several incomplete ones, and they are all pretty good. It's a song that feels like nothing so much as bits and pieces the band had begun to develop but didn't yet know what to do with, and indeed one need only look at the other songs included in the "Jackson tape" to get a sense that that's exactly what was going on. The general strength of these "idea nuggets" pulls in your attention on this piece, but the total lack of cohesion prevents the song from being much more than an interesting historical footnote, not to mention the way it ends abruptly like someone simply shut off the creative faucet and all we got were a couple leftover drips.

I'd like to think that if Ant stuck around, we'd have seen 'Resignation' blossom into a proper song like the others, given that his stamp is really evident on this one. And then I might, perhaps, be writing instead here about one of the best Genesis songs in the discography. Alas, it wasn't to be.

157 - It's Gonna Get Better

from *Genesis*, 1983

Man, what an atmosphere to open up this track. It's so alien sounding, so strange, so striking. What even is that?

> **Tony:** *I just recorded [on the synthesizer sampler] the beginning of this classical album, which was four cello notes, and I'd written the recording to try and get a good string sample, and pressed it, and it sounded awful. But for some reason I pressed four notes at the same time and these incredible interweaving harmonies all suddenly came out, and I thought "This is brilliant! Truly fantastic! I'm doing nothing and it's sounding wonderful!" And so that sort of made me think, and became quite a big feature within Genesis from then on really, using those kinds of ideas.* [3]

Between synth-sampled strings competing over one another's notes, a really compelling bass line, and the haunted keyboard lines coming through, the song conjures up for me images of walking through a foggy back alley and not knowing what's lurking around the corner. It's 2 AM, I'm downtown, the streetlamps are flickering, a dog is barking somewhere in the distance, and I have no idea how safe I really am. It's an extremely powerful sensation of mood, and the boys lean into that well with some of the lyrical turns: "Always fighting and moonlighting, it never ends in the city if you're all alone." Like, that's it. That's bang-on what this pit in my stomach feels like when I hear how this song opens. Masterfully done.

Which makes it something of a minor tragedy that the instant the vocals first come in, that strong, dark mood is shattered in favour of a half-hearted pop hook that's completely wasted on a song like this one. Maybe in a different song altogether that "Reach out" chorus might have some legs, but *this* one is called 'It's Gonna Get Better', and so you'll have to pardon me for feeling a mite put out that it did, in fact, get worse. At least after the initial chorus, the mood is somewhat recaptured in the song's only verse (featuring the lyrics discussed above); those percussive blasts like expulsions of steam from over-pressured vents? Yeah, that's the stuff. Yet here comes a second chorus, ready to wipe away that renewed effort as well. And then the song ends with a swelling, preachy bit of lyrics punctuated by some falsetto lines that don't particularly mesh with anything else the song is trying to do.

Like 'Another Record' one album prior, this is an album closer song that starts off incredibly strong for the first forty-five seconds or so before gradually degrading over the rest of its runtime. Both songs do something really unique and engaging in the Genesis catalogue sonically, at least for a bit, and I don't want to lose sight of that here. As Tony explains above, 'It's Gonna Get Better' was a catalyst song for Tony to delve deeper into the bag of tricks that sampling technology could offer him. Remember that back in the early 70s he had a Hammond organ and really nothing else to work with. Then by 1991 he's recording random sounds in the studio just to see what he might be able to fiddle with and turn into something special. This "eureka" moment with the cello sample on 'It's Gonna Get Better' was therefore a big milestone to further developing the Genesis sound, and we owe it a debt of gratitude for all the doors it opened…but it's still only an average song in its own right, I'm afraid.

156 - The Magic of Time

Demo, 1968

Picture if you will a world where Genesis the band never forms, and the lads complete their Charterhouse education before moving onto whatever mundane careers they might have done instead of music. Chris Stewart would likely have become an author, and I make that claim with confidence because he did, in fact, become an author some time after being fired from the band. Peter might have become a painter instead; I feel like art in some form or another has always been his calling. Mike may have been destined for middle management somewhere, though he was so unruly it's hard to say. But you'd like to think that at least one of "Team Genesis" would continue doing music to some degree on the side, right? Ant, certainly, might end up doing something similar to what he eventually did in reality with his solo career, although he'd be far less successful without the Genesis name to propel initial interest. But in this hypothetical world I'm less interested in Ant and more interested in Tony, who had been classically trained in piano but ended up in a rock band. What if he hadn't?

It's worth bringing up that Tony hedged his bets with the band by attending university for a year. Perhaps that could give us some insight into what direction his life might've taken?

> **Tony:** *I went to Sussex University, originally to study chemistry, but then changed to logic with physics. I wasn't really enjoying the chemistry very much and wanted something that offered me a little bit more, and the new course had a hint of philosophy, which interested me.* [1]

'The Magic of Time' is like a two minute snapshot into this parallel dimension. It's a secret recording some interdimensional traveller made on a phone of Tony playing jazz piano at his daughter's tap-dancing recital. He's making a modest living as a physics teacher at a secondary school, but he supplements his income by teaching piano lessons to the neighbourhood kids, many of whom are also in the room. And though at the moment all the eyes in the room are on the little girl in the fairy outfit toe tapping away, if anybody happened to fix their vision on Tony they'd see him attacking the song with a level of concentration and seriousness far above and beyond what the event calls for. He can't help it. He's locked in and he has to get it right. He is, after all, still Tony Banks.

Tony's old school buddies are singing the lines of the song, doing a competent enough job for a kid's tap-dancing recital (but not much more). Then the music calls for an instrumental break, and Tony really lets loose. At this point a few stray eyes glance his way, impressed by the Piano Dad putting so much effort into what they'd otherwise regard as a relatively throwaway performance. And then the school buddies start back up, and those wayward eyes focus once again on the child with her Tinkerbell wings, grinning ear-to-ear as she clack-clack-clacks away to end the number. The music fades, the other parents politely clap, and a sweating Mr. Banks (as he's known to his students) beams with pride at how well she must have done. You see, while he assumes she performed brilliantly, he can't be entirely sure. He was too zeroed in on his own playing, too obsessed with getting it right to actually watch her.

He wonders, wistfully, what it must be like for those other parents. What if he could simply enjoy the recital? Then he sighs and smiles again. What else can he do? His little girl needed music to dance to, so he had no choice in the end. Yet his smile begins to fade as a small voice comes unbidden into the back of his mind, which will haunt him for days to come: "You know, you missed a few notes."

155 - Tell Me Why

from *We Can't Dance*, 1991

In 1989, Phil Collins released his fourth solo album, *...But Seriously*. The massive success of his first three albums meant he'd already have a head start on selling this one with people buying it on spec, but it never hurts to have a solid lead single out there. As luck would have it, Collins had just that with 'Another Day in Paradise', which rocketed to 1 on the US charts enroute to winning Record of the Year at the Grammy Awards. Despite its success, however, the song wasn't without its critics. Given that the subject matter was the way society ignores the plight of the disenfranchised, and that Collins is/was a multimillionaire, many people found the message to be hypocritical, or at least a bit out of touch. Collins disagreed, of course, but to this day there are those who find 'Another Day in Paradise' a little distasteful for that reason.

> **Phil:** *I'm counting myself as a normal bloke, and how this is just another day for you and me, compared to the plight of those poor souls on the streets with cardboard boxes for beds. In hindsight, I can see it differently: a rock star who has it all, tritely lecturing his fellow jewellery-rattlers...about the travails of the homeless.* [12]

In 1991, Genesis released their fourteenth studio album, *We Can't Dance*. The massive success of their previous few albums meant they'd already have a head start on selling this one with people buying it on spec, but it never hurts to have some solid singles out there. As luck would have it, the band thought they had just that with 'Tell Me Why', which was released as a single two years later to zero fanfare and only a middling English chart presence. Despite its relative obscurity, however, the song wasn't without its critics. Given that the subject matter was the way society ignores the plight of the disenfranchised, and that the band are/were multimillionaires, many people found the message to be hypocritical, or at least a bit out of touch. The band disagreed, of course, but to this day there are those who find 'Tell Me Why' a little distasteful for that reason.

> **Phil:** *We have no solution at hand. But I wrote the song when the Kurds were stuck in the mountains and the whole world ignored them. I happened to see the pictures of their misery on TV at dinner, and I was horrified. Shortly afterwards, a cyclone devastated Bangladesh, after which the disaster in Ethiopia came. Only the politicians could solve all of these problems - when they would finally lift a finger.* [20]

I trust you see my point. 'Tell Me Why' isn't a bad song per se, but it comes off as little more than a band cash-in on a Collins solo hit. Even the music videos are essentially the same. Look, I'm not trying to be insensitive here. I'm not saying that these aren't actually important social issues, and I'm not sitting here rolling my eyes at a music video showing images of the homeless. I'm simply trying to make the point that 'Tell Me Why' was effectively a bleed over of Collins' solo efforts into Genesis - the very thing that soured many "prog diehards" on the band's 80s and 90s output. Usually I think these complaints are ill-founded, but in this particular instance they ring pretty true.

> **Tony:** *The one song [from We Can't Dance] where I wasn't totally happy with the lyrics was 'Tell Me Why', where I felt that Phil had covered that ground before, and I would have preferred a slightly less burdensome lyric. He took it into a field where it didn't need to go and when he was just playing the instrumental and he was "nah-nah-ing" his way through the lyric it sounded great, and we thought it could have been the big single off the album. But with that lyric it was just impossible to release it.* [6]

Obviously they did eventually release it anyway, and, well, Tony was right. This is three minutes' worth of song stretched out to five, and five minutes is a long time to be preached at. And while 'Another Day in Paradise' puts things into narrative form before a chorus asking you to "just think about it," 'Tell Me Why' is lyrically just a series of images spelled by Phil demanding answers. From politicians, from listeners, from God, from anyone really. It feels more accusatory, and maybe that was the point, but it makes the five minutes of 'Tell Me Why' harder on the listener than the same five minutes on 'Another Day in Paradise'. One thing to bring attention to a matter; another entirely to start blaming.

All this said, I don't hate 'Tell Me Why'. It doesn't sound like a *musical* clone of 'Another Day in Paradise', though there are some similarities, and I think Phil's vocal performance is really strong. Mike's playing also stands out to me as a big plus here. But it is the weakest song on *We Can't Dance* for me, and I suppose the fans agreed when they didn't buy the single. A bit sad then that this was the final single of the Phil Collins era of Genesis, assuming we're not counting 'The Carpet Crawlers 1999'. But it is what it is.

154 - Sea Bee

Demo, 1968

In US naval parlance, "Seabee" refers to members of the construction battalions (C.B.) who make up the Naval Construction Force - what is essentially the civil engineering arm of the United States Navy. Created in World War II after the US was drawn in by the attack on Pearl Harbour, the Seabees represented an organised effort to manage naval construction projects with military oversight. International law dictated that civilians who resisted an enemy military attack would be branded guerrillas and subject to summary execution. Given that the US didn't want its civilian engineers to go quietly, but also didn't want them violating international law, they basically said "OK, you guys are military now." It's all very interesting, at least to me.

Of course, Genesis is an English band, and probably didn't care one whit about American naval organization. So it's far more likely that what they're referencing with the title of this track is a cute little boatplane.

There were only just north of 1000 Seabees ever built, as military demand was never particularly high, and not many civilians are qualified to either drive a boat or fly a plane - much less both. The eventual niche the Seabee settled into was that of a marine rescue plane, being dispatched to save those who had drifted out to sea or what have you. This fits at least a bit with the lyrics of the song: one can imagine Pete is singing from the perspective of a lost soul drifting at sea, hoping for a Seabee to swoop down to the water and bring him home.

The music itself isn't terribly impressive, but it's pretty easy to listen to. The melody is mediocre, and like so many other early Genesis tunes, the heart of the song is just Tony plunking away at his piano. If Ant and Mike's strumming were removed, the song wouldn't really feel much different. There's frankly not very much that's compelling about this one. It's just decently pleasant filler material, at a time when filler material is all the band was able to produce.

So then it's probably best I provide some personal context to this, because with the things I've written about this song so far, you might be wondering why I'd ever have it even in the lofty heights of the 150s in this list. Let me start by admitting that I do like this song more than I probably should, and that's almost entirely because of when I heard it. It was at a time when I was starting to get more deeply into the music of Genesis, but in a relatively haphazard way. Streaming internet radio was my go-to for music in those days, so while my general tastes helped drive what I'd hear, by and large I was at the mercy of some unknown algorithms to determine what I'd hear next, or what new music I'd be exposed to.

In this way, 'Sea Bee' became my first exposure to the Genesis of the 60s. I was already very familiar with most of the band's material from *Nursery Cryme* through *We Can't Dance* (though not exhaustively so), but by now you've probably realised if you didn't already know: 1960s Genesis is nothing like any other era of Genesis. Hearing the early stuff for the first time was, you might say, something of a...revelation for me.

So it was that when I first heard 'Sea Bee' my immediate thought was, "Well, this isn't very good." My second thought was, "I wonder who this is." My third thought was, "Genesis? Get out of here." It was only at my fourth thought that I began to concede that the track was very interesting as a kind of time capsule for a band I was coming to truly love, and so I told the algorithm that I was willing to hear the tune again sometime. As the song continued to get occasional play on my personal radio station, it grew on me a little bit more each time. Eventually it led me to seek out and listen to *From Genesis to Revelation* itself, which as we all know is a...unique experience in the Genesis catalogue.

Yes: I can acknowledge that in strictly musical terms 'Sea Bee' doesn't measure particularly favourably even to the better Genesis songs of its own era, but for me it'll always be the song that introduced me to a whole side of Genesis I never knew before. There I was, adrift in the seas of baroque pop ignorance, obvious to the fact that I even needed to be rescued. And then what sound did my ears hear drifting in through the skies? That sputtering engine working so hard to come save me from my own disinterest?

It's a boat! It's a plane! No, it's 'Sea Bee'!

153 - Robbery, Assault and Battery

from *A Trick of the Tail*, 1976

One of the hallmarks of the Peter Gabriel era of Genesis, which is to say one of the hallmarks of Genesis in general for the first several years of the band's existence, was strong character pieces performed by a dynamic singer using different vocal styles. 'The Battle of Epping Forest', 'Harold the Barrel', 'Get 'Em Out by Friday', 'The Musical Box' - you know the kind of song I'm talking about. So naturally, when Gabriel parted ways with the band there was a question among the fans: will the new guy - whoever it ends up being - be able to carry a character-driven song like that? Will Genesis even continue to write songs in that vein?

> **Phil:** *We've written some strong material…'Robbery, Assault and Battery' [proves] there's still a place for the "story" songs for which Genesis are known…[It's] a stand-out and works really well from the off - I add a bit of my Artful Dodger into the vocal delivery. Slowly, I'm showing that I can not only sing these songs but bring in something else. A bit of character, in every sense of the word. I can inhabit them, without resorting to Peter's visual accessories…I can wear a flat cap and Edwardian coat for 'Robbery, Assault and Battery' but that's as theatrical as I'm prepared to go.* [12]

It only took the band one album to put that discussion to bed. 'Robbery, Assault and Battery' has all the character, all the charm, and all the humour of those earlier pieces, proving that Genesis could maintain its identity even without its erstwhile frontman. It's a song that tells the story of, well, a criminal engaging in acts of robbery, assault, and battery. Murder too, but, you know, I guess that crime wasn't important enough to land it a spot in the song's title. And about that title, you know what irks me? Why isn't there a comma after "Assault"? It's called the "Oxford comma" and serves as an important way to break up lists into more readable chunks. The classic example is that a panda's eating habits could be described as "eats shoots and leaves" while a homicidal diner patron might have his behaviour described as "eats, shoots, and leaves."

In this case the song's title describes three distinct charges: robbery, assault, and battery. Now I've had this discussion with some other grammar aficionados before, and the most common defence for Genesis I've seen here is to describe "Assault and Battery" as a single crime. That is to say, rather than denoting *three* illegal acts, this song title only describes *two*, with the second crime being a compound phrase rather than a single word, and the two are separated by the one comma. This seems to be an elegant solution until reading up on British law (at least insofar as a cursory glance at a potentially unreliable Wikipedia article can be considered "reading up") , where assault and battery are indeed considered separate offenses. Sometimes assault can encompass battery, but in those cases you wouldn't see "assault and battery" as the charge; you'd more likely see something like "assault by beating."

The only other time it seems to be grammatically acceptable to omit the Oxford comma is in the realm of journalism. Even that's a little archaic, though. The notion was that you could save money on the ink for those commas if the context made it clear enough what the meaning of the sentence should be. And beyond ink savings, you could also potentially squeeze in an extra word or two depending on how many commas you were able to excise from the article, given the limited space afforded by the newsprint medium. Nowadays in the fully digital age that's less and less relevant, but I suppose back in 1975/1976 those considerations were probably still bigger factors. So one could theoretically argue the song title is like a newspaper headline, where the comma would likely be omitted even though it does properly belong. And so perhaps I should give Genesis a pass on this one.

But it still bugs me.

Commas aside, when listening to this track it's easy to get so distracted by how well Phil handles the back and forth voicings (particularly in live performances like the one on *Seconds Out*) that you might completely miss the great quality of his drumming. Note that even after Phil had recorded the vocals for the album, he still assumed they would hire in a new singer and let him go back to his drum kit full time. If anyone doubts why that was a reasonable thing to believe, they really only need to listen to this song to understand; who would be able to replace him back there?

> **Tony:** *I am not technically the greatest player - and I am not saying that to be modest - and the fast stuff I would always push myself and I enjoyed doing that. Things like 'Robbery, Assault & Battery' are tough: it's in 13/8 and I was always trying to ignore the drums because they were playing off beats all the time.* [21]

It took Bill Bruford casually offering to Collins to handle drums for the tour before Phil felt comfortable with the notion of singing up front.

> **Phil:** *All I'm thinking is that it's a one-time-only deal. As a stopgap I've managed to sing the album, but doing it onstage will be another matter entirely. So, really, we still haven't got a singer... Having explored every other angle, it seems like the drummer is the last-ditch, last-resort-only option. None of us can take this entirely seriously... Finally, a compromise: I might consider this if I can get a drummer that I like, because I don't want to be looking over my shoulder the whole time, checking and quietly critiquing.* [12]

Yet despite the strength of the performance and the clear message it sent Genesis fans about the band's ability to carry on, the music of 'Robbery, Assault and Battery' doesn't really click for me as much as I'm sure it does for most fans. It's fun, jaunty, certainly not unpleasant by any means. But the melody of this song simply doesn't excite me. It's actually all the *other* stuff that really makes me appreciate it. The middle instrumental solo is really strong, which is the only part of the song Tony didn't already have written when he brought the piece to the band. The bass line is strong throughout, and especially near the end of the instrumental section. Steve as always knows his role and textures the track with great skill. But on top of all of that, the melody is just a bit "eh" to me. At specific moments, I daresay I even find it a little irksome.

It's a good song overall I think, but if I were ever to skip a track on *A Trick of the Tail* - unlikely as that might be, mind you - this is probably the one. There's a lot of really high-quality stuff happening, but the core melodic thread of the piece just doesn't much agree with me, and that's the most important element to my personal listening pleasure. I can enjoy most of the song readily enough anyway, but it does mean I tend to like everything else on the album a bit more.

152 - Please Don't Ask

from *Duke*, 1980

There's an alternate universe out there where 'In the Air Tonight' is a Genesis track, sitting somewhere in the middle of *Duke*. You see, after touring wrapped up for *And Then There Were Three*, Phil went off to Canada in an ultimately futile attempt to save his first marriage. Tony and Mike then took the opportunity to make their first solo albums, *A Curious Feeling* and *Smallcreep's Day*, respectively. When Phil came back to England ready to work, Tony and Mike were deep in the middle of getting their albums done, which Phil naturally respected. Bored and depressingly alone, he set up some sound equipment and instruments in his apartment and began writing/recording a bunch of material, which would end up comprising his own debut album, *Face Value*.

When Tony and Mike finished their solo projects, they went over to Phil's place to start working on the next Genesis album. They figured with leftover material they had, plus Phil having done some writing, each band member would get two "individual" songs on the album, and then they'd do the rest as a group. So Phil simply played them what in essence was the entire *Face Value* work-in-progress and said "Pick any two." At this stage he didn't have tremendous confidence in the stuff he was doing, and wasn't really expecting anything out of his material; it was just a way to kill time and work out some emotion while he waited on the other two guys to be done. They ended up selecting 'Misunderstanding' and 'Please Don't Ask' for use on *Duke*, leaving the rest to *Face Value*...

> **Phil:** *Tony Banks claims to this day that I didn't play them 'In the Air Tonight', because he reckons that they'd have chosen it if they'd heard it, but I know I played them everything. I didn't want to hold anything back because I didn't know I was going to make a record at that point.* [1]
>
> **Tony:** *Phil didn't play us 'In the Air Tonight', because if he had and we'd rejected it I'd be very pissed off. I don't think he'd written it at that point, that's why.* [1]
>
> **Mike:** *No one can remember whether we heard 'In the Air Tonight'. I'd like to think that if I had heard it, I would have remembered.* [1]

Whatever the truth of that fateful event, the Genesis faithful would have to wait another year or so for 'In the Air Tonight', while in the interim 'Please Don't Ask' was the Collins tune of the day. A very emotional song; you can tell in Phil's performance that this one means more to him than singing about any of the fantastical stuff so typical of the band's earlier lyrics. One of the common complaints I hear from detractors of the band's more successful era is that their songs sound indistinct from Phil's solo output. While I don't agree with that statement in a general sense, this one literally *is* Phil's solo output, so maybe the naysayers have a point. It's got his trademark vocal harmonies, the jazzy kind of feel to it...basically it's a good indication of the sort of stuff he'd produce on his own over the next couple decades.

More to the point, it's a very outside-the-box selection for Genesis. It's not so much that the band were strangers to ballads or even love songs; 'Your Own Special Way' and 'Follow You Follow Me' can attest to that fact. Heck, even the hallowed ground of "breakup song" wasn't new territory, given the fact that both 'More Fool Me' and 'Many Too Many' exist. But the delivery of it all is just so foreign to what the band had ever put out before.

> **Phil:** *A very personal song, my version of the conversational device David Ackles used in 'Down River'. I thought that was an unlikely choice for the band - it's so intimate, and very unlike anything Genesis have done before.* [12]

I think part of that disconnect comes from the lyrics. Recall for a moment that every song I listed above as examples of Genesis love ballads had lyrics penned either by Mike or Tony, which is to say a couple of public school boys trained from an early age to repress their emotions - particularly the ones that might make them appear weak, like, for example, saying "I love you." Now they did over the years get better at expressing those sorts of things. I'm not going to sit here and tell you that 'Follow You Follow Me' isn't a really solid love lyric. But contrast something like "The part was fun but now it's over / Why can't I just leave the stage?" from 'Many Too Many' to "Oh, but I miss my boy." One is a poetic metaphor. The other is a big ol' punch to the gut.

Before I was a father it was pretty easy to dismiss 'Please Don't Ask' as a lyrical albatross. Just "typical Collins melodrama" or whatever I might have thought in passing along those lines. It's this awkward conversational piece with an ex where you know things aren't going to work out and it's a bit pathetic to hear Phil desperately trying in vain to change that reality. And now I'm a father of two, and instead when I hear 'Please Don't Ask' I wonder what I would do if my kids were taken away from me. What kind of emotional state would I be in? Phil says in the song that he can't really be sure if he even still loves his son's mother, but that he's willing to try to make it work. Once upon a time that was a silly concept to me. Now it's the only thing that makes sense. Anything to be in your child's life. To be able to see him every day, watch him grow, *help* him grow. Oh, but I miss my boy. It's painful to even imagine.

That's the kind of visceral pain that a Tony Banks or a Mike Rutherford simply couldn't summon up. *That's* the kind of raw, heart-on-sleeve sense of loss that Genesis had never quite managed to convey before in such a way. *That's* why, regardless of whether 'In the Air Tonight' was played at Phil's apartment that day, Tony and Mike decided 'Please Don't Ask' needed to be a Genesis record.

Tony: *We liked [this song] a lot.* [1]

Succinct, yet all-encompassing. 'Please Don't Ask' broke new ground for the band and in so doing opened up a number of musical doors that were heretofore closed. It's a song that predates the Phil Collins Solo Career Experience and yet is of one substance with it. Which means that your opinion of this piece probably comes down to how much you like the Phil Collins' solo output in general. I personally am a fan of his music more often than not, so I do actually like this song quite a bit.

Why then is it my least favourite on *Duke*? Well, with an album as consistently strong as *Duke*, *something* has to be last. More specifically, there's no real chorus to sink your teeth into here. I can tell you exactly how 'Please Don't Ask' goes, but it will never get stuck in my head. I also think maybe the music could tap into that well of lyrical pain a bit more, rather than feeling like light jazz at times. Or perhaps I'm just wistful that I never got to hear the full Genesis take on 'In the Air Tonight'. In any case, these are just light criticisms for a song that's grown on me a lot over the years, and may well continue to do so.

151 - In Hiding

from *From Genesis to Revelation*

As I've repeatedly established over the course of this book so far, the Genesis of the 60s was primarily concerned with writing hits. And while the totality of their early efforts can be linked together by a shared kind of vague stylistic quality - and, let's face it, by the overall immaturity of the sound - the songs themselves cover a fairly broad range of audio territory on an individual basis. It's as though the band was throwing a whole bunch of darts, all of different shapes and sizes, experimenting to see which ones would actually stick to the board (the answer, of course, was that none of them did). Already in this book I've written about the Bee Gees pastiche that is 'Silent Sun', the folksy groove of 'The Conqueror', the heavy drive of 'In the Beginning', and the list goes on.

'In Hiding' is notable because it marks the band's attempt at something much more gentle and restrained. It's got no need for a bombastic performance, a big chorus, heavy swells, or anything to make the record pop. It's as though someone in or near the band said "What if it just didn't pop at all?" and the lads replied with a shrug saying, "OK, let's give it a go." It's a song that doesn't give itself any opportunity to offend the listener. Now, granted, that may mean it has a limited ceiling by taking no bold risks or charting any new territory, but it also means that the song's floor is *significantly* raised. Regardless of someone's feelings about the first album or whether it should be construed as "actual" Genesis material when compared to the later catalogue, I'm not sure many people would say this song is actually unlistenable. It's thoroughly pleasant.

Peter's voice falls into that perfect little pocket here where he doesn't have to try to be too saccharine-sweet, but also never needs to exert himself to hit the notes. Everything is gentle and controlled. The same can be said for the backing vocals, which sees the likes of Ant and Tony and Mike - is Mike actually in this vocal mix? I have no idea, to be honest. But in any case, they go beyond the simple oohs and aahs and establish some actual vocal harmony for the choruses. It's not amazing by any means, but it's a level beyond the other stuff they were doing in this era. And when the oohs and aahs do come in over one of the verses, they're very tasteful and well-delivered.

Meanwhile, the arrangement itself is stripped down to make sure nothing ever escapes the texture. No piano or organ here for Tony. John Silver gets to take the day off; there's no percussion whatsoever on the track. If not for the strings added in post-production, the arrangement for 'In Hiding' would consist exclusively of rhythm guitar, strumming away on simple chords to keep the beat. It's like something you'd hear around a campfire just before bed, which is funny because there's another song on the album actually called 'Fireside Song', so I guess they were channelling a certain kind of mood pretty well at this point.

If Genesis never evolved into the band that made *Trespass* and beyond, and instead stayed more in line with their debut effort, this is the direction I hope they'd have chosen to stick with. Of course I'm glad they didn't stay in this direction at all considering everything that came afterward, but one could do a lot worse than being a purveyor of pastoral easy listening tunes. With respect to the band's talent level as writers and performers at this stage of their careers, songs like 'In Hiding' were their real niche: the stuff they were best at. It's a small shame the rest of the album was so much less consistent.

150 - Evidence of Autumn

B-side of 'Misunderstanding', 1980

Though it doesn't sample from or reprise any other track in the band's catalogue, 'Evidence of Autumn' to me feels like an amalgamation of other Genesis pieces that Tony Frankensteined together in some dark laboratory, trying to distil the perfect Genesis song. Like all typical experiments of mad science, the effort showed a lot of promise, even if the results weren't quite as resoundingly successful as the eccentric genius may have hoped for. But hey, that's just the nature of experimentation, isn't it?

For starters, there's a lot of 'Undertow' here, to my ears. Tony plays an electric piano on that 1978 track, and it sounds like he's playing the same instrument here, or at least something that produces a very similar sound. It creates the same kind of atmosphere, at any rate. Then the vocals enter and it's got the big cymbal crashes and chords, like a hint of 'Heathaze' maybe. Though perhaps that's cheating because 'Heathaze' and 'Undertow' are themselves so similar in the first place; more on that later in this book. No coincidence here either; all three of these songs are Tony Banks solo compositions. He clearly had a certain kind of style in this era, didn't he?

Regardless, 'Evidence of Autumn' doesn't boast as strong a chorus as either of those earlier songs. What this song does differently comes from its sole verse, where the vocal melody is doubled by the keyboard, with Mike tossing in a few guitar sparks for good measure. But even this isn't immune to feelings of familiarity, as the verse gives me distinct 'One for the Vine' vibes. That's perhaps a strange thing to say given that the two pieces don't sound anything alike, but I'm talking strictly in terms of feel here. There's just something about the energy and delivery of the music that conjures up that piece in my head, which of course is another Banks solo effort.

Now so far this song has been something of a Tony Banks paint-by-numbers exercise, but 'Evidence of Autumn' does something in the back half that really breaks it from the mould. Perhaps this bit is the "mad" in "mad science." After a bridge section defined by some really intense Banksian chords, in bursts this chipper, up-tempo bit with quirky little synth sounds. It smells slightly of 1977's 'Pigeons', really, before shifting back into a 'One for the Vine' instrumental style segment and abruptly launching back into that epic bridge one more time. Then the piece returns to its chorus, finally ending on more electric piano in that 'Undertow' vein once again.

To be clear, this isn't to say that this song sounds just like any of these other ones at any given time, but that it seems to be taking the atmospheres those other tracks created and pulling them together into a new form. It helps the effort that all those other songs are good-to-great; any individual section of this piece can stand on its own pretty well as a solid listening experience. I just don't think they blend together as seamlessly into one cohesive idea as they'd need to in order to propel this track into the stratosphere. Couple that with the song's relentlessly muddy production - everything sounds slurred and homogenous, especially in the vocal department - and you get something that doesn't quite gel as well as maybe it ought to. As eight snippets of longer songs, I love 'Evidence of Autumn'. As a single song in its own right, however, I merely like it.

149 - Naminanu

B-side of 'Keep It Dark', 1981

I've mentioned earlier in this book that half of *Duke* was originally planned as a side-long epic musical suite. That was the band's initial vision for what eventually became the six tracks that comprise the suite, and indeed they played those tracks sequentially with no breaks on the supporting tour for the album. But on the record the guys became very self-conscious about drawing comparisons to their famous epic 'Supper's Ready', and decided to spread the suite over the album specifically to avoid that. A small shame in my opinion, but at least the songs are all there on *Duke*, in the correct order, and with some custom playlisting or CD track skipping you can still sort of recreate the song that might've been. If nothing else, their repositioning helps the entire album cohere a little bit more.

A year later, Genesis made a different choice for their follow-up effort to *Duke*. While writing and recording 1981's *Abacab*, another epic song suite was conceived and played; but this time they took half of the thing off the dang album entirely. The 'Dodo Suite', as fans now sometimes refer to it, consisted of 'Dodo', 'Lurker', 'Submarine', and 'Naminanu'. There is some contention among fans about the intended order of the pieces, and I'll address that more directly later when covering 'Submarine', but for now, just trust me: 'Naminanu' was the closing number of the suite.

Anyway, while 'Dodo' and 'Lurker' remained joined at the hip and made the final cut for *Abacab* as the aptly titled 'Dodo/Lurker', both 'Submarine' and 'Naminanu' were scrubbed to make room for stuff like...ahem...'Who Dunnit?' and 'Another Record'. Yeesh. Look, I know the whole point of *Abacab* was to radically reinvent the Genesis sound and shun anything that might have sounded like "the old Genesis," but how much stronger would the album be if a couple of its weaker songs were removed and we got the 'Dodo Suite' in its entirety? But that's not what happened, and now instead of closing out a sixteen minute progressive work, 'Naminanu' sits by itself as the B-side to a minor UK hit from the album. How does it fare?

The first thing I noticed is the intensity of the drum work. Phil's really getting after it here - probably his strongest percussive effort in years by this time. Then I noticed the jazzy interlude bits that sound like nothing so much as some of the instrumentals Dutch band Focus put out there. Stick those parts on *Focus II (Moving Waves)* and nobody would find them out of place. Finally, of course, I noticed the vocal drone, which sounds very sci-fi, like the kind of music Mork might find relaxing back on Planet Ork, were Mork a being capable of relaxation. Nanu nanu, Naminanu...hey, I'm just saying. Honestly, that's probably why this track got paired with 'Keep it Dark', given that song's subject matter of an alien abduction.

> **Tony:** *There's a moment in 'Naminanu' when it really takes off and goes into double time at the end. The whole thing's building to that. The track can maybe be a bit irritating and repetitive, but I found it quite exciting.* [18]

All in all, 'Naminanu' is a trip. It's fun, exciting, and very different from most other things the band did, at this or any other point in time. It works better in its originally intended musical suite than as a standalone piece, injecting a metric butt-ton of energy into the lethargy generated by 'Submarine', but it's still a quirky and worthwhile effort in any context.

148 - Illegal Alien

from *Genesis*, 1983

Well then...this aged poorly, dinn't it? Let's not beat around any bushes here: 'Illegal Alien' is a song that consists of wealthy British men making fun of would-be Mexican immigrants to the United States, and the whole concept is absolutely embarrassing at this point in history. There is a bit in the lyrics where the song's protagonist tries to bribe a border official with sexual favours from his sister; just layers and layers of problems. Now I'm normally pretty staunchly against the concept of the radio edit. I'm something of a purist in that regard - I don't care about your ad revenue or the average attention span of 21-29 year olds driving around town. Just play the song the way it was meant to be played, you know? So it says something that in this particular case I think it was wise of the band to omit that section from the single entirely, and therefore from the radio and video versions of the song. But that's faint praise.

> **Tony:** *It is a tongue-in-cheek thing. In fact, it's meant to be sympathetic towards illegal aliens. It isn't about any particular race, though in America you hear about the Mexicans coming across the border on the TV news all the time. Mike Rutherford just wrote some lyrics about it and we did a promotional video as well with us all dressed up for the part...it goes into a reggae feel in the middle, so it's not just about Mexicans.* [22]

Whatever you say, Tony. At any rate, now that I've established that I think the lyrical content is disastrous, I want to attempt to separate that side of things from the music itself. And the music for this one is, for better or worse, super catchy. The opening keyboard riff, the repeated chorus line, earworms all. The instrumental break in the middle features Phil playing trumpet, and is a really engaging section of music that could work well even in a proper prog tune. Plus the flavour of the whole thing does have a sort of street market feel, which is fun in itself.

> **Tony:** *I think the biggest differences [in how I used the keyboards between the 70s and 80s] are that I'm using keyboards...for sound effects. Since you can record anything you like and then play with it, you can get some things that are quite bizarre. 'Illegal Alien' has a lot of that sort of thing - car horns and phones. It was quite fun recording all of it...I've got some great disks full of sounds for that sort of thing.* [23]

Really, I think this tune is a great synthesis of the Genesis and Collins sounds. Obviously Collins is *in* Genesis, but what I mean is that this one feels sort of like a midpoint between the sound of your typical "hit Genesis song" and your typical "hit Phil Collins solo song." It's so energetic, features a little bit of brass, a slick beat, and catchy melodies throughout. That's all very "Phil solo" side of the coin. But then it's also got these weird turns like the sonic cacophony Tony mentions up above, along with the following breakdown section. Yes, that's the section with the line about whoring out one's sibling, but just speaking musically it's a "lean in" kind of bit. Very interesting, especially in juxtaposition to the quirky silliness of the rest of the track, which is itself a very Genesis kind of thing to do.

There's something irresistible happening on 'Illegal Alien', perhaps to the chagrin of those who would prefer to see it buried and forgotten. Genesis and Collins alike would both have plenty of other hits, most of them bigger than this one, and yet I daresay 'Illegal Alien' might just be the most infectious of them all. Why is that?

> **Phil:** *We went through a few different drum parts on 'Illegal Alien'. I initially was trying for a more sophisticated drum part than the song actually required. Eventually I ended up with that basic rock-and-roll part - two and four on the snare, one and three on the bass. That's what made the tune work. I'm happier with my playing on 'Illegal Alien' and 'Mama' than I am on something like 'Dance on a Volcano', in spite of the fact that 'Dance' is a much more intricate part. To me the drums are played much better, and that's the bottom line. I'm not afraid to take off my schooling hat, and I've matured enough to say, "People won't laugh at me," if I play something simple, direct and effective.* [24]

But this brings me back full circle to the crux of the matter. Even as I was writing the previous couple paragraphs I found myself running into the big problem again. When the elephant in the room is this big, it's almost impossible to ignore it. It's amazing how a song can be comprised of so many different interlocking pieces, and how the choice of words can be so minimally impactful to the pure sound of the thing, and yet they often end up defining the song to the listener. I specifically tried to spend several sentences looking at 'Illegal Alien' through a purely musical lens and yet I couldn't help but acknowledge the lyrical side more than once during that time. It's inescapable.

See, 'Illegal Alien' just has that strength of immediacy to it that makes it get stuck in your head. And then you realise exactly what the words that are stuck in your head are saying, and you start to feel a certain sort of way about that. It's a song that you want to be awful so you can dismiss it entirely, but it's got a great hook and a number of other really good things happening, so you just can't, and that disconnect is a little perplexing. "If I like this groove, am I a bad person? If I listen to this song and find myself involuntary tapping my foot, am I a monster?" How does one handle this kind of thing? We're in uncharted, uncomfortable territory. The fun and the revulsion are doing a tango here and I can't easily separate them. Often my personal answer is to avoid listening to the song altogether. "Maybe if I don't hear it," I think to myself, "I don't have to admit I kinda sorta dig it."

When this book existed merely a series of ramblings on an internet forum, one individual asked me how I could feel the way I do about the lyrics of 'Illegal Alien' and yet not rate it as my least favourite track in the Genesis discography, or close to it. I could only reply with the truth: the songs that find themselves at the bottom of my personal Genesis list are ones that I truly wanted to like but couldn't. 'Illegal Alien', on the other hand, is a song I really don't want to like.

But I do. God help me...I do.

147 - Like It or Not

from *Abacab*, 1981

That ascending guitar riff is a fantastic way to open a song, isn't it? It only takes five seconds for 'Like It or Not' to command your attention. And then once that riff disappears and the verse takes over, the thought that comes to mind is "This sounds like a Genesis song from the 1980s." Now, I know. That's a bit of a "duh" observation, but I think it's significant in context. Note that the album here is *Abacab*, where the band was desperate to sound like anything else **except** Genesis. And while they largely succeeded in that effort, what's interesting about the verses of 'Like It or Not' is the way it acts as a kind of sneak preview of the Genesis sound to come. *Abacab* was a departure from the typical sound of the band, yes, and a lot of the album's experimental ideas went by the wayside afterward, but in this song we have the kernel of something more lasting, especially if you also extend that thought process to Mike + the Mechanics..

For *Duke*, Genesis made an intentional move toward more group writing, allowing each band member only two "solo" songs apiece on the album. With *Abacab* they furthered their commitment to that idea, and now each member was only allotted a single track as a solo writing effort. This culminated in the albums *Genesis* and beyond having no solo material whatsoever, which is a pretty remarkable achievement. But here, 'Like It or Not' was the single Rutherford piece to hit the album, and while Phil's 'Man on the Corner' was a stark, stripped down piece compared to the band's usual fare, and Tony's 'Me and Sarah Jane' went much further afield with its sounds, Mike's verse and chorus could sit comfortably in the middle of really any Genesis album of the decade and you wouldn't bat an eye.

Lyrically, it's a song of a lover spurned, going through a progression of emotions from hope, futility, and anger. And through it all, a strong undercurrent of sadness. You can follow those emotions not only lyrically, but musically as well. This stuff comprises the entire first half of the song (minus that initial riff intro). The singer laments his fate, the drums come in with a heavy groove, and it's all just...all right for what it is, I suppose. Decent enough but nothing special or particularly compelling. Taken by itself that's fine, but after the excitement of the opening riff, it's something of a let down.

So the good news is that just past the halfway mark of the song that guitar riff comes back in and the song really begins to shine. What's striking about this is that the back half of the song can be noticeably better than the front while doing the exact same things in the fundamental structure. That drum and bass groove just keeps driving forward in as it always has. Phil's still belting out emotion on what I can only call a semi-melodic line. But there's a difference now. There's backing vocals, there's the occasional keyboard run. Most importantly, there's now a raw power behind it all that makes the music work much better than it did initially.

Ultimately, 'Like It or Not' is a "safe" piece floating in a sea of adventurous ones. The other songs on *Abacab* all try out new ideas in hopes of cooking up some new kind of new and delicious musical omelette. Some succeed wonderfully. Some end up as little more than cracked eggs. Meanwhile, 'Like It or Not' is content to just be a slice of toast, grounding the whole affair. Halfway through the song it realises it needs some butter and dutifully adds it, and that's about all there is to it. It's a taste of normal on an album that needed one, and it manages to get steadily stronger over the course of its five-minute runtime. It may not turn many heads, but it's part of a balanced breakfast all the same.

146 - Run Out of Time

B-side of 'Not About Us', 1998

The core conceit of this book, the thing that gives it its format and hopefully keeps you turning the pages, is that I am counting down my personal favourite Genesis songs. As such - and bear with me on this one - I'm writing about individual songs in their entirety. But what if I went more granular than that? What if instead of discussing my favourite songs of Genesis, I was discussing my favourite Genesis *moments*? These could be larger sections of songs or even multiple songs when played in sequence. For example, the end of 'Entangled' going into the first note of 'Squonk' on *A Trick of the Tail*? Now *that's* a great moment. But moments can also be smaller, self-contained things. They could be fleeting shivers at certain chord changes, or a particular drum fill, or anything else really. What if this whole endeavour was a catalogue of those instead of full songs?

In that hypothetical Genesis book, you would see 'Run Out of Time' show up much, much higher on the list. Perhaps and probably even in the top ten, if I'm being honest. So what's the moment? What is it about this obscure B-side from the late 90s, post-Phil era of Genesis that really grabs me? Interestingly enough, it's that very moment when Phil's successor first makes his presence known.

"Ohhhh, hear me." This is the moment. Ray Wilson's vocals come in and for a brief few seconds everything is pure magic. Tony hits the perfect chord. The bass comes in with perfect gravity. And Ray's husky, longing voice delivers that feeling of need perfectly. It's an atmosphere that conveys in one chord, in one moment, the entire thrust of the rest of the song. It's an emotional progression of caring about someone, hurting them, letting them go, and accepting that you'd do it all over again. Therefore, finally, it's also about deciding to remain alone indefinitely. It's the kind of deep tragedy that can only be generated from deep love, made all the stronger from the surprisingly effective lyrical effort on display.

I'm not sure whether it was Tony or Mike penning the words to the song, but in either case 'Run Out of Time' strikes that ideal balance between sappy and energetic. "Through the light of a candle, through the base of a wine glass, you could almost take me for the real thing." I mean, that's fantastic. Great imagery, great weight.

But then, this book isn't about moments, is it? It's about the full songs, and unfortunately when I pull the magnifying glass back I don't always like what I see. I chose that metaphor with intent, by the way; if a 1930s private eye had a love/breakup song, I imagine it might sound something like this. I could say that's because of the chord progressions, but if I'm honest it's because of the big ol' cheesy faux saxophone sound Tony uses to open the piece. As if inflicting it upon us once wasn't enough, it comes back again after a swelling instrumental section that would otherwise be the strength of the song. Instead, any musical or emotional momentum the piece had is destroyed, and even a high-quality final verse can't save it.

I'm telling you, if 'Run Out of Time' ended after three minutes and change, it'd be utterly brilliant - one of the top ballads in the entire Genesis library. Instead it goes for six and a half, languishing and wallowing and wasting much of its potential in the indulgence. No small irony that a song called 'Run Out of Time' might drag on for too long, yet, well, here we are. It's a shame, yes, but there's at least a silver lining: no matter what, we still have that one precious moment.

145 - Window

from *From Genesis to Revelation*, 1969

In the entry for 'One Day' earlier in this book, I wrote about the way the brass arrangements could at times really lift some of the material of *From Genesis to Revelation* above its weight class. Then, in the entry for 'In Hiding', I asserted that a gentle, more pastoral sound was better suited to the band at this time than the harder stuff they occasionally tried out. So you might at this point be wondering how I'd feel about a 1960s Genesis track that takes those two concepts and melds them together, combining brass arrangements with a gentle pastoral tune. If that's the case, you're in luck! 'Window' is precisely that tune.

Now, you wouldn't necessarily realise that 'Window' fits that bill from the first twenty seconds of the song. For whatever reason it opens with a piano riff straight out of middle school musical theatre. I don't know what that riff is doing here of all places, but I admit that it does at least create a lot of excitement and anticipation for whatever might come next. Of course, what comes next then has absolutely nothing to do with the opening section: that jaunty little riff disappears abruptly, never to return. That's classic *From Genesis to Revelation*, really. Try to write a song, end up instead with an extra little morsel of music that doesn't neatly fit anywhere, slap it onto the front of something else anyway and call it an introduction. I'm not surprised the group of teenagers felt this was a good idea; I'm a little surprised the album's production crew didn't talk them out of it. Either way, let's just put that aside and focus on the remaining three minutes.

It's here that we find out that 'Window' is *not* a twinkly piano dance but instead a gentle ballad. Like some of the other pieces on the album, the song was envisioned pretty much just as a "Peter + guitar" kind of sound, with backing vocals coming in for the chorus. And like those other songs in this vein, Jonathan King and crew decided to fill out the arrangement with strings and brass. The end result is that we get Peter singing a lovely little melody with understated horns, spelling a genuinely pretty guitar sound from Ant, and strings that mostly work well, though sometimes they're a tad too loud in the mix. And then, rare for Genesis in this era, they decide at the end to really go crazy and let drummer John Silver jump in and play a couple measures. "No, really, knock yourself out John! We'll just start the fade-out here, and…"

The lyrics don't do the song any real favours. I've got no issue with the imagery they paint, but they're a bit too wordy for what the piece is trying to accomplish; perhaps the start of a trend, that. That said, they don't detract much from the overall pleasantness of the affair, either. It's an altogether cosy, relaxing affair. At one point the song threatens to build itself up beyond that threshold, but then enters a brief instrumental interlude that serves as a kind of reset, letting us know that it's all right to sit back again.

It's not the most technically proficient song out there, and it's not any kind of major songwriting achievement, but 'Window' is a splendid little picnic song. That's not to say it's *about* a picnic; in fact, I'm pretty sure it's about going to sleep and having good dreams. But it's the perfect kind of tranquil tune for that sort of setting, conjuring up as it does images of clear skies and green pastures. That's gotta be worth something, right?

144 - Shipwrecked

from *Calling All Stations*, 1997

By 1997, Tony and Mike had over fifteen years of experience just jamming together and letting their material blossom out of that. Of course, for most of that time, Phil Collins was there too, but when he departed Genesis and they were left to write as a duo they retained the approach that had served them well over their past few albums together. 'Shipwrecked' came about through one of these jams, as they doodled around for nearly half an hour to see if anything good might emerge. The opening muted guitar riff of this song is what survived that session, and in fact what you're hearing on the studio track is that very improvised moment itself; Tony just sampled that riff from the rehearsal room, stuck it through his synthesizer, and off they went.

> **Tony:** *It was a riff [Mike] played twice in the [improvisation session] and...[it] sounded really good...We just played it back and it had some magic about it.* [25]

Now it stands to reason that if a riff is good enough to build a song around, it'll probably show up pretty prominently within that song. That's true for 'Shipwrecked' and yet also understates what this song does a bit. See, most riff-driven songs use the riff as a kind of springboard into the verse or the chorus. Maybe the riff comes back gloriously in a bridge or outro, or maybe it gets developed further in a solo of some sort. If it plays behind the vocals at all, it's typically during the verse, letting the chorus take that momentum and apply it into something else.

'Shipwrecked' goes a different direction. Tony and Mike loved this riff so much that they both wanted to play it, and play it often. So they worked up a verse melody with a little bit of tension behind it and a vocal melody for the chorus simple enough to act as a kind of highlight or accent to the riff, and then played that riff as grandly as they could every time the chorus came around. The result is that, in a very real sense, the true "chorus" of this song is actually just a repeating five note phrase played on the guitars and keyboards. It's an inversion of typical pop song structure; here the *backing track* is the hook, and it's the vocal bits that are the extra fluff designed to keep the listener somewhat engaged. It's really a fascinating approach to songwriting. Nobody will come away from hearing this song quietly singing "I'm shipwrecked, I might as well be shipwrecked" to themselves over and over. But they very well might come away humming those five notes.

> **Ray:** *It's an interesting song. But yeah, it's a good track and it fitted the style, the way I sang, and I made that song my own.* [3]

Ultimately though, that's also part of the song's downfall. Revolving around this elongated, descending pattern gives the whole thing a lethargic feel. It didn't perform all that well on the charts, and the band dumped the song from their setlist early on in the album's supporting tour:

> **Ray:** *Some songs don't work very well live... We threw it out of the setlist after a couple of shows; it's kind of boring.* [26]

It may be boring as a live track, but it's a really interesting listen for its unique approach to building a pop/rock ballad, so it keeps me engaged from that angle. I also think its positioning on *Calling All Stations* does it a disservice, but I'll have more to say about that later on in this book. I do think it's a little funny to see what Mike had to say about the track ten years later, though.

> **Mike:** *My favourite [track from the album] was 'Shipwrecked'. I think we could've done it a lot better, actually, the way we recorded the backing track. But it's a very, very nice mood. And I like the title...Nice title, 'Shipwrecked'...Had we had a producer who was more a producer - in terms of trying to get ideas and develop songs - we probably could have done a better version.* [3]

What really gets me about this is how nearly self-aware Mike is on this. It's his favourite track from the *Calling All Stations* album, and that's great, but he sees its warts. He knows there's something that just doesn't quiiiiiiiite work about the piece. And rather than figure that he and Tony needed to develop it further, or change the arrangement, or really anything that involves personal responsibility, he calls out producer Nick Davis for not having enough songwriting vision to push Mike and Tony to realise that maybe 'Shipwrecked' needed a bit more time in the oven.

One imagines that, upon hearing those remarks, Nick Davis probably felt a little shipwrecked himself.

143 - Wot Gorilla?

from *Wind & Wuthering*, 1976

Part of what makes progressive music hard for some people to get into is the extended instrumental sections. While fans of the genre tend to love the long solos, virtuoso performances, and overall willingness to let the music flow where it will, casual listeners often lack the patience or desire to let these passages really digest and absorb. So when Genesis say that *Wind and Wuthering* is likely their least accessible album, what they're really saying is that three of its nine total tracks are instrumental pieces.

Bookended by wind chimes that make it sound initially like some kind of companion piece to 'The Waiting Room', 'Wot Gorilla?' instead spends its first thirty seconds as a drum solo before veering off into jazz fusion territory, an area that Phil was particularly passionate about. He had to lobby for its inclusion on the album, and winning Tony over was the crux of it.

> **Phil:** *One of my favourite songs on the whole record, because it was a bit more of my 'Los Endos' thing coming in the door. It was my fusion, kind of Weather Report side of me, where suddenly I was sort of able to make Tony Banks play this stuff. And he seemed to like it!* [3]

> **Tony:** *It was important that Phil tried to steer us a bit in that direction. It's less easy for Mike and myself, but that's not to say we don't like it. That's the advantage of having different tastes in a group: you do pull people in different directions, and you get something out of them they would never do on their own. 'Wot Gorilla?' is a good example. I didn't like it very much at the time, but when I've heard it since I really like it.* [10]

But there are two sides to every coin, and Tony allowing Phil to jump in with a piece meant there was less room on the album for a more accomplished writer like Steve; specifically in this case his song 'Please Don't Touch', which was initially linked to 'Wot Gorilla', sharing a bass drum rhythm.

> **Steve:** *'Wot Gorilla?' was good rhythmically, but underdeveloped harmonically. Dispassionately, I think 'Please Don't Touch' has both rhythm and harmonic development, which is more exciting.* [27]

Evidently Steve learned diplomacy later in life, as I've seen claims that he referred to 'Wot Gorilla?' in the 80s as both "a very inferior instrumental" and "a real doodle of an idea." So for better or worse, 'Wot Gorilla?' has sort of become the poster child for why Steve left the band, especially since 'Please Don't Touch' went on to become the title track of his second solo album. And while I do agree with Steve that this is my least favourite of the band's instrumental efforts (if one counts 'Ravine' as a non-song and considers 'Naminanu' to be a vocal track), I wouldn't go so far as to say it's anything like a bad song. It doesn't particularly *go* anywhere, true, but it's also not trying to.

It's a song about finding a groove and just playing with it for a while, and there's some value and excitement in that effort. This is Tony and Phil just playing their little hearts out, with Steve (begrudgingly?) providing some backing texture and Mike swelling the bass. It's not epic, and it's not incredible, but it's pretty good fun, and is well-placed in the album as a sort of wake-up call from the dreamy and fluffy 'Your Own Special Way'. It deserves better than to be dismissed out of hand - though I have no idea what its title means.

142 - Small Talk

from *Calling All Stations*, 1997

Did you ever play any organised youth sports? I'm not talking about your high school football team or your horseback riding club, either. I'm talking further back, when you were so small you can only vaguely recollect being "single digits old." These were the years when you'd play a sport because your parents thought it was important for you to get some quality outdoor time but they didn't want to have to be responsible for overseeing it. So they'd convince themselves and you that a team environment would be really good for you, even as they dropped you off at practice and drove away grinning ear to ear at having a guilt-free hour away from you.

These were the years where you'd buy fully into the sport, put forth as much effort as you could possibly muster, and learn to deal with the frustrations of all the things out of your control. Like the kid who so badly wanted to be anywhere else that he would sit down and eat dirt in the middle of an actual game because it legitimately sounded like a better use of his time. Or the mother who tried to fill the hollowness in her soul by yelling "BOOT IT!" at all these poor children, thinking somehow that would prove to the other parents that she loved her kid best. Or the fact that you'd often enter a season knowing that no matter how hard you worked or how talented you were, you'd never get a real opportunity to play because your team had a pair of twins and their dad was the coach.

But there was an upside to all that as well. These were also the years of innocence, where winning felt good, but running through that tunnel of parents leaning their hands into one another was the real victory. Where even the worst teammate could be tolerated because his mom is the one who brought oranges for everyone to eat after the game. Where you'd hope for the orange drink, were happy for the red, would settle for a green; just anything but the purple. And it was in this spirit of rewarding kids for tiring themselves out somewhere other than home that the idea of participation awards started to emerge.

I didn't like playing baseball. I was an average player, but in youth sports you're either the star of the team or absolute trash, so I spent my entire youth baseball career feeling like absolute trash. I recall one game where I was made to play left field during a very hot day, which was basically akin to being exiled from the team. Nobody at that age was going to ever hit a ball all the way to left field. So I spent long minutes just standing in one spot in a big uniform under a blazing sun, and after a while I was dizzy and delirious from heat exhaustion. I got pulled from the game because I was incapable of standing still by myself in a grassy field. That was a bit of a low point.

At the end of that season, my coach decided to give everyone an award. These were thin metal plates that had enlarged baseball cards printed on them, and added text naming the award. Essentially they were all participation awards, but jazzed up in such a way that they weren't *called* participation awards. Like one kid got the "Ken Griffey, Jr. Home-Run Hitter Award" because he was good at hitting the ball. That sort of thing. The goal was to let every kid feel valuable and give them a keepsake to remember that feeling, you know?

I got the "Pete Rose Most Improved Player Award". Pete Rose about five years earlier had been *permanently banned from baseball* for gambling infractions, so that already felt like a slap in the face. And then "Most Improved" is really just a kind way of saying "You used to really suck, but now you're kind of less terrible," isn't it? Nobody ever wants to get a "most improved" award. Ever. I'm pretty sure I cried the whole way home. I had toughed it out the entire year being made to feel like I was garbage even though I was pretty sure I was decent, and now my twin-dad coach decided to give me a big metal trinket that said "We really *did* think you were garbage, and we want to honour that by giving you this likeness of professional baseball's number one *persona non grata*."

Y'all, I flippin' hate baseball.

What on Earth does any of this have to do with Genesis? Well, when I began this massive project back in the late summer/early fall of 2019, there were quite a number of the band's songs with which I was only loosely familiar. 'Small Talk' was one of those that I had only heard once or twice previously, in my dad's car while he played it, ironically buried beneath the soundtrack of our own travel small talk. So when visiting these tracks with an eye to making personal critical judgments, I got in the habit of jotting down my very brief gut reactions and impressions of the songs. Maybe one note would say something like "fun, upbeat" while another would read "good riff." You get the idea.

This is relevant because, while the specifics of every individual note elude my memory, I recall explicitly that the note I wrote myself for 'Small Talk' on that first intentioned listen was, and I quote, "SMALL TALK." The only thing I was able to come away with on that first true playthrough was Ray splurting out that phrase like it was a Tourette's tic, and I immediately wrote the song off. "This thing's horrible, let's move on."

> **Tony:** ...*Quite a good character, I think...The best thing about it for me is the line "Small talk" itself, which has just got a great sound to it.* [25]

Does it though? Does it *really*, Tony?

As the project continued in its first phase (creating the force ranking itself), I necessarily had to listen to every one of these Genesis tracks multiple times over. The best way to compare two songs is to listen to them back to back, after all, and with one hundred ninety-seven songs to compare, well: that's a lot of Genesis on the stereo, I'm sure you can imagine. Some songs I was all too happy to come back to, but others came bundled with a healthy dose of dread. 'Small Talk' was in this latter group for me. "Oh, what's next? 'Small Talk', huh? What's my note for that one say? 'SMALL TALK.' Ohhhh that's right. Ugh."

> **Mike:** *Ray arrived late in the process [of writing the album], but he brought some good ideas in, especially on 'Small Talk'.* [1]

Did he though? Did he *really*, Mike?

But listen to it repeatedly I did. And you know what really jumped out to me over the course of that months-long exercise of listening and ranking and listening and ranking? To my great surprise and despite my ingrained bias from that one little note, I somehow liked 'Small Talk' a little bit more every single time I listened to it. Every time I found something new to redeem the song just a bit further:

- "OK, it's not quite as bad as I recall. Maybe I was a little too harsh at first."
- "Tony sounds like he's playing this on Mario Paint. It's straight up MIDI quality. I actually kinda like that aspect of it, actually. It's charming. Or at least not strictly bad."
- "You know, I'm not giving this chorus enough credit. Good melody and counter-melody with the vocals and the keyboards. Maybe this song's even as good as mediocre?"
- "I can't believe I'm saying so, but this whole thing is a kinda funky jam, and it's getting into my bones. It might even be pretty good?"

> **Tony:** *A really good song.* [1]

Is it though? Is it *really*, Tony?
Well, you know...maybe it is. Maybe it is.

And so I find myself looking at 'Small Talk' now through a somewhat different lens. The glasses aren't rose-coloured but they're not eclipsed with total shade, either. I can genuinely say I enjoy everything 'Small Talk' brings to the table, despite my initial misgivings about it. I find it to be a solid member of the Genesis discography, and yet! And yet now and evermore, whenever I think of the song, the first thing that will pop into my head is that daggone note: "SMALL TALK." It's a permanent reminder to me of the place of scorn the song once held in my heart. I can appreciate it for what it is, but in a way that's forever clouded by what it once was. 'Small Talk' is, I'm afraid, the Most Improved Song in the Genesis discography for me.

> **Ray:** *It was a good backing [track]; it sounded a bit 'Sledgehammer'-ish to me, and I thought, "I really like this, I hope I can write something worthwhile." And I felt with the song I almost got it but not quite. It misses a hook for me. If it had one it could have been a great single but it is still a good song and I am happy with it.* [28]

Again, it's a testament to the quality of the band's portfolio that its Most Improved track would be this deep into the triple digits of my personal ranking, but there is a **lot** of strong material on offer from this band. 'Small Talk' an acquired taste; a block of funky cheese that repels you at first, but whose scent you grow to really appreciate if you're locked in a room with it. Maybe that just makes it Stockholm Syndrome: The Song, but Most Improved will have to do.

And in case you're wondering, no: I never played baseball again.

141 - Happy the Man

Single, 1972

The tour for *Nursery Cryme* marked the first time the band had ever gigged outside the UK, specifically heading to both Belgium and Italy in support of the album. They even did a half hour set for Belgian TV consisting of 'The Fountain of Salmacis', 'Twilight Alehouse' (which wouldn't appear again until after *Selling England* had come out), 'The Musical Box', and 'Return of the Giant Hogweeed'. Pretty strong set! Thankfully for the band, the Belgians and Italians loved them, and their European fandom only grew from there.

It was during this span of touring that they decided to release 'Happy the Man', an old concert staple from the pre-*Nursery Cryme* era.

> **Steve:** *Before I joined Genesis formally I had been to see them playing another gig...The band had started the set like an acoustic folk outfit, with a song called 'Happy the Man' that had something of a Cat Stevens feel. They were quieter than most bands I'd seen. They weren't trying to beat you over the head with volume. There was no bluster. They gradually built the energy up and I felt there wasn't a substantial rock tune until...the end [of the set]...Both then and during my time with Genesis in the early days, I used to long for that rock number at the end of the show...I personally would have been happy if the set had been full of those types of numbers and increasingly that's what happened: the band got louder and we gradually ditched the more acoustic moments, but here's me all these years later playing nylon guitar at least as much as I play electric, and I'm very glad for the time we spent tinkling away.* [1]

Rather than tacking it onto their next album, the soon-to-be *Foxtrot*, the band put the song out as a single with 'Seven Stones' as the B-side to capitalise on the goodwill their international touring had created for *Nursery Cryme*. And naturally, the single didn't do a doggone thing in *any* country, to the point where now sources can't even agree on when it came out. That's something of a shame, because 'Happy the Man' is a good time.

> **Tony:** *I didn't have much to do with [writing] it really. I was sort of there if you know what I mean? I was happy with it being a single. I quite liked it actually. That was quite fun to do. Once again, Mike had another tuning on the guitar where everything was tuned to a chord and he played a riff on that that sounded good. I played guitar along with him and we built it from there.* [6]

Steve's guitar strumming, which opens the track and continues throughout, can't be described as anything but "cheery." It's an instant mood of frolicking through a field somewhere, not a care in the world. Peter even punctuates this by banging his bass drum after the line "I don't care!" Nice of the guys to give him a chance to crack that drum on record, even if they padded it so much it couldn't be heard on stage.

'Happy the Man' is a song about being content with where you are and what you have, and it's a charming way to spend three minutes because of that. It was never going to succeed as a single, given that it lacks the kind of true verse/chorus structure that would've gotten it real radio play at the time, but that's all right. It's upbeat, enjoyable album filler that got released as a single instead, therefore predictably going yeah, yeah, yeah, yeah, yeah, nowhere on the charts. Oh well!

140 - *it.*

from *The Lamb Lies Down on Broadway*, 1974

The fourth side of *The Lamb Lies Down on Broadway* is something of a decrescendo. The story is winding down, the imagery becomes more grounded, and the music trends to a more sombre and reserved bent. This isn't universally true, of course, given that the side opens with the quirky 'The Colony of Slippermen' and has the frenetic 'Riding the Scree' in the middle, but the general trend of energy on the fourth side is downward. So when '*it.*' bursts out of the death throes of 'In the Rapids', it really grabs your attention. The song doesn't really sound like anything else on the album. It's an alien entity forcing itself into the end of Rael's journey, arresting the story with a sudden conclusion of energy when the listener thought it would go out quietly.

The lyrics make several referential call-backs to the rest of the album, but beyond that I can't really make any sense of them. The story in the liner notes says that Rael and his brother, who is now also Rael, dissolve into a purple haze and that "It's over to you," the listener. I couldn't begin to tell you what that means, beyond a general sense of "interpret this however you want," but I bring it all up to illustrate that by this point the story of *The Lamb* no longer means anything to me. The narrative conclusion, as far as I'm concerned, occurred with 'In the Rapids'.

So if musically the song feels removed from everything before it, and if lyrically/narratively it might as well not exist, '*it.*' to me is almost like a non-album track that just got attached to the end of the album, and I hear it in that way.

> **Tony:** ...a little disappointing...[it] could have been so good but we were rushing the recording by that time. [6]

> **Phil:** I remember '*it.*' We were really pushed to get the album finished, over at Island Studios, and by this point we had a day shift and a night shift. I was on the night shift with Peter, I think. And the day shift was Tony and Mike and Steve. And we did a mix of '*it.*', me and Pete, and the other guys came in and thought we were mad. Changed everything. There was a bit of friction there, but we were just trying to get it finished and get it out. [3]

Whether the disconnect with the rest of the album comes from the product being a bit overhurried I can't say for certain, but regardless it makes me unable to properly judge the song in context of *The Lamb* as a whole. Thankfully, I don't quite need to, because even as a wholly independent entity '*it.*' stands up pretty well.

And to prove that point, one need only listen to Phil's drumming on this track. Seriously, just play the song and ignore everything but the drums, if you can. Look, Phil Collins was a tremendous singer. The range, the power, all of it. One of the most talented rock singers I've ever heard. I'd put him up against almost anyone else vocally. So I really want you to understand what I mean when I say Phil Collins was a better drummer than he was a singer. And if you run into someone who questions that take, play that person '*it.*' That's the only retort you'll need. The rest of what's happening on the track is fine, and enjoyable in its own right, but this is a percussive showcase through and through. And in that way, I guess you could say *The Lamb* ended with a bang after all.

139 - Harold the Barrel

from *Nursery Cryme*, 1971

This song gets shot out of a gun straight onto your stereo. It's got such a strong energy to it, like they wrote a six minute song and then decided to just play the whole thing at double time and get it over in three instead; sort of a 'That Thing You Do' effect. I'm sure that's not at all what happened, and I'm not even using that as a criticism, but instead to illustrate just how utterly relentless the drive is here. It feels like if you blink you'll miss an entire verse.

And that would be a shame because the lyrics to this song are absolutely worth hearing. Not that they're deep or meaningful; quite the opposite, in fact (well, mostly). This is Genesis at their silliest, telling the story of a restaurant owner who suffers a mental breakdown, chops off his toes, then goes to a high rise with the intent to jump out the window to his death. Now, I get it. Self-mutilation and suicide are less "silly" and more "tragically dark," but hear it in context of the manic music and you'll get what I mean. Lines like "Hasn't got a leg to stand on," or my personal favourite, when Harold's mother is trying to convince him to get down from the ledge, "Your shirt's all dirty, there's a man here from the BBC!" She wants him to live not because she loves him for who he is but because she'd be embarrassed by his dishevelled corpse showing up on the news!

> **Phil:** *'Harold the Barrel' was a good, fun song. It showed the kind of humour that...always has been part of Genesis. People take us very seriously, but we don't. So that was a good thing.* [3]

These playful lyrics are delivered with a lot of oomph as well, thanks to Phil and Peter singing unified lead on the track. The two voices don't merely mesh seamlessly with one another, but they generate a ton of power as well.

> **Tony:** *[Phil's vocal impact] was more on the contributions where he's singing with Peter. 'Harold the Barrel' for example. They sing the whole thing as a duet. Sing it together. In fact they're actually mixed on the tape; you can't separate them...Sometimes it sounds a little Phil-biased, I think.* [3]

> **Peter:** *What happens is that my voice...has got quite a lot of bass content, low content. Phil's, on the other hand, has a much higher element, his sort of centre of gravity, if you like, harmonically. So if you put the two at exactly the same level, you'll read more of his voice than mine. Even though 'Harold the Barrel' was all my song, I think you do hear just as much of Phil if not more in some places. So I think when I left and that voice continued, that was easier for people to get used to.* [3]

It's the kind of song you'd want to dismiss out of hand as an exercise in frivolity and therefore not "real" music, but 'Harold the Barrel' won't let you do that. It demands your attention, and once it's got your attention it demands your respect as well, all the while making you roll your eyes and grin at how ridiculous its whole scenario is. At the end, as the pulsing beat disappears in favour of simple piano chords from Tony over a fading vocal of "jump," you realise that the conclusion of the tale is that Harold actually did jump, turning the tone into something much more sombre. It's enough that one almost feels guilty for having revelled in the whole affair. Almost.

138 - Pacidy

Live recording, 1970

The second of the three *Trespass* era non-album live tracks recorded on BBC's Night Ride radio program to appear on this countdown, 'Pacidy' was something of a turning point for the band from their attempts at writing hit pop tunes to doing something a bit different.

> **Tony:** *I always think of this as the time when we decided we were moving onto the next stage [of songwriting], writing songs like 'Pacidy'...* [1]

This song, like many others of this time period, really highlights just how proficient a player Ant was - and he was only 19 at the time this recording was made! No, there are no flashy solos or big lead parts. It's all just atmospheric acoustic playing, but the man doesn't miss a note. He's clearly the class of the band at this point in pure musicianship terms. So it's not a huge surprise that the mood he and the others manage to create is a sombre, effective one. Lyrically I'm not sure if the titular Pacidy - the singer's love interest - has broken up with him, or died, or suffered some other mysterious fate. But regardless, our vocalist seems to be taking it pretty hard, and the music captures that feeling well.

Of the non-album songs recorded in this era, this seems among the most likely to have made the next Genesis album if Ant had never left the band. Instead, with his fingerprints all over the thing, 'Pacidy' left the repertoire when he did.

> **Tony:** *'Pacidy' sounded good live as well but part of the problem was that we just had too much material - about two hours' worth - and when we did Trespass we could only get forty minutes on the album. By the time we came to Nursery Cryme we were fed up with those songs so we decided to do some new ones instead.* [6]

I do wonder what this song would have become if given the extra little tweaks to make it suitable for release on a studio album. Then again, maybe its exclusion was ultimately something of a mercy.

> **Mike:** *We often made life more complicated for ourselves. Somebody's aunt or grandmother had given us a cello, and I started trying to play it on 'Pacidy'. I couldn't play the cello at all, so I had to put white tape on the fretboard so I could work out where to put my fingers.* [1]

From *Nursery Cryme* hopeful to *Introductory Cello with Mike Rutherford*, 'Pacidy' seems to have fallen hard over a short period of time. Nevertheless, it survives in this live rendition on *Genesis Archive 1967-75*, sans fumbling cello, as another small snapshot into the world of Genesis that might've been had the *Trespass* line-up not changed. Compared to the Genesis sound that would come to dominate over the following years, 'Pacidy' features more intricate acoustic playing, with keyboards complementing that sound rather than overbearing or featuring on their own. It's a quainter, simpler world of Genesis; another foray into progressive, romantic folk music. For that reason alone it would be well worth a listen.

The fact that it manages to be so effective in its moodiness as well? That's just the icing on the cake.

137 - Twilight Alehouse

B-side of 'I Know What I Like (In Your Wardrobe)', 1974

Another live staple from the late *Trespass* era, 'Twilight Alehouse' served as the penultimate song in the band's standard set - a sort of appetiser for 'The Knife' to come, as it were. When Ant left the band they pivoted away from the song ahead of *Nursery Cryme* before coming back to it in the *Foxtrot* sessions. Though it may have fit decently well with the overall *Foxtrot* sound, when the dust settled there wasn't enough space left on the album for it, so the track was set aside once again. One might expect the third time to be the charm, but *Selling England by the Pound* is an album striving for a particular thing: a kind of "portrait of Englishness" that permeates the entire affair. 'Twilight Alehouse' didn't mesh with that either, and so it came to pass that a song written back in 1970 and played live pretty consistently over the intervening years didn't find official purchase on vinyl until early in 1974, when it accompanied the single release of 'I Know What I Like (In Your Wardrobe)' as its B-side.

> **Tony:** *Everybody seemed to want us to record 'Twilight Alehouse' [as a single] but we didn't particularly want to as we didn't think it was as good as some of the other ones [we had during the Trespass era].* [6]

That also makes this song something of a musical anomaly. By *Foxtrot* the band had come a long way as composers from the *Trespass* era. That's not to say the latter songs were strictly better, mind you, but the songwriting dynamic had significantly shifted. It'd be impossible for it to be otherwise, given the involvement and influence of both Phil and Steve at this point. No, they still weren't really writing songs on their own, but their contributions and sensibilities nevertheless helped shape everything Genesis put out.

Yet, since 'Twilight Alehouse' still got regular play in concerts, it didn't dramatically change or evolve over the years alongside the band's overall output. And that's a surprising statement to make given that, as documented in a 1972 performance for Belgian TV, nearly two minutes of runtime were added from the live staple to the version that eventually made it to record. One might assume two minutes to be huge deal, but here the extra time consists merely of another run through the chorus and then some additional flute and keyboard doodling around the main riff of the piece.

> **Ant:** *...A bit of a knockabout track...* [1]

Note that I don't say "doodling" in a derogatory sense, because the flute is my favourite part of this whole shebang. I think the opening verses are splendid; a dark, brooding atmosphere full of uncertainty, with ghostly guitars and little bells. By contrast, however, the chorus does absolutely nothing for me. I don't care for much of anything that happens within it, so the third run-through in the studio recording doesn't do the song any favours, in my opinion. But then the instrumental work feels like a big free flow jazzy improv session, and I can dig that pretty well. So while I don't think it's their most consistent prog effort, when we grant that 'Twilight Alehouse' had effectively six writers, that's probably to be expected. And through that lens, the results are pretty good on balance.

> **Steve:** *It had an interesting verse and a chorus that really aspired to be a blues [number] but I don't think the band were sufficiently prepared at that point to let their hair down... and so I didn't come up with any blues licks for them! I could have played all over it. I could have played the harmonica on it and done it justice.* [29]

...Can't say I'm not curious to hear that hypothetical harmonica version, though.

136 - One Man's Fool

from *Calling All Stations*, 1997

As the very first beats of this song kick in, you might think you somehow turned on 'Tonight, Tonight, Tonight' by mistake. That feeling dissipates rather quickly once the keyboard sounds jump into the mix, but I do wonder if Tony and Mike wanted to use a similar rhythmic base and see what they could build from it. They ended up with a track that has nearly nine minutes of runtime (only five seconds off from 'Tonight, Tonight, Tonight', in fact...), comprised of two distinct halves. The first half is brooding, dark. It's a reflection on the mind of a terrorist and an attempt to wrap one's mind around how someone could be willing to do such atrocious things. The second half then expands those thoughts and feelings into a more philosophical place, delivering a message about the importance of respecting one another's viewpoints whilst remaining sceptical of one's own.

Given how stark the divide between the two is, I think it makes sense to tackle them almost as though they were two different tracks entirely. Along those lines, I think the first half of 'One Man's Fool' has enough legs to have been able to stand on its own. Really, cut the first four-odd minutes of the song and rework the track's linking section into a proper ending, then put it out there with the name 'To All Who Think They Know'. It doesn't need the back half to work. It's a very straightforward, alt rock feeling, dark ballad. Sure, it doesn't particularly *go* anywhere within itself, and in that sense would probably never work as a hit single. But as a B-side or album filler? I've heard worse! The biggest flaw songs like that tend to have is dragging on too long, and in this case the first half of 'One Man's Fool' ends just as you begin to tire of it. So that works pretty well, I suppose.

Yet it's the second half where the song really manages to take off for me. Unlike the first bit, I don't think this second half works quite so well independently, and that puts the first half in context somewhat: it exists because the second part of the song almost mandates some sort of prelude. The sounds are wildly different, but the back half of 'One Man's Fool' is inherently a kind of payoff. There are subsections you could arguably point to as verses or choruses, but from the moment Ray pops back in with some vocals after the instrumental link you feel like you're listening to the final section of some twenty-minute prog epic. Just big, hopeful tones designed to fill you up.

Yes, the lyrics are a little preachy, but it's also anthemic. It's got a pull and gravitas about it. They throw in a darker break before the very end so as not to let that warmth lose its lustre, and it all culminates in the double-time vocals at the end. I think the real strength of this whole section is Ray, but surprisingly enough it's not his lead vocal that I'm most interested in; it's the repeated mantra-like backing vocal of "There are only dreams like any other." They carry a ton of water in giving this section its cathartic kind of vibe.

> **Ray:** *If I [were] going to add anything else from the Calling All Stations album [into my solo live set], it would be 'One Man's Fool', which was a good track...* [26]

Interestingly enough, Tony doesn't seem to feel the same way about it. In what could be a fascinating case study of how market success can change an artist's attitude towards his or her own work, Tony back in 1997 had almost nothing but praise for 'One Man's Fool' and for Ray's vocal performance in particular. Granted, he was doing interviews specifically to promote the album, but he doesn't strike me as the type to just outright lie.

> **Tony:** *I suppose it is the most distinctive Genesis track on the album in some ways. I think it is because it has all the elements. It is quite long, quite a lot of aspects to it and quite a heavy lyric...Musically I thought it was one of the most interesting things, the second half [of the song]...there are some nice little chord changes in there and a strong feel and I used a lot of this octave vocals from Ray which I think sound really strong. It sounds a little like Pete, I suppose when he does that but it has just got a strong character.* [25]

But fast forward ten years later and the situation has changed. The album didn't perform as well as anyone expected or hoped, a tour got nixed, and Genesis was reuniting for a new world tour with Phil Collins, Daryl Stuermer, and Chester Thompson all back on board. So what did 2007 Tony Banks have to say about the song and about Ray?

> **Tony:** *Previously I had been writing either specifically for Phil or for myself, and although some of the songs worked fine when they were transferred to Ray's voice, there were a couple that didn't work so well, particularly 'One Man's Fool'. The first half of the song was good, but the*

second half suffered. If Phil had been there I just know it would have just taken off and gone somewhere else. [1]

Isn't that wild? Tony went from saying the second half was the strength of 'One Man's Fool' in large part because of Ray's vocal contributions to saying that the second half actually dragged the song down because Ray simply didn't have the right voice for it. Now, again, this is marketing of a sort: new world tour coming, gotta get the fans excited and sell tickets, right? Since Calling All Stations was the last time Genesis had toured, I'm sure there was a little bit of trepidation about how much interest there would actually be in the band's reunion tour. Even still, I don't think anyone needs to really hype up Phil Collins, do they? And especially not at the expense of a guy who kind of got stuck between a rock and a hard place and gave it his all anyway.

For me? For me, I think it's all pretty good. I do wish that as a nine-minute composition it were a little more involved than "here's the first half, here's the second half," but that second half has enough of a "soar" to it that the song ends up being a decently strong album closer regardless. Of course, that wasn't the original plan for Calling All Stations, but more on that later to come. Still, when this is the last thing you hear on the album, you probably come away with a better overall impression than if it had ended on most of the other tracks I happen to like more.

Ultimately, 'One Man's Fool' is another track that's grown on me a fair bit since my first attentive listen, and I expect it may continue to do so over the years to come.

135 - Time Table

from *Foxtrot*, 1972

In 1979 Tony Banks released his first solo album, *A Curious Feeling*. But fans who were paying close attention knew that his first solo efforts actually came in the early 70s; they were just released as Genesis tunes with the band performing them. 'Time Table' is probably the biggest example of that - Tony gave the boys a song and they played it dutifully according to his instructions.

> **Tony:** *I came in with a complete piece and just sort of said "This is it," and we did it.* [3]

I like to imagine Tony walking into the rehearsal room with little booklets he got made at the local copy shop explaining everyone's parts. I'd say sheet music, but I'm pretty sure not all of them would've been able to read it. So instead it's like a packet of IKEA instructions, complete with a little confused Swedish man and a picture of drumsticks with an arrow pointing from them to a light snare drum. I'm sure that's not even remotely how it went, but hey, it's fun imagery.

Really, that "prefabricated" nature of the track might actually be part of why this song tends to be the underdog of sorts on *Foxtrot*. Everyone knows 'Supper's Ready' of course, and generally 'Horizons' by extension. It's similarly hard to forget the impactful opening of 'Watcher of the Skies', while both 'Get 'Em Out by Friday' and 'Can-Utility and the Coastliners' have their truly stalwart fans. I've seen people say any of these is their favourite from the album at some point or another.

And then there's 'Time Table', just sort of, you know, also there. It's not epic in length (second shortest on the album behind 'Horizons') or scope. It doesn't feature Peter Gabriel doing funny voices. It doesn't have big blaring chords that drill down into your core. It's just a tale of kings and queens and goblets and lost ideals, played on a tinkly toy piano. It's quaint by design. If *Foxtrot* as a whole was a maturation and evolution from the sound of *Nursery Cryme*, 'Time Table' is the missing link. It feels like it could fit on either album, a thread binding the two efforts together.

> **Steve:** *I detected a slightly sort of Beatle-y feel and so I tried to play guitar in a Beatle-y sort of way. I...just did an arpeggio guitar figure, very underplayed because I felt it was very much more a keyboard thing where the melody modulates...and I felt that all I needed to do was play underneath it. There was a little bit in there...where I go into the area of distortion, and try to give the music some angst that it doesn't have at one point. I think my contribution to that track is fairly minimal, but if you play the track back without me, you would notice the difference.* [30]

Perhaps unsurprisingly, the tinkly piano bits are the best part of this song. I'd imagine if this track were group-written we might have seen some strong new elements emerge, but it's only natural that a song written entirely by Tony would be a piano feature through and through. The vocal melodies are pleasant if not incredible, but the little introspective piano response to the chorus is the real highlight. I don't think many Genesis fans - even the hardcore fans of their early days - would ever choose 'Time Table' as their favourite Genesis song overall, but I also think one would be hard-pressed to find anyone who simply doesn't like it at all. It's a charming little ditty in the midst of a load of thicker stuff, and I think there's a lot of value in that.

134 - Visions of Angels

from *Trespass*, 1970

While we like to think of Genesis as a group where every member (not including the pre-Phil drummers, anyway) is an accomplished songwriter, that of course wasn't always the case. The writing for *From Genesis to Revelation* was dominated by Tony and Peter writing as a pair; Mike and Ant were a writing pair as well, but there was a skill divide there.

> **Ant:** *Peter and Tony were way out front on the first album, no doubt about it. Mike and I were playing catch up.* [1]

This is evident not just by surveying what made it onto that first LP, but also by what didn't.

> **Ant:** *I had started to write on piano, independently of Mike, and so I had my own thing going with a couple of tracks. In fact we did a version of 'Visions of Angels' for [From Genesis to Revelation] which...just didn't work out - a much better version ended up on Trespass... [it] was a godsend.* [1]

See, the final track selection for the debut came largely from the band (and, likely, Jonathan King) deciding which of their pieces were their best ones at that point in time. Ant's 'Visions of Angels' - a piano tune written by a guitarist - wasn't good enough to make the final cut. Which sounds absurd on its surface when comparing this piece to the majority of that first album, but we're not hearing the original version of the song on *Trespass*. The 'Visions of Angels' we ended up with was one that had time to grow and refine, well beyond its initial limitations.

> **Ant:** *That was a very early piano song for me...I couldn't play the piano at all in a conventional way...I think Tony thought I was an idiot, which would be understandable, but like a lot of idiots, sometimes you come up with something that's just a little bit different. I was helped by the fact that I was very limited. A song with too much skill isn't necessarily a good idea...The middle section with Tony's keyboard, the chords and all that sort of glory that it gave it, makes so much difference to it.* [3]

The piano-based origin story for the piece is immediately evident from the moment the song begins. But over the intervening time between its initial writing and the version laid down for *Trespass*, guitars took over a lot of that original piano work. This is good, because dominant piano melodies were one of the primary sounds of *From Genesis to Revelation*, and stripping that away makes 'Visions of Angels' sound much more mature by comparison. More importantly, it allows the middle of the song to feature keyboards as a contrast instead of as a homogenous "more of the same." That contrast in turn really strengthens the entire piece as well.

In a lot of ways, 'Visions of Angels' is the first "real" Genesis song. It's an outtake from the band's first album that, once free of the demand to be a straightforward pop song, was allowed to expand, be rearranged, and develop into a piece with multiple sections. It's got big chords; proto "walls of sound," if you will. It's got a keyboard solo. It's got a pretty good vocal from Pete, no longer trying to sound like pure sugar. "I believe there never is an end" gives me chills - it's a fantastic delivery of a good line. It's even got some pretty solid drumming, which we tend not to expect when thinking about pre-Collins Genesis. This is the beginning of the signature Genesis sound. Not bad for a first outing, boys. Not bad at all.

133 - Eleventh Earl of Mar

from *Wind & Wuthering*, 1976

Much like 'Watcher of the Skies' before it, 'Eleventh Earl of Mar' opens a Genesis album with a swelling, ethereal bit of instrumental playing. This time around though, instead of Tony playing Mellotron, the effect is accomplished through Steve's guitar, soaring like a ghost above the chords flowing below. The intro doesn't linger around quite as long as the one in 'Watcher'; in fact it's about exactly half as long, going forty-five seconds compared to the ninety of that earlier track. But it's nevertheless an effective opening salvo, grabbing your attention and getting you engaged into the album right from the get-go.

> **Tony:** *One of the chords in that is basically a G-minor chord with an A-flat in the bass. That sounds unlikely, but it sounds great in context. A lot of this comes out of improvising - doing things that you originally didn't intend to do and finding that it sounds nice.* [23]

> **Tony:** *I wrote these strange chords and thought it would make a great introduction. It had an atmosphere about it which sets up the whole thing. Steve had the chorus and the chords; Mike then wrote most of the lyrics for it.* [27]

Like 'Watcher of the Skies' before it, the eerie intro doesn't much inform the rest of the song. Both songs move from heavy chords and high atmosphere into something much more rhythmic and - dare I say - peppy. It really makes this song feel like a bit of a bridge between the five-piece era and the three-piece era. And yes, I say that knowing that this song took place during the four-piece era so there's a sense of "no duh" about the statement, but I'm singling out this track in that way because it sounds remarkably like two *other* versions of Genesis within itself. That opening section wouldn't feel out of place on *Foxtrot* or *The Lamb Lies Down on Broadway*, while this primary verse sounds to me like a kindred soul to something like 'Scenes from a Night's Dream' one album later.

> **Phil:** *There's bits of it that...we played [by] listen[ing] to a groove and that is obviously the best way to do it...* [31]

As if that weren't enough ingredients in the recipe, at around the four minute mark the song takes a significant detour into yet another feel entirely. This middle section comes from a piece Steve had been writing on his own, called 'House of the Four Winds'. As Steve had already demonstrated on his 1975 solo effort *Voyage of the Acolyte*, he was very interested in exploring the way abstract ideas might sound. In that album the ideas were fortunes from tarot cards; here the idea is wind itself. Can one capture the "essence" of wind, so to speak, in musical form? While Steve's material didn't always generate much interest from the rest of the band, 'House of the Four Winds' was a bit they were eager to use, so it was pulled into the song where Steve already had a chorus running, and repurposed to be the bridge. Incidentally, this is also where the "Wind" from the album title *Wind & Wuthering* gets its name (the "Wuthering" coming from the titles of the pair of instrumentals that prelude the album's closer, 'Afterglow').

> **Steve:** *One of the reasons we have so many different elements in one song, let alone an album, is that if the listener doesn't respond to one thing, he probably will to another thing. If you're going to lose them there, you'll catch them somewhere else.* [31]

Now, all of that's well and good, but if I absolutely adored this song, it wouldn't very likely be sitting here well into the triple digits of this ranking. So what gives?

In a word: words. It's the lyrics. I just...they're just *awful*, you know? If we think back to 'The Battle of Epping Forest', the lyrical inspiration for that piece came from Peter reading an old newspaper story, fabricating some details, and acting it out like a play. 'Eleventh Earl of Mar' seems to be Mike thinking, "Maybe I can do that, too," and the results are disastrous.

> **Mike:** *The lyrics were inspired by a story I'd found about a near uprising among the old Scottish clans. I knew we'd suffer a bit lyrically without Pete. When you were writing words you'd often be tied by the music to a certain area, but both Tony and I...didn't have the edge of reality that Pete always had. Even when he was at his most quirky, there'd be a harder edge to Pete's lyrics and he'd ground them more in human life and human emotions...but at the time we didn't really allow ourselves to have any of these thoughts: it would have been too depressing.* [14]

It's an inelegant retelling of the failed military life of 18th century Scotsman John Erskine. Depending on which creation of the earldom you're referencing (and this is a wild rabbit hole of confusion you absolutely do not want to go down), Erskine was either the 6th, 11th, or 23rd Earl of Mar, so I suppose "Eleventh" must've just sounded better on tape than "Twenty-third Earl of Mar, couldn't get them very far." I generally like story songs, and I also like history, so one would think a song like this would be a huge winner in my book. Tell me about battles and conquests all, and we're probably golden even if the delivery leaves something to be desired. But 'Eleventh Earl of Mar' doesn't go that direction. It can't, frankly, because its chosen subject is a failed general who is most famous for retreating from a battle in which he had arguably the upper hand, who then spent the remainder of his life branded untrustworthy by essentially everyone who ever knew him. That's neat trivia as far as I'm concerned, but it was never going to work as engaging subject matter for a progressive rock song.

Yet even still, if I were merely disinterested in the subject matter sufficiently that I could simply dismiss the lyrics altogether, that would be fine. But that's not a mercy Mike Rutherford granted me. Instead, inexplicably, the entire lyrical affair is framed with constant interjections along the lines of "DADDY! YOU PROMISED!" That I just can't abide. It's a downright baffling, nigh unforgivable line - and it's the lyrical backbone of the entire song. More than that, it's delivered by Phil Collins in a manner I can only really describe as "petulant yelling." I don't fault Phil for this, I think; the poor guy was just doing what was asked of him and I'm sure he was working outside his comfort zone. But performing those lines *should* make him uncomfortable. On account of them being so terrible.

Mike: *'Eleventh Earl of Mar' had a tremendous energy. It was always good on stage.* [27]

The good news is that the music *does* have that energy about it and does do its best to salvage what the lyrics try so hard to throw away. The intro is bookended by a likeminded outro - there's that 'Watcher of the Skies' influence again - and they do their jobs well, even if the outro has to contend with an echoing "DADDYYYYYY!" in transition. Tony's keyboard melodies are likewise quite strong throughout. Yet I think it's that 'Four Winds' bridge that really what makes the whole thing work for me. Its presence means that rather than five non-stop minutes of "Daddy" yells and incomprehensible "military exploits," the listener gets a chance to breathe with an introspective interlude that makes better sense of the intro/outro and really ties the whole song together. With that in mind, it's hard for me to come away from 'Eleventh Earl of Mar' and think that maybe Steve didn't have a point about his material deserving a bigger spotlight within the band after all.

132 - Nowhere Else to Turn

Promotional release only, 1997

OK, OK, I'll admit it. I'm cheating a bit here. The core concept behind this book was to rank every song that ever received an official release from the band according to my personal tastes, yet 'Nowhere Else to Turn' doesn't *technically* fit that grouping, as it was never officially released. In fact, at the time of this writing it remains impossible to legally "own" 'Nowhere Else to Turn' in any format. So why am I including it in this project?

Well, unlike various early compositions that never made it onto tape at all (and so are necessarily excluded because nobody outside the band or earliest live audiences have ever heard them), 'Nowhere Else to Turn' *was* actually recorded, produced, and prepared for release. It was included on a promotional CD with the other non-album tracks from the *Calling All Stations* sessions and delivered to executives at the record company for the purpose of determining which songs would become the B-sides to the album's singles. There were eight of these extra tracks in total, and ultimately three singles were released from the album, with seven of the eight "bonus" songs released among them as B-sides. With no further singles, this song had - *ahem* - nowhere else to turn, and was allowed to vanish.

> **Ray:** *I don't know why it wasn't used [as a B-side]...it might be that it was crap.* [32]

Yikes! I don't think I'd go nearly that far, Ray. Granted, on a musical level this song is pretty emblematic of all that hardcore fans of Genesis' more progressive works hate about their later efforts. It's got a very simple, straightforward composition. Tony plays some romantic chords, Nir Zidkyahu lays down a basic drumbeat, and Mike strums a few bass notes to hold it together. Above it all is Ray singing a melody without much variation or dramatic range, belting lyrics that are about as vanilla as a love song could be. There's virtually nothing "interesting" happening here. It's an adult contemporary, soft rock song that doesn't make any significant effort to differentiate itself.

But you know what? *Who cares?* People can use this song as the poster child for Genesis allegedly losing their inspiration, or selling out, or whatever other cynical bent they want. And maybe they're not even incorrect, yet I have absolutely no problem turning on a song like this and just enjoying the music. There's nothing exciting, sure, but there's nothing offensive either, and I'm certainly not bored by it. The melody is simple, yes, but it's also really pretty. It's the sort of song I can put on in the background and it lifts my mood even if I'm not actively listening to it. Maybe that's not everyone's cup of tea, but I find there's a lot of value in it. And since I'm not ranking these songs by compositional quality, but rather by how much I like listening to them, I don't feel any guilt for saying: I like 'Nowhere Else to Turn'.

> **Ray:** *They gave me that one to write lyrics to...they did all the backing tracks and didn't know what the hell to do with it, [so] they gave it to me...'Nowhere Else to Turn' was a b-list song and we left it off [Calling All Stations] because we didn't think it was good enough...I certainly wouldn't put it into my set.* [26]

Ray may think this one is utter trash, but he and I (and many of you reading this book, I'm guessing) will have to respectfully agree to disagree.

131 - Here Comes the Supernatural Anaesthetist

from *The Lamb Lies Down on Broadway*, 1974

One of the few tracks on *The Lamb Lies Down on Broadway* where Steve credits himself as the primary songwriter, 'Here Comes the Supernatural Anaesthetist' follows his vein of mostly writing what he knows: guitar. As reflects the rationale behind the typical advice for aspiring writers of words "write what you know" is a way to get set up for success by making the bar easier to clear. There's a kind of "threshold of quality" when it comes to most creative endeavours. Now, that's not to say that an artistic or creative pursuit that doesn't cross that point has no inherent value. Art is entirely subjective, after all, and I'd argue the most important element in artistic expression is whether the product has meaning to the artist producing it. Nevertheless, critical evaluation is a natural human response to this, and while it can be difficult to pinpoint or articulate what makes some art generally successful and other art less so, it's a classic case of "you know it when you see it."

Steve Hackett, for his part, was still a relatively novice songwriter at this point in time. His playing chops were wonderful and his writing was rapidly improving, but at this point in time he was still finding his footing a bit. So it's unsurprising that, when looking over his writing credits before *The Lamb*, we find songs like 'For Absent Friends', 'Horizons', and 'After the Ordeal'. By bringing material to the band that was guitar-centred, Steve was writing what he knew. Maybe a complicated keyboard arrangement wasn't something he could pin down. Maybe drum patterns were still a little troublesome to wrap his mind around. Steve could've brought in a complete piece and told everyone what to do just like Tony Banks did with 'Time Table', but would the results have been any good? No, while he did have major contributions to more band-focused works like 'Can-Utility and the Coastliners', Steve's modus operandi as a songwriter was to write himself some nifty guitar parts to play and let the band build around him. Much easier to clear that threshold of quality that way and produce something that sounds pretty good, all the while building skill for more ambitious future endeavours.

Thus, 'Here Comes the Supernatural Anaesthetist', which consists of twenty-five seconds of Phil and Peter singing high-low harmonies followed by two minutes of guitar solo. The growth demonstrated here comes from the fact that those earlier guitar pieces were almost uniformly gentle in scope. They were all pleasant listening, like Steve was strumming a sunny day into existence. This one, by contrast, is quirky and chirpy and almost alien. Which makes some sense, as the album's story at this point has Rael coming face to face with Death, who is wearing an anaesthetist's costume, and who puffs some sort of gas into Rael's face before dancing away into a wall, as I suppose Death is wont to do. So the music here - though I'm sure it was written before the lyrics and story got attached - is really painting a picture of Death in a silly costume cavorting away. But of course, the picture is fuzzy because the viewpoint - Rael - has been sprayed with a gas that, if not fatal, is at least psychotropic to some degree.

So while still safe in one regard, 'Here Comes the Supernatural Anaesthetist' is also Steve Hackett the Songwriter stretching his wings a bit. Not tranquil, but a breath of silly fresh air on the otherwise serious back half of *The Lamb*; ironic given that it's a puff of anything but for Rael. It works better in the flow of the album than it does as a standalone piece, but it's pretty good either way. It's no wonder that he found the confidence to create *Voyage of the Acolyte* in the year to come; he proved to both himself and the band here that he was capable of more than even he had previously realised.

130 - The Colony of Slippermen

from *The Lamb Lies Down on Broadway*, 1974

The first Genesis song since 'Supper's Ready' to have explicitly defined movements, 'The Colony of Slippermen' is only a third the length of that earlier piece. Moreover, it doesn't musically strike me as three different songs smashed together into one, as might be expected from its stated division of Arrival, A Visit to the Doktor, and Raven. I think the movements are more for lyrical/narrative divisions than musical ones, so that's probably the reason for it - after all, the music on *The Lamb* was written before they had any of the lyrics, for the most part. So my best guess is that this was written as one song with no movements, and then the lyrics came in and a decision was made to split it three ways to support the story being told.

At any rate, this song kicks off the fourth side of *The Lamb*, and while it's connected to the events of side three by the story in the album's liner notes, 'The Colony of Slippermen' begins a five song stretch where the narrative is clear even without the benefit of that extra text. Everything else that happens during side four is a direct result of everything that occurs lyrically in this one song. I say that to make the point that I think this is one of Peter's stronger lyrical efforts on the album from a narrative point of view, providing listeners with a strong anchor point to a story that is otherwise at times utterly confusing. There's a lot to be said for the poetry and beauty of some of those other lyrics, but by this point in the album having a song play out like a fast-paced fiction novel is just what the Doktor ordered.

The musical highlight of 'The Colony of Slippermen' for me is its melody. A song doesn't have to have a strong melody to be good, but that aspect of music is one that I particularly latch onto, so having one really helps me sink my teeth into a piece. Here the core melody is really solid and used in both the Arrival and Raven sections of the song, effectively acting as the "verse,", while the melody of A Visit to the Doktor feels something like a chorus by contrast. Perhaps that's because that section includes a name drop of the track's title, or maybe it's just because of what surrounds that bit of playing: a tense lead-in with the keys acting like a pre-chorus while the section's own ending sounding almost like a bridge.

So the whole piece gives this illusion that it's got a traditional verse/chorus song construction, when of course that's not at all what's happening. For one thing, it's all preceded by over a minute and a half of quirky guitar, effectively conjuring up images of these weird lumpy creatures milling about in some underground city. While I could very easily do without those first ninety seconds personally (they do nothing to enhance or detract from the experience for me), they do produce effective imagery...once you know what kind of images you're supposed to be imagining. Beyond the intro, 'The Colony of Slippermen' also has a big keyboard solo. If we consider this song to be like a stage play where Peter portrays Rael (and the slippermen and the Doktor), and Phil portrays John, Tony is tasked with portraying the Raven. It's a good solo regardless, but much cooler when considered in that context, synths a-flarin' and wings a-flappin'.

So if, other than perhaps that first introductory bit, I really like the musical aspect of this song, why would I put so many other Genesis tunes above it? Well for starters, I'm going to let you in on a little secret: I *really* like Genesis, and I think they easily have over a hundred "good" or better songs. But there's also an elephant in the room whenever 'The Colony of Slippermen' comes up. I've mentioned already that the song is a great narrative anchor for the album, and that's true, but it's also true that by this point in *The Lamb Lies Down on Broadway* I just really don't care for that narrative whatsoever. I've never been particularly interested in surrealism, and *The Lamb* really leans into that harder and harder the longer the album goes on. And then the centrepiece of this song is what, chopping off male organs and sticking them into tubes? Really? It's not the kind of thing I'd ever personally feel like singing along with. I get what's happening and I appreciate what the story is trying to convey on a larger scale, but ultimately 'The Colony of Slippermen' is just completely gross to me, and that can be a little bit hard to get past.

It's not just me, either. On the album's supporting tour, one of Peter's priorities was helping communicate the lyrics and ideas to an audience that hadn't necessarily already absorbed the whole album. Strong visual aids go a long way in helping audience members connect to the subject matter being sung about. That's great for a lot of songs, but it meant that for 'The Colony of Slippermen' the goal was going to be all about lumpy men and their genitalia.

> **Peter:** *I've always loved visual things...interesting looking visuals get a reaction from people. Much in the same way the fox's head and the dress had gotten a strong reaction, the slipperman was a really ugly looking thing. I would crawl out of this phallus which would unroll on the stage, and it was a great moment.* [3]

> **Phil:** *I was starting to feel like the music was being overshadowed by the visuals, which were getting a little bit out of hand...It was very Spinal Tap. Cutting edge, but Spinal Tap. And the*

worst was the slipperman, where he came through this inflatable dick, and dressed in this horrible outfit, which sometimes got a little bit stuck on the way out. And other times when he did make it out, the microphone could barely get near his throat. And then he was out of breath! I mean, there's a lot of words in that song, and he was running around...he kind of hadn't really thought it through, I don't think. [3]

Peter: *Phil's absolutely correct on that. It was bloody hard to sing inside there. We didn't have those little tiny mics, so inside this mask I was trying to hold the microphone and tripping up over things at different points...appearing at different places. But I was just trying to explore things and push it a lot and have fun. Because it was fun. But again...I knew that if everything went to the vote it would die a horrible death.* [3]

Phil: *It's what Spinal Tap was written for. It's funny, and it was adventurous, and it was edgy, and it was like nobody else, and we should be thankful that we were all in the same band experiencing it, but: I didn't think it was very musical, that's all.* [3]

While compiling interview bits for this project, I found that Genesis had very little to say about what went into the music of 'The Colony of Slippermen', focusing instead more on the visuals and logistics around playing it live. Since I'm a big fan of the music but would just as soon the piece have altogether different lyrics (or none altogether!), this was something of a disappointment for me. And yet, it makes perfect sense, doesn't it? These guys lived through that entire tour, night after night, and the tour happened more recently than the writing of the music. We often remember things in reverse order, with the most recent coming to the forefront of memory most easily. For these guys, the visuals and logistics ended up defining 'The Colony of Slippermen' more than the composition itself did.

I guess in a way that's true for me as well. As much as I'd like to forget about the lyrics and their subject matter, perhaps focusing mainly on things like the keyboard solo that survived the years to enter live medleys during the band's three-piece era, I can't help my instinctive responses. And my instinctive response when I hear the word "slippermen" is, simply, "ew." There's a really, really good song buried under all those lumps. Perhaps you'll find it more easily than I did.

129 - Paperlate

from *3x3*, 1982

When Phil Collins was recording his debut album *Face Value*, he got an idea. Really, more like a fantasy - one that happened to come true:

> **Phil:** *Earth, Wind & Fire are one of my favourite bands...I'd wanted to use [their horn section] on some of Duke but I'd thought "No way. Black mafia and white boys? No chance." But when I asked this guy from Atlantic [Records] in America to see what he could do for me they agreed...I think I'd like them for the next Genesis album [as well]. They rang up last week to find out what was happening.* [33]

Having enjoyed working with Collins on his solo album and getting jazzed about the concept of working with Genesis, the only remaining obstacle to getting the Phenix Horns (that aforementioned brass section from Earth, Wind & Fire) was convincing Mike and Tony that they would make for a good addition to the overall sound of *Abacab*. As it turned out, the band happened to have a pair of songs on hand that they felt the horns would go well with. Of those two, 'Paperlate' was excluded from *Abacab* not because the band thought it was a bad effort, but because they thought it was a little *too* good.

> **Mike:** *[This song is likely to be] a BIG hit.* [34]

More to the point though, *Abacab* was an album featuring Genesis at its most experimental, trying to sort of "undefine" what the Genesis sound was all about. That mission statement worked both ways, though. It wasn't going to be enough to simply deconstruct the box that Genesis felt themselves constrained by; they would also need to avoid building an entirely new box around themselves. Thus, while both 'Paperlate' and the other "featuring the Phenix Horns" track 'No Reply At All' were songs the band was proud of, putting them on the same album would undermine the album's impact by driving public perception of "the new Genesis sound" to something horn-driven and altogether poppy. Phil Collins had no such compunctions with his solo work, of course, but for Genesis this meant that 'Paperlate' - which they favoured more as a pure single - had to be excised from the album.

> **Phil:** *I was a bit worried that I was maybe pushing and putting my neck on the line if it didn't work. And Tony had some reservations at the beginning but we're all happy with it now.* [34]

Ironic then that the title of this song that serves to help tear down the band's past is itself a reference to their prog heyday: "paperlate" comes from one of the opening lines of 'Dancing with the Moonlit Knight', though that's the only thing the two tracks have in common. Unlike anything that can be heard on *Selling England by the Pound*, 'Paperlate' is a high energy rock/big band number with a relentless drive and a catchy hook. As this was the start of the music video era, the band made one consisting of their appearance promoting the song on *Top of the Pops*. It gives a good visual sense of the energy of the piece, though naturally the whole band was just miming the performance so in the end all you hear is the studio recording. Still, it's got an undeniable pulse about it.

Between the two Genesis/Phenix collaboration tracks, I personally like 'No Reply at All' ever so slightly more, but 'Paperlate' is still very solid in its own right. How solid? Let's just say it managed to sell the British public on an EP that also included 'Me and Virgil'. Now *that's* impressive.

128 - Lilywhite Lilith

from *The Lamb Lies Down on Broadway*, 1974

He writes as a nearly middle-aged man, with very pale skin, quietly talking to himself. He discovers he is at a loss and asking for a muse. "What's the use of a muse if you've got nothing to say?" ask the readers. "I've got something to say," he replies, "and if you quiet your own critical noise, I'll show you. I'm a creature of habit and I know what I like (in my wardrobe)."
He moves across the genres and they leave the dwellers of prose, who dismiss their departure as certain to fail.

The readers were in confusion - on all their faces furrowed brows
I could almost just hear, a voice unclear mutter,
"The hell's he on about?!"
Said "'Just a Job to Do' or 'Since I Lost You'
Those are choices I could get behind.
Cut another Lamb, the best from the band? You've lost your mind!"

'Lilywhite Lilith',
The guitar is growling and the melody's tight.
'Lilywhite Lilith',
Starting the side off right.

When through the shock, he leads the readers into musical analysis. The riff of the guitar soon fades but the confident steps of the band prevent their stumbling in the darkness. After a solid verse they arrive in what he judges to be a big fun chorus, and he speaks a second time, noting Phil's highly effective backing vocals. It feels like a choral arrangement.
"Readers, listen here. Steve's interlude will come to you soon. Don't be afraid; it's understated but really good." And failing to explain any more, he leaves off. They face their dissatisfaction once again.

When I'd led them through the breakdown, the angry noise began to grow.
They said "You have rated this track far too low!
What do you even know?"
So I pleaded my case that I enjoy this song, they said
"It's one-twenty-eight, and that means that you're wrong."
Then they try to claim they hated this book all along.

'Lilywhite Lilith',
Evolved from an early piece known as 'The Light'.
'Lilywhite Lilith',
This chorus is outta sight.

An interlude is lit up in front of him, and he begins to bob his head. As it grows in intensity, he hears a non-aggressive, pleasant instrumental. The readers are feeling painfully incredulous, asking how this can possibly be better than 'The Battle of Epping Forest' until their voices are lost in a sort of numbing silence.

This ain't just 'bout my rankings,
I've gotta fill, fill the page.
And if you don't like my poetry,
Well at least this chapter isn't 'In The Cage'.
If you flip to the end of the book now,
You'll see what I chose as number one.
But I hope you keep counting down with me,
'Cause I think the surprise is part of the fun.

127 - No Reply at All

from *Abacab*, 1981

When the very first note you hear on a Genesis track is a trumpet punch, you know you're in for a different kind of ride. And though the first single from *Abacab* was the title track, 'No Reply at All' was also released in advance of the album, almost like a warning. BEWARE: Genesis-yet-not-Genesis ahead. Contemporary critical reviews of the album were mostly positive, but that's because contemporary critics tended to hate everything the band had done previously. They called out 'Who Dunnit?' as the highlight of the record for crying out loud, so I'm not sure we can really lean on these opinions as more than historical footnotes. The band's fans, though? Well, safe to say many of them did not care for these bold departures in the slightest.

> **Phil:** *I'd been working with the Earth, Wind & Fire horns. I thought, if we're going to reinvent ourselves, why not have some horns on there? I mean, this is a song here we've written that sounds like kind of a funky thing, an R&B thing, why not have horns on it? Who says we can't have horns on it? It's our fucking record, you know? So we did it. And people hated it.* [3]

But once the initial shock wore off that Genesis had done something so out of left field, many fans eventually did come around on 'No Reply at All'. Which is a good thing, because it's a pretty solid romp. The groove is strong and the melody turn on the chorus still has that trademark Genesis feel to it, where the right chord comes at just the right time to hit you in just the right way. That's good stuff. It's also got a stripped down section halfway through that works really well as a contrast to the bulk of the tune. And for a tune called 'No Reply at All', ending the song with a call and answer between the vocals and horns is something of a brilliant move.

> **Phil:** *It probably sounds like I wrote it because I suggested the horn lines. Prior to that the band wasn't really interested in using horns in our music. The way the tune came about was, like most of our compositions, through improvising in rehearsal. We just get together and play, and if we find something we like we record it. Later I wrote the lyrics for the tune and suggested the horn arrangement...Quite often our music happens by accident. It's a difficult process to describe, other than to say that just getting together and playing as a group and coming up with beats and parts that we like is the basis of our songwriting. I wanted, in 'No Reply', to write something that the Jackson 5 might like to record. I also wanted to steer the group into an area of music that we hadn't tried before.* [24]

But truly, the highlight of the song for me is Rutherford's bass. Usually when talking about a rhythm section one looks to the drummer first. And of course, Phil's drumming remains beyond reproach here, but Mike's doing all kinds of intricate stuff and shouldn't be overlooked. Sometimes he's on the beat, sometimes off the beat. Sometimes he's doubling a melody, sometimes he's doing his own thing entirely. Even if you aren't actively listening to him on the track, the effort subconsciously makes the song much more interesting. The horns are cool, but they don't make this song. The bass does.

Either way, whether because contemporary Genesis fans rejected the experiment, or because the band didn't want to re-tread what by then would be old ground, the prominent horn sounds of 'No Reply at All' and 'Paperlate' only returned once over the rest of the band's catalogue, on 'Anything She Does' - and then only as Tony's keyboards outputting some questionable synthesized brass. I'm ultimately glad they didn't dwell in this sound for longer than they did, but I readily appreciate what we ended up with here.

126 - I Know What I Like (In Your Wardrobe)

from *Selling England by the Pound*, 1973

We live in a musical world today where it's pretty common for a band or recording artist to go three to five years between album releases. If it's a new artist the label is really trying to push, maybe that condenses down to two years for that initial follow-up effort to the debut, which consists of several months of touring in support of that initial release and then perhaps a year of writing and recording. We accept this as the normal timing of things, though as someone engaged in generating creative output myself, it does seem to me like a pretty cramped window of time to hope that brilliance might somehow emerge. Come to think of it, that's likely why "filler" tracks exist in the first place; the label has a deadline for the album but you've only managed to come up with enough good ideas to fill half of one? Better just churn out some mundane tunes to keep your job!

At any rate, it's mind-boggling to me now to look back at the classic rock era and see how those timeframes were even more condensed. For example, fresh off the *Foxtrot* tour in 1973, Genesis' label Charisma decided that the tour and album were successful enough that they could afford to be patient and generous with the band as they recorded their follow-up album, which would be their fifth overall and fourth on the label, which saw their first release in 1970 just a few years earlier. This "generous" span of time off consisted of two or three **months**. And the band actually felt like they relaxed a bit! It's astonishing to me a work like *Selling England by the Pound* could have formed over a single summer but that's essentially what happened. At the outset though, there was some worry.

> **Tony:** *On this particular record, we were a bit stuck for ideas. There were two or three things that we knew we had. There was this riff that Steve had been playing on stage and all over the place, which we thought was really good. And we knew we wanted to do something with that. And we developed that into the song 'I Know What I Like'.* [3]

> **Steve:** *Phil and I used to jam on this thing. And no-one else was that keen. They said "It sounds too much like the Beatles, we're not gonna do it." The following album, Phil and I are still jamming away on the same thing, playing it like idiots. And the whole band joined in, it became a jam, and it became a song, it became a hit. And I remember joking about this to journalists, "Oh you should hear our latest hit single!" As if it was a done deal! And I was just joking, and then it became a hit! And I was thrilled, of course.* [3]

The first twenty seconds of the song have more in common with 'The Waiting Room' than with any pop song, but from there it's every bit as prog-pop as anything that the band put out in the 80s or the 90s. Verse, chorus, verse, chorus, chorus, extended outro. Folks, that's a pop song. The fans who vocally decry the "pop era" of the band tend to give this one a pass, probably because it was written in 1973, but this song has more in common structurally with 'In Too Deep' than it does with 'Supper's Ready'. If, like me, you don't have any qualms about Genesis producing high quality pop material, then that statement won't prickle you.

> **Phil:** *That was us doing our Beatle thing. Which we didn't see any harm in, because we had yet to have a hit single. So nobody else minded either. As soon as we had a hit single, that's when they started to mind about us having hit singles.* [3]

Funnily enough, despite having spent all of the late 1960s desperately chasing singles success, and despite spending the whole of the 1980s as chart darlings, and despite breaking up the band in 1998 because they couldn't pack arenas anymore, back at this exact moment when 'I Know What I Like' began to land on the radar, Genesis had some misgivings about possibly getting *too* famous and diluting their own brand:

> **Tony:** *We knew we had written something that had single potential although we were a bit embarrassed about it as we weren't supposed to be a singles band. Anyway, Charisma put it out and we refused to go on Top Of The Pops! We thought that was enough of a stand.* [6]

It's hard to overstate the importance of the core riff to this song. It's the engine that makes everything work, the very foundation the song was built upon. If that riff is no good, the whole song falls apart. But it had to be good if Genesis decided to finally give it a try after hearing Phil and Steve play it hundreds of times. The band would seem to agree about its quality, having used the riff as the anchor for the ending section of the 'Old Medley' during the *We Can't Dance* tour, allowing their other songs to weave in and out of its flow. Even if you're not a huge fan of medleys in general, it's a pretty cool moment.

> **Phil:** *In the studio the song didn't strike us as particularly "pop", though it was of pop-single duration. We had got hold of a sitar-guitar, something used by The Beatles. Steve played the basic riff, which sounded good, I started to play a Beatle-ish groove, and it went from there. Peter's lyrics came in quite late, because they were influenced by the Betty Swanwick painting (The Dream) on the album cover. On the track, my voice is in there, in a kind of duet with Peter. And that's it. Genesis have their first hit.* [12]

> **Mike:** *You must understand that the word pop - we grew up with The Beatles. It's the best band in the world, and they were pop. This word "pop" has become something different now. A great song is a great song...and I suppose 'I Know What I Like' is one of the first songs we actually were able to sort of take a short, simple idea and develop it rather than...have too many bits in a song, you know. We took one riff and sort of made it into a song. Which is great! It's a real character piece too, with Pete's lyric.* [3]

As for the rest? Well, I can't say it moves me, but I'm not sure it's supposed to. Suffice it to say that I think it's a much stronger groove than melody, and that I generally agree with Peter's own opinion:

> **Peter:** *I never really loved that chorus. Of course I like my sections, but I think that was one of Tony's melodies...and after a while I got very bored with it. But it was fun playing the sort of jerkier and jumpier melodies of the verse and doing that with Phil, and getting into this more floaty, simple chorus line.* [3]

But then, I agree with Tony's summary as well:

> **Tony:** *I had the idea of playing it on the fuzz piano and organ at the same time and because the piano was very out of tune with the organ, the whole thing had a nice quality about it even when I was just playing these very simple chords...I've heard the album again just recently as we have been doing some remastering and that song in particular still sounds very good. It's unpretentious and it's quirky; I'm pretty pleased with that song.* [6]

Unpretentious, quirky, pretty good. Hum de dum de dum.

125 - Hold on My Heart

from *We Can't Dance*, 1991

In a lot of ways, it's surprising that 'Hold on My Heart' was ever a hit. We can all agree that it's more pop than prog, but it's nothing like what we'd expect a pop song to sound like. Typically in pop we expect some alternation of verse and chorus, maybe a bridge, maybe a repeated chorus. Something like an A-B-A-B-C-B-B or even A-B-A-C-A-B song structure, I don't know, just spit balling here. Instead, with 'Hold on My Heart' we get this: A-A-A-A-B-B-A-A. What in the name of Peter Gabriel's ghost even is that? Six verses and a double bridge? What? I just...what?

So that to me is the first major indication that, "Hey wait a minute, maybe Genesis *isn't* actually doing paint-by-numbers, sell-out hit writing. Maybe they're still actually trying to do something different with their music." Forget for a moment that 'Hold on My Heart' performed so well on the charts, that it came in an era where the band was known for hit singles, and that it's easy on the ears to listen to, and just look at that structure again. That's a bonkers way to build a song, as brave and ambitious as anything the band had attempted before, regardless of how compelling you might feel the result to be.

> **Phil:** *It would be good if people kind of remembered that side of it. That that's the same band, like 'Silent Sorrow in Empty Boats' which was kind of like sailing ships, clouds, fog...same band that plays 'Hold on My Heart'. Same band that plays the songs that they say we've sold out on. It's the same band. It's the same mentality.* [3]

For my money, though? The result is pretty good. Of course with a structure like that there's a lot of repetition - practically the point of the song when it's built in such a way. But there are a lot of little, subtle things to differentiate it all. For one, only the first and last verse actually repeat their lyrics, bookending the song. The rest of the words (outside of the titular "hold on my heart" line, of course) are all unique. Try to sing this one back from memory and confusion is bound to follow. "Ah nuts, which verse am I on again? The 'Tell her to be patient' one?" So it's anything but a sleepwalk even from that point of view. But on top of that you have Mike essentially free-form plucking over everything else going on. It's like he's doing entirely his own thing in the verses, but it's all so understated that it's easy to miss if you aren't listening for it specifically. It's that unpredictable element combined with gentle touches like the small cymbal hits in the post-bridge, or the occasional caress of a backing vocal that keeps this track from being boring to me. There's just always something *slightly* different that keeps me engaged from verse to verse.

> **Tony:** *We compromise with each other...I know nowadays that there are certain chord changes that Mike and Phil are not so into. I slip one or two in on the album, really when they're not looking, you know, and once they've heard it enough times they like it. There's a good example of that with 'Hold on My Heart', the opening bit of that, the way it goes into the main song is an example of what I like a lot. When you use unusual chord changes, it just sets the song off on a different motion.* [35]

'Hold on My Heart' may not be the band's finest pop song, but I do think it's a generally underrated one, adventurous in its form.

124 - Alien Afternoon

from *Calling All Stations*, 1997

When Mike and Tony decided to continue on as Genesis after Phil left the band, they hit a bit of an identity crisis as songwriters. While the two had certainly written songs together as a duo before, by the mid-late 1990s it had been ages since they'd tried to write in tandem without Phil Collins in the room. Turns out he was a pretty big deal.

> **Mike:** *Writing with Tony had been a big part of my life but I hadn't realised how far apart we are musically. It had always seemed to me that it was "Mike and Tony's music," with Phil somehow alongside us. What I discovered going in to write without Phil, was that Phil had actually...made Tony and me work well together by pulling on a bit there from Tony and a bit here from me, bringing in his great melodies and lines...There had been something about the chemistry of the three of us that made me and Tony work well together. Now that Phil wasn't there, we had to find our own way to come together.* [1]

It seems to me, looking at the material produced on both *Calling All Stations* as well as its array of extra tracks, that one of the principal ways Mike and Tony found that they could come together was in trying on new styles, like a sort of musical fitting room. And this makes quite a bit of sense, actually. Hearken back thirty years or so to when these schoolboys were first trying to find their musical feet and what do you see? *From Genesis to Revelation* and all its sundry demo tracks, each and every one an attempt to score critical and financial success with a different musical style. That debut album was an exercise in figuring out what kind of music Genesis ought to make, even if only by exhaustively eliminating every kind it shouldn't. Now, though they've been in the industry their entire adult lives, Mike and Tony found themselves on unsolid ground once again. This wasn't the a five-piece or a four-piece or even a three-piece. This was something new. What sort of music should "Just Mike and Tony" be creating, anyway?

I think that's how we get a song like 'Alien Afternoon' showing up on the album as the fourth track, having been preceded by songs that might be described as a hard rock opener, a grunge pop single, and an AOR ballad. All different things, and then here's this track, where the first half (after a sufficiently sci-fi intro from Tony) is essentially "Genesis does reggae." This isn't the first time the lads have gone for a reggae vibe, but it is the longest they've tried to stretch out that feeling. The results are...interesting. Not bad certainly, but I wouldn't call it quite great either. And indeed, if the song were just this four minute faux-reggae jam, it would rank much lower on my personal list. A worthwhile footnote, but nothing particularly compelling in its own right.

Yet 'Alien Afternoon' takes a dramatic turn over a minute-long transitional section. If you're asking whether I mean dramatic in the sense of "noticeably different" or dramatic as in "full of drama," the answer is "Yes." How big a musical shift is it? Well, the band literally switches drummers, if that tells you anything. Goodbye Nick D'Virgilio, hello Nir Zidkyahu. That reggae-like rhythm section gets buried under chords of increasing tension, Ray's voice gets filtered deep into the distance, a keyboard choir starts singing, and before you know it there's a different man hitting the cymbals. This is the band saying, "Make no mistake. These last couple minutes are something else entirely."

> **Tony:** *I had these two bits and I thought that both of them were really strong in a different way. Mike was particularly keen on what ended up on the second part of it and it was just that there wasn't a way you could really make a song out of them and say that's one chorus to the other's verse, they were two separate entities. So the idea was to have a kind of link and I had this odd chord sequence that went with the second half but wasn't really part of anything, so that was used as the bridge between them.* [25]

Ultimately that "something else" ends up being much more traditionally Genesisian in sound than arguably anything else on the album to this point; big, full-bodied chords with some flavourful guitar lines and impassioned vocals. Except in this case, the vocalist is an alien returning to his home planet from a sojourn on Earth, and so they keep some filters on Ray's voice throughout the conclusion of the piece. I think it might be a stronger ending if they let him loose, but to hear Mike speak of it, maybe that wasn't a viable option.

> **Mike:** *The only thing Ray lacked [as a vocalist] was that both Peter and Phil could let rip towards the end of a song. In the last quarter they would improvise, screech, and just go for it.*

> *Ray could never quite do that, it's not his thing. He doesn't improvise and go mad, which has always been part of what we have done with singers.* [1]

Regardless, the alien motif is a brilliant one to slap over this whole affair. You've got a pair of wealthy, middle-aged white guys playing what they believe to be reggae and it's not bad, but it feels, ehhh, a little bit off. Well, yeah: that's because it's an alien trying to blend in as a normal human. You've got big chords showing up out of nowhere, interrupting the song's groove. Well, yeah: that's the alien's spaceship coming to take him home. You've got vocals at the end that sound as though they want to be set free but are instead suppressed by technology. Well, yeah: the alien is getting back into its spacesuit, and besides, it's not human anyway. You've got a fade out instead of a "proper" ending to the song. Well, yeah: that's the ship flying away again into the distance, gradually disappearing from view.

> **Tony:** *It was just a matter then of working out a lyric that would combine the two very different styles...It is very deceptive because it is a very simple pattern and yet somehow, it sounds special and you don't know why that is...just that it has that quality about it. I suppose it is a classic Genesis bit. It has got all the hallmarks and I think that is what we do best. That is what Genesis music is all about...it sends a shiver down your spine at those moments.* [25]

Granted, maybe this was all just a lyrical mask for what were actually the song's perceived deficiencies, but man: that's one heck of a mask. It manages the deft feat of turning those deficiencies into elements of interest, if not exactly pure strengths. And really when you think about it, the lyrics serve as a kind of allegory for the entire album, a fascinating snapshot into a Genesis trying to reinvent itself one last time. The experimentation on *From Genesis to Revelation* led to the band largely discarding most of what they tried and starting to find their core sound on the next album. There was no next album after *Calling All Stations*, so we'll never truly know where this incarnation of the band might have settled in. I suppose all we can do is turn our heads up to the endless blue, open our eyes, and imagine: what would those skies look like if they turned to green?

123 - All in a Mouse's Night

from *Wind & Wuthering*, 1976

Both sides of *Wind & Wuthering* start with big ol' keyboard sounds, but while 'Eleventh Earl of Mar' tends to be remembered fondly for it, I feel that 'All in a Mouse's Night' is relatively forgotten in that sense. It's probably got a lot to do with what happens over the rest of the song, but those opening fourteen seconds are sublime. This isn't a coincidence either; 'All in a Mouse's Night' opens the album's second side, so with this intro Genesis ensured that you'd get blasted with big keyboard sounds regardless of which way you put the record on the turntable. The song goes a different direction from there, but thankfully that grandiose keyboard sound comes back around about two thirds of the way through the track, now accompanied by vocals. It's then allowed to really develop and blossom into a full-blown, longer form solo of rich bass and tasteful guitar flourishes and giant chords. Lovely, lovely stuff, making for an epic ending to a presumably epic song.

> **Mike:** ['All in a Mouse's Night' is] a loud, powerful song which more or less came together in the studio. It's a very simple story about a mouse and a cat. It started out as an involved epic, but we thought, "Fuck this," and went completely the other way. [36]

Shwelp, guess not! Now look, just because the whole song isn't swelling synths and stuff doesn't mean there's a problem. In fact, once the primary riff jumps in after the big intro, it sounds pretty good! The rhythm pattern leans heavily on the cymbals which gives it a certain kind of flair, and the guitar and bass play around an overriding heavy triplet pattern, creating a lot of drive. Meanwhile that keyboard riff helps lock everything down into a pattern that I wouldn't quite call a groove, but that still has a bit of solidity to it. There's definitely enough here to hold listener engagement and form a strong (if perhaps unspectacular) progressive rock song.

And yet, here comes Phil with this wispy, half-falsetto vocal singing lyrics that are essentially a retelling of any generic Tom and Jerry cartoon. You've got this big impressive opening, an even more powerful ending, and a compelling rhythmic motor running through the middle of this song. And you decided that on top of all that you wanted Phil Collins to sing half-heartedly about a mouse getting chased by a cat? I get the desire to subvert expectations and avoid the trap of self-seriousness that can come from building a progressive epic. But this?

> **Tony:** I don't feel it's my most successful track. The riffs were good, but the lyric was a little self-conscious. I don't think it's bad, it's just not up there with my other two [on the album, 'One for the Vine' and 'Afterglow']. It has that humorous element in it, in contrast to some of the heavyweight tracks elsewhere on the album. It's important in that sense. [27]

'All in a Mouse's Night' isn't a bad song - far from it, in fact. But it does indeed sound like a song that was meant for greater things than to be a Tom and Jerry fluff piece. I think with some reworking of the middle "core" of the song, a stronger overall vocal performance, and a set of suitably grand lyrics, we could be talking about this piece as one of the all-time Genesis highlights. Instead, it's here for me, firmly in "good but not great" territory. It's quality album filler, a decent enough prog song on an album with better ones. Try to put aside any wistfulness over what might have been, and you'll find a song that's well worth a listen all the same.

122 - Broadway Melody of 1974

from *The Lamb Lies Down on Broadway*, 1974

This is the first real casualty of the format of this project, being for all intents and purposes the second half of 'Fly on a Windshield'. But for whatever reason, the band decided to split the two halves into two separate tracks, and for consistency's sake I set a rule going into this shindig that "half tracks" such as this one would have to stay apart. I say all this to indicate that if 'Broadway Melody of 1974' were to be re-joined within this countdown to 'Fly on a Windshield', you wouldn't see either for many, many pages to come. As it stands, I believe that 'Fly' is stronger without 'Melody' than vice versa, so the bill has unfortunately now come due for the latter.

    A consequence of being the second part of a whole is that the song "opens" abruptly, and not in a natural way. But it's not really fair to hold that against the track under the circumstances, so rest assured that my personal qualitative judgment of the track doesn't take that aspect into account. Instead, my focus here is exactly what the title of the song might indicate: the vocal melody. 'Fly on a Windshield' opens with some vocals but then "ends" with an instrumental passage, and there's never a chance for a consistent melody to lock itself down. I wouldn't define that as a weakness at all, and I'll have more to say about it later, but what it means for 'Broadway Melody of 1974' is that this follow-up track is able to provide a strong contrast to its predecessor by relying on a consistent melodic line. It's a situation where each "half" of the whole idea is missing one key element that the other one excels in.

    Furthermore, since 'Broadway Melody of 1974' is a song revolving around a vocal melody, I'd argue that the lyrics become more important than they might be in many other Genesis tunes that have different foci. Here Rael is witnessing an alternate universe New York City, with a sort of "it's opposite day" vibe using prominent American figures of the past decades. Famed obscenity comic Lenny Bruce agrees to "play his other hand" and do a clean show. Philosopher Marshall McLuhan, whose legacy is about understanding the impact of the media on our lives, has his "head buried in the sand." Comedy legend Groucho Marx is a comedic failure unable to so much as find an audience, while a white supremacist hate group serves up traditional African American cuisine in a jazz bar. Convicted rapist Caryl Chessman is no longer executed in a gas chamber but instead leads a perfumed parade. This one has an added double meaning; Chessman spent years protesting his innocence to the public, and actually convinced many of them before his sentence was carried out. "He knows, in a scent, you can bottle all you made." In a scent, innocent. I see you, Peter Gabriel.

    Steve: *Very evocative lyrics...I think it's challenging lyrically.* [13]

    It's a lyrical triumph, avoiding Peter's common pitfall of having those lyrics detract from the music of the piece. Quite the opposite really; the vocals and lyrics are what give 'Broadway Melody of 1974' all its oomph, especially in the absence of its partner song. Which makes it even more egregious that some pressings of *The Lamb Lies Down on Broadway* - including, alas, my own CD copy - screw up the track break. They start 'Broadway Melody' at the last 30-some seconds of the pair of songs, making 'Fly on a Windshield' sound like the full piece while this track becomes nothing more than a short interlude into 'Cuckoo Cocoon'. That's a pretty disappointing publishing mistake, because this is a good song in its own right and deserves to be appreciated. Nevertheless, it's only truly outstanding when properly joined with 'Fly on a Windshield', so do me a favour: set my strict rules aside and listen to them together. You'll be glad you did.

121 - Invisible Touch

from *Invisible Touch*, 1986

Ladies and gentlemen, I present to you the 1980s. Which is a strange statement to make, I think, because in large part this feels like a chicken/egg situation. There's this sense nowadays that the *Genesis* and *Invisible Touch* albums sound "too 80s" for the old Genesis faithful. Which means, I take it, that they'd fit on a playlist with other "80s songs" which range from the likes of Duran Duran to Journey to Bonnie Tyler to Quiet Riot, which is to say that they merely were popular songs that released in the same decade. After all, is it ever fair to say that there is some kind of singular, all-pervasive "80s sound" in the first place? I don't think there is, but some would disagree. And I'd wager that when pressed to give an example of what that "80s sound" is, many of these people would point to a Genesis song, 'Invisible Touch' first and foremost.

You see, Genesis didn't "sell out" to "sound like the 80s" and thus find chart success. No, Genesis was instrumental in *defining* the music of the 80s really from *Duke* onward. The one common thread people seem to think of when they hear the phrase "80s music" is synthesizers, and hey, guess what Tony Banks plays? Always at the cutting edge of keyboard music, it's his playing as much as anything else that created the "80s sound" we talk about in the first place. Thus, it's my position that Genesis didn't start sounding like the 80s; the 80s were rather in large, part built around Genesis.

It's also not as though the lads went away individually to try to pen hit songs for the group. Everything on the *Invisible Touch* album was a truly group-written effort, created more or less from scratch.

Mike: *Phil would start with the drum machine. It was always a little bit different, you know. You could play it up and off we'd go. Tony would play some chords, I'd bash around on guitar, Phil would start singing. And this little loop he started with kind of set the mood for something. I had a guitar riff, I think...And on top of it...is the lyric. It's a simple sort of pop song in a way, but the lyric's got a nice little play on words with "invisible touch." I think it's quite strong, that.* [3]

Phil: *'Invisible Touch' is my favourite Genesis song and it came more or less out of nowhere. We would arrive in the studio every day and just start playing. One day Mike Rutherford played a riff on the guitar, with an echo, and I suddenly sang: "She seems to have an invisible touch – yeah!" It came into my head fully formed. I'm sure people have all kinds of ideas about how we wrote these songs they love or loathe, but really our writing process was close to jazz. We improvised.* [37]

Tony: *Originally it developed out of the same jam as 'Domino', but we realised it was such a good little thing in itself that we decided to extract it and make something of it on its own, and just wrote what I suppose is for us is a fairly straightforward kind of rock song. I think it works really well because it's a sort of concise thing. I never think I'm gonna like it, and then when I hear it, I like it. You know what I mean? In my brain, intellectually I'm not too sure about it, but it actually works.* [38]

Mike: *The best songs tend to get written quickly. That's how it was with 'Invisible Touch'. We'd rock up, have a cup of tea, see what happened. On day one, we had no songs, no ideas, and a blank bit of paper. Phil was always keen to fill that bit of paper – he was very organised – and we let him. It's a wonderful song: upbeat, fun to play, always a strong moment in any gig.* [37]

Love it or hate it, it's remarkably impressive that three men walked into a studio with literally nothing and came out a short while later with one of the defining hits of an entire decade. It's no wonder Phil kept coming back to the band between solo efforts when they were able to - seemingly effortlessly - just churn out stuff like this as a group. Yes, it's a straightforward pop song. Yes, it's using a drum machine instead of one of the greatest drummers in rock history. But it's so tightly and expertly crafted that it's hard not to really like. It's got this infectious quality that everyone was able to see right from the get-go.

Tony: *'Invisible Touch' was one of those songs that began an album and which started off as this very simple song which everybody thought was straightforward...some songs were less ambitious; 'Invisible Touch' itself was such a simple thing and it was great fun doing the video and it was a nice moment.* [6]

Phil: *I think we probably all felt that it was a single, or the representative or flagship of the record. But it was number one in America. First number one album and single in America. It was a very big record for us.* [3]

Tony: *It certainly took us to a different kind of level...about a year later [after the album's release] we did Wembley Stadium, four nights at Wembley Stadium. And the album went back up, it hit number two I think again. And it had been in the top ten the whole year. It was just extraordinary really. And I did think when we did those shows at Wembley Stadium, I thought*

"It will never be bigger than this. This is it. We've had an album that's been number one everywhere, and we're selling out these shows four times," and it was a great feeling. I just thought "I'll enjoy it," I think, because I thought it might not last. It lasted longer than I thought it was going to, actually. [3]

For a while there, Genesis and this song in particular were totally inescapable, with the results being that, for a lot of people, Genesis is nothing more than their big hits of the 1980s. To fans of the band's music before 'Follow You Follow Me' ever showed up on the charts, there can be a little bit of jealousy creeping in. "Sure, 'Invisible Touch' is a fun song, but look at all this other great stuff! Please!" As much as I think that kind of possessive, defensive fandom is utterly silly, I've got to admit that I understand it. After all, I experienced some of that myself back in my college years.

See, when I first saw Where in the World is Carmen Sandiego? on my local PBS station as a youngin', something enamoured me well beyond the title character's comically large red hat, or the geography lessons, or even the game show format of it all. That something was a group called Rockapella, who introduced me to the concept that music could consist exclusively of voices and yet not be choral in nature. It kinda blew my mind, as well as my older brother's; who knew that something as simple as "Oooooooh, The Chase!" could be such a revelation?

Fast forward to high school where my brother decided to create an a cappella (Italian meaning "without accompaniment") singing group he called Harmony, in order to have an outlet for he and his classmates to produce this stuff on their own. Fast forward another couple years and I'm not only running Harmony as its President, but I'm also beginning to transcribe vocal arrangements for our use. Then comes college where both my brother and me successfully audition to join the Cheezies, the oldest a cappella group at Miami University. For a year we're singing a cappella music together on stage. Then he graduates and I start pushing myself not just to transcribe but to actually arrange music over my remaining time.

By my last year as a Cheezie, I knew I had a bit of leeway with what I could convince the group to do, as long as I could create a reasonably compelling arrangement and they were comfortable that enough people would know the song. And as at this time I was truly coming into my own as a Genesis fan (alongside some other progressive rock), I started daydreaming a bit about how amazing it would be to do a big a cappella rendition of one of their most impressive songs. You know, just really go after it with a complex arrangement, voices mimicking all the various instruments, soloing like guitars and keyboards over these epic backdrops, just layers and layers of harmonies taking the audience on a journey for eight to ten minutes, itself an unheard of feat of musicianship.

Yeah, that's a nice dream. The reality was that this was a group of college kids rehearsing in their spare time. While they were all quality singers, not all of them were adept at reading music, and more than a couple had issues memorizing the material. Moreover, it was repeatedly hammered into us that our job (as an offshoot of the larger choir, the Miami Men's Glee Club) was to entertain. Specifically, to entertain an audience full of people aged 18-22, where some of them might well be drunk before the concert would even begin. I was determined to get us to do a Genesis song, but a rousing rendition of 'The Cinema Show' was never, ever going to work on any level.

And so, I sat at my computer, booted up my software to create sheet music, and churned out an arrangement of 'Invisible Touch' to take back to the guys at rehearsal. "Oh yeah, I remember that song!" We half-assed our way through learning it, performed it a single time at middling quality because we never completely locked it down beforehand, and discarded it into the ether, forever forgotten by anything except the history you've just read. Regrettably, though a live performance, we did not opt for any F-bombs.

Phil: *I still joke about these lyrics to my son when we talk about people that we know - either have had relationships with or, you know, close relatives - people that have the invisible touch that you're not quite sure, but whatever it is they do you can't get them out of your mind. And the live lyric of the song I sing, "and though she will fuck up your life, you'll love her just the same." It's kind of one of those things that I actually, I like that lyric because for me it's been part of my life, I suppose. The "she seems to have an invisible touch, she reaches in and grabs right hold of your heart." She tears it out but you still go back for more. So I feel quite close to that song.* [3]

It's not what I really wanted deep down, but it was still Genesis and so still worth doing. Given the choice, I'd definitely do it all again. And that's really 'Invisible Touch' in a nutshell, isn't it? It's not the most musically impressive, or emotionally affecting, or deeply rewarding Genesis song out there. But it is among the most memorable, most influential, and most entertaining-to-college-age-women songs they ever did. I can't fault it for any of that. If anything, the biggest problem I have with 'Invisible Touch' is that I hear it a little too often, a victim of its own enormous success.

That's a good problem to have, I'd say.

120 - ...In That Quiet Earth

from *Wind & Wuthering*, 1976

Here we have another example of Genesis taking what is effectively one song and splitting it into two tracks on the album, perhaps in this case simply for one pretty silly reason:

> **Tony:** *I'd always wanted to use an ellipsis in a song title!* [27]

OK! Nevermind that you guys released 'Ripples...' less than a year earlier, I suppose. And given that the next album was officially called *...And Then There Were Three...* one wonders if perhaps Tony hadn't just recently discovered the ellipsis and felt a compulsion to use it as often as he could. Thus, at least in my own fanciful imagining of how this might have gone down, a dastardly idea was born: split the big closing instrumental piece of *Wind & Wuthering* into two parts so that he could use an ellipsis on *both* titles! The schemes!

Unfortunately for Tony's master plan, Genesis' North American distributor wanted no part of that nonsense, originally releasing the album with the two songs combined into a single track, the way God intended. Eventually, however, all releases of the album would indeed split the tracks out as the *band* intended, so I suppose Tony got his ellipses in the end. But as a result of this decision, I'm forced to look at the two halves of this whole separately.

While 'Unquiet Slumbers for the Sleepers...' is, well, sleepy, '...In That Quiet Earth' doesn't line up with its title much at all. It's bubbling over with energy, from Phil's incredible cymbal work, to a melody that weaves back and forth between Steve's soaring guitar and Tony's ethereal keyboards, to a bass line that isn't content to simply plunk away, instead cascading on its own beneath everything else. It's like an ocean of sound washing over the listener.

> **Tony:** *'...In That Quiet Earth' sounds as if it will be a gentle piece but ends as very attacking.* [27]

And then it all breaks out into a very segmented, plodding rhythm section over which Tony plays a foreboding keyboard solo. It's 'Cinema Show' redux for a solid two minutes, and it's really strong stuff (if not quite as strong as its spiritual predecessor). Then things wind down in a hurry as the track prepares to transition into 'Afterglow'. So really, '...In That Quiet Earth' ought to be regarded as the second part of a musical trilogy; the darker, moodier middle chapter where the conflict burns the brightest, in contrast to the wondrous opening ('Unquiet Slumbers for the Sleepers...') and the triumphant, cathartic resolution ('Afterglow').

> **Steve:** *It was very good. You had the fast and the slow – the compelling slow rhythm, setting up all those marching band aspects. You have the implied army coming at you.* [27]

I think it works a lot better in that context than it does as a standalone experience, but it's certainly a strong enough effort to be worth a listen in isolation as well. I like the second half of the song more so than the first half, but the first half is much more interesting to pick apart, which provides a sort of counterbalance. The end result is that I can't say I have many complaints about it as a whole, excepting of course that it's *not* whole. But let's see if we can't do something about that here next.

119 - Unquiet Slumbers for the Sleepers...

from *Wind & Wuthering*, 1976

While '...In That Quiet Earth' sounds remarkably unlike any kind of quiet earth, 'Unquiet Slumbers for the Sleepers...' works much better as a musical rendition of its namesake. Running at less than two and a half minutes, the whole piece is a dreamy, foggy affair; if you had to choose any one song on *Wind & Wuthering* to reflect the album's cover art, this would be the one. It's peaceful, but it's not at peace. Restful and yet restless.

> **Steve:** *'Unquiet Slumbers for the Sleepers'...gave great scope for both instrumentation and creation of atmosphere.* [39]

It's one of the four Genesis tracks that make up the set of short, gentle, atmospheric instrumentals that are often overlooked by the fans. Part of the reason for that may be that the other three are all found on *The Lamb Lies Down on Broadway*: 'Hairless Heart', 'Silent Sorrow in Empty Boats', and 'Ravine' all fit this mould, but are generally viewed as mere linking interludes on an album with grandiose intentions. I think that's something of a shame, because I believe all of these pieces have quite a bit to offer if we just give them the time. And despite strong company there, I'd go so far as to say 'Unquiet Slumbers for the Sleepers...' is arguably the most sonically interesting of that entire batch of songs. There is a melody, but it's not a proper pop/rock melody; you'd never start humming this tune to yourself. It's more of an orchestral motif that runs alongside the windy air of the rest of the instrumentation.

The difference is probably again in the context, though of course to some extent I'm trying to ignore that for this exercise. If you look at the three *Lamb* songs I listed above, all of them are "come down" moments. You have the explosive rage of 'Back in N.Y.C.' followed by the raw vulnerability of 'Hairless Heart'. The emotional high of 'The Lamia' followed by the sombre reflection of 'Silent Sorrow in Empty Boats'. The panicked chase of the raven in 'The Colony of Slippermen' followed by the impotent despair of 'Ravine'.

'Unquiet Slumbers for the Sleepers...' is, on the other hand, more like the calm *before* the storm. It grows rather than diminishes, building tension and excitement but managing to keep either factor from getting out of control. It's allowed to swell and abate like waves on the shore; though the tide inexorably rises, it comes without violence or aggression. You put your toes in the water, stood your ground, and a couple minutes later you're up to your knees in it. There's an invisible but very real kind of power in that.

> **Mike:** *I always loved 'Unquiet Slumbers', which was especially great on stage.* [27]

I think I tend on average to enjoy instrumentals more than most. I love a good vocal as much as anyone, but sometimes those dang singers just need to get out of the way and let a mood speak for itself, you know? To that end I also tend to appreciate the atmospheric instrumental pieces a little more than the bombastic ones on average. I love the idea of being transported away, and these are the kinds of songs that can do that. Hence, 'Unquiet Slumbers for the Sleepers...' here, ever so slightly above '...In That Quiet Earth', though both are solid and of course they're really just one song anyway. I just think it's easy to get so drawn into the complex time signatures and virtuosic drumming and slick solos that we can occasionally overlook the gentler stuff in the Genesis catalogue, which is quite strong in its own right. 'Unquiet Slumbers for the Sleepers...' is in that mould: more than meets the eye but still pleasant on the ear. I dig it.

118 - It's Yourself

B-side of 'Your Own Special Way', 1977

With 'Supper's Ready' Genesis took a song and brought it full circle, ending with reprises of the opening sections of the epic track, giving the whole thing a grand sense of cohesion and resolution. One LP later they closed *Selling England by the Pound* with 'Aisle of Plenty', which applied that same concept to the album as a whole, reprising the opening melodic strains of 'Dancing with the Moonlit Knight' and wrapping up the whole thing nicely. Then *The Lamb* did its own, mostly-cohesive thing that nevertheless included several melodic call-backs, but on *A Trick of the Tail* the band revisited the concept in earnest a third time, expanding it once again into a little ditty called 'Los Endos' - except now, instead of just reprising itself, or reprising the melody from the opening track of the album, the song was a reprise of the entire album itself, featuring bits and melodies from the entire length of the record.

Why would I bring this up here and now, on the entry for a mostly-forgotten B-side from the late 1970s? Well, remember that opening little bit of 'Los Endos'? You know, the kind of twinkly bit that they pretty much always omit in concert. Here's something you might not know about it: *That was a reprise too.* Specifically, a reprise of 'It's Yourself' here, which was written in the *A Trick of the Tail* sessions but got cut from the album and then shelved for a year, eventually being released as the B-side to 'Your Own Special Way' from *Wind & Wuthering*.

It's not entirely clear why 'It's Yourself' was removed from the album, though the simplest explanation seems the most likely: time. At fifty-one minutes long, *A Trick of the Tail* was already pushing the limits of what could fit on vinyl. 'It's Yourself' runs nearly six minutes on its own, which would push the album's runtime dangerously close to an hour. For context, *Selling England by the Pound* ran about fifty-three minutes, already causing concerns about the potential impact to sound quality. Then you look at where 'It's Yourself' may have fit with the other tracks, and the initial thought is that it would probably slot well between 'Squonk' and 'Mad Man Moon', as the final notes of 'It's Yourself' are identical in pitch and pattern (if not octave or arrangement) to the opening piano salvo of that Tony Banks classic.

Anyway, what even *is* this track? Well, it's pretty much three sections: the first is a truly beautiful, emotional vocal bit. This section contains all the lyrics, and it's, for my money, fantastic. Honestly if this section were expanded and became the entire song, I'd probably catapult this up dozens of spots. It's great. The second section is, essentially, the opening of 'Los Endos'. I'm not even sure they're two different recordings. I think - especially when they decided to gut 'It's Yourself' from the album - they just copy/pasted an edited version of the bit onto the front of 'Los Endos' and called it a day. Finally, the last section is just pure atmosphere, with a sitar-inspired bit of Hindu musical mysticism for good measure.

Now this isn't to say the three sections don't transition or blend well into one another, or that there's anything I truly don't like in any of them. But for me the first section is so strong that it's almost a shame the other two sections exist after it; I yearn to hear more of the song's opening stuff. Those bass pedals, those chords during "Where will you go," that heavy drum banging in the second verse… Magnificent, all of it. And it's ironic that it was released as the B-side of 'Your Own Special Way', because to my ears that first section is essentially "What if 'Your Own Special Way' was actually really good?" If you buy that single, you're hearing a meh ballad followed by a glimpse into what could have been an incredible one, which then itself turns into something George Harrison would be proud to put on his stereo. It's a strange ride, and ultimately I'm not at all surprised this track is mostly forgotten. But oh, what might've been!

117 - On the Shoreline

B-side of 'I Can't Dance', 1991

When you spin up *We Can't Dance*, one of the first sounds you hear is this bizarre growly *thing* that immediately grabs your attention. "What in the world is that?" a first-time listener might wonder. Well, it's something the boys call "Elephantus," and it was created by Tony recording Mike's guitar on a sampler, then playing that sample back through his keyboard at a lower register. It's an unmistakably unique kind of sound that really kicks the album off with a bang and helps propel 'No Son of Mine' straight into your consciousness. Whenever a Genesis fan, or even someone casually aware of the band hears that sound, 'No Son of Mine' immediately comes front of mind, and for good reason.

Which is tough luck for our ol' buddy 'On the Shoreline' here, because this thing was meant to be a bit of sonic glue to hold *We Can't Dance* together, a feat which starts by bringing back a touch of that Elephantus all over again. But a touch is all it is - all it needs really, if the song were allowed to sit in the just-past-halfway point of the album like I think it was envisioned to. Just a little call-back to help a very long album cohere a little bit more. Beyond even the brief Elephantus bit in the background, there's a bridge here that sounds rather similar to the chorus of 'Driving the Last Spike'. Not enough to call it a true reprise or anything, but there's a kind of alignment between the sounds that feels as though it's probably not coincidental. So while not anything like a grand conclusion, 'On the Shoreline' could carry a lot of water for *We Can't Dance* as a kind of anchor track in the middle. Not 'Los Endos' but maybe 'Los Centros', if you will.

But that's not what happened, is it? Instead, we got...'Tell Me Why'. Not ideal! So if the call-backs don't work because the song isn't on the daggone album, what have we got left? Well, I think we have the makings of a hit!....in the mid-late 80s. 'On the Shoreline' to me feels like a slice of *Invisible Touch* launched forward five years in time only to find that its audience had mostly gone away. Seriously, put this out as a non-album single in 1987 and I'm convinced it catapults up the charts.

That's not to say it completely delivers across the board for me: the middle "Take me over, lead me through" bit (the aforementioned nod to 'Driving the Last Spike') feels out of place, and the music sort of peters out at the end. But man, when this song is on, it really rips. It's a great vocal performance from Phil throughout, and that section from 0:49 to 2:16 is among the absolute strongest pop/rock performances of the band's career. Their *Invisible Touch* era output in that vein was more consistent, but 'On the Shoreline' has a peak that I'd put up against any of it.

Tony: *'On the Shoreline' is a good track!* [40]

You tell 'em, Tony! Look, if *We Can't Dance* was so doggedly determined to be as long an album as it was, there's almost no excuse for not stripping out 'Tell Me Why' - *especially* given Tony's reservations about it lyrically - and sticking this in its exact place on the track listing. If there was that much push internally that 'Tell Me Why' could be a single, then that's all the more reason for it to soar independently of the album, right? The record would flow just as well with 'On the Shoreline' there; better, arguably. Of course, it's my opinion that stripping 'Tell Me Why' and adding nothing at all would still result in addition by subtraction, but the point remains. This is a really solid if not uniformly spectacular tune, and it deserves better than to languish forever as the forgotten B-side to a song about a lack of dancing skill.

116 - Scenes from a Night's Dream

from ...*And Then There Were Three...*, 1978

Oh, this song. What in the world am I going to do with you? You've got that Banksian intro that sounds good, yet also immediately dates you to 1978 precisely. Look, *And Then There Were Three* isn't a concept album but virtually everything *on* the album sounds like it's *from* the album, you know what I mean? And as much as that album cover doesn't make a lick of sense, that same overarching sound I'm talking about? If you ask yourself how that sound might be visualised in terms of colours and images, the only suitable answer is "Well, I guess it looks kind of like a reddish-purple cloudy sky," and gosh dangit there you are.

So here you have this song that from its very first moments sounds like it's right at home on the only album it could possibly belong to, and then you get this really bouncy up-tempo groove that's just a joy to hear. When the intensity picks up slightly, you get a cowbell so prominent even Christopher Walken's Bruce Dickinson (pardon me, *The* Bruce Dickinson) would be satisfied. It's cheesy, yes - it is a cowbell after all - but it adds to the whimsical, jaunty nature of the whole affair, so in context it works terrifically. Then you also get these little guitar licks over top, a dash of spice on top to flavour the dish. At the end is a fade out that isn't very successful, but hey, we can forgive a minor fault like that, right? Awkward, unsatisfying fade-away aside, 'Scenes from a Night's Dream' is three and a half minutes of really fun, peppy stuff. A real humdinger of a tune. A musical hayride through a childhood wonderland.

> **Mike:** *I think that by cutting down on the length of some of the songs we've been able to get much more variety on this album. This song is a slightly lighter element that might not have got on to the album in the normal course of events.* [17]

But then. Oh, but then. "Nemo get out of bed!"

Let me provide some background here, which I hope you find as genuinely interesting as I do. In 1904, American cartoonist Winsor McCay launched a comic strip called Little Sammy Sneeze for weekly publication in the New York Herald, where he worked as an illustrator of editorial cartoons. The premise of the comic was pretty straightforward: Little Sammy would be in some sort of room or situation with adults present, and as they were trying to get on with their business, he would progressively build up a massive sneeze that would ruin what they were doing and result in his getting punished. Reception to the comic was strong enough that after little more than a month, McCay was allowed to do a second weekly strip for the paper as well: Dream of the Rarebit Fiend. In contrast to the light-hearted mischief of Little Sammy Sneeze, this second strip focused primarily on the dark and repressed thoughts of troubled adults. Each week featured a new person's nightmare, their worst fears brought to life. The unifying thread was that the last panel of each strip would feature the victim waking up, cursing the food they ate before bed (usually Welsh rarebit, hence the name) for causing the bad, vivid dreams.

One of the unlucky characters in Dream of the Rarebit Fiend was a bit unlike the others, however. Not an adult but a child with an active imagination, McCay would take the character he called Nemo and create a third comic strip for the New York Herald in 1905: a synthesis of each of his two previous ones, called Little Nemo in Slumberland. This would follow the titular child not through his daily routines of accompanying grouchy adults like Little Sammy Sneeze, but through Nemo's own wild dreams. Summoned to Slumberland by its ruler, King Morpheus (the Greek god of dreams; popularly also the inspirational namesake of The Matrix character of the same name), Little Nemo would spend every week in a fantasy that changed with his dreams. The comic strip was very influential; its continuing story arc over multiple years, its full colour style and high attention to detail, its experimentation with the comic form in itself...all in all, Little Nemo in Slumberland was remarkably ahead of its time.

Now if you're like me, that little slice of history might've whetted your appetite a bit for the comic strips themselves. To this day, my understanding of them is purely academic; I haven't read more than a strip or two of Little Nemo in Slumberland or either of its predecessors, but I might need to go track down a compilation somewhere and change that. It all certainly seems like something that would be up my alley. But what *doesn't* sound particularly compelling to me is to hear someone describe the comic strip to me in song form, you know? Comics are an extremely visual medium, and from everything I gather this one is particularly so. You can't reasonably expect someone to "get" the thrust of the comic by having it described in dry, non-rhyming poetry can you?

Which means that, I suppose, the only audience that might eagerly latch onto the lyrics of 'Scenes from a Night's Dream' would be people who were already fans of Little Nemo in Slumberland. Now, I guess that audience isn't quite so small as I would've guessed. After all, the comic *was* tremendously influential as I said before. Enough so, in fact, to warrant a film adaptation in 1984 with further ones following, an opera in

2012, and even a mainstream video game on the Nintendo Entertainment System in 1989. But note that all of these things came *after* 1978, when 'Scenes from a Night's Dream' was released. At that point in time, what was the hope exactly? Was there some expectation that there would be significant overlap between the group of people who like Genesis and those who were fans of a 70-year-old newspaper cartoon? I've got to imagine that Venn diagram looking like a circle sitting next to a barely perceptible dot, representing only those very elderly comic lovers who weren't put off by this new-fangled progressive rock stuff.

> **Mike:** *The music is by Tony and the words by Phil. This went through a funny change. We always liked it but Tony didn't like the lyrics he had for it and went off them - more than the rest of us, actually - halfway through. Then Phil came back with some different lyrics, a slightly different melody, and some answering harmonies.* [17]

OK, so the aforementioned elderly *and* Phil Collins, I guess. But you know what really gets me about this quote? *This song had entirely different lyrics.* Holy....I mean, how bad must the original batch have been for Tony to decide that Little Flippin' Nemo was the better option? That's nearly unthinkable. The lyrics to 'Scenes from a Night's Dream' are playful and imaginative, sure, but do they sing well? Are they engaging to anyone who might actually listen to the track? No and double no.

> **Phil:** *I bought my brother a book of cartoons about a chap called Little Nemo from the New York Post...it was very surreal and psychedelic stuff. Basically every day he would have a dream, you would think it was really happening but in the last frame he would be woken up by his mum because he had been shouting. I said, "Why not have a bash?"* [41]

On the one hand, that's a great reason to do something as an artist. Never question the "why not?" attitude, lest all your work become stale and derivative. On the other hand, COME ON.

> **Tony:** *What was wonderful about the song was all the little vocal ideas and I quite enjoyed all of that.* [6]

Even 'All in a Mouse's Night' had better lyrics than this. Look, make this song an instrumental and I'm there; it's great. As it stands? I guess I'm still there...but by golly I'm less enthusiastic about it!

115 - The Knife

from *Trespass*, 1970

From 1970 until perhaps 1974, if you asked any random Genesis fan to blurt out the first of the band's songs to come to mind, 'The Knife' would likely be the most common answer. After all, it was the band's closer and a concert staple for quite a long time; what you might call Genesis' "signature song" of the era. People showed up at shows *specifically* to hear this one track. In fact, this even worked to the band's detriment when they were touring for The Lamb Lies Down on Broadway.

> **Tony:** *In all honesty, whatever anybody thinks, [the show] never went down all that well on stage because people really wanted to hear 'Supper's Ready' and 'The Knife', and here we were playing them this [album] they'd never heard before.* [3]

As a fun little sidenote to the above, it seems at least that the band was pretty keenly aware of what their audiences wanted and, by extension, the potential disappoint that Genesis was inflicting upon them instead. So it's notable that while the shows for The Lamb Lies Down on Broadway Tour were simply the band playing through the entire double album in sequence, they did often include an encore or two as well. Usually this encore was 'The Musical Box', and on occasion 'Watcher of the Skies' got tossed in as well. And while 'Supper's Ready' was far too long to play as an encore to an enormous, intricate stage show like The Lamb, a few times they did indeed toss 'The Knife' in there. So if you were one of the lucky fans to attend one of those small handful of shows, you at least did eventually hear the song you came to hear, regardless of how you felt about the rest of it.

> **Tony:** *'The Knife' was a very popular stage song. And we used to construct our set in those early days, we used to start acoustic - I used to play a lot of guitar - and the first two or three songs I'd play guitar on...'The Knife' was the final song in the set. And it always got the audience; they always loved it...It was a key song for those early days, and it became very much for the first year or two that we were touring the key song, the kind of trademark Genesis song.* [3]

What was it that made this song so popular with the fans, anyway? Well, compare it to the rest of *Trespass* and the answer should become clear. It's a departure of style from everything that comes before it: harder, darker, more solo-centric. On *Genesis Live* you can hear the roar the fans give just from hearing Peter announce the track's title. Now, was that a genuine audience response at that show, or just post-production editing magic to make the album sound better? Who knows? Who cares? The energy is infectious, and it's not a big leap to imagine crowds of die-hard, earnest young men going crazy for a song where they could release all their pent-up aggression vicariously through the likes of Peter Gabriel. Heck, at one show Peter even broke an ankle jumping into the audience because he was so pumped on adrenaline he wasn't quite thinking clearly. The fans had to physically carry him back to the stage where he finished the song on his knees - the show must go on! - before mercifully getting shipped off to the hospital right after the performance ended.

I imagine that if I were a young British man in the early 1970s, attending a Genesis concert, I might feel the same way about 'The Knife' as they seemed to. Unfortunately, "Live at Cheltenham" isn't the context in which I received this song, so my opinions about it tend to be moulded by the studio track on its own merits, rather than the studio track acting as a kind of conduit for my own experiences of hearing the song in person.

On those merits, therefore, how does the song fare for me? On first impression, not so well. See, while there are plenty of people who gravitate toward musical aggression, I've never been one of them. For instance, death metal? Possibly the worst thing I've ever heard. I had a co-worker once who dug the stuff and I asked for some recommendations. I listened to these songs with an open mind. Truly, I did! But I had a lot of trouble finding anything redeeming to say about them. I'm glad people like whatever they like musically, but for me it's a total non-starter.

Mind you, I'm not saying 'The Knife' is death metal or even anything close to it. But the opening verses of this piece? Peter's chosen singing style? Get that right out. The march-like organ is fun and flavourful, providing a quality structure, but those words just spill out violently, providing me with absolutely no enjoyment whatsoever. I get that that's the point - it's a song about violent revolutions and how they inevitably create violent regimes - but it's not anywhere close to my cup of musical tea. In a lot of ways, it's a kind of precursor of things to come from the vocal side of the fence. Things like 'The Return of the Giant Hogweed', for example, which I really don't care for overall.

Peter: *'The Knife' used to be known as 'The Nice' because we were big fans of The Nice...There was an energy...The Nice, not many people know much of their work nowadays...But they were amazing: it was powerful, it was inventive, driving...And there we would be, sitting on stools, twiddling away at 12-strings. And you'd think, where's the balls in this? Let's get something with a bit of energy...something a little dangerous. We didn't have anything like that so I started to try and write something that would have that energy. That's really how things began. Then Tony added a section to it, and obviously the keyboard thing at the end. But I think it was the first sort of peek at a darker energy we discovered.* [3]

Yet 'The Knife' does something different that sets it a rung above those verbal eruptions of the next few albums. While nasal sneering dominates the first couple minutes of the track, 'The Knife' takes the rest of the song somewhere else entirely, to a place that is honestly fantastic. Unlike a song such as, say, 'Watcher of the Skies' that opens and closes with powerful instrumental moments while sticking all the words in the middle, 'The Knife' kicks you in the teeth with its lyrical section and then gets out of its own way. You've got the same march organ acting like part of the rhythm section to form the spine of the thing, except now there's a strong guitar solo interplaying over top of it. You've got a quieter section spelled by flute, which has always been one of my favourite elements of the early Genesis sound. A growing chant of "We are only wanting freedom" does a great job building tension into a stellar duet of guitar and bass, before at last the marching order changes up with the guitars providing that backbone while the keyboard gets to play on top of it for a bit. It's all really, really good.

Peter pipes up again near the end with "We have woooooooon!" and I feel like that dude at a cookout constantly trying to swat a gnat away. Again, I get it, but it's intrusive. Yet when he returns once more moments later to reprise the song's chorus, there's a sort of "Oh, I get it now" moment where I find I don't even mind it anymore. 'The Knife' needs that instrumental stuff to sell the vocals, and simply makes the mistake of putting the vocals in there first. The end result is that the song gets better for me every time I hear it; the back seven minutes are just that strong. It took me years to "get on board" with 'The Knife', and I'm sure for some of you reading this right now I'm still not quite there. I may never connect to this song in the way I might have were I around in 1971, but I'm at least at a point now where I can mostly see past that opening salvo of avalanching lyrics to see the glimmering gem behind.

114 - Pigeons

from *Spot the Pigeon*, 1977

Wind & Wuthering has been repeatedly described by the band as a "romantic" album. When Tony says "romantic" he's mostly referring to the chord structures/progressions used in the songs, but there's more than that here. There's a sort of seriousness about the album, pervading through the entire track list; 'All in a Mouse's Night' notwithstanding, of course. It's that heaviness that you feel not only from the music but even just from looking at the album's cover, lonely tree trying to stand firm amidst a bleak landscape. So one might naturally expect that Genesis found themselves in late 1976 in a certain kind of mood, and that therefore the outtakes from *Wind & Wuthering* would match that forlorn feeling to an extent. That they were most likely excluded because they were treading ground already covered by other tunes on the record.

'Pigeons' takes those expectations and drops fifty tons of denial all over them. It's everything *Wind & Wuthering* isn't: bold, bizarre, driving, and most of all, funny. It's a charming little farce of a song that showed Genesis wasn't afraid to really experiment and do something different. In a way maybe that makes this song a grandfather to 'Who Dunnit?' if not *Abacab* in general; they certainly both do their best to annoy the listener.

> **Steve:** *The thing about 'Pigeons' was that it was possible for the band to play a whole note for a whole thing: ding-ding-ding-ding... And that was unvarying whilst the keyboard changed and Tony tried to do as many different chords as possible. It was obviously a send-up and it was trying to sound like an English musical performer called George Formby. The sound of the guitar was just a little bit like a banjo or a banjolele.* [42]

The difference between a song like 'Pigeons' and one like 'Who Dunnit?' is that the biggest sonic nuisance of 'Pigeons' is also its greatest strength: that incessant rhythmic pulsing on a single note over the course of the entire song. It's like eight tiny daggers launched into your ears every few seconds. Now I know that doesn't sound like a good thing, but here's the rub: those daggers have been coated with a narcotic. They pierce your ears and go straight into your brain, and it's painful at first, but then it gets into your blood. The venom alters your mind until you start to hunger for more of those insidious wounding strikes, creating a vicious cycle from which you can never escape. Listen to twenty seconds of 'Pigeons' and you'll be irritated. Listen to a minute of it and you'll be involuntarily bobbing your head, perhaps looking a bit pigeon-like yourself. Listen to the full thing and you'll find yourself unconsciously queueing it up for a repeat play, like some kind of half-human half-bird zombie. It's downright virulent.

> **Tony:** *'Pigeons' itself was a great track; a humorous track that should have been on [Wind and Wuthering] but we couldn't fit [it] on.* [6]

On the 2007 remaster the lads doubled down on the song's whimsy, adding a sort of old-timey filter on Collins' voice so the whole thing sounds like a 1920s radio report. It's brilliant. All that said, I don't have a strong opinion on whether this track would've improved *Wind & Wuthering*, but maybe it's better for the album's flow that it's off doing its own thing. Because once this little ring-a-ding-ding infects you, there's no going back. The sounds get into you little by little and then, before you know it, they're everywhere.

They're everywhere.

113 - Fireside Song

from *From Genesis to Revelation*, 1969

Previously in this book I've more or less ignored the instrumental snippets that either open or close some of the songs on *From Genesis to Revelation*. As a general rule, I feel like they were understandable attempts at generating some sense of linkage or continuity within the album, working in service of the loose, proto-concept album feel they were striving for. And as a general rule, I don't think they worked much at all for that purpose. In terms of this ranking exercise, my logic was that those snippets, existing only as a futile attempt to help tie the album together, weren't really part of their "parent" songs, and so rightly ought to be excluded from consideration. It's similar in philosophy to the bit at the end of 'In the Cage', which I don't think anyone would really argue is part of that song proper, but was attached to it because it needed somewhere on the album to live - and as an aside, unlike the general *FGTR* fare, I feel that the interlude on 'In the Cage' was actually pretty successful.

So this is where I get to claim my right to be a total hypocrite, because 'Fireside Song' opens with an extended one of these album interludes before diving into the song proper, and you'd best believe I'm going to "count" it in favour of the track, because those fifty seconds are the best stuff the entire album has to offer. It's all just piano, as so many of the instrumental passages of this era are, but it's so good. A dark, sombre mood that somehow manages to still sound hopeful, played simply but beautifully by Tony. The strings come in after to transition to the 80% of the song that comprises the actual 'Fireside Song' portion, but all those last 3+ minutes have to do in order to make the song successful is just *not screw it up*. Tony's already built a winner, so just be palatable and you're there.

Luckily, the rest of the song also delivers better than nearly anything else on the album. It's laid back, pretty, reserved - the exact kind of sound I praised 'In Hiding' for and wished they'd done more of on their debut. Peter isn't overly sugary sweet on his vocals, but still delivers a pure tone. He's less of a lead vocalist here as opposed to one instrument among several others blending together to craft an image of a serene campfire at sunset. It helps his cause that the melody is so pleasant, too. The backing vocals double on him, which hides the occasional singing deficiencies of Ant and Tony while still adding that sense of fullness, of friends sharing a song around the fire. It's good stuff.

> **Tony:** *One of the other tracks which was significant for me was 'Fireside Song'. The verse was something I had originally written using really quite complicated chords and one day I sat down and thought that the melody line itself was nice, but why didn't I just use the most bog standard chords I could underneath to see how it sounded? And I thought. "That sounds actually a lot better." Being a keyboard player you are always a little prone to using lots of funny chords, and over the years I've obviously done a lot of that, but I have also always liked things where everything has been kept really simple, and I think working on that song in particular taught me that.* [1]

Simple and sweet, but never overly so on either point, with a terrifically moody intro. In context, Tony's piano interlude could be the sun going down, with all the fear and uncertainty that might bring, until the fire bursts to life with the strings and all is well again. I'm really impressed these guys wrote this one in their teens, and I could listen to this one any time. For my money, the best song on *From Genesis to Revelation*, and it's not terribly close.

112 - Silver Rainbow

from *Genesis*, 1983

Genesis has a strange flow to it. You've got a longer hit single followed by a shorter one, followed by a classic prog jam on side one. Solid! Then the oft-maligned second side comes in with three consecutive pop rock numbers: a pair of minor chart hits and a tremendously punchy tune that could've been a third had it ever been released as a single. Finally, the album closes with a pair of songs that aren't entirely sure what they want to be. I've already talked about 'It's Gonna Get Better', but 'Silver Rainbow' seems like a song completely immersed in an identity crisis.

It opens with some keyboard noises that aren't even sure whether they want to commit to joining the song's key signature, while Phil warbles some lines that might as well be declaring it Opposite Day in Genesisland. Very hypnotic stuff. And then the drum just goes off like a grenade and blasts all of that away, replacing the whole personality of the track with a pulse-pounding rock vibe. It's the sort of heavy rhythm that you could turn the volume up on and feel in the core of your chest, you know? Just relentless strength. Soon we get "To the land that lies" and you begin feeling as though you're being tugged upward, expecting a grand chorus to release the tension, and...back down into the verse we go instead.

> **Tony:** *'Silver Rainbow' is a real favourite of mine. Phil started playing this kind of Adam and the Ants kind of drum thing with the cymbals, just banging his way through it. I started playing this piano riff on top of it and I thought it was a really strong song, and I hoped it would go a little further than it did actually, but it wasn't sort of recognised.* [3]

When the chorus finally does come, it's just as tense as the verses themselves. The melodies and chords never actually resolve musically. All you want is a dang major chord and it's simply not ever going to be there. The song forces you to the edge of your seat over and over again but never provides any relief. There's no payoff. Even the end just fades out, leaving you hanging one last time. Tony Banks loves to set up fake-outs like that, drawing in your anticipation for a resolution, but his modus operandi in these situations is to *delay* the resolution. Removing it entirely? What are you doing to me, Tony?!

This would all be infuriating but for the subject matter of the song. It's a love song, but rather than being a *declaration* of love, it's a *description* of it: one can only go "beyond the silver rainbow" when one is so enthralled that one is not aware that one is actually beyond the silver rainbow. It's a place where logic and patterns are out the window. It's - dare I say - a land of confusion. And that's, brilliantly, the picture these compositional choices musically paint: you don't know if you're coming or going. You think you know where the song is heading, and then it pivots and takes you somewhere else entirely. If you're thinking about the silver rainbow, you haven't been beyond it. Trippy.

> **Tony:** *I also have a lot of affection for 'Silver Rainbow', which is something of a forgotten track from the second side.* [1]

So when I say it sounds like a song having an identity crisis, that's actually not a bad thing. The identity crisis *is* the identity of 'Silver Rainbow', quite purposefully. I wouldn't go so far as to say it's a hidden gem per se, but it does have a certain kind of allure to it. Maybe less a diamond in the rough and more a really rough diamond? It's hard to pinpoint. Which I guess means 'Silver Rainbow' itself is beyond the silver rainbow? But wait, if I'm aware of that, then it can't be so. And yet surely there's something to be said for the circular nature of the thing, right? I guess maybe if I listen to the song and don't *think* about the silver rainbow? But then again they want me to think about it, don't they? Why else would they make the song this way, you know? Have I ever even been beyond it at all? I think I have...But doesn't that mean I haven't? Oh boy, here we go again...

111 - Congo

from *Calling All Stations*, 1997

'Congo' was the band's final top 40 hit in the UK, peaking at 29 on the charts. It did not chart at all on the US Billboard Hot 100, though it did hit 25 across the pond on the Mainstream Rock charts. Now I don't think you can properly analyse or judge a song based on its chart performance, but I bring these numbers up here because I think they tell us two things about this track. First, that the song is catchy enough to have landed as a mid-minor hit, scoring some radio play and creating general awareness of its existence. And second, that the song is *not* catchy enough to have become an *actual* hit, or have any lasting presence whatsoever in the public consciousness. It's a single that sounds like it ought to be a single, and yet all it takes is one listen to realise that it's missing that elusive "something" that would make it a *successful* single.

> **Ray:** *The single 'Congo' has never been my favourite song, I make no bones about that. It is a bit too quirky for me and I think there are better alternatives, but the idea was that they wanted to establish the band in rock radio, you know. There are so many formats and they wanted to give the band the credibility tag that maybe they had lost with the "pop" element on the last couple of albums, and the feeling was that maybe we could hit the rock radio format with a song that fitted the four minute playing format. So that they wouldn't have an excuse not to play it, and establish ourselves as a rock act again, and the credibility would feed through to top forty radio and so on and so forth...I didn't see how 'Congo' fitted that at all. For me, it's a rock song, yes, but it doesn't have that...aura about it, whatever it is, that just doesn't happen and I don't see the point in selling something to a format that doesn't fit that format.* [28]

What do we make of that? How is it that 'Congo' manages to somehow both succeed and fall flat at the same time? Well, I have a theory, and my theory begins with the notion that 'Congo' is actually two entirely independent songs that, for better or worse, got mashed together into one.

> **Tony:** *It developed out of a loop that I was fiddling around with. I was combining two or three different things together and slowing them down and doing funny things with them and it just had a really good feel to it I thought. So we ended up having two completely different moods on this loop, one of which was very much a happy thing which was kind of more obvious because it suggested slightly African beats or that Caribbean feel and you could see that. The other thing was this much darker thing which was much more straight ahead, more rock and we just combined the two really.* [25]

Taking ideas that are ostensibly different songs and jamming them up against one another into a single piece is a very Tony Banks kind of thing to do. One need only look at 'Supper's Ready' or 'Firth of Fifth' to realise that it's a longstanding trick in the band's history. But unlike those pieces, this isn't a progressive epic; it's a single. You can't typically stick two totally different moods together on a tune made for the radio and expect people to buy in. The obvious solution is to edit the song down so that only one of the two moods remains - essentially acknowledging the fact that you only found yourself in this pickle because you mixed your moods in the first place! But even that remedy doesn't solve all the problems. For one thing, you've got to answer the question of why you combined the two ideas to begin with.

Was it simply a matter of convenience and speed? That is to say, did you have these two bits and, rather than spend the time and effort developing either one on its own, you decided to just run them up against one another and see what happened? Again, that's actually the method Genesis used to construct some of their longer progressive works back in the early 1970s. It wouldn't be unheard of for them to go that route again, but when we're talking potential singles, it's far better to have one honed idea than two or three less refined ones.

Or was it a matter of feeling that neither idea could reliably stand on its own at all? Perhaps this "happy thing" that Tony described just didn't have enough strength to carry the weight of an entire song. And perhaps this "much darker thing" had that core to it, but didn't engender the kind of listener response that Tony and Mike really wanted. The idea that maybe these two bits truly need one another to balance out the piece.

And that leads us right back to the single edit of 'Congo': knowing that the song with both moods couldn't succeed, the "happy" mood from the intro and outro were excised, leaving only that darker middle. Sure, there's a wistful bridge in there to temporarily uplift things, but the fact remains: once you take out the positive vibes you're left with only the negative ones. Sometimes that's OK! After all, 'Congo' is a song about separation and space: "Send me to the Congo" is really just a fancy metaphor for "I'll go away if you want me to." Then you have Ray Wilson's husky voice delivering the lines, which are a great match for the song's darker energy.

> **Tony:** *I must admit that when we were writing this, I had just heard the Stiltskin album and I said to Mike, "This would sound fantastic, get that singer from Stiltskin, this sounds exactly like one he would sing..."* [25]

Unfortunately in this case, music videos are also a thing, and when you combine a title like 'Congo', lyrics like "You say I put chains on you," and strip out any sense of joyous perspective that the intro and outro might bring, you get things like directors who decide to craft the music video for your hopeful hit single around imagery of a modern day slave trade in a shipyard. It not only destroys any goodwill the original song had, but puts your single on very dangerous waters, because this is now the visual that people will associate with your song.

> **Tony:** *It was really the first time ever that we let a director have his way with us, because we had quite a lot of respect for the guy as a filmmaker. It was quite fun to do, although I haven't got a clue what it is about...Certainly nothing to do with what the lyrics are about!* [25]

Regardless, I think the middle, darker section of 'Congo' is all right for what it is. The lyrics are poor and the delivery unconvincing, but the grungy guitar provides a good sound and the melody of the chorus is solid. I even like the backing vocal shout-outs on subsequent refrains. I just feel that 'Congo' really needs that intro and outro to elevate it above the ho-hum filler status, and ultimately, that maybe those sections should've been the core of the song instead. They don't quite cohere to the darker middle section anyway. As it stands, the album version is far better in my mind than the single edit for this song.

> **Ray:** *I've always...hated 'Congo', as everyone knows.* [26]

That might be fair, Ray, but have you ever considered a version of 'Congo' where it's just upbeat and pleasant and you don't have to sing about soldier ants that inexplicably become the artwork for the single? Maybe, just maybe, in that world you think this song is pretty swell.

110 - The Lady Lies

from ...And Then There Were Three..., 1978

Among those aware of the Genesis during the first half of the 1970s, there was a thought - quite understandable, mind you - that Peter Gabriel's departure would mark the end of on-stage theatrics for the band. No more costume changes, no more giant slideshows or swirling snake cones, no more any of it. To an extent, these concerns were well founded.

> **Phil:** *If you're not predisposed toward bat-wing headgear and flying in the air, what do you do when there's no singing? ... I'm not going to be able to do what Peter did.* [12]

Yet the masses here might have been missing the forest for the trees. Peter Gabriel's costumes and other visual aids were always there as a way to provide a sort of conduit for the meaning of the music to be absorbed more readily. It wasn't "bat wings for bat wings' sake" but "bat wings and UV makeup to give a visceral sense of something alien happening, as this song is 'Watcher of the Skies' and people should ideally 'get it' right away." The visuals were there to enhance the performance, yes, but they were not the performance itself. And performance? Well, Phil Collins was no stranger to performances.

Having done a couple runs of *Oliver!* in London's West End as the Artful Dodger, Phil had to get comfortable on stage from a very young age. As a teenager he even showed up on the big screen in the children's film Calamity the Cow as its (human) lead, although his refusal to follow direction led to him getting fired partway through. The point is, Phil had spent years developing his skills at playing to a crowd and digging into a persona, and so costume or no, his ability to captivate an audience during a Genesis concert shouldn't come as a huge surprise.

Even still, when I see footage of 'The Lady Lies' being performed on tour, I find myself amazed out how well he brings the lyrics to life. There's the narrator describing the noble knight, the "maiden" in distress, the demon revealed, and Phil effortlessly jumps between all the characters as though this song were his own personal 'Battle of Epping Forest' in miniature. The music isn't even really that different in the live version. It feels maybe a bit more jazzy on stage, and there's more instrumental stuff at the tail end to replace the studio fade-out, but the performance makes it something a bit different. The jazzy feel in general is surprising, given that 'The Lady Lies' is a Banks piece in its entirety, but Phil is the guy who was always really interested in that jazz fusion kind of direction. For me, though, when I hear this song it always sounds like I'm in a ballroom.

> **Mike:** *The ending was meant to be cacophonous with the sort of jazz style that happens when the musicians get that really happy look. It sounded very strong even after we'd put down the basic track. The beginning is meant to be slinky - a strippers feel to it. Hence the title.* [17]

From the first keyboard riff all the way to Tony's longer solo and beyond, this seems like the kind of song that someone in a big frilly red dress should be waltzing to - a feeling provided by the 12/8 rhythm delivering patterns of three in what sound initially like patterns of 4. It gives the whole track a sort of elegance about it, despite that uneasy feeling that maybe this isn't the "right" way to view the whole endeavour. But then I take a step back and I realise that with this rhythm I'm being entranced by something that seems like one thing, but is actually another thing, the deception making it all the more enticing. And that's when I recognise that the story of the song describes the song itself. Oh, that crafty Banks.

109 - The Grand Parade of Lifeless Packaging

from *The Lamb Lies Down on Broadway*, 1974

Toot toot! No, it's not time to get back to work (unless for you it is, in which case get back to work!), though that is a factory whistle you're hearing at the start of the recording. It's a real attention grabber of a sound effect and a great way to open a song. It's well placed on the album, too, coming directly after the little musical interlude that officially ends the runtime of the epic 'In the Cage'. You've got this big bombastic piece, followed by a meandering little wind-down, and then toot toot! Wake up and let's start a whole new mood. I quite like it.

> **Tony:** *There were just bits that developed out of [improvisation] where great moments just happened in the room...There were three or four positions on the album where we had no song so we wrote a specific song for it which was quite fun; it was on the spot. One of them was...'The Grand Parade Of Lifeless Packaging'. [One] of the stronger moments on the album...kind of quirky and almost written to fulfil a role.* [6]

Like a factory whistle might signal the start of a shift, where production slowly ramps up until the whole place is churning with activity, so goes 'The Grand Parade of Lifeless Packaging'. The entire song is one giant crescendo over nearly three minutes. And not just in volume, though that's true as well. It's also a crescendo of complexity, of layers. At the outset it's just Tony quietly playing a light marching tune, and he's quickly joined by Peter delivering a belting vocal - but that's been run through a suppression filter to keep the volume and intensity deliberately low. Incidentally, this effect was created by Brian Eno and credited on the album as "Enossification" in exchange for Phil being loaned out for a song on Eno's own album at the time.

> **Phil:** *While laying down the tracks, word gets to us that Brian Eno is recording in the studio upstairs... Peter goes up to say hello and asks if we can put some vocals through his computer. In return Eno asks if I can go up and play on a track of his called 'Mother Whale Eyeless'. I don't mind being pimped out... I'm drawn to his way of working. I end up playing on [three more of his] albums...* [12]

Serendipitous talent trading aside, the layering of 'The Grand Parade of Lifeless Packaging' continues as filters come and go. Tony adds a higher harmony onto the keyboard sounds. And now there's a tiny bit of hi-hat, and now a guitar running with some sustained backing notes, and now there's some actual drum hits, and now a deeper voice presaging Peter's own 'Moribund the Burgermeister' comes in, and we've got a bass layer, and now the guitar is soaring ever higher, and now the cymbals are crashing and the belting vocals have no filter at all so they're coming through at full strength, and now there's wailing voices on top of everything else, and then someone presses the red "stop" switch in the factory control room and everything grinds to a halt.

The melodies and structure of the song are fine - nothing terribly impressive but perfectly serviceable. So this isn't a matter of Genesis coming up with an amazing tune and then laying it down, as is the case with many of their other works. Instead this is an achievement of arrangement, in taking something relatively vanilla and building around it in the most interesting way possible. Play 'Grand Parade' at a steady mezzo forte with consistent instrumentation and it's a run of the mill linking track barely worth a notice. Arrange it in this way, though, and it's a fascinating parallel to the general lyrical theme. Not bad for something the guys came up with just to pad out some time, eh?

108 - You Might Recall

from *3x3*, 1982

You want groovy? Genesis has got groovy in spades. Left off *Abacab* because it wasn't quite weird enough for the flavour they wanted with the album, 'You Might Recall' takes a verse vibe from somewhere in between *And Then There Were Three* and *Duke* and then mashes that onto a chorus that's got all the pop sensibilities of *Invisible Touch* but without the kind of instrumentation that might make someone call it "too 80s sounding."

Which isn't to say that nothing sounds "80s" about this song that first came out in 1982, mind you. The opening keyboard riff is what it is, and it comes back in various shades several times throughout the song. But in general when Tony isn't just playing chords for texture in the back half of the song, he's delivering a reserved performance on electric piano. It's really all about the guitar melodies threading through the second half. That's the real "meat" of the piece, even though you walk away remembering the slick vocal melody more than anything else.

And of course, there's Phil's drumming. One of his primary talents as a musician is to make complicated things sound simple; to create an immediacy to the listener that cuts through the intricacies that actually comprise the music itself. 'You Might Recall' is a terrific percussive example of this, in large part because the drumming at the outset of the song *is* fairly simple. But Phil adds hits and layers throughout the song that really fill out the sound of the whole affair, all while maintaining that same simple-sounding core of the beat. You miss it entirely if you're not listening for it. Very cool stuff.

But you know what's not cool? Gutting a solid song like this from *Abacab*. Believe me, I get that the band was going for more experimental songs and trying to include songs that didn't "sound like Genesis." The thing is, while 'You Might Recall' does sound "like Genesis" *now*, it didn't sound like Genesis *then*. At the time this was bold and fresh! Nevertheless, decisions had to be made.

> **Tony:** *When we played [Abacab] to Atlantic in the States, we had a couple of extra tracks to choose between, one of which was a more straightforward, pretty Genesis song called 'You Might Recall', and there was some debate about whether we should include that track or 'Who Dunnit?'. I remember that [Atlantic Records exec] Ahmet Ertegun said, "No, I'm afraid you've got to put ["Who Dunnit?"] on."* [1]

Gosh dangit, Ahmet. One could argue he made the right call given how polarizing 'Who Dunnit?' still is all these years later, and how therefore people are still talking about *Abacab*. But that doesn't do much to salve the wound. 'You Might Recall' is vastly more enjoyable to me, a breakup song that eschews sappiness and melancholy in favour of a really funky groove. Slot this into the second side of *Abacab* and you actually get an album that's listenable all the way through. Isn't that worth something?

The only real issue I have with 'You Might Recall' is that it never really arrives. Sometimes that feeling works to a song's benefit, but here in the riff/verse/chorus structure it comes as a bit of a disappointment. That chorus is a "lean in" kind of vibe, where the tension and excitement builds and builds, causing the listener to start overflowing with anticipation for the grand musical reward that never comes. 'Silver Rainbow' would have this same issue on the very next album, but in that case it actually served the lyrical message. Here that sense of relentless forward motion undermines the core "pop hook" nature of the piece a bit, keeping 'You Might Recall' from reaching even loftier heights.

107 - Guide Vocal

from *Duke*, 1980

1979 for Genesis was spent on solo material for each of the three bandmates, though Phil's debut album itself wouldn't arrive for some time yet. And given that 64% of 1978's Genesis album *And Then There Were Three* consisted of solo-written songs as well, it's not too surprising that a return to the band setting for *Duke* might bring with it a change in mindset.

> **Mike:** *Having been out there doing solo work, I felt, probably subconsciously, it would be good to get back to what we used to do, which was writing together. And with Duke we turned that corner.* [1]

As they jammed, that group effort turned into a side-long thing, a great epic reminiscent of the heady days of the early 70s. And then, to avoid mentioning the heady days of the early 1970s, that side-long thing was split up into six individual tracks, creating a curious kind of anomaly: 'Guide Vocal' is definitively part of the collection of "group-written" tracks on *Duke*, and yet is also credited solely to Tony Banks. That's the nature of the beast, I suppose. "Use my lick here, your chord there, tie on that riff at the end of this melody I came up with..." When you break the big piece into components, you might just end up with an entire individual song when in the larger context it would've only been a case of, "Yeah, that was my bit there."

At under ninety seconds, 'Guide Vocal' clocks in as the shortest song the band ever officially released, but that doesn't mean it doesn't have much to offer. Of course, it offers much more in the album's context than it does on its own, but to see 'Guide Vocal' as nothing more than a precursor to the climactic moment of 'Duke's Travels' is, I think, to sell it a little short. This is more than a pre-prise, if I might coin the term.

Just listen to that emotion in Phil's voice. After 'Please Don't Ask', this is probably his most passionate performance on the album. 'Please Don't Ask' itself is basically a response to divorce by saying "Hey, maybe um, maybe we could, I don't know, you know, maybe we could try again?" It's vulnerable, it's absurdly courageous, it's hopeful in the face of almost certain failure and rejection. 'Guide Vocal' is its emotional counterpart and reflection: "There was a choice but now it's gone...take what's yours and be damned." It's just so *raw* a feeling and statement. And the thing about these thoughts and emotions is that they aren't actually opposites. They coexist together, in cacophonous pseudo-harmony, because divorce bloody sucks and there's no easy way to deal with it.

Take a gander at the track listing for *Duke*, if you will. The album is constructed like a mirror, where each track has a sort of parallel in its opposite position. 'Behind the Lines' and 'Duke's End' as the bookends are obvious, since they're at their core the same song (and were even combined into a single live version called 'Duke's Intro' to open the 2007 tour). Similarly, 'Duchess' and 'Duke's Travels' are the intense, powerful moments at the beginning and end, respectively. Then there's 'Guide Vocal' and 'Please Don't Ask', two sides of the same coin of visceral reaction to this loss in one's life. 'Man of Our Times' and 'Cul-de-sac' also have very similar lyrical themes, and a similar energy about them. 'Misunderstanding' and 'Alone Tonight', well, I trust by now you see the pattern.

'Guide Vocal' may just be a snippet, but it's still a really powerful dive into very deep, very murky waters, and it's a terrific example of how a great band can say an awful lot while saying very little.

106 - Can-Utility and the Coastliners

from *Foxtrot*, 1972

The tale of King Cnut (Canute) and the tide is a popular one, if perhaps dubious in its historicity. The story goes that Cnut, King of England, Denmark, and Norway all, plopped his throne by the sea shore and commanded the tide to halt at his feet. The tide, of course, did no such thing. Unsurprisingly, it wasn't long before Cnut was sitting in a chair surrounded by ankle deep water. The legend goes that he did this to demonstrate to his sycophantic courtiers that the ultimate dominion and command of creation rested not with him, a mortal king, but instead with God, the one true King and only being worthy of proper worship. Over time interpretation of the story shifted, and now modern references often get this bit wrong: many now read the story with the thought that Cnut was being earnest in his audacity to command the tide. It transforms the tale from one of piety and wisdom to one of the absurdity of human arrogance, culminating with Cnut being humiliated in front of his subjects, rather than the other way around.

'Can-Utility and the Coastliners' is the Genesis version of the story ("**Can-Ut**ility" being a playful reference to Cnut and "the Coastliners" referring to the simpering noblemen surrounding him), and as a set of lyrics it seems unsure which accounting of the tale to follow; or perhaps it even forges its own third, unique recounting of events. In the second verse you have King Cnut exasperated with all the undeserved praise being heaped upon him, going so far as to say "We heed not flatterers." That seems very much in line with the "correct" accounting of the legend. As is common to both sides of the quasi-historical coin, "the cause was lost" and the tide rose anyway. This is where the stories typically differ, with the original claiming that Cnut stood up, proclaimed God the lord of all, and permanently retired his crown in order to show proper respect to the true Sovereign. The latter-day account, by contrast, portrays an embarrassed and undermined Cnut in disbelief that nature dared disobey his command.

In 'Can-Utility and the Coastliners', however, the ocean itself begins to swallow the throne while proclaiming the absolute power of God, as all present on the shore knelt before His display of authority. While this dramatic showing would seem to support the spirit of the original telling of the tale, curiously the next lines feature a Cnut who seems disappointed with the outcome. He has to smile through his teeth, finally demanding that nobody in his retinue so much as smile at his misfortune. Is this genuine discomfort, or is Cnut further making a point at the farcical nature of the whole affair? It's unclear, but "soon they dared to laugh" anyway. That takes us to the last couple lines, which are for me the most confusing of all. They describe a "little man with his face turning red," and I have no idea whether this represents Cnut himself getting angry at the laughter, or a severely chastised noble failing to "get" the joke, or something else entirely. It's an ambiguous ending to the tale, delivered by Peter in a kind of choked scream that could just as easily represent a fit of laughter as a fit of rage.

In any case, it's a typical lyrical play by the band at this stage: go grab a classical story or legend, put a slightly comedic twist on it, and set it to some progressive music. This was the band's bread and butter of the early 70s, and I think this song in particular might be one of the best examples of that style. As a set of lyrics it's got strong character and imagery, ebbing and flowing like, well, the waters of the sea that move from calm to stormy. And as a composition, it's varied and interesting. That's the result of another typical Genesis move from this era: taking different "bits" written by individual members and stapling them together. The difference is that 'Can-Utility and the Coastliners' runs under six minutes instead of in the ten minute realm, so it's much more compact with its ideas. This gives each section more impact, though also less of a chance to seamlessly transition.

> **Tony:** *The end section of 'Can-Utility' is really good. Well, the first part's good [too]. It's a really good song. It's just a bit fragmented, that song I think. That's where it suffers slightly. But the last part is a good instrumental piece as well.* [3]

Therefore, when I listen to this song, I can't help but hear it as essentially three distinct sections of music: the initial storytelling "verses" painting a scene of a tranquil ocean being overtaken by a heavenly storm, the heavier middle instrumental as all present are overawed by the divine power on display, and the final human reflection of what it all means. Full credit to Steve Hackett here, whose songwriting was beginning to really develop by this point.

> **Steve:** *It was a joy to write much of 'Can-Utility and the Coastliners'. I realised that by now I was a fully-fledged writer along with the other band members.* [39]

'Can-Utility and the Coastliners' has not one, but two of the best instrumental passages in the early Genesis catalogue. The first is built around a guitar riff and chords that evoke images of the coming sea storm described in the previous section's lyrics. There's no melody here really, just a pervading mood of impending disaster. It's this heavy triplet pattern running up against Mellotron strings, and the tension is almost palpable. Then Peter comes in with a vocal line that rapidly builds to a climax on "where they fell," launching straight into the second big instrumental. This one has two distinct sections of its own: a huge organ showcase and a more playful, guitar-focused bit that resets the focus from the turbulent ocean to the silliness reigning on the seashore. But it's that organ section that stands out to me as the best moment of the song by far - and perhaps even the entire album. Whenever I want to listen to this song, this is the singular moment I'm tuning in for.

The section's in a straight 4 rhythm, but *everything* is playing against that, creating a kind of musical struggle. Phil's keeping the beat on the bottom, but even he's peppering in anticipatory hits that throw off the scent. The main organ riff plays once on a straightforward rhythm but immediately echoes itself with a syncopated, elongated version, and then continues stretching that initial basic pattern in unexpected ways as the notes move from chord to chord, bass pedal ploughing away. Steve's playing his own triplets against the sustained organ notes to mask the beat even further, but after four measures veers off into his own countermelodic playing instead, like a call and answer to the main riff. At the same time, Peter comes in on the oboe, providing the icing on the cake you didn't even know you needed. Some Genesis songs of this time period were overly complex for me, just layers for the sake of layers. Not so with this section, which is eight measures of arranging perfection before the come-down.

> **Steve:** *It didn't get much of an airing [live] in the day. We played it a few times in Italy to literally three men and a dog. We didn't do great versions of it back then, so we retired it. Part of the problem was the fact that it was so sequential, and I had to run to drop my 12-string and pick up my electric...But I still think it's a beautiful song, very intriguing.* [13]

Shame about the stage, but what're you gonna do? The opening section of the song isn't nearly as exciting to me as the middle, but it's every bit as pastorally (nautically?) pleasant as most of Steve's other work with the band. I do think the ending section is a bit weak, though perhaps that's the point - who, after all, can possibly follow God? That middle section truly makes the song for me, and there's nothing wrong with that, though I do, like Tony, wish the individual components of the song meshed a bit better with one another. Still though, I like almost all of 'Can-Utility and the Coastliners', and I absolutely love a major part of it. Can't complain about that.

105 - Man of Our Times

from *Duke*, 1980

"Repetitive" is a word that often gets thrown around in strictly negative terms. It's a ghastly insult among hardcore prog fans, a shorthand of sorts for "soulless sell-out garbage." Call a song repetitive and BAM, you've instantly discredited all the work that went into making it. In this sense it's an arrogant word, one that seeks to take a person's subjective opinion and convert it into universal truth. You can say a song is good or bad, pretty or ugly, pleasant or distasteful, and everybody understands that it's just your opinion; there's no weight to it beyond that. But if you call a song *repetitive*, well, that's a statement of fact, isn't it? "No, listen, this section repeats. It's inarguable." So if you can influence people into associating "repetitive" with "bad," and you can point to a song you don't care for and say - quite factually - that it's repetitive, you've essentially just said "This song is objectively bad," and you have to hope the person you're talking to isn't clever enough to catch onto the linguistic trick you've just pulled.

Why am I diving into all this? Because, simply put, 'Man of Our Times' is repetitive as all get out. You've got a riff running over big cymbal crashes and bass slams, and then it opens up into this massive chord where the guitar plays a melody and Phil wails over it with the title line. There's a post-chorus transition which is almost musically identical to the verse, so that registers in the mind as a repeated section in itself. Then it does the whole thing again. And after that second post-chorus, which again, is essentially the same as the verse but with different vocals, it's another chorus which plays for over a minute until the song fades out. I've talked about song structure earlier in this book, and this one looks like this: A-B-A'-A-B-A'-B^{BBBBB}. This is all pretty factual stuff; you can't tell me the song isn't repetitive because it very clearly is. It's not up for debate.

Now, did you read that second paragraph and think to yourself, "Sheesh, I can't believe this guy hates 'Man of Our Times'"? It's all right, you can be honest. We're all friends here. I'm not judging you, but that assumption is precisely what I'm trying to combat. 'Man of Our Times' is a genuinely *good* song. It's repetitive as all get out, yes, but that doesn't need to be a dirty word. What you have in this track is structurally very simple, but it's musically very dense. There's so much happening in nearly any given second of this song that the repetition actually gives you a chance as a listener to catch the things you may have missed the first time around.

When I listen to this song it feels like it gets stronger as it goes on. That last chorus feels more powerful than the first; the natural inclination is to assume that it added something to the mix, but I don't actually think that's true. I think it's pretty much bang on the same thing, but Genesis is saying "No no, we don't think you really understood us the first couple times around. We're serious. Here, try again." That repetition doesn't undermine the song but rather opens your ears up to the strength that was there from the first beat of the first measure. It's a song you don't need to play on loop because it's already doing that for you. All you've got to do is let it wash over you, and lift you a bit more every time it passes by.

> **Mike:** *In terms of my own songs, Duke was an album of highs and lows, the low being 'Man of Our Times', which was my attempt to be a bit Gary Numan. I had a guitar synthesizer for the first time, which allowed me to write songs with string parts. I wasn't a great fan of synth stuff but...I thought it was important to investigate what was on offer. With hindsight it's a song that's best forgotten...* [14]

With all due respect to Mike, I have to disagree.

104 - Dance on a Volcano

from *A Trick of the Tail*, 1976

When the first words of an album are "Holy Mother of God," you know you're probably in for a good ride. Even more so when those words don't even come until after an introductory section featuring searing guitars, booming bass pedals, and cymbal hits that sizzle like scraps of cloth falling into burning lava. Right from the start, you're just *there*. It's such a strong opener that the band used 'Dance on a Volcano' to kick off the 'Old Medley' sixteen years later on their We Can't Dance Tour, going so far as to play multiple verses of the song before finally transitioning away.

> **Mike:** *It kind of embodied all that Genesis did well, which was majestic, powerful stuff, interesting rhythms, good melodies...the intro had a drama, an excitement, and if you heard it you'd kind of go "Oh, what's that? It sounds great!" That's an important track. I'm not sure the rest of it was always up to scratch, but the intro and the first bit I thought was very strong.* [3]

> **Steve:** *Particularly spectacular opening, I think. I always felt this one worked spectacularly well live. It was always powerful, and of course those bass pedals... The thing about the intro is we were rehearsing it up and Phil had the idea of doing those accents to interrupt the arpeggiating 12-strings, the twinkly stuff, and we all hit the accents together and did this rising thing, so it was a bit like the band working on telepathy.* [13]

So it's a little ironic that with the guys delivering on the "volcano" part of the title so quickly and thoroughly, the song isn't actually one you can "dance" to. Which I guess makes its inclusion in said We Can't Dance Tour that much more appropriate. You see, the song is mostly in seven, which is to say seven beats per measure instead of the usual four. Not only is this effectively murder to the hopes of any would-be dancers, but it also can be a problem for the rhythm section, depending on the personnel. Phil Collins? No problem, let's get nutty! Trick of the Tail Tour (and former Yes) drummer Bill Bruford? Well, that's a bit of a different story.

> **Tony:** *He has to think about things; he has to count things as well. I think he found some of the songs like 'Dance on a Volcano' not that easy: there was a fill in the middle which had to be played in 7, and you could see Bill's mouth counting it all out.* [1]

> **Steve:** *Compelling riff in 7/8; the whole thing is in 7/8, can't dance to it... There aren't many tracks in 7/8 that swing like this...* [13]

So no, the titular "dance" isn't a literal thing. Instead it's the representation of someone trying *really hard* not to fall into a river of flowing lava. "Crosses of green and crosses of blue" mark the remains of those who failed in the quest to trek over the erupting volcano, and everything about the song's music is built to serve the tense, dangerous imagery. There's the steeling of resolve, represented by Tony's big chords after each "You better start doing it right" lyric. There's the guitar spitting little bursts of fire after the line "Blazing hot, the molten rock spills out over the land." An ominous line of "Let the dance begin," followed by the utterly frantic ending instrumental section, wherein we can envision leaping from one sliding rock to another, trying desperately to make it to the other side of the slope before being swallowed whole by the hungry mountain.

> **Steve:** *I wrote the end section, the fast and furious thing that we struggled to play back in the day. I like to think with the benefit of hindsight and experience, I could do a stronger version of that. So I still love playing it live...* [13]

A bit of this hustle and bustle and the music calms down, providing the both the subject of the song and the listener a chance to breathe. Safety at last, you think? No, I'm afraid not. The respite is cut short as the caldera bursts forth anew and the desperate dance picks up once more, down, down and down the peak, until finally secure purchase is found and everyone can finally rest. It's such an exhausting exercise that one imagines our intrepid hero likely laying down for a much-needed nap after the ordeal.

Indeed, if we're paying close attention, we seem to get just that. Notice that there is no mention of "he" or "she" or even any name in this song. It's always "you" and "your", isn't it? That's not just a happy accident. This song isn't meant to tell the story of some *other* person's trials and travails atop a red geyser of death; it's meant to put *you*, the listener, into that situation and encourage you to feel every bit of it along the way.

It's exhausting subject matter, but just try counting along with those seven beat measures the entire way through and you'll find that it's exhausting to listen to in earnest as well. It's not enough to just count the time out straight through, because there are subtle tempo shifts throughout the entire piece, minute speed-ups and slow-downs that throw off your internal metronome and make you feel as though you're in constant danger of being overrun. You see how that just serves the purpose further, yes? And then, when the music at last winds down and you feel too tuckered out to continue, the band serves up 'Entangled', a song all about sleep and dreams. They knew *exactly* what they were doing.

> **Tony:** *'Dance on a Volcano' started off on day one, when Mike, Phil and I were there because Steve was finishing off his solo album. And we came to the studio and we just started improvising. And what became the first part of 'Dance on a Volcano' came out of that. It was at that moment that I felt - having come up with a little bit of trepidation about "What's going to happen? How's it going to be without Peter?" - we wrote that, and I felt "This is great, I'm really excited about this." And I think it set us off in a really good direction.* [3]

What an in-your-face statement this song was for the band. Months of media speculation about how the band could even carry on, articles signalling doom and gloom for the band, for how could they ever survive without Peter Gabriel? And then the new record comes out, sceptical listeners put it on, and the first thing they hear is 'Dance on a Volcano'? Just as this song gave Tony a sense of peace that everything would be all right, I'm sure it must have done the same for a great many contemporary Genesis fans as well, putting them immediately in the shoes of this poor soul on a deadly mountaintop and saying, "Have fun."

Often times lyrics represent music only through proximity: these are the lyrics to this song, so therefore this music is about these lyrics. But it's an arbitrary thing, and if you replaced all the lyrics the song would mean something totally different, and it wouldn't necessarily be worse. Well, 'Dance on a Volcano' is probably one of the best marriages to lyric and music I've ever seen. Though the music was written first, it seems the lyrics were penned not with a mind of "What do I want this song to say?" but rather *"What is this song already saying?"* It's a fantastic example of letting the music speak for itself, despite the fact that there are words all over it. So, even though it's not my personal favourite track off the impeccable *A Trick of the Tail*, I still think it's a masterpiece in that respect, and well deserves the adoration it gets among fans. And if there had been any doubt among fans of the era, they needn't have worried: Genesis was definitely "doing it right."

103 - I Can't Dance

from *We Can't Dance*, 1991

Is there anything in the world more inane than a television commercial for blue jeans? "Here's a guy stripping at the laundromat. Buy some jeans." Or perhaps one that attempts to convince you to buy blue jeans by only ever showing you people's upper bodies. You know...the parts not wearing jeans. It sounds absurd, but these commercials actually existed, one of them featuring a young Stanley Tucci. There's one where a guy literally flatlines on the operating table in an ER because all his doctors and nurses are busy singing a bad rendition of 'Tainted Love' by Gloria Jones (and later Soft Cell). Only cologne and perfume ads are more consistently ridiculous, and you can at least excuse them a bit on the basis that they're trying to sell you a smell through a visual medium, and I acknowledge that that's a difficult ask. But jeans ads?

There's just nothing redeeming about them, even when the models are actually wearing the product; one quintessential TV spot for Jordache jeans had a handful of reasonably attractive people hanging out at the beach, dressed in an *awful* ensemble of denim pants, denim jackets, and red-orange shirts, dancing and snapping in what could only be described as body spasms. No sense of rhythm whatsoever, even as the background music cheerfully repeats "The Jordache look!" It's hard to imagine that commercial selling anyone at all "the Jordache look" when it's so poorly represented. There's zero talent on display. They can't sing (and neither can the ladies on the backing track, if we're being honest). They aren't allowed to talk. They *most certainly* cannot dance. And while we're at it, why on earth are they wearing blue jeans and denim jackets at the gosh dang beach of all places? That's a terrible idea! What with the hot sun beating down, and making you sweat, and so forth.

At any rate, I'm digressing big time. You're not reading this book for my opinions on the state of denim advertising; you're reading it because you like Genesis. So let's shift back on topic. Did you hear about Tony's new keyboard? Tony, tell 'em.

> **Tony:** *I got this new keyboard...a sort of Roland thing.* [3]

Oh, that sounds nice, if a little vague. Does it do anything cool?

> **Tony:** *It had a bass drum that went boom-ch-boom-boom like this and then I started playing these silly sounds on top of it.* [3]

Well that sounds a little out there, but I suppose it could be the start of something. I assume you guys are going to develop this, well, whatever it is at some point, yeah?

> **Tony:** *We thought, "Oh this is really good, we'll do it like that." And what we did was after we'd written it, we didn't do anything to it...And then we said "Well we'll put that song down, the one with the guitar riff."* [3]

Wait, what guitar riff? Mike, what is Tony talking about?

> **Mike:** *Tony had this boom-ch-boom-boom which he played on the keyboard, and I had a guitar riff.* [3]

Well yes, I managed to gather that much so far. I was sort of hoping for something, you know, a little more helpful than that...

> **Mike:** *What I do remember, actually, is that I remember playing it, thinking "Ooh, that's really quite nice," but then I couldn't find it again. I had to go back and find the tape - we'd recorded it - and listen over and over and over again to work it out, because it's a simple riff but it's quite unusual the way it's actually put together.* [3]

Oh, so it sounds like maybe it was a little more complex than Tony was making it sound at first.

> **Phil:** *...a stupidly simple song...* [12]

What was that, Phil? "Super simple", is that what you said? Are you saying there was nothing deeper going on here at all? You just walked in, tossed it together, called it a day?

Phil: *Five minutes work. You know, that was our classic example of "Let's not do this any more. Let's just record this right now." And I remember Mike was doing a guitar part again, and I was writing the lyrics in the corner chair and said "I'm finished!" and we went and did it.* [3]

O....K.... That whole process sounds a *bit* suspect to me, but you guys are the experts, I guess. Doesn't sound like the recipe for a hit, but hey what do I know.

Phil: *We never sort of said, "Listen, we need the money, we need the success, we need the hit singles." We just...didn't need the money. And we didn't need the success 'cos we were all doing all right. We just wrote... as we went along. The three of us just making it up, blank page...let's just do what we do as a group, which can't be fulfilled in any other way.* [43]

All right, I can respect that, even if this whole thing still feels a bit weird to me. Any other inspirations at work here?

Phil: *That opening high burst of the first chorus line -* **ouch***. The reason I wrote that little bit was as a nod to Fine Young Cannibals' Roland Gift, who has a terrific soul voice. But singing that every night… Shot myself in the vocal cord with that one.* [12]

So what's this song called?

Phil: *'I Can't Dance'.* [12]

Interesting...I think… What's it about?

Phil: *It's not about being unable to dance.* [44]

Come on Phil, throw me a bone here.

Phil: *It's about guys that look good but can't string a sentence together. Each verse is a piss-take at the scenario of a jeans commercial.* [44]

Welp, I'm sold. Keep up the good work, gents. Genesis just *gets* me, you know?

102 - Aisle of Plenty

from *Selling England by the Pound*, 1973

The opening melody of 'Dancing with the Moonlit Knight' (and therefore of *Selling England by the Pound* in general) is just gorgeous. I'll say more about it when it that song shows up in the pages of this book yet to come, but I adore that melody and feel it really sets the tone for the entire album to come. It establishes a high bar of quality for the album right from the get-go; a target line to which everything else on the album must measure up or else disappoint by comparison. So the concept of creating a brief epilogue for the album using that same melody as its central focus has me automatically on board. To that extent, 'Aisle of Plenty' doesn't have a lot of heavy lifting it needs to do in order to be a listening pleasure for me; its "parent" song has already done that work for it.

> **Steve:** *'Aisle of Plenty'...perfectly bookends the album, because you get the recapitulation of the theme [from 'Dancing with the Moonlit Knight'], and then [it] just fades out...I think it's absolutely beautiful.* [45]

What strikes me about this song is that instead of trying to live up to the pressure of expectations and inevitably falling short, 'Aisle of Plenty' feels free to just do whatever it wants with its inherited melody, and I really like the direction it goes over its short runtime. It doesn't try to copy 'Dancing with the Moonlit Knight'. Neither does it try to develop the melody into something new. Instead it simply re-establishes that melody, lets it go, and runs the underlying riff for a while as Pete starts shouting out prices like a hawker in a market. It all seems utterly ridiculous when you read it as a description like this, but it's *perfect* for the album: an ideal conclusion for a portrait of Englishness and consumerism.

And even in the span of a mere ninety seconds, there's still a lot going on musically. The interplay of Tony's bouncy keyboards with Pete's almost mournful vocals provide a really powerful and engaging contrast over the track's first third. Then you get Steve doing subtle variations on the guitar riff while the aforementioned street vendor vocals start layering. By the end of the track Pete has three or four independent lines all playing over one another, and they somehow all work in unison to create a harmony of discordance. Individual threads painting a single picture. It's remarkably effective.

> **Phil:** *I know Tony said that he could've done without it. I don't remember it.* [3]

This is the primary issue the Genesis fandom seems to have with 'Aisle of Plenty': "I don't remember it." Perhaps for Phil it just blended in with 'Dancing with the Moonlit Knight' and wasn't involved enough in the recording process to register with him. But among Genesis fans, I've witnessed time and time again a tendency to think of 'Aisle of Plenty' as little more than a coda to 'The Cinema Show'. On the one hand that's completely understandable: in the earliest conception of the pieces, 'Dancing with the Moonlit Knight', 'The Cinema Show', and 'Aisle of Plenty' were all one giant track, and even on the released product the ending measures of 'The Cinema Show' serve to transition the listener back into the 'Dancing/Aisle' melodic mindset.

But on the other hand, have these people actually *listened* to 'Aisle of Plenty'? I get that 'The Cinema Show' is a big attention-grabber and the brief track following it might feel like an afterthought, but it's the summary paragraph at the end of an essay! The heroes walking off into the sunset! The Deutronomy to the Numbers, Leviticus, Exodus, and yes - the Genesis! And so I think to see it as nothing more than the fumes left in the wake of 'The Cinema Show' is to severely - ahem - undersell it.

101 - Since I Lost You

from *We Can't Dance*, 1991

On an album full of efforts to further hone the "modern Genesis sound," 'Since I Lost You' comes as a surprising throwback. The penultimate song on the record, it opens with a big cymbal roll before hitting you with this descending piano pattern that sounds straight out of a 1950s breakup song. I don't think that's a mere accident, either. Too much of 'Since I Lost You' feels designed to channel exactly that vibe: the doo-wop style backing vocals that oooo gently over the verses, then come in during latter choruses with their own sort of swaying harmony lines? Yeah, that's a classic breakup song right there. All it's missing are the snaps, which the snare drum is covering in spirit. Nevertheless, there's a modern influence at play: Mike's little guitar solo is evidence enough of that, as are Phil's drum fills in the back half. It's a piece that deftly straddles two eras of music, pretty impressive in its own right.

But the biggest giveaway for the inspiration is, of course, the choice of lyrics. "But my heart is broken in pieces since you've been gone" is exactly the kind of melodramatic, over-the-top schmaltz I might expect from that bygone age of rock music, where singers were far more concerned with entertaining the crowd than with delivering any kind of meaningful message or life lesson. Yes, it perhaps sounds a bit overproduced, maybe a tad artificial. But isn't that part of the fun of it? Isn't that what the whole exercise is all about, just taking that style of classic song and creating an extreme example of it? So while 'Since I Lost You' might be completely over the top as breakup songs go, perhaps that's kind of the point.

But then. Ohhhhh, but then.

> **Phil:** *This is probably one of the heaviest things I've ever written, or had a part in writing... One night after [Genesis] rehearsal I went home, and a friend rang up, and he said, "Have you heard about Eric [Clapton]?" So I said, "No, what do you mean?" He said, "His son's dead." So I...I couldn't believe it. Because I knew Eric very well; I knew [his four-year-old son] Conor very well. So I called New York, I found out where he was, and I found out that it was true. Well, the next day we went to rehearsals, and Mike and Tony also knew Eric very well, and we'd been writing this song. But we didn't have any lyrics. It didn't have any direction at all, lyrically. And we played this song, because, you know, work went on. And the lyrics to this - the chorus, anyway - came straight away.* [46]

Now this is a different animal entirely. Once upon a time, I thought the opening line of this song was laughable. Part of the charm, sure, but laughable nonetheless. After all, if you're in a relationship with someone, you can typically see the end coming well before it arrives. And if not, then it probably wasn't that strong a relationship in the first place, you know? Besides, there's this eye-rolling kind of feeling, like "How much more can Phil possibly milk his first divorce for material?" And then the pivot. "Wait, hang on a minute. There's something else going on here."

> **Phil:** *Straightaway, I was singing the things you hear on the record. "Cos my heart is broken in pieces, yes my heart is broken in pieces since you've been gone." It wasn't until the lyrics were finished that I told Tony and Mike what they were about. I didn't want to talk about it. Nor did any of us. We would prefer people to think it's just a love song...Now we're talking about it. I'm glad I can. But it still gives you shivers when you think about it.* [47]

"It seems in a moment your whole world can shatter." Oh, God. How do you even deal with that? This song isn't about a significant other leaving for greener pastures *at all*. This is a song about trying to somehow cope with the unimaginable grief of losing your child. This isn't Phil putting on his best soap opera voice and generating false pain. This is a man whose close friend just lost his son in a sudden, horrific accident. This is a man whose daughter turned two years old just two days prior. A man whose older kids were taken away from him to another continent. He's getting a second chance at being a good father; you think he's not getting flooded with involuntary mental images of this happening to his own little girl? I *know* he was, because as I write this paragraph, I'm less than a week removed from my own son's fourth birthday. You know, the same age as Conor was. I can't stop thinking about it, picturing it, mourning it. And I've never even met any of these people.

No, for Phil Collins, this was incredible grief just flowing out. That impassioned, desperate vocal performance? He's not chewing the scenery, man. That's *real*. That's *raw*.

Phil: *And when we finished the song, I took it to Eric to play it to him, because I wanted him to like it before we released it. If he didn't like it, we wouldn't have released it. I sat there, I played it to him, he had tears in his eyes, and then he played me a song. He said, "I've written one for Conor, too. I want to release it as a single. What do you think?" So he played it to me, and I said, "I don't think it's a single. It's a beautiful song, but I don't think it's a single." And that was 'Tears in Heaven', so what do I know, huh?* [46]

Phil: *In his grief, Eric has pulled together something extraordinary.* [12]

Ultimately, the fact that 'Since I Lost You' disguises its meaning gives it more versatility. As a call-back to 1950s doo-wop breakup melodrama, it works. As a vessel for and reflection of a parent's pain, it works. It's a song that competently manages to straddle both realms, which might in one sense make it the most impressive song on *We Can't Dance*.

Now look, that all said, do I think 'Tears in Heaven' is a better song than 'Since I Lost You' overall? Probably, sure. But when I see Genesis fans use the existence of 'Tears in Heaven' to dismiss this song because "there's a better tribute to Conor out there," I can't help but feel like I need to take a shower. What an absolutely gross sentiment to express, as though the two pieces need to be in some kind of competition. My guess is that the people who dismiss 'Since I Lost You' out of hand fall into one of two camps (or occasionally both): people who have never realised what the song is actually about, and people who have never had kids.

I hope, if you came into this entry as one of the people in that former camp, that you can set this book down, go turn on 'Since I Lost You', and have yourself a bit of a cry. Appreciate the song in a brand-new light. I know that was a big turning point for me; seeing the track through a newer, truer lens completely changed my opinion of it, and it might do that for you as well.

If you're in that latter camp, well, I can't help you there. But if you do ever have kids, and discover the new, incredible world of love they bring into your lives, I hope you come back to this book a few years later. At a moment when you can scarcely remember what it was like to live without your child or children, despite their having been around for so short a time, perhaps you'll come across 'Since I Lost You' once more. And perhaps, as I did, you'll find it hits you in a brand-new way.

100 - I'd Rather Be You

B-Side of 'Throwing It All Away' (UK) or 'In Too Deep' (US), 1987

Have you ever thought about the way that kids' cartoons aren't all created equally? I don't mean that some are good, some are bad, and most fall somewhere in between, although certainly that's true. I mean that the kind of cartoon a two-year-old might watch is likely drastically different to what a four-year-old might watch, which is drastically different still from a show made for six-year-olds, which is still pretty far removed from a show for eight-year-olds, etc. The mental development of children occurs so rapidly that, even though at the time they see it all as just pure entertainment, each show has to cater to a pretty narrow window in order to be successful.

You might have a show over here that's just songs and nursery rhymes, trying to engage and not much else. Maybe another show seeks only to educate, doing so with characters that they hope will appeal, but nevertheless a fairly heavy hand in driving critical thinking and learning. Maybe another show seeks to teach important life lessons, obfuscated by the fact that every character is some kind of talking dog. And maybe some cartoons are just plain noise with no redeeming qualities. As a dad of a toddler, I've seen them all.

Where does 'I'd Rather Be You' fit into all of this? Well, with all respect to Genesis as I'm sure this wasn't their intent, I can't help but hear this song as the opening theme song to one of these cartoons, targeting perhaps that 8-10 demographic. I can visualise the whole thing, really. It's probably a show about a group of crime fighting teens; you want the heroes to be older so the little kids look up to them, but not so old they're not relatable, you know? These teens don't have superpowers though - not exactly - but they're highly skilled and have cool tech to lean on, like a combination of Teenage Mutant Ninja Turtles and Power Rangers I guess. Just really ambitious and heroic kids who understand the power of teamwork and how to seem totally rad to anyone who might salivate over their endless lines of merchandise.

Every time Phil sings "I never wanted to be closer" I can see an overhead shot of those cartoon hands zipping into a "Go team!" kind of circle pattern. "It's dog-eat-dog" accompanies a snippet of one of them running down a hill getting chased by a veritable army of the bad guys in one of those stylish perspective shots, like the camera is in front of his face, which has that expression that just screams "GUYS HELP!" It's youngster comedy gold, I'm telling you. Heck, with a title sequence this catchy, I'd probably watch that show, too.

That unrelentingly peppy bass, those playful keyboards, that slightly shouty vocal - it's just begging for a montage of our heroes hopping into their mech suit hovercycles to save the city from the giant rubber monster that the kooky (but ultimately harmless) scientist accidentally made while he was trying to invent a better bouncy ball. You know what I mean? Just zany fun where each episode takes you on a wild ride of action and adventure, so engrossing that you don't realise you're learning something along the way. Maybe one episode is a lesson about the importance of trusting others. Maybe one is about sharing feelings. Maybe another is about the disastrous consequences of not telling the truth. But it's all buried under this facade of teenage do-gooders fighting robots and other ne'er-do-wells to save the city. I mean, what's not to love?

OK OK, so I can tell you might not be sold. That's fine, it's fine. I get that not everyone is going to get the same kind of vibe from this song as I do. But I want you to do me a favour, if you don't mind. If you're sitting there reading this book, sceptical that 'I'd Rather Be You' could possibly double as the soundtrack to a show that would be flagged by the ratings board as "parental advisory for cartoon violence and mischief," yet one you also wouldn't feel the slightest need to actually forbid your kids from watching, here's what I want you to do. Go listen to 'I'd Rather Be You'. However you can manage to do it. Got it all queued up? All right, great.

Now I want you to listen to that pre-chorus build up going on. You know, just groove with it a bit. Good stuff, right? OK, now this time, listen to that part, and then sing along with these lyrics:

> *Why worry when you're holding the aces*
> *Don't throw it away 'cause you know*
> *I'd rather be you than me*
> *Up there looking down*
> *Tell me what do you see, oh*
> *Duck Tales! Woo-woo!*

You hear it now, don't you?

You know you do.

99 - Alone Tonight

from *Duke*, 1980

When 'Follow You Follow Me' released as a single about a month ahead of its parent album, *...And Then There Were Three...*, Genesis found radio success like they never had before. Top ten in the UK. Top 25 in the US. Top 20 in Australia, for all you blokes and Sheilas who typically feel left out of these kinds of chart recaps. With that first success, a new world opened up for Genesis; a band with one hit single would be more likely to have radio stations give them a shot with the next song, which would mean more likelihood of another hit single, and so it goes down the line. Thus, when 1980's *Duke* came around and it was time to choose a lead-off single from the album, Genesis knew that success was ripe for the taking. So what do you think they chose?

> **Tony:** *When we played this album to the record company, they said, "Oh, there's a great hit on there!" We said, "Yeah yeah, we know! It's 'Turn It On Again'!" They said, "Oh no no no. It's 'Alone Tonight'." We said, "'Alone Tonight'?! Oh, god no."* [3]

That's right, it was 'Turn It On Again', which also landed in the UK top ten. But then for the album's *second* single, surely 'Alone Tonight' would get its due, right? I mean, it's got all the hallmarks you would want. Big, bombastic chorus with a catchy hook? Check. Relatable lyrics about love and loss? Check. Radio-friendly runtime? Check. No big instrumental breaks or keyboard solo bits? Check. It's really easy to see why the record company zeroed in on this particular song as the obvious choice for a single. "There's a great hit on there!" I'm betting they were right!

Instead, Genesis opted to put out 'Duchess' as the second single from *Duke*, and I'm sorry, but what? 'Duchess'? You've got to be kidding me. Now don't get me wrong here; I adore 'Duchess' as a song. Assuming you're reading this book in sequence, you haven't come across my entry for 'Duchess' yet and there's very good reason for that. But anyone who listens to 'Duchess' and thinks "Yeah, that's a hit in the making" ought to be institutionalised. Even after gutting more than two minutes from the song (an absolutely brutal edit for anyone who esteems the full version so highly - and they trimmed it down even more for the music video!), 'Duchess' just doesn't feel like the kind of thing that would really take the popular airwaves by storm. And indeed, it stalled on the UK charts outside the top 40.

'Misunderstanding' was the album's third and final single, and you're not going to find me sitting here ripping that decision. But 'Alone Tonight'? Poor, forgotten, flippantly dismissed 'Alone Tonight'? It's easily the best Rutherford solo-written song in terms of being a potential chart darling, probably over his whole career. And here's the thing: the band apparently didn't rate it at all. There's scarce mention of it in interviews. It was never played live. Mike Rutherford wrote a dang memoir and devoted multiple paragraphs *specifically* to talking about his solo song contributions to *Duke* and couldn't even be bothered to name drop the song. What gives, man?

As ballads go it's rock solid, if unspectacular. You get the double verse intro, nice and quiet and gentle, and then the big ol' chorus. The next verse section follows a different melodic arc which keeps it interesting, and then there's a double chorus to close things out. There's not a ton going on here I suppose, but it's all full-sounding and emotional and pleasant to the ear. I can listen critically and say "This song doesn't do anything especially ambitious," but whenever it comes on I find myself involuntarily swaying. And isn't that the very stuff that radio gold is made of? "Ooooooooooooon my own again, alone again toniiiiiight!" I mean, hey: that's pretty good.

98 - Harlequin

from *Nursery Cryme*, 1971

For a song that comes in at just under three minutes, there's a lot to unpack about the way 'Harlequin' came to be. First there's the fact that, despite *Nursery Cryme* being the Genesis debut of both Phil Collins and Steve Hackett, much of the music was written before they were members of the band. This is especially true for Steve, as Phil joined several months before Steve's successful audition, and was therefore involved with these songs for a longer period of time. It's fairly well known, for example, that 'The Musical Box' was more or less a done deal when Steve was brought on board, having been co-written in no small part by Anthony Phillips before his departure. So what does this have to do with 'Harlequin' specifically?

Well, the writing of this time was very much reflective of a Genesis trying to learn how to survive without Ant. I've said it already in the earlier pages of this book, but it bears repeating: while we as fans tend to think of Tony Banks and Mike Rutherford as the irreplaceable core components of Genesis, the guys at that time felt Ant was that solid foundation, the musical backbone of all they hoped to accomplish. And so it's quite understandable that Mike might, after Ant's departure, find himself in the situation of trying to write a guitar-centric song for himself and Ant (his go-to writing partner) to play even though Ant isn't actually there anymore.

> **Mike:** *I tried to play both my guitar part and Ant's on a single twelve-string guitar by tuning the pairs of strings to harmonies. It was pretty dodgy.* [14]

"Nevermind this new Steve fellow, the ghost of Anthony Phillips will assist me!" Well, Mike may have ended up with a bit more geese than ghost on that front, but I still love this little ditty. Dodgy or not, the guitars are lovely; more so in the verses than the chorus, but both are enjoyable. This is also true for the vocals, which is remarkable because they're so dreadfully sloppy.

> **Tony:** *'Harlequin'...was a bit embarrassing. I think the song is alright but the performance is rather poor.* [6]

This isn't 'Harold the Barrel', where Peter and Phil double the same bit over the whole song, so in sync you can get tricked into thinking that they aren't actually doubling at all. Here the precision is stripped almost entirely away as the two alternate between doubling and harmonizing. It's like they're channelling Simon & Garfunkel but can't figure out which one of them ought to be Simon and which one Garfunkel, so they each kind of end up just doing whatever feels good at the time.

> **Mike:** *Not my finest hour lyrically either: "There was once a harvest in this land / Reap from the turquoise sky, harlequin, harlequin". 'Harvest' is a word I've learned not to use in songs.* [14]

When they're on, they're really on - some of these vocal harmonies are really something special. When they're a little bit off, as tends to happen on the chorus, it's still got a charm about it. But rather than detracting from the end product, the imperfection gives the piece a kind of personality and intimacy that's rare from a band with Tony Banks on board. Maybe that's why it holds a special place in my heart; it's a last gasp of full-on folk, warts and all, before Genesis would forever head to more distant lands. The band may be embarrassed by it, but 'Harlequin' is a treasure to me all the same.

97 - Down and Out

from ...And Then There Were Three..., 1978

I've written previously that And Then There Were Three has a distinct sort of sound to it that pervades every song. Fittingly, that exact sound, that distilled "Essence of Three," if you will, is the first thing you hear when you spin up the album. It's not just the instrumentation, but the way it's played. There's something almost-but-not-quite otherworldly about it. And then that riff kicks in, and you think you're maybe getting something a bit different after all, but a few measures later you're firmly entrenched in that inescapable "Three" sound, crawling up your spine in lockstep with Tony's keys crawling up the melody during the second half of the verses.

> **Mike:** *In a sense, I suppose [it's very recognizably Genesis]; it's got some drama. The three of us wrote this while we were rehearsing for the album. We often toy with the idea of trying something totally different to start with but we haven't yet.* [17]

Which is to say nothing of the drum work, crashing cymbals with a reckless ferocity that somehow manages to still hold the 5/4 time signature together. That's no mean feat, as Chester Thompson learned when he started learning the piece for the album's accompanying tour.

> **Mike:** *He just couldn't get that right at first. When we wrote it Tony and I thought of the riff in a different way to Phil. We were looking at the same structure from different directions. And Phil couldn't explain the riff to Chester, which added to the confusion. It's funny because once you get used to a strange time signature it sounds very natural and you forget that other people will take time to get used to it.* [17]

> **Phil:** *The song is basically one of the more instrumentally biased songs. It's complex rhythmically; you can tap your foot through it, but it will come out somewhere else.* [41]

And indeed, when listening to the song nothing feels *wrong*, per se, but something does feel very *off* about the whole affair. It's an alien rhythm overtop an aura of pure otherness, designed specifically to break the listener out of his or her comfort zone - Genesis trying to prove a point that they can still catch you by surprise.

> **Tony:** *We were on tour, so we never spotted [the rise of the punk movement]. Suddenly we came back, and we were apparently yesterday's people...The lyric to some extent had some reference to, possibly, us being out of date.* [48]

> **Phil:** *Lyrically I wrote the words to it, that's why my name is first [in the writing credits]. The idea was to have a song about an American record company - no names just companies - that are quite prepared to toss you out when you become passé. The chorus is spoken from the artist's point of view and the verses are from the company's point of view, basically cut and thrust.* [41]

Can you imagine? There you are, a working musician toiling away creatively to try to produce something that doesn't just have artistic merit, but that can also find enough of an audience for you to make some sort of living. And then, even if you're successful in that endeavour, you have to toil some more on the road. Long months in strange places, playing the same songs over and over and over again, night after night after gruelling night. Time away from the family, your kids getting older as you miss one important milestone after another. Just a relentless cycle of creation and promotion, no chance to focus on anything but entertaining the crowds at home or the crowds at the theatre, and if you do it well enough you can put enough bread on the table to be in position for an even larger tour the next time.

To come back from your latest set of shows in your seemingly continuous eight year run of them only to find this upstart musical movement saying "Get these jokers out of here!" That's got to feel like an enormous kick in the teeth. And in your state of total exhaustion, it would perhaps be easy to think "Well, the writing's on the wall. Tastes are changing and our time might be up." Maybe you scale back your workload, take a breather, trust that you'll retain enough of your audience to eke out a modest income for the foreseeable future.

Or, you can be Genesis and say, "Um, excuse me, but who the hell do you think you are?" If punk was in some ways a rebellion against the musical establishment, 'Down and Out' is the establishment rebelling right back, a message that Genesis would not go quietly. Make no mistake: opening the album with a song like this isn't just a coincidence of track ordering. This is a statement, a counterpunch. Sometimes you'll see or hear the metaphor that punk was "shaking the tree," seeing which apples (bands) weren't strong enough to hold on. In that sense it could be said that Genesis clung fiercely to the branches, but I don't think that's accurate imagery. This apple didn't hold on for dear life; it leapt from the tree to strike punk in the eye then bounced back into the foliage telling the punk movement to find a different tree altogether.

The difference is in intent. A passive Genesis would've kept doing as it had always done and hoped for the best. But *And Then There Were Three* marked a conscious shift for the band, going for shorter pieces, the individual songwriters honing their talents to make commercial success more ultimately attainable. It was an experiment that paid off, as 'Follow You Follow Me' put Genesis firmly on the Top 40 map.

Ironically then, it's 'Down and Out', the band's show of resistance and statement of intention, that they felt suffered most from this change in philosophy.

> **Tony:** *The heavier tracks [on the album] like 'Down and Out' don't sound so good. That kind of song needs more room to stretch out.* [10]

> **Mike:** *That's why 'Down and Out' was never a good live song: over so quickly.* [10]

It's easy to see where Mike and Tony are coming from. With its funky time signature, synth intro, unusual chord structure, and yes, flashy keyboard solo, 'Down and Out' does indeed sound like nothing so much as a "classically" Genesis progressive rock song condensed down into a sub-six-minute package. It's got that "Three" flavour I described at the outset of this entry, and it's got a kind of ferocity or sharpness about it that was lacking in the band's previous canon (particularly with Phil at the vocal helm), but it's still very recognizably Genesis all the same. One might think that would make 'Down and Out' a solid sort of "transition" song that would resonate well with audiences, but indeed: after 1978 the song was never played live again.

And you know what? Perhaps that's a sign that it was Mission Accomplished for Genesis after all. 'Down and Out' was a song that Genesis didn't intend to go anywhere, necessary only until the point had been fully made. That the band continues to tour to this day seems to prove that they had it right.

96 - ⅞

B-Side to 'Shipwrecked', 1997

```
Thank you for calling the Genesis Support Line. If you know the extension
of the party you are trying to reach, please dial it now.

...

If you are calling about accidental 'Who Dunnit?' exposure, please hang up
and dial 911 immediately. For long-form discussion about 'Supper's Ready',
press 1. For inquiries about why your favourite B-Sides didn't make an
album, press 2. For moral outrage that Chester Thompson was declined a
permanent spot in the band, press 3. For debate on whether the band "sold
out" in the 80s and beyond, press 4. For information on ---
```

Ugh, come on already! How many options are on this thing?!

```
--- and other devices, press 5. To pre-order Phil's updated autobiography
Awright, Nearly Dead Now, press 6. For insight into various solos in the
band's catalogue, press 7. For ---
```

Eh, that's close enough!

```
All our representatives are currently unavailable assisting other callers.
Please continue to hold and the next available representative will be with
you shortly.
```

Of course they are. Wha? What was that honey? Yeah, I'm on the phone! They put me on hold. No, I don't know how long it will take. Yeah! ...Yeah, I know! I'll be there as soon as I can!

```
Your call is very important to us. If you would like to leave a call-back
number, ple---
```

Come on, come on! I thought this would be like a two minute call, tops! Huh? Yes honey I'm still on hold! What? No, that's not... No, I'm not shouting at you! I'm just trying to---

Thank you for calling the Genesis Solos Department, my name is George, how can I assist you today?

Yes, hi! Thank you George, hi. Listen, uh, I was just going through some of these B-Sides from the *Calling All Stations* sessions and ---

B-Sides? You'll want extension 2 for B-Sides sir, please wait while I transf---

Wait, wait! No, wait! Please don't transfer me. I listened to the menu, OK? I'm uh, I'm not asking why these B-Sides didn't make the album, but I just wanted to know more about the, uh, middle section of this particular song. Like two...two? Yeah two minutes or so into it the whole texture changes and it's suddenly really epic. Like, don't get me wrong, the rest of it's fine too. But, um, yeah, this part was just really interesting and I was hoping that maybe there was some insight out there from Mike or Tony about it. You know, how they came up with it, or how they felt about it, or why they didn't want to include it on the al--- uh, no! Not that one. But anyway, you know, just hoping for a quote or two so I could put it into the uh, chapter...of my book... Is that something you could help me with, George?

Well sir, I don't really know what book you're talking about.

Oh, no, you wouldn't, I'm still writing it. It's not out yet. I'm just trying to get some quotes so I can make it a little bit better.

I do wish you good luck with that sir, but I don't think I can help you write a book.

Uh, no… No George, I'm not asking you to help me write this book. … JUST A MINUTE, HONEY! Sorry, George, my wife is getting a little impatient with me. Um, I just want to know if you guys have any quotes from Mike or Tony about writing this B-Side. I guess I'll take Ray quotes too, but it's an instrumental so I don't think he was involved at all.

OK sir, just to clarify, are you talking about just a solo section in a song here?

Uhh, no, I guess not exactly. I mean, the whole song is an instrumental, but really th---

Ah well sir, this is the Genesis solos department. You're going to want the instrumentals department on extension 8, sir.

Aw come on George, 7, 8, what's the difference? Like, um, don't get me wrong, your hold music's pretty good, but I just don't have the time right now to call back in and go through those motions anymore. Can't you just help me out?

Of course sir, I'd be happy to transfer you. One moment please sir.

Wait, that's not what I ---

```
We are currently experiencing high call volume. Please continu---
```

GODDANGIT GEORGE! ...NO HONEY NOT YOU! I'M NOT SHOUTING AT YOU! WELL YOUR NAME'S NOT GEORGE, NOW IS IT?! YES, I'LL BE THERE AS SOON AS I CAN.

```
Did you know you can listen to all your favourite Genesis albums on compact
disc? Check your local Sam Goody---
```

WHAT THE F- `<click>`

95 - Silent Sorrow in Empty Boats

from *The Lamb Lies Down on Broadway*, 1974

A running theme I've come to notice not just among the popular music listening world at large, but also even among fans of a particular band, is that instrumental pieces tend to be disregarded. Not disdained, mind you. That would involve a level of active listening and reaction that instrumental pieces of music are rarely afforded. Rather, they tend to be heard, forgotten, and therefore dismissed entirely when considering one's favourite songs. If I'm being honest, that irks me a bit. The same fans who might laud a group like Genesis for something like the longform keyboard-focused instrumental passage at the end of 'The Cinema Show' might look at an instrumental piece like this and say, "Eh, it's nice filler material I guess." Why do we so routinely toss these works aside?

We tend to think of vocal work as being the dynamic element that really sets one song apart from another, but I think that tremendously undersells the range that instrumentals can encompass. Some instrumental songs or passages are designed as grand displays of musicianship. A virtuosic solo here, a mind-bending rhythmic pattern there, complicated inter-weavings of melodies and countermelodies throughout. Others are built to provide a contrast to whatever surrounds them; like a slow piece with a much more energetic instrumental section in the middle; the first bit doesn't work nearly as well without the second. Still other works are experimentations on an idea, jamming around a central theme to just find what sounds good and brings the song to life.

> **Phil:** *[A] piece of ad lib music, things that don't date.* [49]

Genesis has done all of these, and there are examples of them doing all of them extremely well. 'Silent Sorrow in Empty Boats', however, is none of these things. I mean, yes, it is a group piece built around a central theme, but to call it a "jam" just doesn't feel right. No, 'Silent Sorrow' is an exploration of a feeling. It's a meditation on being. It's an impressionist painting for the blind. It's simple, sure, but only in a way that a colouring book's pages come in black and white: it's designed to let you fill it with whatever colours you want. To let your mind fill in the blank spaces of the music. Too much more in terms of complexity and you no longer have a pristine mental canvas to work with. Bear in mind that while this song has no lyrics of its own, the line immediately preceding it on *The Lamb Lies Down on Broadway* is "The stage is set for you." This isn't Genesis' song; it's **your** song, to make whatever you will of it.

Now maybe what you'll make of it is a mental image of an angsty young Puerto Rican male weeping over the dead husks of the snake women who poisoned him with their mind-altering drugs, and who attempted to devour him before they were themselves devoured *by* him. That's certainly one option; it's what Peter Gabriel made of it after all, and the album flows more or less in that narrative direction. But where other songs from *The Lamb* may be neutered or rendered meaningless by removing them from the lyrical context of the album, 'Silent Sorrow in Empty Boats' is instead liberated when treated as its own thing. Once upon a time, this song had no title and no accompanying story. It wasn't written with the imagery from 'The Lamia' in mind. So I encourage you to listen to this song on its own. Ignore any preconceived context, and let the music become whatever it coalesces into for you.

I think it's beautiful.

94 - Match of the Day

from *Spot the Pigeon*, 1977

Is there any song more controversial in the Genesis catalogue? The band wrote it, loved it, thought it would be a big hit. Then it wasn't. Now they all hate the dang thing, and maybe there's a cause and effect sort of thing going on. Maybe once it fell flat with the public they got thoughts like, "Of course this wasn't a hit, it's trash and always has been." There's no consistent fan opinion, either. Some seem to love it, some seem to hate it. It's great, it's awful, it's terrific fun, it's odious garbage. I feel like I've heard every take about this song *except* for "It's pretty good for what it is." So let me be the one to tell you: 'Match of the Day' is pretty good...for what it is.

The music sounds tinny and dated, but I'm pretty sure that's with intent. Those first bars of the song aren't Genesis forgetting how to write a compelling tune; they're Genesis mimicking the sort of bumper music that serves to begin a television or radio sports broadcast. If at the eight second mark the bass never entered and the song just faded out to some guy in a tweed jacket saying "And now it's time for Sporting World Tonight: I'm Chuck Maxwell, and this is your match of the day," you wouldn't bat an eye. So from the very first notes of the song, you're *right there* getting the exact kind of imagery you're supposed to be getting. That's masterful writing.

> **Phil:** *In no way is the music on the [Spot the Pigeon] EP secondary to what we did on the album. We feel as strongly about these things as the rest of the stuff.* [50]

Speaking of that bass line, pretty good romp, yeah? It's emblematic of the song on the whole: joyful and carefree, just you and your mates hanging out at the stadium heckling officials and generally having a good time. What's there to complain about?

> **Tony:** *The...song we all hated was 'Match of the Day', which was just about football and not great musically.* [9]

All right, all right, so maybe you could complain about the lyrics. I'll concede that; they're not terribly good. In fact, they might even be goodly terrible. Phil literally just describes how the sport of football works. Not even describing what's happening in the titular match of the day itself, mind you, but just the general concept of the game and then the atmosphere of being there to watch it. It's not a strong effort, particularly when he claims there are a few things we ought to know and proceeds to simply name off various fouls. But before you can even respond with a "Huh?" he's whisked you off to the pub, where you find yourself suddenly sharing a pint with the lads. OK!

> **Steve:** *Mike was really hoping that 'Match of the Day' might become a single. But I guess it didn't really have the same lilt to it, the easy-going fun aspect that 'I Know What I Like' had...it was an outside shot. There are some songs that are just a bit of fun.* [51]

Even if the lyrics aren't always stellar or even always passable, they still do their job of putting your butt in the imaginary seat of the imaginary stands, showering imaginary abuse on imaginary referees, before complaining to your imaginary friends about how a particular imaginary player isn't living up to his impressively high imaginary salary. What could be grander? It's not a perfect song, but by golly it's a pretty good one...for what it is.

93 - Me and Sarah Jane

from *Abacab*, 1981

The group songwriting efforts on *Abacab* were all intended to shake up the band's status quo, for good or for ill. From horns on 'No Reply At All' to synth harmonica on 'Another Record', from the pulsing of the title track to the intentional troll job that was 'Who Dunnit?', everything they wrote together in this time period veered off in directions hitherto foreign to their catalogue, and that excited them. The entire creation of *Abacab* was immersed in this pervasive mood of reinvention, yet in the midst of that Tony produces - as his one allotted solo writing credit for the album - what might otherwise be considered a pretty typical, progressively-styled Genesis tune.

> **Tony:** *You could call it a piano study, where I started with a two-note riff which I slowly altered to create an effect; the first two or three minutes of the song are just that one idea, followed by a middle section that is very, very romantic and an ending that has a certain finality about it that I like.* [1]

In essence, it's classic Genesis. You've got different sections flowing into one another, taking you through a series of lyrical and emotional shifts, ending at an echo of where you started, but richer for the journey. The structure is all there, yet 'Me and Sarah Jane' doesn't *sound* like classic Genesis at all.

> **Tony:** *In some ways ['Me and Sarah Jane'] has quite a lot of the old traditional Genesis in it. But I hope it also sounds different.* [34]

Tony's doing the same thing he's been doing for years, but now he's accomplishing it with wildly different sounds. It's drum machine, it's electric piano, it's ghostly guitar sirens, it's Phil's nasal shriek of "And now I'm standing on the corner," and it's the carnival-like bass juxtaposed against all the other stuff. 'Me and Sarah Jane' just sounds *weird*, man. So when 4:05 hits and the song lifts into something more familiar, it feels *earned*, somehow. None of the weird stuff is bad - quite the opposite in fact - but having it there amplifies the effectiveness of everything that comes after.

> **Tony:** *It contains some of the most emotional moments on the album, sort of shivers down the spine stuff, which is something we've been noted for in the past, if you liked us. If you didn't I suppose it's a bucket of cold water down the spine.* [34]

It also works perfectly with the lyrics - the singer is someone coping with the end of the world by conjuring up a fantasy woman to spend his remaining time with. That's not something a sane person would do, which is why the first half of the song is so nutty and seemingly random in its lurches between ideas.

> **Tony:** *Originally, I didn't feel very strongly about sort of having the song as one thing like that, going through a series of what, 8, 9, 10 bits. I mean, I was quite happy to take some bits out of isolation and make a song out of them. But the way the rest of the album was going was very much into songs with one mood in them. 'Abacab' tends to stay pretty much in one mood, for example. And so I thought it'd be a nice idea - we all did, really - to keep this song going through a series of moods, because it was sort of contrasting with the rest of the album. And it would definitely stand out for that reason. I think it works, that idea.* [52]

But then, by the "romantic" back half of the song, there's a sense of stability.

> **Tony:** *On 'Me and Sarah Jane' I poured all my flowery, beautiful stuff into one song… probably the last time within Genesis that I wrote a song which goes through loads of chord changes…Our later producer Nick Davis calls these my "terminal songs," where everything's over, it's bye-bye, people walking down the beach and the world's about to end.* [1]

In this way 'Me and Sarah Jane' is reminiscent - to my ears, at least - to 'Afterglow'. But where 'Afterglow' is the tale of one person's loss amidst a much larger crisis, 'Me and Sarah Jane' feels more personal. There's certainly a vague hint of some calamity befalling the world, but it's firmly in the background as we follow the singer down into the maze of his mind. If the lyrics feel at times illogical, well, that's not without reason. This is a guy who "invents a name" of his imaginary lover only to then begin "remembering" all the pain they endured together. Even his dream woman doesn't provide him with a consistently happy relationship. Then there's the murkiness of the details themselves: what kind of clue is he searching for on the sandy shore? Is he actually walking down the streets of the city, or is this a memory? If it's a memory, is it a real memory or just another conjuring with his fictional sweetheart? Who is providing the mocking laughter at the end? Does the sea swallow him?

See, 'Afterglow' is a song about losing what you had, but 'Me and Sarah Jane' is about finding something you can lose. And even though that something ends up being a complete fabrication, there's a sense of healing that occurs. As it turns out, this imaginary relationship, while in one way a sign of the singer losing his marbles, is also precisely what he needed to find his peace in the end. And, possibly, to make his peace with his own end. It's a beautiful thing, conveyed really effectively. We don't understand his journey, but we know that he is - and we are - richer for having undertaken it.

Now, all that said, I do think from a musical perspective that all the changes happening in a compact span of time make it a bit more difficult for any of the song's melodies to stand out in memory. That's not to say the melodies are poor or any such thing, but rather that they never really get a chance to "lock in" and create that lasting link. There's a reason musical artists often refer to melodies as "hooks," drawing analogies to fishing. They need to dangle out there long enough to get you to bite, and once you do, it's in you. 'Me and Sarah Jane' does not dangle.

Thus, if you're like me, you'll never find yourself singing or humming anything from this song. In fact, you might not even remember how it goes if it's been a while since you last heard it. So in the vault of memory it often comes as an afterthought; a kind of "also-ran" on *Abacab*. While understandable, that's a real shame, because even though 'Me and Sarah Jane' might not leave a lasting impression, every time I spin up it leaves a good one.

92 - Deep in the Motherlode

from ...And Then There Were Three..., 1978

Gold has always interested me. Or, more accurately, the *perception* of gold has always interested me. Years ago in my old company break room, the TV was always tuned to one of those 24 hour news channels. And while frankly I think that there is such a thing as being too informed and the end result of this channel selection was a consistent net drain on employee morale, that's not my point here. No, like that person who shows up to a Super Bowl party despite not even liking football, my focus was always on the ads. The news programs at that point in time were just riddled with commercials urging people to invest in gold. No fewer than three different companies, all competing for airspace, all imploring the viewer to call them right away to get a head start on building a Scrooge McDuck style treasure vault.

I remember the CEO for one of these companies was also its spokesperson, and I remember the moment when I saw him appear on a rival company's ad instead. Apparently this dude switched teams in the middle of the Great Gold War of the Afternoon News, which never failed to give me a chuckle. But this guy also had a sort of catchphrase. A selling point he took with him across enemy lines, as it were. He'd look at the camera, make one of those gestures with his hands that politicians do when they're pretending to say something they mean, and then say as though this were the only argument he'd needed all along, "Gold has *intrinsic* value." And I remember hearing that and thinking, "Wait...does it though?"

Don't get me wrong. Gold is a fantastic component metal for electronics: it's resistant to corrosion and oxidation (rust) and conducts electricity really well. It also reflects electromagnetic radiation and can be used for heat shielding. It's got a ton of *applied* value, and I don't want to short-change that. From there it could also be argued that gold's relative rarity on the planet could conceivably make it highly valuable in a monetary sense as well, in that it would become more expensive to acquire gold for use in such scientific and industrial endeavours.

But that's not what this dude meant, is it? *Intrinsic* value? That's saying "Gold is valuable because it just is," and I'm sorry, but while that seems like a truism I'm not buying it. We're all aware that gold has historically had tremendous value financially, as currency or as a currency backer, or in the form of jewellery, etc. It's the stuff pirates dream of unearthing under the letter X. It's the colour of crowns that adorn the heads of royalty. For as long as history has been recorded, mankind has seemingly coveted gold. But I dare you to ask yourself *why* gold has been so valued in this way for as long as we can remember, and I would imagine you'd eventually come to the same inevitable conclusion I have: **"Because it's shiny."**

We're all just a bunch of dumb monkeys in the end, aren't we? We've built, over thousands of years, an entire global economy based at least in major part on the universal principle of "Me like shiny thing." And even if you yourself can claim the high road and truthfully say you aren't driven by this "get shiny thing" mentality, the fact that other people *are* driven by it demands your participation in the exercise. Because if you want to barter with someone, you need to give that person something *they* see as having worth. *Intrinsic* worth. Because it's shiny.

And so, in 1848, when a man named James Marshall discovered gold in California, the rush was on. The discovery of a lode of silver in Nevada in 1859 further renewed the hunt for fortune in them thar hills, and in 1865 newspaper editor Horace Greeley famously advised the youth of America: "Go West, young man, go West and grow up with the country."

'Deep in the Motherlode' is a song about a teenager leaving his family behind on a hopeless quest to find treasure to make for himself and his loved ones a better life. Tony's keys open the song full of excitement and energy - "They've struck gold! It's falling like water, coming down from the hills!" There's a slick groove underneath, and the mandate of "Go West young man" feels more adventurous than burdensome.

> **Phil:** *A rock-a-boogie tempo, really. That's one of the things we try to do, take a song which can be played in various ways and we try to pick feels which we haven't used before. We've got a catalogue of rhythms we haven't used before and this is definitely uncharacteristic of the things we would do.* [41]

And then, darkness. A long, lonely journey to mining spots that have long since been depleted of any precious metals, if there were even any there to begin with. The realisation that he can't go home empty handed, but that there's nothing here, either. Go West young man? Oh, if I knew then what I knew today! Fittingly, the instrumentation here, wailing guitar and all, takes the excitement of the song's opening passages and makes a complete mockery of them. Can guitars sound sardonic? Because Mike sure makes that guitar sound sardonic.

Mike: *This one was originally called 'Heavy' and I think it's obvious why. There's a good mix on this one. Even when there were just the three of us playing we made a pretty good sound. There wasn't much overdubbing necessary. This was where the dreaded bottleneck [guitar playing] came in which became something of a joke at the end of the recording. The first time I ever played bottleneck was when I put that bit on at the end. It took me a while. I even put it on the wrong hand at the beginning. Anyway, bottleneck is quite a precise art and until you've got it right it sounds like somebody playing their violin for the first time. So every time I got the bottleneck out all the technicians started running out of the studio.* [17]

Perhaps Mike's travails with the slide guitar sound are in some ways a light-hearted reflection of his own lyrics about the gold rush. "Everyone else is using this bottleneck sound, I should figure it out too!" And then, despair amongst the audio engineers. "There's no gold in those hills, just a creaky violin being played by a small child!" But bottleneck/slide guitar playing is a skill that can be honed with time. Gold, though? Gold is either there or it isn't, and you've either struck it rich or wasted a chunk of your life. There's not a lot of in-between when you've committed to that leap.

So 'Deep in the Motherlode' is a cautionary tale of following the masses. It's a reminder that the things that are most valuable aren't what you can buy in a shop, or even the currency you use in order to do the buying. It's things like family, like friends. The people, not the coinage. A reminder that maybe the shiniest things were in our hearts all along. Gold may not have intrinsic value after all, but 'Deep in the Motherlode'? Now that's pretty good stuff.

91 - Stagnation

from *Trespass*, 1970

In many ways, 'Stagnation' is the birthing place of the Genesis we all know and love. Of course the band had already released an album before, and of course there were other tracks like 'Visions of Angels' that were more or less done before 'Stagnation' was even a glint in Anthony Phillips' eye, but nothing really set Genesis on the path of progressive rock music quite like this song. Here are some things we tend to take for granted about Genesis now that first truly blossomed in 'Stagnation':

- Length beyond that of a "normal" pop song

    Tony: *'Stagnation' developed out of a piece we had rather pretentiously called 'The Movement', which we'd been rehearsing for a long time before we'd played it on stage or anything, and it developed. This thing at one point was about thirty minutes long, and it got condensed, and bits came and bits left. But the first bit stayed. And so it was always sort of a key song for us.* [3]

- Different moods and feels over different sections

    Peter: *'Stagnation', that was a journey song, as I call it. You didn't follow the normal verse/chorus/verse/chorus sort of structures, but you went through a series of landscapes, and I think right from the word go that was something that interested me, and continues to interest me...I love that, and I think some of my favourite pieces of music are when I as a listener get taken into different worlds made out of sound, and if there are some things that you've never encountered before or blends that you haven't met before, then it pays off even better...So I think that's what we were aspiring to, and I think that's one of the tracks that did that.* [3]

- Using ideas and bits from all the writers in the band

    Ant: *It was really a sort of two 12-string thing that Tony got in on very early, and it wasn't right to say that [Mike and I] sort of did the chordal basis and Tony just put solos on top. It was more than that. I think his sort of cross rhythms and cross harmonies influenced the way that the 12-string harmony went. It was fun, because you have this feeling that maybe we're just going somewhere slightly differently to other people in a very natural way.* [3]

    Tony: *'Stagnation' was the most significant track on the album...[Peter and I] were more keyboard based [as writers] and [Mike and Ant] were more guitar based. Then there were moments when we all met like on 'Stagnation'. That's why that was such a successful song as it became a combination of everyone's best parts.* [6]

- Peter's flute playing

    Tony: *Peter used to play a lot of flute, really. It was nice for us to have an instrument. You must understand those days "keyboards" meant organ and piano really, that's all there was...but the flute which Peter played was a very strong thing. I mean, he wasn't a great flute player - you would never say he was - but it was a lovely touch in there. Things like [how] 'Stagnation' has got the big melody in the end, that big riff that carries on, starts off as a flute thing, and it's a really nice thing. It was a really nice quality to have in there, I think...we could run another dimension to the sound.* [3]

It really is the prototypical Genesis song, in the literal sense of the word "prototype" as being the first of its kind. Now prototypes in that way are typically less refined than their successors, and so it is that I don't think 'Stagnation' is quite as strong as some of the material they'd do even one album later, but it's a massive leap forward from anything they'd done one album prior.

Ant: *It was [a] slightly more sophisticated recording than From Genesis to Revelation, but not a lot...I know that [producer] John Anthony wouldn't let anyone drop in. I remember Mike had*

> *a bit of classical guitar at the end of 'Stagnation' about six minutes in. He had to sit there and listen to the whole track, and of course by the time it got to this bit he was so nervous that he fluffed it, you know, start again! So it wasn't THAT sophisticated.* [3]

Well, a massive leap musically if not in terms of the recording process, at any rate. I do think the production sounds a little muddy, but there's not much we can do about that. Beyond that point, does 'Stagnation' meander a little bit? Well, sure, I'd say it does. Does it try a little too hard at times? Perhaps that's true as well.

> **Mike:** *We were determined to prove ourselves, and...the idea that less is more was completely alien...we should have limited ourselves to two guitars but instead we used about ten. The result was that they all ended up cancelling each other out on record and the final thing sounded so muted you couldn't hear anything properly.* [14]

Nevertheless, there's no shortage of things to like here. I'm a sucker for the 12-string acoustic stuff, so I find the opening of the song to be great. The creepy keyboard solo also works well, and the contrast when the tempo finally picks up and the piece finds its groove is really strong.

> **Tony:** *'Stagnation' is probably the best track on the album, because it showed the way we were developing. I particularly like the way there wasn't much repetition: we went to a section, developed it, and moved onto the next section, which became a characteristic element of Genesis, a kind of storytelling with music. I also had to write a solo for 'Stagnation', which was a totally novel thing for me. I'd never done a solo. It always used to be the thing when we were playing with school groups, jamming on a twelve-bar blues: at some point you'd have to play a solo and I couldn't do it. On this track I liked the idea of deliberately constructing a solo as opposed to trying to improvise one, so that it became more of an instrumental, and I found I was comfortable with that.* [1]

Any way you slice it, 'Stagnation' is a pivotal piece from the band and, while it may be overshadowed for me by the stuff it inspired and enabled, it still stands up on its own as a solidly good listen. The historical merits are just the icing on the cake.

90 - Shepherd

Live recording, 1970

In 1979, when Tony Banks recorded and released his debut solo album *A Curious Feeling*, he opted not to sing anything himself.

> **Tony:** *I had never really intended to be a singer at all ever...I really didn't think I could do it. Every time I tried to sing I couldn't get myself right – the tuning and pitching and everything was terrible. I demoed all the songs for [eventual A Curious Feeling singer] Kim [Beacon] and he said it sounded pretty unpleasant.* [53]

Somewhere along the line I suppose he found his confidence, because by 1983's *The Fugitive* he'd come around completely and decided to sing all the songs himself. The reception to that performance was...mixed, to say the least. I've seen people who absolutely adore Tony's voice and can't understand why he wouldn't sing all of his own material on every album. And I've also seen people like my father, who excitedly bought the album only to literally throw it in the trash because he thought Tony's singing made the music completely unsalvageable.

> **Mike:** *I think to this day Tony thinks his voice is better than it is. In terms of vocal abilities I would say we were about the same and I have a pretty realistic opinion of my voice, but Tony always thought his was better. I tell him to his face sometimes that it isn't, but I don't think he quite believes me.* [14]

I think I fall with Mike somewhere in the middle on this. Is Tony's voice passable under certain circumstances? Sure. Is it strong enough to carry a record? Ehhhhh not so much. I guess Tony got the memo as well, because with the exception of one track apiece from his next two non-soundtrack albums, he didn't attempt to sing lead again.

So that makes a song like 'Shepherd' a really rare treat, featuring as it does Tony singing lead vocal. Rare in itself, but in Genesis? This is the only surviving instance of a Tony lead line, albeit still alternating with Peter. And unlike an album such as *The Fugitive*, where his vocal style is very "put on" in a sense to try to achieve 80s chart success, here he sounds far more comfortable in his own skin. The result is a surprisingly pleasant sound, especially in contrast to Pete's more husky tone. You've got a story with two different narrators creating two different sorts of moods, and I find it rather effective.

> **Ant:** *We used to do a song of Tony's called 'Shepherd' which was a really pretty song...* [11]

Ultimately there's not a whole lot on this track for Mike or Ant to do but strum, though Ant's part is at least a little bit interesting. John Mayhew may have been taking a smoke break or something at the time; he's nowhere to be found at all. No, between the vocals and piano work this song is 70% Tony, with the rest being roughly 20% Peter, 9% Ant doing Ant things, and 1% Mike playing the cello near the end. And you know what? I'm on board. 'Shepherd' works perfectly well as a piano piece with a vocal duet, and I don't think developing it any further would have improved it much.

It's a historical footnote because of Tony's dalliance with singing lead, but the song transcends that and is actually pretty good in its own right. Far and away my favourite early non-album track; the best that Disc 4 of *Archive 1967-75* has to offer.

89 - Just a Job to Do

from *Genesis*, 1983

Barring a couple small exceptions, Genesis have always been pretty good at picking out singles from their albums, haven't they? Which isn't to say all the singles have had success mind you, especially back in the 60s and 70s, but more often than not the tracks the band (and their record labels) selected to be singles were the "right" ones for the job. But by the 80s they had become *so* good at this that quantity started to become a problem. *Invisible Touch* had five singles hit the top 5 on the US charts, and arguably the best pure "single" from those sessions was a song called 'Feeding the Fire', which didn't even make the album. 1983's *Genesis* itself also spawned five singles, though they didn't have the quite the same meteoric level success of the ones from the following album. Still, all five found at least a moderate level of success in one or more territories, which is a lot stronger a showing than most bands could ever dream of. And yet out of all that, here's 'Just a Job to Do', never released as a single anywhere, sounding like nothing so much as an 80s mega-hit waiting to happen.

Did Genesis start to sound more and more like Phil Collins as time went by, or did Phil Collins start to sound more and more like Genesis? Was it just a kind of vicious cycle that fed on itself until the two entities eventually had to split apart just to find themselves again? Certainly a lot of people seem to think so. I'm not completely sold on the notion myself, yet 'Just a Job to Do' has always to my ears sounded musically and thematically very similar to Collins' own 'Don't Lose My Number', a song he recorded for *No Jacket Required* about a year after laying this one down with Tony and Mike. Was 'Don't Lose My Number' just Phil trying to evoke the spirit of a song from a year prior? I think maybe in a sense it was; though rather than taking its concept and evolving or developing it further, 'Don't Lose My Number' feels more like a simplification of 'Just a Job to Do' - stripping it to its most basic elements for an even stronger play at the charts.

Phil's primary strength in Genesis had always been as an arranger, and his attraction to immediacy as a writer went hand in hand with that. As a result, Genesis (with Phil on board) has always had this amazing ability to take really complicated things and make them sound incredibly simple. If you spin up 'Just a Job to Do' and play it in the background you'll hear a straightforward 80s pop rocker with a really sharp chorus and an interesting bridge. But if you intently listen to it, you'll hear that what sounds like the simple guitar riff is in reality Tony riffing on his keyboard, and the *actual* guitar riff is this really intricate thing bubbling under the surface, counterplaying with the equally intricate bass. The drum pattern sounds like little more than simple snare hits on beats 2 and 4, but then you hear all the complex cymbal work happening. There's so much happening here that you absorb unawares unless you're specifically listening with the intent to hear it: the complicated made simple.

> **Tony:** *I don't think 'Just a Job to Do'...[is] very good.* [5]

With respect to Tony, I think this is one that could've been a top 10 hit if there had been space in the band's release schedule to put it out there. Instead it's a largely forgotten album cut that they barely even mention in passing except to dismiss it. A shame, really. Just listen to the explosive power of Phil's vocals as he shouts "BANG BANG BANG!" and try to tell me 'Just a Job to Do' didn't deserve a little more spotlight. It's got a name, and it's got a number. Don't lose it.

88 - Never a Time

from *We Can't Dance*, 1991

Earlier, in this book's entry for 'Hold on My Heart', I argued that despite the song being a hit loosely in the adult contemporary vein, it wasn't very paint-by-numbers. Now there's nothing inherently wrong with by-the-book pop/rock songs, and Genesis could definitely write tunes that qualified for that label structurally speaking: they'd done it multiple times in the years before *We Can't Dance* and even did it again on this album with 'Jesus He Knows Me'. But if *Invisible Touch* was Genesis slimming down and seeing just how strong a pop/rock tune they could craft, *We Can't Dance* was the band experimenting with the form. Less "follow the recipe to make the ideal soufflé" and more "let's throw away the cookbook and find out if there's another way to make a soufflé entirely."

'Never a Time' is among the fruits of that labour. Spin up the song and see if you can figure out where exactly the verse ends and the chorus begins. Is it when the backing vocal harmonies first pop in? That feels kinda chorus-like, right? But hmm, that's not really a new melody and it doesn't do any of the other things you'd expect a chorus to. So maybe that's more like a pre-chorus. So that means the bit starting with "All I know is what is true" must be the chorus, right? No, hang on, I think that's the bridge. Or wait, is the bridge the part right after that starting with "You live your life locked in a dream"? Or was *that* the chorus?

You see, it's all a trick question. There is no verse. There is no chorus. There is no bridge. Not really. There's just flow. It's that progressive mentality of going where the music leads you. It's almost like a stream of consciousness, just floating along for about four minutes before continuing to drift away without you. Not that it fades out, but it doesn't really "properly" end either. Phil sings "I'm gonna tell you right now," and then doesn't tell you anything at all, because the song's done. Or rather, it's left you behind. You were just a temporary auditory passenger for one stage of its eternal journey down an endless musical river. Some say they're still playing 'Never a Time' at The Farm to this day.

It's this transient nature that perhaps most held the song back from being quite as successful as the band thought it would be, doing diddly-poo on the UK charts - though to be fair it did chart pretty well in North America. *We Can't Dance* producer Nick Davis had another theory:

> **Nick:** *We had another song we called 'BB Hit' which stood for 'Big, Big Hit' - because that's what we thought it would be. It eventually became 'Never a Time', but it never did become a big, big hit. We were being filmed by a TV crew who used to come in one day a week - they call them "fly on the wall" documentaries, but I've never seen a fly as big as a camera. Phil is probably used to performing in front of the camera but I know Tony hates it. We did the vocal for 'Never a Time' one day while they were filming and I think the song never recovered from that...The songs you think are really powerful at the beginning of the process are not always the ones which are strong by the end...* [1]

The Genesis: No Admittance documentary did indeed catch Phil struggling to lay down the vocal for this song, and it's a rough watch. But whether because of its overarching ephemeral quality or just TV crews making Tony Banks nervous, 'BB Hit' is now considered by a lot of Genesis fans as little more than a third rate filler track on an album that, at 72 minutes long, could've perhaps stood a bit of a trim. Nevertheless, I really enjoy everything 'Never a Time' brings to the table, and it's always welcome to swing by my stereo on its everlasting, winding voyage to parts unknown.

87 - Keep It Dark

from *Abacab*, 1981

Oh boy. How am I going to dissect this one? I hope you'll pardon me if I get a little bit technical with this entry, because 'Keep It Dark' is a wild ride of musical rule breaking. Nothing about this song makes any sense in itself, and it *really* doesn't make any sense when you mash it all together, and yet here I hold it in fairly high esteem. I have no idea how much music theory you as an individual reading this book might understand, but I'll do my best to explain it all without assuming you're well versed in the subject. I've also transcribed bits of the song into sheet music to help illustrate what I'm talking about, so if you *are* more familiar with the concepts being discussed, you can hopefully get something meaningful out of this too.

The song opens with Mike's riff, but for the sake of analysis I'd like to start with the drum pattern instead. Firstly, the song is in 6 (six beats per measure), which is already a little different from the norm (most pop/rock songs are in 4), though not enough for the ear to feel like something strange is going on just yet. This is especially true because Phil is banging out a pretty standard pattern on his kit: hi-hat cymbals on the odd beats (1, 3, 5) and snare hits on the even beats (2, 4, 6). At this point there isn't anything super weird going on yet. Here's how that pattern looks on paper:

'Keep It Dark' drum pattern sample

I want to call out to the musical theorists out there that while I'm notating this song as though it's in a very slow 6/8 tempo, it may very well be a brisker 6/4 tempo instead. Either way you'd get the same resulting sound, but if you prefer the 6/4 time signature on this one, just mentally double the length of every note and rest you see in the transcription and you'll be all set. For those of you reading this who have no idea what I just said, don't even worry about it! Let's move on.

This single bar of drums pictured above, once it enters in the fourth measure of the song, repeats the entire way throughout.

> **Mike:** *It was a drum loop. Phil played this pattern, straight beat, which there was a moment when he was playing it that it sounded so good - just right - that we actually looped it...It had a great sort of heavy sound and I think the song always kind of worked that way.* ³

> **Tony:** *The inhuman aspect of it is what we liked about it. It became something inhuman and relentless. And when something repeats absolutely like that it becomes almost subliminal, so you don't pay too much attention to it.* ³

So I've covered the drums, but what's a rhythm section without bass, right? Not to worry there: Tony Banks has got you covered. Wait, hold on, what? Yes, despite Mike Rutherford being a bassist by trade, the bass line for 'Keep It Dark' is really just Tony plunking away at a single note on his keyboard until the end of time. In conjunction with the drum pattern, it looks like this:

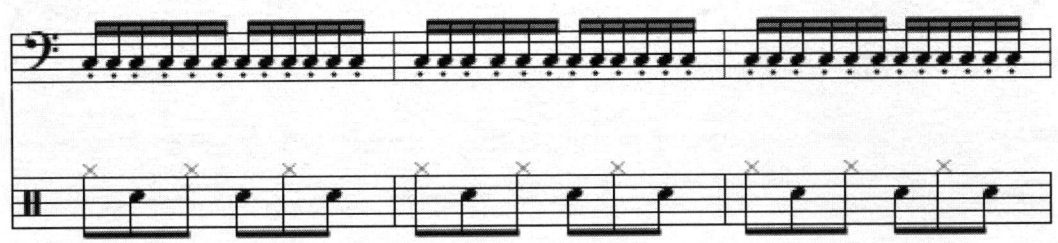

'Keep It Dark' rhythm section sample

Hard to blame Mike for skipping out on plucking this bit himself; that line looks both boring and exhausting to play for an extended period of time. Once when I was arranging a song for my college's contemporary a cappella group, I put in a bass line very similar to that. It changed notes every measure at least, but it was still just a repeating four-measure pattern for virtually the entire song. I thought this was great because the basses in the group wouldn't have to spend a lot of time learning their parts. Figured it was a big efficiency gain. Instead it only took one rehearsal for them to complain about how hopelessly dull it was, and because it wasn't engaging, they often got out of time and destabilised the whole song. They asked me to change it but I felt strongly that the bass line was the glue that held the entire effort together; if it wasn't there intact, we might as well not do the song at all.

We didn't do the song at all.

> **Mike:** *That actually sounded good in the rehearsal room. We got in the studio, and there isn't very much on there. I mean, you know, there's like the drum track, and Tony's playing the bass part with his left hand, I'm just playing one riff the whole way through virtually, and unless you capture some magic or some feeling, it sounds awful. And we had a couple of gos and it still wasn't...happening was it? And then suddenly we got it one day. We managed to capture it.* ⁵²

Here, one assumes that Tony was at least able to program his synthesizer to let him simply hold down the key and have the rhythm play on its own, or else God bless that man's left hand. Regardless of the potential for monotony though, this is still pretty standard stuff all around from the rhythm section. By now you might be wondering where all that so-called rule breaking is, yeah?

Well now that we've established the core rhythmic spine of the piece, let's return to that guitar riff of Mike's that opens the song. The riff itself is six notes long, and most of those notes are exactly one beat in length. And hey, we've established that the song itself has six beats per measure, so this sounds like it's a pretty straightforward thing as well, doesn't it? Plus, when you consider that it's the first thing you hear at the start of the song, you'd assume the riff starts on the down beat (the first beat, or "1") too, right? Absolutely not:

'Keep It Dark' guitar riff sample

Not only does that riff *not* start on the down beat, it doesn't start on *any* beat at all. 'Keep It Dark' begins *between* the third and fourth beats of a measure, on what is known as the "off" beat - the space exactly halfway between two proper beats of the tempo. And if starting on the offbeat isn't enough, the riff actually *stays* there - forever! Of his six note riff, only the fifth note shows up on the beat. Everything else is syncopated, which is a fancy way of saying "off the beat." So now the fact that it's a six-note riff in a six-beats-per-measure song is actually a huge sonic problem - it's as though the guitar and drums are trying to do the same thing but started out of rhythm with one another, and for the next four and a half minutes they'll never get back in sync.

> **Tony:** *And then Mike was playing this riff, which goes very much against [the drum pattern]; the rhythms of the two things are quite strangely positioned. Sometimes you hear it and you go "God, it's all out of time."* ³

Again, since that guitar riff comes *first* the natural inclination is to think it's the rhythm section that's playing things out of alignment or incorrectly, but the rhythm section is typically your source of truth in these matters, isn't it? What you need is an arbiter of some kind. Some extra bit of sound to show you what's actually going on. So you might naturally look to Tony's keyboards to help get some clarity. Maybe he's going to pop in with some chords or something that really highlight where the true beat actually is. You know, clean off the mud so there can be no mistaking it. Well, erm, not quite:

'Keep It Dark' synth hits sample

When Tony does jump into the mix with something other than that repeating bass note, he comes in on the down beat with a series of quick synth hits, lending "credibility," if you will, to the rhythm section's claim on the actual beat. It's not big chords and there's some funkiness going on in that third bar, but there's a little bit of direction to be found. But then arrives something vaguely resembling a chorus shows up and we get this nonsense instead:

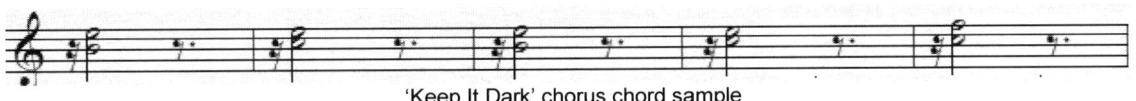
'Keep It Dark' chorus chord sample

Now he's coming in on the off beats with Mike! That's completely unhelpful, Mr. Banks! The chorus is meant to be the part that everyone at home can follow along with and enjoy, isn't it? I mean, the guys released 'Keep It Dark' as a single in late 1981 so clearly they thought there was something that might hook people. So why in blazes are these chorus chords popping in between the beats?!

> **Tony:** *Then the chorus comes in and all the chords are sort of anticipated, and the resulting effect is kind of strange...* [3]

Quite the understatement there. So if the drums, bass, guitar, and keys can't seem to get anything aligned, what's left? Just the vocals, I suppose. Good ol' Phil, he'll come through for us, sort all this mess out. Let's take a look at that vocal melody:

'Keep It Dark' verse melody sample

Hmm...not quite the revelation I'd hoped it would be. Sure, it starts on the down beat with the rhythm section, but it only takes three notes before the melody completely jumps ship and hangs out with that suspicious lookin' off beat crowd for a while. Then, fickle thing that it is, it kind of comes and goes between them for a spell. So we look to the chorus once more. If there's anything at all that can make this song make any kind of sense, it'd be a strong chorus melody. Let's check it out:

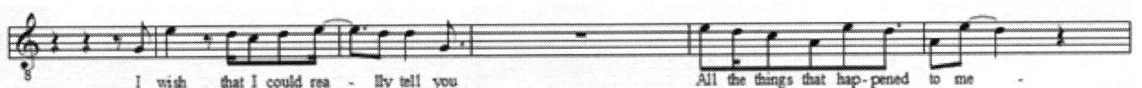
'Keep It Dark' chorus melody sample

Still unhelpful! It's almost like the rhythm section and the guitar are fighting over ownership of the beat, and the vocals are caught between them, somehow trapped in the middle of the dispute. Like the singer is, I don't know, caught somehow between two worlds.

Say, wait a minute...

> **Tony:** *I think the resulting song works really well. It's got very stark verses and very romantic choruses, and I wrote a lyric that kind of did that. So the idea was that this character had to pretend that he'd been robbed by people and that's why he disappeared for a few weeks, when in fact what had happened was he'd been taken up in a spaceship and gone to this fantastic world with everything wonderful and beautiful...but he couldn't tell anybody that because nobody would believe him. So I thought that was a quite nice idea.* [3]

On the next page you can see how the first eight bars of the song look when you put it all together. It's utterly chaotic but there's also a lot of (outer?) space in there somehow. It 100%, positively, should not work. And yet, somehow, it does. No agreement on rhythm, no overpowering melody, no sing-along chorus, Top 40 hit in the UK. Sometimes things just defy explanation, but here's my simple summary: *Abacab* was Genesis at their most experimental, and on 'Keep It Dark' the experiment was a success. That's about all you can ask for.

Keep It Dark

Genesis

86 - Behind the Lines

from *Duke*, 1980

In November 1980 Genesis bought a place called Fisher Lane Farm, which was (as the name would imply) a farmhouse with a cowshed. Over the next few months the band converted the space into a recording studio, which would be their hub of operations for the decades beyond. In 1979 though, they had no such dedicated space, and so when the band said they were going into "the studio" to start writing material for what would become the album *Duke,* what they really meant was they were hanging out in a bedroom apartment leased out to one Philip Collins, which he had converted into a kind of slapdash recording space. It was a fitting scene, as Genesis didn't have a lot to work with musically at that point, either.

> **Tony:** *I think we came in there [to the Duke writing sessions] a little bit barren of ideas, so we sat down and did a lot more improvising...I had this one riff, which was the opening part of 'Behind the Lines'...and I hadn't really developed it. So we sat down and started playing it, and immediately little ideas came, and then the whole song which came from it was actually just a development of that first part. But it wasn't something that I had written beforehand at all, so it very much emerged in the studio from that one idea. And that's how a lot of the things happened with us a bit.* [3]

All three band members had just released or written solo albums (Tony's and Mike's released in 1979, while Phil's wouldn't come out until 1981), so while there were "leftovers" from those efforts that made it onto *Duke*, the album didn't have any real meat on it just yet. Just a little riff of Tony's: dah-dah-daaaah, dah-dah-daaaah! That's nice I guess, but is it enough to build an entire album around?

> **Tony:** *When I hear it now there is still something about the opening of 'Behind the Lines'. It is so optimistic.* [1]

It's funny how creativity can get going. Sometimes even when you expect you're in a rut, all it takes is one tiny thing to give you an idea for the next tiny thing. And those tiny things start cascading out from one another until your paucity of ideas has become an overflowing fountain of them, and suddenly you find that you're not worried about how you'll fill your quota but rather what you'll have to cut. From one riff, a notion: build a sprawling, epic, side-long piece of music, entirely group-written, and have that be the focal point of the new album. The solo tracks that felt like a starting point, a kind of "well at least we have those" at the outset? Afterthoughts, now.

But then a thought, a worry. A doubt creeping in. "We already did a side-long epic before, with Pete and Steve. Oh, the reviews will be merciless. 'Genesis out of ideas, rehash *Foxtrot*.' We can't do a big piece like that again, we can't afford to draw those comparisons! We need to do something different somehow." Yet, this piece is far too good to discard entirely, and it represents too much growth in the trio's joint songwriting chemistry to even bury under the solo stuff.

So, then, a new idea: keep the epic. Keep all of it except perhaps a couple linking bits between sections. Split them into individual tracks. Put the front half at the start of the album, the last bits at the end, and take an expanded version of the strongest linking section and stick it right smack in the middle. No more side-long pieces to draw the eye rolls of the critics, but all the material is still there, largely intact, and defines the entire structure of the album. The solo songs can just fill the gaps in between.

While I personally think the full side-long 'Duke' track could've surpassed even 'Supper's Ready' - and there I go making the comparison, proving the band's point in not going in that direction - I can't argue with what we ultimately got on record. In fact, I only feel that way about the potential epic because the material is such consistently high quality; there's no question in my mind that the group-written songs of *Duke* are, broadly speaking, the best stuff the album has to offer. And a large amount of the credit for that goes to 'Behind the Lines', which opens both the album as well as this so-called "hidden suite."

Immediately that riff grabs your attention. It's got such a drive and positivity about it that you can't help but be drawn in. One of the favourite pastimes among Genesis fan communities is to discuss favourites. Favourite songs, favourite concerts, favourite albums, you get the idea. And whenever I see the discussion in these places turn to "favourite openers," the love for 'Behind the Lines' inevitably starts pouring out. The only other Genesis album-opener that really captures the imagination right from the get-go like this is, for my money, 'Watcher of the Skies' with its haunting Mellotron chords. But 'Behind the Lines' is more than just a riff, too. It's an emphatic bass drone, a grand fanfare, and then a soaring guitar to flavour the mix. It goes up, it goes down, it goes dark, it goes light. In only about two minutes and fifteen seconds, Genesis manage to paint a powerful picture of everything this album is going to be. It's a terrific stage setter.

> **Phil:** *'Behind the Lines', a lot of energy, the live drum sound, the live feeling of everything in the band...that was, to me, the first time we'd started to sound good on record.* [3]

Then, after that big intro, there's an entire song! Light-hearted and peppy, the vocal melody doesn't quite conform to verse/chorus standards, but nevertheless feels like something you ought to be singing along to. Yet even that is just a variation and development on the riff at the heart of the whole affair. The bombast is gone, but the thrill remains. Perhaps that's just a residual kind of feeling from the immensity of the intro, but that's all the section really needs to be anyhow. The entire vocal section of the song is just icing on the cake, when you get right down to it. It's 59% of the song by runtime but only about 20% of the oomph that the piece delivers. It's the long straight rail at the bottom of the roller coaster's biggest hill, allowing the rider to revel in the sensation of speed that persists even after the bottom has been reached.

Which isn't to say the "main song" portion of 'Behind the Lines' is of a lower quality than the intro or any such criticism, but it's a reversal of expectations in a way. We'd typically expect the vocal section to be the main brunt of the song with the instrumental stuff acting as the intro to the "good part," but here all of Phil's singing is just the outflowing of that grand entrance itself, which is the true mission statement for the song and indeed the album as a whole. What's usually the core of a song is instead closer to an afterthought, albeit a really, really good one; all the little instrumental flairs do their best to keep the magic alive, right up until an understated recapitulation of the primary melody at the end. Heck, I can't even fault 'Behind the Lines' for lacking an impactful ending, since it trails off into 'Duchess', a rousing adventure of its own.

From one riff, a song. From one song, an album. From one album, a Farm. From a Farm, sixteen more years of creativity. It doesn't take much, does it?

85 - Duke's End

from *Duke*, 1980

Well now, this sounds familiar, doesn't it? A strange case of déjà vu? Or just one of those good ol' reprises that I'm such a hopeless sucker for? 'Duke's End' is, at its most obvious, a reprise of 'Behind the Lines': that unmistakable bombastic keyboard line, those ambitious drums, that bass that bursts through like the hum of an enormous power generator. It's all there, every bit as strong as it was the first time around.

But 'Duke's End' does more than that, too. Most notably, it trades the entire vocal section of 'Behind the Lines' - that bit I said was relatively superfluous, albeit in a good way - for an interplay with 'Turn It On Again', fusing the two songs into one big ol' showcase of riffs and melodies, bringing both the so-called 'Duke Suite' and the album *Duke* itself to a close with one heck of a bang. It's like a miniaturised version of the 'Los Endos' concept, summing up the suite by covering its most prevalent parts. Yes, 'Behind the Lines' is longer and does arguably more different things, but I just think this blending of the two entities is so strong that I ever so slightly prefer 'Duke's End'.

> **Mike:** *The title of the album is Duke, which came from the original working title [of the song suite]. We were going to do one long epic called 'The Duke Piece' which was all group composition. But it gave a bad balance to the album and we've split the long piece up into different sections, mixing individual songs with group compositions. We might do 'Duke' as one long piece live.* [54]

And indeed they did; on the Duke Tour itself the second quarter of the band's set was indeed 'Behind the Lines', 'Duchess', 'Guide Vocal', 'Turn It On Again', 'Duke's Travels', and 'Duke's End' in sequence, really allowing this final piece to hit with its full might. I can't recommend listening to the 'Duke Suite' uninterrupted enough.

> **Phil:** *A lot of people think that the bloke on the cover [of the album] is Duke, but it's really not like that. There's no overriding concept...Originally when we started this album, we wanted to do a long piece written by the group. The working title for that piece was 'Duke'. We ended up splitting the long piece into sections and interspersing it with solo songs by the three of us, but we ended up keeping the name Duke. We thought of it originally as a working title because there's a fanfare on the first and last tracks, and we thought of royalty. But it's very important to get across...that it's not the duke or the duke of something or some guy's name.* [55]

That "fanfare on the first and last tracks" had another live ripple down the road: on the 2007 Turn It On Again Tour and again for 2021's The Last Domino? Tour, 'Behind the Lines' and 'Duke's End' fused into a hybrid piece called 'Duke's Intro' that Genesis opened the concerts with. This version had no reprise effect since the two pieces are so similar anyway, but the flavouring of 'Turn It On Again' within 'Duke's End' allowed the group to transition straight into that song (the tour's namesake) pretty effortlessly, proving that even when rearranged these puzzle pieces can still form a really effective picture. It was a great way to kick off a show, just as 'Behind the Lines' was a really effective way to kick off an album, and 'Duke's End' a really effective way to end one.

84 - Riding the Scree

from *The Lamb Lies Down on Broadway*, 1974

scree - *noun*

1. a steep mass of detritus on the side of a mountain
2. the loud, high-pitched scream of a hawk, meaning "F you"

The first of these definitions comes from Dictionary.com, a popular and reliable enough resource for finding word meanings online. The second, more colourful definition comes instead from a website called Urban Dictionary, which specialises in defining slang terminology. The definitions are, as one might imagine, very different - and yet both ring true for this particular song. Of course, the setting of the track is Rael, cliffside over a canyon, seeing his brother drowning in the river far below. Making the choice to save him, he commits to a wildly dangerous slide down the loose rocks, skidding downward with treacherous speed in order to have any chance of reaching John in time. So 'Riding the Scree' is, in the traditional sense of the word, quite literal.

But Rael is also only in this situation in the first place because an enormous raven stole his "private property" and flew off to said ravine with it. This whole chapter of the tale of *The Lamb* is the result of an agitated avian flipping Rael the bird, as it were, and Rael having to "ride out" or deal with the consequences. So 'Riding the Scree' can also be taken figuratively: it's the story of a man trying to make the most out of a big ol' Caw-Caw being a right wanker.

That all said, when I think of "scree" as onomatopoeia, a bird isn't the first thing that comes to mind. Instead my mind conjures up images of ghosts and banshees and other things that wail. Things like, say, Tony Banks' keys in this song. It opens with a fiery keyboard solo, which transitions to something more in that wailing tone, then becomes very melodic by contrast. Not to last though: it's all fire once more before finally giving way to the vocals. By now more than half the song is over! It's like an inverse 'Cinema Show' where all the pyrotechnic keyboard work happens in advance of the actual lyrical section.

> **Tony:** *The length of the album meant that I could do three solos on the album instead of one. The 'Riding The Scree' one I enjoyed the most I think.* [6]

Or it would be, except Tony doesn't ever bother to stop. He's still spinning lines over Pete's vocals, and after less than a minute's digression he picks the whole thing back up again. Phil is splashing cymbals and putting drum fills everywhere and Tony just keeps blasting those sonic fireworks up in the air. Then it all fades out so that 'In the Rapids' has room to breathe afterward, but phew, how do you follow that up?

This is a keyboarding tour de force, a brilliant flare of light in the general darkness that comprises the fourth side of *The Lamb*. When you're faced with this much "scree"ness as a listener, how can you possibly handle it?

I'd argue that there's only one way: that's to ride.

83 - A Trick of the Tail

from *A Trick of the Tail*, 1976

Arguably the most straightforward, poppiest pop song the band recorded until the release of 'Follow You Follow Me' two years later, this one tends to get a pass from the snobbier type of fans, probably because the stuff that surrounded it on the album was still peak progressive Genesis. It also helps that it's a breath of fresh air on *A Trick of the Tail* the album, coming after the grandness of 'Ripples...'and right before the ending powerhouse of 'Los Endos'. It's like opening a window to let in the cool breeze: refreshing, even if the temperature inside was already quite comfortable.

> **Tony:** *I had a few ready-made pieces available, which I'd written thinking about a possible solo album...'A Trick of the Tail' was something I'd written many years before, but with Peter's departure, I liked the idea of slipping in something lighter and more quirky.* [1]

Tony's lyrics can be pretty hit or miss with me; even some of his better songs have some lyrics or individual lines that just don't really work. 'A Trick of the Tail' is one of the good ones in my book. It's a fanciful story that teases the imagination, and it's also a story *about* imagination. It would make a terrific children's book, and I don't mean that in any kind of derogatory way. The story is simple and easy to follow, but it leaves a strong impression. There's an element of "don't take what you have for granted," which is an echo of 'Mad Man Moon' earlier in the album, but the overriding message is to be willing to dream, and to believe in the incredible. It's a concept Tony would revisit some years down the line in a different flavour with 'Keep It Dark', but the moral is the same. To me, it's a reminder to not be afraid of my own creativity; to be open to exploring. I really like that message.

> **Mike:** *As Tony and I were ordinarily quite stiff, I always enjoyed making videos...None of the ideas ever sounded so bad at the time, but then you'd see the end results and wonder what on earth any of us had been thinking, like the video for 'A Trick of the Tail', where Phil ended up minimised, hopping around on a piano keyboard.* [14]

> **Phil:** *'Trick of the Tail' is probably the most embarrassing video I've ever been in. There's a very small me running up and down the piano. I mean, you know when you look back and think, "Who told me to do that? Whose lapse of taste was this? Was it mine?" I think it was a mixture of me and the director. And the other guys. Everyone was to blame for that.* [56]

OK, so sometimes indulging your own creative impulses doesn't turn out so well, but hey, that's part of the journey too, right?

The musical side of the equation is a little different. For a band used to playing complex and demanding instrumental passages, there probably wasn't much in the album's title track to really challenge them. It was written long before the album was made, when they weren't quite so accomplished as musicians, but you get the sense that they maybe wanted to do something a little more ambitious by this point. The fact that they released the song as a single but didn't play it live even on the supporting tour is pretty strong evidence, at any rate.

And while I can't fault the band for preferring to play other tracks, as a listener I still really enjoy this one. Leaving the song jaunty and simple gives the mind a bigger canvas to paint whatever picture it wants, and that's really kind of the whole point, isn't it?

82 - Snowbound

from ...And Then There Were Three..., 1978

Typically when we refer to someone as being "snowbound" what we mean is that they're shut inside their home on account of heavy snows. We conjure up images of warm hearths, hot cocoa, knit sweaters, cozy log cabins. It's a cause for children to rejoice, as schools are temporarily shut down and they can play to their hearts' content in the beautiful white canvas of nature.

> **Phil:** *We have never really, apart from perhaps this album, written love songs. We have always shunned away from them for some reason, a subconscious thing. It's getting to the point now when most of the songs can be taken as love songs - 'Snowbound' for instance is very romantic.* [41]

Yet despite Phil's description of the song as "romantic," when Genesis says someone is "snowbound" what they really mean is there's a guy who got trapped inside a snowman outfit and smothered/mauled to death by a bunch of kids who didn't realise he was there.

> **Mike:** *It was an easy one to record, a romantic song about a guy who gets inside a snowman outfit to hide from everybody. He was paranoid, and he gets stuck!* [41]

Yeesh. Talk about grim. And yet somehow the tone of the whole piece is so full of innocent wonder. After all, the chorus is just kids shouting "Hey, what a snowman!" over and over. They don't know there's a delusional soon-to-be-corpse in there, so why wouldn't they be happy? The choruses of 'Snowbound' as a result are this really strange combination of childlike mirth and dark, horrible tragedy. The drums were recorded at a faster tempo and then slowed down in production, and as a result each drum hit has an extreme amount of heaviness to it, every one a core-shaking reminder of what's really under that snowman exterior.

> **Mike:** *There's one or two interesting things on this one. It's very difficult for us to keep trying to be different - to avoid being a parody of ourselves. Here we slowed the drums down to fit the track and give it a slightly different sound. Phil originally recorded them at a much faster speed. His singing is exceptionally good on this song, but then I think his singing has improved all round on this album. With some songs we have to push the singing a bit but this one was the first or second take. He has a lovely breathy sound on the softer parts.* [17]

Ultimately though, despite the atmosphere and imagery it conjures, a chorus that ends every line in the word "snowman" isn't going to be very strong lyrically. The rest of the song doesn't do a lot for me in that regard either, but that's not the point. The lyrics in 'Snowbound' aren't particularly well crafted, no, but they do deliver on their most important job of informing the listener of the song's general concept, which then allows the musical moods to take over and do everything they need to. So they're *functional* lyrics, even if they're not particularly *good* ones.

So from a purely musical point of view, I get what the band means when they call this piece "romantic." They're talking more about tones and feels than anything else, and there's no denying those swelling sounds can really move you. Doesn't make it any less hilarious though! Just, uh, remember to check your snowmen for signs of life next time you're playing outside in the winter, won't you?

81 - Man on the Corner

from *Abacab*, 1981

The first chapter of the Philip David Charles Collins Homelessness Institute trilogy of songs, 'Man on the Corner' is a good deal darker than either of its two successors, and this is probably to its credit. It's also a bit more subtle - if 'Another Day in Paradise' beats the listener over the head with social awareness and 'Tell Me Why' beats the dead horse of social awareness, 'Man on the Corner' beats around the bush of social awareness by contrast. It's a character study of a single individual rather than an attempt to paint a vague mass of people in heterogeneous circumstances with a broad brush, and it's lyrically better for it.

Yet though the song's words might inevitably draw parallels to Phil's big hit from 1989 - as indeed this very entry proves - I'd argue that musically speaking the song is actually an evolution of his first big hit: 1981's 'In the Air Tonight'. They're structured nearly identically to one another, but 'Man on the Corner' makes a few little tweaks to the formula that help to differentiate it and make it arguably more interesting.

> **Tony:** *There was this reaction against songs like…'Man On The Corner' because it was simple and that was seen as being wrong, and yet that has always been a part of Genesis. And there is this illusion that [simplicity] has taken over and I don't think it has taken over at all. There is just a little more emphasis and we do it better than we used to and therefore it gets a much higher profile, because the singles are actually hits.* [6]

Let's start with the ways they're so similar. Both songs open with intro sections focused around a drum machine pattern with restrained synth chords that establish the mood and key signature. Both songs open with an instance of the chorus before the first verse, and then do a second chorus/verse pairing afterward. Each verse ending is built on intensity and anticipation, and while the first verse of each song sustains the tension by going back into the chorus, the second verse of each song releases the tension with a dramatic entrance from the actual drums, along with the first appearance of bass.

> **Mike:** *Phil and the drum machine…it had rather this lovely beat that he does, where until you know where 1 is, you haven't got a clue. The drum machine comes in, and I think if I don't count from 1, and just listen to it, I haven't got a clue where 1 is. And then you find that it's great, but many a night we did it on stage I would see Tony kind of going "Where the fuck is 1?" If you miss that moment, then you can't get it. But, great song.* [3]

But here's where the two songs diverge a bit. While the iconic drum fill of 'In the Air Tonight' sees the drum machine entirely replaced for the remainder of the song, 'Man on the Corner' features a more intricate pattern from the get-go, and keeps it going alongside the real drums. This might on paper sound like excess baggage, but in practice it's something of a necessity; removing that pattern outright in favour of simpler drums (even if they're inherently more powerful) would cause the song to decline, or to feel less complex at this climactic moment instead of more so. Can't have that. Increasing complexity is what it's all about, right Tony? Found 1 yet, mate?

> **Mike:** *The one thing about Tony's mistakes is that he'll never hold his hands up if he gets it wrong. I'll always own up but Tony's technique is to look at me over the top of his keyboard and growl so that I immediately start thinking it's me that has messed up. He used to do it to Phil, too, and it was ages before the two of us were on to him.* [14]

Well keep at it ol' chum, I'm sure you'll figure it out sooner or later. Beyond the drum pattern, there's one other really notable thing 'Man on the Corner' does at this point of the song: it goes into a bridge. This is a brand new section with a brand new melody we haven't yet heard before. It's an attention grabber, which is why it's no coincidence that this is the moment in the song where Collins switches the lyrical subject from the titular man on the corner to both himself and you as a listener, striking at the heart of the matter, delivering his message un-obfuscated for the first time. Look at the pronoun usage over the course of the lyrics (ignoring the repeated phrase "I don't know" in the choruses) and you'll see what I mean.

First Chorus: he's, he, He's

Post-Chorus: him, you (foreshadowing!)

First Verse: he, he, he

Second Chorus: He's, he's, he, He's

Post-Chorus: him, *you, me*

Bridge: *we, We're,* he's, *you, you*

Final Choruses: he's, he, He's, he's, he's, he's, he's, he, He's

One of these things is not like the others! It's a dramatic shift from "Hey check out that guy over there" to "Look at *us*. What are we doing?" The turn is so unexpected - despite its being foreshadowed after the first chorus, even - that it convicts us as it catches us unawares. It's a similar kind of trick as to what George Harrison used in his hit 'My Sweet Lord,' where the backing vocalists echo his melody with sing-along calls of "Hallelujah!", and by the end you catch yourself singing "Hare Krishna" along with the radio, wondering how you got there. Same idea, except instead of trying to spread the message of Hinduism, Phil Collins is trying to snap you out of your complacency. He'd do it again more directly in the future, yes, but I think the subterfuge actually makes this his most effective attempt.

Returning to the musical comparison exercise at hand, both 'Man on the Corner' and 'In the Air Tonight' end with repeating choruses, now bolstered by additional instrumentation and vocal oomph, before finally trailing away. 'In the Air Tonight' fades out with the vocals still in motion, while 'Man on the Corner' allows them to conclude and has the backing music perform the fade-out on its own, but the effect is pretty much the same.

So in a very real sense, 'Man on the Corner' is pretty much the answer to the question "What if Genesis actually had used 'In the Air Tonight' on *Duke*?" It's structurally almost exactly the same song, but there is a little more emphasis on the backing music (Tony's keyboard line is a bit more involved than the simple chords from 'In the Air Tonight', for instance). And wouldn't you know it, 'In the Air Tonight' found its major chart success right before Genesis moved into The Farm to start writing *Abacab* with a certain Hugh Padgham on board as producer...

80 - The Lamb Lies Down on Broadway

from *The Lamb Lies Down on Broadway*, 1974

While *A Trick of the Tail* is obviously the first Genesis album without Peter Gabriel, functionally by 1974 Genesis was a band learning how to survive without one of their primary writers, even if nobody in the group quite realised that was what was happening. Between running off with William Friedkin to try to be a Hollywood "ideas man" and making it through his daughter's traumatic birth process with virtually no support from his bandmates, Peter was starting to realise there was more to life beyond Genesis, and accordingly began to distance himself a bit.

> **Peter:** *As always I had some semi-finished ideas to bring in, but a lot of the jamming which took place [during writing sessions for The Lamb] I was not participating in. I would go off and the others would carry on evolving the music through jamming; then I would come back and try to develop melodies on a piano in another room.* [1]

This emphasis on improvisation and group writing without Peter makes the album's title track something of a last hurrah: Peter and Tony had been, from the band's formative days, a pretty dominant writing pair, constructing much of their earliest material together. Now, faced with a double album and a need for lots of material, we got what would end up being their final effort as a duo.

> **Tony:** *We pooled all the ideas we had. I had one fast piano introduction which Peter and I developed into a song, 'The Lamb Lies Down', the last song that Peter and I ever wrote together, just the two of us. And I think it showed our strengths: it had a good feel from what I gave it but much of the solidity came from what Pete wrote.* [1]

Calling it a "fast piano introduction" doesn't quite do proper justice to the first thirty seconds of the song. It's a musical rendition of watching a scene slowly unfold and then burst into life - one of the more powerful openings to a song in the band's career. And it's not as though the piano goes away after that either: Tony's fingers never stop moving over the whole piece. For a guy known mostly for big chords and walls of sound, 'The Lamb Lies Down on Broadway' is instead a showcase of fluid notes and constant motion. You can *hear* chords, of course, but they're never static. It's always a rapid series of notes and arpeggios oscillating around that central point.

It gives the song a kind of restless, kinetic energy that lends itself to a view of, oh, I don't know, New York City at the start of the day?

> **Mike:** *I think the title track, the opening track is great. The piano riff... And Pete sets up the image. Describing the New York scenes, you know. Early morning skyline, those sorts of lines really paint a picture of the album.* [3]

The bass lines are the emphatic punctuation, like the sputtering of engines beginning their commutes. It's wonderful imagery, which lends one to naturally ask what the image of the lamb itself must represent. Maybe the album's liner notes have some answer.

> *Meanwhile from out of the steam a lamb lies down. This lamb has nothing whatsoever to do with Rael, or any other lamb - it just lies down on Broadway.* [57]

Or maybe not.

The lyrics are part of the magic of it all. Obviously not to undersell Peter's musical contributions to 'The Lamb Lies Down on Broadway' themselves, but there are any number of places that lively piano intro could've gone lyrically, and I'm not sure any of them would have been better than the scene Peter painted for us conceptually. It's not even about the lyrics themselves exactly, though his lines are wonderfully descriptive like they come from a fiction novel rather than a song. But it's the brilliance of hearing that music and thinking "This sounds like a city coming to life in the morning." That's unusual insight.

> **Steve:** *It was entirely Pete's lyric, that one. I think Pete was becoming increasingly less a fan of singing anyone else's lyrics, no matter what they were like.* [43]

> **Peter:** *There's not many books being written by committee. And that's for very good reason. And it really challenged some of the fundamental principles of trying to sort of share things equally.* [43]

I'm not entirely sure whether 'The Lamb Lies Down on Broadway' and its lyrical ideas predate the narrative for the album on the whole, or whether those ideas were crafted because Peter's already-existent narrative required a starting point, so I don't want to overstate the impact of this song on the conceptual whole of The Lamb Lies Down on Broadway as a project. Yet from a *results* standpoint, it's hard to argue that this song doesn't position the album for success.

> **Tony:** *In terms of songs, I always think of 'The Lamb Lies Down' itself being the last song that Peter and I kind of ever wrote together, because we'd written a lot in the early days together. And, you know, it was a pretty good song to end on really.* [3]

I mean, let's face it: while I love The Lamb as an album, I do think it's got some weaker moments, musically and especially narratively. That's really a natural consequence of making a double album, when you think about it. Under normal circumstances, you'd make a single album and then any strong material that didn't quite fit in would get worked into singles and/or B-sides - maybe an EP if you had enough of it - while the weaker excess material would be simply left out altogether, never to see the light of day except perhaps in some kind of rarities collection a couple decades later. On a double album, by contrast, *all* the strong material makes the album, giving the whole thing a bit more heft and impact. But the problem is you might only have three sides' worth of stuff when all is said and done, so despite including even more high-quality material, you're ironically now a little short of a full second record. By necessity, then, you pull in more of the stuff you've created - including material that normally wouldn't be judged as strong enough for release. And so in the end your massive, impressive double album has a few weak moments that you've got to hope don't sully the entire package.

But apparently arbitrary title aside (thanks for nothing, liner notes), 'The Lamb Lies Down on Broadway' itself isn't among the weaker batch on this album by any stretch of the imagination. It masterfully sets the stage for everything to come, and it's no fault of the title track if occasionally the later sides of the album don't quite deliver on its initial promise. I may not care for everywhere this album goes, but I'll take this opening every time. It's a great introduction to a great album. What more could anyone ask for?

79 - Throwing It All Away

from *Invisible Touch*, 1986

>Need I say dee-da-dayee-ay?

>Need I say de-dayee-ay?

One thing that really surprised me when I first started becoming involved in Genesis fan communities was the utter disdain a lot of people seem to have for the live theatrics of 'Throwing It All Away'. Which isn't to say I don't understand the argument; I do. This is a gentle, emotional ballad that loses the very elements that make it so pretty when Phil Collins is up there on a stage in a stadium shouting "lee-da-deh-deh-deh-deh!" over and over. But it feels as though nobody is willing to acknowledge what the song gains in the process of that transformation as well. Audience engagement is a big deal, and if you've ever actually *been* at a concert where Genesis performed this song live, when Phil held the mic out to the crowd I doubt you just stood there with your arms crossed, making a grumpy face, muttering that this isn't "real Genesis." No, you dutifully shout-sang "Dee-da-dayee-ay!" right back at him, and if you're honest with yourself, you were downright giddy about it.

So let's dispense with the notion that the call and answer routine somehow ruins the song. It might make it into a somewhat *different* song, and that's a fair callout, but I for one think it's a tremendous idea and that it works really well. I kick myself from time to time that, when picking a Genesis hit to do with my college a cappella group, we opted for 'Invisible Touch' instead of 'Throwing It All Away', because that call and answer would've been a big hit with our audiences - much more than the relatively bland reception 'Invisible Touch' got us, certainly. When that "dee-ba-day" bursts back in a like a bat out of hell after the big build of the final chorus? Such a strong, strong moment.

>**Phil:** *It turned out to be a great stage tune, actually.* [3]

>**Tony:** *By the time of Invisible Touch, we were putting out songs like 'Invisible Touch', 'Land of Confusion', 'Throwing It All Away', 'In Too Deep', and they were all hit songs. In America they were all big hits, top ten, top five even. It was a great period and audiences were massive. It was a strange thing, a bit of a dream, really. In 1987 on the Invisible Touch tour we played Wembley Stadium, four nights in a row; that's nearly 300,000 people. OK, there might have been a few repeats in there, but I thought at the time, and I still think now, that moment was the peak of our career.* [1]

>**Phil:** *Each one of those songs like 'Land of Confusion', 'In Too Deep', 'Tonight Tonight [Tonight]', 'Invisible Touch', 'Throwing It All Away'...they were all kind of either top 5, top 10 singles in the States. I think that was probably, that...first stadium tour...that was probably our peak in America.* [1]

See? Everyone loves it! No need to be a sourpuss about it anymore. If this book does nothing else for you, may it at least relieve you of any misgivings you have about happily grumbling a cheery "moo-zee-moo-day" right back Phil's way.

Now that we've gotten *that* elephant out of the room, let's talk about the actual studio track. Much more mellow by comparison, this song is easy listening all the way through. Phil's vocals are so relaxed that he almost slurs his words on occasion, and then that lift from Tony's chords in the chorus? Sublime. I also love all the little vocal effects: the harmonies on "watch the world go round and round" and onward, the falsetto singing after it. But I think my favourite little touch has to be in the second chorus, where it sounds like someone snuck into the recording room drinking a crisp, refreshing Dr. Pepper. That blissful whispery "ahh" after each line couldn't be anything else, could it?

Man, I could really go for some Dr. Pepper about now. Several years ago I decided to make one of the shamefully few health-conscious decisions I've made in my adult life and I cut carbonated beverages out of my diet completely. You'd be shocked at what a difference that one change can make if you're a big soda drinker. Getting rid of all those empty calories provides an enormous swing back toward the healthy end of the spectrum, even if you aren't doing all the other things in terms of diet and exercise that you really ought to as well. It's also a big money saver: make note of every time you go out to eat and save two or three bucks on a beverage by just ordering water. You'll be surprised! So I don't regret the lifestyle change at all, and I don't even really miss drinking the stuff anymore.

Except that, occasionally, I'm reminded that there's a drink out there called Dr. Pepper, and that it stole the heart of my tongue many years ago. I miss it still.

Anyway, while the thirst-quenching vocal effect may be my favourite little bit of flair in 'Throwing It All Away', it's not quite the best moment of the song in general. No, that honour goes to the fourth and final verse. Stripped down to a sparser sound, attached to poignant lyrics:

> *Someday you'll be sorry, someday when you're free*
> *Memories will remind you that our love was meant to be*
> *But late at night when you call my name, the only sound you'll hear*
> *Is the sound of your voice calling, calling after me*

That's a grade-A brilliant lyric. It's like the most despondent "screw you" of all time. One can gloss over the words of the previous verses by just grooving along with the song, but the instrumental change here forces you to listen and catch these lyrics even if you've registered nothing else, and they always strike me as really powerful. Then the regular accompaniment returns with Tony's chorus chords, and they just sound so mournful in context here. It's great stuff.

Phil: *One of Mike's riffs; he wrote the lyrics for it as well.* [3]

Mike: *[Assigning lyric-writing responsibilities] was a case of someone saying "I really want to do this one because it excited me." There were certain songs that we knew Phil should be working on because there was a vocal moment that suits his style. Tony would usually work on the longer songs. As for me, I tended to write the simple lyrics like 'Throwing It All Away'.* [58]

Again, great work Mike, great work. Perhaps one of the greatest lyrical passages you've ever written. *Almost* as great, in fact, as a tall, cool Dr. Pepper.

78 - Cul-de-sac

from *Duke*, 1980

If the "Duke Suite" gave the album its name, and was called such because of the regal atmosphere conjured up by the big fanfare introduction of 'Behind the Lines', then it's almost a little surprising that 'Cul-de-sac' isn't part of that suite at all. Here's a song whose lyrics are actually about declining royalty, with all the pomposity one might expect from a king's public address. Now, I've seen rumblings and rumours that the lyrics are actually all about the extinction of the dinosaurs, complete with unsourced and unsubstantiated claims that Tony Banks himself said so directly in an interview at some point in time. Maybe that's true and maybe it isn't - certainly a fun interpretation either way. Regardless, I don't think it matters for my argument here. Whether describing the fall of the kings of men or the kings of beasts, 'Cul-de-sac' screams magnificent nobility all the way through. In that way it nestles in right at home on *Duke*, an extra bit of thematic ammunition to keep the listener from losing the overall grandiose feel that the album inspires from the get-go, even if the track sits mired in the midst of the solo-written middle cuts of record.

> **Tony:** *'Evidence of Autumn' and 'Cul-de-sac', it was a choice of which one went on the album and I think we went with the right one really.* [6]

But in another sense, 'Cul-de-sac' is a really foreign piece, sounding somehow different than everything else that *Duke* has on offer. I think it's largely because the big progressive work of *Duke* - going through multiple changes of moods, time signatures, and melodies - is broken down into six different tracks, and of those component pieces only 'Duke's Travels' really has that shifting, journeying feel within itself as an individual cut. Granted, 'Behind the Lines' and 'Duchess' have two distinct sections apiece, but that's not quite the same thing. And then every other solo-written song on the album has pretty much its own uniform feel; they're true individual songs. Heck, to this day I still see people on occasion surprised that 'Turn It On Again' is itself part of the "Duke Suite" because it sounds so much like its own thing to the point that it was a bonafide hit single.

It's in the midst of all that where we find 'Cul-de-sac' barrelling through, hitting three distinct moods within its first sixty-five seconds alone. First you've got the very gentle initial vocal line and subsequent piano intro, a kind of Calm Before the Storm. This transitions into the very sounds of self-importance themselves: (synth) trumpets blaring, the red carpet being rolled out, throngs of peasants gathered to witness. And then that's all shattered by this heavy groove, a sort of biting, rhythmic sound that makes mockery of the entire scene. The choruses of the song then blend these two disparate sections - Fanfare and Caustic Rock, let's call them - into one unified sound that shouldn't work at all, but miraculously does.

After the second round of verse and chorus, we hit a bridge which serves as a fourth mood. Quiet, introspective, reflecting on the finiteness of one's own potency. The section builds in lockstep with the singer's anger as invading armies encroach, and Phil is literally just screaming by the end of it. It truly is the Beginning of the End. From there we transition once more into a sort of corrupted reprise of the Fanfare section, something we might call Crumbling Empire. Then one more chorus in true Fanfare fashion, then back to Crumbling Empire, and finally one last kiss of that gentle piano to cap us off. If I wanted to paint this out with named sections, 'Cul-de-sac' might look something like this:

> **i.** Calm Before the Storm
> **ii.** Fanfare
> **iii.** Caustic Rock
> **iv.** Beginning of the End
> **v.** Crumbling Empire
> **vi.** Fanfare (reprise)
> **vii.** Crumbling Empire (reprise)

Now please, allow me to remind you: this song is only five minutes long. It's a true progressive journey, similar in form even to 'Supper's Ready': gentle intro, powerful section to be reprised near the end, groovy rock stuff in the middle, and a big build to that aforementioned reprise. But of course, 'Supper's Ready' takes upwards of twenty minutes to accomplish all of that. Don't get me wrong: that extra time is of course put to good use, and being able to explore each section more fully is a huge boon to it. I'm not trying to argue that 'Cul-de-sac' is a *better* version of 'Supper's Ready' or anything of the sort. What I *am* saying is that in my mind 'Cul-de-sac' is like the fun size candy bar version of that seminal epic, and honestly, I'm here for it, even if Genesis themselves weren't fully on board.

> **Phil:** *I felt I was pulling in a different direction...there was one track on Duke called 'Cul-de-sac' by Tony, and Tony's a very white writer. As soon as I have trouble playing something, he knows he shouldn't have played it [in the group] and he should have kept it [for his solo career].*
> [59]

It's not too difficult to see where Phil might have been a bit resistant to this song. The melodies are very Tony: meandering with a focus on enhancing the underlying chords rather than built around a steady hook that might pull a listener in. And from the rhythmic side, it's a lot of heavy cymbal work. Tony has Phil using the actual drumskins for accents and flairs, and the crashing metal as the beat driver in a kind of reverse of the typical style anyone might expect from a more concise song. That is, except when he doesn't: during the verses Phil has to shift back and forth between "standard" playing and this "reverse" playing as the melody churns on. To his great credit, he nails every aspect of what he's asked to do, but it must have felt pretty strange indeed.

Ultimately this is a kind of grand experiment for Tony, I think. We know he likes to wander in his songwriting a bit and really let the music spin out as long as he feels it needs to. And we know that with, for example, his material on *...And Then There Were Three...* he made an attempt to write more concise, focused pieces. 'Cul-de-sac' feels like the true hybrid of those two ideas, indulging Tony's need to get lost in the woods for a while yet not taking up half the record to do so. That it found a home here, on an album built around the very themes and expressions the song exemplifies, is simply the icing on the cake.

77 - Not About Us

from *Calling All Stations*, 1997

Wait, this is Genesis? I've seen the sentiment many times that *Calling All Stations* doesn't feel like a "real" Genesis album, and perhaps should've even been released under a different band name. I've always thought that was a little bit silly, but 'Not About Us' is a track that gives me pause, as it's pretty unlike anything else in the band's entire catalogue. It's not just that it's a gentle, romantic sounding ballad; Genesis has plenty of those over the years with 'Carpet Crawlers', 'In Too Deep', and 'Hold on My Heart' to name just a few. But 'Not About Us' is fundamentally different from all of those.

> **Ray**: 'Not About Us'...is a nice song. It sounds a bit like a Mike + The Mechanics song as well unless you try to play it, and then you realise that there are so many chords in that song – it's actually very Genesis when you play it. But when you listen to it, it's actually kind of Mike + The Mechanics. [26]

The key is in the instrumentation. Listen to any of those other songs and what you'll hear are emotional pieces driven almost entirely by keyboards. They may be moving and twinkling like in 'Carpet Crawlers', or they might be dense, heavy chords like in 'Hold on My Heart'. Maybe, like 'In Too Deep', they're somewhere in between. Heck, even 'Your Own Special Way', which was much more guitar-centred, still had a fullness to its sound that only Tony could provide. And yet here is 'Not About Us', opening with a sound that's entirely stripped down to just acoustic guitars.

> **Tony:** 'Not About Us' was all of us really, but Mike...every time he played the opening sequence which, once again, was very simple...a couple of chords, but it just sounded very good, very evocative, and...so we wanted to keep that acoustic feel. [25]

I mean, yes, there are synth chords and drums that come in later, but they're not the meat of the piece by any means. One needed only to watch the promotional appearance the band put in on VH1 to see just how un-Genesis a song 'Not About Us' fundamentally is. Ray stands in the centre of the stage, acoustic guitar hanging from his shoulder. Mike and Tony flank him, both seated, both also with guitars in hand. Tony's got a keyboard in front of him, sure, though it's just a single unit instead of his big "cage" of synthesizers. That said, he doesn't even bother to touch them for this song. And then there's poor Nir Zidkyahu, a really energetic drummer, looking like he's not sure why he's even there. He's standing in the back with a shaker in one hand and a drum stick in the other, occasionally striking a tambourine.

Folks, this isn't a Genesis designed to put on elaborate stage shows full of lighting effects and costumes. Nor is it a Genesis that would be at home in stadiums and arenas, inviting audience participation from crowds of thousands. This is a Genesis built to play in the corner of a coffee shop before being shuffled off the six-inch-tall stage, collecting polite spurts of applause as they depart just in time for some overenthusiastic young woman smelling of patchouli to go up and read a poem she just wrote about her cat. If I didn't know any better, you could play me 'Not About Us' and tell me it was the B-side to Howie Day's 'Collide', and I wouldn't bat an eye.

> **Tony:** I wrote the chorus part, the chords, and everything for it to go with but a large amount of the melody on this during the verses came from Ray...when he was auditioning...we were making him sing...on top of these various bits we had written and one of them was that piece and he pretty much sang what became the first verse. So, to a large extent we used that, and Mike wrote a chorus to go with it, melody and stuff. A lot of people like this track because...I think it is less of a typical Genesis song in many ways, and I think it takes us more towards mainstream. [25]

You know, though it sounds laughable now seeing how much of a commercial flop *Calling All Stations* was, including the single release of 'Not About Us' itself, I don't think Tony was that far off. The late 90s were chock-full of ballads like this one, weren't they? What's 'Truly, Madly, Deeply' by Savage Garden got that 'Not About Us' is lacking? Is there really something so iconic about Duncan Sheik's 'Barely Breathing' that meaningfully sets it apart from this incarnation of Genesis and songs like this one? Not that I've necessarily got anything against either of those songs, but my point is that it's easy to listen to the kinds of things that were getting massive pop radio airplay and chart success around that 1997 timeframe and feel like 'Not About Us' fits right at home with them. Just because the song (released with a whimper as the album's final single, in 1998) didn't enjoy the same kind of success doesn't mean Tony was wrong; this was definitely a more mainstream effort.

Which leads us to the main reason, I think, that Genesis fans tend to trash on the song, and the album in general. *Doesn't sound like Genesis.* I've seen plenty of statements over the years such as "This sounds like any given late 90s band could've done it," and indeed I've spent this entry largely offering my affirmation of that statement. The difference between myself and these fans is, I suppose, that I simply don't care. So what if it sounds like something that could've been released by The Verve, or even The Verve Pipe? Does that make it an inherently worse song? Shouldn't the fact that Mike and Tony managed to become such sonic chameleons something impressive rather than disappointing?

On top of that, I'm not even sure 'Not About Us' *does* sound completely unlike Genesis. I mean, it's totally understandable that people would say this sounds like almost anyone *except* them but listen to those choruses in the studio version of the track. What in the live setting is a lot of straightforward strumming is, in the actual released song, a series of very Banksian chord changes. He's got his foot off the gas, letting everything breathe, but the influence is there if you know what you're listening for. But ultimately, sounding different is precisely why this song exists in the first place. Yes, it "takes us more mainstream," but the mentality was not one of "Let's do what everyone else is doing." It's a mentality of "Let's do something we haven't really done much of before," and that's the way Genesis has always really operated.

Now, if you're the type who thinks pop ballads are trash unworthy to carry the name of Genesis, then sure, there's not much here to like. But if you, like me, happen to enjoy a good adult contemporary ballad, then hey, good news for you: Genesis does it better than most. It's a really pretty tune with good lyrics, and I daresay I'd enjoy it just as much on an album from any other late 90s artist as I would here on *Calling All Stations*. That's not a crime; it's just a good time.

76 - Sign Your Life Away

B-side of 'Not About Us', 1998

In order to talk about why this B-side from 1998 appeals to me, I want to go back to 1970. And if I may be so bold, I'd like to quote someone who not only was no longer with the band by the time this song was released, but whose replacement had *also* departed for greener pastures. Here's Peter Gabriel on the band's mentality going into writing *Trespass*:

> **Peter:** *We were trying always, I think - whether it was church music or whatever the influence, whatever the passion - to try and blend it. Nowadays that seems nothing special. Everyone takes whatever they want. But at that time, music was very segregated. I remember sitting in some...record company, and they were saying, "You have to decide what you want to be. You're a folk group, or you're a blues group," or whatever. "You can't try and cross all these borders and barriers." And I feel that's what I've been doing my entire musical career: whenever someone puts up a barrier, I try and find a way through it.* [3]

Now Peter doesn't always speak for the likes of Tony and Mike; it's pretty clear to me that they've all got different personalities and motivations. But in this I believe they were all on the same page. *Trespass* was the result of a unified band deciding to stop trying to be a pop singles act and to instead begin moving in their own uncharted direction. It was, in essence, a complete re-founding of the band Genesis, now built upon the principles of musical exploration and genre agnosticism. And we see throughout the band's discography, even well after Peter had left, that this mentality never wavered. That's how we got the instrumental focus of *Wind & Wuthering*, the bold experimentation of *Abacab*, and yes, the slick pop sensibilities of *Invisible Touch*.

That leads us to this point here, nearly 23 years after Peter left Genesis - and a few years after Phil Collins had left as well - where we get a song that at first blush seems like an abandonment of those core Genesis ideals, but upon further review actually embodies them as well as anything that came before. Let's dive into the song so I can show you what I mean.

The first sound you hear on 'Sign Your Life Away' is a grungy sort of guitar, very unlike any kind of typical Genesis sound. If anything it sounds like it could be ZZ Top, Billy Gibbons just grinding away. It's nearly thirty seconds of these fuzzy chords, sounding remarkably unlike any Genesis music that's come before. And then the verse starts and the feel changes entirely. The guitar drops out, replaced by understated, beat-keeping chords using a totally different tone. The rhythm evokes memories of reggae; certainly the repeating guitar chord throughout the length of the verse has that kind of structure about it as well. Yet the keyboard work over top of the rest unmistakably carries an 80s pop influence. Just dancing, textural notes that dispense with delusions of melodic grandeur in favour of twinkling atmosphere, complete with the occasional swell of synth choir for dramatic effect. This by itself *is* something Genesis has done before, but in this way? Over that guitar and rhythm pattern? No, that's quite unusual.

Then the chorus hits and that fuzzy guitar sound roars back in. The keyboards continue briefly in their 80s pop vein, though now there's something more about them, like the dancing notes themselves are creating a proper chord that you're just hearing in a non-simultaneous manner. It's hard to describe, but they quickly drop away, leaving the guitar to buzz on its own. Yet then in the second half of the chorus, the keys are back again, this time with a hollow, flutelike synth tone that sounds more New Age than anything else. What is this song, anyway? Is it like instrumental Mad Libs? Did Mike and Tony just write a bunch of sounds and styles onto little strips of paper and then pull them one by one out of a hat until they had something approximating a song?

> **Ray:** *I mean there were bits and pieces of the additional songs that were OK. There was something in ['Sign Your Life Away'], but not enough to justify going the whole way with it. And I think it's great that these songs are available as B-sides or whatever, but they should remain that way.* [26]

Another verse and chorus come and go, normalizing this strange potpourri of sounds, crystallizing the song into its own distinct, decidedly non-Genesisian entity. But wait, what's this bridge? Gosh darnit, *that* sounds like Genesis! The guitar tones, the chord structures, the emotive vocals, the keyboard arpeggio sounds that could be straight out of a Tony Banks solo effort...this is eminently recognisable! Twelve bars of "Ah, I know this band," signalling perhaps a turn back into familiarity...but no. Mike rips back in with the guitar, running a simple riff that might as well be leftover from Van Halen's cover of the Kinks classic 'You Really Got Me'. So...nope. Not quite the Genesis sound after all.

Ray: *Mike wrote that one. I think it was about a dodgy salesman.* [32]

Lyrically I don't find 'Sign Your Life Away' remotely impressive, but musically? Musically this one is something else indeed. Realise that *Calling All Stations* was intended - until Mike called it quits on the band, anyhow - to begin a brand new era of Genesis. With that came a return to the band's ideological roots: pull from the sounds you like, regardless of genre, and put them together to make a piece of music that, by virtue of sounding a little like everything, sounds counterintuitively unique. It is a shame about the lyrics though; the title line sings really well, but on the whole they're a weak effort. Words aren't everything, but a solid set of well-performed lyrics might have catapulted this one much further up my personal list of esteem.

Still though, it's compelling music, and I'd add my voice to the (perhaps relatively small) chorus of fans who would have loved to see where the band might've gone from here had the Third Era of Genesis been allowed to continue. If 'Sign Your Life Away' is the kind of song we got from a first effort, one has to wonder: what strange-yet-effective hodgepodges of sound did we miss out on altogether?

75 - Watcher of the Skies

from *Foxtrot*, 1972

'Watcher of the Skies', to me, is like a bizarro-world sandwich. Think for a moment about the best sandwich you've ever had. I don't care what kind it is: turkey and cheese, chicken salad, veggie delight...doesn't matter. The point is it's the best sandwich that *you've* ever eaten in *your* life. Now think about what made that sandwich so spectacular in your mind. Was the temperature of its contents just that absolutely bang-on ideal value? Did it have exactly the right ratio of ingredients straight down to the condiments? Was the quality of those ingredients impeccable to the last? Was the sandwich packed so fully and evenly that every single bite was sheer perfection?

Whatever it was that stood out to you most, I'm guessing your answer wasn't "really good bread," but *that's* the exact kind of sandwich 'Watcher of the Skies' is for me. It's a decent batch of filling; I like almost all the individual foods that comprise it (could do without the pickles though, if I'm being honest), and they seemed like they'd really go together well. But things didn't quite work out that way, and I don't think I'll be making a sandwich exactly like this one again. Something similar, perhaps, but changes will absolutely be necessary. Wasn't bad per se - some people might really dig it! - just not really my thing personally.

But oh, that bread! Lightly toasted but never burnt, substantial yet never too thick, more flavourful than it has a right to be, and yet somehow doesn't fill you up like you'd expect it to. That's some of the best bread I've ever tasted, and I really hope it wasn't the last of the loaf because I really want to use some more of it on a different, better sandwich. Oh, no? That was it? Those were the last two slices? Well, that's a real shame. Still, I'm glad I got to experience it, and I suppose I'll always look back fondly on that sandwich as being the one and only home of some of the greatest bread I've ever had..

What on earth am I going on about sandwiches for? Well, the bread in this case is the intro and ending. They're the bookends that contain the "proper" song, and they're some of the strongest stuff Genesis has ever done.

>**Steve:** *Those well-known opening chords, to my mind one of the great Mellotron moments of the 20th century, and into the 21st...* [13]

>**Mike:** *[Foxtrot] opens with that 'Watcher of the Skies' sound, which I remember hearing Tony playing those chords...on Italian tour, one of those big sort of Palasports [venues] with the echoes booming, it sounded fantastic. The band was getting some darkness, I think, into the music. I look back on 'Watcher of the Skies', fantastic intro.* [3]

>**Tony:** *People had never heard a big, big sound like that before...I had been searching for chords that actually sounded good on the Mellotron because of its tuning problems, and I happened to settle on these two chords that sounded great, even though they were way out of tune. There was an atmosphere about them that I really liked.* [1]

>**Steve:** *I have come to realise what my effect was on Genesis, particularly with tracks that I didn't write, although influenced in a way that just... gave them a puff of wind, or something. Gave them a little more cohesion or something or other. For instance, 'Watcher Of The Skies', I remember being the one who said "We've got to get a Mellotron, we've got to get a light show..." So...unless I pushed, I don't think we would have inhabited that Mellotron/orchestral region and I think my contribution to that was not harmonically but dynamically and conceptually, if you like.* [30]

Perhaps you, reading this, are of sufficient age, geographical location, and sustained fandom to have had the privilege to have seen Genesis perform this song in concert back in the early 1970s. But chances are you didn't have that opportunity, in which case: can you imagine? Can you imagine being in a darkened theatre ready to see a rock band and then having the auditorium fill up with *that* sound? It must've been unlike anything most of these people had ever experienced at a live show.

>**Tony:** *...It was a great beginning to a live show...We would start off with...that big atmospheric keyboard intro, and Peter would wander on with his bat wings glowing in the UV light and with the eyes shining through. I don't think the audience had ever seen anything like it. I'm a big fantasy fan and I liked the way we were able to create a fantasy on stage.* [1]

> **Peter:** 'Watcher of the Skies' was a very important track to us...Tony was sort of the lead writer on that, with particularly the Mellotron chords, and I did some work on the verses and chorus, but the vibe was sci-fi meets prog, I think. [3]

> **Steve:** It was sort of rock music meets classical music meets a great story, because the idea of the alien aspect...something very compelling about it. It's quite a journey. I always felt that when this was played in large spaces like Italian Palasports for instance, it used to literally shake the foundations, and you did feel as though you were aboard some kind of alien craft. [13]

It was that very alien feeling of the chords that led the band to develop out the middle the way they did. In pursuit of the otherworldly, here's Phil Collins with an interesting rhythm, creeping into the chords, catching the listener entirely by surprise as he breaks the spell that Mellotron holds over you.

> **Phil:** Seems funny to say it now, but I was still going to see Yes every Wednesday at the Marquee, and I was still trying to bring a little bit of that musicianship into the band, the kind of tricky arrangements that they used to have. I said "It's a shame we can't do stuff like that," so I think 'Watcher of the Skies' ended up, certainly the intro was all Tony of course, but that [rhythm], that probably came from somewhere near my drum end. [3]

> **Tony:** Phil started playing a kind of riff in 6/4 underneath while we kept the chords going and tried to develop a song on top of it. [1]

> **Mike:** Rhythm's great...I think that buh-ba-da-bum-bum-bum-bum is a nice sort of groove under those chords. [3]

This is doubtless an exciting way to begin engaging with the "meat" of this sandwich, the entire four minute stretch from 2:18 through 6:19. That crescendo-ing rhythm quickens the pulse and builds fantastic anticipation for what comes next. And what comes next is indeed interesting, if nothing else. It's rhythmically engaging, it's progressively adventurous...and also it's only merely OK. Like an hyperactive frog that can't sit still, the core of the song feels restlessly "jumpy" to me in a way that's almost distracting. It doesn't feel like any of the mini-sections within this extended main body have a chance to coalesce into anything before they're onto the next bit.

That's to say nothing of the lyrical and vocal efforts, as well. With lyrics written by Mike and Tony as a team but delivered by Peter, there's already something of an inherent disconnect there. That's not necessarily a bad thing, though, given the main conceptual thrust of the song.

> **Tony:** Mike and I wrote a sort of sci-fi fantasy lyric... [1]

The ethereal Mellotron chords, the pounding rhythm in an uncommon meter, the stilted delivery of high-falutin' words by a man who didn't write them...these are all elements that do indeed lend themselves well to the notion of an alien being visiting the planet. But does in itself make the music *good*? Ehhhhhh, I'm not so sure.

> **Mike:** The words are a bit suspect. They're kind of OK. Tony and I wrote them. But looking back, it's a little too busy...As the years go by, I think I've learned...you can't just use the words you want to say; they've got to sing well. Those are interesting words, but they didn't sing very well. "Watcher of the skies, watcher of ALL!" That's a STIFF lyric. But a good musical song. [3]

Mike's got it right here, I think. As with some other pieces of the era, the band felt compelled to cram as much "stuff" into this sandwich as they could, and it made the balance of the thing all wrong. Too many things in the mix. Too much of one kind of thing, not enough of another, ingredients that might be tasty by themselves but don't quite taste right in conjunction with one another, all resulting in a sandwich too big to even fit in your mouth anymore. You can take a picture of it and people will say "Whoa, that looks like the best sandwich I've ever seen!" But you who tried to eat it know better.

Look at it this way: if 'Watcher of the Skies' were just a four-minute band piece with those keyboard bookends stripped away, you'd have been reading this entry much earlier in this book. Just one more song lost in that mire of overly busy vocals and a complete lack of space during that five-piece classic era. That's a shame, but also a testament to how outrageously strong the opening and ending of this song are. That "really good bread," those scrumptious bakery delights, they elevate the song so substantially for me that I can overlook a lot of what I otherwise don't care for about 'Watcher of the Skies' in the first place.

The band seems to agree with me. In 1976 on the Trick of the Tail Tour, they closed their set with a medley of '*it.*' and 'Watcher of the Skies'. Except, notably, they cut out the entire central section from 'Watcher' and let those Banksian bookends stand on their own, one pushing straight into the other. Do yourself a favour and check that track out on *Three Sides Live*. It's incredible. What a way to end a show. Inject that stuff straight into my veins, man; if this ain't addition by subtraction I don't know what is. That transition between the intro with the building rhythm and the end section is just so powerful. And then Phil's climactic yell at the end? Mmph. Give me that *every time* over what showed up on *Foxtrot*.

Tony: *I don't think the song ever quite lived up to the promise of the introduction...* [1]

No, Tony. No, it didn't. But in the end, this is the sandwich we have in front of us, complete with some of the best bread that's ever been baked. Is that enough to eat and enjoy it? Well, I can only speak for myself, but I'm feeling pretty darn hungry.

74 - Cuckoo Cocoon

from *The Lamb Lies Down on Broadway*, 1974

I want to tell you about a dream I once had. This was probably, gosh, closing in on 20 years or so ago at this point, but I still remember it vividly. The first thing that was notable about this dream is that, within the dream, I was asleep in my own bed. This is perhaps the most disorienting kind of dream; when the setting of a dream is identical to what is actually occurring in real life, the boundaries between the two can start to blur. Events or visions that might otherwise be regarded as fun or fanciful can instead seem frighteningly real. Keep that in mind.

Now, in this dream, I was sleeping. I was not Dreaming While I Slept so much as Sleeping While I Dreamt, I suppose. At any rate, I then heard an unusual sound that startled me out of my slumber. I opened my eyes and saw only my relatively dark bedroom, looking exactly as I'd expect it to. There was a trickle of moonlight coming through the half-shaded window which, combined with my darkness-adjusted eyes, allowed me to visually discern my surroundings pretty clearly. Seeing that nothing was amiss, I simply listened, trying to see if I might hear again the strange noise that summoned me back to consciousness. If I did, I thought, I could recognise it for whatever mundane thing it may be and, satisfied, return to the depths of sleep. I can't recall how long I listened. Perhaps it was a few minutes; perhaps it was only a few seconds. Either way, I didn't hear the sound repeat - not exactly, anyway. I couldn't have told you what the sound was, but I knew what it was not, and I never heard it again. Yet I did hear something else. Another sound, similar but not exactly the same. If the first one could have been loosely described as a bump, this one was more like a shuffle. A distant, muted kind of shuffle, as though someone were downstairs in the living room, moving an object around on a table or shelf.

As my brain wrapped around this auditory hypothesis, the implication began to prod urgently at my subconscious: *there is an intruder in the house*. More guesses of logical deduction followed: *this individual must be actively searching for valuables*. What other explanation for the noises could there be? My mind flashed briefly to the cat and tried to envision him atop the furniture, playfully pushing a stand-up picture frame across the glass surface of the table that adorned the entryway. *It's not the cat; the cat would be meowing*. My instinct had it right: the cat was old and going out of his mind, and his night time adventures were invariably accompanied by his unmistakable senile braying. No, this was a human being acting with intent. *Do something*.

Here I must remind you that this occurred at a time before cell phones were ubiquitous, so it was not at all unusual that I didn't own one. Unfortunately the nearest landline telephone to me was out of my bedroom, down a hallway with clear view to the living room below, and into another room entirely. Moreover, the floors were pretty creaky on the second story where I was, and it sounded as though my intruder had now made his or her way to the base of the stairs, the hunt for spoils leading to a bookcase adjacent to the landing. *You have to do something*. What could I do? Given the circumstances I almost certainly couldn't sneak out unseen or unheard to call the police, and if this intruder were armed I'd be in a world of trouble. What valuables are worth more than my life? *Do nothing. Don't move.* Ah, now my subconscious had started to come around to my way of thinking; or perhaps it was just too afraid to offer any further input. But I took the advice: I stayed put and resolved to stay vigilant, waiting for an opportunity to make for the phone when and if it presented itself.

Naturally, that's when this burglar began slowly creeping up the stairs. I could tell that they were trying to be quiet about it, but these stairs were old and unsubtle by nature. Every slow step marked a new announcement of the individual's progress towards the second floor. Sometimes when we're so afraid, so intensely focused on one thing, the strangest, calmest thoughts come to us unbidden. So it was that I remember thinking at the time that this burglar was making a really bold move, as climbing the stairs would risk waking anyone who might be up there. And then I recall thinking that it was strange that I should have that thought at that time, scared witless as I was. As I thought about my thoughts, I became suddenly aware of the passage of time; the home invader was now only a couple steps from the top. My bed faced my open doorway, and though I hadn't moved an inch, I could see the frame clear as day. *Don't move. Feign sleep.* But will my open eyes be seen? I hadn't seen any light; didn't that mean the burglar's eyes were adjusted to the dark as well? Would the intruder see that I could see? But wasn't it better to see so I could react, rather than close my eyes and hope for the best, unsure of what was happening? My mind raced circles around these thoughts, coming no closer to figuring out the better option.

It was around that, my most terrified moment, that a new kind of awareness pierced through a veil in my mind: **you are still asleep**. I don't understand precisely *how* I knew, but in that instant I was positive that what I was experiencing was not real. For the briefest of moments I felt an incredible sense of relief. Yet on the intruder came. Only one stair to go now. *Hide. Pretend to sleep. Do not get caught.* You see, a tricky thing about fear is that it doesn't simply disappear without a trace, even when you can rationalise away its source. It's an emotion marked by distinct physiological changes (like an elevated heart rate, for example) that persist even after the original source of the fear is gone. There's a kind of "come down" period to get back to normalcy. In my case, apparently this calming period was going to be marked with a continued potential threat against my life from a phantom attacker, and that just wasn't going to do at all. So I did what I think most reasonable people might try if they found themselves trapped within a lucid nightmare: I resolved to wake up.

It was a good plan, but the problem was that I couldn't seem to execute it. I tried to rouse myself out of bed. I attempted to lift my right arm...nope, no good. Wouldn't budge. My left arm? No, that was stuck too. Legs? Total dead weight. I could feel my muscles straining with exertion but nothing was moving at all; I couldn't even lift my head the slightest fraction. I was sure that if I could just **Get. Up**. then that would end the dream, but I couldn't make it happen. Another creak at the top of the stairs, a shadow in the doorway, and I knew it wasn't not real, but the terror remained. *Why can't I wake up? Why can't I move?*

Finally, whether the trigger was simply an end to my REM cycle or something else, the dream world collapsed all at once. Simultaneously, my poor body shot out of bed like a cannon, what with every muscle having been straining to move and then all that potential energy being released at once. I probably flew a good three feet off my bed onto the floor, creating a very real bump in the night, and had no small amount of embarrassment for it. I would later learn that I experienced a phenomenon known as "sleep paralysis," and that it is well documented as creating harrowing visions. I'm just lucky I've only experienced it two or three times in my life, and that the other times were far more benign than what I've just shared with you.

Anyway, 'Cuckoo Cocoon' is quite a bit like all of that, except it's slightly less scary and features slightly more flute.

> **Steve:** *I wrote most of...'Cuckoo Cocoon'.* [39]

Thanks, Steve!

73 - More Fool Me

from *Selling England by the Pound*, 1973

Tony and Mike have both said more than once - and some of these quotes will appear later in this very book - that when Pete left Genesis they had a lot of confidence in Phil's ability to sing a portion of their material. Specifically, the more pastoral, gentler, romantic side of the band was something they had no doubt could carry on with Pete left, and 'More Fool Me' was their Exhibit A for why that sort of sound could remain successful.

> **Tony:** *Well I think initially what happened was that we sort of thought at a certain point that Phil could probably sing some of the songs. He'd obviously done things like 'More Fool Me' and done a lot of backup singing to Pete on various songs prior. We knew he had a lovely soft voice.* [3]

Of course, Phil had sung lead on one Genesis song prior to 1973 as well: 'For Absent Friends' from *Nursery Cryme*. But that song was the result of Phil and Steve doodling together as the so-called "junior members" of the band. 'More Fool Me' instead came from the mind of Mike Rutherford, a "senior member" with a bit more sway. This was Mike taking the proven concept of "Phil can sing a gentle song" and working with the drummer to toss a song together specifically for him to sing, working to really integrate Phil's voice into the "core" Genesis sound, at least inasmuch as Mike's writing represented a more meaningful chunk of that larger whole as far as the likes of Genesis themselves were concerned..

> **Mike:** *'More Fool Me' was a song that Phil and I wrote, and which Phil would sing on stage. It was the first thing Phil and I had written together, and although Phil had come into the band with no desire to write, it felt easy, intuitive. Nothing was ever laboured with Phil: he'd work fast, he'd write fast, he'd record fast. He was completely opposite to the rest of us.* [14]

> **Peter:** *Phil wrote all the lyrics and Mike did the music - it's a little love song which is quite a breakthrough.* [60]

In my previous entry for 1997's 'Not About Us' I lightly insinuated that that song was essentially the band's first foray into a true acoustic ballad. While that assertion was only half true from the Mike side of the fence for reasons dealing in differences of style between a song like 'More Fool Me' and that latter effort, for Tony it was true through and through. After all, his involvement on 'More Fool Me' was literally non-existent.

> **Tony:** *'More Fool Me', I had nothing to do with that. I didn't even play on it but I quite like it.* [6]

And of course, I wasn't really counting a song like 'Horizons' in that claim either, being as it is effectively a Steve Hackett solo number with the Genesis name attached. But here's 'More Fool Me', right in the heart of the peak progressive era of the band, featuring Mike and Phil creating this wonderful little acoustic ditty with a tasteful touch of backing vocals from Pete. It's a terrific bit of fresh air amidst the often complex and at times overcrowded music of the early Genesis library.

> **Steve:** *[A] little acoustic track, just one acoustic guitar and Phil Collins singing. But because Genesis had two extraordinary lead singers at that time and they had similar voices - they both were powerful rock singers - people thought that that was Peter Gabriel. So good in one way, but in another I guess that might have been a little bit miffing for Phil back then...Compared to modern day progressive stuff, I think there was tremendous emphasis on the romance of those songs.* [45]

The band must've agreed about its merits, because they even played it live! One imagines Tony sitting at his Hammond organ just surreptitiously doing a crossword puzzle while Phil wanders out in his overalls to sing countertenor. It's bizarre but so pure and magical.

> **Mike:** *The first time Phil came out front from behind his drum kit to sing, he put on a white jacket which, because he was wearing white dungarees, made him look like a painter, but from the word go people liked him. Before he even sang a note, people cheered.* [14]

> **Phil:** *I'm not going to go onstage for the first time as singer wearing something not* me. *Workman's overalls it is.* [12]

Ironically considering the import I'm giving this song as a foreshadowing of things to come, I think my favourite element of 'More Fool Me' is those previously mentioned backing vocals courtesy of Genesis' *actual* lead singer of the era. We've heard Phil singing harmony to Pete any number of times, of course, and on things like 'Harold the Barrel' they're doubled up for pretty much the whole thing. But here instead of cloning or doubling we get really strong two-part harmony lines like "except when things weren't going your way," followed then by some even stronger three-part harmony: Phil overdubbed on the lead and high lines, Pete on the low ones. Meanwhile the guitar lands at a layer between them all, which makes the thing sound rather like a full *four-part* harmony. I mean, at that point you're basically a choir, right?

As a former long-time choral singer myself, that sort of arrangement really gets me jazzed, and the boys sound uniformly great throughout. The hesitance, choppiness, and tuning issues that defined the band's attempts at strong vocal harmony during the *From Genesis to Revelation* are long gone now, and thank goodness for that. If anything from the five-piece progressive era of the band feels like it could have flown out of the same songwriting veins as the stuff on that debut, 'More Fool Me' is probably it. It's amazing what a little skill, experience, and polish can do for a sound, even a mere few years later.

That said, I'm not sure I'd go so far as to say I wish Genesis did a bunch more songs *like* 'More Fool Me'. Give me ten albums of this kind of thing and you'll probably lose my interest somewhere along the way. But I'm extremely glad they did *this* song, and that it sits where it does on the band's timeline, right in the middle of a progressive masterpiece where listeners are forced to reckon with it. Frequently overlooked on an album of greats, I think Phil's second brief stint as frontman ought to be considered a classic in its own right.

72 - Mama

from *Genesis*, 1983

And now, an oral history of 'Mama', told in the band's own words.

Tony: *This time, we didn't play each other anything we'd had before. And the songs just kind of evolved. We started putting things down on tape as soon as they took any kind of shape. It was an exciting way to work. You can get more spontaneity that way. Sometimes, when you get a song beforehand and go into rehearsals with it, develop parts for it, and end up changing it, you overwork it. This time we didn't really develop things in quite the same way. We tended to try and get them down in the freshest form possible. That's why some of 'Mama' is so simple. We started from a drum box and everything else was added to enhance that.* [23]

Mike: *When we were in the studio, we had a drum machine because it was nice for Phil to sing as well as just play the drums. The way it worked was the drum machine would start with a little loop or pattern. It kept us in time and gave us a feel.* [58]

Phil: *I suppose 'Mama' is a song that most people, because it's drum machine based, everyone thinks it's my thing, but actually Mike was the one who came up with that early Linn drum machine sound, with it going through the gated reverb.* [3]

Mike: *The tune had begun with a drum loop I'd written in the soundproofed spare bedroom at home. I put it through my Boogie amplifier and distorted it so much that it nearly fell off the stand. That was something an American musician would never do, I always thought. Take a sound and really fuck it up.* [14]

Phil: *Typical Rutherford, really, you got the beat on the wrong part of the bar. So instead of being on the back beat, it was like this: oozh ku-GAH oov-oozh ku-GAH... And you know, it was an extraordinary sound.* [43]

Tony: *These poor little amplifiers just jumping over the ground...but it produced this fantastic sound. It made the drum machine sound really, really good.* [3]

Mike: *We had got the drum pattern playing in the studio and Tony started with his dark, low sustained chords, and then we just jammed on it for half an hour, recording as we were playing. We had known that if we caught the song as it came into being we might catch some magic.* [14]

Tony: *Once we heard it we knew, "That's a good song, we don't really need any more." I added a dark, atmospheric drone down at the bottom of it and a spooky sound on one of the synthesizers.* [1]

Phil: *It was the early days of taking a MIDI cable out of the back of the drum machine, plugging it into a keyboard. So if you had a cowbell going [on a rhythm], and Tony put his hand on the keyboard, it would just play the rhythm [while Tony] play[ed] the notes.* [3]

Tony: *We had various versions of it. We had the drum machine part, and then just sort of, bass pedal, put all these sounds on top of it. We had an atmosphere going which we knew was going to be strong, but we didn't know quite what the top line was going to be. It could've been a lot of things and still been good.* [3]

Phil: *I was into this John Lennon 'Be-Bop-A-Lula' echo thing, "I...can't see..."* [3]

Tony: *I had this way of pulsing the keyboard in time with the drum machine, and when we put all those ingredients together and Phil bluesed some vocals on top of that, it sounded really strong.* [1]

Mike: *Phil would just sing and improvise and little things came out like lyrical sounds and phrases. The word 'Mama' is a great example of one of the sounds that came out. Sometimes the words are there right from the start and you carry on from that.* [58]

Tony: *Phil was sort of singing along as we went. That phrase, "can't you see me, mama" was there quite early. So it all evolved together. That's one advantage to using rhythm machines when you haven't got an actual drummer in the group. Phil can sing and you can still get a feel for where everyone's heading right from the word go.* [23]

Phil: *A lot of the lyrics just came because of the sound of the voice with the echo. That's, you know, those were the lyrics. "But I knooooow you're always there. Oh to tou-ch!" It was the "tou-ch!" that set the echo off. And it's kind of, you play with the sound, and that's how the words were written.* [43]

Tony: *It was slightly simpler, sustained a mood perhaps. But I still felt it was an essentially Genesis kind of thing, sustained chords, and dramatic, which has always been Genesis' thing.* [43]

Phil: *['Mama'] is just about a young teenager that's got a mother fixation with a prostitute that he's just happened to have met in passing and he has such a strong feeling for her and doesn't understand why she isn't interested in him.* [61]

Tony: *I remember playing it to my wife and she goes "You've got to lose the laugh, it's terrible." I said, "No, no! That's the key! That's the hook!" And I think it is! I think that's sort of ultimately the thing that people remember about that song.* [43]

Phil: *[Our producer] Hugh Padgham had brought in this record that had just come out by Grandmaster Flash [and the Furious Five], which was 'The Message', which he put on. It's hard to believe now, but it's the early days of rap, so no-one had really heard this stuff. [Lead rapper Melle Mel] had this [line] "It's like a jungle sometimes, it makes me wonder how I keep from going under...ha-ha, ha!" And we all thought it was great, you know this laugh, with such character.* [3]

Mike: *The evil laugh was Phil's idea. He had said he wanted to do something like 'The Message'...* [14]

Phil: *We just happened to be going back into the studio after having listened to it, to do 'Mama'. And so we were improvising our way around [the song] and then every now and again I'd go "Hah-hah, heh!" The guys would laugh...* [3]

Tony: *It was just a sort of joke and it sounded so good we had to put it somewhere and it soon became a feature of the song. I love moments like that, where it is not even written.* [6]

Phil: *It became a thing! It became kind of the hook of the song. And it's all because of Grandmaster Flash [and the Furious Five]. You ask most Genesis fans that and that would be a million miles away. But that's how it happened.* [3]

Mike: *Phil was always more musically aware than Tony and me, and would get out and see bands much more than we did...I saw our insularity as a strength: when we played and wrote together we realised how unique each one of us was musically, and how unique we sounded as a band.* [14]

Tony: *'Mama' was one of those songs that obviously had to build. It was a question of what to build to. My idea was to have very minimalist chords throughout the song and then at a certain point bring in these massive major chords - I thought that would do the trick.* [1]

Mike: *'Mama' is a great example of...how the album worked. The version of 'Mama' that's there was recorded very early on...so you captured spontaneity for the first time, actually. You captured us kind of writing things and playing them very early on. And recording them, rather than finishing the song and going in to record them somewhere else later.* [3]

Phil: *This was a period of continual rise.* [1]

Mike: *['Mama' is] the best song on the album...too brave for American radio, but I was very gratified when it came out in the UK and went straight to number 4.* [14]

As for me, some of my own fondest Genesis memories are of driving home from work, playing my "official bootleg" of the 2007 Turn It On Again Tour show I attended, and irresponsibly shredding my vocal cords by belting along with 'Mama', creepy laugh and all. This happened with quite a bit of regularity; my voice would become hoarse and I'd need to take a few days off from car-singing to give it a rest, and then as soon as I felt it was in decent shape again, "HA-HAH HEH!" If my ill-fated singing career hadn't already been over by then, it almost certainly wouldn't have survived my 'Mama' commutes.

No regrets!

71 - Squonk

from *A Trick of the Tail*, 1976

It's nearly impossible to overstate the importance of 'Squonk' to Genesis, and by extension to anyone who is a fan of any of the band's music after Peter Gabriel left, because 'Squonk' is the song that propelled Phil Collins into the lead vocalist role. This also means it's nearly impossible to talk about 'Squonk' without getting into the vocalist transition. While I don't want to make that the focus of this entry, it is a story worth summing up, so I'll let the band handle that work.

> **Tony:** *We thought things like 'Ripples' and 'Mad Man Moon', things like that would be great for his voice. We never even contemplated that he'd be right for 'Squonk' or '[Dance on a] Volcano', these things that require a bit more power. And yes, we'd obviously recorded the song, and we did get this singer that we liked, and he came in and sang on it.* [3]

> **Phil:** *He was our big hope...So we laid down all the backing tracks and invited this guy in to sing. 'Squonk' was the first one.* [3]

> **Mike:** *The poor guy battled through but it was never going to work.* [14]

> **Phil:** *The first line of that vocal is a bitch: "Like father, like son..." We don't ask for his key or range. We just give it to him... Poor guy. It's not remotely his key... Looking back, I feel bad... I've been that soldier that has to sing the song in the key I'm given. In those days, though, we didn't even consider that an issue.* [12]

> **Steve:** *The guy had a perfectly good voice, he just wasn't right for the part. And so, I remember Mike and Tony saying to Phil, "What do you think Phil?" and he said, "I'll tell you what I think; I think it sounds fucking average. Let me have a go..."* [30]

> **Phil:** *I knew I could do it but I didn't want to force the others into letting me do it.* [62]

The rest is history, but rather than talk at length about what finally pulled Phil out from behind the drum kit for good, I'd like to talk about 'Squonk' as a bit of music. It's no surprise that this was the song the band chose to try out new singers: if you as an aspiring lead vocalist can nail 'Squonk', you can do pretty much anything the band might ask you to. The problem is that nailing 'Squonk' is an almost unreasonably high bar for a potential frontman to clear. Heck, Phil only got the job because he was *close enough* and could sing in the same key as the song, not because his voice was bang-on perfect for the job.

> **Mike:** *It sounds strange to say now, but Phil's voice then was not the voice it would become...The truth was that in 1976 Phil had a pure, choirboy voice, whereas Pete had an R&B raunch, which was what you needed for a song like 'Squonk'. After a little more unchoirboy-like living - life on the road, drinking and drugs - Phil got the raunch too, but back then he was still a bit too healthy.* [14]

This isn't to say Phil sounds even remotely bad on the track, but the song opens with that big drum and cymbal flare surrounding that pounding bass pedal. It's an atmosphere of pure oomph right from the get go. And likewise the vocals come straight in on the highest note of the whole song. That's extremely unusual; vocal parts tend to climax in a bridge or somewhere near the end of a song, and higher notes, when produced with the chest voice as opposed to a gentler falsetto, will generate more power. So it's pretty typical for a song to begin in a lower vocal register then slowly build in vocal intensity until that climactic moment where the highest notes are delivered with as much strength as the vocalist can muster, before the song scales things back down.

'Squonk' has no interest in any of that. It's gonna hit you in the mouth with the rhythm section at the start and then knock out any remaining teeth when the singer jumps in hitting his most powerful notes right at the start. Turning on this song is like standing behind a jet engine that you thought was a regular desk fan. It's an unexpected and potentially excessive blast of force hitting you, and that leaves an enormously strong impression.

> **Steve:** *I remember doing Madison Square Garden, we were using ['Squonk'] as an opener. And I remember going on stage, and the whole audience standing up as we kicked in with the first strains of that. That was a really powerful live number.* [3]

There is a drawback, however, to opening a song by unleashing everything you've got, and that is that it can be difficult for the rest of the song to hold up. Any ultimate reduction of power over the course of the runtime and the result is that the track peaks in its first few seconds, leaving the listener feeling as though everything after the start was weak by comparison. Think Ozzy Osbourne's 'Crazy Train'. Great song all the way through mind you, but does the bulk of it ever manage to live up to that fantastic introduction? I don't think it does; the moment the verse comes in you've already experienced the best the song has to offer.

> **Tony:** *For 'Squonk', Mike and I had been driving in a car somewhere in Germany and heard this song on the radio. Not being people who keep our ears to the ground, we said "This is fantastic, the drum sound is just so good," but we didn't know who it was. Afterwards we found out it was 'Kashmir' by Led Zeppelin, from the Physical Graffiti album. I'd never heard anything like this and I thought, "I want our drums to be that big." Mike and I played it to Phil and asked him to try the sound on 'Squonk'. We didn't quite get the sound we wanted but we did capture the slow tempo feel which produced a song that worked very well live, better live in fact than on the record.* [1]

So you can't let the power decline, but you've opened with everything you've got, so by definition you also can't increase it. This leaves you with very little choice but to attempt to *sustain* the power of the first few bars over the remaining length of the song. Indeed this is the choice that Genesis made. It's an unenviable task that they made quite a bit more difficult on themselves by having the song run for six-ish minutes. Now that extra time did allow them to block off some softer sections for contrast - places where the power is *expected* to be lessened with the hope that returning to the powerful bit will carry the same weight of impact as it did initially - but this is a bit of a fool's errand. Trying to deliver the full oomph all the way through a song that long is a noble but fairly unobtainable goal. That Genesis even mostly succeeds with 'Squonk' is a testament to their songwriting chops.

> **Phil:** *'Squonk' was a musical standout. I've always liked that. That was always our [Led] Zeppelin kind of song. Kind of a bit of 'Kashmir', a bit of 'When the Levee Breaks'. When you listen to it, it doesn't sound like that, but that's what it was meant to be. These heavy guitar chords, me with my John Bonham hat on. So I think that's probably one of the standout tracks [of the album].* [3]

I think on some level they realised this themselves: 'Squonk' doesn't try to carry that power all the way through its ending but instead takes a surprising, pleasant, happy turn with its final measures, fading out on joyous strains that tell the listener the barrage is over. Which is perhaps an ironic choice, given that the subject matter of the tune is a North American cryptid so ashamed of its own ugliness that it weeps incessantly, providing a track of tears that a skilled hunter can follow to capture it. Like the creature of myth, the titular squonk of this Genesis number dissolves into a pool of its own tears when captured, leaving no trace of its existence but the moisture left behind. I mean, the final lines of the piece reflect on the notion that the squonks are nearing extinction as a race, that the world is a cruel and unfair place, and that the chief constant of the squonk's life is that it will always be miserable.

Perfect material for a cheery little fadeout, right? Ah well, I suppose Genesis was simply in a good mood in late 1975 and nothing was going to break them out of it.

> **Mike:** *By the time...we'd also written the start of 'Squonk'...I knew we were going to be okay. If we could write this sort of stuff, any doubt I had - that any of us had - about carrying on [without Peter] was dispelled.* [14]

I think this is all why I really like 'Squonk' but don't quite love it. The transition on *A Trick of the Tail* from 'Entangled' into 'Squonk' is so incredibly strong, and then we get a song that tries desperately to maintain that energy, but falls just a little short of pulling it off. It's got an interesting lyric about a fantastical creature, though between Phil's semi-strained vocals and the reverb effects it can be hard at times to make sense of them. "He's a shy one, he's a sly one...doo-be-doo?" And then there's a bit of a mismatch between the emotional tone of the lyrics and the music itself, especially at the end.

Still though, what 'Squonk' lacks in these areas for me it definitely makes up for in others. It's got terrific drive, a good melody, a strong identity of sound, and an opening bar that will blast you into the next room over. That's more than good enough for me.

70 - Counting Out Time

from *The Lamb Lies Down on Broadway*, 1974

Genesis is a band that never took itself too seriously. About the quality of their music, sure, but the music itself never needed to be serious along the way. This was especially true during the Peter Gabriel years, with lots of character pieces and silly concepts driving material from 'Harold the Barrel' to 'The Battle of Epping Forest' and everything in between. Songs like 'Pigeons' and 'I Can't Dance' proved that this levity was a feature of the band and not Gabriel specifically, but no Genesis song is as purely funny in my book as 'Counting Out Time' from Peter's swan song with the band.

Chronologically the first song in the story of Rael (despite being the ninth song on the album), 'Counting Out Time' is a flashback to a simpler time. It's a time before aerosol paint and chain gangs and hairy hearts, and a time long before ravens and ravings and ravines. It's a time of innocence, when Rael was so nervous about his first sexual encounter that he bought a book and tried desperately to follow its "instructions" to the letter. The lyric "I'll get my money back from the bookstore right away" is a tremendous punchline, always deeply amusing no matter how many times I've heard the track.

Musically it sounds pretty straightforward when you listen to it, despite the first half of the verses being in a sneaky 13/8 time. While some might register that as a criticism, I think the ease this song exudes is perfect for it.

> **Steve:** *I think 'Counting Out Time' was the nearest thing to a single on the album, but it was a trifle risqué...Possibly not as strong as it could be musically. I think you need a bit more of a hook than just [the riff of] da-dum-da-dum-da-daaa-dum.* [3]

> **Tony:** *Well I think 'Counting Out Time' is played because it's a pop song...that was a song of Pete's, actually. I think [it's] a good little song. It's good in context of the album, because it's simpler compared to a lot of the other things.* [3]

It's got a bouncy, jaunty rhythm going, exuding anticipation for the coming events. There's no real chorus contrasting with a verse, so much as a Section A and Section B that alternate between confident excitement and intense concentration on making sure all those diagrams are hit in sequence. If they don't quite flow perfectly into one another, well, that's all right too: chalk it up to the nerves and inexperience of someone's first time. Then you get Steve's guitar solo acting as a stand-in for the act itself, and the guitar sound is just as laughably ridiculous as one imagines Rael's performance might be.

> **Steve:** *The guitar synthesizer called a Hi-Fli, it's excellent for little jokey sounds. I used it in the thing on 'Counting Out Time'...people wondered what it was, if it was a synthesizer or a voice, or if it was a kazoo. I said, "No, it's a guitar solo." The particular sound that I got...had a setting where you would hit a note, and it would alter the actual pitch of the note: ride it above, and then below. So it would be like a vibrato.* [63]

Nothing here needs to be complex, so nothing is, but that simplicity allows the various moods to take the fore. It's a much stronger song as is than it would be with a long, proggy section anywhere in the middle, or a grand intro, or a guitar solo that sounds "good," and not like a set of tuned whoopie cushions exhaling in sequence. I don't think *The Lamb* really needs 'Counting Out Time' narratively, but musically and lyrically? It brings a much-needed lightness to the album, and a smile to my face.

69 - Dusk

from *Trespass*, 1970

All right, let's all be honest with ourselves for a moment: if the triangle as a percussion instrument disappeared completely from the history of the music, would you even miss it? In search of justification for the triangle's existence, I searched out a video tutorial on how to play it. Surely, I thought, there must be some hidden techniques that only masters of the craft know. The video was two minutes long, and the primary thrust of it was "hold the triangle and hit it with the metal stick." I was disappointed, but not exactly surprised. Now, that isn't to say there is no such thing as skillful triangle playing: I watched another video featuring an individual who couldn't be called anything but an accomplished percussionist, and this guy was really maximizing his instrument. Clasping the top of the triangle to mute the sound or let it ring, landing all the striking angles both inside and out, playing complex rhythms at speed... but come on. Who are we really fooling here? In the end it's still just "shades of ting," right? There's footage of famed conductor, composer, and educator Leonard Bernstein rehearsing with an orchestra, beside himself because the triangle doesn't sound the way he wants it to and apparently never will. Fans of Nintendo games probably most closely associate the triangle with a dopey gorilla named Chunky Kong, who played it solely for comedic effect in a game called Donkey Kong 64; yet the audio soundbite the game played found a way to be annoying anyhow.

Why am I going on and on about triangles? Because it's the only thing 'Dusk' really gets wrong in my eyes. Each tinny little dagger is a piercing distraction from the otherwise masterfully idyllic scene being painted; everything else about this track is just splendid. Ant and Mike are both playing their 12-string guitars - that's 24 strings total for those of you counting at home - and weaving a really well-defined atmosphere out of them. This entire song is a *[TING!]* mood, and it excels in that vein.

> **Peter:** *The folk sound of it was definitely from Ant and Mike and this 12-string combination. I think that was really quite innovative, and I loved it and tried to encourage it from my point of view. They'd do these things where they'd get a composite chord - this is getting technical here - but one guitar would be playing one chord, and [the other guitar] another chord, and you'd read the final chord as a composite of the two. Very boring for most people, but the effect of that was to give us a sound that was I think quite unique, and early on we had one local paper who described us as "folk/blues/mystical."* [3]

For all that interweaving of guitars, the standout element of 'Dusk' to me is the chorus, if you can even call it that. Providing wonderful contrast to Pete's emotional yet reserved vocals during the verses, the chorus is, well, choral. Pete's still there in the mix but his voice is blending almost seamlessly with Ant's and Tony's. Mike might be in there too; he's credited on the album with backing vocals but I can't tell if he's in this particular mix. At any rate *[TING!]*, it's gorgeous. We like to rag on the guys behind the lead for their vocal prowess or lack thereof, but this performance is just mesmerizing. Perhaps the key is to just only let them sing in unison.

> **Ant:** *Mike and I had already written the basic parts of 'Dusk'...We sat and played in a circle and people would come and sit and listen in the middle which is a great way to listen to a band because you have a completely equal sound. After the summer of doubts, we were in a very positive frame of mind.* [1]

And of course, there's the instrumental section at 2:05. It's got drive, it's got flute, it's got...triangle...ugh...and it's got a few different little feelings of its own. While not as drawn out as we might expect a true "progressive instrumental" bit to be, it doesn't lose anything for the brevity. Quite the opposite in fact: its self-restraint gives the song just the right amount of contrast without ever fully losing sight of the magic that defined the piece initially.

Perhaps because there are only a few sections in play here, on a song that runs merely four minutes and change, 'Dusk' also transitions between bits remarkably well for its place in Genesis history. A lot of the musical transitions in a more progressive-oriented work, especially this early in the *[TING!]* band's career, can be abrupt. "Just mash this section up against this other section and call it a day." If there seems to be a sense to the transitions, it's often only because we as fans of the song have come to expect those transitions to come, and thus they "feel right" because we're already so accustomed to them. The instrumental break in 'Dusk' is different because it "feels right" on the very first listen. When it enters there's just a sense of "Ah, here it is." And then it departs very naturally as well, going straight back into the final verse before it's overstayed its welcome.

Tony: *[Some of the songs on Trespass] don't quite do as much for me anymore as they once did. I always felt 'Dusk' was a bit of a B track, though it sounds OK.* [3]

I often see 'Dusk' called out by both Genesis fans and Tony Banks alike as the weak point of *Trespass*, and I suppose it's easy to understand why. Songs like 'Looking for Someone' and 'Stagnation' dove further into that progressive mould. 'The Knife' was a huge live standout. 'Visions of Angels' was at least a holdover from the late 60s, so it carried with it a feeling of real growth for the band. 'White Mountain' had a lively organ part for Tony to play. Amidst all that, here's 'Dusk', shortest song on the album by a full two and a half minutes, committing fully to its nature as a sort of prog folk haze, dwelling in a *[TING!]* mood and content to not try for much more. For fans of more adventurous fare (and keyboardists, I suppose), maybe this song doesn't have that much to offer.

For me, though, 'Dusk' is affirmatively a highlight of *Trespass*. Not exactly my favourite off the album - the mosquito-like nuisance of the triangle makes sure of that - but a highlight all the same.

68 - Back in N.Y.C.

from *The Lamb Lies Down on Broadway*, 1974

In this entry I'm going to talk about album flow. This is maybe a little bit of a dry subject, granted, but I think when you're a band faced with creating a double LP consisting of 23 tracks, it's a major consideration. And we already know that there were cases on *The Lamb*, some of which still to come in this book, where a piece of music was written specifically because two *other* pieces of music needed to be linked together. So I feel this is a worthwhile discussion to have, and I want to focus specifically on how the four sides of *The Lamb Lies Down on Broadway* cohere to one another. What better time to do that than now, with the first track of the second side of that grand album?

The first thing we've got to remember is that these were the 1970s. Even a single album running a mere 30-40 minutes was required by sheer necessity of the vinyl medium to be cut in half. Listeners couldn't just stream the whole thing or even pop in a CD to get the entire album at once. Thus, mindful bands had to think about how to arrange their albums' track orders so that each "side" was both coherent and not overstuffed with music; too much runtime on one side and you'd jeopardise the sound quality. Outside of that general consideration, up until this point in Genesis' history their primary consideration in album construction had seemed to be "Open each side with something strong." The idea is that someone starting the album halfway through (whether by choice or just putting the record on the turntable upside down) would still get some kind of immediate aural treat, even if not quite as strong a one as they would with the album's proper opener.

But concept double albums are a different beast, aren't they? They're by their very nature all connected, and so you ideally want some sort of "sonic glue," if you will, to hold the sides together. Later bands would take this to the extreme: British progressive act IQ (a personal favourite of mine, and if you're reading this book, likely you'll enjoy them too) split their 1997 concept album *Subterranea* in half by literally taking the same song and playing it two different ways, once at the end of the album's first half, and once again to open its second half. But of course, that was in the CD age when a double album meant only one break. Genesis in the vinyl hey-day of 1974 needed not one link between two halves of the musical whole, but *three* links between *four* quarters. A much more difficult thing to manage effectively.

Sides 3 and 4 of *The Lamb Lies Down on Broadway* have arguably the weakest linkage between them, existing only in the album's meta-narrative. Rael's encounter with the lamia of Side 3 is the catalyst for the physical transformation he experiences in 'The Colony of Slippermen' opening Side 4, but beyond that detail there isn't much of a segue into that final block of music. This may be part of why Side 4 feels at times to me like a bit of a let-down, meandering and disconnected whereas the first three sides of *The Lamb* feel much more focused.

Sides 2 and 3 tie together more overtly, thanks entirely to the effort of 'Lilywhite Lilith' to make them work in tandem. That song opens with an immediate musical climb that makes it feel not like a new song is starting but like we're joining a conversation mid-sentence. It puts you right in the midst of what's going on, aided further by the fact that the lyrical setting hasn't changed; we find ourselves still in the previous track's titular Chamber of 32 Doors. The first line of 'Lilywhite Lilith' reinforces this explicitly: "The Chamber was in confusion..." This is Genesis making *absolutely sure* they haven't lost you while you were re-sleeving one record and lining up another one. "We know you just spent 30 seconds fussing with that needle arm, but don't worry, you haven't missed anything! We pick up precisely where we left off..."

But what about that break between Sides 1 and 2? Well, that one's a bit more subtle in its delivery, but I'd argue it's the strongest transition of them all. Let's start with the very first thing you hear as Side 2 of *The Lamb* begins. Though the notes are different, that low, rhythmic bass line that opens 'Back in N.Y.C.' has an identical pulsing pattern to the one that kicks off 'In the Cage' from a couple tracks prior. This is no coincidence. It's an intentional call-back that evokes that "caged" kind of mood, though it's stealthy enough that most listeners won't be consciously aware of it. It's a form of aural manipulation, really, putting the listener into a state of mind that they've been trained to reach through the introduction to that earlier song. And for these purposes, it's a thematic link that makes 'Back in N.Y.C.' feel immediately familiar and of one mind with the album's first side.

There's something bigger that I want to talk about here too, a much larger framework that Side 1 of *The Lamb* sets up so that 'Back in N.Y.C.' can deliver on it. This gets down to the skeletal structure of the songs themselves. See, the first quarter of *The Lamb* exists as a kind of ebb and flow of aggression, with the title track encapsulating that feeling within itself - the aggression peaks with "I'm not your kind, I'M RAEL!" and valleys with "The lamb seems right out of place..." A fine way to construct a song certainly, but if we step back a bit and look at the bigger picture I think we'll find that the other tracks of Side 1 display that same pattern on a larger scale: 'Fly on a Windshield' starts off mellow and then cracks with a fierceness, before blending back into the moderation of 'Broadway Melody of 1974', and then the gentleness of 'Cuckoo Cocoon'. Then 'In the Cage' itself opens with warmth and tenderness before it too blows up in musical panic.

A non-track interlude at the end of that song brings us down once more only, for 'The Grand Parade of Lifeless Packaging' to start anew, building up from nearly nothing all the way to a peak of ferocity that ends the side.

Note that I use the term "aggression" here instead of something like "intensity" or "power," because you can have something very intense or very powerful that is inherently joyful. There's not a lot of pure joy on *The Lamb* to go around, however, so while they're related concepts, they're not identical. Now, if you were to take Side 1 of *The Lamb* and chart its musical aggression over time (an admittedly subjective exercise, in part), you'd see the very series of peaks and valleys I've been discussing. And indeed, I think this visualization is so worth seeing that I've created one for us:

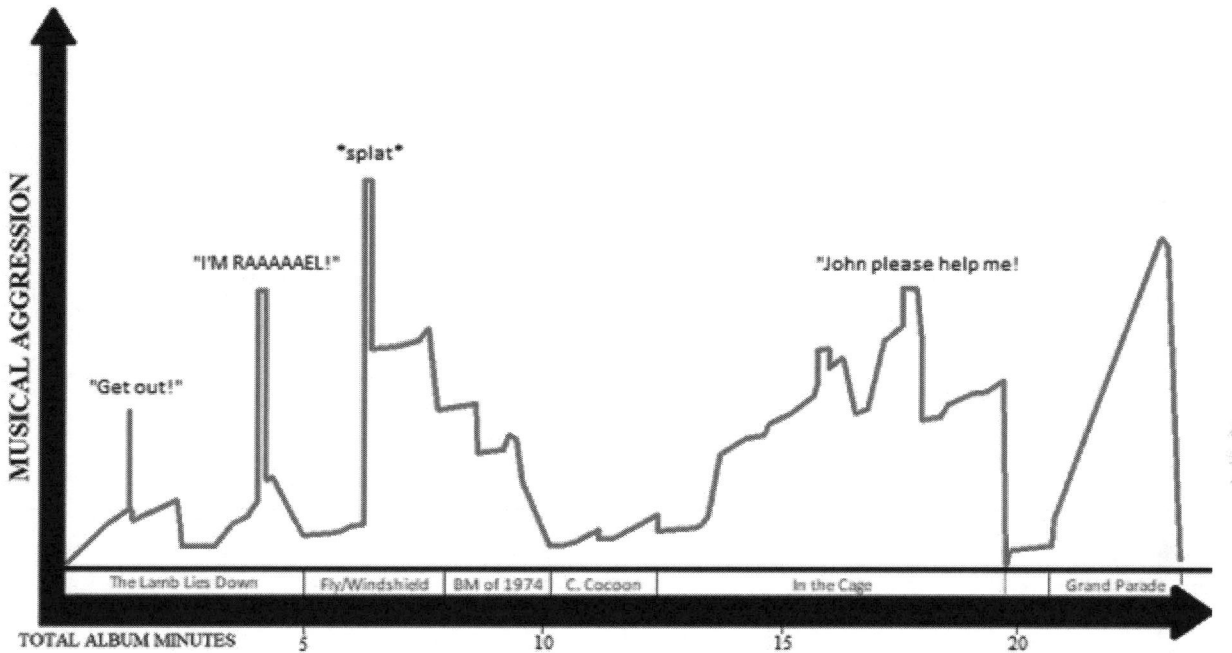

Your first thought might be "Hey, this looks super messy," and you'd be right. I tried to catch every change in aggression over the album's side, no matter how minor, so there are lots of tiny spikes and bigger hits; the biggest ones I've labelled so it's clear at a glance what's happening at those moments. But I figure a simplified view that smooths out all those tiny spikes would probably be useful too, so I went ahead and made that as well:

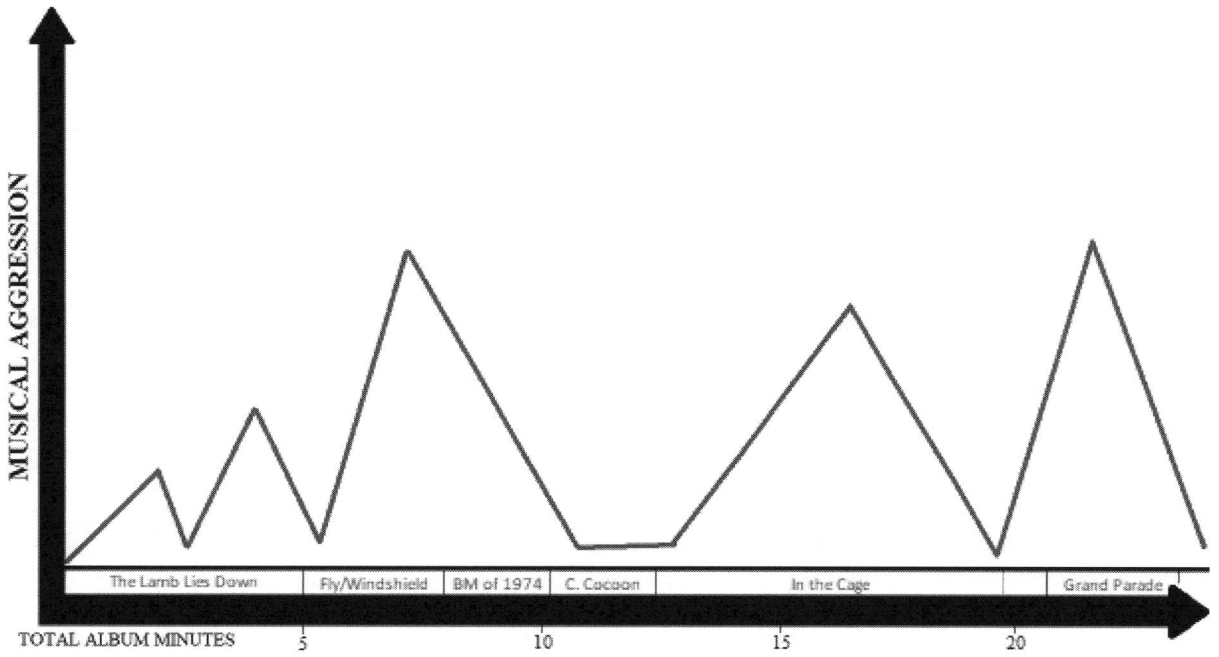

Now it should become a little more clear what's happening over the course of the whole of Side 1: there is an initial build-up to a small peak in aggression, then a relaxation, then a second build to a higher peak, then another relaxation, and then a third, bigger peak (albeit this time without much build-up at all; 'Fly on a Windshield' takes no prisoners). This all occurs between the opening track and the first half of 'Fly on a Windshield'. The second half of that song eases off the throttle - it has to, after a "bang" like that - and we get an extended valley where 'Cuckoo Cocoon' is allowed to dream peacefully for a spell. From there the pattern returns yet seems to stretch, with a higher starting point than the first time around: a higher peak with a more gradual build and a correspondingly longer decline, then once again a taller peak still. We aren't actively aware of it as listeners, but after that second "new" peak (the end of 'The Grand Parade of Lifeless Packaging'), we're now *expecting the pattern to continue.* That is, we're expecting another big valley and then the third peak in the pattern, and we're expecting that peak of aggression to be bigger than anything of the others we've heard so far.

And so, on Side 2, we get 'Back in N.Y.C.' delivering the most aggression on the entire album. That its graph looks sort of like a big city skyline is just a happy coincidence, but it's a highly appropriate one that I'm sure the Genesis lads would be all too happy to take credit for. "Oh, yeah, we definitely wrote that song to 'look' like a city skyline, you got it!" In any case, one thing is pretty clear: 'Back in N.Y.C.' is a very "spiky" song in general.

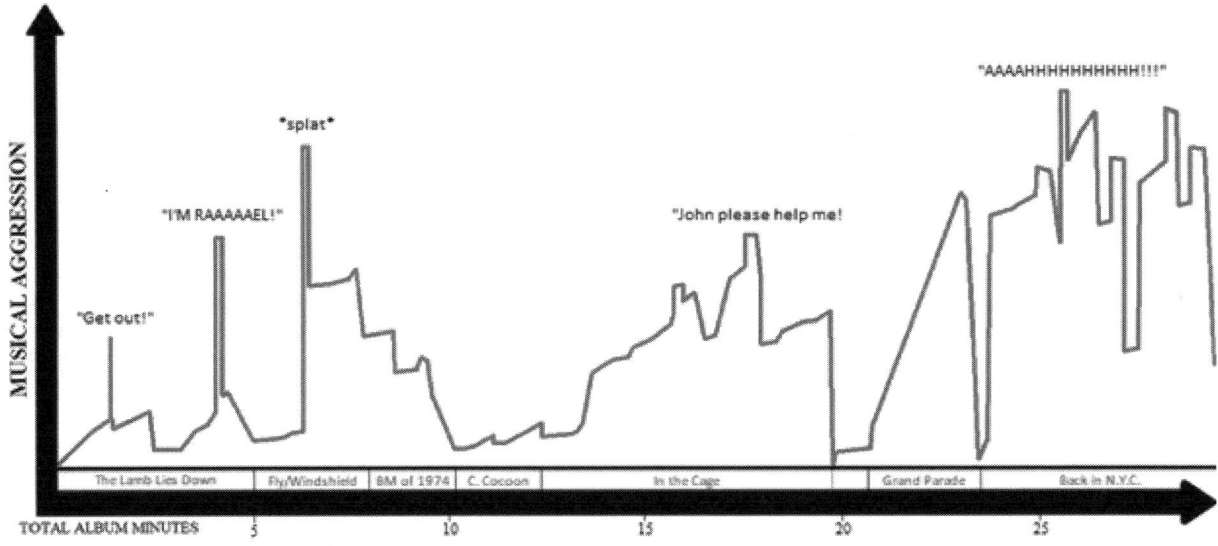

Given this extra song, what happens when we simplify the view once more by smoothing out all those rough edges? Well, wouldn't you know it? There's our pattern again.

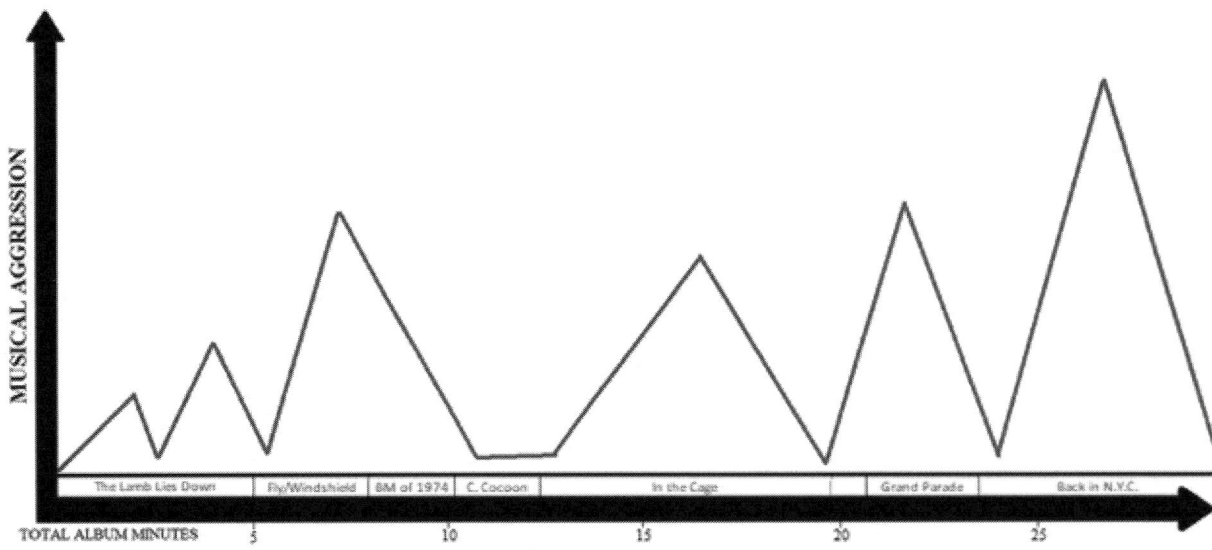

A series of three shorter peaks and valleys, then a rest, and then another series of three more extreme peaks and valleys. "Do the thing, then do it bigger." That's an old Genesis trick of songwriting (used on 'Fly on a Windshield' itself, even, though more on that to come later in this book), applied here to a full quarter of a double album. The only thing that might not quite line up between the two patterns is that 'Grand Parade' ends suddenly and 'Back in N.Y.C.' only takes a few seconds to kick into gear. Thus, it might be argued that there's hardly any "valley" present, and thus it's not quite the same pattern.

But that's the genius at work here: *the valley of musical aggression is you having to get up and flip the record over*. 'Grand Parade' ends like a factory shutting off all the machinery, and then the turntable's spinning literally comes to a halt as well. You as a 70s listener are therefore without any music whatsoever until you go through the process of resetting the record to start the second side. It's a built-in "cooldown period." Then, once you've set the needle again, you have a quick "build back up" at the start of the second side's opening track, and you don't feel like you "missed" anything along the way. In other words, *the musical pattern accounts for the limitations of the medium*. I think that's the coolest thing in the world.

> **Mike:** *I love 'Back in New York City'. That was just a weird track, just out there. It was so heavy for us. I think I wrote it with the band...a lot of jamming, a lot of improvising. At the time we thought, "It's a shame that Pete want[s] to move on, because this is sounding really good musically." Very strong. And I think at the end it's still a strong piece.* [3]

As far as opinions about the track itself go, I don't always absolutely love Peter Gabriel's vocals, but I think they're just fantastic here. For a lot of Gabriel-era tunes I believe you could slot in Phil on vocals and not really lose too much, and I feel that *Seconds Out* proves this point to some degree. Despite that, I can't imagine anyone but Pete on this one. He really smashes this track all the way through. Which is great because it leaves Phil to deliver the "No time!" backing vocals that are way better than I ever see them get credit for, particularly at the song's ending. That perfect segue into 'Hairless Heart' puts a smile on my face every time.

> **Tony:** *That started off as a riff that Mike had; this idea of playing six string bass, this riff on it, and we sort of developed that as a song. And Pete just did this sort of shouting type vocal on it, which was at the time quite surprising. I think it works pretty well. Again, I think the song is a bit more complicated than it needs to be. There's a couple extra bits in the middle there, probably courtesy of me in fact. Would've probably been better off if they weren't there, but they are there, so that's what you've got.* [3]

Those "extra bits in the middle" are a point of contention among fans, as pertains to the way this song was mixed in the 2007 remasters. Notably, the "As I cuddle the porcupine" vocal effect was completely changed and those sections were significantly rebalanced. I have mixed feelings about this, as I liked the personality of the effect, but it made the sounds so muddy that I couldn't properly hear or appreciate all the other things going on until the remix made everything clearer. So I can see both sides. Certainly I don't agree with Tony that it would be a better song if they weren't there at all.

> **Phil:** *'Back in New York City' has been covered by a couple different bands recently...Just from my point of view as a player, I mean, I was PLAYING. I went to see The Musical Box play this [album] in its entirety, and I was amazed at just how complicated it was. And this guy was playing it well, but I mean, I must've played it better. Because I wrote it! And I mean, my drum set was like...it wasn't like a big drum kit, it was just like lots of noises here, lots of things there, and I was whizzing around it...It was probably the height - between that and the next 3 or 4 years with Brand X and Genesis - it was probably the height of my playing. But a lot of inventive stuff from everybody. Steve got a great sound, Tony was getting the maximum out of what he had, we were onto the double-neck kind of thing with the guitar and bass...seemed to be a surge forward, really.* [3]

A surge forward indeed. At any rate, *The Lamb* stops following this "triple peak" pattern after this song, with 'Back in N.Y.C.' instead providing the kick-off point for Side 2's own distinct journey into Rael's past and current emotional limitations. It's the end of one thing and the start of the new thing, or in other words, the perfect concept album link. Doesn't get much better than that.

67 - Turn It On Again

from *Duke*, 1980

One of the traditional hallmarks of progressive music is that the music will not only change styles and moods during a song, but might also change time signatures. And for many progressive rock fans, there's a positive correlation between how unusual a time signature is and how much they enjoy the song. This attitude is only a couple small steps away from sliding uncontrollably into the territory of pretentious snobbery, but there's something to be said for the way weird time signatures can pull people into a more active listener role, which in turn allows them to more fully recognise and appreciate all the other stuff the song is doing as well. It's a big part of why progressive music never went beyond a niche audience; casual listeners tend to just want a good hook or rhythm, something mindless to pop on in the background while they focus their attention on another matter entirely.

Genesis, as a pioneering progressive rock band, know a thing or two about funky time signatures. And if we're going to talk about them here, why, there's no better place to look than their second top 10 UK hit, 'Turn It On Again'. Wait, what?

Yes, it seems to be fairly common knowledge among the Genesis faithful, but if you're reading this wondering to yourself what weird time signatures are in 'Turn It On Again', don't feel bad: Peter Gabriel thought the exact same thing! During the band's 1982 reunion concert, he offered to play drums on what he likely regarded as the band's most recent "simple" hit. And, well, it didn't go as smoothly as he probably hoped.

Tony: *It was typical Peter: "Oh, I can play this." But once he started playing, he kept looking around going, "Oh fuck!" 'Turn It On Again' does funny things; it's truly a Genesis song.* [64]

Heck, even Mike didn't get it, and he wrote the riff!

Mike: *[Phil] said to me, "Do you realise that it's in 13?" I said, "What do you mean it's in 13? It's in 4/4." He says, "No it's not. It's in 13."* [43]

Phil: *It's actually in 13/8. And yet you'd never know it was in 13/8. That was the good thing about it, because obviously no one would buy it if they knew it was in 13/8.* [43]

And even *Phil* didn't get it because the riff in question is *actually* in 13/4! That's a tomayto-tomahto sort of distinction, but it matters because what gets lost in the shuffle when people talk about this whole 13/8 business is that there are actually two *other* time signatures in this song as well, and one of them is, in fact, 4/4 time. See, the tempo of the song never changes, so either that 13/8 is actually 13/4, which seems most reasonable, or else we'd need to think of the 4/4 section as actually being 8/8, which strikes me as a bit silly.

Tony: *The second part of 'Turn It On Again', the "I can show you" bit [was a leftover from A Curious Feeling]. Mike wrote the main riff on 'Turn It On Again', which is really what is best about the song. We kind of put that bit – the bit he didn't use on Smallcreep's Day, curiously enough – with the bit I didn't use on A Curious Feeling, and put these two together. We made it much more rocky, both bits became much more rocky, my bit was a bit more epic, and Mike's bit was a bit slower and a bit more heavy-metal. And then Phil gave it a much more straightforward drum part that perhaps neither of us would have ever thought that we would want. And it made it into something much better, I think.* [53]

That whole "I can show you" section kicks off in 4/4, and stays that way until near the end of the "I get so lonely when she's not there" bit. But then, just to throw you off again, the measure right before Tony's big keyboard riff has an extra beat. Yes, that's right, out of nowhere it's one measure of 5/4 time. Then the keyboard bit itself leading back into the verse is three measures of 4/4 followed by one more measure of 5/4. And then, of course, right back into the main 13/4 groove where they'll run the whole sequence around again. It's madness.

Tony: *At the time when we were talking about [making a side-long epic], the bit 'Turn It On Again' was just a link. We went once around the whole sequence, the two bits, and then went on into 'Duke's Travels'. And we did it and recorded all this stuff, and went "That's much too strong to just do once," so we did it twice!* [3]

So how'd they pull that off? How do you have a song with a primary basis in 13/4 time, add in little sprinklings of 5/4 time, and somehow Jedi mind trick everyone into thinking the whole thing is in straight-up, common 4/4 time? Well, you hire Phil Collins to be your drummer, I guess. See, Phil's a sneaky little rascal and contributes a couple key elements to the aural deception that is 'Turn It On Again'. The first is its tempo.

Mike: *I had this guitar riff, which I was playing much slower actually. And Phil said, "Just try it, pick it up a lot, and try it like this." I was going [about half the final tempo], at one point with sort of Queen harmony guitars. I don't know why I got to that point, I was just messing around with it.* [3]

Tony: *My bit was slow too. So we were playing it more like that. And then Phil was kind of, I don't know, there was a certain kind of mood in those days. The drums are what make it. Absolutely the drums are what make it. It's a key thing. That's why it's so much a group song, even though musically it came from [me and Mike]. It just gave it an energy and something that we hadn't seen in it at all originally.* [3]

This is Guy "Skitch" Patterson counting off 'That Thing You Do' at double the speed Jimmy Mattingly ever wanted it to go. There's terror, there's indignation, and then there's the audience dancing along and the makings of a hit. Sometimes drummers just have that incredible instinct to be able to see the magic lurking beneath the mundane and figure out how to get it to surface. In this case the tempo also masks the time signature; it's harder to notice an extra beat when everything is so high energy and exciting, isn't it?

But Tricky Phil wasn't done there, and his most devious contribution was in a way his most simple. Faced with 13 beats in a measure, there's a question that needs answering about how the song might account for the extra beat. Phil's solution to this problem was to *pretend it didn't even exist.* Listen to the drums under that riff and you'll hear that he plays this thing with a bog standard, mainstream beat: bass kicks on the odd beats, snare hits on the evens. This is just about as basic as it gets. Your brain immediately registers that as a 4/4 pattern, and since measures are 13 beats long, you get what feels like three full measures of it (12 beats) before anything different happens. So you'd expect that 13th beat to come as a surprise and throw you off, right?

Wrong. For the 13/4 sections, he just hits a snare again on beat 13. That's it. That's the whole trick. It's like a déjà vu thing where your mind eats up that snare as though it was the snare on 12 which you also just heard. It's the the same concept as to how you probably didn't notice that I typed the word "the" twice at the beginning of this sentence. Your brain just autocorrects it, processes it, and moves on. Then, when those sections transition into the *actual* 4/4 parts, he doesn't actually change anything about the drum part. He's doing the exact same stuff, except now he doesn't need to add that extra snare hit anymore. So your ears are fooled into thinking nothing ever changed, and since this part *is* 4/4 you're convinced the song was *always* 4/4. By merely pretending that the "extra beat problem" doesn't exist, he counterintuitively ensures that there is, in fact, no problem at all.

Phil: *[People] can't dance to it. You see people dancing to it and every now and again they get on the off beat and they don't know why!* [43]

Dastardly. But what about the 5/4 lines? Well, when the 5/4 measures come in, the entire piece is in a syncopated state. Nobody's really playing anything on the beat, so unless you've been counting along for the song's duration (an exercise I had to consciously do in order to write this entire entry), you've lost the cadence completely. Which means the lads can throw in an extra beat here or there and you'd never know the difference! This works especially well again because they have heavy syncopated sections during the 4/4 measures as well, and since the time didn't change there, why would it change here? It's like musical gaslighting. "No, you didn't hear an extra beat there. Don't even worry about it."

Phil: *It's got a good drum part that makes it sound simple, rather than making it sound as complicated as it is. So that's one of the reasons it could be a single, I think. If you told the record company it was in 13/8, they'd go "No, that couldn't be a single."* [3]

This is Genesis doing Genesis things: take a bunch of tricky time signatures, mash them all together, and fool the world into making it a top ten hit in their home country. Heck, they'd done something very similar several years prior on 'Counting Out Time', but without the "scored a big hit" part of it. They're pretty good at this sort of thing. Helps as well that 'Turn It On Again' is one of those songs that doesn't hit the title line until the very end, where it just repeats forever and gets stuck in your head.

Phil: *The catchy part came at the end, you know, "Turn it oooooon, turn it on, turn it on again." It then became a stage classic, and then much to the annoyance of most Genesis fans I think, we did a Blues Brothers parody at the end of it. Which they'll be pleased to know we've ditched for this last tour. [Author's Note: the tour in question here was aptly named the Turn It On Again Tour].* [3]

When you look at all the elements that comprise 'Turn It On Again', it's a wonder it was ever even remotely successful, much less hugely so. Yet when you simply play the song and let it run in the background while you focus on some other task entirely, it's no wonder at all. In the end, Tony was right about this song: it's much too strong to only be heard once.

66 - Submarine

B-Side of 'Man on the Corner', 1982

To be honest, when I was initially working through the listening exercise where I first force-ranked all these songs, I found that I had rated 'Submarine' even more highly than I have it here - just barely outside my top 25 Genesis songs, in fact. I realise that statement might sound like a criticism in context: "Golly, this song plummeted 40-odd spots in his estimation!" Therefore I want to clear the air and state emphatically that the change in ordering is less an indictment of 'Submarine' itself, but more an indication of just how close together all these tracks are for me by this stage. Precious little actual personal enjoyment separates 30 from 70 for me, and it was only through repeated listens to the other Genesis instrumentals yet to appear that I began to feel that maybe I like those ones ever so slightly more. And as I tended to feel more strongly about their positioning in relation to the songs around them, it made sense to allow this one slide quite a ways back.

You see, 'Submarine' can be a little difficult to pin down, because, more than perhaps any other Genesis song, it's highly dependent on the listener's frame of mind going in. If you're in one kind of mood, 'Submarine' might be one of the best things you've ever heard - as I suppose it was for me during that first foray into my ranking exercise. If you're in a different kind of mood, however, you might well regard it as mere fluff - in one ear and out the other.

> **Tony:** *'Submarine'...was an instrumental thing of mine.* [6]

See? Even Tony doesn't have a lot to say about it. You might think I'm editing that quote down for the sake of a joke, but I assure you I am not.

> "Tony, can you tell us a little bit about 'Submarine'?"
>
> *"Oh that track? Yes, I wrote it."*
>
> "Ah...anything else?"
>
> *"I'm sorry, what was the question?"*

But again, I don't think it's because 'Submarine' is lacking but because of what it inherently is, and therefore also what it inherently is not. To make sense of that statement, let's put ourselves in the mind of a 'Submarine' detector. What criticisms might we expect to be laid against this song? For one, we might point to its status as a linking track. Earlier in this book in the entry for 'Naminanu' I indicated that there was a so-called "Abacab Suite" included in the band's original vision for the album. That suite consisted of 'Dodo', 'Lurker', 'Submarine', and 'Naminanu', in that order. Some fans argue that 'Naminanu' provides more punch as an opening track than a closing one and prefer to listen to it in front of 'Dodo/Lurker', and that's their prerogative as listeners, but the argument that the band intended it to come first holds no weight when measured against the band's own words.

> **Tony:** *Both ['Naminanu' and 'Submarine'] didn't get on the album but I really love them...There was a possibility of 'Dodo/Lurker' to have gone into other bits and pieces like 'Naminanu' and 'Submarine' on the album, but we decided in the end not to do that. We thought we should go the shorter, more direct route.* [18]
>
> **Phil:** *We have removed these two tailing pieces ['Submarine' and 'Naminanu' from the 'Dodo Suite'], because ultimately the organ sound was too close to older material, even Trespass.* [65]

Now that we've established the order, realise that 'Submarine' is the third chapter of a larger whole, meant to bridge 'Lurker' to 'Naminanu'. A critic might point out that it works fine for that purpose, sure, but has a bit of trouble standing on its own. Pull the song out of its home context and it suffers for the switch. That doesn't have to be the case with linking tracks, of course. The previous entry in this book, 'Turn It On Again', was itself a linking track that was so independently strong that the band expanded it and turned it into a single. So the 'Submarine' critic must then move onto point number two: the song doesn't actually do very much. It just repeats a section or two of organ stuff repeatedly while it gets louder. There's just not much there that could hold one's interest, you know?

If I might now respond to these imaginary criticisms I invented here for the sake of my own self-serving sophistry, in my experience the first criticism does somewhat hold up. It's difficult to imagine listening to no music at all, then spinning up 'Submarine' all by its lonesome, then right back to no music. Again, you sort of need to "prime the pump" musically to get the most out of your listening experience. I'll fully grant that. That said, I don't think it's quite dependent on 'Dodo/Lurker' and 'Naminanu' *specifically*, either. Plop this song into the middle of *any* playlist - especially a Genesis playlist - and it'll work pretty well. The ending feels somewhat abrupt without another piece to transition into, but otherwise I think it's quite functional. Nevertheless, while I don't entirely agree with the complaint, I can see in this case where someone might be coming from with it. The second phantom criticism, on the other hand - that the song is inherently uninteresting - finds no footing with me. This is prime Tony Banks material here.

The slow, continuous build is a concept taken straight from multiple tracks on *The Lamb Lies Down on Broadway*, but here it comes packaged with an overwhelming heaviness, like, say, the weight of an ocean pressing in on you. The melodies and bass pedals combine in this same vein to create an atmosphere of (literal nautical) depth and beauty. Put this song against high-definition footage of an active coral reef or something, and you'll get what I mean. It's a world that continuously expands, bringing in ever greater, ever more unknowable discoveries as one plunges yet deeper. Thus, what you're hearing shouldn't be considered as simple repetition, but rather *descent*.

The perils and wonders of the ocean make for very powerful imagery. It's a concept that English band Keane, perhaps themselves influenced by 'Submarine', would explore again in their own instrumental, appropriately titled 'The Iron Sea'. The crashing of waves, the passing of creatures, the call of sirens...it's all really strong stuff, transporting you to a place and a mood, and holding you there until the storm passes. And Tony Banks did it better than most.

As a forgotten stand-alone B-side, 'Submarine' can perhaps underwhelm. But I urge you to take it instead as a series of images and moods, and seek it out when you're in the right kind of mindset. I think you'll find yourself surprised by its gravity in that context, and perhaps as I did you'll allow yourself to admit: this piece is actually quite strong.

65 - Hearts on Fire

B-side to 'Jesus He Knows Me', 1992

Do you have roughly an hour of free time right now? Have you ever seen The Rutles: All You Need is Cash? If the answer to these questions are "yes" and "no" respectively, please put this book down, find and watch the film, and then return here when you are finished. I promise you it's the best hour you'll spend all week. Don't worry, I'm happy to wait. Not going anywhere. See you in a bit.

Now, for those of you reading this without the time to spare at the moment - and I implore you to view that short film as soon as you are able, because it's simply fantastic - The Rutles was a project conceived by the team of Neil Innes and Eric Idle. You may know Idle's name from his time with the Monty Python troupe, but Innes has some roots there as well on the musical side. You may even know his face as the minstrel happily singing "Brave Sir Robin ran away" in Monty Python and the Holy Grail. Anyway, the two of them teamed up on a *different* sketch comedy show in the 70s, which spawned a bit called "The Rutles", an affectionate parody of sorts to The Beatles. This in turn spawned the musical comedy film I mentioned above, with an entire soundtrack written by Innes to be a pastiche of The Beatles' sound over their career. If you're unfamiliar with the term "pastiche", here is its primary dictionary definition:

> **pastiche:** a literary, musical, or artistic piece consisting wholly or chiefly of motifs or techniques borrowed from one or more sources

So why am I bringing all this up here and now on this semi-obscure Genesis B-side? Well, because pastiches sort of bookend the Genesis discography in a really fascinating way. The first song the band ever officially released was, of course, 1968's 'The Silent Sun'. This was specifically written as a pastiche of the late 60s era Bee Gees (the disco era Bee Gees still being a decade or so away). It was Genesis trying to sneak into the music industry by exploiting the tastes of their would-be producer, and it worked. With a record deal in place, they wrote more music in a somewhat similar vein (though no longer truly pastiches themselves), until they broke those shackles completely for *Trespass* and never looked back.

While musical changes and influences abound, no true pastiche appears again in the entire Genesis catalogue for the next 24 years until 'Hearts on Fire', which sounds like nothing so much as Phil Collins doing guest vocals for The Police. Incidentally, this would be the final new song to be released by the band in the Phil Collins era, meaning that if you exclude *Calling All Stations* (as I'm sure many of you might like to do), the discography of Genesis begins and ends with the only two pastiche tracks they ever recorded. Kind of trippy when you think about it.

'Hearts on Fire' is a reggae-infused rock jam where Phil's vocals stick around in that upper register with just a hint of reverb. In other words, it's the sort of thing that would arguably fit in better on *Zenyatta Mondatta* than on *We Can't Dance*. And yet here I think the pastiche quality is most likely unintentional or subconscious. It's 80% Police, yes, but the other 20% is distinctly Genesis. The "Can you take me there" section keeps that hot beat going but the chords have the name Tony Banks written all over them. And yet after the final one of those they slap a very Sting-esque fadeout on the whole affair. It's like they were playing with ideas as they always have and somehow stumbled headlong into another artist's wheelhouse, then said, "Well, this place looks interesting, let's stick around for a spell."

> **Phil:** *'Hearts on Fire' I REALLY like...* [9]

There's something to this, I think. Tony and Mike dipped their toes lightly into reggae for 1983's 'Illegal Alien' and would again for 1997's 'Alien Afternoon'. If you're picking up the pattern here it's that to them, reggae-style rhythms are inherently "alien." Not so for Phil, who stuck one reggae section into 'Jesus He Knows Me' and now goes on record as professing his love for 'Hearts on Fire', which manages to sound unlike any of those other reggae efforts, or any other song Genesis has ever recorded, period. That's a running theme here in this series, because Genesis is a band that was never satisfied to remain locked into a sound. I suspect that's a big part of why we're all fans.

It was also potentially the source of a bit of conflict, as one group interview to promote *We Can't Dance* revealed. Here's Phil yearning for these funky rhythms and beats, and Mike and Tony going along with him only to a point. When asked if there were any songs they'd recorded that wouldn't make the album, this exchange occurred:

> **Tony:** One of them's called 'On the Shoreline', and the other we called what? 'Hearts on Fire'?

Phil: 'Hearts on Fire', yeah.

Tony: 'On the Shoreline' is a good track!

Phil: *[annoyed]* So is 'Hearts on Fire'...

Tony: *[unconvinced]* Yeah...they're both good tracks!...

Mike: What's the second part of the question, before they start arguing? They're about to fall out. We had a slight disagreement over which two songs to leave off, if any, but we...2 against 1.

Phil: We don't agree on everything, but we're man enough to sort of back down occasionally, and Tony was man enough to back down in this particular instance. [40]

With only three members to account for, Genesis had a simple rule: if two of the three members didn't want a track on the album, it didn't get on. Looks as though Tony stumped hard for 'On the Shoreline' and Phil for 'Hearts on Fire', with neither of them quite caring for the other, while Mike didn't much like either. What cracks me up about this exchange is the way Tony and Phil got mad at one another for not endorsing the "other guy's" song, and nobody's mad at Mike, who poo-pooed them both!

Alien or not, album cut or not, 'Hearts on Fire' is worthy in my book of the *We Can't Dance* name, proof that even after multiple line-up changes and a quarter-century's time, Genesis could still churn out a good pastiche if they wanted to. As for The Rutles, kings of the art? They proved so popular that Innes and company penned an entire follow-up album, and so effective in channelling the Beatles' musical energy that Innes found himself sued by the then rights holders for the Beatles catalogue for plagiarism and/or copyright infringement, forcing him to hire a musicologist to prove that his songs were actually original works and not mere copies. Now that's a pastiche master at work.

64 - Phret

B-side to 'Shipwrecked', 1997

Back in the entry for 'Stagnation' I included a quote from Peter Gabriel in which he referred to that track and other similar progressive works as "journey songs," and what he meant by that term was that the music takes you from one place to another, using different sections and sounds to move you from Point A to Point B to Point C, and so on. Often these kinds of songs additionally feature a lack of repetition as well; there may be peaks and valleys but the path being travelled is usually linear in nature. Yet this isn't a universal property of journey songs, as some might have circular features, such as the way 'Supper's Ready' returns to itself in the end, or repeated motifs as with 'The Musical Box'.

In any case, if several of Genesis' classic progressive works can be said to be journey songs that whisk the listener away with the music in this vein, 'Phret' to me is a journey song as well, but in a strikingly different mould. It's not the classic "Come with me and let me tell you a tale of times when kings and queens sipped wine from goblets gold" kind of journey. Rather, 'Phret' to me is a third person view *of* a journey. Of someone *else's* journey. We aren't the ones being taken along for a ride so much as we are witnesses to another's quest, already engaged. That might at first blush seem somehow less appealing - "*I* want to be whisked away, me, me, me!" - but I think this alternate approach can hold a surprising amount of emotional power in its own right, just as one could read a book and become deeply concerned about the fate of a favourite character.

'Phret' opens with a distant drumbeat, a sustained single bass note, the sounds of wind, and a dark keyboard melody that reveals the bleak landscape. It's an image of a barren vista, ravaged by cold, devoid of companionship. But eight bars in, the music shifts into major tones. The landscape is the same, but now we are seeing the determined face of our traveller. This is someone not easily cowed, and at that point I'm immediately invested in the tale the music has conjured up in my mind. Six bars reflecting upon this curious newcomer and then the two moods blend. It's like a film that begins with a wide shot of an open desert at night. There's a small figure shuffling across the sands, and because of the context typical to these kinds of shots, we assume that they're about to collapse. But then it cuts in close and we see the figure's eyes, fiery and resolute, and we know instantly that this is not our victim but our hero. And finally, the camera zooms back out halfway. We again see the shuffling figure, now knowing their movements to be filled with purpose. But we also can still see that there is no end in sight to these hopeless dunes and wonder what will become of it all.

Then, a minute in, sunrise. Light returns to the world along with warmth, and there's an added vigour to the journey. It's a section that screams "I'm your chorus," except there are still no vocals, still no real hook. This is, after all, still a wasteland. There is hope, but not accomplishment. Warmth, yes, but a dangerous warmth, and still no signs of life anywhere nearby. Instead there's only a keyboard and a guitar, with very little difference in sound to tell which is which, rolling through the melody: a foreign element in an inhospitable place doing its best to get by.

Then night rolls in once more, and the cycle repeats. In the end, the hero's fate is never known. The journey presses ever onward through night and day, despair and hope, ice and fire. It's not *our* journey, no, but we bear witness to it, and there is still something quite profound in that. Regardless of whether the traveller ever reaches his or her destination, we will remember. We will remember.

As for the track's title, I can't find any sources that I can provide as clear evidence, but I strongly believe it to be a reference to a late 19th/early 20th century children's tale called "Phuss and Phret":

> *Have you heard of the land called Phuss-and-Phret*
>
> *Where people live upon woes and regret*
>
> *Its climate is bad, I've heard folks say*
>
> *There's seldom, if ever, a pleasant day*
>
> *'Tis either too gloomy from cloudy skies*
>
> *Or so bright the sunshine dazzles one's eyes*

'Tis either so cold one is all of a chill

Or else 'tis so warm it makes one ill

The season is either too damp or too dry

And mildew or drought is always nigh

For nothing that ever happened yet

Is just as it should be in Phuss-and-Phret

It's a case of a song sounding simple and straightforward - just two different primary sections that repeat once apiece - but within that simplicity 'Phret' is able to paint a compelling picture on the canvas and really engage the listener on a much deeper emotional level than one might first expect. That is assuming, of course, that the listener is willing to be so engaged. Are you?

63 - The Carpet Crawlers

from *The Lamb Lies Down on Broadway*, 1974

Ah, '(The) Carpet Crawl(ers)'. What am I to do with you? I go back and forth on this song all the time. It's a little confounding, if I'm being honest. I know I quite like it, of course, or I'd have written about it much earlier in this book, and yet I think it's fair to say I don't esteem it quite as highly as the average prog-era Genesis fan does. And that is in itself confounding, because this is a song that puts to the lie everything that prog snobbery is about.

Those who hold that prog is king and pop is formulaic garbage are, when confronted with 'Carpet Crawlers', almost uniformly revealed to be pretentious hypocrites. Here is a song that, introduction aside, has about the most boring compositional structure imaginable. 4/4 time throughout, 8 bars per section, Verse, chorus, verse, chorus, verse, chorus, verse, chorus. I mean, I nearly fell asleep just writing that. This is the *exact* sort of thing the Prog Snob rails against and brands unlistenable. But get into a conversation with one about music and say a kind word about 'Carpet Crawlers', and I all but guarantee you'll hear waterfalls of praise begin to gush forth.

> **Steve:** *It's a lot of people's favourite, this. Compelling chorus...One of Pete's great vocals.* [13]

> **Tony:** *It just worked really well. It's one of those things where it's very simple, and I think that's half its charm. Sometimes with Genesis it's overworked, we put too much into things. Something like this which was a bog standard chord sequence in a way - well, the chorus is a little bit different - but it just gave it somewhere to go...Why audiences like it, I don't know really.* [3]

Is there something so incredibly special about this song compared to the pop songs - often more adventurous in form, even - that Genesis wrote into the 80s and 90s? Something that truly sets this one song so far above what came after that all its structural mundanity suddenly becomes a non-issue? No, I don't think so. Frankly, I think the Prog Snob forgives 'Carpet Crawlers' simply because it came out on a concept album with the "classic" line-up. Or, more to the point, the Prog Snob disdains the later pop works simply because they *didn't* come out on a concept album featuring Genesis' "classic" five-man line-up. What a shame!

> **Tony:** *There were two or three points [during the writing of The Lamb] where we had no music but Peter had written a storyline, and we had to create something on the spot. One was...'The Carpet Crawlers', where we had no starting point at all. Mike and I sat down and developed a chord sequence in a simple D, E minor, F sharp minor with a roll from the drums flowing through it, and Pete wrote a beautiful melody on top of that. It proved that you can slave for hours trying to get a song together and then, almost spontaneously, you develop one of the best tracks on the album.* [1]

See, my point here isn't that 'Carpet Crawlers' isn't a great song. My point is that if we're willing to concede that it's a great song, that ought to tear down a lot of barriers we've built up in our minds about what a good song can or should sound like. Tony's not wrong that it's one of the better songs on *The Lamb Lies Down on Broadway*, and it's competing for that distinction against a number of tracks that are far more complicated. If not for Mike drinking himself through the audio review, who knows if it would've even seen the light of day.

> **Mike:** *We jammed for hours, recording everything we'd played - Phil was the keeper of the cassettes, being a collector by nature - and then listening back to what we'd done each evening. That was how we found the start of 'Carpet Crawl': I was sitting in the kitchen one night drinking beer, playing back one of the jam tapes of the day, and there it was - one of those bits that at the time we hadn't really rated but, with renewed perspective, was potentially quite interesting.* [14]

So yes, compositionally this song *is* pretty dull, and yes, at times when listening to it I do get a touch of listener's fatigue from it. Occasionally by the end I'm just ready for it to be over, a feeling that's a bit more pronounced when listening to *The Lamb Lies Down on Broadway* as a full album, because there every loop of the end chorus is keeping me from the masterful opening of 'The Chamber of 32 Doors'. But catch me off guard and ask me out of the blue if I like 'Carpet Crawlers' and my answer will almost certainly be, "Yes, of course I do, why would you even need to ask me that?" So what is it about this song that pulls me in? Is it the introduction that serves as a call-back to the album's opener and title track?

> **Tony:** *We skip the intro [live], because it doesn't really belong to the song; it's an in-between bit...The album had a lot of those bits between the songs and this one obviously was a reprise from the song 'The Lamb Lies Down' itself...But it's another song. It really starts this way. The intro makes it more complicated.* [66]

No, pretty as that is, Tony's right: you strip it out from the live versions and there's not really much harm done. So there's got to be something inherent to the core of the song at work here. Hmm... Well then, is it the lyrics? ...No, I'm certain that's not it. They're just...well, Tony:

> **Tony:** *'The Carpet Crawlers'...works [out of context of the album] because it's got a chorus that kind of could relate to anything. I mean, the verse lyrics are pretty strange when you listen to them, but there's lots of lovely imagery in there as well, so I think that works well out of context.* [3]

Tony beats around the bush here, but let's call a spade a spade: 'Carpet Crawlers' is lyrically a graphic description of the act of sexual intercourse with an aim toward procreation, told in part from the perspective of a sperm cell. It immediately follows 'Counting Out Time', itself a jovial song about sex, and, well, if you've never made this connection before I encourage you to just go read the lyrics for 'Carpet Crawlers' with this notion in mind. I don't necessarily want to dwell on the lyrics here and turn this entry into an anatomical lesson, but the sperm's gotta get in (to the woman) to get out (as a baby), and when you realise that, you start to catch onto the hidden meanings behind things like the "red ochre corridor," the congealing liquid "that has seeped out through the crack," and so forth. Again, I've probably already said too much, but the point is that the lyrics of 'Carpet Crawlers', though grandly poetic in their imagery, are little more than an expanded metaphor for sex. Sure, we can take them at their literal face value as pertains to Rael's surrealist journey, and that's valid, but come on. Peter knew what he was doing. Yet since the song has evolved in audience impact beyond its original role in the album, the band would prefer to keep that "this could be anything" mystique around it. They all play coy, but we know better.

Anyway, suffice it to say, the lyrics aren't even remotely the thing that does it for me in regard to this song. So then...is it the instrumentation?

> **Steve:** *Very distant guitar part. With the guitar part, I was trying to sound like a distant violin. There was an effect I'd heard on a Yardbirds track years and years ago where I felt Jeff Beck had sounded very much like a distant violin. Almost inaudible, but tantalizingly in the background.* [13]

Maybe...maybe. I do really like the combination of Tony's rapid arpeggios and Steve's gentle guitar textures. The drumming is pretty straightforward - rare for Phil in these days - and the bass line is pleasant but not incredible. So the rhythm section in itself isn't the draw. The vocals are pretty good too, but I wouldn't put this among Pete's top performances even on the album. But there's something in there, maybe...Could it be in the way the song continues to build?

> **Tony:** *I think the fact that the song slowly crescendos, it sort of just creeps into you like that. It's got a very strong chorus hook as well.* [3]

Ah, now I think maybe we're getting somewhere. Earlier in the same album, 'The Grand Parade of Lifeless Packaging' was built around the concept of a continuous crescendo, from sparseness to cacophony, and it worked really well. 'Carpet Crawlers' is sneakily the exact same idea, but in the form of a gentler ballad. The first verse is just Pete, Tony, and a hint of Mike on bass. Pete sings the first chorus in a soft, low register, allowing Phil's backing vocals to wisp away on the main line. When Steve comes in it's so subtle you might not even know he's joined the party. Then the second verse adds drums. The second chorus builds volume. The third verse picks up the bass while Pete jumps an octave, adding intensity. He doubles Phil now on the chorus main line, adding power. Steve plays more throughout the fourth verse, and Tony's volume hits its maximum. Then of course the vocal interplay at the end caps it all off.

It's boring *compositionally,* yes. It's boring *on paper,* yes. But the *performance* keeps you engaged, drawing you in a little more each time. I think we're almost there. For me, though, I think it comes down to the melody.

> **Peter:** *I love the melody of ['Carpet Crawlers'] because I worked my ass off on it...I spent hours and hours honing that melody, and then the lyric.* ³

Gorgeous from start to finish, blending perfectly with the textures of both verse and chorus, the melody of this song is one of Pete's crowning achievements with Genesis. I'd argue *that's* the reason the song has taken on a strange life of its own among the Genesis fandom. *That's* the reason the band used it to close their 2007 tour. The melody is so good it transcends the lyrics and becomes something somehow every bit as intimate as its subject matter.

> **Tony:** *It shines out a little bit from the album in terms of its solidity. Confidence, I think. The other songs, they're all a little bit more meandering. It's one very sort of bright spot in the middle of the album. Which at the time we wrote it, we had no idea it was going to be picked out. We played the album to people, and we thought that if there was going to be a single, it would be 'Counting Out Time'. And everyone said, "No, 'Carpet Crawlers' is the one."* ³

It's the connection of the band's artistry to its recipients. It's a bond between creator and listener that neither side can quite explain. When I saw them play in 2007 on that tour, Phil introduced the song by saying "This is a very special part of Genesis' history, and we offer it to you." Nobody can tell you why, but this is something else now. And maybe that's why, despite being able to tell you that it may not be the perfect song, I can also tell you that I don't really care.

62 - Anything Now

B-side to 'Not About Us', 1998

When I was but a wee little lad, I went to an amusement park, brimming with excitement that I was finally tall enough to ride one particular roller coaster that I had been greedily eyeing for years. This was a wooden coaster, so I was warned in advance that the ride would be a little less smooth than the steel kiddie coasters I'd been stuck on before. I didn't really worry much about that, however, as I'd also previously ridden a different, less intense wooden coaster. Full of my ignorant pre-pubescent hubris, I felt like I had a pretty good idea what I was in for; all these well-meaning cautions from the adults could take a hike. I just didn't care about anything other than the fact that I was finally going to get on the big ride and go really fast. What else could possibly matter more than that?

It was a busy, hot summer day, so the nearly two hour wait must have been a bit of a pain, but I was so excited that I can't even recall feeling bothered by it. There was a misting area about halfway through the line branded as the Cool Zone (brought to you by Coca-Cola®), and for me that was part of the adventure to be relished almost as much as the ride itself. You could see the relief in the queuers ahead entering the shaded tent spaces where the water spritzes kept flowing, giving you a tantalizing milestone to reach while the true prize remained firmly out of reach. Yet once the line progressed through that Cool Zone, it was all eyes on the prize. Shade was more plentiful in the back half of the line as it wound under the elevated station platform, building anticipation with every rumbling train that rolled in overhead. An ascent of the old wooden stairs and then finally, at long last, I buckled into the ride. I was so giddy I could barely sit still in the train car - this was truly a dream come true! - and out of the station we rolled. Clink, clink, clink, clink up the chain lift hill, going higher than I'd ever been on a thrill ride to that point in my life, seeing the tops of trees all around and catching glimpses of the lightly wooded area we were about to plunge into: this was bliss.

That first descent was pure exhilaration, everything I could've hoped for and more. As the roller coaster zoomed onward over foothills and between the semi-sparse trees, my smile must've been a mile wide. How could anything in life ever get better than this? Two minutes felt like thirty, and before I knew it the ride was entering its final leg: a big, banked curve that looped around twice through a dark, suspended tunnel. The first bank took me by surprise and I was jolted slightly by the car's sudden tilt into the turn, but hey, they said it wouldn't be smooth! All part of the fun!

It wasn't to last. The second bank came, fiercer than the first, and I found myself being whiplashed hard to the side. Unfortunately, as an older roller coaster, comfort and safety weren't quite the orders of the day. While the car was sturdy enough and the seat restraints functioned well to prevent any disastrous ejections, there was no padding to speak of around the car's metal frame. And though I was tall enough to ride, I was regrettably the precise height necessary for this whiplash effect to send my head careening into that uncovered side of the train car: mercifully blunt, but nevertheless built of unyielding steel. When I entered that tunnel, I was grinning ear to ear. When I left I was bawling my eyes out with pain, dizziness, and no small feeling of betrayal.

There was a walkway bridge for general park foot traffic that looked over the final portion of that roller coaster, where people often liked to stop for a moment and watch the trains speed by. Of course, this was a two-way affair: riders on the roller coaster could also look up and see the people on the bridge, should they be so inclined. So it was that I vividly remember seeing other kids watching me from that overlook, gasping things like, "Mommy, Mommy! That boy is crying! Why is he crying?!"

A lot happened in an instant. First, it dawned on me that not just one but many complete strangers were witnessing my anguish. My older brother (esteemed veteran of this ride that he was) must've sensed it as well, as he turned toward me from his adjacent seat in the train car to ask what was wrong - as the ride was still in motion! I felt utterly humiliated, which only made me cry harder. This then triggered a sympathetic response from a number of the small children watching from the bridge, whose own joy and excitement transformed into abject terror before my watery eyes. "Mommy, I don't want to go on the ride anymore!" Who could blame them? I was the only kid their size and I was clearly miserable. Who would wait hours in line for *that* outcome? And yet deep down I knew that my experience wasn't the norm. As exasperated parents pulled their screaming children away from the vicinity of the roller coaster, guilt welled up within me. My day might be irrevocably ruined, but right had I to ruin theirs as well? So I cried even more. What else could I do?

I held a grudge against that roller coaster for years, refusing to ride it again out of a combination of fear and anger. The bitter memories were simply too much to bear. Eventually though, I found myself back at that park with a large group of others, and everyone wanted to ride. Faced with the prospect of either sitting alone for well over an hour or standing up to my demons, I managed to get back on. I told myself things would be different that time: I knew about the danger and would be ready for it. I figured I could lean the opposite direction into that turn and avoid the issue. Besides, I was taller by then, so even if I did whip to the side, I probably wouldn't hit my head again, right?

I hit my head again. Same exact way. I was bigger, with a higher pain threshold and a better ability to manage my emotions, but it still hurt like the dickens and I am not ashamed to say I was mighty peeved. But I learned. I determined not to let this daggone roller coaster beat me. I've ridden it many, many times in the years since, and you know what? It was worth it. Somewhere along the way, too young to even understand the wisdom of the epiphany, I realised that if I let this one flaw, this negative interaction colour my entire attitude about something I otherwise thoroughly enjoyed, I'd be robbing myself of something special. And that would be quite the shame, now wouldn't it?

'Anything Now' is a piece about getting over it. It's *Shit Happens: The Song*. It's about seeing oncoming change - to your expectations, your reality, your circumstances, whatever - and shifting your thinking to be able to view that in a more positive light. One could guess that maybe Genesis wrote this one about the start of their third phase with Ray, though when Ray was asked if the song was about Phil leaving the band, his answer wasn't very helpful.

> **Ray:** *I honestly don't know [what it's about], Tony wrote the lyrics to that one.* [32]

Regardless, it's a burst of optimism, left off an album that probably could have used some. It wastes no time coming in with joyful major tones, soon spelled by what I affectionately refer to as "Tony's little keyboard diddles." The chorus isn't quite catchy, but it's definitely buoyant. And then from that positive launch point the song hits a *lot* of different moods: the bluesy rock vibe of the verses, the powerful tension of the pre-chorus chord sequence bolstered by Tony's keyboard countermelodies and the perfect splash of backing vocals, the noir-like jazz lounge Tony wanders into with his piano in tow, the epic final keyboard solo, and of course that chorus of sheer positivity peppered throughout.

> **Tony:** *We have DATs all the time of things as we go along and there was a little bit in [the jam session that produced 'Shipwrecked'] that became 'Anything Now'...It was [part of]...a long, twenty-five minute improvisation.* [25]

Taking a jam session that produced a bunch of great ideas and honing them into a single track that still manages to accurately capture the breadth and impact of all those ideas individually? Yeah, that's the Genesis we all know and love right there. This is high quality music from the highest quality band, exemplifying the very attitude that they needed in order to persevere into the late 90s and beyond. This was great things beginning to take shape, a palpable excitement in the air.

> **Tony:** *We feel quite strongly that ['Anything Now' is] as good as anything on the album really, particularly the instrumental part...it's a pity it couldn't get on the album.* [66]

> **Ray:** *I've never been to America or Canada yet. As much as I've been everywhere in Europe, I've never been outside. And to arrive in Canada and North America to do your first Genesis concerts...what a way to arrive, you know? "Hi, I'm here, and by the way I sing with one of the most famous bands in the world, let's go!" That is a really exciting prospect.* [67]

Ray said that in 1997 as Genesis were rehearsing for their upcoming world tour. He was positively bubbly in the interview. Dreams coming true. And then, out of nowhere, the end.

> **Tony:** *The feedback was that [Calling All Stations] was going to enter the American charts at number two. We put together another massive tour. It was a mistake. The album was released and it came in at number forty-seven or something...We had to cancel the US leg of the tour.* [1]

Mike and Tony had lived decades of success with Genesis. Year upon year of steady growth before being catapulted into superstardom. *Calling All Stations* was never going to reach the meteoric heights they had found with Phil Collins in tow, and ultimately they couldn't handle the disappointment. Tony, a man whose solo efforts always struggled to find the spotlight, was willing to rebuild a bit from the ground up as the "new" Genesis, but for Mike it seems 47 was no longer acceptable territory. In a way, perhaps Tony always knew this going in. Back in a 1987 interview, he showed alarming prescience for what might happen a decade later.

> **Tony:** *We never thought we would get as big as this. But then you start to get greedy, you see; this is the trouble. You have a 1 single, and you want the next one to be a 1 single. And now we want a 1 album. I can stand back sometimes and say, "This isn't really what it's all about," but you get caught up in it. A prime example of this happened with Mike's record*

> *['Taken In' by Mike + the Mechanics]. It did an about-turn at around 40 on the American charts. He said, "Only 40? This is terrible." I said, "Look, if two years ago I had said to you, 'You're going to have a record that's going to be 40 in the American charts,' you would have been ecstatic." But he'd had two Top Ten hits just previous to that, so 40 didn't seem as good.* [68]

So accustomed to success that merely making the music and making a living were no longer enough, Mike phoned it in. And with that writing on the wall, Tony threw in his towel as well.

> **Mike:** *Tony and Ray were keen to carry on but...To me it felt right to just stop there - no real harm done.* [14]

Anything now could've been there for them with a little perseverance and a more positive mindset. Yet despite sending out the message so effectively in this song, it seems that they weren't quite willing to receive its wisdom themselves.

> **Ray:** *I was never involved in the decision not to do a second album. Tony and Mike were afraid that it might not sell at all and that that would ruin the good name Genesis had built up over thirty years, and I can understand that. But they never should have tried it in the first place if they weren't prepared to see it through...If they didn't have the balls to do it they shouldn't have done it at all. And they didn't have the balls to do it, that's it in a nutshell.* [1]

Tony and Mike were those kids on the roller coaster, crying that they'd bonked their heads around the final turn, while Ray Wilson watched them from the overlook bridge. As the media buried the band and irritated mothers dragged their screaming children away, Ray's was the quiet, brave voice saying, "But I still want to ride."

> **Ray:** *A lot of people thought that ['Anything Now'] should have been on the album quite honestly, and it will be a B-Side but it will be a waste of a B-Side because it had more of an EP feel to it and there are a few [leftover tracks like that].* [28]

"This deserves more than to be a B-side. More than to be an album cut. This should be featured." But instead, it's a lost, forgotten track, piled under a painful history. But its message remains strong to this day, and deserves to be heeded. While never officially a full member of the band, I want to share this quote from *Calling All Stations* session/touring drummer Nir Zidkyahu as well:

> **Nir Zidkyahu:** *When it became clear after the end of the Calling All Stations tour that there would be no follow-up album, I did feel frustration and disappointment, especially as I thought that in the final stages of the tour, the band had begun to glue together, really started sounding like a band...I have to be honest, there was some anger at the time. But I came away with many positives, and I learnt a lot about myself, and with ten years' perspective I realise that what was meant to be would be. That's the way it is.* [1]

Whether you want it or whether you hate it and try to battle it out, someday you may just come to discover it was all for the best.
Nir gets it.

61 - Fly on a Windshield

from *The Lamb Lies Down on Broadway*, 1974

With 1981's *Abacab*, Genesis made a conscious decision to move away from pre-written songs and focus more on group writing efforts, encouraged as they were by the strength of the group material on the previous year's *Duke*. By 1983 this mentality had completely taken over, and they called that year's album *Genesis* to reflect the fact that, for the first time, the songs were all entirely group written, having emerged in the studio from jamming sessions and the like. This defined the approach to every Genesis album afterward, including *Calling All Stations* after Phil had left and there were effectively only two writers collaborating anymore.

But even though it wasn't until the 80s that Genesis fully embraced the group jam as the best and only way to produce material, working together to invent something out of nothing was always part of the band's DNA. 'Fly on a Windshield', in fact, sprung into being in a manner very similar to the game "Scenes From a Hat" from improv comedy show Whose Line Is It Anyway? The idea of that game is that someone draws a card at random from some sort of container (most often a hat, as you might imagine) then reads the phrase on that card, which serves as the title of the scene to improvise. All the players then set in motion accordingly, making the whole thing up as they go along. So it was with 'Fly on a Windshield': Mike said "Pharoahs going down the Nile," played a couple chords, and they were off.

Tony: *Instantly the rest of us would conjure up that particular mood.* [69]

The difference is that instead of a host with a buzzer suddenly ending the creative outpouring out of deference to network advertisements, here the band had a chance to develop the ideas further and make something really great from them.

Tony: *We were sat down just sort of playing fifths, and just mak[ing] it sort of like the Egyptian army coming across the landscape.* [3]

Steve: *With 'Fly' we were influenced by the "ramming speed" scene in the film Ben Hur... the march of death to accompany the suffering of a million ancient slaves.* [70]

Peter must have sensed this too, given that the dust cloud that drives the narrative of this piece is described in the lyrics as a "wall of death." Not much wiggle room there; this approaching barrier of tightly compacted fine debris is a sinister thing, practically sentient and full of ill intention.

Steve: *I like this very much. It's largely an atmospheric piece, but very powerful. Particularly powerful live, of course...The chords are very Tony. I think of the influence of Respighi, and that idea of the legions coming to life that you get with so much classical music: Respighi, Mussorgsky...again it's got those wide dynamics that's characteristic of so much beloved progressive music.* [13]

So we've got this really heavy atmosphere here. Foreboding dread, impending doom, calm-before-the-storm type stuff, all-coloured with a vaguely Egyptian flavour. Pete's leaning into that by painting a verbal picture of an evil, ever-encroaching death cloud. Inexorable, unavoidable, cold, emotionless, oncoming destruction. What happens when it arrives? Eventually it's got to arrive, right?

Tony: *'Fly on a Windshield'...starts as a very soft little thing and then this huge crash comes in from the drums with the guitar and the Mellotron. It's one of the strongest moments in Genesis, a physical "pow" that really gives you that feeling of a fly hitting a windscreen.* [1]

Steve's guitar screams through the haze as everyone's volumes kick up and it's the kind of sound that raises the hairs on your arms.

Steve: *I wanted the guitar to sound like distant cries - the death agonies of prisoners.* [70]

Yeah, that'll do it all right. It's such a jolt of lightning that it's easy to miss precisely what's happening behind it: more of the same. The other guys are doing the same kinds of things they were all song long (though Pete's singing has stopped as Rael has become enveloped and encrusted in the dust), but now there's just so much more OOMPH behind it all.

Tony: *We had a quiet one and a loud one, and we just sort of butt-joined them. But then with the lyric, this idea of this fly coming and hitting a windshield, which comes in with such a big*

> *bang, which is probably the single best moment in Genesis, I think. That moment when it comes in, that first chord. After that it's just downhill, but it's just a wonderful moment I think.* [3]

Tony's not wrong about that "bang"; while I'm not sure I'd definitively call it the single best moment in the band's history, I'm having trouble picking out anything else as being distinctly stronger, so I suppose it's as good a pick as any. Which isn't to say that I agree with Tony about the rest of the song being weaker, mind you...though he delivered that comment somewhat wryly, so it may have just been self-deprecating humour. The strumming guitar and Mellotron choir that open the piece work so well together to set a mood. It's every bit as easy to envision it as some sort of soundtrack to Ancient Egyptian suffering as it is to visualise the ominous sight of a dust wall about to smack the everlovin' stuffin' out of you.

> **Mike:** *'Fly on a Windshield'...had real size and power.* [14]

Similarly, I think the "loud one" that follows Steve's big guitar wail works brilliantly too. Again, it's ostensibly the same stuff: same chord structure, similar rhythms, etc. But Steve's just allowed to let loose on top of it all, and of course the drums are now crashing around too.

> **Steve:** *I was trying very, very hard to get my guitar through the mix a lot of the time...very, very dense keyboard structures, and I'm always trying to do something to highlight and try to do something sympathetic in the background. Although you've got guitar moments like 'Fly on a Windshield', where you've got the guitar doing something where it sometimes comes to the fore, rises and falls, and so I think that is a lovely piece of music. So as a guitarist, I loved that.* [3]

It transforms the entire communicated mood from one of dread to one of chaos, panic, and impact. It builds, and builds, and builds, and then finally it breaks as 'Fly' ends and 'Broadway Melody of 1974' takes over.

> **Steve:** *I went for Egyptian phrases as we made the same modulation from E to F that roughly parallels the modulation on Ravel's 'Boléro' at the end; a tone up, in other words. It gave the piece that tonic lift and I suppose what would be trite in a [pop] song you know, when the chorus goes up like that, in an instrumental piece works really well. That came together spontaneously.* [30]

That break is interesting because it's not the typical "ray of light piercing the veil," major chord, victorious sort of shift that one might expect. The tones are still very dark and things are still decidedly unwell in Rael's world, yet the tension has lifted. The storm has passed and now you find yourself amidst the damage it left behind.

> **Steve:** *The triumphant chord change... with a victorious sense of a shift into a new dimension, at once beyond good and evil... When nowadays I play that piece of music, it's because of its timeless power.* [70]

This is why these two tracks, more than any others except perhaps 'Home by the Sea' and 'Second Home by the Sea', were the most disappointing to me to have to break up for this exercise. 'Fly on a Windshield' and 'Broadway Melody of 1974' together are a true powerhouse of a pairing, but I felt it was important for me to stay consistent in my methodology for this exercise. The difference in the way I esteem them individually is that, for me, 'Broadway Melody of 1974' loses a little something for not having 'Fly on a Windshield' in front of it. 'Fly on a Windshield', by contrast, *gains* something for having 'Broadway Melody of 1974' come after it. It's a subtle distinction but, I think, an important one.

> **Steve:** *Orchestral keyboards, Mellotron, RMI piano, brassy effect, the chord change...going up a tone to a major...I think still very beautiful...It's really a piece that I love. It's Genesis at its most orchestral in spirit...It's got all of that and much more. And of course the band on the instrumental section, we were all playing live [on the record]. So it's absolutely what you hear is what you get, so I think that's also very honest. Very magical, still love it.* [13]

That's it right there. This piece has it all, really. The lyrics aligning with the tone of the music and then getting completely out of the way, the introduction of a musical theme and its development into something stronger, the orchestral-like arrangement of its varied sounds in order to generate an incredible mood... 'Fly on a Windshield' delivers it all, letting listeners to *The Lamb Lies Down on Broadway* know very quickly that they're in for something truly special.

60 - Taking It All Too Hard

from *Genesis*, 1983

Ever heard someone utter the phrase "I'm my own biggest critic" or something along those lines? There's a temptation from the outside, especially when we're fans of the subject matter, to dismiss such statements as false modesty, isn't there? If you could ask Leonardo da Vinci about the Mona Lisa, what do you think he'd say? Would he agree that it was one of the most important and influential paintings of all time, the masterpiece that we seem to universally regard it as being? Or is it more likely he'd look at you with a hint of guilt-tinged confusion, shrugging his shoulders and muttering, "It was just a commission I wasn't able to finish on time?"

Creating is this weird, constant give-and-take between pride and shame. It's that excitement over having an idea or vision in your head, the thrill of getting some of it out into the world, and the solitary disappointment that what you produced is almost inevitably worse than what you had in mind. If you're lucky, your work is good enough to have fans, and in their eyes what you created might be something truly impeccable and lasting. And that's gratifying to hear, and certainly the kind of reaction a creator hopes for, but it doesn't quite silence that little internal voice that highlights all the ways in which you feel you fell a little short. "I'm glad they like it, and I think it turned out pretty well, but I could've done so much better." It sounds like false modesty until you've been there yourself, and then it's a feeling you'll get to know far, far too well.

Thus, when we hear Tony Banks talk about some of his songs and it sounds as though he struggles to muster much enthusiasm for any of them, I can sympathise. He's not trying to take this tune out behind the old woodshed because he's incapable of joy; he simply has a bit of trouble moving beyond that little perfectionist voice inside of him. He can't distance himself from the work like we fans can, no matter how much he might want to. If you want an example of that in action, you need look no further than 'Taking It All Too Hard'.

> **Tony:** *I had this little piano piece and we just played around with it and it came out well in the end. Mike wanted to do the lyrics, and I was happy with that as I didn't have any ideas for it. It was a nice track, but for me the lesser track on the album.* [71]

First off, I want to point out that last sentence in particular. Note that Tony didn't say he felt that 'Taking It All Too Hard' was *a* lesser track on the album, but rather *the* lesser track – which is to say, the worst song on *Genesis*. Now, I don't think this is necessarily a condemnation of the piece, as he still also acknowledges that it both "came out well in the end" and "was a nice track." One could charitably read into this quote that Tony appreciates 'Taking It All Too Hard' but simply likes everything else from that 1983 effort a little bit more. Yet I don't think that's the whole picture. I believe there was something else about this piece that must've niggled at Tony in that classic creator fashion; after all, as it originated as his "little piano piece," he could well be said to have been the "prime writer." So how did Genesis handle 'Taking It All Too Hard' after finishing the track?

As with every other Genesis album since the debut, the lads went on tour to promote *Genesis,* playing many of its tracks during those shows. Yet this so-called Mama Tour notably did not include 'Taking It All Too Hard', indicating that perhaps Tony had already pegged it as something he wanted to move on from. By the tour's end in February 1984, he probably thought the song was out of sight, out of mind forever. The band's record label, however, had other ideas. Sensing the radio potential for the track with American listening sensibilities in mind, 'Taking It All Too Hard' was released in June 1984 as a US-exclusive single. That wouldn't be notable in itself had the single performed poorly; the band and their American audience could just forget about the song equally.

That single went to 50 on the US charts, getting a bunch of radio play along the way. 50 is not a *massive* hit, granted, but it was sufficient that one can still hear the track from time to time on the radio (or perhaps the local supermarket) in the States to this day. It was certainly big enough to enter the public consciousness. And yet despite that initial burst of success, the band opted not to capitalise. This was the beginning of the golden age of MTV, where a strong music video could catapult a tune to new heights on the sales charts. To have a minor hit and not try to bolster its performance with a video bordered on negligence, potentially costing the band quite a lot of money and further fame. Were they too busy to throw together a two-day film session to support the song's presence on the radio? Were they truly satisfied to merely ride out whatever small wave of success the song could muster on its own? Or was there a bit of upturned nose at the thing, like a snobby sniff of disbelief: "They like *that* song over there?"

In 1985, while Genesis themselves didn't put out any new material, there was a major new player on the pop/rock scene: a little outfit called Mike + the Mechanics. Working as Mike Rutherford's second attempt at a solo career, the Mechanics found success immediately with multiple big hits. Tony Banks, one could say, took this a little too hard.

> **Tony:** *Getting an audience beyond the Genesis audience—or even a major part of the Genesis audience. That was the challenge I never managed to surmount...I just want to be loved!...Yes, I had fantastic success with Genesis - the sort of success most songwriters could only dream about, so I really don't want to over-emphasise the disappointment. But if you ask me, "Would I like to have been more successful as a solo artist?" The answer is "Yes." I say that because I think a lot of the music on my solo albums is as good as the stuff I did with Genesis. So, I would like it to have had a higher profile. There isn't anything wrong in wanting that. The salt was kind of rubbed in the wound by the success of Mike + the Mechanics. Phil's stuff was successful because he's a singer and all the rest of it. But with Mike + the Mechanics, it sort of made me feel like I was very much the third member. It would have helped just a little bit - for my own ego, I suppose - to have had solo success...I had great hopes for some of the albums. But it was a bit disappointing and depressing to put out a record and hope something would happen with it and then not have it happen. I have to be honest about that. I can't deny it.* [18]

One imagines, then, that returning to Genesis and their ever-increasing levels of success came as something of a relief to Tony, who dove into the new material with true relish, eager to move on from the relative failures of the recent past. This again proved awkward for 'Taking It All Too Hard', whose late release meant it was (in the United States) the most recent Genesis song on the airwaves before 'Invisible Touch' hit in 1986. It was still very much part of the Genesis pantheon when the band went on tour again, so it wouldn't have been unreasonable for a concertgoer to expect to hear it. For many newer listeners, one assumes, 'Taking It All Too Hard' might have even been their favourite Genesis song! Yet the song itself was nowhere to be found on stage. Of course, *Invisible Touch* itself was proving to be bigger than anything that had come before, so it certainly made a bit of sense to push some other pieces aside in order to make room in the setlist for its tracks, but one can't help but feel that this piece wasn't getting its due.

Alas, by the We Can't Dance Tour the song was a distant, fleeting memory deemed unworthy even of consideration for inclusion, and so it is that Genesis have *never once* played this song live. Whether because Tony's negativity toward the piece was contagious or because he had his own issues with it, Mike seemed to share Tony's general opinion when talking about *Genesis:* they both agree that love the first side of the album ('Mama', 'That's All', and 'Home by the Sea/Second Home by the Sea'), but don't venture to make much mention of the second side at all. While it's certainly hard to argue with the quality of that first side, the implication is that the album's second side falls a bit short. And that might *also* be true in a general sense, but it's like, you know US radio hit 'Taking It All Too Hard' is on that second side, right guys?

Tony's little piano piece. Mike's lyrics. And neither of them seems to really want to "own" the song. As a fan, it's frustrating. It feels as though they made this terrific song blending up-tempo rock sensibilities with a ballad-like structure, utterly unique and compelling, and then the Men In Black showed up with their trademark red flashy thing, "neuralysing" their minds and implanting a suggestion that the whole thing was trash. What other explanation could there be? How could they not see how good it is? It was a (minor) hit! People liked it!

But perfectionism and internal criticism aren't rational. They're a complex web of determination, achievement, annoyance, fear, pride, joy, and regret. You and I can listen to 'Taking It All Too Hard' and hear all the things that make it so successful in our minds. There's that terrific piano groove. That chorus you can listen to on repeat without it ever becoming tiresome. The understated bass, the powerful and pleading lead vocals, the "oooh no no!" backing line, even the little drum machine hits that sound like someone's clacking a toddler's wooden blocks together - all of it works. It's outstanding. Even the gentle wall of sound in the background makes you feel right at home, those Banksian chords delivering as they always do.

But that's not what a Tony Banks or Mike Rutherford hears. They were mired in the work and hear only the flaws. The verses don't have quite so strong a hook. The keyboard work is more interesting, sure, but the melody isn't quite as seductive. There's a lot there for a so-called muso to appreciate, but to the casual fan, probably not so much. They're hearing all the ways it could be different, or better, but time constraints and lack of other available material forced them to stick it on the album as-is anyway. For us it's an 80s Genesis pop music work of art. For them, perhaps it's little more than a barely finished, failed experiment.

It's hard to understand the mindset unless you've been there, but once you have, you get where they're coming from right away. I wish the band liked this piece much more than they do, because I really do think it's a stellar pop number. Regardless of how the band might feel about it, for me 'Taking It All Too Hard' will always be the "yes, but" of *Genesis* as an album. As in, "Everyone knows Side A of *Genesis* is better than Side B."

"Yes, but..."

59 - In Too Deep

from *Invisible Touch*, 1986

Our poor Tony just can't catch a break, can he? In the previous entry I mused that perhaps the lyrics of 'Taking It All Too Hard' could have made him more sensitive about his lack of significant solo career success, and now there's 'In Too Deep', rubbing his nose in it once again. Confused? Allow me to explain.

Back in 1978, Genesis was approached to score a horror film called The Shout. Well, the producers *actually* wanted David Bowie for the gig, but as he blew the whole thing off, Genesis served as the backup. Not great timing for the project since at this point Phil was unavailable, but Mike and Tony decided to plough ahead with it on their own. Not that it ended up mattering in the end; the music they composed found itself eventually being billed as merely "incidental music" in the film. Moreover, the sound design of the film left much to be desired from a musical point of view, given that various sound effects during scenes were layered over the music, preventing the primary theme of the score - itself a development of *And Then There Were Three*'s 'Undertow', and later to become 'From the Undertow' on Tony's own *A Curious Feeling* - from even really being heard.

Understandably, this whole affair soured Mike on the movie business well enough, but Tony was not so easily deterred. He came back to the soundtrack scene to score 1983's The Wicked Lady, released a few months before *Genesis*. The film had a very small budget to the point of having to pay its actors in revenue percentages, which would've been great for them except the movie completely bombed, failing to make back even 10% of its meagre production costs. This naturally meant that nobody saw the dang thing and our old friend Tony Banks gained diddly squat for reputation in film scoring circles.

Lesser men would've bowed out right then, but instead Tony came right back for 1984's sequel to the Kubrick classic 2001: A Space Odyssey, called 2010: The Year We Make Contact. Someone had miraculously spotted his work on The Wicked Lady, was suitably impressed with it, and asked him to do the music for this film as well. Eureka! A big-scale film with a built-in following? His work would finally be known everywhere! This could open up heretofore undreamed-of avenues of fame and success for Mr. Banks. An Oscar some years down the road? Perhaps! Who's to say?

Hilariously, tragically, Tony then got fired:

> **Tony:** *I'd originally written music for a scene in the film 2010, which I was summarily sacked from at a certain point, because the director didn't quite know what he wanted.* [18]

The film was a mild success, but of course dear old Tony Banks didn't get to experience any of that. Instead he hopped straight to another film project, Lorca and the Outlaws, later retitled Starship because nobody was going to watch it anyway.

> **Tony:** *Suddenly I had nothing to do for a few months, and I was very frustrated with that. After 2010 fell through, I took the first film that came up, which was an English film called Lorca and the Outlaws. They had no money to pay me, but I just wanted to do something. It was such a low budget thing...After 2010 I was loath to come back to Hollywood, I must admit. I felt that I was rather badly treated.* [68]

What a low point. "They had no money to pay me." How desperate must he have been? This downtrodden and hapless yet immensely talented man takes an unpaid job because he's bored and dead set on breaking into the film industry, and once more gets absolutely nothing for his efforts? Man, what a series of gut punches he's been through. Hard to imagine anyone sticking it out even as long as he did. Surely that's got to be where he threw in the towel, right?

Amazingly, no! No it's not! In 1986, four months ahead of the release of *Invisible Touch*, a flick called Quicksilver came out starring Kevin Bacon, scored by - you guessed it - Tony Banks. But hey, Kevin Bacon is a draw, right? This one SURELY went better, right? Of course not! Panned by critics and theatre-goers alike, Quicksilver was yet another box office disaster with the Banks name attached. Worse, while Tony did score the film, the soundtrack at large was bloated with pop-rock jams, the film production's attempts at scoring a chart hit to help the movie gain exposure. Seeing an opportunity in this clout-chasing, Tony dutifully wrote one such song of his own for a key scene as well. They didn't bother to use it.

Tony: *One of the songs that didn't appear in Quicksilver I recorded with the English singer called Fish, who's with the band Marillion. I think the song would've worked great in the position I wrote it for, but they decided on [someone else's] song...They'd thought they'd got a sure-fire hit. They put it out as a single and it was a big flop, because it's a lousy song, and it didn't work well in the film either.* [68]

Tony is straight up firing shots here! The sad thing is, I'm not even sure he's right; it's unclear which song from Quicksilver he's talking about here, but the movie's main theme 'Quicksilver Lightning', featuring Roger Daltrey of The Who, was a minor hit in the States. Moreover, the song Tony recorded with Fish, 'Shortcut to Somewhere', is irredeemably awful. In any case, right after Quicksilver came and went in a flash, Tony released his album *Soundtracks* so that at least his own dedicated audience might hear his music. Then finally - mercifully, after years spent in varying degrees of failure - Tony Banks swore off the soundtrack business for good.

So it seems a right swift kick to the nads that when Tony Banks finally managed to co-write a hit song famous for being featured in a film, Phil Collins got all the credit.

To all the would-be Patrick Batemans out there, no, I'm not talking about American Psycho. Believe it or not, 'In Too Deep' was actually written for a British film called Mona Lisa. It's a surprisingly complex story about a guy who falls for a prostitute...though come to think of it, the infamous scene in American Psycho featured prostitutes as well. What does that say about 'In Too Deep'? ...Anyway, my point is, Mona Lisa isn't like the movie version of 'Mama' or anything. But I guess it was close enough that the studio rang up Phil Collins to see if he'd write a song for them.

Phil: *The song was [already] there. Ray Cooper, who is Elton John's percussionist and also production manager at HandMade Films, he rang me up...and he said, "Did I have a song, could I write a song for this film?" And I said no, because we're working on the Genesis album, doing a group project. But I said maybe, because we had such a lot of material, that maybe we could find something that would suit. So he sent a cassette of the film along, a video of the film, a rough cut, and I saw it, and [Mike and Tony] saw it too...Anyway, we had this song written. We were just writing anyway. And there was a song that would suit the film. And the lyrics, I just changed it - because I wrote the lyrics to that particular song - I just changed the lyrics so that it would work for the story of the film. It wasn't actually written for the film but it was written with the film in mind.* [72]

How do you write a love song to a prostitute without coming off creepy and laughing maniacally into a spotlight, anyway? Well, 'In Too Deep' is probably about as close as anyone will ever get. You're trying to hit that mix of genuine emotion, caution, self-doubt, maybe a little self-disgust too, but all tinged with a hint of hope. How in the world do you pull that off?

The answer Genesis had, I think, was to just take all the various sounds of their career and mix *them* together as well. It's sometimes easy to forget by the soaring chart success of 1986 that they hadn't actually lost their chops elsewhere.

Mike: *It seemed realistic to me to assume that if you'd got into Genesis in the early days you probably wouldn't be so keen on Invisible Touch [the album]. Fans are always going to prefer the era when they first discover you and assume that any change is for the worst. It's a problem common to all long-lived bands.* [14]

Tony: *We tried writing singles [in the past]; we just didn't seem to be very good at it. And not just that, but we couldn't get them played on the radio. I don't know what it was, perhaps they didn't sound right. But it took us a long time that way...Our strength has always been our variety. We don't want our eggs all sort of tied up into this one single. Every time I'll apologise for it, I'll say, "Well that's okay, that's one side [of what we do], but we do this as well."* [73]

'In Too Deep' manages to combine real drums with a drum machine. It's got big chords mixed with actual melodic lines from the keys. It's got classic, booming, sustained bass sound mixed with little spritzes of adult contemporary style lead guitar. It's got Phil mixing his gentle mid-70s falsetto and pure tones with the sort of throaty angst he could only conjure up from *Duke* and beyond. It's got a pop structure but a bridge where the guitar and keyboards each play a totally unique melody - to one another as well as the rest of the song - to create something more intricate than pop typically dares to go.

Tony: *With the songs, say, off The Lamb Lies Down, maybe they're lyrically more complex, but in terms of the songs themselves - 'Carpet Crawlers' or 'Counting Out Time' - they're all* *attempts at the same sort of thing. Even our first album, From Genesis to Revelation, which goes back to 1969, was all short songs, all attempts at writing hit singles. And all failed. Now we have an album where we've got shorter songs, and because we have an audience, we have hits. I think we just got better at it.* [68]

And that's just it, really. 'In Too Deep' isn't the sound of a prog band abandoning everything that got them there so they could go make some money. It's the sound of a prog band finding their footing, improving in an area that had always somewhat eluded them.

Tony: *We got better at condensing things and being confident enough in the idea that we didn't feel we had to immediately do it and then change it and go to something else.* [2]

That's probably not going to be good enough for prog purists, but it's certainly good enough for me. Now if only we could find Tony a hit, too!

58 - If That's What You Need

from *Calling All Stations*, 1997

One day, 'Follow You Follow Me' was walking through a lovely little park on a cloudy day. It looked as though it were just about to rain, or maybe as though the rain had just recently stopped. Either way, the ground was damp; it *had* been raining quite a bit here recently, in any case, so 'Follow You Follow Me' was grateful for the brief dry spell to go outside and stretch her legs. She started walking but soon found herself unconsciously skipping down the path, as elegant and graceful as always. It wasn't something she could help; the outside air was just so invigorating. All she wanted was a little bit of exercise, a touch of light breeze, a glimpse at the greenery. But in the end she found so much more than that.

You see, at roughly the same time 'Follow You Follow Me' entered the park from the west entrance, 'Shipwrecked' came rushing in from the east. He was always something of a languid guy, always looking ahead to the next thing with a head full of worry, and so never finding himself in a hurry to reach it. Crippled with a deep-seated fear of missing out, 'Shipwrecked' had somehow gotten it into his head that it was best to be habitually late for, well, everything. "If you're not early, you're late." That's what his old school instructor had repeatedly drilled into him, and though at first the statement almost made sense, now when he stopped to think about it he found the mantra so ridiculous it was laughable. If you're not early you're late? No, surely it was much better to be late and smell all the roses along the way than to be early and miss the scents altogether.

This might normally be all well and good, but on this particular day 'Shipwrecked' had a job interview, and thus found himself in something of an uncharacteristic hurry. Well, a hurry by his standards, at any rate. And so, as he typically never moved quickly enough to need to multitask, he found it difficult to divide his attention between getting the perfect Windsor Knot on his tie and actually watching where he was going. Thus, 'Follow You Follow Me', her smiling face turned upward at a delightful little pair of lovebirds in a nearby tree - cuckoo to you! - walked smack into 'Shipwrecked' and they both took a most unfortunate tumble into a muddy bit of grass.

It took several stunned moments for reality to set in for dear old 'Shipwrecked'; his suit had become so filthy that the job opportunity might as well already be lost. But at the same time, who was this angel sitting next to him? She must have fallen from the sun and impacted him on the way down, because beings such as this surely didn't walk on their feet like the unhallowed souls below. And he'd gotten her all covered in mud! No, no, this wouldn't do at all! Not being a particularly clever or charismatic man, 'Shipwrecked' couldn't think of anything to say other than "Oh no" and "I'm sorry." But what he lacked in creativity he liked to make up for with quantity, so he dazedly found himself just repeating those two phrases over and over and over again to the beauteous soul before him.

And then, to his utter shock and bewilderment, she laughed! 'Follow You Follow Me' actually laughed! And not just one of those polite, awkward, "please get away from me you overbearing creep" kind of laughs either, but the real, genuine article! See, 'Follow You Follow Me' was a big believer that the universe has a strange way of pushing people together. And wouldn't you know it, she had *just* been looking at those happy little birds and, for the first time in a long time, felt a tad lonely. Yet before she had even had a chance to dwell on it, wham! Here's this guy in an ill-fitting suit like he's dressed for a date (or at the very least something quite important), now totally covered in mud because of her own inattention, plans ruined, and all he can do is apologise to *her*? It helped that he was sort of cute. Well, OK, maybe not *traditionally* cute...OK so he wasn't cute at all, but he *did* seem really sincere and the way he looked at her, well. That was enough to make anyone feel special.

> **Tony:** *'If That's What You Need' was another song that somebody developed out of one of those loops in a similar situation to 'Shipwrecked'. Just a little bit which we made something of and wrote the chords on top of it. Again, Mike wrote a kind of romantic lyric on top of it and I suppose it is more in the tradition of 'Follow You Follow Me' and that kind of thing, more than other things. But I think it works, and I actually prefer that to 'Not About Us' myself. I think it is a better song, but they are both more straightforward things.* [25]

Over the next few years, 'Follow You Follow Me' had a wonderful time with 'Shipwrecked'. She wasn't too fond of all the in-laws, though at least she got along decently well with little sister 'Not About Us'. But none of that truly mattered in the long run, because at last she had a family, someone to stay with her. And 'Shipwrecked', well, he still couldn't quite believe his good fortune. He hadn't exactly thought too much about it before, but it took finding the love of his life to realise just how long he'd been feeling helpless and alone, drifting out to sea. He had been so busy patting himself on the back for his relaxed approach to life that he never realised what it actually was: total lethargy. But now he had someone. Someone beautiful, yes, but also someone active and full of life. And he realised now how much more he could be with her by his side. He couldn't believe what she meant to him, and if this was love, he realised he never should have been satisfied to be a single.

> **Ray:** *'If That's What You Need'...I regard...as being [one of] the best single option[s] but if we'd started with that it would have given the wrong impression, and made people think "More fucking middle of the road Genesis, here we go!" and really the album isn't middle of the road, it has got a lot of stuff on it that is definitely not middle of the road, although there are one or two songs there that are.* [28]

On the 1st of September, 1997, 'Follow You Follow Me' and 'Shipwrecked' had their first and only child, 'If That's What You Need'. And while the baby may have gotten a couple of bum genes from his dad along the way, all the well-wishers would always say the same thing to 'Follow You Follow Me' whenever they'd see her out and about with the stroller: "Oh, what a little darling! He looks just like his mommy!"

"I know," she'd beam.

57 - Banjo Man

B-side to 'Congo', 1997

By 1997, there wasn't much left on the musical hors d'oeuvres tray that Genesis hadn't taken a nibble of. Saccharine-sweet 60s pop, hippie rock, symphonic progressive, acoustic folk, jazz fusion, avant-garde, adult contemporary, straight pop, reggae, hard rock, country/western, R&B, easy listening...in essence if you name a genre, Genesis probably had at least one track that tapped into it to a meaningful degree. But there were two major exceptions to this, on radically different ends of the musical and cultural spectrum: hip hop and bluegrass. While the former of those was at times an inspiration, especially to Phil Collins, the band mercifully spared us any attempts to create their own rap anthem. Not so for the latter, where Ray Wilson came on board and helped them pen a bluegrass style number about, fittingly, a guy playing a banjo.

'Banjo Man' has no business being any good. Ray wrote it and hates it. Genesis scrubbed it from the album at the last minute because they apparently hate it. My dad even hates it. There's a very good chance that you, reading this book right now, probably hate it, assuming you've ever even heard it in the first place. Maybe I ought to hate it too. Two middle-aged wealthy, upper-crust Brits and a post-grunge Scotsman trying to channel Appalachian roots? What could possibly go *right* with that idea? It's horrible on every level.

> **Ray:** *With regard to...'Banjo Man'...I mean, that was a load of shit, to be honest with you. And the guys of Genesis had the same opinion...I mean if you take the song 'Calling All Stations' and try to compare it with... 'Banjo Man', I just don't think there is any comparison.* [26]

And yet! From the first second of the piece I'm somehow 100% in. Mike's just pickin' away on this killer riff; I'm not even sure if he's using a real banjo or not, but it doesn't particularly matter to me. It *sounds* like it could be a real banjo, and that's all you really need. It gives way to more traditional guitar in the darker sections, but once Ray says "emotion" he starts pluckin' again with a fury. You can almost see the stalk of wheat in his teeth, the tattered straw hat on his head, his faded overalls catching the sun on their buttons as he leans against the post of his dilapidated porch. But on top of this performance sits Tony's chordplay, coming in with big swells on 2 and 4 alongside the drums, creating the kind of anticipation that true bluegrass music thrives on. I'm telling you, this combination is way more effective than it's got any right to be.

Then you can add to all of that Ray's vocals, which don't even approach his finest hour on a technical performance level, but which really strongly paint the picture of a struggling busker sacrificing his ambition just to get by:

> *Always play just what they want me to*
> *Everybody wants the same song*
> *If only I could do it in my own way*

One wonders, knowing how excited Ray was about the direction of his own musical career before joining Genesis, how much of this song is like his secret diary about his feelings in the band. "I should just say no and play them what I want to" smells strongly of Ray lining the lyrics with his own suppressed frustration at not having the freedom to do more writing in the group, hoping that Tony and Mike might hear this performance and come around, but allowing him plausible deniability if they didn't. That may be far off base from reality, but my point in the musing is to say that even if the vocal performance won't floor you with its power or skill, it sounds like it comes from a very real place, and it's accordingly emoted quite well.

> *They feel my emotion*
> *Emotion*

There's a sense of darkness about the whole affair. Where bluegrass music can sound lonely and mournful in its playing, it's rarely got the sort of shadow hanging over it that 'Banjo Man' produces. Despite my praises for Mike's playing and the images it conjures up in my head, I would never hear this song and consider it true bluegrass or think it came from an actual bluegrass outfit. It's distinctly "Genesis does bluegrass," and maybe that's another reason people don't tend to like it. Maybe it just feels too artificial or put on, and there's a sense of discomfort in hearing a favourite band trespass into lands where they might not quite belong. Personally, I think the song is better for the foreignness of it. Those darker chords of Tony's carry all that emotional weight of the song, lifting it out of "meaningless fluff" territory and into someplace much more impactful.

Even still, as I was working through my ranking exercise and even again as I've been writing all these entries, I've continually wondered if there was something I was missing about 'Banjo Man'. Some better reason to hate it that everyone else seems to get except for me. And so, bizarrely, I've listened to the song more over this whole endeavour than perhaps any other Genesis tune in the catalogue. Moreover, most of the time I was listening with the express intent of searching for flaws. "How can I rank this lower while still maintaining my integrity? Because surely I can't leave 'Banjo Man' this high. I mean, it's 'Banjo Man' for crying out loud. I must've had a moment of weakness, or been in a strange mindset before. I'll listen to it again, get confirmation that it's not as good as I thought, and then I can send it a bunch of spots down on the list and feel better."

I really can't make no sense of it
As hard as I try
Is it something I do wrong?
Please won't you tell me why

Dear reader, *every single time* I tried to put a dagger in 'Banjo Man' I instead came away thinking, "Got dang, 'Banjo Man' is a *jam*. I wonder if I should rank it even higher?" I can't resist this song. This simple melody is all I have. Please send help.

56 - Afterglow

from *Wind & Wuthering*, 1976

You know, one thing that has always drawn my attention a bit when people refer to Genesis' live medleys is the way they are commonly named. Now, obviously when a medley has been given an actual title, like the 'Old Medley' from the We Can't Dance Tour as immortalised on *The Way We Walk, Vol. 2: The Longs*, we use that name. And when medleys are contained entirely within a given song, like when the band decided to close their concerts by stuffing 'Turn It On Again' full of snippet-length covers of various rock hits from other groups, it's easy to say something like "Oh, that's the 'Turn It On Again' medley" without any hesitation.

But of particular interest to me is the so-called 'In the Cage' medley that the band performed in several different flavours from 1980 all the way through to 2021, with the Last Domino tour likely being the final time we ever see such a medley on stage. Here is every permutation of it the band ever performed, along with when they were played:

- 1980 - Duke Tour - *In the Cage / The Colony of Slippermen / Afterglow*
- 1981 - Abacab Tour - *In the Cage / The Cinema Show / Afterglow*
- 1982 - Three Sides Live Encore Tour - *In the Cage / The Cinema Show / The Colony of Slippermen / Afterglow*
- 1983/84 - Mama Tour - *In the Cage / The Cinema Show / ...In That Quiet Earth / The Colony of Slippermen / Afterglow*
- 1986 - Invisible Touch Tour - *In the Cage / ...In That Quiet Earth / Supper's Ready*
- 1986/87 - Invisible Touch Tour - *In the Cage / ...In That Quiet Earth / Afterglow*
- 2007 - Turn It On Again Tour - *In the Cage / The Cinema Show / Duke's Travels / Afterglow*
- 2021 - The Last Domino? Tour - *Fading Lights / The Cinema Show / ...In That Quiet Earth / Afterglow*

Now don't be fooled by the track listing of the *Three Sides Live* album: it's not called 'In the Cage Medley' there but rather 'In the Cage (Medley - Cinema Show - Slippermen)'. The idea is that when seeking a track, this marks the start of 'In the Cage', which then goes on into other songs as a medley. You also won't get clarity from *Live Over Europe 2007*, where the track is listed with just the songs comprising the medley itself - again, no appellation.

Still, on first glance, I get it: for twenty-seven years 'In the Cage' always opened the medley, was the only song that appeared in every single iteration of the medley, and it was always played in its entirety as well. But I contend that this could also be called the 'Afterglow' medley, and that such an appellation might be even *more* appropriate. 'In the Cage' in this context alters its studio ending by replacing the fade out with a run into one or more snippets, but those snippets inexorably find themselves leading right back into 'Afterglow', itself *also* always played in its entirety. Indeed, it's so important a piece that it gets its own track listing on each of those two aforementioned live albums. It's the release that the instrumental middle bits of the given medley - whatever they might be at the time - all build up to, themselves built upon the inherent tension that 'In the Cage' creates and never disperses on its own. 'In the Cage' is played as a nice throwback to an bygone era, but 'Afterglow' is the *actual* focus point of the musical endeavour.

Mike: *'Afterglow'...was a big highpoint on stage. We'd have a huge arc of magenta lights behind the drum riser going out into the crowd.* [14]

Tony: *You could get great beauty out of [the Vari-Lites] by putting a bit of smoke through them, which created a dreamy and lovely effect which worked really well on a song like 'Afterglow'. Sometimes we'd incorporate an effect that was absolutely stunning, but use it only once in the course of a show. We'd get comments like, "You've got all these bloody lights and you're not using them," but if you could hold the effect back until three quarters of the way through the show and suddenly something happened that no one had ever seen before, that was visually very powerful.* [1]

And indeed, if you check the setlists for the 80s tours, you'll see that this is exactly where 'Afterglow' always hit: just ahead of the first closer before the encore, or in other words about three quarters of the way through the set. Despite this, I must admit to one glaring fact that provides the strongest argument against reconsidering the work as a so-called 'Afterglow Medley': there is, undeniably, that single iteration of the medley listed above that doesn't include 'Afterglow' at all. But is this really a problem, or is it the exception that proves the rule?

A closer look reveals that the Invisible Touch Tour had a whopping seven legs (North America, Oceania, North America again, Japan, Europe, North America a third time, and finally Europe a second time), and the end section of 'Supper's Ready' only closed the medley for the very first leg before the band went "What are we doing?" and reverted back to 'Afterglow' forevermore. This is key, and I want to stress it again: they tried to pull 'Afterglow' from the 'In the Cage Medley', replacing it with what they likely considered to be the strongest closing section of music of their entire careers, only to discover that they *actually* had an 'Afterglow Medley' all along - one that just so happened to always begin with the song 'In the Cage'.

If further evidence was needed, we got it with the 2021 Last Domino tour, where a decision was made to include the medley, but now for the first time *without* 'In the Cage' at all. Perhaps because of a desire to spend some time fondly looking back on their careers or saying goodbye, or perhaps because the demands on the vocal performance were too high for Phil Collins to adequately perform, 'In the Cage' was dropped in favour of 'Fading Lights'. Yet there was 'Afterglow' at the end of it all, the ever-present rock of the thing.

> **Mike:** *'Afterglow' is still a classic. I think it still sounds great.* [3]

Why do I care so much about this? Well, if you seek out video recordings of any of the live performances they did of the medleys over the years and you'll see what I mean. You'll see how the lights shift to warm colours just as the warmth of the song itself takes over. You'll see how a 2007 crowd cheers wildly as the opening strains of 'Afterglow' reach their ears. You'll perhaps argue that they were really cheering Phil's drum performance during the stellar instrumental sections of 'Duke's Travels', and I think that's true as well, but they're also cheering his return to the microphone, because hey - it's 'Afterglow', man. I think it strikes me a certain way because I was at one of those 2007 shows, so there's a sense of nostalgia, but also I have a very real memory of how powerful that transition was. The audio recordings from the various live albums are great too, of course, but the pure atmosphere the song creates in person is really something else.

Yet for all my talk about 'Afterglow' as a live piece, it's not one of those like 'Throwing It All Away' where the song's form dramatically changes live compared to what's on the album. It's pretty much the same exact thing, right down to its status as a cathartic closer, though I do think it sounds better live than on the album. *Wind & Wuthering* ends on a three song suite of 'Unquiet Slumbers for the Sleepers...', '...In That Quiet Earth', and 'Afterglow'. Unfortunately I needed to break them all apart for this exercise, but in practice this mini-suite flows like a soft, atmospheric instrumental piece that explodes into bombast and nervous energy before all the pent up tension is released by, you guessed it, 'Afterglow'. It's a very unusual way to end an album, but one nevertheless quite reflective of the band's mindset at the time.

> **Steve:** *It was an album uncompromised by the need to have a hit single. I don't think there were too many of them on there. I think 'Afterglow' perhaps could've made that hit single...But, you know, we were making an album at that time. There weren't the pressures of having to do three minute songs that were going to be acceptable for video, et cetera, so I do think it's the band at its best, doing perhaps what it did best, at least with my inclusion in it. So I am very fond of [Wind & Wuthering].* [3]

'Afterglow' itself has a familiarity about it too, but perhaps that's just because the subconscious can sometimes register it as certain classic Christmas carol.

> **Tony:** *'Afterglow' I really wrote in just about the time it took to play it. I just sat down and...fancied using that chord sequence and just started singing on it. I was really excited by that, because I don't normally do things like that. But a couple days after I'd written it I thought, "Shit, what I've done is I've written 'Have Yourself A Merry Little Christmas' again. It's a terrible thought! I was thinking "Have yourself a..." and [feeling immense dread], and I listened to that particular song and realised it WASN'T the same, and I could get away with it. But it was a terrible moment, when you think, "God, I'll never get away with it." But, 'Afterglow' became a big stage favourite, was just a very strong kind of anthemic piece, which I think closed the album really well. So I was very pleased with it.* [3]

Hey, maybe there's something to that, yeah? Christmas carols work because they've got those singable melodies, right? Well, 'Afterglow' has a flow that falls right in line with that same kind of ease.

> **Tony:** *The basic song is in G and the chorus is in E flat. The relationship between those two keys gives the whole tune a more wistful feeling. Then when you come back to the big chorus*

at the end, we change from E flat to C, which is a very dramatic kind of change. There's a lot you can do with key changes to make a song more interesting. [23]

Not that it's just a la-la-la, children singing at your door kind of vibe about the piece. There's real emotional weight as well.

Tony: *'Afterglow' is simple but still has elements of that splendour prog rock has...It's about a reaction to a disaster and the realisation of what's important to you, in a slightly cataclysmic way. As I was writing the melody, I wrote that first verse and made the chorus the essence of what the person is actually thinking.* [27]

Phil's vocals get progressively more desperate as the song continues, ending on the simple but impactful gut-punch of a lyric, "I miss you more." Then massive amounts of vocal overdubbing (replaced live with keyboard choir samples) join with the climbing bass and glimmering guitar to create a sound best described like, well...can music cry? Is it possible for a tune to shed a waterfall of tears? Because that's how this has always struck me, as beautifully haunting as anything I've ever heard. It's like Tony found the musical formula to create feelings of sympathetic loss in his listeners and, being a mad, evil genius, said, "Yeah, let's try it." It's powerful, powerful stuff, though separating it from any other tracks reduces its impact somewhat.

Mike: *'Afterglow' comes as a peaceful, relaxing moment after some epic moments.* [36]

Without those epic moments, it's not really a release *from* anything, so it loses quite a bit of the emotional oomph it otherwise has when the "disaster" bits Tony referenced still occur in front of it. Nevertheless, it's good enough that I'm often willing to play something else in front of it just for the sake of getting the payoff of 'Afterglow' at the end. Something like, say, a medley.

55 - Jesus He Knows Me

from *We Can't Dance*, 1991

Slick. In a word, that's 'Jesus He Knows Me' and everything surrounding it. From the music to the production quality, from the way the words all scan really smoothly to the personalities of their subjects, this whole endeavour is just *slick* from start to finish. Let's hit these aspects in order, shall we?

We begin with the music, now as always the most important thing. It kicks off with this opening keyboard riff, but like 'Keep It Dark' a decade prior, the riff can't be bothered to start on the down beat. Instead, the song is built around beats 2 and 4. That's where the snares hit when they come in, but unlike that alienesque *Abacab* track, here the rest of the instruments follow suit. Thus, this riff actually starts on beat 2, and falls on 4. Again, the brain expects the hits to come on 1 and 3, so starting on 2 tricks you into thinking that's where you are. It's only when the bass kicks in on 1 proper that you start to realise what's going on. As a result, you get something played in straight time, maybe relatively ho-hum in composition, but sounding like it's always driving forward. This is aided in no small part by the song's tempo, which is a blistering 180 BPM (beats per minute) or thereabouts, meaning that a full three beats - or 75% of a measure - pass by *every second*. It's like a hot red convertible blasting down the fast lane; very rare speed not only for Genesis but for pop songs in general.

The chorus has strong chords that come in on 1, by contrast, which is why it's so dang catchy. Nobody walks around singing the verses to this song, but the chorus? That's something else. It's still flying at a hundred miles an hour, and that snare is still kicking on the even beats (as snares are wont to do), but now the ear can follow it all along. More than that, the drive of the verses has created such a strong sense of kinetic energy, you almost *need* to clap along, right? Or is that just me? Either way, the motion is infectious - *slick*, you might say - which leads us to the middle break and the second area I wanted to cover: the production.

We Can't Dance saw the band dismiss Hugh Padgham, with whom they'd worked since *Abacab*, in favour of a fellow named Nick Davis, who had done some work with both Tony and Mike in their solo careers. Yet it didn't take long at all before Nick, excited to work with this band he loved, started sweating bullets.

> **Nick Davis:** *We were working on 'Jesus He Knows Me'. We had done a take during the day and after everyone had gone home, I stayed at the studio with the assistant, listening back to the track. I heard one drum fill that either wasn't that good or was dreadfully out of time, and thought, "Oh God, I'm going to have to tell Phil Collins that I'd like him to do that again." I had only been working with them for two or three days. The next morning he came in and I said, "Phil, by the way, I think there's a bit of a dodgy drum fill in the take we did yesterday." He went, "Oh, it's going to be like that, is it?" He said it tongue in cheek, but my immediate reaction was "What have I done?"...He listened back to it and said, "Yeah, that's terrible. Good. Well spotted," and from that moment on we were fine.* [1]

Not only did he help get the drums cleaned up, but he even helped push the musical direction when the band wasn't sure which way to go.

> **Nick:** *'Jesus He Knows Me' didn't have a middle section at the time and I remember suggesting to Phil, "Why don't we try a downbeat, reggae feel," which he tried out and which stuck.* [1]

That "reggae feel" is a great trick. It sounds like it's going half the speed as the rest of the song, but the pace is in reality no different; they're all just playing longer notes. So you *hear* a shift in tempo and *feel* a sense of relaxation, but it's all illusory. When you have a producer determined to make the most out of an album to the point of influencing the music itself, that can either be stifling or liberating. Here it's the latter, and everything about how this song sounds on record is just, well, *slick*.

> **Phil:** *It makes a difference whether you just let the music splash past you or if you listen carefully. Maybe there is more to it than you think.* [20]

'Jesus He Knows Me' is no lyrical slouch either, though it emerged from another one of Phil's trademark, off-the-cuff improvisations.

> **Phil:** *'In the Air Tonight' was totally improvised. I sang what came out of my head and wrote it down afterwards. And because it worked for that first record, that's what I've always done. When I'm singing along the phrases come out. You can hit higher notes singing some words or if your throat's in a particular position. You're improvising with your voice in the same way you would improvise on a sax...that's how I came up with the chorus of "Jesus he knows me and he knows I'm right"...* [1]

Do me a favour. Say '"Cos Jesus he knows me" aloud, over and over, really fast. It sounds almost like a buzzing bee, doesn't it? Over that tempo, over that sense of frenetic motion, Phil instinctively invents a phrase that itself just zips on by. And from there the rest of the lyrics have a starting point. You've got this core phrase that just meshes *perfectly* with the overall feel you're creating musically, and now you can build the rest of the words around that theme. Coming up with a theme and then trying to hammer in whatever old words you want to say, regardless of whether they sing well or not? Clunky. Letting the music dictate the perfect words to sing? *Slick.*

Which takes us to the subject matter itself, naturally: American televangelists, particularly of the deep south.

> **Tony:** *I like 'Jesus He Knows Me', which is a much more cynical song - more cynical than Phil normally is. He's normally a bit more genuine. I'm a bit of a cynic myself, as you've probably spotted, so I like the cynical approach of that song. I like it a lot. And it sounds good, too. That's the other thing: a lyric's got to actually sound good when it's sung.* [35]

> **Phil:** *In Genesis, I write a lot about things that I've observed. For example, 'Jesus He Knows Me' is about an American TV priest and how he turns people's beliefs into money. When I first saw the man on American television, I was totally fascinated. These people are hypocrites, total hypocrites!...These people build an empire with their double standards and even get away with it. The whole thing is a hypocritical farce!* [20]

These guys are popular targets for lampooning in the internet age when their daytime broadcasts have been expanded beyond the intended audience of poor and desperate rural folk, but there's a seriousness about what these guys are doing: they're con men - often very successful ones - typically preying on the people who can least afford it.

> **Phil:** *I don't know how they get away with it, to be quite honest...There's a guy called Ernest Angley...and he gets people to send in a hundred dollars for a "personal prayer" that obviously is not a personal prayer at all...This guy, for example, has trucks, you know, like we go on tour with 12, 15 trucks. He has the same thing!...He has seen the video [for 'Jesus He Knows Me']...he thought it was very flattering. It wasn't meant to be sacrilegious, it was just meant to be, "Listen people, wake up!" These people are fleecing them.* [74]

In a word, they're *slick*. Slick hair, slick suits, slick messages, slick schemes. And now, in context, the rest of the song slots even more firmly into place. The speed of the music, like the cars they drive or the fast-talking they do on air. The fact that the verses are just off enough to keep you from fully buying in, but the chorus is exactly what you want to hear, so you check your reservations at the door. The middle section that is built upon a rhythmic lie, but you groove to it anyway. And you realise how masterful this bit of pop really is.

Luckily though, Genesis weren't quite content to let the structure of the music speak for itself and deigned to bless us with a music video. While other Genesis videos may have more accolades or be more popular, none for me top what they did in 'Jesus He Knows Me', dressing the three guys up as *slick* TV preachers and begging viewers to touch the screen to be healed - but only if Preacher Phil gets eighteen million dollars by the weekend. You get to see Mike and Tony struggle with lip syncing. You get a telethon-style family scene where Tony wears a wig that makes him look like Robert Tilton, who would later become the "star" of the satirical Farting Preacher videos. It's a hysterical video; the best they've ever done.

> **Mike:** *Phil, Tony, and I were whooping it up making the video in the guise of [tel]evangelists, and having a small insight into their lifestyle. The filming started with a jacuzzi filled with Californian babes...and us, of course. The next scene was of me having a four-hand massage - non-pornographic - with even more babes. The filming took longer than expected, although no one was complaining. Except I did have to call home and say I wouldn't be home as this wretched filming was running overtime. I'm not sure [my wife] Angie felt too sympathetic once she saw the video.* [14]

> **Tony:** *The record is undoubtedly accessible because over the years we have always tried not to sound as esoteric as before - we just never had a penchant for aggressive guitars. But there are moments of anger and a feeling of discomfort that we want to express in our songs...We have always been a very emotional band. It's even one of our strong points - building moods and manipulating people's feelings. But we also wanted to show humour on this album because if a record is too serious it will be boring.* [20]

Real humour combined with a real message combined with a real hook and groove. That's 'Jesus He Knows Me'. In a word? *Slick.*

54 - For Absent Friends

from *Nursery Cryme*, 1971

Genesis during the Gabriel years were an often contentious lot, as every one of them will freely admit. The primary culprits were Tony and Pete, best of friends and bitterest of enemies all at once. Each one had very strong visions of where the band should move musically, and though they were often aligned similarly, when those two visions came into conflict, it really blew up.

> **Peter:** *Tony was quite used to getting his way and I was probably the only person who would take him on, on any issue...When there was a discussion about whether a solo should last for twenty minutes, if you said "No" you had to decide whether you were prepared to take the next four days of argument to justify your position.* [1]

By virtue of necessity Mike had learned to navigate these murky waters over the previous few years, arguing his case as necessary to one or the other fellow Charterhouse alum, or else simply joining one side of the squabble so it could reliably shout down the other. You know, really healthy stuff.

And then here come Phil Collins and Steve Hackett, wondering what on earth they'd just signed up for, understandably forming a bond with one another over the "Can you believe this?" kinds of conversations that would naturally - but quietly - result from witnessing someone storm out of a house because they didn't get the chord sequence they wanted. And while Phil at this point had no internal drive to write any music of his own, Steve was feeling keen to dip his toes in the water a bit, just to see what would happen, and felt like having a partner might be beneficial.

> **Steve:** *I was aware that Phil and I were the new boys in the situation and it was often easier to get one person on board with an idea first, and then present it to a committee that had been together since childhood!* [70]

The result was one of the most purely pleasant songs the band's ever put down on record. I say "the band" here, but I'm not sure that anyone else even performs on it besides Steve and Phil. I'd thought Pete did some backing vocals for a while, but after listening repeatedly I find myself doubting that and I think it's all just Phil tracking over himself. Makes sense in a way, given Steve's reluctance to even play Peter the song in the first place.

> **Steve:** *I think I was too shy to present it to the lead singer. "Hey Pete, do you fancy doing this?" Because Pete was very much the star; very open, friendly, approachable, et cetera, but at the same time I think maybe the fact that we were the two new boys - Phil and I - we sort of wrote that thing together. We wrote the lyrics together; I came up with the music for it. It was a pleasant little ditty.* [3]

> **Phil:** *Steve and I did write the song because we were the two new boys and kind of felt, "Well why don't we see what we can do?"* [1]

One can only avoid the inevitable for so long, however. Steve and Phil now had a tiny little song and, if they ever wanted it to see the light of day, were faced with the daunting prospect of playing "show and tell" with the more accomplished songwriters who hired them.

> **Steve:** *I felt it was good to join up with Phil as the other new boy: Collins Minor and Hackett Junior, going off to a corner somewhere and presenting the senior boys, the prefects, with our humble efforts.* [1]

> **Phil:** *To acquaint the guys with the lyrics and melody, I open my mouth and go for it...a bit. I'm not sure about this - to me, my voice sounds soft and tentative. But the guys like it, and that's good enough for me.* [12]

It almost certainly helped their cause that this was a song coming from a place completely external to the traditional power struggles of the group. Neither Steve nor Phil had been around long enough yet to offend anyone, and it's perhaps easier to take a leap of faith in a couple guys you already decided were good enough to be in your band than it is to put aside a history of occasional bad blood. The fact that the song clocked in at under two minutes would only make it more palatable; a very small sacrifice in album time to let these guys feel like full contributors to the group.

> **Mike:** *I could have done without it on the record, but because it was something that the pair of them - the new recruits - had written together it seemed right to have it there.* [14]

> **Tony:** *It's not my favourite moment, I have to say, but [Phil's] voice sounds very nice, very pure. It almost had a James Taylor sort of quality in those days before he got this great big rasp that was to come later. But it showed that he had it. I think because he had a nice voice we thought it would be great to sort of feature it as a solo thing, and that was it. I think Pete was quite happy with that actually. Just showed another side to the group, I think.* [3]

> **Mike:** *Any formation of the band has always been, anyone that can do something, bring something to the table, you know - singing, playing flute, oboe - we encourage it! Whatever you've got, you use. I think Pete enjoyed having Phil singing.* [3]

> **Phil:** *The fact that it was on the album I guess is because it was very different from anything else. I think we were quite happy to have that variety.* [1]

The so-called "senior boys" may only be lukewarm on this track, but Phil is right on that 'For Absent Friends' stands apart from everything else they had working at the time, and that's a big part of its appeal to me. Some songs take you on an epic journey from Point A to Point Z and everything in between. Some songs give you a great beat and catchy chorus so you can dance and forget about your cares a bit. Still other songs come at you with power, with force, perhaps less about creating a mood and more about inflicting that mood upon the listener.

'For Absent Friends', by contrast, is like a Bob Ross painting in song form. Now, I know, Bob Ross is all about landscapes and this song is about people, but I'm talking style and feel here. This is a song that just effortlessly generates imagery in simple brushstrokes. A chilly day in the park; a little girl pushing her baby sibling along; a simple church service led by a friendly, familiar face; the comfort of consistent companionship with a dear friend who shares in your circumstances. It's not flowery, gorgeous imagery. It's not psychedelic, surreal imagery. It's not grand, majestic imagery. It's a grounded scene, painted with details, strikingly believable and all the lovelier for it. It's a snapshot that ends as soon as the pair of widows board the bus that ambles down the street, because the frame of the painting only provides us a window into this single street corner.

> **Steve:** *We were trying to devise a song where the cast of players would have a different relationship to the traditional one of boy/girl so we dreamt up the idea of a couple of old ladies whose husbands had passed on, and concentrated on very English imagery, a park with padlocked swings and generally the kind of "keep off the grass" feel that I was to explore with future songs. I guess it was our idea of producing a lyric that was quintessentially English.* [1]

The exploration of what is "quintessentially English" would define *Selling England by the Pound* just two years later, so even if Tony and Mike felt as though they were simply doing the new boys a favour by allowing 'For Absent Friends' on *Nursery Cryme*, its style and message must have struck a chord along the way. This was new ground for Genesis and eventually they became unified in their desire to explore it. 'For Absent Friends' planted that seed.

> **Steve:** *I felt we were writing our own 'Eleanor Rigby', with imagery like the abandoned swings symbolic of the harsh greyness of British life.* [70]

Here's the most striking thing to me, given the love for more sprawling, complex tunes that Genesis was known for in this "peak progressive" era: if 'For Absent Friends' were any longer, or tried any harder, it wouldn't be nearly as strong. Its brevity and simplicity give the song a kind of unexpected gravity all its own. It's there, and then it isn't - a momentary snapshot of something very real and all the more poignant for its pure and unembellished reflection of reality. Inadvertently, Steve and Phil discovered something important about constructing and balancing albums here: that on a record full of myths and monsters and magical musical boxes, it's good to have a track that pulls your head back down out of the clouds...even if only for a couple minutes.

53 - Inside and Out

from *Spot the Pigeon*, 1977

Have you ever been falsely accused of something? And no, I don't mean like "I was at a party and the dude next to me passed gas, and then he tried to blame me for it by having an overdramatic reaction, pointing at me like, 'WHOA, that stinks, man!'" That's certainly not cool, but it's also pretty small potatoes. No, what I'm asking is whether you've ever been falsely accused of something *serious*. I have. It's, uh, not a fun situation in which to find oneself. Here's my story.

 In my late teens I became aware of a girl who attended the same church as I did, though our paths didn't cross a whole lot as we generally hung out with different groups of people; she went to an all-girls private school, and I was a couple years older than she was as well. At that age, that's enough to be essentially different worlds completely. Yet despite that, when we actually did meet we seemed to hit it off pretty well and we acknowledged the strong mutual interest we shared in one another. But I was also keenly aware of the fact that her prom was coming up in a month or two and I became a little suspicious: is this girl *actually* into me, or is she just trying to get an older guy to be her prom date for the "prestige" factor? The age difference wasn't significant, but any time you're in high school and dating anyone out of your grade level, it's significant. Besides, I had no insight into the culture of her high school. How much of a status move would that be for her? Did her classmates and friends care about that kind of thing? Did *she*? I realised I didn't know her all that well.

 Not wanting to end what seemed like a promising relationship before it could even get off the ground - and being a believer that open and honest communication is the cornerstone to any successful relationship - I voiced my concerns to her. She assured me that what her peers would think of me was the absolute furthest thing from her mind; she just wanted to date and see what happened, and the timing of it was completely coincidental. So that's what we did, and things seemed to be going well enough, as teenage flings are measured. We hung out multiple times, at least one proper date if memory serves, and the mutual interest appeared to remain strong. Then came her prom. I still wasn't completely over my fear of being used, and debated taking a "prove it" stance with her. You know, "I'm your boyfriend but I'm not taking you to prom because I don't fully trust you." If you read that and think "yikes" then you're completely right; I'd be torpedoing the relationship myself, in that case. Thus, despite my reservations, I dutifully attended the event.

 Now, I need to mention here: big parties aren't really my thing, and hanging out with a bunch of shallow, clique-y high school girls really was *definitely* not my thing either - not to say my date fit that description, but rather when you go to an all-girls high school prom, that's the environment you're walking into. I made sure to meet her friends, dance a little, make some jokes - you know, "good date" stuff - but I think she may have sensed that I was out of my element a bit there. I did have a pretty good time overall and (in my mind) made the most of the evening, but though I wanted to spend time with her, I didn't *really* want to spend time at her prom, and perhaps that came through more than I'd have liked. I thought she mostly had a good time, but there were moments I could feel her disappointment: that maybe I wasn't quite the shining life of the party she hoped for, and that maybe her friends weren't all that impressed with me (and therefore with her for bringing me).

 I wasn't too surprised to get the phone call a few days after prom night, though it bummed me out nonetheless. "I don't think this is working out." As if that cynical voice inside of me needed any more fuel, right? "Trust your gut on these things! You *knew* she was just using you for prom!" We had a nice conversation as these things go, helped by the facts that we'd only been together a short while, and that I had instinctually retained some emotional distance for just this eventuality. We wished each other well, I cursed my own stupidity, and I thought that was the end of it. Until, that is, a couple months later when a mutual friend of ours I really respected (and still do) reached out to me and started asking me some very pointed "hypothetical" questions, chief of which was this: "Would you ever hit a girl?"

 I was flabbergasted by the bizarre line of conversation and sensed that something was afoot. After humouring him with some answers (I could tell this was very important to him) and a bit of goading, he relaxed. I could tell he was relieved by what I had to say, and he then came clean: my ex had been casually accusing me in conversations with friends, *at church,* of physically abusing her while we were together. I was absolutely staggered. She wasn't "reporting" anything to anyone in any official sense, but an accusation that serious nonetheless eventually works its way up the church leadership channels. Before long there was a quiet inquiry to see if actual legal authorities needed to become involved. I never did get summoned to the principal's office, as it were, because thankfully when the church leaders talked to my ex, she realised how out of control the situation had become and admitted she made the entire thing up.

 Over the days and weeks that followed, I had lots of conversations. Only a short one with my accuser, where she almost tried to double down before thinking better of it, but many with other individuals. All a bit too gossipy for my tastes, but I had to know what was behind this lie that could've ruined my life. Here's the gist of what I gathered: call it a working theory, I suppose.

Essentially, I was a fairly well-liked guy in that community, and I had been open with my friends about my reservations regarding potentially being used as a "trophy date" for a prom. They knew that I put myself out there, deciding to trust this person anyway. Some of these friends even personally vouched for her character: "I get it, but you really don't need to worry. She's not that kind of person." To this day, despite that cynical voice inside me, I'm *still* willing to believe that our brief relationship wasn't a ploy, but just a bad coincidence of timing and failed chemistry. But here's the thing: when people asked her why she broke things off with me, she felt that if she said something like "I just didn't feel we were a good match" - a perfectly valid response! - people would assume the worst of her because of that timing. She was worried about her reputation, which is a really tough situation for her to have found herself in. "I can't even break up with a guy without getting labelled one thing or another?" I don't envy her position there. But because of this fear, the gears started turning in her head. "How can I make sure I'm not the bad guy?" The answer, of course, was to make *me* the bad guy instead. "How can I do that?"

"Say he beat you."

I have to believe she felt awful about this, despite the partial apology she gave me. I think she never intended me to find out about it. Her friends would just tell her how strong and brave she was, call me a jerk, and everyone moves on, right? I'm glad my church family took this kind of accusation more seriously than she thought they would. I'm glad there was a yearning for the truth, for justice, and that there was to be zero tolerance of violence against women. I'm glad for their response, but man: I really wish it hadn't been directed at me.

I virtually never saw her again after this episode. She certainly stopped going to our church; I think maybe there was just too much embarrassment there at that point. In fact, I'd bet some of her old high school friends who weren't part of the church probably still think I'm guilty. So much easier to just let the lie fade away. It's a real shame, because she had a pretty solid support network with that community, and in the end no truly permanent harm was done to anyone. But that's the thing, isn't it? I got lucky.

'Inside and Out' is a tale of someone who didn't get so lucky. It's a tale of someone who offers to give a lady a lift home, gets seduced by her, and loses years of his life to a false rape conviction and its corresponding prison sentence. Good gracious, it's a downer. And though my personal story doesn't have anything to do whatsoever with sex, having been on the receiving end of a serious accusation - however brief-lived it was - makes this song really resonate with me. It brings back to life memories of those feelings of betrayal, and confusion, and anger, and helplessness. It terrifies that part of me that can forgive but never quite forget.

Steve: *Obviously, the outstanding track [from Spot the Pigeon] is 'Inside And Out' which was really a jam. I seem to remember that Phil wrote the lyrics which was quite rare for him in those days.* [42]

The track's title itself doesn't seem particularly clever at first glance, but there's a little more to it than meets the eye. See, 'Inside and Out' is a musical dichotomy. It's two pretty distinct things, differentiated in a number of ways. The first half (well, 60%, but who's counting) is all melancholy guitars spelled by sombre chords. Even the really pretty chorus has an air of sadness about it. And that makes sense: this section of the song is the entire story of the fateful night, the accusation, the trial, the sentence. And strikingly, hauntingly, the fact that even release and freedom won't dispel the shadow. That the protagonist of the song will forever be a convicted sex offender with all that that carries. Lyrically it's all told in a theatre style, something the band hadn't done since Peter Gabriel left the group, so that's semi-remarkable in its own right. Other than the chorus, the whole story is told in words *other* than the victim's, and the chorus itself is more or less just his testimony from the courtroom. But that style allows us to see the impact not just to the victim, but also his loved ones. A mother just lost a son, a brother just lost a brother. It's heart-wrenching.

Steve: *I think it was one of the stronger tracks that didn't make it onto [Wind & Wuthering]. I think it should have been because it has a very beautiful sound to it. Right from the word "go" it's got that Genesis multi-jangle thing where it sounds like one guitar, but it's a whole bunch of guitars all playing the same thing.* [75]

And then, the other side of the coin: flaring keyboards alternating solos with dancing guitars, driving tempos, major tones. No more words - a total shift of moods. Finally, this is the view from the victim's eyes. This is a musical rendition of finally finding your long-awaited freedom. It's the exhilaration of being, simply, *somewhere else*. An exultation in the mundane, because even the mundane is fresh and different. There remains baggage, yes, but in the moment who cares? *I can have a life again.* The anger and sense of loss are tucked away in the background - you can still sense them if you try - but this section is an overwhelming joy pushing them down for the moment. Powerful stuff.

> **Tony:** *The first part, I think, is a better song than 'Your Own Special Way', and the second is an exciting piece of music. Both Steve and I were going quite eccentric with the solos.* [27]

Thus, the first part of the song is the victim in prison, and the retelling of the tale: 'Inside'. The second part is the victim being released and the flood of emotion that comes with it: 'Out'. It's essentially two distinct pieces of music butted up against one another, united by the lyrical theme. 'Inside' and 'Out' combine: 'Inside and Out'. Such a simple thing, but pretty cool nonetheless.

52 - There Must Be Some Other Way

from *Calling All Stations*, 1997

Imagine, for a moment, that you are Ray Wilson in the mid-1990s. You broke onto the scene, if you could call it that, as the frontman for a small-time band called Pink Gin, playing clubs to a bunch of unemployed Scotsmen nursing their depression with booze. Beginning to feel a bit depressed yourself by this, you start a new band called Guaranteed Pure, whose only album *Swing Your Bag* might as well have been released directly into a bottomless pit deep in an unmarked cave. Aggrieved but undeterred, you answer a host of ads in Melody Maker, eventually landing a gig with a new outfit called Stiltskin, which turns out to actually be little more than a vehicle for an upstart multi-instrumentalist songwriter to cash in on the song he wrote for a blue jeans ad. That song, 'Inside', somehow manages to claw its way past legendary ditty 'Mmm Mmm Mmm Mmm' by the Crash Test Dummies and hit 1 on the UK charts. Suddenly, you're headline news. Your album may not be breaking any sales records, but it's doing pretty well, and your "band," such as it is, is in the process of working up material for another one.

Instead, 1995 comes and goes and Stiltskin dissolves because it was never truly a real band at all. But that's all right, because you've been writing your own music and that project created enough Ray Wilson brand awareness that you can probably put this stuff out and find an audience for it. You work furiously through the start of 1996 on this material and by the summer you've got it all written with a recording deal in place. You're ready to start the process of getting your material down on record and seeing where your promising young career may take you, tremendously excited to open this next chapter of your life. Then your phone rings.

> **Ray:** *It was Tony Smith, saying, "I am Tony Smith, manager of Genesis. Phil Collins has left, we're thinking of getting a new singer, and the guys have heard your voice on the Stiltskin record."* [1]

How do you process this? Could you really go from singing in blue jeans ads to singing with the band whose recent hit 'I Can't Dance' was expressly about mocking blue jeans ads? It's so out of left field, so foreign to any kind of trajectory you might have expected your career to take, and it would also mean dropping everything you're doing.

> **Ray:** *The initial reaction was, "Wow, what a strange call to get and a strange situation to find myself in." I guess soon after that when I started to think about it, I thought, "Is this really for me? I'm not really a big fan of Genesis. I don't really know all that much about them. Is it something I should be doing?" And I'd also been writing an album, the first album after Stiltskin's record, and I'd just finished it, so I was really quite passionate about what I'd been writing and didn't want to stop. But of course you're faced with singing with one of the biggest bands in the world or just carrying on in your kind of small career.* [3]

So you make the only sane choice you can see at the time and show up to the audition. But you hedge your bets a little. You're still totally unsure if this is right so you decide to maybe try to tank the audition before it even starts, just to see if the likes of Tony Banks and Mike Rutherford will make the decision for you.

> **Ray:** *I remember standing in front of Mike and Tony and Tony Smith saying, "Look, the bottom line is I've done my own album, I've got a deal organised for it, so it's not really that important to me whether I sing with you guys or not. What's important is that it's right." I was very confident about it, deep down probably not feeling that way, but certainly coming across like that.* [1]

"Maybe they'll just kick me out now and I can get on with my life." But to your surprise, they appreciate your candour, your arrogant "I don't need you anyway" sort of attitude. You open your audition with 'No Son of Mine', and it's not quite in your prime vocal range, so you think you probably blew it. Blessing in disguise after all? But then you get the follow-up call that they loved the audition and want you back for more. Is this actually happening?

> **Tony:** *Ray has a great voice...When we let Ray have his reins, like on the title track and 'There Must Be Some Other Way', he really sounds strong.* [18]

Now at your second audition, you're hearing the new material they've been working on. They ask you to just make up some words and sing along. "Can I do that? How does that even work?" But you dutifully try, and something happens.

> **Ray:** *Even at my second audition we had been working on some of the material for the new album, with me singing away, making stuff up, "bluesing away" as they call it. From that second audition a couple of songs developed, 'Not About Us' and 'There Must Be Some Other Way'.* [1]

They're...receptive?

> **Tony:** *We did definitely use a couple of [Ray's] ideas. And we thought he had a fantastic voice...We'd get him to blues along sometimes and used that as a basis for...the main line in 'There Must Be Some Other Way'...We should have had Ray more involved sooner so we could have got more ideas going...I felt he and we could work well together.* [1]

Before you know it, you've landed the gig. You're still not even sure you want it, but here you are, trying to fit in with a couple men from another world.

> **Ray:** *I felt our working relationship was good. It was painfully obvious, however, that that was where it ended...It was kept strictly business and I can understand where they were coming from...During one recording session I'd been singing 'Calling All Stations' or 'There Must Be Some Other Way', one of the songs that took a lot of energy. I came back through from the control room, my face all flushed because I'd put so much into it. And I found Tony Banks doing the Times crossword and Mike ripping some paper into about fifty different pieces to create a little ball he could throw in the bin...* [1]

This is OK; after all, you were just a sing-monkey for someone else's music in Stiltskin, too. But you slowly learn that this nonchalance isn't disinterest; it's trust. If you'd sounded like garbage, they'd have told you. By doing crosswords and playing paper toss, they were really saying, "Keep it up lad, you're doing great!"

> **Ray:** *[Songs like] 'There Must be Some Other Way', they aren't middle of the road songs. They are rock songs of a Genesis type for me.* [28]

And though the songs are basically all finished, your input is still being valued.

> **Ray:** *'There Must Be Some Other Way' is quite a good soundtrack to write to.* [26]

It's 'Tonight, Tonight, Tonight' ten years on. It's got that same kind of structure, and that same kind of darkness about it. This is walking through a dark, damp alley, hearing the sound of water dropping into puddles from a rusty pipe coming out of some building's exhaust steam. It's got a chorus that you can groove to, drawing on your grunge roots. It demands all you have to give vocally, and now Mike's adding little guitar touches that really elevate the whole thing a cut above.

> **Tony:** *'There Must Be Some Other Way'...in some ways is one of my favourite tracks on the album. I think it is really a big ballad with an extended instrumental middle section...There is a bit...in the middle of this [song] that is recognizably Genesis... It is a song with a very sad lyric really, about divorce and things like that...I wrote the lyrics to this but I used what Ray came up with on the chorus fairly spontaneously again, when we were doing this improvisation early on... and he just sang... "There must be some other way" and it sounded so good and I thought, "I have got to use that as the basis." And so we did, and we thought what it could be about and modified it a bit to make it work. It is what you might almost call a piece of straightforward rock singing on the chorus... it is not original but it is something that he does so well you have just got to use it. You have got to harness it. And you don't need to write a great melodic line; it just sounds so good and it has a lot of passion to it.* [25]

> **Ray:** *I discovered from working with Tony and Mike that the quality of their writing is that it is never predictable; the second verse is not quite the same as the first verse. It's similar, but something subtle has changed. That for me is particularly a quality of Tony's writing.* [1]

Again like that 1986 prog-pop hit, the guys run free with an extended instrumental interlude. It's less Monkey Zulu and more Funky Voodoo, but Tony's brought melodies to spare, and this session drummer from Israel is just nailing it on the drums. "*This* is why I signed up for this gig," you smile to yourself before delivering your final verse and shredding your voice for the last chorus and outro. But you've got that prickling feeling running down your spine, and you're not sure why.

> **Ray:** *My character is such that as soon as something good happens I'm always thinking, "OK, well, what bad is round the corner?"...I was always suppressing my emotions all the time, never allowing myself to enjoy anything. I didn't find out there wouldn't be another Genesis album for maybe eighteen months, which is a long time.* [1]

The album sales a disappointment, the US tour cancelled, Genesis itself cancelled. So you go back to that album you were making before, trying to find your passion again. You release this project, Millionairhead, under the pseudo-band moniker Cut_. And you realise it's too late.

> **Ray:** *Its moment was when I'd come out of Stiltskin and I had a particular fan base, and a level of media interest. Five years on I'd moved away from that. I'd become a part of Genesis, and I hadn't realised just how big a deal that was. The album I'd written didn't fit the Genesis audience.* [1]

What would life have been like if you'd only said "No" to Tony Smith? There must be some other way things could've turned out. In the end, you did something worthwhile, yes. But at what cost?

> **Ray:** *I think in hindsight a big part of me wishes I'd carried on with my [kind of small] career.* [3]

51 - The Light Dies Down on Broadway

from *The Lamb Lies Down on Broadway*, 1974

When is a reprise not a reprise? When it's *two* reprises, of course! More than simply a re-imagining of the album's title track, 'The Light Dies Down on Broadway' goes a step beyond to create a deeper sense of cohesion for the album itself. That's a big deal, because *The Lamb Lies Down on Broadway* has a terrific sense of musical flow in itself already. One song into another, into the next, perhaps into a brief non-track interlude, and then on again. Each transition feels pretty natural, except perhaps 'In the Rapids' to '*it.*' at the very end. As every song ends and the next begins, as a listener I sort of go, "Yeah, that sounds right." And that's not because I'm simply used to the album structure after listening to it however many times by now. I felt that from the very first time I played the album all the way through; heck, it's what drew me in to listen again (and again and again and again…).

But what really jumps out at me about this achievement is that there's very little melodic repetition happening. If you look closely you can find very small call-backs in the rhythm sections, perhaps, but on a front-facing melody level there's less connection here than you'd expect. Essentially, you have 'The Lamb Lies Down on Broadway' opening the album, its gentler section repeated to open 'Carpet Crawlers', and then here on the final side of the thing you get 'The Light Dies Down on Broadway' as one more call-back to the album's beginning. That's basically it. Two recapitulations of two different musical themes, each of which originating from the same parent track.

It's remarkable that that's mostly enough to tie the album together, but 'The Light Dies Down on Broadway' serves a critical function by pulling double duty: it's also a reprise of 'The Lamia' from the album's third side. That song's chorus becomes the verse of this one, while the chorus of 'Light Dies Down' is naturally a reprise of the chorus of 'Lamb Lies Down' before it. Thus, we get a song that apparently follows a verse/chorus format, but in reality is just alternating choruses all the way through. In other words, it's got the biggest hooks from *both* parent pieces, giving the piece an incredible kind of "genetic" strength. Despite that, it's somehow still subtle enough that I didn't even register the 'Lamia' connection until it was pointed out to me by another fan. Yet it's so important for everything the track tries to do and the role it serves on the album.

Think for a moment about what those previous two songs represent within the framework of *The Lamb Lies Down on Broadway* as a whole. 'The Lamb Lies Down on Broadway' is a stage-setter. It's the opening scene, the establishing shot, the introduction to this world. But for Rael, it's something much more personal and meaningful than that: "My home!" What we see as the hustle and bustle of the city, sights and sounds serving as the descriptive paragraph of a fiction novel, Rael sees as his place of belonging. It's the home he loves and the home he's lost over the course of the album's narrative. Hold that in mind.

'The Lamia', on the other hand, represents the other end of the spectrum. By that point in the story Rael has journeyed through multiple caves, tried and failed to escape the dreamworld, and gotten lost within its twists and turns. The melody of the 'The Lamia' is utterly seductive, as befits the characters the tune reflects, but again for Rael there's more happening than what meets the eye. He's not simply seduced by the lamia themselves in this song; he's seduced by the dream itself. Up until this point in the story (flashbacks aside), Rael has been striving for a means to get back home, single-minded in his focus. Here the dream offers him up something that obviously can't belong to his beloved real world, and yet he embraces it. From this point on, Rael forgets about his quest to go home, completely absorbed in the dreamscape and its events.

That is, until 'The Light Dies Down on Broadway' happens, revealing a portal back to New York City and presumably out of the dream entirely. *That's* what's happening in this song: the two worlds are clashing, vying for Rael's attention. The 'Lamia'-inspired verses try to hold him in and force him into remaining; Rael first notices Brother John drowning during a verse section. Meanwhile the 'Lamb Lies Down'-inspired choruses try to pull him through the portal back home, causing Rael to hesitate even to save his brother, calling out a desperate "Hey John!" in hopes that maybe John will simply save himself and accompany Rael through the closing window.

Unsurprisingly, then, 'The Light Dies Down on Broadway' isn't a chipper affair. If you were to describe the overall emotional feel of the album's title track in a single word, which would you use? Exciting? Energetic? Invigorating? Maybe you get a different pull than I do, but that's where that song takes me. It's just bursting with life, except for the middle section, which I'd probably describe as "sleepy." But what about 'The Light Dies Down'? What words come to mind there? For me it's words like "defeated," or "forlorn."

But more than that, the song is *nostalgic*. Here's Rael, having suffered a series of really bizarre agonies, catching a glimpse into the world he left behind. Oh, how he misses it! And yet there's John, flailing in the water at the foot of the cliff, doomed if Rael doesn't render him assistance. He can't have both. So he makes the choice to stay. It's the *right* choice, but that doesn't make it an *easy* one. Thus, the mood is not only nostalgic, but *wistful*. It's fond memories of a beloved home that you may never be able to return to. It's the yearning for comfort, familiarity, and safety locked in battle with the crushing weight of responsibility, tinged with an unhealthy lingering desire for the nightmare itself.

That's why this song does more for me than the album's title track. The first song is a description of a man and a city, and while it energises me it doesn't really move me. Here by contrast the emotional stakes are very high, with the instrumentation and alterations to the song's cadence really hammering all that home. The gorgeously haunting melody of 'The Lamia' is the icing on the cake I didn't even know I needed. I think part of why it works so well, interestingly enough, is that this is the only song on the entire double album for which Peter didn't write the lyrics. Though they were mandated to maintain the story, I do think Tony and Mike perhaps felt a little closer to this one since they got to be involved on that lyrical level instead of being shut out entirely as on the rest of the album.

> **Mike:** *We were...incredibly behind schedule [writing the album]. The music was on course and we even had a recording date booked, but Pete's lyrics were nowhere near ready. Things got so bad that Pete eventually had to ask Tony and me to write the lyrics to 'The Light Dies Down on Broadway'. He gave us a brief so what we produced was much less flowery than our usual style, and I felt it ended up being quite in keeping with the album. Obviously, it was a token contribution, but at least we could feel we'd done a song and wouldn't have to live with an album that had "All words by Peter Gabriel" written on it.* [14]

Either way, there's no question for me that this is the highlight (skylight?) of *The Lamb*'s fourth side, and arguably the most emotionally effective/affecting song on the album. Who would've thought that the best thing to happen to Times Square would be a splash of darkness, eh?

50 - Follow You Follow Me

from ...And Then There Were Three..., 1978

This is the granddaddy of all Genesis songs for me. If you're wondering what in tarnation that means, the explanation is simple: I'm not using "granddaddy" idiomatically here, but instead referring to a sense of lineage. You see, my dad was loosely aware of Genesis thanks to a college roommate of his, but didn't actually become a fan in any real sense until 'Follow You Follow Me'. That song, and by extension the *And Then There Were Three* album as a whole, were his effective entry point into the band as an active listener. From that moment on - as you reading this book must also realise - there's no turning back. I myself was then raised with Genesis tunes in the background, and I've got some fond childhood memories of them, some of which I'll share as this book continues. This early Genesis exposure then conditioned me in my own college years to be receptive to their stuff when I myself was in an active listening frame of mind, thus initiating my own fandom proper, beginning a journey that would eventually lead me to this gargantuan undertaking. We haven't hit "the" song for me personally yet - my own Genesis daddy tune, as it were, that locked the band forever into my conscious memory - but without 'Follow You Follow Me' bringing my own pops into the fold, this book almost certainly wouldn't exist..

And it's pretty easy to see why this song gripped not only my dad but also countless others on its way to the UK top 10 and the US top 25.

> **Phil:** *It was our first real hit. Genesis had been trying desperately to write pop singles for a long time. Everybody was a fan of the Beatles and the Kinks and the Stones, but we didn't have a very good editor in the band — it was hard to write songs shorter than 10 minutes. But 'Follow You, Follow Me' was a game-changer.* [44]

> **Mike:** *It's one of those songs you hear now on the radio and for some reason it's not sugary. It could so easily have been a little bit soppy. It's the way Phil sang it; the combination of everything. It sounds convincing.* [76]

That's it exactly. When you hear this song, it doesn't sound like just another typical love song, even though it kinda sorta actually maybe is. There's something different about it. It's tough to cynically dismiss out of hand like a person might do for 95% of other love songs that come and go, or for that matter even other love ballads by Genesis themselves. There's just some intangible quality about 'Follow You Follow Me' that helps it avoid that fate, and I'd like here to try to figure out just what that is. After all, for the first time in the band's history, there were *girls* at the shows!

> **Mike:** *Until 'Follow You Follow Me' our audience was very strongly male. After it, all the guys were able to say to their girlfriends, "Here's that song you like." So they'd come along, and of course they'd enjoy the whole evening. It changed our audience ratio and we got more women after that. Out of the blue we had our first hit single [in the States]. In America we were a popular live band with a cult following, but we struggled at radio. Then suddenly this song came out and people liked it and bought the album. It was nice to have a little bit more recognition from people who didn't like us before. People were drawn in by it.* [76]

> **Phil:** *It was just another step on that ladder that made us a bigger band than we were before. Playing to more people, more interest, more play on the radio, suddenly a few girls in the audience, you know...I remember when Chester Thompson joined the live band playing drums, he said that on the Weather Report bus, they always used to play that song. And I thought, "All right! God, we've done SOMETHING right if Weather Report like it."...For me, I was always sort of...why can't we do something edgy? Why can't we do something that's kind of cool and hip? Anyway, it looked like we HAD done something, although then it became a pop single, so it kind of took the edge off the edgy/cool/hip thing. But, you know, it's still played on the radio today. It's a lot of people's favourite song from that period.* [3]

So what is it about 'Follow You Follow Me' that really sets it apart? To answer that question, I think we need to put ourselves in the Genesis songwriting mindset as they worked on this track and its parent album.

> **Tony:** *I just felt that when I was writing on Wind & Wuthering and And Then There Were Three on 'Burning Rope', I felt that maybe I had already done this before and that maybe I should try*

and shorten it a bit, you know. And then the idea came up of trying to avoid doing the long songs and keep them shorter and see where it leads us. I think it was a good experiment to try but I don't think it produced... it probably produced one of our less satisfactory albums apart from two or three tracks where there was slightly more expansive stuff. [6]

Mike: *Because we'd written so much material for Wind & Wuthering that we didn't have space for, we decided that on this new album we'd have no long songs. The record suffered for it.* [14]

We know that *Duke* and *Abacab* both had planned suites that were scrapped on the basis of the band not wanting to pull comparisons to 'Supper's Ready', but here we see that even back in 1978 there was still a conscious effort from the group to avoid what they considered to be re-treading old ground. These were guys who yearned to do something new so that they could remain invigorated and enthusiastic about their music. But unlike *Duke* where the "new" was a mix of jamming and distinct solo works (made more striking by Phil's emergence as a songwriter), and unlike *Abacab* where the "new" was a bold, radically experimental musical direction, *And Then There Were Three* sought the "new" by slimming down. "Can we do what we've always done, but more concisely?" As you see above, the answer as far as they were concerned appeared to be "no," but maybe that's because the approach was too individualistic.

Tony: *I think that the group at that point was probably its most fragmented with most of the tracks written by individuals...* [6]

Mike: *In those days we'd just work on bits and put them all together...We were never really good at writing short songs...We were an albums band. And it's quite an art to write a song that works in three and a half or four minutes.* [76]

An art which, as the band will all admit, they hadn't come anywhere close to mastering by this point - certainly not individually. It's easy to forget that even the previous album's single 'Your Own Special Way' had a runtime of over six minutes. Brevity, thy champion is not Genesis. So, with all members sensing this mild frustration - consistently getting material that was pretty good but maybe not quite great - whenever they'd hit on an actual moment of greatness during a writing session, they figured they'd better expand on it so as to not "waste" the quality of what they were hearing.

Mike: *Like most of our things it was an accident. I remember 'Follow You Follow Me', at the time we saw it as being a longer song. We were going to take that riff and make it into a solo or something; it wasn't going for a [shorter] song especially.* [3]

I think this is the key component for why 'Follow You Follow Me' works so well. Here you have a Genesis trying to write shorter songs in the progressive mould, finding themselves disappointed with the results, and then saying, "Screw it, let's just make a longer one that'll actually be really good." Listen to that rhythm track. That's not simple pop-rock fare. Phil's cymbal work is so light and so smooth, but it's anything but a straightforward beat. There's so much jazzy syncopation happening that it's stunning to think it could result in what sounds like a basic love song. Meanwhile, Mike's bass hits some longer chord-type notes in the choruses, but otherwise chimes in with the odd phrase here and there. There's not even a true pattern to it. It's all pretty free-flowing, going constantly back and forth between synchronization with Tony's either left hand or else Phil's right. This is *exactly* the sort of thing that made the Apocalypse in 9/8 section of 'Supper's Ready' so engaging, except that there it was Phil as the middleman, bouncing between the keyboards and Mike's bass riff. Now Mike's in that flex role, and because those roles are reversed within the rhythm section, and because we tend to notice drumming a little more easily than bass playing, the effect is more subtle. But it still tickles the subconscious; it still makes you "lean in" to the music.

Even Tony gets in on the action with a true keyboard solo, which has hitherto been reserved primarily for longer, "proggier" works. That the solo is only eight bars/twenty seconds long doesn't make it any less of a classic Genesis thing, and the colour it adds shouldn't be understated. Heck, when that solo kicks in (and again during its reprise in the extended fade-out), I'm immediately beset by images of the Far East. Without any words, that sound and its delivery produce a setting for this track; "Oh, the singer has found love in a foreign land," or "Oh, this is a romantic getaway set to this kind of scenery." That's pretty impactful writing.

That's all without even mentioning the core riff of the piece, which is what steals your attention right from the get-go. Now that's not to say that riffs are inherently "prog"; far from it, perhaps, as a good riff is often what can elevate a ho-hum pop track into a good one. But it's the colour and tone of the riff here that makes it such a standout. It's not an acoustic feel, and it's not an electric feel. Instead it's this distinctly *other* feel, generated by a flange effect, which is the exact kind of experimentation of sound that one would expect to see out of a traditionally progressive group.

> **Mike:** *I'll look at a song and think, now what really matters here? And certain sounds are, you realise, crucial. For example, 'Follow You Follow Me' starts with a guitar riff with a very, very heavy flange on it, and you have to get that flange sound just right. Nothing else but the perfect one will do.* [77]

Then came the song's most defining decision. Realising that they had this longer, proggy thing that sounded really, really good before they developed it further - again, in part *because* they intended to develop it all along - they decided instead to just leave it alone.

> **Phil:** *If a song feels good three minutes long, then we'll leave it at three minutes, because there are some things you can't just stretch out for the sake of it. It just feels right at that length, and so therefore you leave it that length. And 'Follow You Follow Me', if you ask our ardent fans what they think of it, they'll say, "Oh, that's the group's single. It's obviously a commercial single." But to me it's one of the hippest things we've ever done. The way it was written, it was out of improvisation. It was a blow, basically. It just sort of honed itself into this verse chorus verse chorus chorus verse. The attitude behind it was totally on the level. But to the punters, I suppose they see it as their band trying to get a hit single. We've never really needed that.* [78]

> **Tony:** *The most exciting moment for me in the studio was when Mike played a big flanged guitar riff and I started playing a few chords along to it; suddenly the combination sounded fantastic, this very simple little thing, which became 'Follow You Follow Me'. And having worked it up, we decided, "Let's keep this really simple." Mike went off and wrote a very simple love song lyric on top of it, trying not to move away from the flavour of the piece, because it was a song that made you feel warm. It was a happy song - which is something that we're not really very good at - and it needed a love lyric where everything went right. It was a whole new experience.* [1]

That's the other thing: the lyrics and their delivery. It was another departure from the past, but this time in a really healthy way:

> **Phil:** *A lot of people probably think that I wrote the lyrics to this, because it's a love song. The guys were starting to come out and say things like "I love you," having had this repressed public school upbringing where "You didn't say 'I love you,' that's a sissy thing to say!"* [43]

> **Mike:** *I had always found it difficult to put my emotions on paper. [My wife] Angie, however, had encouraged me to be more open. The song captured how I felt...It's an up, happy song that makes you smile without being sweet - not an easy thing to achieve - and the lyrics flowed so fast when I wrote them...* [14]

> **Tony:** *I'd just written a simple love lyric for 'Many Too Many' and I think Mike was keen to try the same thing. Maybe 'Follow You Follow Me' was almost too banal, but I got used to it. I think we find it much easier to write long stories than simple love songs.* [10]

> **Mike:** *Easiest song to write lyrically I've ever written in my life. It took me about ten minutes. I sat down, and it just came out very easily. They're not astounding words, but I think being simple and not being embarrassing is often quite hard. I thought, "It can't be THAT easy. They're so simple. 'Stay with me...'" We'd come from a much more complicated background of lyric writing, and I thought, "I can't just do that, can I?"* [3]

One can easily imagine Tony and Mike sitting high on a building, looking at the landscape below, and then feverishly going back and forth trying to write the lyrics to 'Watcher of the Skies' in an effort to catch that flash of mutual inspiration. One can easily imagine them agonizing over what the right words to use might be, how they'd fit over the rhythms, the kind of story they'd want to tell. And then one can flash forward several years and easily imagine Mike, lonely after touring, simply sitting down with a piece of paper and sighing, "I miss my wife." It's so simple, so pure, so genuine.

I think one part of the lyrics that helps them not seem trite is the relative lack of the word "love." That word appears twice in the entire set of lyrics, and even then it's like a Yoda-style poem: "my love I hope you'll always be" followed by another appellatory use of "oh my love" to close the verse. Compare this even to the Beatles, where 'Love Me Do' says "love" 24 times, or 10 times in 'And I Love Her' with an extra "lover" thrown in for good measure. Now don't get me wrong, I'm not ripping the Beatles. I'm just using them as a famous example of how easy it can be to fall into the trap of "I'm writing a love song so I'd better talk about love" and just start peppering the word everywhere to the point that it's hard to take seriously. 'Follow You Follow Me' deftly avoids that pitfall, and so never feels contrived.

> **Tony:** *When we were recording it, the guy who was our engineer/producer at the time Dave Hentschel, didn't rate it at all. He was a bit dismissive about it. And so we did a mix of it which wasn't terribly good, I don't think. Then we played it to the record company, and they said, "That's a hit. You've got to do it." And so we went back and remixed it, and got it a little bit better.* [3]

A hit indeed. 'Follow You Follow Me' was a huge opener of doors for the band. Not only did it help break down gender walls within their fandom; not only did it help them get a high level of radio play; not only did it score them meaningful financial success; not only did it give them sufficient name recognition that both Mike and Tony could release debut solo albums the following year; but all these things happened at the precise moment when the band's very existence was being threatened by external factors. It's not much of an exaggeration to say that 'Follow You Follow Me' is the song that saved Genesis.

> **Tony:** *You must remember this came out in the middle or just after punk. It was kind of a strange thing, we were sort of still surviving. Couldn't quite work out why, because everyone else had gone. ELP had died, Yes had died, and everything like this, and we were still going along! And we were lucky to perhaps have had this hit single which came out in the middle of all this, and we were OK.* [3]

A prog song, converted to a love song because the song itself demanded it. Lyrics that are about love, again because the song itself dictated that direction, but that don't dwell unnaturally in the overwrought zone, and delivered with a gentle sincerity that makes the whole thing gel. It's no wonder this song propelled Genesis to newfound heights of fame and success. It's no wonder it captured my dad's attention decades ago. And it's no wonder I'm so fond of it now, as well.

49 - Dancing with the Moonlit Knight

from *Selling England by the Pound*, 1973

Good evening everyone, and welcome to tonight's programme. Tonight on Genesis Talk Live, we're going to be discussing one of the band's hallmark pieces, the opener from what many fans say may just be their best album, *Selling England by the Pound*. Yes, it's the song with the line that gives the album its name, the one and only 'Dancing with the Moonlit Knight'!

<applause>

Yes, yes, a marvellous track to be sure. Now, before we dive into our feature segment of the evening, let's turn to the screen here and take a brief look at what the band themselves had to say about this track, starting with the incomparable Mr. Tony Banks.

> **Tony:** *I like the way it starts very much, but it's not my favourite song, although I know a lot of people like it very much. It's a slightly weak track for me.* [3]

<good-natured booing>

Ha, quite the inauspicious start there, now isn't it! Don't worry though, folks, Ol' Tony does lighten up from time to time.

> **Tony:** *Some of 'Dancing With The Moonlit Knight' was nice, particularly at the end.* [6]

<conciliatory applause>

There, see? If you look really closely, you can *almost* pretend he had a slight smile on his face when he said that!

<mild laughter>

Anyway, back to the video, yes? Maybe the other Genesis lads will view 'Dancing with the Moonlit Knight' more favorably, hmm?

> **Mike:** *Although...Selling England by the Pound had a Labour Party slogan as its title and was partly about increasing commercialization and the sense that something was being lost, our music was still more about moods and atmospheres...I often felt our music was a form of escapism.* [14]

> **Peter:** *I think there was a growing sense of confidence, and with that particular track, which I started off writing, I was trying to get a folk reference. And, if you like, sort of protect and preserve some of the Englishness. So it was, in the opening part particularly, trying to capture something that had more reference to Henry VIII than it did to America and song music. And then with the lyric it was in a sense about the commercialization of English culture.* [3]

> **Phil:** *'Dancing with the Moonlit Knight', I was starting to listen to Mahavishnu Orchestra, so I was trying to put my weirdness, my weird time signatures into anything that would move, anything they would allow me. So 'Dancing with the Moonlit Knight', some of the instrumental stuff was me and Steve there.* [3]

<polite applause>

Well, quite informative if nothing else! And a nice segue there from Phil, because we have a special surprise here tonight for all of you - and for the viewers at home. As many of you may know, we've spent years trying to convince the members of Genesis to join us on the programme, thus far to no avail. Tonight, however, it is with immense pleasure that I can say we've finally managed to overcome that hurdle.

<audible gasping>

Yes, you heard me correctly. We have with us a member of Genesis here, in the studio, tonight! So without further ado - this is really a treat for me to announce - please allow me to introduce you to: a highly accomplished member of the band's "classic line-up" and a prolific solo artist with roughly thirty albums to his esteemed name... Here to help me present and discuss 'Dancing with the Moonlit Knight', ladies and gentlemen, let's have a rousing round of applause for none other than Mr. Stephen! Richard! Hackett!

<thunderous applause>

Steve: Hello. Guten abend. Dankeschön. [42]

<laughter>

Ha! Charming! Charming. First of all Mr. Hackett - may I call you Steve? - first of all Steve, I just want to thank you so much for agreeing to be here tonight.

Steve: It's great to be here, absolutely wonderful. I am in danger of talking too much. [42]

Oh, nonsense! I can assure you that all of us in attendance tonight would love to hear everything that you have to say, wouldn't we folks?

<vigorous applause>

And there you have it! Well, let's just get right into it, shall we? Now, I want you all to know something from the outset: no matter how much you might claim to absolutely adore 'Dancing with the Moonlit Knight', I *promise* you that you aren't more enthusiastic about it than Steve here. Isn't that right, Steve?

Steve: My favourite Genesis track from my favourite Genesis album. For me, it reigns supreme of all Genesis songs because it goes through so many different styles. [13]

Well Steve, that's quite an introduction, and lofty praise indeed. And speaking of introductions, 'Dancing with the Moonlit Knight' features what might be my favourite opening to any Genesis song. That opening line, unaccompanied, is just so...

Steve: You've got Pete doing this kind of Scottish Plainsong thing at the front, this a cappella thing, which then goes into the strangest atmosphere. And it retains that strange atmosphere right through to the end. [3]

...yes, precisely Steve, that's the section I'm talking about. But what's especially compelling about it is the way...

Steve: When it starts out, you really don't know where the song's gonna go, do you? [3]

...No, no, I suppose you don't. But if I may here, what I've been trying to say is that it's some of the starkest stuff the band has ever put on record. To open an album with a voice and absolutely nothing else is really bold, and the entry of the instruments beginning with the line "it lies with me" and on beyond... well, it just works brilliantly. The gentle guitars, the dancing keyboards. Beautiful, beautiful stuff.

Steve: It starts off with Scottish Plainsong at the front, "Can you tell me where my country lies?" And then it's into that Elgarian thing, "Citizens of hope and glory." The Land of Hope and Glory, addressing all the Brits, the idea of corporations taking over. [13]

Yes, I agree with you Steve, great lyrical work there too, really setting the stage for everything to come.

Steve: Nostalgic and wistful... [79]

Just so! Then, after that nearly perfect first minute and change, we get a really compelling central guitar riff in there, too. Was that a bit you brought to the table?

Steve: Pete wrote [that riff] on piano, and it mainly becomes a guitar figure throughout the song. Someone else's melody, interpreted on guitar in two different ways. [3]

Very interesting! Not what I would have expected, because I must say, you play it quite well. It sounds very natural on the guitar. That riff, combined with those vocals...

Steve: And Tony had just gotten the voice tapes on the Mellotron, so we had that choral thing as well we were able to do. So we could sound like an orchestra, we could sound like a choir... [3]

...Yes, that's exactly what I was about to mention! All stellar stuff there. In fact, I might like that beginning section a little *too* much, because when it ends...

Steve: Then it bursts forth, it fights off its shackles, really takes off like a rocket, into another section, which seems to borrow from something that sounds more Russian in a way. It's European, but then at times, it turns into the jazz that I liked originally - but big band, with the accents. [79]

...No argument there really, but I think what I'm trying to get at is that the "chorus" as it were was always a little disappointing to me.

<good-natured booing>

Now, now, friends! I'm not saying I think there's anything wrong with it whatsoever! Merely that it marks the end of those very sublime opening passages, which to me are the absolute highlight of the song, and perhaps the second-best bit of music on the entire album.

Steve: I think it's a lovely tune but it grows into so much more. By the time it gets to the instrumental, it doesn't just waffle off into that, it goes into something that has aspects of...you hear the voices in the background, overhanging...those Mellotron voices have got a hint of Mozart's 'Requiem', and then you get into this very angular riff played on Mellotron cellos and distorted piano...there's all of that and then you get the guitar moments, tapping, sleeve picking, octave jumps, and I think the whole thing's bound together with Phil's extraordinary drumming. A jazz rock drummer let loose amongst all these different styles that are going on: you've got part rock, part classical... [13]

Oh, definitely. Again, making absolutely clear for our passionate audience here, there's nothing wrong with any of it. In fact, after that first "chorus" and the inevitable sensation of loss I feel during it, there's a great lift again as the song really takes off, just like you described.

Steve: Furious drums, great ensemble playing. [1]

No doubt about it. Then it comes back to the chorus again, and I think once again I feel a slight let-down. Now don't you lot go and boo again!

<laughter>

I think, Steve, that in the end I really just wanted a recapitulation of the opening strains of the song, which of course doesn't come until 'Aisle of Plenty' at the end of the album. I read somewhere that originally there was a three-song suite consisting of 'Dancing with the Moonlit Knight', 'The Cinema Show', and 'Aisle of Plenty' - that they were all connected originally. And that they then got split out to sort of bookend the album. Is there any truth to that?

Steve: If you listen to Phil Collins' drumming, you've got this sort of jazz drummer playing along with stuff that's got Elgarian references, and all the very British stuff, and then you've got this stuff that really predates jazz rock to a large degree. You've got something that's arguably fusion before the term was being used. [45]

Yes, I agree that the drumming on this track is consistently phenomenal, but I was actually asking about the concept of a kind of 'Selling England Suite' and whether...

Steve: I think 'Dancing with the Moonlit Knight' has got a lot of great moments on it. [3]

Ha, ah, yes, Steve, yes it does. But can we return for a moment to my question about that opening melody a bit and a multi-song connection?

Steve: By the time it comes to the end of the song, you've got this kind of...almost like garden gnomes fading out on the very end. [13]

Yes, yes, but I'm aski...Wait, what? Did you say gnomes?

Steve: That lovely bit on the end that we used to call 'Disney', which they've started using for some reason on gardening programmes these days. Shot of a gnome and there's this tinkling twelve-string and you say, "Ah! That's Mike's bit there." This sort of repeated chord pattern. [3]

Oh, I see, not that it sounds like gnomes, whatever that might mean, but rather that if you've seen one of these gardening shows, you can make that visual connection. I follow you now. I'm sure you can understand my confu-

Steve: But we all operated with rock instruments, but not like a rock group: we all sort of faded ourselves in very, very gently, and we're all being very pastoral. [3]

Sure, sure, that section is certainly atmospheric. Not quite a payoff, per se, but still quite enjoyable in its own right. Why 'Disney' as a working name though?

Steve: A very floaty, drifty, pastoral exit from the song...the idea of a still, tranquil lake with each player slightly disturbing the surface: Pete using the reed from an oboe to make duck noises, over beautiful Mellotron chords from Tony and an arpeggiated twelve-string figure from Mike holding the whole thing together. True fusion. [1]

OK, I suppose that... mostly...answers the question, I guess. Well it looks like our time is rapidly coming to a close here, so Steve, I really want to thank you for comi-

Steve: *Selling England by the Pound* has always been my favourite Genesis album. [39]

...Yes, great, thank you Steve. And thank you so much for joining us tonight to talk about 'Dancing with the Moonlit...

Steve: I love the album. It's completely bonkers from end to end...I believe that Mike and Tony are not as fond of that album, but I felt we'd made this sort of leap forward as players. We were doing stuff that was difficult to play and using techniques that no one else was employing, so this was very good. [3]

Right, terrific, thanks again Steve. Let's hear one more big round of applause for Steve Hackett, everyone!

<applause>

Well, we've got a thrilling show lined up for you all next week, with special gue...

Steve: ...My favourite track, which for me epitomises Genesis at its best... It begins with the magic and primitive feel of Scottish plainsong and sweeps through the anthemic Elgarian English melody with a choir that conjures the bygone Baroque age before revving up as it pitches ever faster forth via a flight through time into a wild fusion of sound. [70]

Oh dear, he's really going after it now, isn't he folks?

<awkward laughter>

Steve, I'm afraid we're out of time, but again, thank you ever so much for...

Steve: It runs the gauntlet of styles and is like a musical time lapse...clouds fly by, flowers grow faster but also decay before your eyes, the old world passes, giving way to the new urban concrete jungle - angular, detached, disconnected and cubist. By the end it's practically post holocaust. [70]

Post-what?! A-haha, haha, oh Steve, very charming, thank you so much for your time. We'll uh, we'll see you all next week for...

Steve: The end conjures water to me... an ultimate tranquillity beyond the maelstrom in the remnants of civilization, the flotsam-&-jetsam of it all. There's something of Mozart's 'Requiem' in it - the loss of the personal touch in favour of big business and the sense that every civilization must pass. [70]

<awkward laughter>

Listen, my apologies, folks. As you know, this is Genesis Talk Live, and as a live show, well, we can't always predict what might happen. But, ah, we thank Steve for his passion and his willingness to share that with us, and we...

Steve: It encapsulates the repeated theme in Genesis of the passing of time, and the memory of an era high on chivalry. It was an amazing hybrid between classical and rock. I don't think that any other band has written anything quite like it. It was a quantum leap forward for us. [70]

All right, I think we're done here. Good night everyone!

Steve: I particularly love 'Dancing with the Moonlit Knight'... [39]

YES, THANK YOU STEVE SO MUCH FOR YOUR TIME.

Steve: Thank you very much. Dankeschön! [42]

<cut>

48 - Calling All Stations

from *Calling All Stations*, 1997

It's a tired old adage, but it's stuck around so long precisely because it's true: first impressions matter. My first day on a certain job, I was taken by my new manager to a large, interdepartmental work meeting that happened to be going on that day, and found myself meeting a number of future colleagues. I wouldn't end up working with most of these people for quite some time, and the afternoon was a bit of a whirlwind, but two of these interactions still stick out strongly in my mind. The first was that when I was introduced to one high profile co-worker and my role was explained, the response was "OK fine, but I don't want to talk to him. I want to talk to X." X was the employee working on this person's pet project, you see, and that was that. No "nice to meet you," not even any eye contact. I simply didn't matter whatsoever. So, first impression locked in: "this person is an egomaniac with zero social skills and I hope we never work together." The second interaction was perhaps more bizarre. Immediately after meeting me, this person (who happened to be a woman) asked me for my personal cell phone number on the basis that "it might be needed for future collaboration." I felt deeply uncomfortable about this, especially as a married man, but she was heavily pressuring me and I had no concept of her role in the organization. I feared that refusing the request would send ripples that could lead to my employment being terminated for not being a team player or some such, and I really needed this job. Thus, I found myself giving my private number away to a total stranger who I may or may not even work with in the future, who may or may not have been on the level with the request. First impression locked in: this person abuses her authority to stalker-like levels.

    Now, first impressions aren't the end of the story. I did eventually work extensively with both of these individuals, and in both cases when I retold to them the tales of our initial meetings, they were embarrassed but also didn't have any recollection of the event. I eventually discovered the first individual to be fun and warm in addition to the hyperfocus I'd already seen, and the second individual was simply a quirky personality who meant no harm. To both of them the interactions with me were just business as usual, but it took a long time for me to get past that initial burst of negativity and build a trusting working relationship with either of them. Those first impressions weren't accurate - well, not *completely* accurate, anyway - but I weighed them far more heavily in my mind than I did any of the subsequent positive interactions, until I was finally forced to admit that maybe I didn't have all the information that first go-round.

    This is just human nature at work, and I saw the same kind of thing happening when I first presented these essays to the Genesis fan community online. I know my taste for Genesis music isn't quite mainstream among hardcore fans, but one of the earliest impressions people had of this project was me saying "I don't really care for 'Return of the Giant Hogweed'," and the reflexive assumption that a lot of people made from that was "This guy doesn't like classic/progressive Genesis at all." We like things to be defined in a neat and tidy way, so it's a very natural reaction to say, "This thing is this way, so it must *always* be this way." A number of users then wrote off the project entirely on the basis that the posts held no value to them if they didn't agree with my opinions. For them, that first disagreement was evidence enough that they would *never* agree with my opinions about *any* Genesis song, so why bother? It's just human nature at work: your first strong impression informs your beliefs about someone or something more than any of us probably care to admit.

    It's no different with albums. You can spin up *Foxtrot* and those first Mellotron chords of 'Watcher of the Skies' tell you you're in for something unlike anything you've ever heard. "Oh, this album will be something else." Genesis has always been pretty good at opening their albums, but by 1997, they were perhaps more keenly aware of this phenomenon than ever.

> **Tony:** *We started the album with 'Calling All Stations', which is a slightly more ambitious track partly to give that feel. You should have a slightly more kind of intense feeling, I think, than perhaps...you know, you start an album like Invisible Touch with what is a quite straightforward song, and you go "Oh, this must be a straightforward album!" But then you still have things like 'Domino' and 'Tonight, Tonight[, Tonight]' on it, which were more substantial tracks. And I still think this [album] is a mix. But Ray's voice naturally makes everything sound a little bit darker and more dramatic, I think.* [67]

> **Ray:** *It's the title track of the album. It's the first song with me on it, the new front person and stuff, and the song has to have that kind of "Wow!" thing about it.* [28]

    Even *We Can't Dance*, a return in many ways to writing more expansive songs, opened with 'No Son of Mine', *itself* pretty expansive but also the lead single from the record, released a week ahead of the album. Easy enough to say "Just more top 40 radio fodder" and be done with it. They weren't going to let that happen this time, if they could help it.

> **Mike:** *I think the opening track was meant to be something that showed our dark side. That kind of melody really suits Ray's voice, I think.* [3]

Thus, the very first thing you hear on both 'Calling All Stations' the song as well as *Calling All Stations* the album is this razorblade of a guitar riff, *fiercer* than anything else the band had really done before. It's allowed to distort, allowed to come and go, slicing and dicing its way over Tony's brooding chords, occasionally wailing out. It's got a kind of grungy, industrial, alt rock feel about it, making sure you understand that *this* Genesis album will be different. It's not what you expect. When Ray jumps in it's not even that surprising. His voice just *fits* the sound they're creating, even if it's not anything like a typical Genesis sound. Which is ironic, because the heart of Genesis is still beating strong within it.

> **Tony:** *Dramatic kind of traditional Genesis, I suppose, in terms of the chords and the rhythm and everything about it. And then a vocal that, not really rare for us, but it doesn't really repeat all that much. Perhaps it echoed slightly more earlier Genesis, this sort of feeling. Ray had a very dark voice. I think towards the end of the song it really lifts and it gets a fantastic sound about it. I'd have liked to have lifted a little bit earlier on, I think, that's my only feeling about that song. It needed to lift a little earlier. But it's still a song I'm proud of; it works really well.* [3]

Yet as soon as you start to feel like you understand the song's direction, the guitar sound changes completely to a sort of romantic Spanish guitar. The brooding is all still there, and even the razorblade comes back briefly, but now there's a kind of dim light about the piece. A bit of that lift Tony is talking about, I suppose, but then again, maybe not: The song drifts darker again, and then darker still, and Ray's voice builds, and builds some more.

> **Ray:** *My favourite song on Calling All Stations has to be the title track. It just had an energy about it; it just sounded like an authentic Genesis song to me, and I sang it well. I really, really enjoy that song...It was like the 'Mama' track on the album. 'Mama' was always one of my favourite songs, and 'Calling All Stations' for me had that same drama about it...I remember with these songs, I'd sing them two or three times, and then [producer] Nick Davis would kind of comp it together, the best from each take. 'Calling All Stations', the last take I did I seem to remember was the one that just took everything I had. I was singing from the pits of my stomach. And singing that song live was a real challenge. A bit like 'Mama' was for Phil, I think. He sang that in the studio, it sounds amazing! But try reproducing that one live: it's hard. And 'Calling All Stations' was like that for me.* [3]

And now a break; sparseness and echoes and 'Tonight, Tonight, Tonight' style creepy keyboard sounds. A fuzzy guitar solo? Sure, why not! That's when it starts to hit you: this isn't a pop song! It's not even a single! It's an outpouring of ideas that doesn't backtrack, doesn't repeat. And hot dang does it have this ineffable *strength* about it!

> **Tony:** *This is very much a chord sequence based piece and all these chords just sounded really good on it, you know, dramatic types of things. It was a question of trying to put them in an order that gave some kind of sense as a song because there's virtually no repetition in the song. There is a little bit of repetition at the end but for the first four or five minutes of the song there is no actual repetition and yet it seems to hang together very well. I think it is a dark and dramatic and slow tempo sort of piece...We wanted to put this first because it gave a slightly heavier elemental edge to the album and first tracks make a lot of difference. We wanted this to come across more as a rock album, so it has got a heavy guitar riff at the front of it and as I say, lots of dramatic chords. Mike wrote the lyric on it and melodically Mike had various vocal ideas, and we got Ray singing them, and then we tried to make it so that his voice sounded right on them. We were very much experimenting with his voice to see what we could get out of it and some melodic lines were better than others so we shaped the melody very much around his voice.* [25]

It's the same sort of "let's see where this goes" that drove the band to make *Trespass* and much of what came later. It's 1997, and it's a band that's had overwhelming commercial success, trying to prove to the masses that they've still got it even with a new singer, opening their album with a song that clocks under 6 minutes. And it sounds *nothing* like you'd assume it would from that description. I was listening to it while writing this and my arms went cold from the intensity of the thing. This isn't pop, it's progressive post-grunge, absurdly powerful in its delivery. While the rest of the album didn't always live up to the expectations this song created, it's one doozy of a first impression.

> **Ray:** *I brought a bit of balls to the band's music. I don't know whether that was a good thing for the fans. It was for me.* [32]

Heck yeah, Ray. You tell 'em.

47 - Misunderstanding

from *Duke*, 1980

It's 1979, Tony Banks and Mike Rutherford are putting together solo albums, and Phil's sitting at home with a drum machine he doesn't really want and nothing to occupy his time.

> **Phil:** *I'm just playing, in every sense of the term. Tinkering. My ambitions are low...I program some pretty simple drum-machine parts, and I mess about on the eight-track...Over a year these doodles of mine slowly take shape. But they are doodles. Nothing is really prepared, or finished. Yet nonetheless, gradually, without me even noticing really, doodles become sketches become outlines become mini-portraits. Become songs.* [12]

While out of this process would come a cathartic release of pent up emotion through songs like 'Please Don't Ask' and 'In the Air Tonight', the first fruit of these sessions was something a little bit lighter.

> **Phil:** *The first real song I finished [writing] was 'Misunderstanding'. And that one came at the beginning of this period when I was to write what would become Face Value, but that was just writing songs.* [73]

It makes sense, really, when you think about it. 'Misunderstanding' is lyrically mired in confusion and frustration. It's about your significant other cheating on you and you trying to come to grips with it. Phil has said this song has nothing to do with his personal life, but come on now. Your wife cheats on you and leaves you and then this is the first song you write and you want to tell me they aren't in any way related? This is very much autobiographical, if fanciful in the details. But at the same time, there's still a distance here. It's a distance created by those very same fanciful details: the framing of the song in the form of a relatable story, the reduction of the relationship from a marriage to a casual dating relationship where the guy gets stood up. It's someone who's smitten and really looking forward to watching a movie with his new girl, but she blows him off. The stakes in 'Misunderstanding' are way, way lower. Low enough, I suppose, that Phil could convince himself it wasn't even about him.

And that's the point, I think. Phil wasn't quite ready to put all of himself out there just yet. He'd opened the pressure release valve a little, but most of it was still bottled up inside. Maybe it was a lack of confidence, or maybe he just needed to dip a toe in the water with 'Misunderstanding' before plunging into the deeper, more personal waters that would come later.

All of this is to say that I think the emotional restraint, intended or not, works heavily in this song's favour. Again, thanks to inexperience with writing, Phil decided to start working from a familiar rhythmic place:

> **Phil:** *'Misunderstanding' was a song that I'd written based on a kind of rhythm. It was a little bit between 'Hold the Line' by Toto and 'Sail On, Sailor' by the Beach Boys. You know, I love that kind of...'Rocky Mountain Way' by Joe Walsh, that kind of rock thing when it's just in the right place. So that's how I'd written it; I don't want to say it ended up being as good as that.* [3]

Interestingly enough, despite citing three other pieces as rhythmic inspirations, Phil doesn't mention any melodic ones. This feels like a huge oversight, given that the primary riff of 'Misunderstanding' is lifted nearly wholesale from 1969 Sly and the Family Stone single 'Hot Fun in the Summertime'. Interestingly enough, 1979 would see this note progression appear once more in Led Zeppelin's 'Fool in the Rain'. While the respective timings of that piece's release (late 1979) and Collins' writing of 'Misunderstanding' (early 1979) preclude any claims of plagiarism, it does make me wonder if Collins and the Zep boys were listening to the same kinds of stuff or even in contact with one another about what they were listening to at the time.

Historical footnotes aside, the point is that 'Misunderstanding' is much less "let me invent something out of nothing" and more "let me try to recreate this specific feel I like and spin it into something new," which is, I'd wager, how nearly every songwriter starts out. As a result you get this rock solid groove that forms the song's backbone, and there's an inherent lightness and joy about the thing.

> **Mike:** *The songs that Phil brought to Duke, 'Misunderstanding' and 'Please Don't Ask', had a lovely sense of space and ease about them, a feeling of not trying too hard. Tony and I would always try quite hard and when it worked, it was great. When it didn't, it didn't. Phil was always able to let a song breathe; he also had an empathy for what was right musically. Whatever he said, you listened.* [14]

Do me a favour and sing these two lines to yourself, but in the tune of the chorus of 'Misunderstanding':

> Oh if you told me that you were drowning (oo-wooooo)
> I would not lend you a hand (woooo)

Doesn't work so well, does it? You simply *can't* have too heavy a lyric sitting on top of this kind of groove because the music itself rejects it. Collins instinctively got that, tossing those doo-wop style backing vocals in there because they themselves act as a lightening agent for the whole emotional pie. Suddenly, these lyrics - that, though maintaining a kind of emotional distance still come from a very hurt place - are transformed in style into a sort of "Look at this poor sod!" We're invited to have a laugh at the singer's expense, this stooge who's too blinded by his puppy love to realise he's been unceremoniously dumped.

> **Phil:** *I was gonna have it on Face Value and then I played the stuff to the guys, and Tony and Mike really liked that because of the same reasons [that I did]. They liked the Beach Boys kind of rock thing...So they took that song and we recorded it, and I guess because it had "SINGLE!" written all over it, in America it was the first single.* [3]

Now, suddenly, you've got a potential hit on your hands. Catchy groove, fun chorus, lyrics that mean something but you don't have to think too deeply about, a great piano rock sound backing it all up? Yeah, we'll eat that up over here.

> **Tony:** *'Misunderstanding', it seems to me, proves that Americans are suckers for anything that goes boom, boom boom, boom boom. Maybe that's unfair...It doesn't misrepresent us but it's definitely just one zone of the group. I think when you have a single it's probably always that.* [10]

Tony and Mike had been searching for chart success for a while, and now their singer/drummer plopped this in their lap? As one of the first things he's ever written? It's a wonder they were surprised that *Face Value* did as well as it did, if Phil Collins could seemingly write hits in his sleep like this one.

> **Phil:** *'Misunderstanding' was our first American hit. 'Follow You Follow Me' kind of grazed and bruised the charts, but 'Misunderstanding' was a top ten hit. [Editor's Note: 14, but who's counting?] So that was great for me as a songwriter, but in terms of the band it sort of led us to a bigger audience.* [43]

Savvy move, boys. This is how legends are born.

46 - Dodo/Lurker

from *Abacab*, 1981

The only two-for-one song this grand undertaking didn't have to break up, it's a mercy to this exercise that Genesis decided to keep 'Dodo' and 'Lurker' together on *Abacab* as a single track. In fact, this track is a mercy to classic Genesis fans in general, coming when it did amidst the big shift that defined *Abacab* as a whole:

> **Tony:** *It has a very distinctive quality about it. I think what it did for us was it took us, having gone in a certain direction a certain way, we then went quite a long way a different direction. And perhaps after that we kind of came back a bit, but brought a bit of that in with us from then on. I think it was an important move, really.* [3]

This is true, and important, and good, and also doesn't really describe 'Dodo/Lurker' quite as much as it does the entire rest of the album. *This* piece is sort of the last bastion of the old sound on *Abacab*; yes, 'Me and Sarah Jane' has some traditional Genesis stuff happening near the end, but nobody would listen to the first half of that song and think, "Yeah, this sounds just like *Foxtrot*." So if you were coming off *And Then There Were Three* and then *Duke* thinking, as many fans did, "Those were pretty good, hope we get even more prog next time," when *Abacab* arrived you probably just sat through Side A in stunned silence. "Do I even like this stuff? Is this even Genesis?"

But then Side B opened with 'Dodo/Lurker', something of a shining island in the darkness of the sparse album sound, and you probably didn't have to think twice about it. "Well, at least *that* one's a winner." And yet, somehow it still feels completely at home on *Abacab* as well; this isn't one of those instances where someone could suggest tossing it on a different Genesis album and thus "sending it home." It's already precisely where it belongs, thank you very much. It's this mystifying blend of both old and new, extremely compelling in its juxtaposition.

For example, those big opening chords sound like a cross between the first strains of 'Watcher of the Skies' and of 'Squonk', but unlike either of those earlier tracks, 'Dodo' gets out of its own way quickly. See, 'Watcher of the Skies' taught the band that opening a tune with a heavy atmosphere is great, but that dwelling there too long risks the rest of the song falling short by comparison. And 'Squonk' taught them that unleashing "maximum chord power" was highly effective, yet unsustainable. So instead we get 20 seconds of that "blast your clothes off" level of force, but it's then allowed to dissipate before we get used to it, settling the song into a solid groove instead. Then when the cannon comes back for the final twenty seconds of the 'Dodo' section as well, the piece is neatly bookended in pure oomph. Much more efficient than trying in vain to hold onto that power for the whole tune. Old thoughts, new mastery.

Similarly, Mike's guitar work here has shades of Hackett sensibilities for me. Steve was of course capable of some pretty soaring lead work, and he had his very pastoral side as well. But I think Steve's tenure as Genesis guitarist is perhaps best defined by his ability to become part of the band's texture. There are times you wonder if he's even playing, but if his guitar were mixed out completely you'd feel his absence. This song is a great example of Mike following that path of playing: 'Dodo/Lurker' is undeniably a keyboard-focused work, and apart from a few little lead phrases, you might not ever really notice the guitar. But it's there, picking away, doing its own weird little things that you don't really notice because it's a weird little song to begin with. Old ideas, new execution.

The vocals follow this pattern as well. Character pieces and Peter Gabriel's performance of them were a big part of the early Genesis style and sound; heck, they devoted an entire concept album to that idea! Even when Phil took over the lead vocal role, those types of pieces didn't completely go away, because they were core to who and what Genesis was. 'Robbery, Assault and Battery', 'The Lady Lies', even 'Match of the Day' had a little bit of that quirky kind of stage show energy. But those songs all came before Phil's voice went Super Saiyan, now didn't they? Finally, in the combination piece that is 'Dodo/Lurker' we get a Phil who can play multiple roles, put on multiple voices, and really just kick your butt while doing it. Old ideas, new talent.

> **Tony:** *The 'Dodo' track, the lyrics were ones which sounded good when a person sang them rather than worrying about what they actually meant, and that is true of quite a few of the tracks [on the album] in a way. That is why we haven't got the lyrics written on the album because we have wanted to steer things away from the emphasis on what they mean and put it on what they sound like...that's not to say that the lyrics don't mean anything; in the case of 'Dodo' it's more like the phrases that mean something. There is a prevailing theme in them and in the main it was designed thinking around the way Phil would sing it and how it would sound good.* [7]

"Heck, we won't even let little things like lyrics get in his way. Just sing any old thing, Phil! We believe in you!" The sound as always was the most important thing, but gone was the need to tightly craft the words to create some kind of epic tale or meaningful message. Old ideas, new abandon.

Even the song's core structure bridges eras for the band. After all, transitioning from one song into another was nothing new. In fact, it was *such* an old trick the band had repeatedly tried to avoid overdoing it since 1972. But now instead of following their initial inclination to connect four songs together, they just scrapped the final two entirely.

> **Tony:** *Originally we had four tracks which we joined together, of which ['Dodo/Lurker'] are the first two, and the other two we decided to shelve because they weren't very strong and so in a way we consider them as separate songs. In fact there is a definite break point and then you are into a different kind of feel.* [7]

Furthermore, instead of developing 'Lurker' into its own big thing that could stand alone, they just made a silly rinky-dink of a keyboard solo and attached it to a riddle that didn't mean anything.

> **Tony:** *It's very interesting, this, because we're now in 1997 and I wrote the lyric to that in '82. You may say there's been a lot of discussion about what the riddle is, but I've never actually been asked that question in an interview. Because no one asked me, it all fell a bit flat! Now all these years on, I'm afraid I have to say really that there is no real solution. You can search for your own one if you like. It was a bit of a joke. When I was writing it I honestly didn't really have a specific idea in mind. If you find out what the answer is, perhaps you could tell me!* [5]

"Let's just leave it where it is and let it stand as a fun little thing. No need to build it into something dramatic." Old ideas, new restraint.

The rhythm section is absolutely wild, too. I've written a few times about how Genesis - and Phil Collins especially - have the ability to take the complicated and make it seem simple. Here on the verses of 'Dodo' the opposite effect happens: everything going on rhythmically is actually fairly simple, but it's done with such style, such flair, that it sounds incredibly complicated. Just check the bass line when that groove gets going. It's an even beat pattern again as I've mentioned in other pieces, but it hits that 2 beat with such sheer force that it throws you off the scent a little. Then the 4 beat isn't a single hit, but a climbing pair of notes that makes the listener expect a resolution on 1. Which of course doesn't come, so you miss it, and then get smacked in the face by that big ol' grunt on 2 again. And hey, while we're speaking of getting thrown off the scent, here's a noodle for you: that bass isn't even Mike.

> **Tony:** *The thing that's important about it is that the fuzz box becomes part of the sound. Often, you'll put something through a fuzz and you get one sound down there and the fuzz sound somewhere up there. They don't knit together too well. Fuzz boxes are better for those heart attack kinds of sounds...that's what I used for the bass on 'Dodo'.* [23]

Meanwhile, Phil's pounding away at a rhythm that sounds heavily syncopated and complex, but that's something of an illusion too. He's still just playing around in standard time, but he's doing something different on each beat to get there. If you're not musically trained, let me share some "vocabulary" with you: when counting rhythms and beats in a measure, you count the numbers themselves as the quarter notes. They're the beats: "1-2-3-4". When vocalizing the half beats, you say the word "and," sometimes stylised like +. So counting the measure in eighth notes (each note half a beat long) will go "1+ 2+ 3+ 4+". Sixteenth notes (each note a quarter of a beat long) are a little funky, spelled out like "1 e + a", where that last "a" is pronounced like "uh". That's all a bit hard to take in from prose, so here are a couple diagrams to help illustrate what I mean.

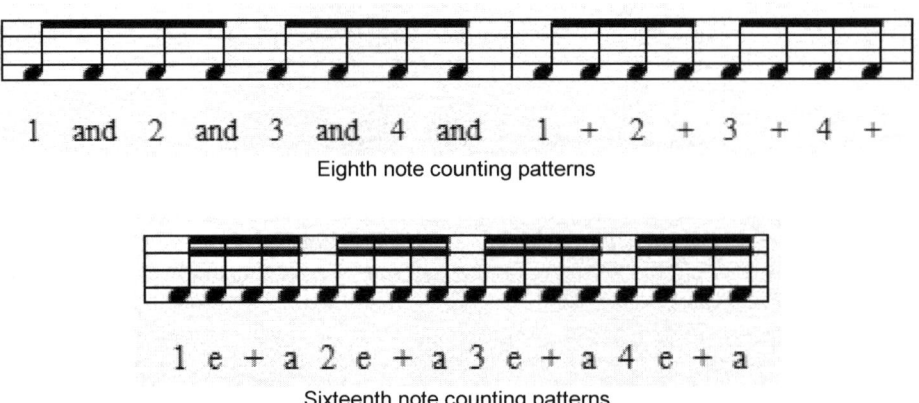

1 and 2 and 3 and 4 and   1 + 2 + 3 + 4 +
Eighth note counting patterns

1 e + a 2 e + a 3 e + a 4 e + a
Sixteenth note counting patterns

Clear as mud? Great. So here's what Phil's playing there in the 'Dodo' verse. He's got two eighth note bass kicks on 1, then a snare hit on 2. Beat 3 is the one that really gets you though: he hits sixteenth notes on three of the four sub-beats, but skips the half beat entirely, before hitting the snare on 4 again. This is important because he's also rocking that hi-hat cymbal (or is it a ride cymbal? I admit I can never quite tell the difference) on the half beats of the first two beats, before coming back to the primary beats with it on 3 and 4. So in practice, if you combined all the drum beats and cymbal crashes into one unified percussion pattern, here's how the drum riff would be counted out: 1+2+3e a4e+.

'Dodo' verse drum pattern (simplified)

In other words, he's giving you every single main beat with bass kicks on the down beat just like you'd expect, snare hits on the "heart attack" 2 beats like you'd expect, and again on the 4 beats, just like you'd expect, while acknowledging beat 3 along the way, just like you'd expect. But he's also trained you to expect something to come on 3's half beat, and instead gives you silence. That ONE little rest, that singular missing half beat, makes the whole thing sound tremendously complicated despite Phil otherwise delivering on your every rhythmic expectation along the way. Old ideas, new space.

Well, I admit I didn't start out writing this with an aim to get into deep detail on drum riffs, but hey, sometimes these things take on a life of their own, right? Which is perhaps a tad ironic, given how 'Dodo' is ostensibly a song about everything dying. Or more to the point, man in his capriciousness killing everything around him. Or is it Genesis, in their own capriciousness, laying waste to their past by honouring it one final time before detonating a 'Who Dunnit?' sized atom bomb over all their fans' lofty expectations? Either way, 'Dodo/Lurker' is so good that it often dwarfs the rest of the album for me, title track excepted. I guess sometimes when you want to get out of your own shadow, you've got to start by tearing down the monolith that's creating it in the first place. Out with the old and in with the new.

45 - Many Too Many

from ...And Then There Were Three..., 1978

'Many Too Many' is, to me, a three and a half minute window into the tangible musical growth, not of Genesis as a band per se, but rather of each of its individual members in various ways. Here I'd like to touch on each of them in sequence so I can better explain what I mean.

Mike's Story

And Then There Were Three, as the title implies, is the first album in the Genesis catalogue where the band lacked a dedicated guitarist. Mike Rutherford and Anthony Phillips were songwriting partners in the early days, and after Ant's departure the band actually had to pull the plug on Mike auditioning Ant's replacement. The problem was that Mike had such a strong idea of how the guitar should sound - namely, that it should sound exactly like Ant played it - that when a promising candidate by the name of Steve Hackett turned up in an ad, Peter and Tony figured they ought to go check him out so Mike wouldn't reject him out of hand. Then years of that signature Hackett sound and style later, Tony and Mike are faced again with the prospect of replacing a guitarist. And again Mike has this very clear idea of how he wants the thing to sound, only now the band has already managed to cover a major departure by having one of the surviving members pulling double duty; Phil successfully taking over the vocals figures to have been a catalyst for Mike's shift of thinking. "Maybe we don't need a fourth. Maybe I can just do both."

> **Mike:** *I wouldn't have felt bad about bringing someone in, but we learned you can do so much more in your camp than if you bring in someone from outside. There are so many problems that come with that.* [10]

Of course, maybe this would also simply mean less lead guitar parts in general.

> **Tony:** *We hadn't used that much lead guitar. It wasn't like we were Van Halen; lead guitar wasn't that important in the group. I don't want to underestimate Steve's contribution, but we could do it differently.* [10]

> **Mike:** *Apart from the lead parts a lot of what Steve used to do was accompanying by picking, which I'd been working in before so that part didn't worry me, but actually playing lead guitar was an area I'd never touched before...We went through various changes over what we wanted to do, but in the end the others decided to give me a shot at it. Obviously I think it works but I feel a lot more confident now than I did during the recording.* [17]

On 'Many Too Many' you can pretty much hear Mike learning how to fill this new role as he goes. When he arrives in the second verse, he's got a colour about his sound, but it's almost tentative in the background. Luckily, that sound works really well with the texture of the song in general, so no harm done. The lead lines that punctuate the vocals throughout have *just enough* flair on them, and of course they're still characterised by that same overarching *Three* sound I've made reference to in previous entries of this book. All of this culminates in a minute-long true guitar solo to end the piece that never sounds clean. But again, that messy, fuzzy texture is pretty much the ideal for the album's sound, and lines up swimmingly with the lyrical context of getting dumped and abandoned. It's the "mascara running from my tears" of guitar solos. What better fall-back cushion for learning a new craft?

Phil's Story

One thing that really strikes me about Phil Collins' drumming over the band's progressive years is just how intricate his playing can be. He turns the drums from a simple time-keeping device into a true musical instrument, with emphasis on the word "musical." Pull up any old Genesis piece that runs five minutes or more and listen to the drum part. You'll hear fills, stray hits, weird little rhythms...all stuff that might pass you by on first listen but really add heaps of personality to the pieces they support. There's always a lot going on with a Phil Collins progressive drum track, and it's a big part of why he's (rightly) so highly regarded among aficionados and peers.

Now listen to 'Many Too Many', keeping an ear to the drum track, and tell me what you hear. Or, perhaps, tell me what you *don't* hear. See, the other thing you always hear people say about Collins' percussive sensibilities is how he's got such a mind for space. It's a defining hallmark of his solo career and would become a similarly defining hallmark of later Genesis tunes as well. 'Many Too Many' marks a sneaky kind of turning point in this way: there's an awful lot of space in this one. It makes the actual drum strikes much more impactful when there are fewer of them, and those slow, heavy fills do a lot more emotional damage than some fast-firing technical display might. Phil hadn't started writing songs yet, but his predilection for creating space was already beginning to influence his bandmates.

> **Mike:** *I think we just started to sort of, maybe relax a bit actually. You know, we were always very intense young men trying to prove that we were the best and the greatest at everything, and suddenly, I don't know. You get a bit older, you had kids, and maybe you just start to, in life, not try so hard. Songs like 'Follow You Follow Me' and 'Many Too Many', for example, don't feel like anyone's trying at all. I think that's why they work well.* [3]

But Phil had two roles in the band here, and I don't think his growth was limited just to the drumming. It's a pretty common sentiment among fans - and both Mike and Tony have expressed similar thoughts as well - that it wasn't until around *Duke* that Phil really came into his own voice. And indeed, if you listen to *A Trick of the Tail* and immediately then listen to *Duke*, you'll hear the difference straight away. But 'Many Too Many' seems to me to be Phil's real coming out party.

Sure, it doesn't have the rough, soaring power of something like 'Duchess', but there is a depth to his vocal performance previously unheard in the "love songs" recorded by the band before. Compare this track to 'Your Own Special Way' just one album earlier and I think you'll hear what I mean. The emotive power of his voice was really coming to the fore, with strong technical displays as well like the seamless transition from chest voice to falsetto in the song's choruses. Then, of course, there was the bit about overcoming his own insecurities in being able to sing the lyrics in the first place:

> **Tony:** *All I remember about 'Many Too Many' was at the time we were doing it, trying to say to Phil, "Yes, you CAN say 'mama'! It's all right! It's all right! You can sing 'mama'!"...I said, "Stevie Wonder uses 'mama' in his lyrics all the time, so you can do it." Because he was so against, you know, he felt very self-conscious about doing it. Of course, a couple years later there was a song we did which was called 'Mama', where it's the main lyric all throughout the song, but at the time perhaps he felt a bit self-consciously that we were trying to be what we weren't.* [3]

You wouldn't know from the way Phil belts out those "mama" lines that it was something he had anxiety about. Or maybe he just channelled that anxiety into the performance so that it translated into the intended emotion of the song, into the loss experienced by its subject. Whatever the case, I think this was a big step on the road to Phil finding enough confidence to eventually open up his own heart and pour it into *Face Value* and everything beyond.

Tony's Story

Take a look at Tony Banks' songwriting output to this point, both lyrically and musically, and what do you find? On the verbal side, it's pretty much just storytelling. From mythical minglings to medieval musings, from undinal songs to spires of gold, from mice to men and back again, Tony always spoke to us through metaphor and allegory. Even 'Afterglow', his most direct lyrics to date, were couched in a narrative context of searching for a loved one amidst the debris of some kind of cataclysmic event. But 'Many Too Many' is different, and Tony recognises that, too:

> **Tony:** *The other one that I like a lot is 'Many Too Many', which again is a love song, and again I wrote the lyrics. I was obviously coming out of my shell here.* [3]

Yes, Tony, you were. This, like 'Afterglow' before it, is a pleading song about coping with loss. But here there's no "What if a bomb went off and you lost somebody?" kind of thought experiment. Here it's just "I got dumped by someone I thought was the love of my life. Now what?" It's so much more relatable, and while Tony is still not communicating from a deeply personal place lyrically, he's inching his way there.

Musically this song rides a similar historical line. Again, Tony's pieces were often longer developments: keyboard ideas mashed together until he's bringing in a ten-minute piece, telling the guys "Play this song in precisely this manner," and getting angsty when they don't deliver exactly according to his specifications. It was always about the way the keys could flow, be it big solos or just chord changes he really liked. Some of the best stuff in Genesis history - Apocalypse in 9/8's "Six-six-six" vocal or the guitar solo in 'Firth of Fifth', to name a pair - came because someone did something unexpected on top of Tony's expansive keyboard part and he found himself conceding that it actually worked.

So if 'Afterglow' was Tony finding that he could, with seeming effortlessness, write a song that didn't need to develop into an epic, 'Many Too Many' was a further maturation along those lines. Now he could write a song that not only was compact enough to be a single, but he was deferring his end melodies to a guitar solo because he realised that would sound better - and this was with a comparatively fledgling lead player in tow, to boot! Heck, at one point he even considered pulling in instruments from outside the band entirely:

> **Mike:** *The basic track for this was piano, bass, and drums, so once we put that down we'd still no real idea how it was going to work. We needed more arrangements. There's a very convincing string sound which Tony did on the Moog. We did actually talk about using orchestral instruments at one stage but somehow we never got round to it.* [17]

It didn't happen, but this was a Tony beginning to consider that perhaps he didn't need to carry the full weight of the Genesis sound on his shoulders. 'Many Too Many' is a keyboard-driven track that sounds like a guitar-driven track, because that's what works best for the song. It's only a slight reduction of ego, I suppose, but without even that small concession do we really think the Phenix Horns would've ever shown up on 'No Reply at All' or 'Paperlate' a few years down the line? If Mike and Phil grew by learning how to step up and take on more musical responsibility, Tony showed his growth by beginning to let go of some of his own. It was a necessary kind of relaxation if everyone was going to thrive.

Genesis' Story

And thrive they did. Some of the best lead guitar bits in the Genesis discography come from Mike's output in the 1980s and beyond; 'Many Too Many' helped catalyse that growth. Some of the strongest vocals in the Genesis discography came from Phil's increasingly confident output; 'Many Too Many' was a huge leap of faith that helped him more fully embrace the lead singer role. Some of the strongest rhythm patterns in the Genesis discography came from drum machines and simple repeating patterns; 'Many Too Many' was a "less is more" milestone that helped the band become more flexible with their ideas of what their music could be. Some of the strongest pieces the band would record over the next two decades were songs that developed out of initial ideas from members other than Tony; 'Many Too Many' helped him become more comfortable with being *a* member of Genesis instead of *the* member of Genesis.

As for 'Many Too Many' itself?

> **Tony:** *Still a bit weird; it's not totally straightforward...But I think it sounds good. I know no one at the time ever felt that it didn't work from that point of view.* [3]

It's dark, romantic, grounded-in-reality pop that's nevertheless sufficiently off the beaten path that it's right at home on an album defined by ethereal, almost alien textures. "Still a bit weird" when you put it that way, I guess, but hey: it sounds good.

44 - Looking for Someone

from *Trespass*, 1970

Have you ever had writer's block? I don't necessarily mean anything as extreme as "I'm a professional author and can't figure out how to start my next book and my publisher is getting restless," mind you. But have you ever found yourself having to write a paper for school, or a document for work, or even just something on your own for fun? Chances are you have. During any of those times, have you ever found that the mental faucet simply wouldn't quite turn on? Heck, this isn't even limited to writing, but for any creative endeavour. Have you ever followed your passion to make something only to become paralyzed by a lack of inspiration?

There's a sense of frustration at that, right? To focus in on writing again, if what you're trying to write needs to fit in a certain kind of box, there comes with it a particular sense of pressure, and perhaps no small amount of terror. How do I create something that meets these specific requirements? Where do I start? And say, to your great relief, you *do* manage to finally figure that out. What if now you need to make *more*? Just keep churning this stuff out. How do I do that *again*? And how can I do it without endlessly repeating myself along the way?

This is a real issue that almost anyone who's ever tried to create anything has faced. I sat here looking at the blank page for my 'Looking for Someone' entry and inevitably found I wanted to distract myself by doing something - anything - else. Where do I start? And this wasn't a new sensation. I had this feeling many times over the course of writing all the words in this book, and it was always the same thing. What am I going to say *this* time?

One imagines the Genesis of 1969 in a similar rut. They'd written some songs, hoping to score a hit somewhere. Given the quality of their very first batch of songs the outlook was dim, so they made another attempt, more targeted this time. That coalesced into a single, which went nowhere. So they did another single. And then a whole album. And now they needed to make a second album, and how do you face that monster again? How are you going to write another entire batch of pop songs without hopelessly repeating yourself, both in terms of the music and the lack of success?

Ultimately, Genesis had the same solution I've used myself repeatedly in my own struggles. *Do something completely different.* Stop trying to write into this box. Be brave, and bold, and let your creativity wander where it will; you can always rein it back later if it wanders too far. Don't let yourself be defined by what you did, but rather by what you can still do. Though obviously not part of the band yet, Phil Collins might've expressed this philosophy best.

> **Phil:** *I'm as good as the next thing I do rather than the last thing I did.* [1]

> Do something *different*, and maybe magic will happen.

> **Peter:** *That was another one that sort of felt like you've got a song which I brought to the band, and the band had then extended. A soul-influenced piece. But it then went into this sort of folkier journey, and I really was pleased with that mixture. It was fun to sing. I've always liked to try and have, in the different voices I work within, to have a bluesy one. And that was more sort of soul-influenced.* [3]

And what a magical coming out party this song is for Genesis! At first blush it seems unimaginable that the band could put out *From Genesis to Revelation* in 1969 and follow it up in 1970 with *this*. Not that I'm saying *FGTR* is a bad album (I am sort of saying that), but the first two LPs don't even really compare. They're not only completely different genres - that tried and true cure for the creativity blues - but the growth in musicianship and songwriting prowess is also astounding. It's one thing to decide to go in a totally different direction, but it's another entirely to have the skill to pull it off, especially with so little experience.

So how did they do it? Well, for one thing, they got a new drummer. Out with John Silver, who resigned from the band to study overseas, in with part-time carpenter John Mayhew. Yes, I know, John Mayhew isn't a name to set the world on fire, but listen to him on the kit here in 'Looking for Someone' and try to tell me he's trash. I don't buy that; this stuff sounds really strong. No, the issue with Mayhew that caused him to be replaced was the time it took him to learn the parts; his lack of natural instinct. Once told exactly what to do, he could bang them drums as well as any group of ragtag 19 year old kids could ask for.

> **John Mayhew:** *I realised that what I had been able to do was to provide a solid platform on which they could set up a repertoire and sort themselves out for a move into the professional world. And if I was that steadying force, then I'm glad that's what happened.* [1]

> **Ant:** *He was a good drummer. But we were very demanding. Very, very demanding. And I think he always felt he came up short. He didn't, really. He did a fine job. The trouble is history*

> *hasn't treated John well because his successor happens just to have been one of the very, very special drummers. Not only a drummer, but a singer and all the rest of it, a brilliant musician. So I think had they found a sort of more prosaic drummer afterwards, then history would speak more kindly about John. But he's cast in a rather dim light, which I always think is rather unfair.* [3]

But *Trespass* and 'Looking for Someone' can't be explained simply by the band simply swapping their Johns around. It's also a big step forward in playing for the established members. Ant's able to jump seamlessly between textural and true lead playing. Mike's got showy bass lines, coming into his own probably for the first time. Tony's playing organ, and playing it well, but he also is more willing to be part of the ensemble instead of "the" guy. Peter's voice has an almost unrecognisable level of confidence compared to the band's first outing, and if that weren't enough, he apparently learned how to play the flute in the interim as well. And of course, the songwriting itself is light years ahead of the amateurish attempts at hit-writing that marked that ill-fated debut. You can look at the track listing for *Trespass* and see that there are only six tracks, and the opener is over seven minutes long. This is something else entirely.

> **Tony:** *'Looking For Someone' was always a high point for us...There was the heavier sound which I think came from Peter and I...We were more keyboard based and [Ant and Mike] were more guitar based...As a lead guitarist, Ant was obviously very much a part of things like...the improvised sections of 'Looking For Someone', but the essence of that song had already been established by our side of the fence. We were very much two writing units.* [6]

So again I'm struck by the timing of it all and how so much could've happened so quickly. But when you break it down a bit, it does start to make a little more sense. *From Genesis to Revelation* was released in March of 1969, yes, but it was *recorded* in late 1968, and *written* in part as far back as late 1967. So what seems on the surface to be a rapid growth in nary a year is really about two and a half years of incremental progress unmarked by studio releases, but forged in the fire of live playing and fuelled by a desire to push beyond the boundaries their debut had so neatly set up for them. It's no less remarkable an achievement, but at least it now seems somewhat human.

Trespass, and 'Looking for Someone' in particular, is a shedding of expectations. It's a band that says "Let's see what happens" instead of "Let's try once more to write a hit single." We can't face this crusty old box anymore; let's do something *different*. The resulting sonic freedom has a grandeur about it far beyond anything that a few barely-adults should be able to produce. Those opening moments of the song are very much a kind of sneak preview of 'Dancing with the Moonlit Knight'. Here's Pete and Tony, putting forth a powerful vocal bit with a striking amount of space, that then is allowed to develop into this big instrumental journey featuring everyone in the band displaying how far they've come.

> **Mike:** *One of the reasons why our early songs were so long: we'd just keep adding bits. Long songs might appear clever and hard to write, but for us they were easy. We'd just take bit A and bit D and segue them together. What we didn't realise was that it was generally better if you didn't try to use the whole alphabet every time. A prime example was the opening track on the album, 'Looking for Someone'. It started with Pete's idea and began with just simple piano chords and voice - such a Pete thing. If I had it now, it'd be a fabulous song as I could make something out of just the first couple of bits. Back then we rambled on with another eight minutes, throwing in bits and pieces...Pete always realised that space in a track was important.* [14]

> **Ant:** *Long, long track with lots of sections - what became characterised as "prog rock." What we were really doing was sellotaping one section onto another. There's not necessarily anything wrong with that...* [1]

Nothing inherently wrong with that, no, especially when there isn't a weak section of music anywhere to be found on this song. These kids got a bunch of ideas and decided to throw out the formula and try them all, and somehow they all work. Whether they all work perfectly *with* one another is perhaps a matter of some debate, but they were exploring, happily honing their craft, unknowingly preparing to join their inspiration King Crimson as foremost purveyors of blissful symphonic prog. And they were learning to do it all in tandem, combining their writing talents to get a whole that was greater than the sum of the parts.

> **Tony:** *There was an extended instrumental section at the end of 'Looking for Someone' that predicted a lot of what happened in the later albums...also a group-written piece.* [1]

I often see a lot of praise for 'Stagnation' and 'The Knife' when it comes to *Trespass*, but for me 'Looking for Someone' just has that special *something* about it. Its arresting opening, its bold instrumentals peppered with solid melodies, its vocal reprise near the end, its triumphant ending with that lingering final chord. It's the first place my mind goes when I think of this album, which is fitting since it's the first thing you hear when you put it on.

In the end, they did something *different*, and that's what made all the difference.

43 - Home by the Sea

from *Genesis*, 1983

Early Genesis was a band of moods, you could say. The technical musical proficiency wasn't there at the start (they were only teens, after all), and was a bit of a slow build over the years of incessant work between writing, recording, and performing. The boys were tossed into a crucible through the early 70s, where their playing had to get up to snuff or they'd risk fading into obscurity. They delivered, of course, but because they were writing music they knew they'd have to go out and perform, and they knew the limits of their own playing chops, virtuosic playing took a back seat in the songwriting room to generating a feeling.

Sometimes a song would sit in one mood, like 'Dusk' from *Trespass*. Sometimes it would go through multiple moods, like 'Get 'Em Out By Friday', to name just one of the band's longer progressive works. Sometimes you'd have a happy and carefree mood like, well, 'Happy the Man'. Sometimes you'd have a downcast mood, like 'Silent Sorrow in Empty Boats'. Maybe there's a mood that channels comedy, like 'Counting Out Time'. Maybe there's a mood that channels anger, like 'The Knife'. And though the musicianship improved, the songwriting sensibilities didn't change when Peter Gabriel departed. You have the sleepy mood of 'Entangled', the adventurous mood of 'Deep in the Motherlode', the self-important mood of 'Cul-de-sac', even the frantic mood of 'Who Dunnit?' - and those are just several examples.

> **Tony:** *If you go back to albums like Nursery Cryme you'll find short and simple songs, but they weren't hits. They didn't get much emphasis...Then there's 'Home by the Sea'... on the new album...* [23]

Now consider that by 1983's *Genesis*, the guys are no longer bringing in any solo material to work with. They haven't gone off and written their individual songs, coming in saying "I've written this song and it fits this particular mood." But they're all still sort of thinking about it, because that's the way this process has gone for the whole of their professional careers. They're jamming, improvising, figuring out what works and what doesn't, and then trying to develop a mood from there.

> **Tony:** *When we were writing the song, Phil had this one phrase he kept singing: "Home by the sea, home by the sea." And as I was writing the lyric to this thing, I thought, "Home by the sea, what does that conjure up?"* [3]

You have a lot of options with a phrase like "home by the sea". Maybe it's a quiet retreat from the busy city life; this idyllic, remote chateau overlooking a tranquil ocean, one's own little personal sanctuary. Maybe it's a bustling port, a home full of activity, sounds of fishing ships and their captains at the docks nearby, hauling and hawking their wares. Maybe it's a summer home, a place to take the kids on vacation, hallways full of giggling and romping, and of course afternoons of great fun in the water. Almost any mood is possible with a simple prompt like that, and Tony as the lyricist got to choose where it was going. And, given the band's penchant for avoiding anything that called back too heavily to the past, it's not a stretch to imagine Tony reflecting on the Genesis catalogue to date, trying to find a mood they hadn't managed to capture yet. And then it hits him.

> **Tony:** *I thought, "Well, let's have a spooky home by the sea!"* [3]

Suddenly, this concept of a home by the sea, which naturally lends itself to positive imagery, has become something sinister. Ideas form. What if the home itself were alive? What if the home by the sea isn't just a place but this sort of supernatural entity? What if it looked normal but the walls were actually solid conglomerations of ghosts? And then, the maddest idea of all: *what if the house and its ghosts were the protagonists of the story?* The idea of centring the song around the ghosts all talking with one another was perhaps a bridge too far, so it was necessary to have some actual person end up in this haunted house. But how do you make sure this hapless victim isn't your hero? How do you subject him to the terrors of the home by the sea without making the listener sympathetic?

> **Mike:** *'Home by the Sea' is a song I could've seen us doing six or seven years ago but we've done it in a way that makes it sound even better...we were a lot more flowery in the early days.* [80]

What if...what if he's the *villain* of the story? What if he *deserves* everything that comes his way? More ideas form. What if he's trying to rob the place? He's doing it with a practiced hand, so we know this isn't his first heist. Done me wrong, same old song? Oh, we'll do him wrong all right.

> **Tony:** *The idea of a burglar going in there and actually getting enveloped and suddenly being with these ghosts surrounding him and everything just quite appealed to me.* [3]

But this definitely wouldn't be the same old song. If you want a spooky mood, you've got to really go for it with the instrumentation. Booting up something called 'Home by the Sea' expecting a lovely vignette like 'For Absent Friends', are you? Right, let's open with a grating guitar sound as though someone just activated an emergency warning system. Let's give those snare drums some punch. Let's really dwell in this minor key realm.

> **Tony:** *And also some of the melodic, some of the little keyboard things that happened also felt a bit ghostly. I thought that was quite a nice thing to do.* [3]

While we're at it, let's take a sheet of sandpaper to Phil's vocal cords!

> **Phil:** *There were certain songs in the Genesis set-list that I'd be dreading coming down the pipe. 'Home by the Sea' has a lot of lyrics...Tony Banks wrote that melody, and those words, but he'd never thought about how it would sound; he'd never sung it out loud.* [12]

Hard to sing? *Perfect.* Let's have him just rend the air while he rends his voice, delivering that ghostly command: "SIT DOWN!" What's this burglar gonna do, not sit down? It's a simple line delivered with terrifying authority. And then let's force this guy to listen to us, forever.

> **Tony:** *And the idea that we're telling our life story through our songs, which is sort of represented by the third verse of the song, "As we relive our lives in what we tell you," I think is quite a strong thing. It's sort of what you do in a group, I think.* [3]

> **Phil:** *'Home by the Sea' and 'Domino' are mainly Tony-biased songs which I found I enjoyed much more fifteen years on.* [1]

It takes fifteen years for this to sink in? *Brilliant.* Why? *Because Genesis are the ghosts.* The home by the sea is their catalogue. And we're the hapless burglars hoping to nab one more little ounce of pleasure from the music, only to find that the music has captured us for the rest of our lives. We'll spend the remainder of *our* lives listening to the art that defined *their* lives, and we'd better learn to like it because we won't get away. No, with them we will stay. For the rest of our days.

SIT DOWN.

(to be continued...)

42 - The Dividing Line

from *Calling All Stations*, 1997

It's no secret that *Calling All Stations* is seen among large swaths of the Genesis fandom as their nadir, an abyss of quality from which the band could never recover. It's should also be apparent by now that I don't agree with that notion in the slightest. In my experience, people who have never heard the album dismiss it out of hand because of everything they've heard *about* the album. And the people who *do* decide to give it a listen are often doing so with a thought process of "Let's see just how bad this is," which of course puts up a conceptual block to the music before it's even begun. I think this is really the crux of why the album failed in the first place.

> **Ray:** *The problem is...especially in America, Genesis this time round are a little bit under dig-ish. Phil has gone and quite frankly even if Phil was still here it would be quite difficult because the mood of America has changed towards more established artists - people like Bon Jovi, Bryan Adams, Tina Turner...and I am not saying that Genesis are in that genre, but they are still an established group...we are struggling like fuck in America, really struggling.* [28]

Look at the 1997 US pop charts and tell me what you see. There's a wide variety of music there, but the common thread (outside perhaps the growing influence of R&B/hip hop on the mainstream) is that the music was all coming from new artists. This was the year of the Spice Girls, of boy bands, of poppy alt-rock like Matchbox 20 and Third-Eye Blind and Sister Hazel. These were the critical and commercial darlings of the time. You think music critics were *ever* going to give any weight to a new Genesis album in this era, especially when Phil Collins has jumped ship? The bad reviews were always going to pour in, regardless of the actual quality of the music. And then bad reviews mean less radio play. Less radio play means retailers don't want to stock the album. No album stock means no sales (my own dad's copy is clearly printed as the store's "display-only" reserve copy, which they nevertheless didn't mind liquidating). No album sales means no US tour. No US tour means Mike feels a wee bit miffed. And Mike feeling a wee bit miffed means no more Genesis. It was always going to go down this way, and it's my strong opinion that it's not the album's fault.

But then there's a significant group of fans who actually *have* listened to the album and insist they've done so with an open mind, who still don't care much for it. And when discussing its shortcomings with these fans, one complaint tends to arise again and again: all the songs fade out, as though the band were too lazy or too idea-starved to ever write proper endings for them. There's a kernel of truth to that, albeit with an understandable explanation, at least according to *Calling All Stations* producer Nick Davis.

> **Nick Davis:** *The weakness of Calling All Stations is not the songwriting, but not knowing who was going to sing the songs or play the drums. It was a weird situation, because the album was virtually written, but there we were auditioning musicians to play on it. With the drums, for example, although I think the drums sound pretty good, we had used a drum box throughout the writing, which means they had never written an ending for any of the songs, so unusually every track on that album fades out.* [1]

True as that may be, it seems to me that Tony and Mike took what was a limitation and tried their darndest to make it into a strength. Look at the album title and its cover art. Note the ellipsis at both ends. Not *Calling All Stations* but *...Calling All Stations...* And then the echoes - ripples? - of that title running down from there. There's an implied before-and-after here, where the album sits in the middle. It's an album that was intended to start a kind of "phase three" of Genesis, crossfading from what came before ('**Fading** Lights', for crying out loud!) and into what comes next. It's not a concept album, but it *is* a themed one; ironically the album they couldn't get on the radio is an album that uses radio as its overarching motif.

This is the thing about the album I think most listeners miss. Every song is a new "station" being tuned into, locked in, and then tuned away again. They tip their hand at the start of 'Shipwrecked', where the first several seconds are radio static and a guitar riff that sounds like it's coming through a lo-fi speaker. The playful African chants of 'Congo' themselves fade in like you're turning up the volume dial, and the dichotomy of moods within that song kind of feels like you're changing between a couple different radio stations, too. I think that's what we're missing. It's not that the album is bad or that the fade-out endings are inherently a problem, but that *we're hearing the album out of order*.

I believe 'Shipwrecked', in all its schmaltzy glory, was originally intended to be the opening track, and I think that radio static cut-in is the giveaway. I think that was then going to run into 'Congo', and that the tracks would continue to amplify in intensity from there.

Tony: *The album tends to get heavier as it gets going, I think.* [25]

The lynchpin of this theory, however, isn't 'Shipwrecked' at all, but rather 'The Dividing Line'. Notice that 'The Dividing Line' is the **only** song on the album that does not fade out. It's the **only** song with a "proper" ending. This isn't a coincidence; you see, 'The Dividing Line' is actually *Calling All Stations*' closing number.

Tony: *We originally thought...I was in favour of having 'The Dividing Line' at the end but the feeling was that a lot of people didn't listen to albums as consecutively as they used to, and in that context we wanted to make sure that they got to that song not too late because it is the most strongly instrumental and playing kind of biased song on the album, and so we swapped 'One Man's Fool' and 'The Dividing Line'.* [25]

Logic like this ("let them hear some of the strongest material earlier on") also led the album's title track, itself quite heavy, to be catapulted to the front of the track order instead of what I'm guessing was its originally envisioned place as the penultimate number. Thus, when listening to *Calling All Stations*, it's my belief that the ideal listening order is **not** how the album eventually released, but instead as follows:

- Shipwrecked
- Congo
- Alien Afternoon
- Not About Us
- If That's What You Need
- One Man's Fool
- Uncertain Weather
- Small Talk
- There Must Be Some Other Way
- Calling All Stations
- The Dividing Line

It completely eschews the traditional album flow of balancing lighter songs with heavier ones in favour of a continual build. It's a gradual shift from malaise into excitement, a listener continuing to progressively tune the dial from the easy listening stations over to the pulse pounding rock of 'The Dividing Line', where, satisfied, the radio is finally turned off. To me it also answers the question of why such solid songs like 'Anything Now' and 'Sign Your Life Away' were left off the album even though the band felt strongly that they were good tracks; once you've committed to this light-to-heavy flow, there's nowhere to put a pair of peppy, upbeat numbers no matter how great they might sound. Again, this setup doesn't flow in the traditional way, and that's a large part of why the concept was abandoned, but it's a brilliant idea, now buried under the rubble of the album's failure and the band's subsequent collapse.

So when talking about 'The Dividing Line' I actually approach it from the standpoint of that album closer role. It's not the song's fault that it got shunted up to the midway point of the album - indeed, that only happened *because* it was so strong! And when you "tune into" this song, it doesn't take long to find out why.

Ray: *'The Dividing Line', that was a great song...it's quite a good live track. Some songs don't work very well live...but that one did.* [26]

That first 1:40 of 'The Dividing Line' is one of the best things Genesis ever put on record, full stop. It's the rhythmic feel of 'The Brazilian' mixed with guitar that's allowed to sound rough and unpolished. It's edge-of-your-seat chords and a keyboard main line that may as well just be an IV drip of adrenaline straight into your arm. Now I don't mean this in a disparaging way against the other six minutes that follow, but if that first bit of the song had spun out into something a little bit different, something that had better held onto that frenetic energy, there's no doubt in my mind we'd be talking about a top 5 all-time Genesis track.

Tony: *It has a great rhythm track, but lyrically, it's a little bit simplistic. Melodically, it could have been better. But it was great fun to do the rhythm part. It has great drumming throughout, and particularly during the drum solo.* [18]

Of course, it doesn't do that, and instead goes into a vocal bit backed by what sounds like Tony playing a rousing game of Simon in the background. Ray's vocals are well-delivered, and the lyrics are...fine. Mike's still on that grungy guitar but mainly just there to accent the thrilling rhythm section, not really exploring the space much on his own. The whole thing works pretty well but would be a huge let down from the opening section if not for the fact that session drummer Nir Zidkyahu simply CANNOT. BE. STOPPED. on that drum kit.

> **Tony:** *'The Dividing Line'...is the strongest instrumental and it particularly features the drummer, Nir. When we originally did this with the drum machine we originally had a very clattery sort of drum machine part that worked really well and the working title was 'NYPD', which was because of the way the drums were very fast!* [25]

I mean, good grief. Obviously replacing Phil as a singer was the biggest fan concern, and to that end Ray Wilson performed admirably within his abilities. Replacing Phil as a *drummer* though? As longtime Genesis fans would tell you, that's an even tougher feat. So it says a lot that after the album's tour, Tony wanted to take Nir (along with touring guitarist Anthony Drennan) into the studio to write together as a full-fledged five-piece. He fit right in, musically.

> **Nir Zidkyahu:** *'The Dividing Line' is a pain in the butt! It was just one of those experimental jam sessions in the studio and I have no idea what I played and before we started rehearsals I said "OK, let's listen to it now..." There is a lot of movement there, a lot of toms and there's a drum solo in there and it will probably be longer in the live show!* [28]

Show up, make stuff up, immediately forget what you played, somehow bang it out live like it ain't no thang anyway. That's Genesis tradition right there. No wonder they gave the guy a big extended drum solo in this song, unheard of in a Genesis studio track to date.

> **Nir:** *Beforehand, when I had listened to the classic Genesis tracks, these masterpieces, I had imagined that every bar and every note must have been precisely arranged. I am open and emotional in my work. I'm the type of musician who likes to play what I feel without planning it out too much. But when I arrived in the studio I discovered that they had a much looser way of working than I had imagined. I found myself jamming with songs, experimenting. I could go with the flow...I found I was working with two artists, two musicians, and the music was a journey, every time...My time with Genesis was a bitter-sweet experience, although a lot of fun, and I am proud of my performances on tracks like 'The Dividing Line'.* [1]

As you should be, brother! Well done. Unfortunately, when the drum solo closes out the song feels like it's not sure where to go, so it kind of hangs in the air for a bit. Eventually it stops loitering and dives headlong into a reprise of that epic opening section, which is probably the best choice that could've been made. It's not the smoothest transition by any means, but a second taste of that electricity, a second drip from that IV bag, well. That was what we wanted all along, so we'll forgive the stumbling along the way.

If you're someone who doesn't hate *Calling All Stations* but never really thought it worked, I encourage you to try it again in the reworked track order I've suggested, keeping the radio dial concept in mind. Of course there's a chance you'll still find it completely unworthwhile, but I've heard from other fans that this idea helped the album finally click for them; maybe it will for you, too. Either way, you'll at least get to end your listen on 'The Dividing Line', and it's pretty hard to complain about that.

41 - Living Forever

from *We Can't Dance*, 1991

I have a couple friends...or rather you might call them a friendly couple. They're married, you see, but I've known them both for many years. Some time ago they, like so many other people in modern Western civilization, reached a point in their lives at which they decided it was time to lose some weight. Not that either of them was particularly large, or that I'd want to ever make that judgment on another person's behalf to begin with, but they announced to us and other friends that they were going on something of a weight loss journey together, and asked for moral support. Of course, I happily obliged along with everyone else. That's what friends do.

However, delivering unwavering support was made a little bit difficult by the fact that the diet they chose to propel them to their weight loss goal was *borderline insane*. I don't know all the specifics, and if they ever told me the name of the diet program it went in one ear and out the other, but the gist was this: each day they could eat three meals, but each meal consisted of, essentially, nothing. A "meal" might be three small florets of broccoli, to give just one example. This portion of the diet would continue for either 30 days or 45 days, I can't quite recall. My friends referred to this period of the program as a "cleanse," but any rational onlooker probably would've opted for the term "starvation" instead. After this intentional shrinking/shrivelling of the body and stomach, the dieter was then to reintroduce healthy foods in gradually increasing quantities until a sort of equilibrium was reached, at which point said dieter would be healthy forever™.

What's maybe the most shocking thing about this diet is that this couple jumped on board with it after a recommendation they received from a *different* mutual friend, who couldn't say enough about how great it was for him. All three of these people are intelligent, well-adjusted individuals. And all three of them thought something along the lines of, "Starve myself for a month? Yeah, that's brilliant!" What seemed so ridiculous and counterproductive from the outside looked like perfect sense from the inside, because when you're on the inside, you can get laser focused on the results and forget about the importance of how you get there.

Which is probably why, after all three did in fact lose a significant amount of weight over that first month - again, they were literally starving themselves, so weight loss was pretty much a given - they felt absolutely terrible in the process. "That's the cleanse working the toxins out," the diet logic claims, so suggestions like "You should probably eat a little more" would be seen as unsupportive, as undermining the end goal, like a little devil on the shoulder trying to trick the dieter off the path. This also helps explain why, after the weight inevitably came back within a few months of the diet's programmed conclusion, these individuals decided to do it *again*. "The problem wasn't the diet, it was my own discipline! I *did* lose weight, but I just need to keep it off!"

> **Tony:** *I think it's a present day people's obsession, diet and things like that, because you can do exactly what you like. It's for the people who tell other people what they are supposed to be doing; that I object to most of all, because they've got this great new thing that they think is good. I'm so sceptical about this because there is no doubt that every five years the information gets reviewed and renewed and I don't really like... I mean like when I was writing this lyric, the Labour Party brought out a plan of what you should be eating and what you should do for a healthy thing and then the Tories brought out their own one and I thought, "I don't want to be told by the Government what I should be doing," in a sense...You know, you have to use a bit of common sense.* [81]

This anecdote is an extreme example, but diets are everywhere, and seldom consistent. Want to lose weight? Obviously, you need to eat fewer fats. Go for those (more expensive) reduced fat and fat free options. Can't get fat if you don't eat fat, right?

No, no, wait a minute, your body actually *needs* fats to operate the right way. So what you really want to do is eat healthy fats and avoid the unhealthy ones. Maybe you should go vegan! We were never meant to eat animal products in the first place, right? Nothing healthier than nature's bounty!

Hang on, turns out animal products are actually pretty nutrient-rich in ways that are difficult for plants to replicate in reasonable quantities. So we should eat veggies AND meat, but get rid of the REAL problem, which is grain. Cavemen didn't eat grains, why should we? Gotta stick to the stuff that got us here in the first place, and that means drinkin' juice and boilin' goose...right?

'Living Forever' is the dieting experience crystallised into musical form. Feel how happy it sounds right from the get-go? How upbeat and peppy it is, with those airy, high chords, that chipper little brush pattern on the drum machine, that playful guitar riff? It's sort of like the distilled emotion of starting a new diet. That elation we feel that we're finally taking our lives into our own hands and making a positive change. That hope and confidence that we've got the secret answer now that's finally going to get us over that edge, that miracle solution that lets us get the body we want with minimal effort. What could be better?

It's so innately attractive, and yet. It's almost *too* perfect, you know? We know somewhere inside that this sounds too good to be true, but there's no pooping on this party. The first chorus ends with Phil's bending backing vocals going into a downturn. It feels like it's going to be a drop, or perhaps just a dimming of the light, but who has time for doubts when you've got a few broccoli florets to tackle? So the second verse is just as joyful as the first, despite the fact that the lyrics are all about doing a complete 180 on the dietary front. You can hear the energy in Phil's lead vocal pretty easily, but if you listen closely you can hear how quiet, weary, and disillusioned the backing harmony vocals already feel. Are we really doing this again? *This time it's the right way for sure, huh?*

That second chorus bends down again, but now follows through to the natural musical and emotional conclusion: this radical diet stuff actually kinda sucks! Which is why when the third verse goes back to the upbeat feel - now with lyrics about wilfully ignoring any and all dietary advice - the backing vocals are now energised too. "So I might be a little bit overweight. Who cares? Better that than wasting away with anxiety over every calorie I take in." It's the same lightness, but now coming from a place of freedom instead of the shackles of ever-changing dietary fads. Punctuated, of course, by the last line of the song. The first line of the first chorus is "I'll live forever." From there it goes to "Living forever," with a single "And live forever" in the midst for good measure. That last chorus, though, replaces these bits with "Just till tomorrow," and finally "Do you really want to live forever?" and they're the happiest lines of the whole song.

Then, of course, the extended keyboard solo. I like to think of this as the artistic rendition of the internal journey to self-acceptance. As such, the solo starts off in a very dark place.

> **Tony:** *On the first bit, when there was a bit of menace, I was playing all kinds of diminished notes....when you first get into this solo, it sounds very dramatic.* [82]

This is a representation of the body image struggle many people deal with on a daily basis, and with which society on a whole gives us almost no support. But instead of gradually working the solo to a more positive place, Tony goes for a sort of zen switcheroo; just think positive, and problem solved! It's not so easy as all that in real life, but it works really well in the song here.

> **Tony:** *Suddenly it goes happy...the natural feel of the bit was more light. At some point I knew I'd have to change, so I thought I'd make the change quite suddenly - a change in tone, from the VFX to the Wavestation [keyboards], and a change in notes - and immediately bring in a different feel. I just wanted to keep this a lightweight solo, a breezy sort of thing, without being too intense, because I knew I had a more intense solo later on the album.* [82]

It's worth noting as well the programmed drum brushes driving the rhythm track for most of the song.

> **Phil:** *The original working title for that song was 'Hip-Hop Brushes'. I had gotten some new disks for my [Emu] SP-1200 [drum machine]. One of them was a jazz kit, and while the regular drum sounds didn't interest me, the brush concept did seem original. So I wrote a pattern with them that happened to be a hip-hop kind of thing. I tried to make it sound like what a drummer would actually play. Then we started playing off of that...To be honest, the drum pattern on 'Living Forever' took me ten minutes to write. Normally at a writing session, in the moments of silence between one idea and the next idea, I'll very quickly program something at random. That's how this pattern happened. All our drum machine parts happen quickly. You have to get something going before everybody puts his instrument down and goes for a cup of tea.* [82]

The solo section is also where these "hip hop brushes" get supplanted by the real drums; the "fakeness" of the first half of the song has been replaced by a sense of authenticity. It's, well, refreshing. And once all those pieces are in place the solo itself just sounds so...happy. You get some nice chords on top of the groove after a little fancy finger dancing, and when the song sounds like it's going to take a turn for the truly epic, it instead just pivots back to a reprise of its intro section. Notably, unlike other, similar Genesis three-piece songs with back half instrumentals such as 'Home by the Sea' or 'Fading Lights', 'Living Forever' doesn't ever bring the vocals back in. It's going that classic 'Cinema Show' route where it's said all it needs to say directly; the music can stand on its own from there.

Looked at another way, 'Living Forever' is a really brief, enjoyable pop song joined at the hip to a really brief, enjoyable instrumental prog bit. But it works so well because each half is a different angle of the same thing, and the overall message is really positive. Hard for me to listen to this one and not just, I don't know, enjoy life a little bit more. And while it's always tough to find the time, I encourage you reading this to do what you can to get some - any - exercise. Ultimately, there's no healthier option than that.

40 - In the Cage

from *The Lamb Lies Down on Broadway*, 1974

I got sunshine in my stomach, like I just rocked my baby to sleep.

> **Peter:** *We had our first child...it was, as it is for anyone really, suddenly the most important thing in your life by a long way. We were all set for a sort of natural birth, putting [the baby] on the breast.* [3]

I got sunshine in my stomach, but it can't keep me from creeping sleep

> **Peter:** *[My wife] Jill had taken an epidural and got an infection from the needle. [Baby] Anna had the cord round her neck.* [1]

Sleep, deep in the deep

> **Peter:** *For the first two days the medical staff wouldn't let Jill go down to the premature unit because they thought Anna wasn't going to survive and they thought at that time it was kinder for her not to make the attachment. It was a nightmare...* [1]

Rockface moves to press my skin

> **Mike:** *We were so unsupportive...we gave him no help at all, actually. Which I'm sure must've been hard.* [3]

White liquid turns sour within

> **Peter:** *There was a sense of frustration and anger and poison building in the room sometimes...* [1]

Turn fast, turn sour, turn sweat, turn sour

> **Steve:** *Life had been relatively simple before, but we were all now growing, expanding and evolving into adult lives.* [70]

Must tell myself that I'm not here

> **Peter:** *I was making these sort of long pilgrimages...I would be based here [in London], and whenever things looked better [with my family] try and zoom back to Wales for the recording.* [3]

I'm drowning in a liquid fear

> **Steve:** *Pete was particularly worried.* [70]

Bottled in a strong compression

My distortion shows obsession

> **Peter:** *I just lost it in lots of ways, because I felt this is so obviously more important than an album or anything else. This is life and death, and it's central to my family, and that's where I need to be.* [3]

In this cave

Get me out of this cave

> **Steve:** *[Headley Grange] was falling apart. In fact, on the day that we left, I'd been washing at the sink, moved back three feet, and as I did so the floor gave way and in front of me was a gaping hole where there had once been the ceiling of the room below.* [1]

If I keep self-control, I'll be safe in my soul

> **Peter:** *They would discuss some of the lyrical stuff with me...but I was pretty anal about hanging onto some lyrical flowthrough and being able to put a stamp on it. I really wanted a*

sort of tougher edge to this record than we'd had previously, and I didn't think there was anyone else in the band who was going to deliver that. [3]

And the childhood belief brings a moment's relief

> **Peter:** *We were excited by the music. I still think it's one of the best things that we did together.* [1]

> **Tony:** *One of the bits I was most pleased about became 'In the Cage', something I'd seen as quite a rather dramatic piece in 3/4. But when Phil started playing the drums, he played against it, playing 2s instead of the 3s which made it much more driving and more exciting.* [3]

> **Mike:** *The songs had such effective moods…'In the Cage'…was claustrophobic and suffocating.* [14]

> **Peter:** *I think it's still some of our best material of the period when I was there…That's one of the things looking back that I feel proud of. So there is, I think, quite often this irony when you get really shitty things going on in life and yet the creativity that comes out of it can still be strong, interesting, and move people.* [3]

But my cynic soon returns and the lifeboat burns

> **Tony:** *We weren't prepared to make quite the time for him that was necessary. The concept of him staying away for more than a day after his child was born was alien to us. And it just got more difficult. The magic had gone out of it.* [1]

> **Peter:** *There was a lot of resentment about that, so I think the seeds for the beginning of the end were sown at that point.* [3]

My spirit just never learns

> **Peter:** *It was a dark time, I think. So it felt as if we were still living that dream of isolating yourselves and being in a supposedly nurturing creative environment, but yeah: it wasn't working on lots of different levels.* [3]

Stalactites, stalagmites shut me in, lock me tight

> **Phil:** *We arrived [at Headley Grange] to find…there were rats everywhere. You'd be walking down the corridor and a rat would stop and look at you as if to say, "What the fuck are you doing here?" and they would carry on walking, no scurrying, just sauntering.* [1]

Lips are dry, throat is dry

Feel like burning, stomach churning

> **Tony:** *The place was absolutely filthy. There was human excrement on the floor, absolutely disgusting.* [3]

I'm dressed up in a white costume padding out leftover room

> **Peter:** *I realised, "I'm part of this machinery and I don't feel this is where I should be or who I am."* [1]

Body stretching, feel the retching

> **Steve:** *It looked as if we only had half a singer. The level of commitment to the band seemed shaky at that point. So for me it cast a pall on proceedings.* [3]

In the cage

Get me out of this cage

> **Peter:** *I could feel the pressure mounting and I had to punch my way out through it.* [1]

In the glare of a light I see a strange kind of sight

> **Peter:** *On the back of the Genesis Live record I had written a story which I used to tell in between songs, about this woman stripping in a tube carriage: she starts playing with herself and pulls her skin off and what you're left with is this column of light.* [1]

Of cages joined to form a star; each person can't go very far

> **Steve:** *Robert Fripp came along to one of the shows and said, "It seems obvious to me that the band are pulling in different directions."...I had to agree with him.* [1]

All tied to their things

> **Peter:** *I think I started to have some frustration at not being part of the keyboard side of things. I have very strong ideas on how things should sound and how you mix things together, and so I think there may have been some frustrations in that department.* [3]

They're netted by their strings

> **Mike:** *Pete wrote nearly all the lyrics...There were often times when he would be doing the words upstairs in the bedroom while we were downstairs working on the music. It was purely to do with time pressures.* [1]

Free to flutter in memories of their wasted wings

> **Steve:** *Something changed in the mood of the band between Selling England and The Lamb Lies Down...I felt that Genesis by the time of The Lamb was almost like a vehicle travelling along a road and all the tires have got uneven pressures. Everybody had their own agenda.* [1]

[keyboard solo]

> **Tony:** *There are the bits [that are] technically difficult to play and I sometimes think that I never played them right. Sometimes you just build up to them, I suppose. Things like the 'In The Cage' solo which, when I hear it back, it is not surprising it was difficult because it is at triple speed, and it wasn't tied to anything, and it was so fast!* [21]

Outside the cage I see my brother John

> **Peter:** *William Friedkin...was THE hip and happening director because The Exorcist had just exploded, so he had carte blanche to do what he wanted. He thought he could revolutionise Hollywood and bring in a whole lot of people who had never been involved with film before.* [1]

He turns his head so slowly round

> **Peter:** *Friedkin saw [my story] on the back of the album [Genesis Live], called me up and said, "I love the way you're thinking."* [1]

I cry out, "Help!" before he can be gone

> **Mike:** *I think Pete felt, "I'd like to do this and I can't do this with Genesis."* [1]

And he looks at me without a sound

> **Peter:** *At the time it was seen as a kind of betrayal because there was a work ethic that you had to sacrifice your life in all sorts of ways...in order to show you were part of the band. A military logic, really.* [1]

And I shout out, "John, please help me!"

> **Peter:** *This was very exciting for me and something I wanted to pursue. I said to the band, "There's this great opportunity. I don't think it need take that long." I think we were talking about six weeks.* [1]

But he does not even want to try to speak

> **Phil:** *William Friedkin sort of [goes], "I didn't want to split the band! I don't even know if this is going to work! This is just an idea!" So Peter comes back.* [3]

I'm helpless in my violent rage

> **Mike:** *So Pete came back and finished the album but I think those few days off had put the idea into his head - and our heads - about what might come next.* [1]

And a silent tear of blood dribbles down his cheek

> **Peter:** *These external opportunities on the one hand and family life and crisis on the other were loosening the ground on which I stood.* [1]

And I watch him turn again and leave the cage

> **Steve:** *He was seriously considering leaving the band so he could follow his own path freely, as well as giving his family more time.* [70]

My little runaway

> **Peter:** *All of the worldly stuff was going in the right direction, but for me internally it was more repressive and darker.* [1]

[keyboard solo redux]

> **Tony:** *It appears there's something about the slightly longer, more extended tracks that suits the live format better. There's no doubt. I don't get any pleasure out of going to see a group, even if they're very good, who just play a string of three-minute hits one after the other. You get bored. Extending songs makes them feel more like you're attending a live performance. Of course, the light show helps...For me, the solo is as much a part of the song as the melody line. You could vary from it, but it's kind of difficult, because either you've got to change it completely because of the way the bass and the drums work with it, or you've got to leave it alone. Playing the same thing has never really worried me. I see it as part of the composition. I don't get particularly bored...I think '[In the] Cage' is a good song, so it's nice to do it...We've been doing 'Cage' since 1978, probably...and it's become one of our classic songs.* [23]

(Raindrops keep falling on my head, keep falling on my…)

> **Mike:** *There was a tug-of-war going on within himself.* [1]

In a trap, feel a strap

> **Steve:** *The idea that we were still trying to employ the philosophy of everyone going away together and living together cheek-by-jowl. You know, but there were families, there were children; it really wasn't a healthy kind of environment for everybody.* [3]

Holding still, pinned for kill

> **Peter:** *The Lamb was...part dealing with alienation, repression, rejection, and trying to get a through-line to some transformative experience and hopefully some wisdom at the end of it. Nothing too heavy.* [1]

Chances narrow that I'll make it in the cushioned straitjacket

> **Mike:** *I think something happened when he left for a bit. In your mind you're thinking, "Wait a minute, maybe he's going to pull somewhere else, a different direction...outside the band."* [3]

Just like 22nd Street when they've got me by my neck and feet

> **Peter:** *I didn't feel able to control, or that I was in charge of my life.* [3]

Pressure's building, can't take more

My headaches charge, my earaches roar

> **Mike:** *Pete had always been inside the Genesis camp - one for all, all for one - and suddenly he was the one going outside the box…* [1]

In this pain

Get me out of this pain

> **Peter:** *I finally told the others I had to leave.* [1]

If I could change to liquid, I could fill the cracks up in the rock

> **Phil:** *My first feeling when Peter left was "OK, well, the vocals get in the way anyway, let's just do it instrumentally!* [3]

I know that I am solid

> **Phil:** *Of course, that was poo-pooed, quite rightly.* [3]

And I am my own bad luck

> **Tony:** *Pete was...getting too big for the group. He was being portrayed as if he was "the man" and it really wasn't like that. It was a very difficult thing to accommodate. So it was actually a bit of a relief.* [1]

Outside John disappears

> **Peter:** *The William Friedkin venture had fizzled out of its own accord. I think he had run into some problems, which was normal: often people start talking in a great revolutionary mode and then reality has a strange habit of setting in soon after.* [1]

And my cage dissolves

> **Mike:** *I never thought to stand in Pete's way if he didn't want to be part of the band anymore.* [1]

Without any reason, my body revolves

> **Steve:** *Peter said he would honour the touring commitments of the band, and more and more shows were put in because nobody wanted to say goodbye to him.* [1]

Keep on turning, keep on turning, turning around

> **Phil:** *The fact that we were touring with someone in the band who was going to leave was a very strange situation. I can't ever imagine saying "I'm leaving" and it being known and then going through those motions.* [1]

Just spinning around

> **Peter:** *The others didn't really understand why I would want to go when we were just about to achieve something we had worked so hard for...People did accept my decision after a while, but I did have that Judas feeling that I'd betrayed the cause. However, I knew that I didn't have any other option.* [1]

39 - Do the Neurotic

B-side of 'In Too Deep' (UK) or 'Throwing It All Away' (US), 1986

> **Tony:** *A lot of people felt we should have put 'Do the Neurotic' on Invisible Touch and not 'The Brazilian'. We put 'The Brazilian' on it because we liked the quirkiness of it. It's a much simpler piece than 'Do the Neurotic'. I think 'Do the Neurotic' is the wildest thing we ever did. I listened to it the other day. It's incredibly complicated and has some really wild moments. You have to remember we were really playing these songs. There was no kind of cheating going on there, in which someone might have been dropping things in after the fact. I think 'Do the Neurotic' is probably the best we ever played together as a unit and it sounds really, really good. Given that we were only a three-piece, it's a very exciting piece of music. Looking back at it, I would have preferred it to have been on the album.* [18]

Director: All right lads, glad you could all make it. As you know, this is a pivotal scene in this Invisible Touch film, so we want to use this here script reading as a chance to really see how you guys want to play these characters and make all this work.

Mike: There's uh, no words on these pages?

Tony: There's plenty of words, Mike.

Mike: You know what I meant, Tony. No lines. It's bloody empty.

Phil: Aww that's great! Who needs words anyway? We can do it all like mimes!

Mike and Tony: Shut up, Phil!

Director: OK guys, let's all just settle down for a moment. You're both right: there are no lines but there are plenty of words in the form of stage directions. What we want to do is see how you interpret those, improvise, and build this scene, rewriting as we go if we need to. Remember, this is a pivotal part of the movie we're making. We're trying to make something new and interesting, but we want to prove to the audience that you guys still have what it takes to make it in this business.

Mike: But there's no fucking words though, y'know what I mean?

Phil: Perfect!

Mike and Tony and Director: Shut up, Phil!

Director: Let's just walk through it and see what happens, shall we?

> *(The scene fades in on an empty room. It's elegant looking, perhaps upper-middle class. The furniture is neatly arranged, with a lovely vase of flowers on an end table near the window and a hutch of fine diningware against the wall. The sofa table is set for afternoon tea.)*

> *(The door opens and **Phil** enters the room. He seems elated.)*

Phil: Oi, mates! M'here! Got some whiskey in me socks, hey guvnah?!

Tony: Oh god, drunk Artful Dodger *again*?

> *(Phil stumbles, knocking over the hutch. There's a big bang and clatter as the dishes hit the floor one by one, shattering. **Mike** enters from the kitchen to see what all the noise is.)*

Mike: Ah, um, hello Phil. Do you need some help with, um, something?

Phil: *(sobbing)* Ahhhh I'll be so careful! I promise not to 'urt you anymore, lil' plates! You won't feel nothin'! I know it's yer first time!

> *(As **Mike** looks on aghast, **Phil** struggles to regain his footing, knocking over the tea set to more crashing and clattering. Mike begins to get angry.)*

Mike: Now now, uh, Phil. If you don't, uh, settle down, I may become cross!

Director: Mike, can you try to put a little more intensity into it please?

Mike: Oh, sure. Um, I really mean it, Phil! Was that better?

Director: OK, OK. Let's uh, let's maybe have Phil play it a little less drunk, and -

Phil: Still cockney though, yeah?

Director: ...fine...and let's get Tony in here too, OK? Let's just go back and pretend all the shattering stuff didn't happen. Maybe Phil, maybe you're just really excited about something, OK?

Phil: Awright.

> *(The door opens again and **Tony** walks in, spotting **Phil** excitedly telling something to **Mike**.)*

Tony: Can I brood?

Mike: Ugh...

Director: Uh, no, no brooding just yet please. We're really going for "excited" here and you don't even know what Phil is trying to say yet.

Tony: All right, sort of just a little bit broody then.

Phil: So anyway Mike, there was this big guy wearing nothing but a leather jacket right, we called him Bison, and there was smoke and stuff so you weren't sure if it was actually this gangbanger from New York y'see, and so the next thing that happened was

Director: You know, why don't we have Mike and Tony lead the conversation in this scene?

Tony: OK great, so Mike, here's how this scene really should go. I actually quite like the tentative attitude you're playing with, that's great. So keep that, and I'll just sort of handle the main part.

Director: Well Tony, this is supposed to be a group effort here...

> *(The door opens and **Tony** bursts in wearing a crown and purple robe, accompanied to great fanfare.)*

Director: He what? That's not in the...OK, who mucked with the script?

Tony: Wasn't me.

Mike: Could work. Maybe someone is outside with a boombox. Bass turned up, really popping, you know.

Director: Let's get back on track here. The point is your two characters need to be having a conversation.

Tony: Right. Mike, would you like to start?

Mike: OK. Ahem...So Tony, nice of you to come, we were just chatting about how to -

Tony: OK great, now it's my bit! I like Phil's energy, sort of really great, maybe I can use a bit of that.

Mike: Sod off, Tony, I wasn't done yet! You're ALWAYS like this, EVERY TIME we -

Tony: WELL IF YOU WEREN'T SO BLOODY M-

Tony and Mike: *[incoherent shouting over one another]*

Director: That's it. We're finished. This will never work.

Phil: ...but really, who really knows what it means? It was just something that was on my mind all the time, you know, a phrase that scanned well, that's all. Is it a girl, is it not a girl, that's not the point mate! The point is how does it *sing*, is what I've been trying to say, but I guess just sue, sue, sue, me

Director: Wait, that's it! If we want this scene to work, we just need to make it an argument scene! It'll be so natural! Guys! GUYS!

Mike and Tony: Wha?

Director: Guys, I've got it. This is a big blow-up scene! It's an argument!

Tony: That's actually sort of not a bad idea, I have to be honest.

Mike: I don't know. Umm...Could work. Could work. Not too busy though, y'know what I mean?

Tony: OK Mike, you should start. Not too intense at first, remember that we want to build up.

Mike: All right, Phil, could you help out here?

Phil: ...up to something, I'm sure of it. They don't tell me nothin' o'course, I'm just an ordinary bloke, but I find out what I can. I can't see it but I *feel* it, right? Like it's right outside my door

Director: I don't think he hears you.

Mike: OK, well here goes anyway....Ahem...TONY YOU MISERABLE LITTLE

Tony and Director: Whoa!

Director: Whoa, let's scale it back just a little here Mike, we don't want to use up all our energy right away.

Tony: ...I'm not *that* miserable. They sort of just won't buy my records. But that's not my fault. The material's great, it's fantastic. It can't be my fault. Can it...?

Director: Mike, Tony seems to be distracted a little bit, going through some motions over stuff he's already done...I don't know, can you bring him out?

Mike: Tony! Hey Tony! Bloody...TONY!

Tony: What's the point? Why keep spending years of my life putting out this really great material - sort of obviously loads better than anything you guys do without me - when nobody's even going to hear it?

Mike: Tony, fucking get over it man! We're supposed to be having an energetic scene here and you're really bringing it down. If you want an easy hit, just rip someone off. It worked for that guy who did that Ghostbusters song. Phil, come on, help me out here.

Phil: ...and I says, I says, "I really ain't bothered what you think of me," right? Guys like that, they want nothing more than to just get under your skin. Ya gotta just tell 'em that you don't care what they say, that you never did believe them much anyway, right? Even if it's not entirely true

Director: Can we PLEASE refocus here?

Tony: Should I start another band, too? I need a sort of catchy name like "Mike and the Mechanics" where my name is there but not *really* there. That's the ticket. That's what I've been missing. It's all so clear now, how could I have missed it? Music doesn't matter, singer doesn't matter, sort of just the name...

Director: Guys, I'm really starting to think this just isn't going to work out.

Mike: Tony, I said get over it man! You can worry about all that baggage later! We're on the clock here and if we want this scene in the movie I'm really going to need you to get it together.

Tony: What, the argument scene?

Mike: YES!

Tony: Do we really need that?

Mike: Wait, do we? Suppose it *is* a bit dodgy...

Tony: I'm just saying.

Director: If you want to see any royalties from this showing up on your bank statement then yes, you probably want to do the scene.

Tony: !!!

Mike: Tony, are you OK? You're grinning from ear to ear. It's, um, a little unnatural.

Phil: ...and I KNOW it's only words, but I figured maybe we both could learn, right? Otherwise it's just the same old sitting here, wasting time, just staring at the phone, and I'm just trying to say that I can't wait forever

Tony: No no, it's fine, fine. I'm fine. Just had a sort of idea is all. I think I'm finally going to get my due, that'll be quite nice.

Mike: OK, but can we finish the bloody scene?

Tony: Just do whatever you want I guess. I don't really mind anymore, I think.

Mike: Fine by me. So I've got some ideas, and...

Director: You know what? I think we're done here after all. We're just going to cut the scene. I'll, uh, I'll call you guys later.

Phil: ...poof, just gone. Unbelievable, really. No evidence was found. They kept searching through the day and into the night, they said they wouldn't stop 'til they found him. But see, they didn't know him and they didn't understand 'cos they never asked him why

Tony and Mike and Director: SHUT UP, PHIL!

Phil: Eh, wot?

38 - Horizons

from *Foxtrot*, 1972

Genesis have always been a forward-looking band. Makes sense, really: that's what "progressive" means, after all. And though we've now turned the term "progressive" into a label we can put on some songs but not others, or on one set of albums but not another, at the time Genesis wasn't thinking in those terms. How could they? The label didn't exist yet, as such, and without a word to box a concept in, the concept itself necessarily remains nebulous. Thus, Genesis of the early 70s weren't actively "making progressive music" so much as they were making music that brought them forward to the next thing.

Trespass blossomed when the songwriting buds that defined the hit-starved efforts of *From Genesis to Revelation* were finally allowed to open freely. *Nursery Cryme* evolved from a further exploration of organ, as well as the new soundscapes made possible by bringing on a different guitarist, a quality drummer, and a backing vocalist with actual vocal talent (sorry, Tony and Mike, but you know I'm right about this). *Foxtrot* then was a further expansion; into side-long pieces, yes, but also into extra theatricality, and a widening of sound.

In the midst of all this, Steve Hackett was ready to take his own giant step forward - out of Genesis. We all know Steve would eventually do just that, after a solo album and some angst about album credits, but all the way back here? What was going on?

> **Steve:** *Well, I was fairly shattered at that time. You know, we'd done a lot of touring and I think every now and again I would threaten to leave, and so would Phil, and luckily on day one of the recording of Foxtrot, Mike and Tony sat me down and said, "We don't want you to leave, Steve. We really like your guitar playing." Now, strange as it seems, I hadn't really understood that at that point. I think there was a stiff upper lip thing in the band; we didn't compliment each other very much. So I felt very insecure as one of the new boys, and I thought, "Well, better to leave before I get sacked." But this was a revelation to me. I think there was lots of great stuff on Foxtrot, so I'm pleased they asked me to stay.* [3]

It's the happiest ending to a "You can't fire me, I QUIT!" story I've ever heard. Invigorated by the Charterhouse boys' willingness to tell him he was doing something right, Steve then took a different kind of step forward as well. Having conjured up 'For Absent Friends' an album prior, he started to feel a little bit emboldened as a songwriter.

> **Steve:** *By the time we were doing Foxtrot, we were all well into our stride...I realised that by now I was a fully-fledged writer along with the other band members.* [39]

He's contributing bits to 'Supper's Ready', he's churning out half of 'Can-Utility and the Coastliners', and then he's also got this other standalone bit he'd like to demo. They said they like my guitar playing, right? Well, here's a bit of guitar playing.

> **Steve:** *I was amazed that the guys let me put it on the album, to be honest. I remember playing it to them in rehearsal one day, and Phil said, "It sounds like there ought to be applause at the end of it." So thank you Phil for that, because otherwise perhaps it wouldn't have made it onto the album. It's very nice. I was thinking along the lines of Tudor composers like William Byrd writing short pieces like 'The Earle of Salisbury', very short pieces: one minute and thirty seconds. Perfectly good enough for a Tudor composer, but for rock and roll? In those days nobody told you that you couldn't.* [3]

An awkward golf clap from the boys and suddenly Steve's got a solo piece on the record. Of course, they'd put it on the album's second side right in front of 'Supper's Ready', and they'd inexplicably toss an errant apostrophe into the name in the printing, and for vinyl time constraint reasons they'd minimise the space between the two tracks, so everyone would immediately discount it as a sort of prelude, but hey, that's all right...right?

> **Steve:** *It functioned like the introduction to 'Supper's Ready' because it just went straight into 'Supper's Ready', so people just assumed it was part of 'Supper's Ready'. That's fine, but it was one minute and thirty seconds of me coming up with something...* [3]

Well, no hard feelings, at any rate.

> **Steve:** *My piece 'Horizons' worked well as a palate cleanser to 'Supper's Ready' with its reflective simplicity, and a sense of the sun coming out.* [70]

'Atta boy, Steve. Embrace it. But now here's the thing that really strikes me about 'Horizons': while everything else in Genesis was all about moving forward - including, in many ways, the song's writer himself - 'Horizons' is a piece that very much looks back. Virtually everything about this song is retrograde, a total antithesis to the 1972 Genesis mission statement. One can start with the instrumentation.

We'll get to the actual makeup of 'Horizons' here shortly, but at the heart of the matter here is this: 'Horizons' is a song played on a single, unaccompanied acoustic guitar. It's gentle, lovely, light. Pastoral, even. Sort of like, oh, I don't know, the stuff that characterised the sound of *Trespass*. That was a different guitarist and an eternity of two albums ago, but slide 'Horizons' in between 'White Mountain' and 'Visions of Angels' and I don't think anyone bats an eye. For a band so committed to relentlessly driving forward, this is one hundred seconds of surprising throwback. It's hard to imagine the gang in 1980, hyper-aware of their own legacy as they were, being willing to put something on record that - even if unintentionally - called back so strongly to their recent past. Genesis goes forward. Steve goes forward. But 'Horizons' is looking back.

This is true of the production, too. See, after *Nursery Cryme*, Genesis wanted a change at the recording helm. Out with the old, in with the new: progressive. So they got some recommendations and brought in a guy they were excited, initially, to work with. Unfortunately, things soon soured.

> **Tony:** *A producer called Bob Potter was brought in because Charisma thought he'd done a good job on Lindisfarne...But when he arrived he hated, for example...the introduction to 'Watcher of the Skies'. I thought this was one of the things we were all about so if he didn't like this, we were in trouble...* [1]

> **Peter:** *I don't think he particularly liked our material: his tastes were more towards the American songwriter folk-rock vibe and prog wouldn't have been what he played at home.* [1]

> **Steve:** *I don't know whether there was some kind of culture clash with him...He said after one or two numbers, "I can't work with these guys."* [1]

Just one or two numbers in, and Bob Potter's collecting his pink slip. Out with the old, in with the new, Genesis progresses yet again. Except...

> **Steve:** *I had managed to record 'Horizons' with him - an acoustic guitar piece - and I got it in about the fourth take. He said, "I can work with you, but I can't work with the others."* [1]

Steve, playing by himself. Steve, on just acoustic guitar. Steve, sounding like the second coming of 'Dusk'. And a producer unable to follow the band forward to new sonic heights. "But you, you I can work with." *Foxtrot* is an album of six tracks, five of which were recorded by Dave Hitchcock. And then there's 'Horizons', the recording product of a fired producer, sitting on the album, already a relic of the past.

But 'Horizons' gazes back even further than all of that, too. It's a short piece, but it wasn't a short process; this 1972 track began noodling around in 1971.

> **Steve:** *I believe I wrote it over a period of about twelve months. I wrote it very, very slowly for such a short piece!* [30]

Those roots go deeper still. See, Steve, passionate guitarist that he is, was tuned into the work of British virtuoso Julian Bream, who had by this point already been playing and recording for nearly twenty years.

> **Steve:** *I had been influenced by a piece that Julian Bream played, in fact, and I didn't know who wrote it...I transposed it to another key.* [30]

Now, I've searched through Bream's *extensive* discography, and I can't seem to find where he had a proper recording of this, but somewhere along the way Bream played a song that would've been billed something like this: 'Prelude in D Major'. Likewise, I don't know when the footage was recorded - likely during the 70s but sometime after *Foxtrot* - but I did track down a video recording of Bream playing that very piece, so at the very least we know it definitely existed.

Hearing the beginning of Bream's performance, it's pretty clear: apart from the key, the first several seconds of his piece are almost identical to the primary melody of 'Horizons', the bit that's played twice at the beginning and then again at the end of that latter Hackett tune. Steve sustains the bass note a bit more, and the tempo is a little bit slower, allowing the music to breathe some, but it's pretty much bang-on the same thing. "Oh, this piece is nice, I'll have what he's having!" Now, the Bream recording goes off from that intro in one direction where 'Horizons' goes another, so it's not quite plagiarism, but we're talking two developments on the same basic concept here.

'Horizons', a piece that recalls a bygone producer, a bygone Genesis sound, and a recording of a virtuoso guitarist popular in the 1950s and 1960s. Yet 'Horizons' isn't content to only stretch back multiple decades. The 1950s? Child's play. To really get to the heart of the matter, we have to go all the way back to the early *18th century*.

Johann Sebastian Bach is widely regarded as one of the most influential composers of the Baroque period, and with good reason. I don't need to dwell on him here. But perhaps he should be regarded as an influential composer of the early 70s progressive rock boom as well.

> **Steve:** *I found out years later that it was a piece by Bach...Bach tends to figure highly on my list of all-time favourite composers.* [30]

See, Bream didn't write that guitar piece. Rather, he was taking the Prelude to a suite that Bach had written for cello, the appropriately named '(Cello) Suite No. 1 in G major', and transcribed it over to guitar, and into the key of D. Steve, of course, decided when writing 'Horizons' to take what he'd heard Bream do and switch it to a different key. He settled, for whatever reason, upon the key of G. Thus, Steve Hackett unwittingly took the guitar version of the Prelude from 'Suite No. 1 in G major' and *restored it to its original key*.

To put it all together, go seek out a recording of the Bach Prelude on the cello, in the key of G, exactly as originally written (famed cellist Yo-Yo Ma definitely has one, but there are certainly others as well), then ask yourself if it sounds familiar. Anyone who isn't a Genesis fan would hear that and think nothing of it. But a Genesis fan hears the start of that Prelude and there's no helping the reflexive thought: "Hey, is that guy playing 'Horizons' on a cello?"

> **Steve:** *That was the only totally solo track I performed with the band on a Genesis album...I played that piece to them on an electric guitar, although I had written it on an acoustic steel guitar, and really it should have inhabited neither of those regions, but the nylon!...I have been interested in people's reactions to it over the years, and most say that it conjures up a picture for them, and it is either that it felt like a boat on a river or a punt on a summer's day. I was very surprised by the reaction to it after all - it is a very short piece, and very reflective.* [30]

A band looking forward. A song looking back. A piece that wasn't intended to be a prelude, except that it is, essentially, the Prelude. It takes us to the distant past, all the way to the heart of classical music, while also to the future, previewing an independent career in the years to come for its sole writer. It's a short song, yes - only a hundred seconds. But those hundred seconds have a reach that spans two horizons.

37 - Abacab

from *Abacab*, 1981

> **Tony:** The letters were originally the three parts of the song but when we finally put them together it spelt something completely different and unpronounceable.
>
> **Phil:** C is Friday.
>
> **Mike:** It's no use saying why it's called 'ABACAB' and then saying that actually it's not. Let's just say it's called 'ABACAB'.
>
> **Tony:** But it doesn't work!
>
> **Phil:** C is Friday.
>
> **Tony:** B is the Stones and A is the main bit. But it still doesn't work!
>
> **Phil:** A is Booker T and the MGs. B is the Rolling Stones and C is 'Friday on My Mind', OK? [34]

What in tarnation are these guys talking about? It seems that even in interviews around this time, Genesis were trying to be as abstract and unidentifiable as possible. "C is Friday" sounds like some kind of spy speak you'd use to make sure the guy in the park with the trenchcoat gives you the correct dossier. "The rooster crows at midnight." "My hovercraft is full of eels." "C is Friday." You get what I'm saying.

> **Tony:** *It just sort of felt quite good. And then when we were thinking about titling the album - and the song, really, but particularly the album - we wanted to get across this more abstract nature of it. We felt this was the most unromantic thing we'd done, whereas Wind & Wuthering only three albums before had been so romantic. This was much less romantic. A lot of the album tracks were very stark, and had a much more straightforward approach, I suppose. And we wanted to get that across with the cover, so we went with a totally abstract design on the cover. It's not definable; just kind of nice shapes and colours. And gave the title 'Abacab', which means nothing at all, really, as a title. So the thing was like an abstract painting, the way I saw it. And that was the final effect. So you didn't really get any particular kind of thing off the album [cover] at all before you heard it. You just knew that it wasn't going to be goblins and fairies.* [3]

Yes, abstraction was the name of the game with this album, and the title track - first in the running order - was meant to exemplify that in every way, right down to its name.

> **Phil:** *Well 'ABACAB' originally was a way of remembering the sequence of the song. "A" was the verse, "B" was the chorus, "A" was the verse [again], "C" was the bridge. So it went verse, chorus, verse, bridge, verse, chorus. We didn't do the song like that in the end. But our way of remembering it was, "It goes A-B-A-C-A-B, all right?" The way we did it in the end was unpronounceable. But the name stuck.* [3]

If we get out our Ovaltine secret decoder ring and set the key to "C is Friday," we can surprisingly make some sense of this. As you may have been able to glean from the wink and a handshake Phil gave above there, what he meant with his repeated mantra was that section C was the section where he played drums in a style consistent with the song 'Friday on My Mind' by Australian rock group The Easybeats. And when you listen to the groove in the chorus of that song, and you line it up to the actual 'Abacab' track, you find that it seems to match up pretty well with the chorus; you know, the "You're never there" part and all its trappings.

So if we accept that C is Friday, and Friday is the chorus, then B must be...the bridge? "Do you want it, you got it, now you know," well, that whole bit *does* sound a little Rolling Stonesy, now that you mention it. That leaves A, "the main bit," as Tony called it, remaining in its verse spot. Thus, A-B-A-C-A-B actually ended up as A-C-A-C-B-A-C. Not quite unpronounceable, though 'Acacbac' doesn't exactly roll off the tongue. But of course, if just for the sake of coherence you flip the C and B around in that finished product - referencing their *actual* order now instead of the *original* order - you still end up with 'Ababcab', which is *almost* the same thing they started with. Unless you add in the intro and outro and then still keep the chronological ordering of the sections and then get something like 'Abcbcdbce' but now I think we're too far afield for anyone to really care anymore.

Which is all to say, why on earth does any of this matter? Well it matters because, quite simply, none of it matters at all. Take everything you think is important in defining and identifying a Genesis track. Then crumple it up and throw it away.

> **Mike:** *I can't imagine us playing the same kinds of music and sounds that we did back in the 1970s and not changing anything. To be honest, the journey's been interesting, as a writer and recorder of music. And I think if we'd stayed in the same place I'd have been bored stiff years ago. You've got to move all the time, I think.* [3]

Fanciful lyrics that tell a great story? Gone.

> **Tony:** *On this album the lyrics are much less upfront. We're not even putting them on the album [sleeve]. They are meant as a more abstract thing, more a part of the sound. We've tried to take some of the emphasis away from them.* [34]

Textural, complementary drumming? Gone.

> **Tony:** *We also had these great drum sounds that Phil had cultivated, particularly with Peter Gabriel on 'Intruder' and later on Face Value. It was such a big sound and so exciting in and of itself...So, that was the approach...We went small and junked everything apart from the drums. I think it was quite successful from that point of view.* [18]

Big honkin' keyboard sounds? Gone.

> **Tony:** *A lot of the size of the tracks [on Abacab] are created by the drums rather than by the keyboards. We'd always had the big keyboard pad come in on the chorus, it was wide and everything, but this...The drums themselves, just by bringing out the ambient sound of the kit just gave it such a big size, very exciting effect I think. I really liked it.* [3]

> **Mike:** *There's a lot of space in that song. People tend to think of Genesis as a wall of sound but that's a thing of the past for us, I think.* [34]

Powerful choruses that hit you right in the feels? Gone.

> **Tony:** *Abacab was definitely a kind of break for us. We got away from the big choruses and went somewhere else that was a little bit more straight-ahead.* [18]

Virtuoso solo performances? Gone.

> **Tony:** *There was a definite, very conscious decision to try and break with the Genesis traditions, really. Get rid of the reprises, the extended solos...* [3]

Tight, well-structured compositions as finished products? Gone.

> **Tony:** *I was trying to avoid reiterating some of the things I'd done in the past. It was an interesting exercise, and I think pretty successful too, particularly the track 'Abacab' itself...* [1]

And with the stripping away of the past necessarily comes new stuff. They don't want big keyboard sounds, but it's not as though Tony's going to spend the whole song sitting on his hands. So out come these fuzzy synth lines, and chords that don't linger, and two-or-three note accents to the vocal line. They don't want folksy acoustic guitar, but it's not as though Mike's going to sit there on the floor playing bass pedals with his butt and doing naught else. So out come these electric licks, often in the background but occasionally hitting the fore. They don't want big romantic vocals, but going fully instrumental would *also* hearken back to the past, and that's a big no-no. So out come these call and answer falsetto bits, and this vocal percussive sort of "jet jet jet jet jet jet jet jet" over the final verse.

> **Phil:** *It's very much a group song. There are bits from everyone on that.* [34]

And then, after the core of the song is through, an ending, right? No? Well, how about an extended, almost random improv session instead?

Tony: *At the end we just jammed until the tape ran out.* [34]

Develop the instrumental bit into solos with a grand ending? What is this, 1976? No, we'll just play and play and play until the recording equipment dies, and then tell everyone, "Here you go, this is the record."

Tony: *We had lots of bits - phrases and things - that we used in the original version, which was 15 minutes long. We edited out two 10-second phrases and then faded it out. We were quite keen to put out the whole 15-minute version because it all sounded good, but you never know...You've got to [edit down] for the dreaded "album can't be too long" question. We don't like doing it, but I know that the shorter you can get a thing and still have it work, the stronger it's going to be...I think what really matters is that you still get the tune across.* [23]

'Abacab' is a track without rules. Its very name is obsolete because they couldn't be bothered to hold to the structure, and certainly couldn't be bothered to give the track anything beyond its working title. Slap some lyrics on there - about nothing at all, naturally - and eh, let's chop it down and release it as the lead single. And it worked!

Tony: *We were very pleased with the result...for us it was crucial and I don't think that the band could have carried on...if we had done another album like Duke, another album in the old tradition. I don't think we would have made it.* [6]

I love this song because it's Genesis at their most relaxed. This is just a trio of musicians sitting around, making it up as they go along, exploring new directions, wandering aimlessly in the studio, violently doing away with their past, and not caring one whit what you think about it.

Mike: *I think it's very important - and this almost sounds rude to your fans, and I don't mean [it that way] - but what I've always felt...It's so important that when you sit down to write an album, that you don't actually care at all about what audience is gonna think about the next batch of songs. Because if you do, you're going to start worrying and pandering about it. All you can do is to write what YOU like, and if you like it the chances are most of them will, because they've quite liked it so far. That's always the way we've done it, and I've never, ever felt any loyalty in that sense. It's not being at all rude. I've never felt I've owed them anything, any fans in terms of the next album. I just gotta write what I like. If they like it, great. If they don't, I'm sorry: because it's what I like.* [83]

Mike Rutherford ain't got time for your opinions, man. They don't matter. None of this matters. What's 'Abacab' mean?

Who cares?

36 - White Mountain

from *Trespass*, 1970

Trespass is an album that's only six tracks long, but it seems most people only ever talk about two: 'Stagnation' and 'The Knife'. Sure, there is occasionally the outspoken fan of 'Looking for Someone', and occasionally one might hear a disparaging remark cast in the direction of 'Dusk'. But for me the most intense, gripping, mesmerizing song on the album is the one that I almost never see get mention, even among Genesis fan circles: 'White Mountain'.

Look, I love Steve Hackett as much as the next guy. You can't argue against his contributions to the Genesis sound, nor against the compositions he brought to the table. I wouldn't try to. But listen to 'White Mountain' and then imagine a Genesis where Anthony Phillips can grow musically alongside his bandmates and tell me you're not just a little bit wistful that never happened. *Trespass* marks the era where Ant and Mike discovered that they could not only play 12-string guitar but could both play it together.

> **Ant:** *Mike and I had started writing on two twelve-string guitars....By complete accident we found that for the first time in our lives we weren't really copying anybody. We used to love it. One of us would play a chord and the other would play a different inversion and we'd marvel at this dual sound. It was like we were entering a magical new world.* [1]

> **Mike:** *With our two twelve-string guitars we were busy creating a distinctive, unusual sound, coming up with new, interesting chords and experimenting with tunings. A new tuning would be a great way of finding inspiration: it'd be like turning over a new page. We were taking folk music and developing it into another area, I felt, and we'd often carry on when the others had finished for the day.* [14]

Ant and Mike were the best of friends at this time, just as Pete and Tony were themselves best of friends. This, naturally, split the band's writing efforts into two distinct camps: Ant/Mike on the one side, Pete/Tony on the other.

> **Tony:** *There were very much two sides to the sound, one of which came from Ant and Mike in the form of the acoustic guitar sound. That was demonstrated best on track like 'White Mountain' and the early part of 'Stagnation'... It's funny, as things were not really planned to be that way but that's the way it happened... I think the sound was a very important aspect of the group. The longer songs tended to develop out of the two guitars playing together.* [6]

All well and good, but while both camps produced some very high-quality material, there was a distinct difference in how they achieved it.

> **Mike:** *Pete composed on the piano but he wasn't allowed to play it: that was Tony's territory. If Pete wrote something, Tony would have to learn to play it himself. In many ways they were the best of friends, but Tony was competitive and there was a friction between them that didn't exist between Ant and me.* [14]

That's the heart of it. Pete and Tony were like flint and knife, a complementary pair, but one that had to constantly generate friction in order to get a spark. When they did, it could catch fire and become something amazing, but there'd be a lot of wear and tear along the way. Mike and Ant, meanwhile, not only lacked this territorial bent, but actually relished the idea of occupying the same territory at the same time! If Pete and Tony were fire, Mike and Ant were water, undulating back and forth between their two guitars, flowing downstream into something that just clicks into place. They were in that really rare place where two people seem to be sharing a single musical mind, producing stuff that neither could do alone.

> **Ant:** *In fact, I've got a tape somewhere of us playing the first part of 'White Mountain' and you can hear Mike's girlfriend saying, "Ooh, that's nice."* [1]

I bet she did! The song is utterly compelling from the very first strummed notes, an atmosphere of, say, a snow-covered sacred glade. The subtle background humming *really* sells this. It's not hard at all for the mind to take this aural backdrop and conjure up an image of a single shaft of sunlight hitting an ancient sword embedded in a pedestal, or perhaps a sceptre and crown, or whatever objects might suit that metaphor from a wolf's perspective.

Now, even if 'White Mountain' dwelled *only* in this sort of feel for its whole duration, I'd still really like it. It's a great musical mood. But the dual 12-strings find purchase beyond that serene-yet-dark introduction, discovering a kind of intensity that works perfectly for Pete's expressive vocals, describing the album's titular trespass. It's great, but ironically it's Tony's organ that takes this folk-acoustic-turned- prog piece to its true heights. Building on 24 strings of tension, Tony's here with a 'Fountain of Salmacis'- esque dancing organ line that acts as the kind of embodiment of, well, wolves in chase.

This is all juxtaposed with some gentler sections. More twinkling guitars, but also some really prominent flute playing from Peter. If you've been reading this book in sequence so far, you've probably realised by now that I'm a hopeless sucker for that flute, and here it works as brilliantly as you'd hope for. So you get this feeling of restless, desperate motion, and then these periods of uneasy rest, like the music itself is trying to catch its breath. While the transitions themselves aren't always the cleanest, the effect is still quite strong.

> **Tony:** *It's deceptive, Genesis. Sometimes, you sort of see them as one thing, but in fact there's this other thing going on, right from the early days, I think. We've always had those two sides to us. It may vary a little bit in terms of how you define them, but there's a romantic side and a sort of more aggressive side. It's a very important part of what we do.* [3]

I think the song is captivating lyrically, as well. It's told in a really unusual way: Fang (son of Great Fang) is the song's protagonist, the one we follow throughout all the vocal passages - which is to say, for the first five minutes of the song. We know Fang committed a crime against his fellow wolves, but hey, he's the protagonist! Yet in the final verse, there's an unexpected shift. Fang's primary pursuer, old One-Eye, is declared the song's hero. At first this line, "But Fang fought the hero in vain," seems to just be a call-back to One-Eye's description from earlier in the song as "an old hero conquered by none." Just an appellation describing his past. But the end of the song paints a different picture.

Fang, branded a traitor, is slain by One-Eye, who is rewarded with laurels on his head and goes off to live in harmony with his pack. It's not Fang, but One-Eye who gets the happy ending. Not Fang, but One-Eye who restores balance and tranquillity. He wasn't just the old hero, he was the song's hero, too, in a sort of musical/lyrical sleight-of-hand. Then, after some prominent whistling, of all things - perhaps they're the birds shouting their witness to the song's events - we return to the mood of the introduction. That solemn, sacred glade, where now the crown and sceptre are being re-hidden, that none might sin again. The song is laid to rest along with the artifacts, and our true hero, the would-be antagonist, lives out the remainder of his days in peace.

I don't know who penned the lyrics to this one; one assumes it was either Ant or Mike. But it really is a sort of preview of the epic storytelling to come in the Genesis catalogue. A simple story, yes, but one with an unexpected ending and one that matches the ebb and flow of the music in a very natural way. Not fire, but water. Or perhaps, in the case of 'White Mountain', a bit of ice. Hard not to be a fan of that.

> **Tony:** *Other songs on the album don't quite do as much for me anymore, as they once did…'White Mountain', we used to do that live, and that was quite nice live, quite atmospheric. But I don't think it's as strong as what was to come.* [3]

Well, unless you're Tony Banks that is. I wonder why Tony might feel that way about a song as good as this one is.

> **Tony:** *I felt I contributed less to that album than most of the other albums…'Dusk' and 'White Mountain' were really Ant and Mike's work…* [1]

Ah, that probably explains it.

35 - The Chamber of 32 Doors

from *The Lamb Lies Down on Broadway*, 1974

At the top of the stairs he finds a chamber. It is almost a hemisphere with a great many doors all the way round its circumference. There is a large crowd, huddled in various groups. From the shouting, he learns that there are thirty-two doors, but only one that leads out. [57]

1) What a wail of a guitar solo to kick off the song, eh? Guitar solos in any song are typically reserved for the bridge, or perhaps as a way to end something on an epic feel. Though I suppose you could also be like neo-prog outfit Pendragon and just solo for 75% of your song, including steamrolling right over the vocals when they come back in because who cares about vocals it's a guitar solo woooooo!

2) Seriously, I'm not kidding. Go check out their tune 'Breaking the Spell' from their 1993 effort *The Window of Life*. Literally three quarters of the song is one endless guitar solo. And it works! It's fantastic!

3) But I digress. My point is that it's unusual at the very least to stick your big guitar solo right at the very *beginning* of a song, but, well, Genesis are something of an unusual band, aren't they? What's more, there's a lot of space in this solo. It's backed by some orchestral sounding chords, yes, but this isn't a band jam with the guitar taking the lead. It's just a moaning guitar in an echoing room, sustaining a cry before a big smash of sound, like it was 'Fly on a Windshield, Jr.' or something. Super strong.

> **Steve:** *I always thought the original was good, but I always wanted to improve on the guitar work.* [13]

4) If you, like me, can't get enough of the intro to this song, why not check out Steve's updated version from his 2012 LP *Genesis Revisited II*? It's the same, except, you know, better. Expanded and made somehow even more impactful. He knew it too, which is why he sequenced the track as the opener for the entire double album.

> **Steve:** *I always felt that Genesis was unfinished business. Being a detail freak for me means getting things totally right. 'The Chamber of 32 Doors' for instance would have been great if the original had that extra level of controlled playing and sustain. The guitar needs to be accurate to create anything like the impression of a voice. But I know I got there on the re-recording of that song.* [70]

5) Anyway, we're getting off track again. From the guitar solo the "proper" song begins and it's already a vocal treat. Here's Peter and Phil singing in perfect, subtle harmony. Not a doubling up like 'Harold the Barrel' but more like "What if 'Harlequin' was in tune?" It's a groovy little jam, but that harmonised vocal gives it an eerie kind of edge. Almost like, say, echoing in a big chamber?

> **Steve:** *What must have been obvious even to the deaf was the fact that both [Phil] and Pete had such similar and sympathetic voices that when they were singing together it sounded like doubletracking. Wonderful harmonies [too], on tunes like 'The Chamber of 32 Doors'...* [1]

6) Whoa, wait, obvious to the deaf? I get what you're trying to say here Steve, and I appreciate the enthusiasm, but, like, this is the one thing that absolutely would not be obvious to the deaf, you know? I don't mean to be the idiom police or anything, but this might be one exaggeration too far.

7) Oops, getting off track yet again. Terribly sorry about that. Back to the verses. See, the verses aren't really straightforward here. You've got the bouncy bit with the Pete and Phil harmonies like I talked about, but from there the bottom drops out again. You're back in this empty expanse of a room, but now instead of a guitar solo filling the space, it's just Phil with a really sleepy rhythm section.

8) Well OK, Steve's there too, droning a little bit in the background. At least, I think that's Steve. It could be Tony. So often they're disguising their playing somehow to sound like the other one that it can be hard to really know. I can't find video footage of Genesis playing the song live, but ah wait! I managed to find a clip of Steve's own band playing it in concert instead. Ah, looks like both Steve *and* his keyboardist are playing during this section. Likely then that Genesis had the same arrangement. Glad we figured that one out!

9) Uh, where was I? Oh! The stark second bit of the verse. So that happens, really making you feel the overwhelming space and loneliness of the titular Chamber, right? And, though it's not delivered quite as emotively as I'd hope for in the studio version, the line "I need someone to believe in, someone to trust" is quite the heart-tugger, isn't it? We've all been there at some point or another, I'm sure. Strange area, strange people, nothing familiar, in desperate need of aid but too afraid and vulnerable to seek it out amongst the crowd. This is relatable stuff.

10) I remember one time, I was going to a...wait, hang on. No...no, nevermind, that wasn't me.

11) But this *other* time, I was...was I? Y...eah....yeah, I'm sure this one was me. So I was in Germany, and suffice it to say that's not my home country. But I was wearing a denim jacket, and I guess at the time that was, like, German Fashion 101. So everyone I'd see in Germany *thought* I was German, even though I wasn't, see? This became something of an issue when I needed to go to a bank to deal with some hangups surrounding my (perfectly valid, thank-you-very-much) traveller's cheques. If you're reading this thinking, "What on earth is a traveller's cheque?" then maybe you already spot the problem. See, debit cards weren't quite as ubiquitous back then, and I didn't have one yet, but traveller's cheques were also starting to get phased out, so a lot of banks wouldn't cash them in.

Anyway, I go into this bank and the teller quite happily greeted me with a smile and a friendly "Guten Tag!" I Gutened his Tag right back, before following with my own cheery "Sprechen Sie Englisch?" Folks, this man's smile didn't falter even SLIGHTLY as he gave his reply with a joyous little lilt: "Nein." I tried to wave these cheques around to get it figured out, but he just kept on smiling, shook his head, and returned to his work. At that moment, man, I really needed someone to trust.

12) RIGHT, RAEL. I'm so sorry that this keeps happening. I'll try to stay focused, all right? We're up to the chorus now, yeah? That sounds right. OK, so, the chorus: haystacks and straw hats, am I right?

> **Steve:** *It's as if you've got these classical influences in rock, and then it gets into a chorus that sounds almost like - well, reflecting the lyric - country music. So if you trust the country man rather than the town man, I can understand why.* [13]

13) Steve's right, it does sound pretty country here. Not that I'm a particular fan of country music, but in college I worked summers for a local contracting firm, and among the regular employees there, country was king. You almost couldn't go to a job site without the radios blaring the stuff. Then, after a few years I left that summer job for a different one, hired to serve as restaurant staff for a 50s throwback joint. I was really looking forward to it, as much as one could reasonably look forward to a summer job flipping burgers. Classic rock, sharp uniform, an upside-down paper boat on my head? Sounds great! Of course, first day on the job I show up and they say they screwed something up with the paperwork and the place I'm about to work at has *actually* just been converted to a celebration of all things country-western, including a 30 song playlist of modern country hits set on continuous loop for the entire summer. I grew to envy those burgers and their sweet release of melting on a sizzling grill.

14) So...uh, what was my point again?

15) Oh! Right! It's that I agree that the chorus of 'Chamber of 32 Doors' sounds kinda country, and I should really know, even though I wouldn't mind never hearing another country song as long as I live. But the addition of piano gives it a saloon kind of vibe, which is a nice little flavour, and the percussive chimes ringing out like mission bells puts the whole thing firmly into "old west" country instead of the sort of stuff you'd see on music videos featured on a channel like Great American Country.

16) Well, I say that, but has anyone else noticed that every TV channel is gradually being taken over by shows about people buying houses? What's with that? Like, take the aforementioned Great American Country. That's a channel that was formed with the *express purpose* of playing country music videos, right? Right, well, here's their programming line-up as of the time this was originally written:

- Docked Out
- Extreme Homes
- Flea Market Flip
- Flippin' RVs
- Going RV
- Great American Playlist

- Hawaii Life
- Lakefront Bargain Hunt
- Log Cabin Living
- Mountain Life
- Off the Map with Shannen & Holly
- Top 20 Country Countdown
- You Live in What?

That's thirteen shows and by my count TEN of them are about people buying houses in some way. Only two pertain in any way to country music. What's happening? I'll tell you what's happening: the country men are turning into town men, that's what's happening. They've abandoned their fields to go look for bargains on the lake.

17) How is there such a big market for this stuff, anyway? Who is sitting there for hours on end watching people with unreasonable budgets buy real estate? I go to my doctor's office and there's HGTV on the television, playing another endless marathon of people fixing up houses. Who on earth watches this stuff?

18) My wife, that's who.

19) I just...hold up. We're way off course again, aren't we? How does this keep happening? I'm trying to work toward the end of the song and the post, honestly. It's just difficult. There's just so many paths I could take this thing, you know? How do I know which one is the right one to develop?

20, 21, 22, 23) Jim Morrison, Ray Manzarek, Robby Krieger, John Densmore

Like, see? Four more Doors right there.

24) But OK, OK. So after talking about who (whom?) he'd like to trust, we return sonically to that same echoing room once more. Sparse sounds again, a mourning cry, and one of my favourite moments of the song: the blending of Pete's sustained note on the word "through" into the return of the dramatic guitar. Man, what a sound. Where does Pete stop and the guitar begin? The world may never know.

> **Steve:** *One of the best songs, I think, from The Lamb. Unfortunately Peter Gabriel's swan song with the band. I think his work on it was exceptional, of course. Pete wrote all of the lyrics and the story; the rest of us were really doing the music. It's a very strange track.* [13]

25) And then we're off again into another verse, with renewed energy and a sense of purpose. Go on, breathe that in. It's a refreshing puff of clarity amidst the confusion. There's momentum, there's detailed observation, there's active thought. It's weird to say that the most profound bit of a piece could be something as mundane as the start of its second verse, but in a way, that's what's happening here. Rael has just finished singing the line "Every single door that I walk through leads me back again," and then boom, here he is, back where he started. Same room, same feel, but he's seeing different people, presumably because he arrived from a different angle. In that way, the song's structure *is* the chamber itself.

26) Of course, then there's another half-verse that descends straight back into indecision and uncertainty. But that's still on brand: it's another door entered, another winding passage to destinations unknown, another retreat into lonely despair. Can't trust anyone, so just pick a route and go where it takes you. Hope it's out of this daggone room.

27) Hey, speaking of priests and magicians, this whole chamber concept is so interesting that I reused it for...well, do you, dear reader, happen to play Dungeons and Dragons? Nerdy a bit, I know, but then again you're sitting around reading a collection of essays about the band Genesis, so "throwing stones in glass houses" and all that. Anyway, I designed an entire DnD dungeon around *The Lamb Lies Down on Broadway*, and The Chamber of 32 Doors was the centrepiece room of the whole thing. Which meant, naturally, designing 32 passages and rooms off it. Well, maybe a little less; see, I cheated a bit and had a few of the doors lead to passages which would wind back and exit through *other* doors, returning you to the chamber itself. The other ones were all dead ends, save the entrance and "correct" exit.

28) But what was challenging, and also the most fun part of the exercise, was that DnD is a game played over a text medium. Even in the ideal setting of playing in person with a group of friends, rooms are still (other than perhaps some abstractions on a piece of grid paper) just text descriptions orated to the players, allowing their minds to imagine the scenes from there. This meant that I needed each of the doors to be distinct in some way, both to draw the players' attention and also to help keep them straight in my own head. Sometimes they'd even inform the encounters beyond. So it wasn't just the passages and rooms, but also the 32 doors themselves that needed to be unique and interesting, and I think I pulled it off. I was really proud of that dungeon, which is a really unusual sentence out of context.

29) Unfortunately, at some point when transferring the file with the dungeon data on it (layout, encounters, maps, everything) over to a new computer, I somehow inadvertently deleted the entire thing, and it's unrecoverable. I was devastated. I put hours into that thing and was eagerly looking forward to running it with a group at some point, but it's nothing but silent sorrow for me, I guess.

30) I'd give you all of my dreams if you'd help meeeeeeeeeeeeeeeeeeeee restore that file.

31) Huh? Who? Oh, Lilith? That's a nice name. What happened to your eyes? Aww gee, I'm really sorry to hear that. Must be tough. Yeah, sure, of course I'll help you out. Say, Lilith...you ever played DnD?

32) Buh-duh-duh-dum, duh-duh-duh duh duh-dum, buh-duh-duh-dum, duh-duh-duh duh duh, always the same, it's just a shame...

34 - That's All

from *Genesis*, 1983

The year is 1968. Tony Banks and Mike Rutherford are back at Charterhouse School, having spent the end of their summer vacation in a studio recording their album *From Genesis to Revelation*. It'll be months before the album is released; after all, if it's successful, they'll need to be available to play shows to support it, and they can't very well do that from the confines of a boarding school. Meanwhile, another teenage lad named Phil Collins is on the set of a film called Chitty Chitty Bang Bang, cast as an extra, but then cut from the finished film in what was becoming a running theme.

> **Phil:** *This is a further nail in the coffin of my enthusiasm for acting. And quite frankly, I couldn't give a fuck.* [12]

Phil, you see, is embarking on his own musical journey, playing tiny gigs with his friend's parents and drumming for an amateurish band known as The Charge. It's good experience, sure, but he's not getting anywhere. Thus, though they've never met, Phil has something in common with young masters Banks and Rutherford: *time*. Time to listen to the music of the day. Time to hear what successful artists are doing, and time to dream about doing the same.

The year is 1968, and The Beatles have just released their self-titled LP, which will come to be known colloquially as "The White Album". It's a monstrous double record, pushing the boundaries of pop music even further than The Beatles had done on their previous record, *Sgt. Pepper's Lonely Hearts Club Band*. And there, sitting right in the middle of the second of the album's four sides, is a little ditty called 'Rocky Raccoon'.

The year is 1983, and Genesis are congregated together at The Farm, writing and recording their self-titled LP, which will come to be known colloquially as either "Shapes" or "The Mama Album", depending on who you ask. They're all just kind of doodling away, tinkering, improvising, trying to get something that works. But what Phil and Mike might not realise is that while they're toying around on their own, Tony is surreptitiously recording them on his rig.

> **Tony:** *I sometimes just record what is going on in the studio, and that's what happened with 'That's All'. I recorded Mike just fiddling about and he was playing this riff...I played these three notes at the same time and again they produced this semblance of a riff and Mike basically learned it and it was the basis of the song. It is quite a useful writing tool.* [21]

And in that riff, all three hear something familiar. A glimpse into a world of fifteen years ago, when everything was much more difficult yet also somehow so much simpler. They'd all referenced The Beatles with one another before, and thought of various songs throughout their shared Genesis careers as being "their Beatles thing," borrowing small ideas and grooves, tiny little feels that inevitably evolved into other, different things in the end. But this time, they really go for it.

> **Tony:** *Like 'Rocky Raccoon', I always think of it, which is a song I liked a lot by The Beatles. Great feel, really. I started playing that piano riff and then Phil started doing this drum riff, and we knew we had a feel. Didn't quite know where it was going. And I just purposefully kept all the chords very simple. I didn't want to go miles in any direction; I wanted it to kind of stay where it was, because it felt very good.* [3]

Now if you're hitting play on 'Rocky Raccoon' to see what Tony's talking about and you just don't see the connection whatsoever, don't fret; Tony's referring to a specific section of that song rather than the whole thing. Skip ahead to about 1:55 in 'Rocky Raccoon' and you'll hear a lively little saloon-style piano bit. Recognise the groove and rhythm pattern on that bit? You oughta; it's 'That's All'.

> **Tony:** *Quite a distinct track in our collection, almost Beatle-ish.* [1]

> **Mike:** *'That's All' is what I always call one of our little Beatle-y chug songs, you know? Boom-duh-duttle-eh-duh-duh like sort of that Beatles sound they have...thought it was a sweet little song, really.* [3]

> **Phil:** *When I'm playing a song I'll often think about how another drummer might play it, and try to be that player in my performance of the song. Often I'll think, "How would Keith Moon play*

> *this?" And I'll don my Keith Moon hat. For another song I'll think about John Bonham, or even on occasion Stewart Copeland, but more often than any other drummer I think about Ringo. 'That's All'...is a Ringo Starr drum part.* [24]

The year is 1983 and Genesis, so invigorated by their radical reinvention of *Abacab* a couple years prior, are feeling a little nostalgic.

> **Mike:** *Abacab had proved to be a transitional album, but a necessary one. I always felt that one of our strengths as a band was to go a bit too far off in one direction, realise that we had, and then get back on course again.* [14]

They still don't want to repeat themselves too much; though they've been doing this for fifteen years, that feeling will never go away, even after fifteen more. Yet at the same time, they yearn for something familiar. Something that feels like the hot meal at the end of a long day's journey.

> **Tony:** *I think we felt with Abacab we sort of like cleared out all the furniture, you know? And so with Genesis it was a question of redecorating a little bit. And I think we had some areas we hadn't been in before.* [3]

So they stumble on a piano riff that conjures up images of an album they all loved during an eventful, formative, yet frustrating year of their teenage lives. They have a basis for a song. And they shop for new furniture. And if it happens to look a little like the old furniture, well hey - that's all right, isn't it? Tony's not using his Hammond B-3 organ here, after all...just something that's designed to, you know, sound like it.

> **Tony:** *That old style organ solo on 'That's All' was all done on the Synclavier and it's probably the best organ sound you could ever get - it's perfect.* [84]

> **Tony:** *That's my great [Hammond] B-3 sound. It's better than what I got out of the real B-3...The Synclavier does a very good imitation of the instrument. It's absolutely spot on.* [85]

And hey, a lot of this furniture is still brand new, too, right? Phil's vocals are brimming with confidence, riding this riff up and down, snapping like a crocodile on the phrase "one bite" - never gonna get that one consistently live, but that's OK too. Mike's got a bouncing little bass line that only shows up in spurts, and that's sort of new too. Speaking of Mike, what's that guitar solo at the end? That doesn't look like the same recliner we had back on *Wind & Wuthering*, that's for sure!

The year is 1983 and the music charts feel like chaos. It's a year where seemingly anything goes - even a taste of the retro. In January of that year, Phil Collins' re-recorded version of 1966 Supremes song 'You Can't Hurry Love' hits 1 in the UK and the US top ten. The 60s, it would seem, are back in. In October Genesis release 'That's All', which breaks into the US top ten itself within a few months.

> **Mike:** *I was kind of surprised it turned out to be a big hit in America. I suppose it's got a sort of catchy little phrase Phil had on the words "that's all," but...I think it was just [that] our time was right in America. I think right around that album things just started working on the radio. We'd been playing the States for years and years and suddenly...we got better at writing shorter songs.* [3]

> **Phil:** *Our first US Top 10 single...At this time we're just very lucky. Whether it's my thing or the Genesis thing, it just keeps getting bigger. One profile is reinforcing the other, and our songs seem to be exciting more and more people.* [12]

The year is 1983, and Genesis are still living in the same house on the same street that they always have. But now the neighbours are a bit more friendly. Now the interior is a bit more clean. Now, perhaps, it feels a little more like home again.

33 - Uncertain Weather

from *Calling All Stations*, 1997

A day of uncertain weather...

> **Tony:** *After the relative lack of success of Genesis' Calling All Stations, I was going to be 50. I thought, "Well, maybe that's it. Maybe it's time to either do something else or do nothing." I'd done all these solo albums and not had much success. Genesis looked like it was fading away. So, what was I going to do?* [18]

'Uncertain Weather' isn't the final song on *Calling All Stations*. And if you use the playing order that I suggested in the entry for 'The Dividing Line' earlier in this book, 'Uncertain Weather' moves even closer to the middle of the album. And yet, to me, this is the last bastion of "classic" Genesis to be found on an album anywhere. Again recalling the case laid out in the entry for 'The Dividing Line', my claim is that *Calling All Stations* was initially intended as a themed album built around an overarching radio tuning concept, following a progression from lighter to heavier fare, and as such the final songs on the album have that extra bit of 90s rock edge to them missing from the album's opening side: 'Small Talk', 'There Must Be Some Other Way', 'Calling All Stations' itself (when moved from its actual release position as album opener). The album's front half, by contrast, is much more oriented toward romantic ballads and adult contemporary pop stylings.

'Uncertain Weather', meanwhile, occupies that niche right in between the two styles. It's teetering on the edge, inches away from romance, inches away from pure darkness. It's characterised by haunting verses with an airy synth, but also by sweeping passages of the most emotionally powerful keyboards to be found in this incarnation of the band, punctuated by Nick D'Virgilio's expert drumming. He's so on point, in fact, that the band failed to fire him.

> **Tony:** *This is one Nick D'Virgilio does the drums on which are really nice and I think we ended up using his part. We did get Nir over at one point to try... we thought at one point we would only use Nir and copy the part but it didn't sound nearly as good as when Nick did it. It is a lighter touch which seemed to work really well on this song I think.* [25]

Captured in a frame forever...

> **Tony:** *The album was an interesting thing. Obviously, if it had been a fantastic success, I'd probably be as happy with it as anything else we did.* [18]

And those big, big choruses. My oh my. Now that's a throwback. This is the swelling majesty of Genesis at their very peak: the grand Rutherford choruses, the grand Banks keyboard chord structures. Such a big sound, but now unmarred by problems like shoddy production. *Calling All Stations* features a few attempts at getting this big sound, notably in 'Shipwrecked', where the whole effort just feels leaden - and perhaps that's the point when given that song's subject matter. 'If That's What You Need' marks a second attempt to hit that high, and it gets closer with a lovely melodic sweep of a line, but it never quite arrives like this. 'Uncertain Weather', especially when following those other two tracks, feels like Tony going "Ah, yes, that's right," and then getting his fingers all locked into perfect position on the 'boards, as though he just kind of needed to fiddle around a bit until the old master could conjure up the memory of how to broadcast directly into your soul.

A face in a faded photograph...

> **Tony:** *When we made the decision to call it a day, my first thought was not to rush into anything at all. I wanted to spend time at home and not feel the pressure to get into any particular project...nothing seemed to be happening...* [1]

The lyrics aren't mind-blowing or anything, but they're certainly far from bad. It's a portrait, in a way quite literally, of a forgotten soldier, dying a meaningless death in a meaningless war. Nobody knows his name, and he'll never be remembered. This song acts as a sort of stand-in for the non-existent memories of any individual people who might have once been able to testify that this man existed. It's the Tomb of the Unknown Soldier in lyrical form, accompanied by music that sounds exactly like the respect-tinged-with-regret you'd expect, yet also like the inescapable emotional distance which brings its own minor twinges of guilt that one feels when visiting such a place. And if that doesn't quite make sense to you, I'd venture a guess that you've never been to a monument like that yourself. It's...confusing. Uncertain, perhaps.

All gone long ago...

> **Tony:** *At that point, I considered leaving the music business totally.* [18]

I really, really like Ray's performance here, too. This isn't his soulful voice like he delivered in 'Not About Us'. It's not his intense voice like what was on display in 'There Must Be Some Other Way'. It's not his light voice like he donned for standout B-side 'Anything Now'. This is its own distinct thing, a wispy kind of insubstantiality that aligns completely with the song's message. And then, in those giant choruses, it's just *mournful.* Sustaining notes, becoming part of the wall of sound instead of trying to stay above it, truly using his voice like an instrument. I love it.

But my favourite vocal moment has got to be the bridge in the middle, situated in a highly unusual position between the first chorus and second verse. It's not even singing...not really. Ray is just kind of droning in rhythm on a certain note, but doing it at two octaves. It's such a simple thing: one low, one high, but it works so well. It's like a rumbling, distant thunder rolling through the middle of the song, rich and deep on the low end but windy and transient on top. Overcast and ominous, yet still dry. It is, in essence, the vocal representation of uncertain weather itself, bringing with it images both literal and figurative as we're taken on the emotional ride through the song's subject matter. And then, as it passes, we're right back into the sombre verse, feeling changed for the experience.

Leaving no trace...

> **Tony:** *I was happy for two or three years to go by while I played some more golf, did some gardening - the things I love doing apart from being a musician - but I would still play every day.* [1]

And you know, despite being able to rationalise *why* this album sees every song but one fade out in the end, I'll admit that I'm not completely immune to the "Ugh, just get off your butts and write an ending for this song!" sentiment that is so prevalent among *Calling All Stations* listeners, especially because producer Nick Davis admits it was a shortcoming of composition due to the timing of the songwriting and recording sessions. But even so, this particular song is an exception: I wouldn't have 'Uncertain Weather' end any other way. Looking at the song's lyrical and musical content, how could it do anything *but* fade out? A "proper" ending would undermine the whole thing. But this fade out here, with that message, with these themes? Fantastic.

> **Tony:** *'Uncertain Weather' is what you might call a more traditional Genesis big ballad type thing really; strong chords...And yes, what can I say about it? I think it is a recognisable Genesis-type piece.* [25]

'Uncertain Weather' is indeed the last hurrah of classic emotional Genesis. After a couple sputters at recapturing that lush sound, it bursts in for one more goodbye, the "first final farewell" before the band scatters like dust. This was the last time Genesis would ever sound quite like Genesis on record: lightning striking twice, and then never again. I love it.

Disappearing like smoke in the wind...

> **Tony:** *I asked myself, "What would I really like to do if I was never going to do any more music again?", and my feeling was I would like to work with an orchestra...* [1]

32 - Domino

from *Invisible Touch*, 1986

Well, this has been a good run talking about things like love, loss, and grand fantastical tales, but I think it's time this book finally got political.

If you're anything like me, you may have read that last sentence and felt yourself overcome with dread. "No, no, you've got a good thing going here! Why would you throw it all away? *Why would you risk saying something that would make me not like you?*" Such is the sharp reality of political discussion. While in modern times we like to think we have a monopoly on divisiveness, the truth is politics have always divided, tapping into that instinctive tribalism that none of us quite care to admit we still possess. It owns a bigger portion of our unconscious thinking than I believe any of us are really comfortable with. It's the same story as it's always been: us vs. them, all the time, for all of time.

But you needn't fear, because this isn't actually a political essay. It's not even an essay *about* politics, per se. If anything, I'd like to hope that this book can provide a nice refuge for you from the inundation of political noise I'm sure you probably experience on a near-daily basis, whether you'd like to or not. I've no intention of jeopardising that, so please forgive my misdirection at the outset of this entry. My intent was simply to make the point that politics and music are pretty strange bedfellows. Allow me to elaborate.

Music is often referred to as a "universal language," given that it can be absorbed, understood, and created by any culture that has ever lived. Mathematics can also make this claim, though maths isn't intrinsically creative. Maths is rather a reflection of the supremacy of logic, driven by the existence of absolute truth. Nevertheless, the claim of maths being universal rings true and bolsters the argument for music: for what is music but applied maths and physics as related to vibrations and sound? Anyway, we're veering too technical here; my point is that music is a *uniting* force. Politics, on the other hand, are a *dividing* force. That the two would mingle is probably inevitable given our nature as human beings, but that intermingling carries a strange effect.

Have you ever heard a song you really liked, and then you read (or else finally heard and registered the meaning of) the lyrics only to find that they were in such opposition to something you believed in that you sort of had to throw the whole thing out? It's a sort of "Man, I really like this song, but these words make me feel dirty" conundrum. I won't give specific examples here, but I trust you see where I'm going with this. When you take a political stance with your music, you are potentially alienating a subset of your fans. Every time. And you might think, "This message is important, and if they're alienated by it then I didn't want them as fans anyway," and that's perhaps fair, but it is a reality that the *one* thing that unites your fans across all their disparate backgrounds - your music - is now becoming the very thing to divide them once again.

The other pitfall of politically driven music is that taking a political lyrical bent almost always sacrifices the ability of your music to be timeless. In fact, the more specific your political position ("I'm against X regime in Z country and I want everyone to know it!"), the less your song will mean after that position is no longer relevant. It'll be an interesting historical footnote, a trinket plopped into the time capsule for that moment and place, but it will struggle to reach anyone once that moment and place aren't in the forefront of the listeners' minds, which is to say, for the rest of human existence.

Why in the world am I spending so much time talking about the potholes to be found on the road of political music? Well, two reasons. For one, Genesis made it through the first 81% of their album discography before getting anything more than tangentially political ('Dancing with the Moonlit Knight' and 'Man on the Corner' are both social commentaries but neither is precisely political). And at this point in this book, we're through a similar percentage of the discography, so there's a pleasant kind of symmetry to having the discussion here. But mainly I bring it up because those political snares are ones that Genesis - in their *two* political forays on *Invisible Touch* after having never really gotten into the subject matter before - somehow deftly managed to escape. Neither 'Land of Confusion' nor 'Domino' stumbles into the classic traps of political music, and I wanted to spend some time examining how that feat was managed and appreciating just how rare a feat it is.

> **Tony:** *Because Invisible Touch produced so many hit singles it's slightly strange for me: my favourite track on the album, for example, is probably 'Domino', which was not a single. I thought the album showed a real confidence, and as a writer I'm very pleased with that: lots of good songs, well done. It is a simpler album, which is maybe why I particularly like 'Domino' - which is more complicated, and less well-known. If 'Land of Confusion' was Mike's anti-war moment then 'Domino' was mine - and I always take a lot longer to say things.* [1]

Me too, Tony. Me too.

Anyway, what both of these songs do really well is this: *they avoid specificity*. In both cases the lyrics are clearly identifiable as political, "anti-war" messages, but they're also painted with such a broad brush that they could describe nearly any political situation of any era. Now, some might complain that this boils the songs' messages down to simple, low-impact statements like "violence bad," but remember that so much of what makes music powerful comes from the listener rather than the artist. With a relatively blank canvas like this, we can apply these concepts to our own time, and our own experiences, and our own current situations, whenever and whatever they may be. It's that timeless quality all over again, because human problems are never going to simply disappear. Now, 'Land of Confusion' threw a lot of that flexibility out the window with its music video - more on that later in this book - but 'Domino' was never going to show up on MTV so it didn't have that problem, either.

> **Mike:** *This time, on this album, I think I got very conscious of what was going on [with] the public perception of us. Because MTV was in full swing now, we were having hit singles and videos and doing well, [and] I think the profile you get with a hit single was so huge it dwarfed everything else. So I think people forget there were long songs on this album like 'Domino'. There's always this thing about "You were a progressive band with long songs and then you ended up doing shorter songs"...we didn't ever really stop doing the long songs. They were just dwarfed perception-wise by the power of television, really. And funnily enough, when you see us live, that balance is so different. I mean, I think when you see us live, the long songs are probably as big a part of the audience's enjoyment as the short songs. And the balance is very much half and half. So I think in a way, songs like 'Domino' get rather forgotten until we go on stage.* [3]

> **Tony:** *Well to me it's a very important track, 'Domino'. It's more meaty perhaps than the others [on the album], in a way. The lyrics [are] mine. I was trying to get across a political kind of message...Politicians don't sometimes think through what they've started off. They do something, and the fact that all these people are going to be, you know...husbands are going to be killed, and all the unexpected consequences that occur when you start something off. And people tend to think very sort of blinkered about a thing; they think, "We've gotta get rid of this guy, we've gotta do that," and of course everything else happens. And that's what the song was all about, really.* [3]

"But wait," you might be thinking, "the song is called 'Domino'. How is that not specific?" Given the timing of the song (the heart of the Reagan era) and circumstances (renewed Cold War concerns), it's easy to assume the title of the song came from the "domino theory" that drove US foreign policy for decades. The idea was that if one country adopted communism, then those around it would "topple" as well, causing the rapid spread of communism throughout the world, threatening the United States and other western capitalist nations. These principles led the US to do things like, say, send people to Vietnam for years on end, not anticipating all the husbands being killed and other unexpected consequences like Tony was talking about. It's a very natural and understandable connection to make, really.

Yet this song isn't about that. Tony was thinking along much broader terms.

> **Tony:** *The idea I had in mind was not the communist Domino Effect, but those huge Japanese domino patterns: one falls over, and there's nothing you can do to stop it. Sometimes with these politicians I don't think they really know what it is they have set in motion, and that's what worries me.* [1]

Musically, what 'Domino' excels at is communicating this uncertainty and tension. The perspective of the lyrics during the 'In the Glow of the Night' half of the song is actually very personal. It's a first-person account of someone who doesn't know whether tomorrow is coming. You *feel* that right from the get-go. The opening keyboard line bleeds anxiety, and it's accompanied by a drum machine that punches strange rhythms at odd intervals, sounding a bit like muted gunfire; shootings happening a couple blocks away. It's such a sparse sound, putting you into a cold room in the middle of the night, trying to make yourself small, hoping those sounds outside don't suddenly become louder than the pounding of your own heart.

And then, of course, the music kicks into gear with big, violent chord hits that are anything but melodic. You wince from their impact: "That could've been me." When the bass hops in and we're in a chorus proper, it's something of an exhale. Those terrifying sounds outside have stopped...for now, anyway. Am I still here? Are you still here? Are my friends still here? Our home? It's damage assessment, picking up the pieces. And then another verse, another violent outburst, and another examination of the dust on the floor in the aftermath.

> **Tony:** *Mike just played a guitar riff and...if Mike's fairly static on quite a simple little riff, then it gives me a chance to play any chord I like. And I like that. And I just sort of played every chord that would fit over that riff, I think; put them in a certain kind of order and you get a certain kind*

> *of result. The second half - the two halves were not the same song originally - developed more out of a jam which we called 'Hawkwind' because it reminded us of an English group who used to do a lot of kind of psychedelic jams. Just keeping a sort of thing going in the bass...going all the way through it, and then just making funny noises on the top. You know, an excuse to use certain of those almost Hammer horror film chord sequences that I always liked very much. Not so much dramatic as melodramatic...I think right from the word go Genesis always quite liked putting soft bits next to loud bits because...louder bits sound louder against a soft bit. I mean, it's a simple technique but it seems to work quite well.* [38]

Your mind can't process the enormity of what's happening all around you, so as a defence mechanism it hones in on the details. Sheets of **double glazing**...**foreign** city sirens...**nylon** sheets and blankets...these descriptive words and phrases don't actually matter in themselves. Instead they're a distraction, something to focus on so you don't have to think about the bigger picture stuff that would stop your breath. *This is a political song,* but it's not actually *saying* anything political at all. It's just forcing you, as the listener, into a night in this person's shoes, and once you're there you realise, "This is *horrifying.*"

> **Mike:** *Tony never did understand how to make words flow. His words are the reason why he'll never write a hit single, although sometimes you have to admire his bravery: he's the only person who could ever get away with writing a lyric about double glazing and nylon sheets and have Phil make it work.* [14]

Mike's right: it *is* clunky, but somehow it *does* work. It works really well, in fact. But then, perhaps because nearly eleven minutes of straight nightmare is a bit much to ask of any listener, the song switches perspectives halfway through. Now a section called 'The Last Domino', this second half puts us back into our own shoes, albeit with a transitional section in between. You get this pulsing guitar riff, chords of swelling darkness...honestly this connecting section of music could be the soundtrack to a boss battle in Doom and I wouldn't question it.

> **Tony:** *It was a nice, big, long song, gave you an opportunity to have a bit of fun both lyrically and musically. And also it's very strong, the end section's a very strong bit. You've got a strong guitar riff, and it works.* [3]

Phil is wailing about children playing with boats in a literal river of blood, for crying out loud. It's energetic, it's entrancing, it's sickening. It's the camera panning outside of that small household so we can see what's happening in those violent streets themselves. It's making us witness the death and destruction before panning back over that same cold house. A musical motif recalling the poor soul trapped within, and then the camera zooms out even further to reveal that the whole scene is actually transpiring on a television set.

> **Tony:** *The second half of the song took a much more detached viewpoint about our attitude to seeing war or bloodshed on television, the awful fascination.* [1]

This is us, now. We're watching our news programs, and our violent shows and films, and though we decry it on the outside, we can't quite look away. We're almost revelling in what's happening, eating it up as must-see TV. And here's the dark truth at the heart of politics in a more-or-less democratic society: *we are responsible.* The politicians may be the ones making these decisions, but they're only there because we put them there. We may claim to hate the results of those decisions, but here we are eagerly ingesting all the horrible fruits of those labours every chance we get. *This is a political song,* but *we* are ultimately the ones causing the problems. We have to look inward before we can look outward if we're ever going to stop the madness.

"Do you know what you have done? Do you see what you've begun?" These lines are meant for us at least as much as any nameless politician. And *that* is how you make a political song a timeless one. Because if there's one thing thousands of years of human history have taught us, it's that human nature doesn't change.

That makes it almost feel somehow inappropriate that the song is such a fun live staple, doesn't it?

> **Tony:** *Classic stage song ever since, I think. In a funny way, from a stage point of view it's one of the best songs off the album, because it gives you more room to breathe. The longer songs tend to work better on stage, I think.* [3]

> **Phil:** *There was a moment with 'Domino' during the [2007] New York rehearsals when we started the song and I didn't know what to sing. I couldn't remember anything. We put the CD on, I listened to it and I thought, "I'll never be able to remember this," but suddenly it came back, and this time it was much more fluent. I was even fine with the famous "double glazing"*

and "nylon sheets and blankets" lyrics I'd had problems with before. They're not the kind of lyrics that I would write, but I realised, "I can find it, I can see it now, I can do it." And that was a pleasant surprise. [1]

From what I can tell, live songs tend to fall into one of three buckets. Let's call them Buckets A, B, and C. Bucket A is where the song just doesn't work at all live, and the studio version is the best way to hear the track. Any song that was never played live falls into this bucket by default, naturally, but some other pieces can show up here as well. Bucket B is songs that are transformed live into something different altogether; songs like 'The Waiting Room' or 'Throwing It All Away' being good examples. And then you have Bucket C, full of songs that are functionally the same as their studio counterparts, but that gain something intangible on stage.

'Domino' is not only firmly in that Bucket C category, but also stands out to me as one that somehow got better every single tour over the first twenty-odd years it was performed. And it's not just Phil's pre-concert audience engagement; silly fun that it is, it actually distracts a little from the core thrust of the song's message I've been discussing here. But between the lights, the energy of the musicians, the electricity of the crowd, it just thrives live and gets better with age. On the Invisible Touch Tour, Chester Thompson added a big drum fill near the end, right before the "In silence and darkness" line. That wasn't there on the studio version, and it's a solid addition. Then on the We Can't Dance Tour, lighting and screens really supercharged the performance, with flashes of turning spotlights in the violent hits and Phil basically teleporting into a space vortex.

Tony: *Some of that stuff is very easy to do and looks VERY effective because people had never seen it before. In that situation I felt we could get away with some very simple ideas; the most obvious one being the "2001" effect and I thought, "Why not?" It is a very simple thing to do; it is all computer generated, and the lines come towards you and you get the effect of traveling into a thing. I had always thought that effect would look great in 'Domino'...and then there was the idea of sticking Phil up in the middle of it and suddenly he was where you weren't expecting him and it worked.* [6]

Did you think you were getting out of this without a mention of the Calling All Stations Tour? Wrong. Sure, by then the screens were gone because the whole endeavour was a little bit scaled back, and sure, Ray at times sounded a little too happy just to be there instead of properly emoting the song, but advancements in instrument technology made the music the best it had ever sounded up until that point. The bass in particular sounded great, Tony found creepier wailing noises, Nir Zidkyahu did some fancy cymbal rolls, and he also sported a fantastic electronic drum sound that transformed the fills in the middle of the piece into something really powerful.

Finally, the Turn It On Again Tour in 2007 brought it all together. The improved instrument sound quality was retained from the Calling All Stations shows, but Chester was back, Phil was back, and the screens were back and bigger than ever. That time around they were sort of shaped like an eye and that vortex in the middle of the song used a full circular tunnel effect instead of the two-dimensional stuff, and...was that Phil's disembodied head in the middle? Crazy stuff. What's more, while the official live CD of that tour featured recordings from the European leg of the tour, when they came to the States later that year, it sounded even better. Remember that drum fill of Chester's I mentioned back from the Invisible Touch Tour? Stateside it had that great electronic drum sound of Nir's tacked on and, at least at the concert I attended, it was played absolutely *perfectly*. What had been a ho-hum moment on record evolved and became the highlight of the song for me. It's that good.

Genesis must've agreed, because when they decided to reform once more in 2021, they went so far as to call the tour itself The Last Domino?, cheeky question mark and all. Thus it was no surprise to hear 'Domino' itself again acting as the centrepiece of the back half of the set, though truth be told I don't think this rendition quite measured up to the versions of past tours gone by. For one thing, the key had to be lowered to such a degree for the sake of Phil's voice that the sound quality suffered. For another, Phil himself still struggled a bit with the piece anyway, to the point where I have to wonder whether the band would have included it in the set at all if they hadn't felt as though they needed it there as a live staple - especially since they were already cutting long-time concert stalwart 'Los Endos'. While Phil's son Nic Collins handled the drum work with aplomb, the electronic drum sound was lost and that perfect fill along with it. Lastly, I found the visuals to be a step down from previous years as well, mostly focusing on generic computer animations of giant stone dominoes falling over repeatedly.

It's a shame that the song went out with more of a whimper than a bang, but that shouldn't detract from its legacy. Again, if they're naming a tour after you, you're probably doing something right. And for twenty-odd years, 'Domino' was a song that could do no wrong.

31 - After the Ordeal

from *Selling England by the Pound*, 1973

Welcome, friends, to another edition of The Dividing Line, the only Genesis debate show on the air. Last week's episode "Best Pedals: Mr. Bassman or Moog Taurus?" set a record number of viewers for us, so we'd like to thank all of you for continuing to tune in. Tonight's subject is quite a bit less technical and more straightforward, and here it is.

"Is 'After the Ordeal' a Good Song?"

Taking the "pro" side tonight we have Mr. Stephen Hackett, co-writer of 'After the Ordeal' and guitarist for Genesis through much of the 1970s. Welcome to The Dividing Line, Mr. Hackett.

Steve: It is very, very touching to come here. [42]

Yes, thank you Mr. Hackett, and taking the "con" side in tonight's debate we have Mr. Anthony Banks, founding member and eternal keyboardist of Genesis. Welcome to The Dividing Line, Mr. Banks.

Tony: <polite half nod>

If you're a first-time viewer, here's the format of the show. We'll introduce the subject and get our initial perspectives from our guest debaters, then provide additional context, go a little deeper, and challenge both perspectives directly. As always, by the end we'll have a determination of who presented the more compelling case and declare a winner of the debate. Clear? Great. So with that, let's jump right in. Mr. Banks, how do you feel about the album *Selling England by the Pound* in general?

Tony: I probably don't have as much time for this album as the previous one purely because I'm not as fond of some of the things... [3]

Ah, well, looks like you're trying to go straight to the point here, but judging from his earlier appearance on Genesis Live Tonight, I would say Mr. Hackett has quite a fondness for the album, isn't that so Mr. Hackett?

Steve: We think [*Selling England by the Pound*] is the best thing we've ever done. The best played, the best material. [86]

Tony: I have ambivalent feelings about *Selling England*...not so sure about the record; I thought maybe it was a bit too tricksy at times. [1]

Steve: I was very pleased with it. For me it was a more comfortable-sounding album and I liked being a guitarist in the band at that time. There were plenty of moments for a guitar to strut its stuff. Perhaps because it was a more riff-driven album, and less song-driven, more rock and less pop. [1]

Fascinating. So it seems that even at the broader, whole-album level there were disagreements about the direction the album should take?

Tony: We had a few arguments about this at the time, because there was too much material to go on the album. [6]

I see. And how would these disagreements typically get themselves resolved? Did you have "council meetings" or something to that effect?

Steve: Things would still deteriorate sometimes into a locker room punch-up over the most unlikely things. Suddenly it would go tilt and you suspected that there were issues from 1963 that hadn't yet been resolved: you swiped my wine gums back in biology, you always were a rotter. [1]

Tony: We were talking about what we should include on the album, something we had generally agreed about in the past. [1]

Oh, so not quite so mature, unfortunately. Well let's get into 'After the Ordeal' specifically. Now this song is one that Genesis fans don't often agree about, and it seems clear that you two gentlemen also have differing opinions about the quality of the track. Mr. Hackett, you were one of the primary writers of this track. Can you give us a little bit of background?

Steve: There was all this emphasis on writing songs, and I hadn't really written any songs for the album at that point. There were things going on in my private life that made it almost impossible to do that. And so really, I just had lots of guitar licks, and I used them all on the album. That's the thing...I had a great time just being the guitarist, not trying to be a songwriter. I think I'd only come up with one thing as a song, which was 'After the Ordeal'... [3]

Tony: 'After the Ordeal' was the track I really don't like. I've never liked it. And I would've liked it to have not been on the album... [3]

Sounds as though you weren't getting entirely too much support for the track, then, Mr. Hackett.

Steve: Chaps like me need encouragement. I need to be told that I'm better than I am. Flattery goes a long way with me. [1]

Tony: 'After The Ordeal'... is actually our worst song we've ever recorded. [6]

Steve: I think it was very, very beautiful... [45]

Tony: A weak moment, pseudo-classical without any real spirit...my least favourite Genesis piece. [1]

All right, all right, let's all regain some composure for a moment. Before we go deeper into the realm of pure contradiction, let's review the history and structure of the piece a bit for our viewers at home. Now Mr. Banks, you referred to 'After the Ordeal' as "pseudo-classical" just now, is that right?

Tony: I really didn't like that. I don't like the whole sort of pseudo-classical thing at all. [6]

Right, well, is that such a bad thing really? I was under the impression that the genre of "symphonic prog," as Genesis is commonly classified, was built in large part around the attempt to get a rock band to operate more like classical music with a different arrangement, rather than the typical rock fare. If there is a song that is in itself flavoured in that classical vein more directly, is that actually a negative? So I think I'd agree with the term you used there, but not in the same disparaging way you meant it.

It's odd in a way, isn't it? Here's this song called '**After** the Ordeal', a pleasant, semi-romantic, semi-classical little thing meant to sonically wash away all the mud and violence of 'The Battle of Epping Forest' right before it, and yet in the background it was the most contentious bit of the entire album. The album might as well go from 'The Battle of Epping Forest' straight into 'The Battle of Chessington' - uh, that's where the writing sessions occurred, for those of you at home - for all the barely-restrained animosity you seem to have for it, Mr. Banks.

Tony: I wanted that off and Peter wanted that off as well. [6]

Mr. Hackett, do you believe you have any insight as to why Mr. Banks here might feel this way about the track?

Steve: ['After the Ordeal'] started out as this electric [guitar] thing. And it plainly didn't work as an electric melody; nobody could make it swing. Ended up being this kind of acoustic thing that had an electric bit on the end. [3]

Ah, now, this doesn't sound like much but it is rather revealing. We were able to recover some of the rehearsal tapes from the *Selling England by the Pound* sessions, and thanks to them were able to hear what the song sounded like in that early electric form. Let's all listen together.
   <plays the tape>

There's Mr. Hackett meedly-meedlying away on the electric guitar as expected, but Mr. Banks is also quite involved here. He's got some chords running alongside the guitar and then he jumps in on the second loop of the melody with this really active and exciting organ bit. The organ still isn't the featured sound, but there's a little bit of a dual solo feel to it. The back half of the song here is more or less the same as the finished product, albeit less refined. But Mr. Banks, is your distaste for this song coloured in any way by the loss of the active organ section from the early recording?

> **Tony:** We could have got it off the album without any trouble as we shouted about it quite loudly at the time! [6]

Mr. Banks seems to be quite riled up at the moment, so we'll continue on along this train of thought. Now, Mr. Hackett, do you feel that perhaps reducing the impact of the keyboards in the final, acoustic version of the track was a mistake?

> **Steve:** Really I'd written [it] as a rock guitar instrumental, but it seemed to work much better as an acoustic track, especially with Tony doing very, very florid piano work on it. So I played nylon guitar. I deferred to that. [45]

Ah, I see! The keyboard part is not actually reduced at all in the album version of the song; in fact, I daresay the switch from organ to piano has really flavored it all up pretty strongly. So again I feel a need to ask you, Mr. Banks, what is it *specifically* about 'After the Ordeal' that you take issue with?

> **Tony:** But Pete also said that he wanted to get rid of the instrumental bit at the end of 'Cinema Show' and I said, "We can't have that, it's great and it's got all the best bits!" So we ended up with a compromise which was to keep the whole bloody lot on. [6]

It would seem that Mr. Banks is no longer willing or able to participate directly in this debate, so I'm afraid we have no choice but to award the debate to Mr. Hackett. Let's get those results on the screen, please?

"Is 'After the Ordeal' a Good Song?"

YES

> Marvellous. And Mr. Hackett, congratulations to you on this fine result.

> **Steve:** It is a very pleasant surprise for me. [42]

As the victor, you have the right to make a final statement in favour of 'After the Ordeal', summarizing your opinions on the subject, without fear of rebuttal. So please, Mr. Hackett, take it away!

> **Steve:** The first Genesis track that I used a nylon guitar on. In fact, I've got a feeling I might've double-tracked it. With [the 2008] remix, you can hear both of them. Played it many times live [as a solo artist], sometimes acoustic concerts, and more often recently with electric gigs. Played it with electric [guitar] for convenience's sake mostly, so that I can play the other bit at the end. Originally I had some idea that this would make a rock guitar number. I don't know what I was thinking at the time, because when we rehearsed it, it just didn't swing. It just didn't work. The phrases were fine, but in terms of timing. It worked much better as [acoustic]. And Tony Banks came up with a very florid piano part to support it. So it's one of those anomalies on an album that is essentially an electric album. But Genesis always had those moments. In fact, when I first joined the band in 1971, I would say easily half the set was acoustic. We wouldn't have been able to do [a song like] this. Real pianos weren't on offer in those days, pickups hadn't really been developed for those sorts of things, and then - much later, course - people used virtual pianos; samples are very good of this sort of stuff all these years later. The [second] section...essentially is written by Mike Rutherford. First bit's mine, and then into Mike's bit, but I'm [playing] the lead again on this. And then it goes back to my bit at the end. I think of it as a palate cleanser on an album full of epics. A small song, but a sweet memory nonetheless. I hope that's sweet for you, as well. [13]

Thank you very much for that moving tribute to the song. An interesting mention there of the back half writing credits. It doesn't seem obvious on a listen, but once you learn that Mike Rutherford wrote the main melody of that bit, it's very much an "oh, of course" kind of moment. For all we like to think of Mr. Banks here as the "wall of sound" guy, Mike Rutherford is the one with the penchant for big, romantic choruses. This is no different, except that it's a chorus without any vocals. But it produces the same feel, possesses the same instinct to drive the electric melody. And then it transitions so smoothly back to Mr. Hackett's melodies in the end. With a little icing on the cake that is the flute work of one Mr. Peter Gabriel. Delightful.

One must here wonder: would Mr. Banks have liked this track if the band had ever figured out how to "make it swing" as a fully electric thing? Who knows. But I for one greatly appreciate the split between acoustic and electric; really, that's what makes the song for me. You've got all this energy in the first half, and stuff that's high energy is often described as being "electric," but instead that section is what's totally unplugged. The dreamier, floatier stuff in the back half is what you'd expect to have a more pastoral sound on, but that's where the electric instrumentation takes over. You end up getting this really yin and yang kind of effect on the tune, where the two halves cross into one another's traditional territories, subverting expectations. It's very engaging to me for that reason, and of course the melodies themselves are still lovely. This is a wonderful little instrumental ditty, two halves of really fun guitar playing.

Speaking personally here now, as someone who isn't a particularly big fan of 'The Battle of Epping Forest' - as our viewers are frequently keen to remind me - 'After the Ordeal' is a real highlight of *Selling England by the Pound*. More than just a calm after the storm, it's like coming home after a long day and smelling a favourite dish cooking on the stove. Like a warm shower after a long morning shovelling snow. Like a rush of breeze coming into a stuffy room. I may ultimately prefer a couple other songs on the record more than it overall, but I find when I put the album on, there's no track I look forward to more.

That's all the time we have here tonight on The Dividing Line. I'd again like to thank our guests, Mr. Banks and Mr. Hackett, for their generous time coming to speak with us about 'After the Ordeal'. Please be sure to tune in for next week's debate, "Was It You or Was It Me?", featuring Mr. Phil Collins playing both sides. You won't want to miss it. Good night!

30 - Ripples...

from *A Trick of the Tail*, 1976

"Actually, we'd like to apologise for that last song," Phil said to the giddy crowd after the final echoes of 'Mama' died away in the rafters, "for being so disgusting, and the lyrics being so naughty and filthy...we apologise for that. And so we won't ever play that song again..."

Unable to continue under the protesting roar of "NO!" from the crowd, Phil recanted. "Well, not tonight, anyway." A collective sigh of relief amidst laughter.

"But we would like to try and make that up to you by taking you somewhere completely different now. Somewhere...where virgins live. Nowhere near here, don't worry." The crowd was settling a bit now, most of them wondering where on Earth Phil was going with this brief monologue. "A place of innocence, and purity. Where butterflies fly all day, and birds sing in the trees." What could this be, they wondered? And though one boisterous man in the crowd who had memorised the set list beforehand started shouting a word, nobody was paying *him* any attention. "A really boring place." Some awkward, confused laughter. "No, we're going to take you there, and it's a place where the blue girls live," Phil concluded to a gentle sound of guitar tuning.

Such was the way Genesis brought 'Ripples' back into the consciousness of a sell-out crowd of thousands in 2007, a return to the innocence of 1976. A time before divorces, before solo albums, before hit singles. A time where an unapologetic progressive rock album could soar to 3 in its home country with a new frontman. It seemed an odd choice at the time; surely there were other Genesis songs, even of the classic 70s era, that were perhaps more well-known, or more in line with the musical sensibilities of a crowd that showed up as much for the likes of 'Invisible Touch' as anything else. And indeed alternatives were, in fact, suggested.

> **Tony:** *We played everything we knew [in rehearsals] and thought about a couple of other songs we might do...I was also keen to do an older song...I suggested 'Blood on the Rooftops', a song I've always loved, and 'Many Too Many', but I also said, because I knew 'Blood on the Rooftops' doesn't go down well with everybody, "Let's do 'Ripples'," which we hadn't played for a long time.* [1]

Tony wanted the obscurity of 'Blood on the Rooftops' but was happy to go for 'Ripples' because, in his implied words, 'Ripples' goes down well with everybody. Well, OK, maybe not with Mike's guitar strings.

> **Mike:** *I had all kinds of weird tunings on older songs like...'Ripples', and it got so complicated. When we'd come back to tour after a break, I sometimes couldn't remember the tunings, so I finally said, "Right—I'm done with that." The one thing I always do, however, is tune the low E down to D. That makes the minor chords sound harder, and the rest of the chords sound richer, which really suits the character of most Genesis songs.* [58]

But outside of that little hiccup, 'Ripples' seems to have universal appeal. To fans of slower, prettier melodies, and fans of bigger, louder sounds. To those who want epic progressive composition and those who just want to hear a good chorus. To the band, to the audience, to the UK and Europe and the US alike.

> **Tony:** *We may change [the set] for America...For the rest of the [European] tour we probably will do what we're doing now...'In Too Deep', that's the one we might do in America, because it's much more popular in America than it was here while 'Ripples' was less popular in America.* [66]

Spoiler alert: They never did make that change. In the end, the question was "Should we play these people our popular top 5 hit single, or should we play them this album cut from 1976?" And the answer from Genesis was "Ah screw it, they're getting 'Ripples'." And let me tell you, as a fan in the US who just so happens to really like 'In Too Deep', my reaction to that decision can be summed up in one word.

Good.

This is a Mike and Tony song, coming together seamlessly as a duo in a way seldom seen before or since. It's Mike doing his *Trespass* 12-string thing over a compelling melody, a taste of Genesis from 1970 propelled forward in time with a new singer and new sensibilities; nothing on *Trespass* ever had a chorus quite like this one.

> **Tony:** *For me it really evokes that first period when Phil took over the vocals.* [1]

Steve: *You've got to remember that this [album] was Phil Collins' first attempt at singing lead vocals with Genesis. Of course, I knew he had a great voice. We auditioned a lot of other singers, but really to have a singer of this quality within the ranks was an opportunity that was too good to pass up on...So to be able to write iconic choruses, or things that sounded like choruses - didn't necessarily repeat the words, but "Here comes the big bit!"...the big moment is Phil singing "Sail away," that whole thing, which I think probably influenced Enya later on with "Sail away, Sail away" [on] her first big hit single 'Orinoco Flow'.* [13]

And then, just when you think you've got the sense that this is just a grand evolution of Mike's *Trespass* sound, a lush and beautiful preview of his pop sensibilities to come, here comes Tony's bit. This is a sonic landscape he relishes working in.

Tony: *I loved the more 'Ripples'-type things that Mike might do.* [18]

Arpeggiating pianos a la 'Carpet Crawlers' soon joined by Steve's haunting guitar, sounding gorgeous but somehow unnatural.

Steve: *There's an instrumental section which features guitar work from me but it sounds like it's backwards! But actually it isn't. It's [the guitar effects unit] Synthi Hi-Fli, which lopped off the beginning of the note, making it sound backwards. And then Tony's keyboards kicking in, so you've got synth [guitar], you've got it backed by piano. Maybe the sort of poignancy of the song comes from this section.* [13]

This feels like it's going to be a guitar solo, but after about thirty seconds it becomes clear that it's really a duet. Steve is going to explore one melody on his guitar over this way, and Tony's going to explore a completely different melody over here at the same time. The two rise and fall, interweaving but never joining, complementing but never converging. It's an entrancing dance of instrumentation, spelled by a rhythm section comprised entirely of impeccable cymbal work. Nothing is in-your-face about this, because that's not the point. The point is to drift, to sail, away and away.

Steve: *I felt...moved by the beautiful and gentle songs. I loved 'Ripples'. I wrote the guitar melody I played in the middle section...* [70]

There's a classic Banksian trick in this section as well, one he used to great effect a few years earlier in the iconic *actual* guitar solo of 'Firth of Fifth': after about a minute into the instrumental section, there's a clear shift. Major tones start creeping in, those arpeggiating pianos start hammering on chords, and the piece feels as though it's building to a grand sun-bursts-through-the-clouds moment. And then, on that very moment when you anticipate just that kind of release, what you get instead is a bellowing bass tone as the guitar and keyboard plunge back down to continue their flirty, mournful dance with renewed intensity. The cymbals become full drums. It's the same, but not the same; more powerful, more dramatic. The expected lift was a false one, only there to reinforce the tension. Which means when it comes around again, you're now a little wary. "(More) Fool me once," and all that. And of course, that second time *is* the release, and your skepticism allowed it to catch you with its full force, as you were now counterintuitively less prepared for it than you were the first time around. You've been bamboozled, and you don't even care.

Steve: *I think that's really important, that Genesis had this ability to have quiet moments and then loud moments, the dynamics of which I think characterised the band very much in those early days...There's so much that's typically Genesis of this.* [13]

It's got such strength that the band, while cognizant that the song would probably never succeed as a single, nevertheless went ahead and made a music video to promote the song and the album. "Nobody's going to buy this song on its own, but *maybe* if we market it well enough, people will come buy the whole album to hear it." It worked.

Mike: *[On] our...video for 'Ripples'...Steve, Tony and I seem to be going for a velvet-and-tassels look; Phil is wearing a beanie and may have been making a point. Whatever it was, I'd say it was a good one.* [14]

Tony: *It was a time to reassess, put it like that. And we were also lucky that at that particular time you didn't need a hit single, because obviously there was no hit single on this album. And*

> *I think a lot of the existing fans really liked it. And we got some new fans, and it just seemed to sort of take off, I suppose. I think the previous album having been a double album as well meant this album had a chance...it was a bit easier for people to take in...and with songs like 'Entangled' and 'Ripples' which have got very strong choruses, I think it works on a lot of levels.*[3]

Back in 2007, the final chorus closes, the spirits of the unsuspecting audience descending back into the arena in which their bodies have remained the entire time. They laughed and cheered and danced with 'Mama', yes. They chuckled apprehensively as Phil introduced something "boring." They weren't at all ready to be taken where the blue girls live, but once there they never wanted to leave. It was a fleeting moment, a glimpse into something beautiful and grand, and though they may have showed up that night for 'Hold On My Heart', now they wanted nothing so much as one more look at that deeper something they just experienced. They want to dwell in that moment, just a little bit longer. But alas, it's too late: ripples, you see, never come back.

29 - Seven Stones

from *Nursery Cryme*, 1971

Luck, be a lady tonight!
 Lyrically, 'Seven Stones' is a metanarrative of three smaller tales. The first sees a tinker lost in a storm. He finds seven rocks under a pile of leaves, takes it as a sign, and sure enough finds shelter within the seventh house he comes across. The second tale is of a sea captain unknowingly making a beeline for disaster, only to see a single seagull over what appears to be open water. He thinks, "Well that's odd," and turns the boat just in case, never knowing for sure whether he just saved the lives of everyone on his ship. And the final tale is of an inexperienced farmer trying to buy wisdom, only to have his money taken with no answers. He did buy wisdom in the end, if only the certainty that wisdom can't be bought.
 These stories are pretty different things, but they're all framed within the song's lyrics as being told by a singular old man who laughs at grief and grieves at mirth. He's passing his own brand of wisdom onto the listener, as each story has a different but related moral to it. The first, that pivotal things can happen totally out of the blue. How unlikely is it that at the exact moment of despair, this tinker finds an apparently meaningful marker on the ground that actually leads him to safety? The second moral is that we can never know what roads other decisions may have led us down. The sea captain didn't know there was a rock there; he never truly will. He makes his decision and moves on, never looking back to second guess it. And finally, the third story tells us that all our meticulous planning for the future is useless. A farmer who doesn't know when to sow wants to schedule his whole crop cycle, but for his trouble is only cheated of his cash, because what answer could the old man possibly give? You live with your choices and you learn from them. That's all any of us can do.
 This is an odd thing for Genesis - well, almost certainly Tony Banks, at any rate - to be writing about, isn't it? To be sure, they'd by now proven their penchant for fanciful stories and drama that would befit some kind of Age of Legends, but 'Seven Stones' isn't quite that.

> **Peter:** *A step into the shade, if you like. There's more sort of sun shining in Trespass, more sort of folky feels and outside stuff, and we'd [now] gone indoors on Nursery Cryme.* [3]

It's not a grand tale of kings and betrayal, or a description of a pastoral scene, or even a channelling of a particular emotion. It's just a kind of proverb, told as a set of smaller proverbs, about how the world is ruled by randomness, and that to an extent simply believing in the power of good fortune can almost will it into existence. Where did this come from?
 My theory is that it had a lot to do with the uncertainty the band had experienced over the previous year, how much stronger they came out of it, and how outrageously unlikely all of that was. Let's take a walk down memory lane, and as we go, I encourage you to continually ask yourself: how incredibly fortunate is it that *this* happened?
 The trouble started, of course, with Anthony Phillips' departure from the band, which initially seemed to spell the end for all parties. Peter and Mike figured they could roll on, but were having trouble getting buy-in from Tony. Which is when old schoolmate (and part-time cook and part-time roadie and full-time 1 Genesis fan) Richard Macphail told Tony he couldn't let this drop.

> **Tony:** *Anthony Phillips left, and so we had to make a decision. As I said before, Anthony I saw as group leader in many ways. Certainly the most influential person in the group. And I thought when he left we probably would split up, actually. And then we had a conversation: Mike and Pete were very keen to carry on, and Richard Macphail - who was our roadie, but a good friend, sort of a big fan and everything - said, "There's no way you should [break up]. You must carry on, you've got something going here." So all these things came together.* [3]

From Genesis to Revelation didn't sell. *Trespass* didn't really sell. The band was gigging, but no money was being made. They were making inroads at a few venues, but if they left, would anyone really miss them? How lucky then that they could have such a supportive and unflappable fan in their midst, who could talk to the band's most stubborn member and convince him that this was worth doing?
 Of course, Tony was still Tony, and thus put a condition on the whole thing: find a new drummer in addition to Ant's replacement on guitar. Which led to auditions at the Château du Gabriel, where a guy named Phil Collins showed up early, but just so happened to be placed last in the audition order. Out of hospitality, the Gabriel parents cheerfully offered that Phil could take a swim in their heated pool. He hadn't brought trunks, but (free spirit that he was) on a whim decided, "Sure, that sounds like fun." And this pool, naturally, happened to be right next to the auditioning area.

Phil: *We've arrived a couple of drummers early and, as I'm splashing about, I hear my rivals go through their paces. The standard is decent and I quickly appreciate what I'm up against. I keep my head down in the water a bit longer, calming my nerves...I'm the last drummer that day...* [12]

Peter: *It was a painful and really time-consuming process, so we thought, "OK, we'll throw some different tests at these drummers and see how quickly people pick up these ideas." Phil arrived early as he often does...listening to the other drummers run through these tests, so by the time he sat down, he knew it.* [3]

How fortunate for Phil that he got there early! That he was invited to swim! That he was placed last! That he could hear the other drummers playing and surreptitiously memorise the part before his own attempt! All of these little things landed in his favour that evening. Does Phil Collins get the Genesis gig without the extra leg up over the competition? We'll never really know, though to hear the band tell it now there was never any doubt before the "tests" even began.

Tony: *Of course everyone's going to say, "Oh, I thought Phil was the best," but Pete and I definitely thought he was. Phil had something about him that was kind of special.* [1]

Peter: *I was convinced from the first moment. I knew when Phil sat down on the kit, before he'd played a note, that this was a guy who really was in command of what he was doing, because he was so confident. It's like watching a jockey sit on a horse.* [1]

From Genesis' perspective, they felt really lucky to have had a drummer of this caliber - he'd recorded at Abbey Road! - show up to their audition. From Phil's, he felt really lucky to finally be in a band that actually got work.

Phil: *I try to play it cool, but inside I'm jumping. I've finally found a band; or a band has found me.* [12]

Ant: *There was a huge silver lining for Genesis which was that me leaving meant they had to have a time of reassessment. They got Phil. I mean, come on, it's got to have been worth it to have got Phil. I feel sorry for John Mayhew, saying that, because John was a decent drummer, but what an impossible act to have preceded, if you like.* [1]

It wasn't completely sunshine and roses, however: Tony, Mike, and Peter were auditioning guitarists as well, of course, and likely felt some disappointment at not being able to find a suitable one in those poolside sessions. Phil had even brought along to the audition his friend, fellow Flaming Youth member Ronnie Caryl...but the guys didn't feel he was a fit. A bummer, it seemed at the time, because prior commitments and the need to earn an income meant the show must go on. The band was therefore forced to go gig for a while as a four-piece, without any guitarist at all. Yet, as simply removing the guitar parts altogether would severely damage the integrity of the songs, Tony found himself picking up the slack.

Tony: *We went out as a four-piece for about two or three months, I think, which taught me a lot, because I ended up playing - I had this piano I put through a fuzz box - all the guitar parts that Ant had played. Well, all the ones I could, anyhow...and at the same time playing the organ parts! So suddenly I was doing this two-handed stuff, which I had never really done before, but it made me mature as a musician a great amount.* [3]

Yes, the missing guitarist appeared to be a problem, but as time would reveal it was really a blessing in disguise. Not "how disappointing we didn't get one sooner," but now "how surprisingly beneficial this turned out to be!" Not that they wanted to carry on in this vein indefinitely, however; they didn't stop looking for a guitarist, after all. Or at least, Mike didn't stop looking. Yet he still wanted Ant, or at least the closest approximation to Ant that he could find. Someone who could produce the same kind of sound, intertwining with him on 12 strings and really just doing "the Genesis thing" as he'd come to know it. So it probably felt like defeat that after months of fruitless searching he came down with a stomach ulcer.

But wouldn't you know it, at *precisely that time* a young guitarist going by the name of Steve Hackett put out an ad for a band. How serendipitous!

Mike: *In truth, I was too set on finding "the son of Ant." I still missed him...For Pete and Tony, however, it was much less complicated: we needed a new guitarist, simple as that. And so* *when I fell ill with a stomach ulcer, they simply went and got another one...Steve was different...His real strength was doing the most amazing, unique, quirky-sounding things on guitar - he brought something to the band that Ant never would have done and I fully appreciated it.* [14]

If Mike is healthy, does he reject Steve like he did all the others? Does stopgap player Mick Barnard end up sticking around the guitar stool for entirely too long? Does *Nursery Cryme* as an album really come together in the same way, and inform the future of the band as strongly as it did? Who can say?

Mike: *Fortunately Steve fitted in really well and it's much stronger now than it ever was.* [87]

Fortunate indeed. And this new five-piece, assembled by a series of increasingly unlikely rolls of the dice, was expanding the band's sound and presence both ever further.

Tony: *Phil and Steve's contribution, particularly at this stage, was to bring a bit of musicianship into the group. I was still learning very much as a musician. I mean, it was OK, but nothing brilliant. And Mike was certainly still finding his way as a musician. Whereas Phil came and was a really high quality drummer right from the word go; he's got a brilliant sense of rhythm. And Steve obviously was technically a better player than we were at that time. And that's what it really gave us: a bit of technique in there as well as everything else. Gave us a better chance to do things.* [3]

Peter: *Phil definitely just lifted the foundation of everything, just with great grooves...and I think Steve, it was colouring. He was a colouring agent in lots of ways. And it was this sort of dark, contained personality that was struggling to get out. I think that's partly why we connected with people, because there was this yearning, longing build up of some compressed energy that needed to explode and get out, and we didn't always get it out, but people could feel and touch those sort of vibrations humming beneath the surface. And Steve definitely had a good dollop of unfulfilled frustrations, I think, that gave it a good personality.* [3]

Heck, even the American press kit for *Nursery Cryme* admits that this was all really just a good deal of a hand, a fortuitous shuffle of the deck. And that claim goes back even further to the band's discovery, as they weren't sure how they were going to escape the grand chasm of listener indifference generated by the efforts of their debut (emphasis mine).

*A group whose considerable talents left them a bit sprawling, Genesis had the **good fortune** to attract the attention of the head of Charisma Records, Tony Stratton-Smith. Smith put them together with a "benevolent and indulgent" producer, John Anthony, and paid a considerable tab for studio time at the Trident Studios in London. This was a wise and necessary investment. The results are Nursery Cryme...* [88]

"Well, these guys were pretty good, but they also kinda sucked, but along came Tony Stratton-Smith to give them a record deal anyway! Fate must've been smiling upon them!"

And now, the final piece of the puzzle: audiences still had to dig their sound. A sound like we hear on 'Seven Stones', with its big organ, sauntering bass line, and effortlessly light drum rolls with clean vocal harmonies delivered from the band's new drummer. Its melodic interplay between keys and flute. Its lead vocal delivered with a gravitas beyond the singer's years. And of course, its dramatic yet still textural guitar, putting a heavier edge on the sound than listeners were accustomed to from the band. And the audiences loved every bit of it.

Peter: *Our style has changed a lot - evolved in the last year. It changed when Phil came along and Steve joined on guitar...Originally we tried to do folk type numbers, and it's all worked up to a crescendo. Now we've got an act [where] we've started to take control of the audiences.* [89]

Mike: *'Seven Stones' was very much Tony's song. It was a great example of what I've come to call Tony's cabaret chords: his big, schmaltzy, music-hall chords which Phil and I struggled with but he loved. In the end we had to make a rule: Tony could have three or four per album and no more. We always wondered what happened to the ones we'd turned down. Then in 2011 Tony released a wonderful classical album and we found out.* [14]

What are the odds?

28 - Land of Confusion

from *Invisible Touch*, 1986

If you progress chronologically through Michael Jackson's singles discography, you'll notice something curious, and I daresay that something is a huge part of what cemented his enduring musical legacy. What am I talking about? And why am I talking about it at all? To find out, I need to ask you to join me on a quick walk through his young career. So take my hand; we're off to Never-Neverland.

Jackson of course started his career exceptionally young as a member and, rapidly, frontman of the Jackson 5. Motown legends with several big hits of their own, the Jackson 5 eventually split and Michael went solo while only 13. He had some hit singles in these teenage years, still deeply entrenched in that Motown mould: 'Got to Be There', 'Ben', a cover of 'Rockin' Robin'...songs that may vary in energy, but all fit snugly into the Motown feel and label. By the time he starred in the 1978 film The Wiz, Jackson had followed a natural evolution into soul and R&B, which would be fully realised on *Off the Wall*, his landmark 1979 album and first away from the Motown label. Big hits again - 'Don't Stop 'Til You Get Enough' and 'Rock With You', to name a couple - solidified him as an R&B great, such that once 1982's *Thriller* came around he was able to rope the likes of Paul McCartney into duetting with him on 'The Girl is Mine', which topped the American R&B charts. 'Billie Jean' continued his meteoric success, blending funk with those now signature R&B elements.

And then, seemingly out of nowhere, there's 'Beat It'. An unapologetically pure rock-and-roll jam, complete with an Eddie Van Halen guitar solo so blistering it literally caused the studio monitor speakers to burst into flames (seriously, this is a true story and worth your effort to look up). Where did this come from?! Rock is a realm reserved for those who live and breathe it, right? The dudes and dudettes who can chew up a piece of iron and spit bullets back out at you. What right does this Motown/R&B star have to make a hard rock song? Moreover, what right does he have to make it *so dang good*?

'Land of Confusion' is THAT song for me in the Genesis canon. Sure, they'd by this time amassed a number of hits, and in some cases hits with a bit of darkness or a slight edge to them, but this is a band known for noodly prog passages and radio-friendly pop dalliances. They're the folks who made a big surrealist concept album and then evolved into the guys who can kick out a nice pop ballad or the odd piano-centric hit. Heck, from *Invisible Touch* itself the band released the title track, straightforward 80s pop as it was, and then 'In Too Deep', a beautiful and well-crafted but equally straightforward-sounding ballad. And now...pulsing drums and edgy guitar riffs? A thumping bass line with an almost shouty vocal, full of reverb? Genesis can straight up *rock*?

> **Tony:** *You know, when we came into this business back in [the late 60s]...God, I'm old...we did [From] Genesis to Revelation. We were with Jonathan King, we were trying to do hit singles. That's what we were trying to do, just trying to write hits. And no one would do them, and we didn't appear to be that good at doing it. And then I think we were sort of shown the way by groups at the time like King Crimson, Family, and Fairport Convention - another way of approaching music a little bit. And that's why we went toward the progressive thing. And we found that we were kind of able to do things in that area that no one else was doing. Whereas in the pop area, we weren't so original. By the time we got to this stage [in the 80s], I think we just felt we'd kind of almost gone as far as we could in certain directions, of going into deep progressive music and extended solos and the rest of it. The idea of trying to craft songs a little bit more was quite appealing.* [3]

I mean, hot dang. And I know this isn't just me feeling this way, because 'Land of Confusion' even got a proper cover in 2006 that *itself* hit 1 on the US Rock charts.

> **Phil:** *A Chicago band called Disturbed had done a cover version of 'Land of Confusion' and taken it into a heavy metal/grunge area. We thought we would bring a little bit of that into the song as well [for the 2007 tour], to acknowledge the fact that it could sound a little bit different, more modern.* [1]

And indeed, if you listen to that 2007 live version you'll find that they followed through; the guitars are noticeably heavier there than on the original studio track. Genesis recognised they had a pure-blooded rock song on their hands and felt they hadn't really been leaning into that enough.

Where did this come from? In the Michael Jackson case, his producer simply said "You should do a rock track on this album" and Jackson went "OK" and spat out 'Beat It'. That's incredible, but it's also just one person. Genesis was a three-man writing team, which by now was splitting their responsibilities evenly across the board.

> **Tony:** *I'm proud of every song on this album. I feel very strongly that all the songs are products of the combination of the three of us being in the same room at the same time.* [85]

What this tells me was that, unlike in the case of 'Beat It', 'Land of Confusion' wasn't even a conscious effort to go down the heavier rock channel. Which means that somehow all three members of Genesis must've been on the same mental page to guide their music further down this path than it had really been before, and they somehow managed to do it with astounding expertise.

> **Tony:** *By the time of Invisible Touch, we went in with such confidence: everything was flowing out of us. We were writing songs left, right, and centre. The improvisation was producing results. I think we were working really well together; we knew our strengths and weaknesses, but we were still challenging each other. We weren't complacent. We suddenly got really good at writing these shorter songs. There's virtually no song on that album you could say was by one person rather than another. It was very much writing as a totality, three people writing almost as one. If you listen to a song like 'Land of Confusion' you might think, "How could three people write a song like that?" And I can't really answer that question, but that's how it was.* [1]

And while I'm sure this sounds like a crazy statement and almost nobody reading this will agree with me, I don't even think the song sounds that dated. I get why that opinion sounds ludicrous: the choruses are punctuated by rapid-fire synth notes, the drums pop in that very Collins way, heck, even the entire bassline is just pushed through Tony's keyboard.

> **Tony:** *The secret of using sequencing well is incorporation. [On 'Land of Confusion'] I use a whole sequenced bassline. Originally it was an addition to the song but it ended up being one of the major aspects of it. I find that quite exciting, I must admit.* [85]

But it's somehow still timeless to me. Part of that is the lyrics, which, as mentioned before in the entry for 'Domino' fall in that mode of "I'm mad and want to channel that energy into this music" but also "I don't really want to say anything TOO offensive." And again, while I'm sure some people would much rather these lyrics be a more specific, scathing take on this or that, the song endures precisely because it's not.

> **Mike:** *I thought it was time for a protest song. I thought the time was right, after all these years. But done in a very subtle way, you know. Actually, I remember this was the last lyric to be finished, I think. And I was behind schedule, late as usual. [Phil had recorded vocals for] one of the other songs, actually, and I hadn't finished [this one]. Phil works at a great tempo in the studio, which is great; pushes it along, you know. And I remember I was actually in bed with a horrendous sort of flu thing, at home because I was sort of delirious. And he came around and sort of sat in the bedroom, I think. This is how I remember it, I'm sure. And I gave him the lyric, thinking, "I don't know if this is any good." I was in a bit of a fever, a temperature, thinking, "I think it's all right," you know what I mean? And then he sang it. I wasn't there at the time when he sang the first version of it. It really kind of worked.* [3]

Mike in a fever dream, not sure if what he's put on paper is even coherent. Phil just making it work anyway. What a unit these guys were.

> **Mike:** *It was a bit of a protest song, you know. I mean, a bit simple, yeah. "The world's a great place; what a mess we're making of it."* [43]

That idea is just as relevant in now as it was in 1986. I have no idea what the current year is for you, dear reader, as you read this book. But I feel pretty dang confident that we'll still be making a mess of the world, somehow and in some way. You'll be able to put on 'Land of Confusion' and apply it to the current struggles of your world and it will work just fine. But "Cold War bad?" No, that doesn't carry anywhere near the weight now that it would've at the time, and it will carry even less the further into the future we go. Which brings us to the award-winning music video for 'Land of Confusion' and the way it sacrificed timelessness for sales; a decision I'm sure the band would probably make again, but still!

> **Tony:** *[Music videos] sort of became a thing you had to do, almost. We weren't naturally inclined to do it...Mike and I could do it as best we could in the background...The songs that were most difficult in a way were the ones that didn't have any particular thing to act out. A song like 'In Too Deep', for example, was quite difficult to do - it was just a performance video. We did a few of those, which was OK. But if we could get a little idea to do something to hang it on, and hopefully with just a little bit of wit, as well, that was what we were after.* [90]

How do you improve upon a bland performance video? How do you counteract the awkwardness of having Mike and Tony on camera pretending to play music in the background? A stroke of genius - take them out of the video entirely!

> **Tony:** *Well 'Land of Confusion' was a lyric that Mike wrote. Obviously it was a sort of much more straightforward political message, and being a more instant song and more of a hit, it probably had slightly more effect [than 'Domino']. And the video was great fun to do for that, you know. I mean, it's the best video we ever did, far and away, because we're not in it! It's as simple as that.* [3]

> **Mike:** *It was intended to be slightly tongue-in-cheek...The video was taking a satirical look at President Reagan and I have to admit they portrayed him as a rather useless president. The final scene showed him in bed, suffering from dementia, and accidentally pressing the red button to start a nuclear war instead of the nurse's call button.* [14]

Of course, the Cold War ended while the US was under the administration of Reagan's former vice president, and of course, Ronald Reagan eventually died of Alzheimer's Disease, so the music video today not only feels like a potential political whiff, but also like a really heartless and cruel jab at a person who lost his life to a terrible illness. Nobody could have known any of this at the time, naturally. It just felt like your everyday, run-of-the-mill political mudslinging. But that's sort of my point here: non-specific lyrics may be milquetoast, yes, but they also never make you look like a total jerk in the end. So I really think Mike had the right idea here lyrically, not to overcommit to too specific a time or place.

Now we look back on 'Land of Confusion' as simply one of many Genesis radio hits, one more checkmark in the "prog no more" box for the critics. But it's easy to forget just what a big deal it was at the time, and how much it elevated the band's perception within its own era.

> **Tony:** *'Land Of Confusion' was something that really worked for me and it was great taking something that was really simple and making it work and getting what we were after. We had always done simple songs in the past but missed it... things like 'Your Own Special Way' for example, we didn't get out of it what we had put into it.* [6]

> **Mike:** *What happened round about then - the Mama album and Invisible Touch - is that videos came out. And so the profile of a hit single was so huge that any other tracks on the album were just overshadowed.* [43]

> **Phil:** *This is the tour on which we start to have underwear thrown at us onstage. Prior to this we'd get the odd shoe - were people limping home? - but now it's underwear. Why?...Tom Jones isn't touring this year?* [12]

> **Tony:** *We did get to the stage around Invisible Touch and just after when we were a big band. So you become the kind of thing that everybody goes to see because you're in town, rather than particularly because everyone's a fan.* [43]

> **Touring drummer Chester Thompson:** *I remember a couple conversations about that, where the Genesis concert was "the event." This is where you went if you were really hip; you had to be at the Genesis concert. And you know, when that happens when you've been used to like, real fans there, then I think that takes a bit away from it.* [43]

Chester's right in that something is lost when you migrate from the intimate nature of theatres to the uncountable crowds of arenas and stadiums, where hundreds of people at any one time might be milling about aimlessly instead of actually tuning into the music. But that's the price of resounding success, I suppose. And 'Land of Confusion' was - and still is - a resounding success. A timeless rock song, elevated yet simultaneously undermined by its landmark music video, serving surprisingly as one of the most enduring legacies of a pioneering progressive outfit. Land of confusion, indeed.

27 - Blood on the Rooftops

from *Wind & Wuthering*, 1976

While it might be said that choosing 'Wot Gorilla?' for *Wind & Wuthering* over 'Please Don't Touch' was something of a straw that broke the camel's back in terms of Steve Hackett finally leaving Genesis, 'Blood on the Rooftops' seems to be Exhibit A for the argument of "Why wouldn't you use more of this guy's material?" Now, things are always more complex than they seem, and the ever-diplomatic Steve isn't going to say anything unkind about this period if he can help it.

> **Steve:** *I felt I was coming up with far too many ideas for the band to fully explore, and in order to develop I felt I had to work with some other people. I already was working with great people in Genesis. I realised at this point that they were a great band and they were great at what they did and they'd done great things, but I felt to prove or to attempt that level of greatness for myself, I had to do that outside of the band. I felt that I needed to paint pictures on my own which would not be seen as a threat to the established order, almost. It was perceived as a threat however, and it was basically a two year decision. I didn't make it lightly; it didn't happen overnight. I think I perhaps underestimated how difficult it was going to be but nonetheless, even now I still think it was the right decision for me...* [30]

But as much as 'Blood on the Rooftops' is a fantastic example of how strong Steve's songwriting could be, it's also a pretty good case study for why he might have needed to leave. For one thing, it represents the peak of his confidence during his time with the band; while Phil Collins would continue on in the "junior member" mould for another album or two, Steve felt he'd already grown beyond that.

> **Steve:** *Probably throughout the whole of the period with the band, I always thought, "What would it be like if I wasn't with the band?" I mean, I used to think that the band were very accomplished songwriters, and I very often used to find it intimidating working with people who were so gifted, and who were so quick and brilliant. And it took I think a long time for my confidence to get to the point where I felt like an equal. I think it probably didn't happen until Wind & Wuthering, really.* [3]

> **Tony:** *He'd kind of been growing in confidence I think over the years with Genesis. You know, you must appreciate that when we started off, that both Phil and Steve were very much junior members, particularly in relation to the composition. And I think at this stage, with Mike and I perhaps being dominant on Trick of the Tail, and we probably were on Wind & Wuthering as well I think, but he definitely had more moments when he came to the fore. This was particularly true I think on 'Blood on the Rooftops', which I think is a lovely track.* [3]

For another, a lot of what Steve was bringing to the table, brimming with confidence though it might have been, was stuff that the other three guys in the group just couldn't really connect with. These pieces felt, perhaps, a little *too* wild and adventurous for where the group wanted to go.

> **Phil:** *A lot of his things - 5/4, 7/8, 9/8 bits - were all over the place. It wasn't really happening...Songs have to turn us all on. There might be exceptions, but 99 times out of 100 each song appears on an album because everyone likes it.* [10]

> **Tony:** *Or at least they can contribute to it. We felt we couldn't do much with Steve's songs; I know Steve found that difficult to accept.* [10]

So why did 'Blood on the Rooftops' work for everyone where the other material fell flat? I think it's probably because it wasn't a fully-formed idea coming into the group. Instead it was more like a couple different, smaller ideas: a classical guitar introduction and a dark, haunting verse melody.

> **Steve:** *I felt 'Blood on the Rooftops' explored new territory as it was subtly different structurally with a long guitar introduction. I was starting to incorporate nylon guitar into the picture much more, which I felt gave the band an added dimension: unusual for rock.* [70]

> **Steve:** *[The nylon guitar intro] sets the song up and it's very personal. There's an aspect of classical, which establishes the scene for something stark...I was thinking of Jimmy Webb and some of his more unlikely melodies.* [27]

Indeed, the opening guitar is very intimate. It's a call-back of sorts to 'Horizons', that moment in time when a Genesis track was able to consist of just Steve, an acoustic guitar, and a dream. And just like that track, this is a completely captivating little bit of music, pulling you in. The difference here is that after only a minute and change, vocals enter and a larger song begins to form.

Tony: *He had written a great introduction and a beautiful verse, but again it was just a wonderful piece of music with no chorus.* [1]

Wonderful is a great adjective here; the verses carry on that classical guitar feel in a buttery smooth transition, but everything around that core acoustic guitar sound is this dense, foggy stuff that creates a truly compelling atmosphere which swells and declines in a manner not unlike the sleepy breathing of some great beast. You're full of wonder as you listen, unsure of where these inhales and exhales are taking you.

Tony: *'Blood on the Rooftops' was one of the best pieces of composition Steve ever did with us...I love that song. It's a beautiful song and because I had nothing to do with the writing of it, I can be a little more detached; it still moves me when I hear it now.* [1]

But at the time, those deep breaths weren't taking you anywhere at all. As Tony indicated, there was no chorus. Nowhere clear for these gorgeous verses themselves to lead a listener. And what this meant was that the piece would need to be finished by the band, rather than Steve - "junior member" that he was - coming in and telling everyone else precisely what to play, as he would've likely done in the rehearsals of 'Please Don't Touch'. Instead, they had a canvas to work with, an avenue by which the more senior writers of the band could contribute. Yet in the end it was fellow junior Genesisian Phil, of all people, who had a complementary bit just laying around.

Phil: *I had the chorus for ages, just the chorus and nothing else.* [31]

Steve: *The chorus musically of 'Blood on the Rooftops' was Phil's. And the idea for the title of the song was Phil's. 'Blood on the Rooftops'.* [3]

Tony: *Phil had a simple chorus that sounded good, with the line "blood on the rooftops" but no other words...* [1]

It's a strange kind of foreshadowing of what would come with Phil in the 80s and 90s: here's Phil, by his own admission not anything like a songwriter, coming up with a really strong chorus hook and splurting out a line of "blood on the rooftops" out of nowhere, for no apparent reason other than an inexplicable instinct of sound. And as lovely as the song's intro and verses are, it's the chorus that really makes the song work in the end.

Steve: *Tying the two together appeared like a complete botch...The number didn't work in the rehearsal room. It was one of those numbers which never work in the rehearsal room. You just have to accept it can work in the studio and just rehearse the parts in the rehearsal room.* [31]

And yet, even though it didn't quite appear to come together at first, and though they didn't do any primary writing on the piece, now that it wasn't strictly a Steve solo effort Mike and Tony felt a bit more at liberty to add their own touches to the song as well, which dramatically increased their buy-in. Tony's tossing in those big floaty keys, Mike's tossing in a particularly melodic bassline to make that chorus even more powerful...no wonder they got fully behind the thing.

Tony: *I had a lot of fun with the arrangement. I was trying to make it into an enormous orchestrated piece using the Mellotron. The combination of everything works really well.* [27]

Mike: *It was great. Steve and Phil was a nice combination, it really worked. And you can see Phil starting to get a handle on melodies.* [27]

Tony: *The chords are much more sort of expansive, if you like. And the way they change is sort of more yearning. This is about as far away as you can get from sort of straight ahead, three chord rock. I like a bit of that myself, but this album is far away from it.* [3]

Steve: *Luckily the band went to town on it, and we had the Mellotron and everything. It's pretty dark. Very English sounding tune...* [3]

From there, all that was left was the lyric. Phil's random, off-the-cuff phrase of "blood on the rooftops" was too good to discard - again, a portent of things to come from him - so Steve figured with such a pretty song, he'd find a way to make something romantic of it.

Steve: *The lyrics probably glued it together...[They] were done as a love song, believe it or not. [But] when I heard the other lyrics on the album there was a bit of a romantic twinge anyway so I decided to go right the other way and decided to make it as cynical as possible. There's also some political references too, which we normally stay away from.* [31]

Welp, out with that idea I guess. Instead, the song functions as a little vignette, a view into a father and son enjoying some quality time with one another in front of the television. The dark imagery, the contentious lyrics, the titular blood on the rooftops? Well, that's all stuff that's *on* the TV, and stuff which ol' pops doesn't much care to see.

> **Steve:** *I came up with this song with the idea of all the levels of action happening on the TV...[There's] something about the song...very much a song in black and white...I think it defines this very black and white album known as Wind & Wuthering.* [13]

> **Mike:** *We tend to write romantic, fairy tale lyrics but on this one Steve has tried to come out a bit harder, and it's about the juxtaposition of various television images. On TV is the news, and in the background someone is making the tea.* [36]

> **Steve:** *English TV, limited channels, but channel surfing nonetheless. When composing the lyric, all these references to different characters and scenes. But essentially, it's two guys, father and son, watching TV together. The son is pretty much open to watching anything, but the father - having lived through a World War or two - really doesn't want the news. He doesn't want death and destruction...I was trying to be controversial when I was writing the lyric, and there are many things that I'd heard in conversation [that] I thought, "I wonder if that can work in a lyric?" You know, the idea of "when we got bored we'd have a world war."* [13]

It all just gels supremely well. It's a gloomy, overcast, maybe rainy day. Not much to do but make some tea and see what's on the telly. But everything in the real world is basically awful, so let's watch something detached and mindless. This is great son, innit?

> **Steve:** *I enjoyed writing lyrics contrasting the claustrophobic, safe world of TV viewers with the range of world events they glimpse.* [39]

> **Steve:** *I wrote the verse picturing a man and his son avoiding reality through the world of television - as with people in Plato's The Cave, only being able to experience life through watching shadow puppets move around a cave wall.* [70]

This is 'For Absent Friends' all grown up. That one was a lovely little painting of a quiet street corner; simple, elegant, charming. Now Collins and Hackett are back again delivering another painting, just as stunning, yet not quite at peace. Complex now and cynical, but no less elegant. It's not Hackett Goes Wild: The Musical. It's, well, Genesis.

> **Tony:** *That was the first time that Steve's writing had really fitted into the band and it was Phil's chorus with Steve's verse so it was both of them...* [6]

> **Mike:** *'Blood on the Rooftops'...was quite important. Big part of Steve on that one. And it's a lovely song. It's a forgotten song, and every time you hear it you kinda go, "Wow, that's nice. I didn't rate that so much." I think it's one of Steve's best moments, actually, on the writing side.* [3]

Steve had to leave the band because in order to make Genesis music, he needed Genesis. And for as much material as he was amassing on his own and yearning to record, it simply wasn't really "Genesis music." 'Blood on the Rooftops', however, is not only Genesis music, but some of the absolute best Genesis music there is. It's a fitting swan song for the four-piece era and its guitarist, but bear in mind the silver lining as you wave your tearful goodbyes: that chorus is still Phil's, and he's not going anywhere anytime soon.

26 - Way of the World

from *We Can't Dance*, 1991

I sit at my computer, silent except for the distant sounds of play from my children downstairs, and I have a vision. In my mind I can already picture the army of heavily furrowed eyebrows. I can almost hear the quiet grumblings, the sharp exhales of furious disbelief. If I close my eyes, I can see a wide variety of readers, diverse in demographics, but united in their bewilderment. Their comments are all the same: "I get you like this song, I guess, but *above 'Song X' I personally happen to like even more?! What's wrong with you?!*"

This is a track almost universally panned by critics - even those who generally liked *We Can't Dance* on the whole. It's one of the most common examples cited by Genesis fans as a case of CD-era bloat; a filler track that would be a semi-decent B-side *at best* but that somehow sits in an unearned place on the album, soiling the overall product by its mere presence. That a person might rank it here, near the top of the mountain of a song catalogue so rich with material that is so *obviously* better - by leaps and bounds! - than this yuckamuck snoozefest of pop nonsense is downright offensive. So again, they ask as they shake their fists at the sky in consternation: "What's *wrong* with him?"

It's fitting, then, that 'Way of the World' is basically 'Deal With It: The Song'. It's a lyrical showcase of really interesting hypothetical metaphors being used like proverbs to make a point. "Take the danger out of a naked flame and what have you got?" Or, in other words, "If you could get the change you're clamouring for, you wouldn't be too pleased with the results." I particularly love the final line of the last verse: "Could you swear if you had that second chance you wouldn't do it again?" It's such a strongly convicting line, because we're all guilty of that. Think about a big regret you have, something you've always wished you might've done differently. If you found yourself in a similar situation again, would you choose a different path? Would you *really*? Or would you look at the situation in the same way because you're the same person and thus make the same choice because it still seems the most reasonable one at the time? And then regret *that* too, afterward? I think to some degree or another, we've all been there.

This lyric is just Mike Rutherford calling us all out, isn't it? More specifically, he's calling out Phil Collins, if secondary sources are to be believed. If you've been reading this book from the beginning, you've probably realised by now that I pride myself on providing primary-sourced quotes from the band wherever I'm able. Video and audio transcriptions, direct quotes from books written by the band members, official interviews in all manner of media - I've used 'em all. But for 'Way of the World', all I could really find is reference in a couple different places to a radio interview the band did in late 1991 to promote the album, for which there is apparently no surviving audio or official transcription, and therefore no way for me to independently corroborate and source the quotes. But if the "word on the street," is to be believed, Mike Rutherford stated that this song's lyrics were a response to Phil's own 'Tell Me Why'.

That's hilarious to me, because 'Tell Me Why' was a preachy bag of hot air, Phil's third and most oppressively overbearing attempt at reminding the world that poverty and strife exist. And while I'm sure Phil thought this was a great and noble thing - he wrote it after all - he might have been the only one. As cited in that song's entry earlier in this book, Tony was pretty gung-ho about the song until Phil's lyrics ruined it. Heck, even on tour for the album he was still enthusiastic:

> **Tony:** *I still think the best single on the album is 'Tell Me Why', which we never released. And, you know, apart from Europe, never looks likely to get released.* [38]

You can't see it in the text transcript there obviously, but Tony was frowning at the end of that statement. He was frowning because he correctly sensed how things were going to play out. 'Tell Me Why' was indeed eventually released as the sixth single from *We Can't Dance*, but only in Europe, and its overall chart performance was worse than everything that came before it, because everyone had already heard Phil Freaking Collins telling them to solve the world's problems twice before.

Meanwhile, returning now to those somewhat dubious secondary sources, Mike was penning a rebuke to 'Tell Me Why' long before listeners ever got to vote with their wallets. "Tell you why? Here's why: because that's how it is. That's how it always has been. Deal with it and move on." In the aforementioned radio interview, here's what Mike supposedly said.

> *It's good to try to put things right, but you shouldn't forget there will always be a balance of highs and lows in the world...[Phil's] the caring one and I'm the uncaring one!*

For the record, despite not being able to verify it, I totally believe this was said. It's just such a very Mike thing to say, and such a very Mike attitude to have. And I love the fact that 'Way of the World' is not only on the album but that it also comes after 'Tell Me Why' in the track order. It's like the ultimate clapback to Phil here: "OK, you can bloviate a bit if you want to, but then I'm going to force you to vocally contradict yourself on a much better, much more catchy tune, and that's what people are going to hear second and better remember." It's like one last pulling of rank, a final "know your role and shut your mouth" from senior to junior Member of Genesis. It's such a devastating power play that in my own head canon it basically made Phil quit the band.

> **Phil:** *I was flying somewhere with [Genesis manager] Tony Smith, and I told him the way I was feeling. "I think I'm leaving it now. I don't think I want to go to that group situation where I have to sing lyrics that I didn't write…"* [1]

That's a K.O. my friends, Rutherford over Collins in the 12th round. Zip zap zow, ya gone. Score one for callous disregard!

And the thing is, 'Way of the World' *is* much better than 'Tell Me Why' musically. It *is* much more catchy. *We Can't Dance* is a twelve song album where literally HALF of them were released as singles, and this wasn't one of them, yet it's the catchiest dang thing on the record. Heck, I'd go so far as to say it's possibly the straight-up catchiest song Genesis *ever* did. What is this thing doing as album filler? Get this sucker on the radio, man! Back before I really knew the ins and outs of the band's discography, I always assumed this actually *was* a single, because how could it not be? For crying out loud, I'm getting super pumped just frickin' writing about it!

WE ALLLLLL AGREE. AS FAR AS WEEEE CAN SEE. OO [oo] [oo] [oooo] IT'S JUST (IT'S JUST) THE WAY OF THE WORLD. AND THAT'S HOW IT'S MEANT TO BE. (MMHMMMM) THERE'S RIGHT (THERE'S RIGHT!), AND THERE'S WRONG. THERE'S WEAK, OHHHHHHHHHHH AND THERE'S STRONG! OO [oo] [oo] [oooo] 'CUZ IT'S JUST (IT'S JUST) THE WAY OF THE WORLD. AND THAT'S HOW IT'S MEANT TO BE OHHHHHHHHHH

I'd say I'm sorry for that caps-locked lyric spam, but I'M NOT because THIS IS THE SONG OF GIVING ZERO FLYING CHUCKLEDUCKS. Y'all can sit there and chew on this little Tony synth guitar mini-solo for a while and think about how much you're missing by choosing not to fall in love with this song. I was gonna sit here and write about how the whole blue sky/red sky thing was a great, still-relevant metaphor troubled political times, and I was gonna sit here and write about this popping snare beat, and I was gonna sit here and write about how pristine this production is and all the little layers, but NOT NO MORE YA FOOLS. I gots jammin' to do.

> **Mike:** *To be honest, I don't really think about an audience…I don't care what they think, really. It's very important that you don't actually give a damn about them.* [35]

WE ALLLLLLLLLLLLLLLL AGREEEEEEEEEEEEE…

25 - Tonight, Tonight, Tonight

from *Invisible Touch*, 1986

If anyone ever asks me how I feel about radio edits, I snarl, whip out an oversized boombox from my pocket, shove in a cassette tape of *Invisible Touch* I happen to have on hand, politely ask them to wait a moment while I fast forward past the title track, shove nine-ish minutes of 'Tonight, Tonight, Tonight' in their face, and then I say, "RADIO EDITS BLOW!" and storm off with my giant pocket boombox. This has happened like eight times in my life in precisely this way, so you know I'm not just making this story up to make a point. The single/radio edit of 'Tonight, Tonight, Tonight' cuts out flippin' half the song. HALF! It's a song with a runtime of 8:50 that gets reduced to 4:32 in the single cut, and no, I won't accept excuses about ad breaks and pop radio listener attention spans because I'm a man of principle. The edit doesn't simply cut out a measure here or there, oh no. It scraps the WHOLE MIDDLE OF THE SONG. It's all Monkey with none of the Zulu. What's the point?

> **Tony:** *We edited it down as a single, and it was a big hit in the States particularly. And it was a hit here [in the UK] too, actually. But obviously the extended version has quite a long middle eight. It's more like a traditional Genesis song: it goes through lots of changes and there's this very ethereal middle part, which is a very nice piece of music actually, but it didn't make it onto the single. It's, you know...I guess I can't put my finger on what it is, really. Obviously Phil had become more established as a singles act. That opened a few doors for us in terms of radio...[they] were prepared to sort of listen to it, I suppose. But I think the songs were there anyhow.* [3]

> **Phil:** *It's kind of still one of those journey songs. It went through different changes. You know, it was outside the kind of format of singles. We were just writing how we felt like at the time. And we weren't trying to have hit singles, we weren't trying to be commercial; I just think that's the way it just happened to have turned out on that record.* [3]

Yeah, you hear that? Not even trying to be commercial. But let's gut this Monkey anyway, yeah? It's outrageous is what it is. But I suppose I should back up here a little bit and explain a couple terms here, as I'm sure there's a good chance you're reading this and wondering, "Monkey? Zulu? What is he even talking about?"

Oh I'll tell you what I'm talking about. I'm talking about the footage that's out there of the band putting the verse section through its paces before any vocals were added, where you can see the three guys just really going after it. Tony's strutting out his head and neck like some kind of majestic keyboard pigeon. Mike's slow dancing with what appears to be a little toddler guitar (actually a Steinberger). Phil's off in his own world, grinning and daydreaming because his electronic drumkit is basically just an extension of his body that he doesn't even need to think about. He's playing a pattern that feels very jungle-drummy. Sort of Tarzan-esque, a full decade before he'd actually be making Tarzan music with Disney. And all of this is happening while they're wearing sweaters over their collared shirts because they're too dang classy for rock and roll. It's...it's beautiful.

> **Tony:** *The first part was called 'Monkey' and the second part was called 'Zulu'. I think it was just because Phil, when we were just improvising words on it, he was just going "ya ya ya, la la la, lala monkey," you know. So that sort of stuck, I think. And the second part, I don't know why it was called 'Zulu'...I think it was the drum rhythm. It just sort of had a feel like that.* [38]

So there you go. 'Monkey' and 'Zulu', sitting in a tree, K-I-S-S-I-N-G and then you get 'Monkey/Zulu' and then that gets words and becomes 'Tonight, Tonight, Tonight', OK? So now you know what I'm talking about. 'Monkey' is everything except the big instrumental break (i.e. the entire single edit) and 'Zulu' is the instrumental break itself. I've dwelled on these working titles to emphasise the way Genesis was working at this time. The improvisation was just flowing almost effortlessly from these sessions, and 'Tonight, Tonight, Tonight' in particular is a great example of what can happen when the old Genesis mentality of "I've got a bit here, you've got a bit there" is mixed with the hivemind of improvisational songwriting they had working at this time.

> **Tony:** *I think one that was sort of always going along pretty early was 'Tonight, Tonight, Tonight', which we sort of had a lot of confidence in from the word go. But the actual shape it...a lot of it we kind of left fairly open until we were recording it, and then we sort of said like, "Well I'll do something on those thirty bars there," or something, and then the thing starts to take shape a bit.* [73]

Mike: *'Tonight, Tonight, Tonight' I think is a prime example of that phase of writing where Phil would start with this great little sort of loop thing, you know, drum machine with echo sound on it. So when the song starts, before we've even played a note - myself or Tony - you've got this atmosphere. That's sort of setting the stage. And then Tony plays some chords, and off we go, I think. That's a very strong song, I think. It's very unique. There's nothing else we've done quite like it. There are certain songs you can liken to other songs before, but 'Tonight, Tonight, Tonight', the sound I think is very original.* [3]

The recording process itself was wild, too.

Phil: *The way we record is a peculiar way, really. After we've decided that we've got all the components for the songs, or this particular song we might be working on, we'll then go and put the track down. Now the track consists of a drum machine, which is a rough. You know, one mix out, a rough because I'm gonna put drums on it afterwards. I'll put a vocal down with it, which'll be rough, purely for reference because there's no words. I mean, there's lyrics, but not completed lyrics. Then Tony will play a guide keyboard part, which will be a rough. And then Mike will put a rough guitar part down...and then we say, "Right, well that's that!" So we've done the backing track, but we're gonna keep nothing of it. We then go back and put the drums on. Then we put the keyboards on properly, bits and pieces at a time if that's what we require. So we end up doing a backing track that we don't actually keep! It's a peculiar way of working, but the idea in the end is that it sounds as if it was done like that. And if it doesn't sound like it's done like that, then we go back and do it again, or do aspects of it again.* [73]

Can you believe that? They make a bunch of stuff up, just finding what sounds all right. "Oh, these chords are nice, we'll use them." Then they fill out that idea with the other parts. "Say, that's a nice guitar accent, and I like that bit about the monkey." Then they start shoving multiple such bits together. "Hey, maybe this can go into that intense sort of bit I've got that sounds like a warrior tribe going off to battle." Then they rehearse it all, as seen in the clip above. Then they record it all, and then record it all again to get a finished product.

Except here, as Tony said, they *didn't* have a finished product when they started the recording process!

Tony: *The middle section of that we had to leave blank because we had to think of something to go in there, and those are the kinds of things that appeal to me.* [6]

What you're hearing on record is raw creativity, pretty much in the moment. "We're laying this down now, so I'm gonna just do whatever and we'll see how it turns out." It's such a far cry from the meticulous crafting that went into a lot of the band's earlier work, but as a result it hits you with some really unexpected things. Tony's finding all these random, obscure sounds on his rig and playing them over the top of this riff, and somehow they all just work; they all produce more of that same musical smoke that obscures the song in a fog of menacing disquiet. It's a terrific atmosphere, and one that might not have been possible to create back in the 1970s.

Tony: *On 'Tonight, Tonight, Tonight' it's a MIDI thing with a marimba all the way through, but at the same time I was playing the Prophet 10 on Drone so the chord would float over from one part to the next - so you're never quite sure where one stops and another starts.* [85]

These technology advancements were especially vital to playing the song live.

Tony: *I tend to divide the keyboard up so that the notes I'm not using as part of the melody have the other parts on them. For example, on the song 'Tonight, Tonight, Tonight' there's a bit in the middle where there are a couple of string lines and an oboe part. I was also playing a chord at the same time through all of this, which means I've only got one hand to do the rest. Since it's in G minor, rather than splitting the keyboard with strings up here and oboes down there, all the notes in G minor are strings, and all that aren't are oboes. As long as you keep your head, you're okay. Of course, the wrong notes don't sound as bad as they might normally, because I've put them in G minor too, but still you've got to keep your head. I try to keep it logical, so that it works out to being in E natural minor, or A natural minor, or something when I'm playing the oboe parts, but there's one time I can't do that - there's one note I have to drop altogether, so the phrase I play on the keyboard isn't actually logical unto itself. But it means that I can actually play the whole part without doing jumps - it sounds awful if you do it like that. I have to use a sustain pedal to keep the last note going. Then I can play the next phrase so that it all overlaps...When we're making the record, I've got all these disks totally separate. When I've got to play the thing on stage, then I work out how I'm going to split the keyboard up. Performing that way probably sounds more complicated than it is; all you've got to do is learn what you're doing. You can't improvise, obviously, but it's fantastic to be able to lay out the keyboard parts like that.* [68]

For a translation of the above, Tony can program different keys of the keyboard to do different sounds, meaning he doesn't have to jump his hands around the keys or even to multiple other keyboards at all to play the song, which was borderline unfathomable back in the 70s. But what it also means is that the creativity didn't end with the songwriting itself. At least for Tony, writing and recording the song was only the first step; from there he had to be creative again in figuring out how to program his instrument to do all the things he needed it to, and then actually relearn the entire song under a new configuration to make it all work live. It's really incredible to think about.

Of course, the song did suffer live later, going from a 9 minute epic - they're seemingly improvising in that 'Zulu' section even on the Invisible Touch Tour - to a token inclusion in a mini-medley, barely recognisable as they repeatedly lowered the key over the ages. I mean, it's understandable: if you watch footage of the band playing Wembley Stadium in 1987, you can see how hard Phil's working to sing the chorus, and they were already performing the song in a lower key than the album. But after a while you just can't drop things any further, you know?

> **Tony:** *The only problem when we played that song live was that we had to take it down a semitone, but if we tried to take it down a [full] tone for Phil's voice, the marimba would just sound awful. So we couldn't do it, and that was the problem with that album: you could push it as high as you wanted - and it was the same with Peter - [but] when you got this stuff to the stage, you couldn't really do it and you had to try and change the keys. It could be a nightmare, but of course, with modern technology you could do that with a button.* [21]

Technology makes it possible, but I've got to agree with Tony here: that three-note flavour pattern is so pivotal in making this song work, and it just sounds downright horrible when lowered down to accommodate Old Man Phil's deeper voice. By the 21st century the stage version of 'Tonight, Tonight, Tonight' was committing *both* cardinal concert sins: lowering to an unworkable key AND editing down the song. I mean, when 'Invisible Touch' runs longer than 'Tonight, Tonight, Tonight', something's very wrong, isn't it? At that point I'd rather the song not be in the live set at all than be thrust out there as 'Tranquilised Monkey', but what are you gonna do? The fans want the hits, I suppose.

But for me anyway, this is a studio track through and through. It's a nine-minute snapshot into the tortured mind of an addict growing increasingly desperate for that next hit. It's not just a lyrical thing, either; the drums on this song are very sneakily the representation of that hunger. You've got that twitchy drum machine pattern going for about a minute and a half, all the way through the first chorus before any real snares pop in. Now bear with me here, but I think that drum pattern is actually the measure of sanity - structured and rational - while the actual drums are by contrast craving-induced *in*sanity. When the snares first come in, it's just a four-shot blast and then they're gone again. An arresting burst of need, perhaps. That same four-shot comes back again mid-verse, but on a different, weaker drum sound. Still urgent, but now less clear, and in an inconvenient place. Then you get a faint drum roll into the second chorus, where the snares start hitting once per measure, on the third beat. It likely doesn't even register, but you're slowly getting accustomed to hearing a real drum sound on the song now through this bit. The need is more frequent, but still feels under control somehow: it's only once a measure, that's not so bad!

The 'Zulu' middle then kicks off with a double snare hit in an act of ominous foreshadowing before disappearing in favour of the electronic heartbeat pattern that underlays the entire stressful exercise above. Synth strings build along with percussive sounds of all sorts, so out there and distracting that we don't really register the significance of that actual drum coming back in at around 4:30. It's now hitting on the second and fourth beats, which is twice as often as it was when last seen. There's one stray fill in there, and then the big fill going into the vocal return, at which point the drum machine *disappears completely*, having been wholly supplanted by the real thing. And why not? It's a big, epic bridge and that demands big, epic drum sounds, right?

Except then we're back to the verse, and the drum machine pattern is still gone. The real drums are here to stay. It took about six minutes, but the actual drums gradually took over the entire song, and you never really even saw it coming. There is no more rational thought; only the need, the craving. 'Tonight, Tonight, Tonight' isn't just a song *about* addiction, it's constructed *like* addiction. Super cool.

> **Tony:** *I was happy with every track [on the album]. My favourite one is probably 'Tonight, Tonight, Tonight' because it has the atmosphere and it has the chords in it! Here...the drum box helps make an intense song out of it...A little bit more expansive I suppose, and more in the mould of the traditional Genesis.* [6]

As a side note, the word "tonight" appears 43 times in this entry, from the initial title down to this very sentence. And when you look at that word 43 times in rapid succession, it stops looking like a real word at all. It's unsettling. Maybe that's just me, or maybe it's just the atmosphere the song created colouring my feelings on it. But I'm ready to not see the word "tonight" for a good, long while. Dangit... there's number 44.

24 - The Fountain of Salmacis

from *Nursery Cryme*, 1971

Sometimes all it takes to turn a crummy idea into a good one is a new arrangement. Can changing one instrument truly, dramatically change the flavour and feel of a piece in such a radical way? To find out, we need only look to our good pals Genesis and the year 1968. With *From Genesis to Revelation* recorded but unreleased, and not knowing what the future might hold for the band, Tony Banks did what any good Charterhouse lad was supposed to do: he went to college.

> **Tony:** *I went to Sussex University, originally to study chemistry...I was really too shy to make the most of university...I had one or two friends, and it was fine, but I don't think I had a fantastic time...The one thing I didn't get to do...was meet girls. There were plenty of them there, but having come out of Charterhouse, and not really knowing what a woman looked like apart from my sisters, I didn't adjust very well and I certainly didn't make the most of my time. The trouble with science was there were only three girls doing science - one of whom was very pretty actually - but if you could imagine one pretty girl amongst 500 young gentlemen, it certainly wasn't going to be me who was going to win.* [1]

Tony with the ol' self-bunsen-burn there. At any rate, since girls weren't part of the equation, Tony had a lot of time to get familiar with his new Hammond organ. Making up for the lack of experimentation below the belt with experimentation on the keys, as it were. And among the things he came up with during this period was a titillatingly fast little bit of back and forth. Really compelling. So when 1969 came and the band decided to not only press on but also get rid of Jonathan King, who had become something of a creative noose around their collective neck, Tony threw this idea forward and the band played around with it.

The result by 1970 was an unfinished song that received the title of 'Provocation' when it was attached to a painting by that name as part of the soundtrack for a BBC production that never made it to the air. You can hear 'Provocation' on the box set *Genesis: 1970-1975*, complete with a very recognisable organ line at the start of the piece. But what's notable about 'Provocation' and this opening organ bit in particular is that it doesn't last long. Only a minute (and is that an accordion elsewhere in the mix?) before it abruptly stops and goes into a wholly different style and mood, never to return. That longer section, arguably the core of the song, is also recognisable as belonging to 'Looking for Someone'. That song, as we all know, ended up being the striking opener for the band's sophomore effort, *Trespass*.

What this means is that Genesis, democracy that it was, felt that 'Provocation' was worth developing into a fuller, more realised song - and that they needed to drop that useless organ dance at the start to make it worthwhile. Not that Tony didn't still like the bit, but he'd have to find it a new home if it was ever going to see the light of day.

> **Tony:** *'Fountain Of Salmacis', the first main part was something that I wrote when I was at university; I had that bit in the back of my mind for a long time as something to use...* [6]

Meanwhile on *Trespass*, the band had been able to use a Mellotron for the first time, having rented one for the recording sessions. Nothing major: just a couple short, subtle bits here and there. But they were excited enough by the new instrument's possibilities that they decided to actually take the plunge (deeper into debt) and buy one of their own.

> **Tony:** *We decided to buy a Mellotron, that was it. Because we loved the sound, and we used [one] a little bit on Trespass, and we loved the first [King] Crimson album, which had used it extensively. So we actually bought one of the ones off King Crimson, actually.* [3]

And now, going into the writing of their third album, armed with a new toy, Tony revisited his little idea held over from his single year of higher education.

> **Tony:** *I had this piece that I'd written while I was at university, which was just this little organ part really, quite a simple little rundown...And this little riff I'd started off in university, I then tried it with using Mellotron and the organ. And it really developed these great big swells on this thing. And it sounded fantastic...* [3]

> **Steve:** *For me, although the rest of the song is lovely, I find that the song is really characterised by that introduction...it's a Mellotron moment that's supreme. You know, you've got the organ, those lovely chords, the crescendos...* [13]

Listen to the beginning of 'The Fountain of Salmacis' and then listen again to the beginning of 'Provocation'. Tony's left hand is playing essentially the same sequence of chords it was before, but the difference in sound between using the organ and using the Mellotron to play them is really night and day. Such a powerful effect. So much so that now when he plays that same cast-off lick back to the band, the attitudes towards it are suddenly much different.

> **Tony:** *It wasn't until we got things like the Mellotron and realised the things that it could do that it really took shape.* [6]

> **Steve:** *Once we had the Mellotron we were able to do songs such as 'The Fountain of Salmacis'. A combination of keyboard, Hammond organ, and Mellotron together sounded magic. I was keen for us to get an RMI keyboard, which could sound like a harpsichord, but at other times an organ. All these things together added to that special Genesis sound where people often couldn't tell what the sound source was. Was it guitar, was it keyboard? It was very much a calling card of the band.* [70]

And then, that's the other thing, isn't it? Anthony Phillips, one half of the Phillips/Rutherford voting bloc, was gone. In was this new guy who was passionate about doing something really different. Prog folk music? Yeah, that's fine I suppose, but what on earth is *this*?

> **Tony:** *Steve was now an ally in these kinds of areas. I had a chord sequence which became very much a Genesis trademark, where we would be in E minor and go to the chords C and D, often keeping the bass note down on E. Over the years I've done something similar a great number of times. Taking this little sequence and then adding the Mellotron sounded really good and made me realise that you could take what was almost a classical piece and make it sound very exciting, which was a significant realisation for me. The rest of the song was built around that introduction.* [1]

> **Steve:** *I threw myself into it completely. I wracked my brain to come up with the most interesting things and I tried to sound like a keyboard player...I was doing the fading-in of notes. I was eliminating lots of things and trying to play very melodically. I was trying to be the icing on a very fully formed cake.* [29]

Tony's in, Steve's in...

> **Tony:** *Peter had this idea of writing a song about the tale of Hermaphroditus, and we wrote the lyric together.* [1]

Tell Pete he can make the song about sex organs and he's in, too. Phil's the jovial new drummer guy; you know he's just gonna go with the flow, yeah?

> **Phil:** *The problem for me was in the recording. We always sounded really edgy live, and bright, and then when we went into the studio it all seemed to get rounded off. There was the classic moment on 'The Fountain of Salmacis' - take thirty-one. A drummer's best take is usually the second or third take, and I never go past that on my own records. So on take thirty-one you're playing everything safe because you don't want to fuck it up and then at the end of the take everyone says, "That's the one, that's the best take." And then they all go off and replace their own parts, and suddenly I'm the only one who's left with my thirty-first tired take! So I never thought we ever sounded good on record, to be honest, until The Lamb...* [1]

Ooh, not ideal. But hey you like that edgy live sound, right? Just imagine the concerts!

> **Phil:** *'Fountain of Salmacis' was a huge stage song.* [3]

Yeah Phil, it'll be great live! No worries there mate, you just focus on that, and now that's four out of five on board, and at that point, "We're doing this? We're doing this."

Tony: *So we then developed from that opening part into a complete song out of that, a lot of jamming from the rest of the group and everything. But it produced a very strongly romantic sort of thing.* [3]

Steve: *I enjoyed it, especially the allusion to Greek myths. Things like 'The Fountain Of Salmacis' were often more of an odyssey than a song. I call them odysseys because you didn't really know where you were going to end up. The structure doesn't vary that much and this was very important; each song was an adventure, it was a journey.* [29]

That organ opening really sets the tone, but it doesn't work without all the other band input after it; remember that none of that stuff really existed back in 1969/1970. This was Tony's seed, but the plant growing out of it belonged to all of them. New melodies over the organ lines, an active bass line, great textural guitar playing, entire new sections with lots of energy of their own. Including, yes, a big guitar feature in the middle from the band's newest member.

Steve: *'Fountain of Salmacis' required a melodic, atmospheric approach, which perfectly suited my guitar part.* [39]

What's fascinating to me about this song and this section in particular is that this part feels like the natural climax of the thing. You've got this big guitar solo with its caresses of flute, a lyrical bent about the bodies of the two characters intertwining, you've got the drama-building descending backing vocals, and then the big chords coming out of it. But instead of a grand ending, the fountain overflows and the guitar spills out some more before the piece resets itself and drives on for another two and a half minutes.

Steve: *I think it's a fantastically beautiful track, Greek mythology, wonderful story, poetic lyrics, and that gorgeous keyboard stuff - nevermind my guitar contributions, which aren't bad.* [13]

What we get is something of an epilogue, then, where lyrically the "big thing" has already happened and now the fountain is just going to be cursed for all time. And *then* you get the big, grand ending. The musical climax comes about two minutes *after* the lyrical one, which is really strange but somehow still works. And then, to top it all off, that guitar one more time.

Steve: *I remember one night we were working on this song: it was about midnight and...normally we didn't do that...Once the sun had gone down, that was usually it. But for some reason we were all up for it. We were rehearsing...and we were doing what became the end of that song, and I think we were all relaxed after a few drinks, and right at the end it just seemed like the perfect moment to do a guitar solo over it. So I steamed in with that, and I felt that there were no bands really around that were doing anything quite like that, you know. Fairly classical chord sequence, and a rock guitar solo over the front that's maybe got a little more to do with the violin in spirit than the guitar.* [3]

Playing over Tony's big chords? WHY I NEVER well hey that actually sounds pretty good I guess. As you were, Mr. Hackett.

Steve: *One of the times when the band clicked was at the end of 'The Fountain Of Salmacis' where Tony played those chords and Mike kept his foot down on the bass pedals and I played a guitar solo over the top of it and that's how it came out.* [30]

Tony: *We gained a certain quality on 'Fountain of Salmacis' from having a fluent guitarist...* [10]

Steve: *A new kind of music was being born. A huge leap forward, my notes bending on top of Tony's beautiful chords on keyboards, sounding like orchestra with choir. It was pure spirit. All my emotions went into my guitar solo. I felt I was able to add significantly to the song's romance and wide range of extra colours.* [70]

I'll say. Tony and Steve, a match made in heaven. Surely this must be the start of an unbreakable musical alliance, right? Anyway...

23 - Anyway

from *The Lamb Lies Down on Broadway*, 1974

Well, well, ain't this a coinkydink? Just one entry ago we talked about the evolution of 'The Fountain of Salmacis' from its inception to its inclusion in the proto-song 'Provocation' and onward into its big evolution a year later for *Nursery Cryme*. And now for our next dissertation, we set our conversation destination to the hibernation and mutation (well, some might say gestation) of a Pete and Tony combination: that musical sensation (I say with reservation) that avoided circulation due to TV cancellation 'til released on compilation, the piano perambulation known only as 'Frustration'.

> **Mike:** *I do think...if you look at musicians and the way it works, no one thinks about someone's career. I mean, you know, the idea that jazz musicians or even folk or other musicians, they have a career. Everyone expects them to start off not so good and improve and get better. And I think that the way [record] companies work these days...there isn't much chance for that. People never think about this young artist, who maybe he'll do a couple of OK albums and then slowly, suddenly blossom and develop. Which I think we did! We were a bit flaky to start with, definitely. And I think it's a shame! You know, you need to have this sort of long term approach.* [91]

The differences between the 'Provocation'/'Fountain of Salmacis' connection and the 'Frustration'/'Anyway' connection are pretty stark. 'Provocation' contained only a fragment of the epic that would later close the band's third album. A crucial fragment, to be sure - arguably the heart of the whole song - but still just a fragment in the end. Meanwhile, 'Frustration' effectively already *is* 'Anyway' for the most part. Let's look at the ways!

- They both have a brief piano introduction before the primary piano melody kicks in. These introductions are a little bit different from one another, but the concept is the same.
- The primary piano riff/melody itself is already fully formed back on 'Frustration'. Same chords, same runs; it's pretty much note for note the same thing across both tracks.
- The vocal melody of 'Anyway' is itself already in place as well. The words would mercifully change - "I am the mad, mad scientist" doesn't do this song many favours - but Peter's singing melody is again essentially fully formed here.
- The first verse ends with the same sense of space, on a "down" energy if you will, on both tracks.
- Even the second verse of 'Provocation' still starts with the word "anyway"!
- After the second verse, both songs enter the same sort of dark breakdown, with the same piano frills, ending into the same chords that propel them into the next thing.

From there the songs diverge significantly: 'Anyway' has a guitar solo and returns for a third verse, while 'Frustration' briefly clips the old demo 'Hair on the Arms and Legs' before wandering off into its own thing. But even still, that's a *lot* of surviving music over the intervening years. So how is it that 'The Fountain of Salmacis' with all its massive developments could emerge from 'Provocation' in about a year while 'Frustration' could sit forgotten for four years and four albums before finally seeing the light of day, despite being very nearly a completed idea already?

Well, I think it's likely that we never see 'Anyway' at all if not for the grand ambition that drove the band to create *The Lamb Lies Down on Broadway*.

> **Peter:** *We had come up with a ton of music - we were talking about doing a double album - and I thought all this disparate stuff with no real purpose or glue would be much stronger if we could make it cohesive. The concept album was still a revered item in some quarters.* [1]

> **Mike:** *We had decided to do a double album from the outset, which gave us the space to improvise some of the longer, jamming pieces; an opening out, more freedom.* [1]

The mentality here is really admirable. They're a group of three and a half songwriters (Steve being the half and Phil being as yet disinterested), they've got some decent ideas already, and they also just want ample time to improvise, play together, and write as a unit. "One for all and all for one": The Three and a Half

Musketeers. And indeed, amidst the turbulent, difficult backdrop that is the making of this album, many of those group musical moments did coalesce, and I've written about many of them throughout this book.

But I think there's also a trap to double albums. Many bands or artists find they have ample material for a single album, and further creativity to spare, so they commit to the double album, only to find that after all the easy stuff is in place they've still got roughly a quarter of the album's space yet to be filled. You've got too much material for one album, but not quite enough for two, and now you're in a pickle. I think this is why sprawling double albums often have some distinctly weaker segments, as the bands find themselves cobbling together whatever sort of works by the end, purely to fill the space. A cynical view perhaps, but in any case, I think that's the impetus behind the resurrection of 'Anyway' here. I can almost envision the anxiety setting into the rehearsal room as the band members crunch the numbers and realise they're running a little bit short. "Anyone got anything we can use?"

So forward comes the piano-driven 'Frustration', passed over for *Trespass* - didn't fit the folky feel of that album; ignored for *Nursery Cryme* - "Guys check out this new Mellotron!"; forgotten by *Foxtrot* - dinner is served; completely abandoned by *Selling England by the Pound* - that's just old stuff we wrote as teenagers, and we're much older/wiser now. But now, on *The Lamb*? Yeah, I suppose there's room for a dark, piano-centric piece on here after all.

> **Tony:** *I think it is the best album from that early period...During the writing of the album we brought in all these little bits that we had and worked on them and for me they were such fun to do.* [6]

Imagine the thrill Tony must've had in taking a song that was basically five years old, written at a time before 40% of the current band were even in Genesis, and watching it grow. There are so many little things about 'Anyway' that elevate it far, far beyond what was there in 1970. The drums kick in right as the verse starts instead of waiting a bit. Speaking of drums, Phil Collins vs. John Mayhew? 'Nuff said there, I think. The bass sound is so much richer, Pete's vocals sound so much more mature, and his lyrics are incomparably better this time around, both in actual words and in the way those words carve out the melodic phrasing. How wonderful to be so profound!

Then, of course, there's the big change of the break near the two minute mark. The quality of the tense lead-in is itself head and shoulders above, but the payoff is much, much better as well. Would we rather a reprise of a weak demo from 1968 followed by random noodling? Or a tight guitar, baying like a trapped animal, brief but powerful? I don't know about you, but I'll take the latter, please and thank you.

And honestly, that whole middle instrumental section is a great bit of songwriting, even back in 1970 where it has its roots. I'll let Tony explain further.

> **Tony:** *In other people's music I suppose over the years, I've always liked music that kind of doesn't always do exactly what you expect it to do, you know. I mean, a lot of modern pop music, it seems to me you set up a chord sequence, and you don't just use it for the verse: you use it for the chorus as well, with a different melody. That's an old trick, because it means the audience sort of heard the chorus before they hear it. They think they know it! And it works very well! I mean, there's been a lot of good songs written in that form, you know. The Beatles were always good at the way they would kind of have a key change for the second bit and everything. And even in simple songs like 'From Me to You' and everything. And I find that really exciting, and that's sort of what I've kind of tried to follow. Some of my favourite composers: people like Burt Bacharach or Brian Wilson...would sort of always do those things, unexpected things, but make it somehow sound right.* [2]

On the one hand you've got something like Billy Joel's 'Piano Man', where the verse and chorus are literally the same daggone thing. Great melody and feel, sure, but that's an example of an audience tricked like Tony's talking about...although Tony's talking about changing the melody of the chorus, and 'Piano Man' doesn't even bother to do that! But 'Anyway' is a great example of hitting the listener with the unexpected in a number of ways. First, it's a song clocking in at 3:17; great length for a single, but of course the actual song is anything but. Far too dark for all of that. The verse rolls through, but then the tempo unexpectedly slows at its end, as though the entire song is grinding to a halt. Then right back into the second verse, and as it concludes, what comes next? You'd expect a third verse if the pattern continues or, perhaps if you're still in that "single" mentality, you're thinking a chorus might pop in here after the second verse.

Nope! Just a big, grim, bangin' chord to rattle your bones. And from that big, plodding set of chords, I'm not sure what you'd expect. Probably not a groovy syncopated bass riff, but there you go. But once you have that riff, you'll explore it a bit, right? Nope! Two bars and then we're off to solo town. Well hey, guess this is a Genesis prog track, so we're just gonna let Steve loose here, yeah? Nope! The guitar solo is actually just a middle eight! We're heading straight back down for a third verse. Still aching for a chorus, or at least, a big sweep of an ending? Nope! Just a subterranean doorman with a cheeky "Kept you waiting, huh?" as the song anticlimactically ends and Rael is whisked away for a dance with Death. You go into this expecting a song with some semblance of pop sensibilities, but instead find it's more like an instrumental interlude...just, you know, one with words and stuff. It's a continual subversion of expectations, and that makes it extraordinarily compelling.

It seems to me that 'Anyway' is often overlooked among Genesis fans, especially when talking about the great songs from *The Lamb Lies Down on Broadway*. I've almost never seen this one get anything more than an afterthought, which is perhaps poetically appropriate, mirroring the way Genesis themselves overlooked it for years before finally allowing it out of the vault to see the light of day. Doesn't help that it never survived as a live number.

> **Tony:** *When we played The Lamb on stage there were quite a few pieces we never would have played live, had we not been trying to perform the whole album. Another problem I had was that at the time there was no real piano sound. None of the electric pianos had touch sensitivity. The RMI piano I was using was OK on a number like 'Lamb Lies Down' itself, but trying to play 'Anyway', which has a much stronger classical feel, sounded awful. That probably left a slightly bad taste in my mouth.* [1]

But hey, who knows, maybe sitting on the song for years is what allowed it to finally thrive in the end, with the benefit of different and more mature musicians guiding it along. Either way, for me this is one of the absolute highlights of the adventurous *Lamb* album, and I wish everyone - the fans and band alike - would give it its proper due. Though maybe that's just my own frustration talking.

22 - No Son of Mine

from *We Can't Dance*, 1991

Back in the entry for 'Follow You Follow Me' I mentioned that we had yet to reach my personal Genesis "daddy" song, which is to say the first Genesis song that really embedded itself indelibly into my consciousness, planting the seeds of what would blossom into a lifelong fandom. Well, here we are. A bit ironic that a song called 'No Son of Mine' might be my Genesis father-tune, but I've found that life is full of little wry grins like that one.

I was pretty young still when *We Can't Dance* came out, but it seems my (human) dad didn't waste much time in picking up a copy on cassette. This was the beginning of the CD age, but it would still be several years before we'd own a CD player of any sort. Around that time it was a fairly common occurrence for me to be awakened on the weekend to the sound of Dad's portable stereo going off as he hung out in the kitchen, either sitting at the table or else sizzling up some cornmeal mush on the skillet.

> **Mike:** *I was playing a guitar phrase and Tony sampled it and turned it upside down and slowed it down. Which is that kind of strange elephant noise which starts the track. And that's really how it started in fact, with a kind of elephant-noise-stroke atmosphere.* [92]

In a very real way, this "Elephantus" was the alarm clock of my childhood. The tick-tocking that opens the piece can sort of fade seamlessly into one's dreams, and while the heartbeat pulse can (with enough bass boost) begin to stir one from slumber, it's that signature growling sound that would blare at full volume, reverberating throughout the house, and get me out of bed on a Saturday morning.

> **Tony:** *Sounds like an elephant being sick. It's just a very distinctive sound, you know? Again, I always like to try and get a sound in there if I can. And this was again just sampling noise in the room. And it was just Mike, actually...sort of thrashing around and I just cut out this little bit in the middle of it. And then slowed it right down and just used the front end of it, and stuck it with this E-minor chord. The effect was fantastic. "Well this is great, I love this." And immediately then Phil started warbling on top of it, and we thought, "We've got a song here. This sounds really good."* [3]

So here's little me, rubbing my eyes, trudging down the stairs, the music getting louder as I get closer to its source. I'd usually arrive in the dining room to see the tape player sitting on the table, just in time for the song's first chorus.

> **Phil:** *We were sitting in that room writing, and we came to the chorus - what was to become the chorus. I was singing, "No son, no sonna mai, ya no son, ya no suh..." and Mike said to me when we came to writing the lyrics..."On that song, it sounds like you're singing 'No son of mine.'" And I don't know what I was singing, really. I was singing something like that. But then suddenly he put that in my mind that that's what I'd been singing, and so at that point I went and wrote the lyrics that made sense of what I'd improvised.* [35]

Out of the fuzzy sound of the overloud stereo, through my juvenile ears, and into my sleep-befuddled brain, I might as well have been hearing something even more nonsensical than what Phil initially improvised. But I interpreted what I heard as "King Osho of mine," and any dissatisfaction I might've had at being roused out of bed by a dying pachyderm was quickly washed away by how much I loved that chorus. Ask me at that time what my favourite song was, and Tiny-Me may well have happily replied, "King Osho!"

Little kids are funny that way, able to let annoyance roll off them as quickly as it came. I've got a couple boys of my own now, both younger than I was when "King Osho" was storming through the charts, and when the older one wakes up there's never a plea for "five more minutes" or anything. It's usually just, "Play with me now?" They fall down, they get hurt, they cry, and then they scamper off in laughter a few minutes later. Kids don't have much past, so they don't bother dwelling on it. Theirs are eyes that look forward, excited for the next wondrous thing they might encounter, hopeful that the best is always yet to come.

Knowing that, and knowing how outrageously blessed I was to have a family like I had growing up, and knowing the boundless love I have for my own sons, this song now just absolutely breaks my heart. That my most defining memories of this piece could be so happy and carefree feels almost like a violation of some obscure kind, as though I'm guilty of something profoundly disrespectful by associating this track with joy in my mind. I'm sure this one hits many other people on a very, very different level. It's so moving because, tragically, it's so real.

> **Phil:** *The story is that this is a young boy, I don't know how old - maybe 11, 12 years old. Who basically, he lives in a family of abuse. The father is the bad guy, and [the boy] just can't stand it anymore. The friction in the house, the fact that every night the guy comes home drunk and just either molests him, or abuses his mother. That's really what it's about. Because the boy as he gets older, he realises that he misses his family, and can't believe that his father was all that bad, and he goes back and sees his father, plucks up the courage to go back home. Knocks on the door with his heart in his mouth not knowing what the reaction's gonna be, and his father is exactly the same.* [35]

I mean, just...what can I possibly say to that? It's not directly relatable in my own personal life, but still has that ring of truth to it. As I said, kids don't dwell in the past; they don't hold grudges in the same way that adults have learned to through years of hard experience. Your heart screams for the boy in this story to never go back. But you can completely understand why he would, and after showing such courage, you root for him to have this happy ending, this catharsis he's needed all his life. "And his father is exactly the same." Of course he is. We knew this would happen all along, but for the boy's sake - and perhaps in some cases for our own sake too - we allowed ourselves to hope otherwise. That the ending is predictable doesn't make it any less painful.

> **Phil:** *We all somehow see ourselves as screenwriters. We sit down and design a script or story. We have always done this.* [20]

It's a magnificent script, but the words are only one part of the equation.

> **Tony:** *I think it's the best lyric that Phil ever wrote for the band. 'No Son of Mine' I think is really strong. Because I think it means something, and yet it also sounds really good. And that's the key, you know...Which is the more important of those two things, I don't know, but if you can get them both together, it's really good.* [43]

How do these words just *fit* so well into this song? Let's rewind a bit, and address once more the elephant in the room:

> **Tony:** *I've often got a mic set up on the Emulator, and every now and then I switch it on without telling anyone what I'm doing. I'll just sample around 18 seconds in the room and see what happens. In this case, that was what I did, and that sound, which is like an elephant trumpeting, is what sets that whole song in motion. Sounds like that don't necessarily end up on the track, but they can set you off on an idea and change the mood.* [82]

You get that sound, on top of those particular chords, and before Phil sings a lick you know exactly what this song is trying to communicate.

> **Tony:** *If you can just set up an atmosphere sometimes, that's what it's all about. You just get a sort of feel going. And funnily enough, what you do after it sometimes is not so important. Once you've got that initial mood, it carries you for a long, long time. So I was very proud of that one.* [3]

> **Mike:** *I think 'No Son of Mine' is probably one of my most recent favourite tracks. Because once again, it's sort of, it's almost like the start of what we could be doing...the next sort of stage, you know what I mean? It's...once again a dark atmosphere.* [3]

They're both right, of course. 'No Son of Mine' is a track that runs nearly seven minutes long, and it consists of the following pieces: verse, chorus, verse, chorus. That's it. That's the whole song. The verses are long, yes, with a pre-chorus bit in there each time, but essentially this entire song is just a basic structure run two times around. There's no big instrumental solo. There's not even a bridge. It's too simple for prog, too extensive for pop. But it *works* because the atmosphere it exudes is so gripping that we stop caring about "my song structure!" and become deeply invested in the story the band is telling us.

>**Tony:** *We felt this song had all of the strengths that represented Genesis, and it also contrasts well with things that are going down [musically] at the moment. It's so different to anything you're going to hear on the radio.* [92]

By the time the drums kick in with their arresting snares, the lyrics have already told us that this is a child trying to find a place to hide. Somewhere the badness couldn't reach him. Good grief, that's hard to even type. As those snares hit, punctuating every sordid detail of the kid's home circumstances, the guitar sound opens slightly too. As the story unfolds, so too does the music itself unfold alongside it, adding layers and depth until we hit the chorus where everything finally spills out like years of tensions and blame finally being expelled onto this poor soul, now a victim twice over.

>**Tony:** *In the old days I used to [brighten the keyboard sound for choruses] a lot on the filter with Polymoogs and stuff like that, but on this song I used a simpler method, which was to play one pad and, through MIDI, fade a second one in. I had an ooo-ey sort of sound on the Wavestation, then I faded up a brassy VFX sound. It's more controllable than opening up the filter, which I was always desperately trying to do not too fast. Also, it's easier to do in the rehearsal room. The idea came out of the improvisation while we were writing the song. All the sounds on the record are pretty much what I played when we were first working out the ideas.* [82]

This is a really technical description of how Tony manufactures hope in the lead-in to the chorus, building anticipation with "positive" sounds so that we can really experience the deflation of the shout-down when it inevitably arrives. It's brilliant, it's effective, and I'm a little upset at him for it.

>**Tony:** *'No Son of Mine' is certainly one of the best songs we've ever done...Our self-confidence was at a level where we played the record company just one track, 'No Son of Mine', and said, "This is the single."* [1]

>**Phil:** *After making the decision to leave, of course I sometimes missed the environment of being in the band that wrote 'No Son of Mine', because it is very, very special to come up with a song like that out of thin air, sitting in a room with nothing written and Tony playing something, me singing something that goes with that, and Mike reacting to what I'm singing. Something fantastic emerges from the fog for a minute, and that minute becomes the nucleus. It's very difficult to achieve that kind of chemistry.* [1]

>**Tony:** *It's probably my favourite song on the album in many ways. We play it on stage and everything, it still sends shivers down my spine. It's just a [relatively simple] song. If you can do it all with a few chords and a simple rhythm, then I think there's nothing to be said against that.* [3]

Indeed.

Postscript: About 15 years after this song was written and recorded, Phil began his own downward spiral into drink. To his immense credit, he was never accounted as abusive. But then, around 2012…

>**Phil:** *The boys are worried, too. In Switzerland they had seen me drinking. Once Nicholas had wisely suggested to [his nanny] Lindsey, "I think we have to stop buying drink for Daddy." A gut-wrenching thing for Lindsey to hear from a ten-year-old boy, and an awful image for his dad to process.* [12]

Phil was likely able to channel his own "daddy issues" from childhood, revolving around not being completely accepted by his father when he decided to go into music, for the lyrics to 'No Son of Mine'. It's easy to imagine how he could've found the emotion to sing the song convincingly, and I'm sure he never even remotely conceived that he might have more in common by the end with the song's father figure. It's telling that during The Last Domino? Tour, 'No Son of Mine' was one of the most successful songs of the concert. Maybe that's just because its brooding atmosphere was better able to weather the storm of being dropped down several keys. But maybe it was also a matter of Phil, singing the song on stage while Nicholas himself drummed behind him, having a deeper perspective than ever before.

21 - Burning Rope

from ...*And Then There Were Three...*, 1978

It's been said numerous times by the band members who "survived" to the three-piece ensemble that they have different approaches to songwriting. Here's one of many potential example quotes.

> **Phil:** *The three of us kind of had the best of all worlds, if you like. Because, you know, I'm pretty immediate. Tony's kind of a little bit, you may not know it at the moment but you'll probably be singing this to yourself in a couple weeks' time, you know? And then Mike is somewhere in the middle of that. He'll write things that are not THAT immediate, but then, you know. I mean it's just the kind of...it makes the things deeper. It makes the stuff deeper when you've got the three of us writing.* [3]

In-your-face Phil, meandering Tony, "eh whatever" Mike. It's a really strong combination; an undeniable chemistry that produced not only the band's biggest hits, but also some really effective longer tracks. The title of the album *And Then There Were Three* could therefore be seen not as a depressing eulogy, but as a triumphant announcement of a band entering its most cohesive and successful phase. Not "And Then There Were Three: Uh Oh" but "And Then There Were Three: Here We Go".

Of course, regardless of the bright future of communal songwriting the album's title portends, *And Then There Were Three* is still a transitional album. Only three of its eleven tracks were actually jointly written, and with Phil still a year away from doing any meaningful songwriting on his own, that meant Mike and Tony bringing in their own pieces and telling the others what to do. Yet even despite that, the songwriting influence they each were beginning to exert upon one another was already apparent.

For example, here comes Tony, waltzing in with this big ol' progressive piece. It's got a bunch of sections, runs probably ten minutes or more, crafted down to the last detail, and he's ready to command his minions to play it and help him realise his epic vision. But then he gets to thinking: "Do I really want all that?"

> **Tony:** *I wrote...'Burning Rope' on this album. Which is kind of like...it looked like when I was writing it [that] it was gonna be like 'One for the Vine'. And in fact there were other sections that were in the song. And then I decided to kind of abbreviate it and not make it quite such a long thing. A, because I didn't want the comparisons to that, and B, I thought, "Well I've done that. I think I'll just leave it [shorter] for this album, and not do that." So we could get more different ideas [on the album].* [3]

Without even realising it, the band was already absorbing some of that Phil Collins instinct for immediacy and brevity, albeit from a philosophical point of view rather than in terms of melodies and hooks. Indeed, this attitude blanketed the entire endeavour, not just on 'Burning Rope' itself but also the album as a whole.

> **Tony:** *The idea of trying to keep the songs a little more concise to get more ideas on the album was quite appealing. It was something we sort of wanted to do regardless.* [3]

Which makes it amusing that the song Tony specifically trimmed down to fit this philosophy ended up being the longest song on the album by over a minute anyway. Tony Banks is still Tony Banks, after all. He can only self-censor so much. But it's *what* he censored out that really makes the difference. He says there were originally extra sections to this song? Obviously it's hard to say what got removed from the song, but there's a lot to be gleaned from what survived the culling.

First, an intro bit. Opening a song with a drum fill is bold, and also happens to work really well when your drummer is Phil Collins. This is like the orchestral overture of the song, previewing what's to come in later sections. It lasts about 45 seconds on the dot, which is suitably long to get a taste of everything to come, but still short enough to stay focused. It's setting the stage, whetting the listener's appetite.

Next comes a chorus, and it's remarkable that you immediately *know* it's the chorus even though it's still completely instrumental. There hasn't been a single syllable uttered yet, but when this thing comes in, it's instantly recognisable as the main thrust of the piece. You've got Tony's slurry synth belting out the top melody, but this bit allows you to spend a while listening to and getting an appreciation for all the musical stuff that's going to soon fall underneath the vocals. What's really interesting to me about this first minute-plus of 'Burning Rope' is that, probably because it opens the song, it's not something you'd ever peg when talking about big instrumental breaks in the Genesis catalogue. We tend to see this whole thing as an introductory passage and so maybe don't give it quite enough credit for being a stellar bit of instrumental playing in its own right.

Now finally we get a "proper" chorus, with Phil taking over on that top line, singing lyrics that sound really poetic but don't actually seem to mean anything - yet. Tony's still there of course, pounding out chords on the piano, filling out the sound of the thing. And now follows a verse, full of strange poetry of its own, and then what you sort of instinctively know to be a pre-chorus, perhaps because you've already heard the chorus before. And now finally the lyrics start to make a little bit of sense, as the pre-chorus makes it clear this song is about the transient nature of things, punctuating it with the final line of "The only survivors on this world of ours are," as the chorus kicks back in with the same poetry of words, now empowered by having a comprehensible meaning.

What follows is a brief reprise of the intro, although if we are thinking of the intro bit in overture terms, then it's probably more accurate to just call it a return of that earlier motif. In any case, Tony pulls his old trick again here (mentioned earlier in the entry for 'Ripples') of ramping up the excitement, building the instrumentation to something big, and then faking us out instead with something else. Here that something else is a tender keyboard moment laced with some tasteful guitar. Then it ramps up again, bigger and bigger until the tension is allowed to break in the form of a big guitar solo. It's a substantial ask of someone who was essentially just trying out that lead role for the first time, and everyone felt the pressure.

> **Mike:** *I was so preoccupied with trying to play lead guitar on that album that I can't remember what we were doing. Our direction was almost secondary. I couldn't play very fast; it's probably something I never will do.* [10]

> **Tony:** *Mike's playing was a little thin on And Then There Were Three, I think. There was one guitar solo, on the song 'Burning Rope', which I had written the line for. If Steve had been playing the solo, I would probably have hoped to have gone further and expanded it, but Mike just played the notes - and it still sounds all right. He obviously needed to gain confidence to feel comfortable in the role, and by the time we got to, say, Abacab, his guitar playing had really improved and he was able to contribute fully as a lead guitarist in addition to everything else that he did.* [1]

Abacab this ain't, but it's really impressive to me not only that Mike was able to manage a solo this good with so little experience under his belt, but also that Tony was able to write a guitar solo this good on his own in the first place. In the past, it had usually been Steve coming up with guitar solos in key spots, or bringing in his own guitar bits and the band working them in, or else just having a melody written for a different instrument get rearranged over to his side of the fence. Here, as with 'Many Too Many' on the same album, Tony's beginning to think outside his keyboards and write some really high-quality guitar bits. Again, the group songwriting sensibilities are evolving, even though this is anything but a group-written piece.

> **Mike:** *It was [a challenge for me] but I'm very pleased with the way it's come out. I think it's the best solo on the album. This is also the longest track on the album. It goes through more moods than any of the others. The basic track was drums, piano, and bass, which didn't really excite anyone. Tony did a lot of building up on the keyboards later on. You have to use a lot of imagination when you're building up from the basic track, which can sometimes be very basic indeed. This album differed from the last couple in that as soon as we'd put down the basic track with one or two overdubs, Phil would put a vocal down. Sometimes he wouldn't have any lyrics and would just la-la-la his way through, but at least it meant that we knew where they were and we didn't crowd them. It's such a good idea I don't know why we didn't do it before.* [17]

From the gentle outro of the guitar solo, it's back into another verse/pre-chorus/chorus combo, the lyrics really hammering home their poignant message of fleeting time and fleeting legacies. Phil's got some layered backing vocals over this final chorus. Sometimes it's harmonies, sometimes some sort of counter-melodic phrase whose words I've never been able to make out, but it all makes the whole thing that much more exciting. Even more so when that final chorus pushes straight into a reprise of the ending portion of the guitar solo, after which the song ends on a wistful, gentle note.

So what are the definable sections of this song in the end, and what kind of layout do they make? Well, in the name of succinctness, let's combine the verses and pre-choruses, since they're often seen as two halves of a whole anyway. Once you've done that, the song structure looks like this:

Intro, Chorus (x2), Verse, Chorus, Solo, Verse, Chorus, Solo

And this means the song only really has four *unique* sections of music, with one of those being an instrumental introduction which, as I've said before, serves less like its own thing and more like the outline page for the thesis to come. Why is this significant? Well, because when your song essentially consists of a verse, a chorus, and a bridge solo, you've essentially made something approximating a pop/rock song, haven't you? Particularly when you've got that ratio of two verses to four choruses; that's pop sensibility through and through.

Now obviously 'Burning Rope' isn't a pop song by any means, and I have no idea what the sections that Tony removed from the piece might've sounded like, or what structure that longer form of the song would have ended up taking. But by going for that sense of conciseness, Tony ended up with a seven minute song that *still has immediacy*. Phil is right that Tony's work often takes multiple listens and a fair amount of time to sink in, but 'Burning Rope' grabbed me from the first time I heard it, and I think this is why. I think this is also why Genesis, from 'Follow You Follow Me' into *Abacab* and beyond, started to become more successful writers of hits. Tony Banks solved the puzzle back in 1978; he just never realised he did. It took Phil's emergence as a songwriter to bring that song-sense fully to the fore, but I think 'Burning Rope' is a semi-conscious drift in that direction already.

Finally, to loop back briefly to that guitar solo, it's probably for the best that Mike wasn't all that confident in what he was doing, if you've ever cared about Genesis as a live act.

> **Mike:** *Part of our thinking at the time was to decide whether we should bring in a bass player or a guitarist, or maybe somebody who could handle both so he and I could interchange...and it seemed that really what we needed was a guitarist who could play some bass.* [1]

Mike, fledgling lead guitarist, learning the entire Genesis back catalogue on guitar? Had he been more self-assured, that may be the route the band went. Instead, Mike figured "Let me play the stuff from this album since it's fresh in my mind, and let me get back to my comfort zone for the rest of the set." And that's how we ended up with Daryl Stuermer, the musical backbone of touring Genesis since *And Then There Were Three*. How fortunate for us!

> **Tony:** *Daryl, it was immediately obvious, could play anything and he could adapt to what we were doing: he was a very lucky find...He could play by ear and pick up everything extremely quickly. When we were running the rehearsal sessions for the tour, Daryl knew the stuff better than we did. We kept asking him, "Hey, how does that bit go?", so we knew that if something went wrong on stage, it was never going to be Daryl's fault...Having a guitarist of probably even greater technical ability and fluency than Steve meant we could do things we'd never have tried before.* [1]

Shoot, Daryl is so locked in he even catches everyone else's mistakes on stage.

> **Tony:** *Sometimes the simple things can be difficult [when playing live] because you forget and you relax, and there have been some classic cases. I was pretty good at making it look like it wasn't me who had made the mistake, it was somebody else! I remember playing 'Dodo' once and I kept going on the verse and I should have [gone on to] the chorus and Phil was looking going, "It's me, it's me!" and I just carried on! But Daryl looked across and Daryl always knows!* [6]

Got to wake up pretty early in the morning to pull one over on old Stuermy. But that kind of precision comes with a cost.

> **Mike:** *Not knowing anything can make you more adventurous as a writer. When the band were jamming together it was those...wrong notes...that led to our most original and interesting ideas. You write by making mistakes. That's the reason why Daryl Stuermer, our new touring guitarist, wasn't a writer: he couldn't play a wrong note if you paid him. But because we were paying him not to, it worked out pretty well.* [14]

'Burning Rope' is one of the best guitar solos Genesis has ever done, but it's one that the arguably most technically proficient guitarist in Genesis history has never been allowed to play. Sorry, chum! You're great, and we love you, but this is Mike's shining guitar moment for the band, and nobody can take that away from him.

As you were, Mr. Rutherford. As you were.

20 - Dreaming While You Sleep

from *We Can't Dance*, 1991

Space. The final frontier. These are the voyages of the rock group Genesis. Its continuing mission: to explore strange new sounds. To seek out new riffs and new instrumentations. To boldly go where no band has gone before!

Exploring space isn't really something Genesis was known for back in the 1970s, but by 1991 the band had evolved its way of working significantly. Gone were the days of penning a song by oneself in a room. Gone were the days of competing with one another to compose the most intricate portions of a song and then throwing them all together to see who would "win." Gone were the days of trying to fill every fraction of every measure with some sonic tidal wave meant to drown the listener.

Instead, space. Room to breathe. Room to let music grow - not because there's more of it in the mix, but because the absence of excess allows the remainder to have a much greater impact. This was unthinkable in the earlier days and years of the band.

> **Phil:** *The less busy Tony has gotten over the years, the more enjoyable it has been to play with him. But we all went through that. If you listen to our earlier efforts, we're always going hell-for-leather behind the vocalist.* [82]

It's hard to overestimate the importance of maturation and restraint here, but there's another significant factor that would've made this level of space much more difficult to achieve back then: the evolution of drum machines.

> **Phil:** *When Genesis were in Japan [for the last leg of the And Then There Were Three Tour] we were offered, gratis, the newest drum machines by Roland, straight off the conveyor belt...the forefront of emerging music technology. I'm told this is the sound of tomorrow...Mike and Tony took one each. But I'm a drummer. Why would I want a drum machine, a future that would consign me to the past? I said, "Thanks, but no thanks."* [12]

It was 1978 before Genesis really even had drum machines to play around with, and the rhythmic heart of the band didn't want anything to do with them. But fast forward thirteen years and four platinum Genesis albums later - to say nothing of any solo recording success - and the drum machine is the foundation of much of the band's improvisations. They put down a pattern and improvise around it. Sometimes Phil lays down real drums to replace the pattern, and sometimes he lays them down on top of the pattern. But sometimes, he doesn't need to bring them in at all.

> **Phil:** *It's all based on the drum machine...The real drums didn't sound good on the verse. They weren't necessary, because the drum machine pattern held its own. It was one of those patterns that set up half the atmosphere of the song. Then, where the big change came in with the smooth chords at the chorus, I started playing along on drums. You then say, "Okay, that part sounds right. Now let's get a sound for it that makes it sound good." Of course, it all has to get past quality control.* [82]

So let's get one thing clear here. The particular drum machine pattern for this track, with its bass drum thump, light snare, and pitter patter of toms is really, really good. In fact, the working title for the song was 'Rolling Toms', strong evidence that the band thought of the drum pattern as the irreplaceable core of the piece rather than a throwaway placeholder. A lot of people might have a distaste for anything that isn't a "real" drum sound, but Phil's right: the atmosphere of this tune is a product of that pattern. You ditch it for real drums, you lose the whole thing. But as it is, you've got a backdrop with plenty of open space, and your mood is already there. It's just a question of what to put on top of that mood.

Musically, 'Dreaming While You Sleep' features two very different explorations of this space. The first, which would become the verses of the song, feature some sequenced marimba parts, which add tones but free Tony up to do something else with his hands. That something else consists of short chord runs: little wah-wah-waaaaah-wahs that flavour the melodies without infringing upon them. Mike can then add his own subtle lines with the guitar, which come and go, fading in and fading out, just distant accents that never get in the way. Indeed, for reasonably long stretches he might not even be playing at all.

But then there's another section too. Big chords, big bass, big sound. This is a different approach to handling the space. If the verse sections are a matter of leaving some space wide open for the listener to hear, this chorus is an exercise in disguising that space from the listener. Nobody's doing anything particularly complicated here. There's still a ton of space in the *arrangement*, but you can't *hear* it anymore because the sound itself is so big. Yet you can still *feel* the space as you listen. This isn't an endless barrage of notes competing for your attention, but single sustained notes or chords that cover the shell of the thing. It's sonically hollow, if you will, a wall of sound surrounding nothing at all.

The band liked both these improvisations on the drum pattern, both techniques at producing something sparse without sacrificing quality. They knew they wanted to keep each idea, so from there it became a question of connecting and developing the components.

> **Tony:** *We had one drum machine pattern going all the way through. There were no drums added when we did it. Really, we had two very different feels going on the one rhythm. We were all improvising things. I was playing on one sort of keyboard sound, then I started playing a few chords. At that point, Phil started singing a melody line. We had this chorus bit that sounded great; it was just a question of trying to organise the improvisations that ended up being the verse and all the other parts of the song to fit with that chorus. So the whole thing was there; it was never a decision to make the dramatic transition between the two.* [82]

Genesis don't tend to say a whole lot about their transitional moments within songs. Sure, they'll acknowledge them by saying "We needed to find a way to link these two bits" or something to that effect, but the actual process of doing that is a topic seldom broached. But the transition sections in 'Dreaming While You Sleep', running from 2:30 to 2:48 and again from 5:17 to 5:36, are so expertly built up that they deserve some extra mention. And again, it's all about space.

> **Tony:** *When I'm [covering the bass notes], I'm just playing the bottom parts. Since most bass guitar parts are put on afterwards, it's very important that Mike doesn't disturb the chord emphasis, because it's so easy to change that with a bass. We have one chord in the song 'Dreaming While You Sleep' where there was no bass note, so he doesn't play one. Any bass note would give the wrong impression to the chord. This is why the bottom note of a chord is often just part of the keyboard part.* [82]

You can hear this specific chord as the elongated third sequential chord in each of these transitional sections. The first two chords feature bass notes from Mike that are gentle, yet definitely present in the mix. The chord structure descends from the first to the second, and you might expect it to resolve on the third chord, but instead it lifts unexpectedly. To describe the progression in emotional terms, it's like a kind of mourning that suddenly gets tinged by a fearful hope. And Mike's bass is nowhere to be found. As Tony indicates, that hopeful lift is the entire point of the chord, so it simply *has* to have a sonic floor that's elevated from what came before. Near the end of that stretching chord, Mike does re-enter with a brief run of his own, and then the three chords repeat again. Except this time, on that third chord, even as Tony performs that hopeful lift in identical fashion to the first time, Mike plays a note that matches the expected musical resolution of the two chords before. So to be clear, it's the exact same chord, and the *only* note that's any different is the one coming from Mike's bass, and he's playing the note that resolves the chords. So you'd expect this to sound somehow warm or fulfilling.

But it doesn't. It sounds like despair.

> **Tony:** *Chords are my specialty. The thing that I understand best is the way chords fit together. You can't just add or subtract notes.* [82]

So you've got this thing that's undeniably groovy, sort of an electronic jazz feel, and you've got this thing that's big and sweeping but still sort of empty in a way, and you've got this sequence of chords linking them together that sounds like the death of hope itself. What kind of lyrics do you put with that?

> **Mike:** *'Rolling Toms' is now called 'Dreaming While You Sleep'. It started off, Phil used to sing "dreaming while you sleep," and actually Tony was gonna do the lyric. 'Cause we kinda pick out songs we want to do, and he felt [he wanted] to do that one, which was fine by me. But then I had an idea driving home one day about a guy who hits a girl. A hit-and-run, really. Didn't see her in the car headlights, night in the rain, and didn't stop. And he drives off and leaves her. But then he can't escape the fact that he hasn't told anybody, and he can't live with the guilt. So he kinda goes back to the hospital where she's lying in a coma for...ever, I guess. I mean, she's still in the coma when the song finishes. And he kind of becomes attached to her. And his life gets linked up with hers, and he can't escape really. I had this idea, and then I persuaded Tony that I was gonna do it. I mean, he wanted to do it. But I said, "Well I have an idea. Let me try it, and if it's good, fine. If not, if it's not a great idea, then you have a go."* [14]

It's probably not a big surprise that a song about running someone over and putting them in a lifelong coma came from the same lyricist who penned the one about a guy getting trampled to death in a snowman outfit; Mike can go to some really dark places at times. But there's such a huge gulf of impact between those earlier 'Snowbound' lyrics and these. Just like with the drum machine technology, he's had thirteen years of maturation here to explore these darker themes. And this one hits *hard*. I have no idea what direction Tony's lyrics for this one might have taken, but I have to imagine when heard Mike's effort he felt he shouldn't even bother to try.

Groovy, jazzy, rolling toms? That's driving in the night time rain, man. That's feeling yourself start to drift off and then the burst of alertness that comes from nearly hitting something. If you've ever driven late at night when you're tired, you've probably had a similar experience. I once drove onto a highway exit ramp because I was tired enough to think that a certain road sign actually meant the exact opposite of what it said. It was super late and the roads were empty, so the worst that happened was me panicking and driving back over the median to the adjacent on-ramp once I saw that "WRONG WAY" sign. But you'd better believe I stayed hyper-alert for the rest of the 25 minutes home. I was lucky to be off in Nowheresville at an hour where most people aren't out and about. Yet it's easy to imagine all the things that could've happened had circumstances been just a little different. Things like, perhaps, hitting a pedestrian and causing serious harm.

Linking chords of anguish? That's guilt, man. That's knowing that you could've stopped - that you had a *duty* to stop - and deal with the consequences of your actions. That's knowing that you made a mistake that anybody could've made, that you never intended any harm on anyone, and that you're too afraid of the consequences of doing the right thing to admit any of it. It's the sound of despair, yes, but also of self-loathing. What kind of *monster* would just keep driving? Would deny the crime for years on end, leaving a family to grieve in ignorance? "Me, that's who. *I'm* that monster."

Big sweeping chorus? That's regret, man. And hey, I'll tell you what: now that this song is about "getting away with" vehicular assault, how about some real drums after all? They ditch the drum pattern for this section, despite it being the driving force in writing it in the first place, blasting heavy, accusatory snares instead. And hey, let's get Mike off that lead guitar and back onto some heavy bass, yeah?

> **Mike:** *During the chorus of 'Dreaming While You Sleep' I tried playing a bass guitar because we wanted a low, powerful sound from the bass end where the drums are a very big part of the song.* [82]

Phil belts his heart out about how really, he hasn't escaped the consequences at all. They've just taken on a different hue. No time served, except the eternity of obsessive remorse that will never wane because there's never going to be enough courage to confess. Two lives ruined, not one, even though one walks free. What an emotional wreck this chorus can make me. I find myself overcome with sympathy for this figure, spending every waking moment just hoping that someone else can have a waking moment too. Your heart breaks, and then I remember that *he's* the bastard who put her into this situation in the first place, and who is *still* dodging justice, and then I myself start to feel like a jerk for feeling bad for him in the first place. And yet, what if he had come forward? Does that make her magically not in a coma? How villainous is he, really?

It's so effective a story that it can even take what on the surface are just the bare minimum in lyrics and make them remarkably powerful. Consider the ends of the verses, before the instrumental prechorus, where the lines are just a repetition of the phrase "dreaming while you sleep." Maybe there's a "memories to keep" in there too depending on the verse, but you get the idea. This is easy to dismiss as somehow lazy, but it's a matter of shifting perspective. Consider that the first verse's "dreaming while you sleep" stanza is a reflection of the driver's state of mind while driving, the concept of the real interweaving with dreams as he chugs along the road, too tired to tell the difference. The second verse's "dreaming while you sleep" still focuses on the driver, now miles away and in bed suffering the nightmares of what's just transpired. Crashing to unconsciousness after crashing someone else into (permanent) unconsciousness, as it were. There's a hopeful attitude of "Let me sleep this off and it'll go away by morning," but the first chorus makes it clear that it will never go away at all.

Post-chorus we get another quick pair of "dreaming while you sleep" lines, which act almost like a mantra to keep the enormity of the situation at bay. "It was just a dream, just move on, forget it ever happened." So then the third verse comes and goes and the mantra is repeated with increasing intensity, and along the way it transforms. It's no longer about the driver, but about his victim.

> *Dreaming while you sleep (forget about it all)*
>
> *Dreaming while you sleep (how can I possibly forget about it all?)*
>
> *DREAMING WHILE YOU SLEEP (oh god, what have I done to you?)*
>
> *ARE YOU DREAMING WHILE YOU SLEEP???*

How chilling is that? The entire situation royally stinks. Everyone's a victim. And now I'm a victim too, any time I hear this song. Which is a lot, because gosh dangit I'm a sucker for these guys tugging on my heartstrings. I think I'd be willing to go so far as to say that the chorus of this song is the most emotionally affecting bit of music for me in the Genesis canon, and I don't even personally identify with the situation beyond being able to loosely imagine it in a "what if" kind of scenario. Then put it on the We Can't Dance Tour where we have to watch Phil emote the whole thing out? Stop, I can't take it. Yes, more please.

Speaking of "yes, more," the studio track concludes with a chorus with new lyrics ("I'll be haunted by..."), followed by an even more intense second chorus with the first lyrics again ("You lie silently there..."), followed by a third chorus that's mostly instrumental, which then fades out. You'll notice on most quality live recordings that the second loop through that chorus is altogether absent. But this wasn't always the case. The We Can't Dance Tour began with rehearsals in Houston, Texas, followed shortly thereafter by three true concert dates in Texas, including Houston itself, before the band took a week off to evaluate and prepare for the start of the tour proper in Florida. It was during these rehearsals, then, that they came up with the ending for the song: run the semi-instrumental chorus back into the "dreaming while you sleep" funky bit with the drums intact and then suddenly stop after the fifth utterance of that line, making it a full-rotation-plus-one through the bit. But they hadn't actually *removed* anything yet.

That makes any bootleg recordings of the Texas shows significant and worth tracking down, as only through them can you hear the song in its full glory, with the full three final chorus loops plus a proper ending, the way it was intended. Unfortunately, intentions and physiology often find themselves at odds.

> **Phil:** *Now that I'm playing so many shows, solo and with Genesis, and increasingly in large venues, I live in fear of losing my voice...After the opening night...we move on via Houston to Florida. I develop a sore throat...The next night in Tampa, I only manage one song...before apologizing and exiting stage left, my singing voice in tatters...I scuttle back to the dressing room and cry. It's just too intense. I've let everybody down, from fans to crew to caterers to the entire team working in and around the stadium. It's a very heavy responsibility, a very heavy moment. It's all on me. One week in, and in my mind I've already scuppered Genesis' biggest-ever tour.* [12]

> **Mike:** *There's a lot of pressure when you're playing to 70,000 people a night, and Phil felt that most of all. I could play a concert if I was ill and half dead, but if Phil caught a cold it would be a big deal because he was concerned about his voice. We would always have to worry if he caught a chill going to the plane in his robe; he'd have to wrap up, he wouldn't be able to talk, he wouldn't be able to go out for dinner after a show...The voice was like another person on tour - the fourth one of us - and I think that got to Phil. It stopped being as much fun.* [14]

> **Tony:** *The increasing size of Genesis tours brought some additional problems...There were more and more interviews and these terrible meet and greets before the show. Phil would say, "I can't do this meet and greet, because I've got to look after my voice," so we'd troop out there and of course the only person they wanted to meet was Phil...It made you feel somewhat superfluous...* [1]

After that episode in Tampa, the second chorus was excised from 'Dreaming While You Sleep', never to be heard again. The song itself was then cut from the entire European leg of the tour, only to return triumphantly just in time for a London show, before it was cut once again because it was demanding too large a toll. Then, likely because of its inconstant presence on the tour, it was excluded from both volumes of *The Way We Walk*. But if all we had was one moment in time, I'm glad we had it at all.

Now let's find out what stage nightmares the band has!

> **Phil:** *Dreaming you go on stage is like the schoolboy one where you go to school...but you've got nothing on apart from the shirt and jacket. Nothing else. No pants, nothing. That's a famous schoolboy nightmare, I think. Or a male nightmare, anyway. And I think that's quite a common one. On stage it's usually that kind of thing: you're standing there, you're singing, and you look down and actually you've got nothing on! Or...there's no leads. The leads are plugged into the wrong things.* [35]

> **Mike:** *When I get out on stage...it's a fairly standard dream I think. I hit the first chord, and there are no guitar strings.* [35]

> **Tony:** *[The keyboardist's nightmare is] you're trying to do a song with all the wrong keyboards and stuff, and the sound is just completely wrong.* [35]

In summary, their worst fears are the following:

> **Phil:** I'm naked!

> **Mike:** My guitar is naked!

> **Tony:** Who mucked with my keyboard?!

Never change, Tony.

19 - Feeding the Fire

B-side to 'Land of Confusion', 1986

Whenever you start a new endeavour, the first fruits of the labour often have an outsize impact. This impact can be both wide-spread and far-reaching, often informing not only the direction of future efforts but also the way you view the entire project. Kick off with something lacklustre and it can really squash any enthusiasm you had at the outset, a case of reality cruelly stamping out your idealistic goals. On the other hand, if your first effort is rewarded with something of quality or is at least something well-received by an intended audience, it can feel like a big burst of energy - a doubling down of the passion to create, and often to create more in that same sort of vein.

This concept can apply to really any endeavour at all, be it manufacturing a product prototype, getting to a first playable build of a video game, or embarking on an extended journey of writing about something you love. Making a music album? That's no exception.

> **Phil:** *Genesis balances my life. And I think that's how we all feel. I like to go on tour with my own band for a year, then maybe make a film in between, but suddenly I think, "Let's try Genesis again." It is always an interesting experiment to meet again after a while and see if it still works.* [20]

> **Mike:** *We'd go into The Farm with nothing, sometimes having not worked together for a year or more and plunge into the unknown. Compared to other bands it was a weird way of working, and there'd always be a nice kind of fear about it. What were we going to do? Would it work?* [14]

> **Phil:** *I don't know any other band that works like we do, sitting round, improvising together, until something forms. Every other band seems to be more organised - more boring - than that...We have something special here.* [12]

So they jam, and improvise, and cross their fingers. They have no idea what will emerge, but assuming something does, it's likely to colour the look and feel of whatever comes next. Maybe they'll get something gentle and beautiful, and end up with a more romantic album as a result. Maybe they'll get something really complex and end up with an album that trends towards complicated arrangements.

Or, maybe they'll get something really angular and fierce, and make an album with five chartbusting hits.

> **Tony:** *One that wasn't on the album was the first [completed song], wasn't it? 'Feeding the Fire'...* [73]

OK, reader participation time now! I want you to put this book down for a moment and make a list of what features your ideal, perfect pop/rock song ought to have. You can include as many or as few things as you want. Just grab a piece of paper and a writing utensil, or maybe just open up a text editor; whatever works for you. I'm sure your list will be unique and interesting, given that we all have different tastes and preferences. When you're done, come back to this book and we'll compare notes. Don't worry, I'll wait. Take your time!

Welcome back! All set? Great. I'll share my own list here as well. For me, a perfect pop/rock song meets the following criteria, listed in no particular order:

- Really strong central riff, rhythm, or repeated phrase; essentially, a great hook under the vocals
- Electricity; I want my rock songs to energise me just as I want my ballads to move me
- A catchy chorus that'll run through my head periodically long after the song is over
- A "cooldown" section to accentuate the harder edges of the main bit while giving me a chance to breathe
- Cohesive main thrust that doesn't get lost along the way
- Long enough runtime to let me savour what it does
- Lyrics that aren't entirely throwaway

- Really rippin' guitars
- A powerful, forceful lead vocal
- A few "POW" moments
- More there than what's immediately obvious on the surface, rewarding future listens

Did we line up on any ideas? Any places where we're not even close to having the same opinion? That's the fun of the exercise! Now, there are a **lot** of great rock songs out there that check a lot of these boxes for me, but I'm not sure I've heard one that really scores a clean 100%. After all, we're talking here about ideals and perfection, and then holding up actual works created by actual people against those unattainable measuring sticks. It's just a matter of how close you can get, really.

So with that in mind, let's return to the mid-1980s. Genesis go into The Farm, fiddle around, and come out with a song called 'Feeding the Fire'. How does this one measure up?

- ~~Really strong central riff, rhythm, or repeated phrase; essentially, a great hook under the vocals~~ ✓

DUN! DUH-DUN! DUH-DUN! DUH-DUHHH-DUHHH-DUN! DUH-DUN! DUH-DUNNNN! This thing's got grooves so tight I involuntarily pucker my lips into a Billy Idol sneer and bob my head to the beat like an angry strutting pigeon whenever I hear it. So, uh, check. Which sort of goes hand in hand with...

- ~~Electricity; I want my rock songs to energise me just as I want my ballads to move me~~ ✓

Them big drum fills, that dirty riff, yeah. Lots of energy to spare here.

- ~~A catchy chorus that'll run through my head periodically long after the song is over~~ ✓

"'Cuz you're feedin'! The fiyah! Oooover which you'll be roasted!" I'm gonna be singing that bit in my head for weeks; I just know it.

- ~~A "cooldown" section to accentuate the harder edges of the main bit while giving me a chance to breathe~~ ✓

This song actually has a couple of them, one longer than the other. They're significant enough that it might be better regarded as a "hot and cold" track, honestly, rather than a heater that spends eight bars off the gas pedal. It's got a bigger ratio of cold to hot than I'd normally expect to want in a rocker, but either way it still gets close enough in my book.

- ~~Cohesive main thrust that doesn't get lost along the way~~ ✓

Opening with a verse that's actually basically the chorus in disguise is a great way to set the tone. Then you repeat it, end with it, and toss another into the middle so you never lose sight. Masterfully structured. Again, those gentler bits comprise a whopping 42% of the track, yet they still never threaten to feel like they're the main point of the song. That means the *actual* main point must be very strong indeed.

- ~~Long enough runtime to let me savour what it does~~ ✓

At nearly six minutes long, there's plenty of rock to go around with this one; both sections really get their due.

- ~~Lyrics that aren't entirely throwaway~~ ✓

Some great Tony-isms here about setting oneself up for failure and being too ignorant, insulated, and/or malicious to realise it. Of course, they also have the pitfalls of Tony-isms in terms of awkward phrasing at times, but we'll forgive that. These aren't lyrics that mean anything to me on a deep, emotional level, but they are at least engaging, which is all I'm really looking for here.

- Really rippin' guitars ✗

OK, so you can't win 'em all. Don't get me wrong; I love the guitar tone here. I just wouldn't quite say Mike is really rippin'. We'll count this as a near-miss.

- ~~A powerful, forceful lead vocal~~ ✓

Awwwwww yeah. Have you heard Phil on this track? Good grief man. It's like his voice was fired out of a cannon. A cannon covered in leather and spikes. Maybe it's a good thing this did end up a B-side; he'd never be able to crush this thing live night after night. People talk about 'Mama' as being perhaps his strongest vocal effort, and I don't particularly want to dissent, so much as just maybe slide these people a copy of 'Feeding the Fire' and watch them say, "Well hey, wait a minute…"

- ~~One or more "POW" moments~~ ✓

"OHHHHHHHHHHHHHHHHHHHHHHHHHHHHHHHHHHH!" If you're dancing along to this song because it's so good you can't help yourself, 4:32 is the exact moment where your dancing stops and you strike a dramatic pose while you raise your eyes to the ceiling and shout from your imaginary mountaintop. You know what I mean?

- ~~More there than what's immediately obvious on the surface, rewarding future listens~~ ✓

All the little background stuff that you're too busy doing a billion push-ups to notice when this song comes on? Well…it's all there, if you, you know, can stop running through brick walls long enough to hear.

So…yeah. For my money, this is the best pop/rock song Genesis ever recorded. It's got nearly everything I could ever want in a bangin' rock tune, and the fact that it's Genesis is just the surprising icing on the cake. It's them taking that natural inclination they have to put "loud bits" next to "quiet bits," but the loud bits are extraordinarily aggressive and the quiet bits are still bubbling over with an intense kind of energy. Like, you wouldn't expect a background vocal of "Dibbi, duh-dip-dip…dip dibbi-doo" to be a line that really works on *any* level, but it works *super well.* I have no idea how they did it.

> **Tony:** *It's a little bit Tears For Fears-y. I think it's a strong song and I was rather pleased with the lyric. The basic riff is really good. I liked using the idea of "feeding the fire" as a way of describing how people cause their own downfall. I'd quite like to have had it on the album, but there were a lot of choices to make.* [18]

And from a launching point like that, *Invisible Touch* was born. More extended soft intensity in the middle of 'Tonight, Tonight, Tonight', more sharp edges in 'Domino', more synth riffing in 'Anything She Does', more deep grooves in 'The Brazilian', and so forth. Hard not to feel good about what you're producing when this is the first thing that crawls out of the ether and into your laps. So why isn't it on the album? Maybe it's because they had another banger of a rock tune in 'Land of Confusion' and didn't think it made sense to put them both on the record. Hard to fault that decision, given all the money that song made them, but if I didn't know any better it would be hard for me to pop that single in my player and not wonder which side was the A side after all.

18 - Hairless Heart

from *The Lamb Lies Down on Broadway*, 1974

You know, much has been made over the years - and indeed in this very book as well - of the disconnect between Steve Hackett and Tony Banks. There was the tension over whether 'Wot Gorilla?' or 'Please Don't Touch' better earned a position on *Wind & Wuthering*. That was just part of the larger feeling that Tony kept shelving Steve's music indefinitely for the band while by contrast his own songs kept "just so happening" to make it onto the records. There was also the fact that Tony was the only current Genesis member at the time to not appear on Steve's *Voyage of the Acolyte*. There was Tony's reluctance to explore the core riff of 'I Know What I Like' until he had to admit he didn't have any better ideas. And of course, there were the particularly hostile soundbites in regard to 'After the Ordeal', with Tony apparently feeling that even his piano part couldn't salvage the song.

After all that friction, particularly in regards to 'After the Ordeal', wouldn't it be nice if we could finally get these two to see eye to eye? Wouldn't it be refreshing to see them working together for a change? Wouldn't it be a welcome sight if they could team up and create something beautiful together - something they could both champion for the record? Wouldn't that be something?

Well, breathe that sigh of relief, because it's time for After 'After the Ordeal'. It's a song about taking all that prickly egotistical hair on your heart, that barrier of aggressive pride, and shaving it right off. It's a song about lowering your defences, letting someone else into your world, sharing it with them, and perhaps finding that it's better together. Steve and Tony were at odds before, and they will be again, but for now let's take some time to revel in this wonderful moment of unity. Let's bask in the conciliatory glow of this song, where the magic of friendship at last can thrive.

> **Tony:** *Steve would probably agree that there were a couple of sides to him that the rest of us weren't really interested in. But where we did coincide it was fantastic. I did an awful lot of duet playing with him, the two of us playing lead together or in harmony, swapping parts.* [1]

'Hairless Heart' is, at its simplest, a song comprised of two alternating bits.

> **Steve:** *The first melody's mine, second bit is Tony's.* [13]

It's fitting in this new era of cooperation that while the first bit you hear is Steve's, the first instrument you hear (after the distant and dissonant chord marking the transition from 'Back in N.Y.C.') is actually Tony's. You get these keyboard twinkles going on before anything else really happens, Tony introducing Steve to the listener. It's a lovely stage-setter for Steve to come in with his nylon guitar, at which point everything else is gone. Now it's *only* Steve and Tony, combining their sounds and nothing else. And, well, it's gorgeous. You wouldn't think it'd be enough, but it is.

> **Steve:** *Lovely playing from Tony: the organ with repeat echo. Nylon guitar from me. The next bit of the melody fades in with volume pedal. Fuzz box, Echoplex...I'm always asked about what equipment I was using then.* [13]

> **Peter:** *Steve wasn't a full-frontal guitarist flashing his crotch. He was a more introverted guy who dug his particular vein with a trowel rather than a spade. What had attracted me to his playing was that it was about mood and sound and colour and added a slightly darker element, more brown than black.* [1]

We loop the Steve melody again, now adding a layer. Tony's still just twinkling away in the background, but now there are two guitars. Steve's swapped out his nylon for an electric but is playing the same melody on it. Now instead there's another acoustic sound - Mike on his 12-string - strumming the chords. This in itself is a really unusual arrangement for Genesis. If there are chords to be played, one would almost certainly expect Tony to be the one playing them. That's sort of his thing. Instead you've got Steve relinquishing the nylon's dual role of chord master and melody driver, yet still not actually giving the chords over to the keyboards.

> **Steve:** *Mike shimmering away...Strange division of labour with Genesis.* [13]

This changes the nature of the thing a little, because now instead of this second loop sounding like a development and expansion of the first - which it is, mind you - it sounds like a transition into what's coming next. It's retaining that acoustic sound but subordinating it to an electric melody, so as the phrase ends your ears expect a further shift in that direction.

Naturally, that shift does indeed come as Tony's writing takes over. It's such a simple melody here: just a walk up the D minor scale with occasional steps back down, but it's somehow still breath-taking.

> **Steve:** *One of those lyrical moments from The Lamb Lies Down on Broadway which had a very kind of experimental, abrasive thing. But there were always these interesting keyboard lines.* [13]

> **Tony:** *I think it's quite a difficult album; it's very dark. Quite dense. But I think if you try it, it still works really well. I think it's rewarding. Perhaps it takes a little bit more to get into it in the first place, and maybe for that reason people - once they've got there - hold it up like that.* [3]

It seems absurd to refer to Tony playing a basic D minor scale as experimental or interesting, but maybe that's the point. Steve's melody was in D minor too, you see, and over the course of that section he also hits every single note in the scale. I think that's why these two sections don't feel like they could've even come from different writers; what Tony's doing by playing a scale in sequence is basically just "unscrambling" Steve's melody from before. That's also why this section feels almost triumphant in a way, despite still possessing that darkness Tony referenced, something inherent to minor keys. Steve's melody starts high and then spends most of its remaining time descending. Tony's scale just goes up and up until the very end, which is a resolution to the minor third, and so it doesn't even feel like a descent of its own. Of course, having Phil jump in on drums and Mike enter on bass pedals doesn't hurt one's chances of attaining sonic grandeur, either.

Steve got two loops on his melody, so Tony takes two of his own, and then just like that we're back to the twinkling sensation and a repeat of Steve's "electric loop" with one notable change: Phil is still playing. There aren't any big fills or flashy rhythms here. He's just playing on the beats in the most basic way possible. It's utterly simple, but just like Tony's own utterly simple bit previously, this adds so much texture and meaning to the piece. You see, Phil isn't actually playing the *drums* here; he's beating a heart. This pattern is not a backbeat but a pulse. We couldn't hear it at the beginning of the song, but that's because the heart was still covered in its muting hair. Now it's been at least partially shaven, so the heartbeat is audible once again.

Phil never does achieve full flight in this song, nor should he: that's not the point of the thing. But he does thump-thump a little quicker near the end of the piece. As the heart is fully cleared of its self-defeating debris and the song is making its final journey towards the "romance" of 'Counting Out Time', Phil starts jumping the beats.

> **Steve:** *[The] accent there [is] very Phil Collins. Getting to the end of the bar very quickly. Sometimes works with things in 7/8, [though] this is in 4/4. There's the accent, the push as we used to call it.* [13]

Anticipatory cymbal crashes, drum fills that would feel lethargic in other songs but make perfect sense here. It's not the most impressive playing on a technical level, but from an artistic standpoint this stuff is top notch, and the best musicians always know when to take their feet off the gas.

> **Steve:** *It's a short song, in some ways a palate cleanser between the noisy ones.* [13]

'Hairless Heart' is a song performed by four people and written by perhaps the unlikeliest combination of two from that group, yet it sounds like it came from one mind.

> **Tony:** *Some of my favourite bits [of the album] are the instrumental moments...* [1]

> **Steve:** *[My music is] a gigantic experiment, but it doesn't matter to me whether it succeeds or fails; I'm more interested in creating unlikely constructions. I suspect that Genesis operated in the same way...Music is this potential time machine, a vehicle that can convey you to all manner of times and places.* [1]

This track has a runtime of 2:10, or 130 seconds total. Of that time, Steve's writing portions comprise 66 seconds and Tony's comprise 64. Consciously or not, they split this thing right down the middle into two halves that need one another in order to truly come alive. And come alive they do; more than any other song in the Genesis catalogue, 'Hairless Heart' is proof to me that it's not the length of the thing that matters: it's how you use it. And this tune is just jam-packed with aural treats. I want it to be longer, but I also know it's exactly as long as it needs to be. I could do with an ending chord resolving to the minor root, sure, but that's just nit-picking. There's more here than meets the eye, and it couldn't have happened without Tony and Steve coming together in this unprecedented way.

> **Tony:** *I think he always thought that for some reason I had it in for him, but I really didn't. It's just my way. I always appear to be like that. I actually used to champion him; I remember a few times championing him against Peter, who wasn't quite so sure.* [1]

It's a shame it didn't always last, but there's good news: these two divergent souls had at least one more miracle in them still to come. Hair always grows back, but this new heart would last for a little while yet. We'll see you again, friends, one last time before this section of the book draws to a close.

17 - Mad Man Moon

from *A Trick of the Tail*, 1976

GABRIEL OUT OF GENESIS?

Such was the way Genesis found out that news had leaked to the press that Peter Gabriel had quit the band. They were a few weeks into rehearsals on the album that was to become *A Trick of the Tail*, having just gotten Steve back into the rehearsal room after he'd finished his first solo album, yet still with no idea who was going to be their primary singer. This wasn't the way the news was supposed to break, but it was going to happen sooner or later, and perhaps it was for the better to have it come out early and then be done with it.

After all, "Peter Gabriel's Backing Band" had been churlishly grinding their teeth for quite some time.

> **Phil:** *There are frustrations and disappointments. The reviews of the band are upsetting. One national paper devoted most of its review of the band to explaining that Peter's wife was the daughter of the Queen's secretary...it's a problem that you can't put into words... I find it incredibly frustrating to play say very well one night, not very well the next, and for people not to know the difference. I'd like to get booed on an off night! Of course it's a good thing that the show can get across by the visuals, but a lot of people don't listen to the music. That's a bit of a drag... I'd like to see Mike and Tony [appreciated] more. After all, they started the band for the songwriting. It must be frustrating for them when they write a lot of the music and get very little out of it.* [93]

> **Tony:** *There was an imbalance in the writing. Mike and I tended to write a lot more than Steve and Phil at the time, and I was getting a bit fed up with [the lack of recognition]. I felt I wrote a lot on Foxtrot, and I suggested to Mike that we receive individual credits on that album. I just felt it wasn't an equal contribution from all five of us; it was a little silly to pretend it was, but somehow it blew over. Lamb was more of a group album, but on A Trick of the Tail...we decided to give individual credits.* [10]

> **Mike:** *If we'd been credited individually with the songs by the time Pete left people would've said, "Well, there's three of them left. They wrote those, and he wrote that." They would have seen there was still a strong writing team there... We were saying, "We can write well...we're gonna make sure we show it."* [10]

The band was jamming, working on pieces like 'Dance on a Volcano', but instead of three writers all expanding equally to fill the departure of the fourth (bearing in mind that Phil still wasn't writing songs on his own at this stage), Steve Hackett had gone off and done a solo album.

> **Steve:** *I'd just come off the back of having done a solo thing, so I was fairly dry of ideas, and I was having to think on my feet. It wasn't really until the following album, Wind & Wuthering, that I'd amassed a lot of stuff to throw at everybody.* [3]

Grumpy and determined to prove his songwriting chops with a piece that would just say "Banks" on the record sleeve's writing credits, Tony dug into his catalogue of solo pieces.

> **Tony:** *I had a few ready-made pieces available, which I'd written thinking about a possible solo album, including a complete version of 'Mad Man Moon'...but had made the decision that if we were going to carry on with the group we would need to pool everything.* [1]

It's hard to say exactly when Tony had finished writing 'Mad Man Moon', or when precisely he wrote its lyrics. But tell me if this hypothetical timeline sounds as plausible to you as it does to me:

> 1) Peter Gabriel tells the band he's leaving Genesis.
> 2) Tony Banks come up with a song that opens with piano and flute,
>   and which continues for the remainder of its first minute with only piano/keyboards and vocals.
> 3) Genesis start rehearsing for an album without Peter, where Tony finds he's the only one bringing in complete ideas, while the others are relatively "dry."

4) News leaks that Peter has quit the band and the press declare Genesis dead.
5) Tony and Mike insist on individual writing credits for the album.
6) Tony pens lyrics to 'Mad Man Moon' built around an extended desert metaphor, grappling with the regrets and perils of leaving someone behind in search of some kind of nebulous greater joy.

You feelin' me now?

'Mad Man Moon' is like the middle ground of Tony's lyrics; he's not yet quite comfortable writing things that are open and vulnerable like 'Many Too Many' a couple years later, but he's also moving away a bit from the pure fantasy of the past. So instead we get something in between: a really poetic, artistic extended metaphor for something very real. The lyrics have always appealed to me in themselves as a broad kind of message about not taking what you have for granted, a fable of the follies of wanderlust. But I think they may well have come from a very personal place, as Tony just watched his best friend turn his back on the band they built together. And for what?

> **Peter:** *The hidden delights of vegetable growing and community living are beginning to reveal their secrets. I could not expect the band to tie in their schedules with my bondage to cabbages.*
> [94]

Peter was only being only slightly tongue-in-cheek here; he really did quit the band to move into the country, grow a vegetable garden, and try to integrate himself into some community or another (one commune was ironically even called Genesis). Was this Pete pretending to have wings for his arms, flying away from his support and security only to soar too high and free fall like Icarus before him? Was he relishing the thought of being freed from his perceived shackles only to become lost in an endless desert, forced to reminisce of what he'd left behind in his hubris?

It seems Tony may have thought so, and the lyrics - gorgeous as they are - take on a sort of juvenile jilted lover aspect when viewed through that lens. "You'll be sorry!" But the emotions are real, and the imagery is still very compelling, so I can hardly fault them. And as I said before, they're still disguised in this fantastical kind of fog, so I suppose it wouldn't have been hard to sell his bandmates on the words. Or the song, I guess, given that they needed material. In walks a very hurt-but-not-going-to-show it Tony Banks telling them how things are going to be, and who's going to tell him no?

> **Tony:** *We did 'Mad Man Moon' straight like I'd written it.* [10]

And as much as one might look at that flute sound that bookends the piece and come away thinking Tony wrote this with images of Gabriel dancing in his head, he also knew straightaway that this was going to be a Phil Collins tune vocally.

> **Tony:** *We had always thought Phil would sing a couple of the softer songs like 'Mad Man Moon' and 'Ripples' because we knew he could handle them...* [1]

Knew better than Phil himself, even.

> **Phil:** *The studio environment was great, allowing us to hammer away at it until the vocals worked...Some songs are especially demanding. 'Mad Man Moon' is one of Tony's, and his melodies are out of my usual comfort zone, especially if you have to learn them on the fly in the studio. I would get used to this over the next few years.* [12]

Discomfort or no, Phil just nails this vocal performance. Not just the notes, but the way he accents certain sounds in the middle section, his enunciation, and most importantly the emotional heart of the whole thing. It's all masterfully done.

Now take that vocal with those lyrics and put it on top of a piano-driven melody composed by a brilliant writer who's got something to prove. The way the piano interplays with the keyboard chords, with Steve's distant, ethereal guitar, with even the layered backing vocals - it's all terrific. And then, in case you didn't get the point by the end of the first chorus, an instrumental break featuring an array of tight percussion, reverberating bass, and a piano solo. Not a keyboard solo, mind, but an actual piano solo that then adds in keyboards partway through. The guys never played this live, and maybe that's because Tony would need four arms to do it justice, because this whole section is just *mesmerizing*.

> **Tony:** *I never quite know what makes one chord progression feel better than another. I think a lot of it is done by how it feels on the keyboard. Some things just feel lovely to play. One example is the main chord sequence in 'Mad Man Moon'. It fit on the hands so well. I like there*

> to be something unusual in a chord progression. It doesn't have to be bizarre, just unusual... One of my favourite chord changes of all time comes at the end of 'Mad Man Moon', coming out of the middle section and into the last verse. It goes from E♭m7 to Gm7 with a D in the bass. It's an uplifting sort of change. And there are lots of those changes lying around that we only use once. [23]

"Uplifting" is right on. It's so energizing coming back from that section into the up-tempo vocal using wordplay and word associations to take you from the sand to a cell to the football field and all the way back to sand again as the song, like its subject, comes back down to earth. It makes that final verse and outro so poignant. "The grass will be greener 'til the stems turn to brown, and thoughts will fly higher 'til the earth brings them down." Tony is a hit or miss lyricist, but these are some of the best he's ever done.

Tony: *It's a funny thing really, because at the time we did it, things like 'Volcano' and 'Squonk' and everything were the ones I really liked. But coming back to it, I actually prefer all the soft songs, I think. I mean, 'Mad Man Moon' has always been a big favourite of mine I suppose; it was a song I wrote on my own completely. And I was very pleased with some of the things. I mean, the middle is not played as well as it should be, but the verse parts and everything. It's just nice; the chord sequences and chord changes and things like that. I was very pleased with them at the time, because they're sort of like...they're unusual, but then don't necessarily sound too unusual. I always think that's a good thing about a song... It's very romantic, I suppose. I think that works very well.* [3]

If I listen really closely, I can almost guess at which parts Tony is saying aren't played as well as he'd like them to be. Almost. But to my ears, this song might as well have been played flawlessly from end to end. I'm moved by 'Mad Man Moon' every single time I hear it. It's just a beauty of a song in every way, semi-forgotten among an album full of greats. And if you look really closely inside the album cover, you'll see a single word under the track's title: "Banks".

Mission accomplished, Tony. I think Genesis will be just fine.

16 - Duke's Travels

from *Duke*, 1980

It's common knowledge by now among Genesis fans, but *Duke* was intended at the outset to be an album where one side consisted of two solo songs from each member of the band. A kind of musical appetiser of sorts. Or I suppose the after-dinner mints, if the solo stuff ended up being the albums' Side 2 instead.

Either way, the real meat of the album was this side-long, group-composed behemoth with the working title of 'Duke', from which the album itself eventually took its name.

> **Phil:** *At one point I think we thought that we could revisit the idea of doing a long side...like 'Supper's Ready'. You know, something that was like a body of work. And I think we kind of...I mean, that's why there's 'Duke's Travels', 'Duke's End', because we still liked those titles...that's what's left of that idea, really.* [3]

> **Tony:** *They would've gone 'Behind the Lines', 'Duchess', 'Guide Vocal', 'Turn It On Again', 'Duke's Travels', 'Duke's End'. Which is actually how it was performed live; we tried it. One reason we didn't do it [on the album] is we didn't want the comparison with 'Supper's Ready', and felt maybe it wasn't the moment to do a totally combined thing like that. As it is, there is quite a lot of linkage between those tracks anyhow; the first three are linked.* [3]

> **Phil:** *The group compositions are the strongest. A lot of that is down to the rhythms...But the group compositions are definitely breaking new ground...I wanted to do a long song with some substance...So basically we put a lot of things together between us...'Duke's Travels' and 'Duke's End' were riffs that we wrote as we went along. We intended it to be one 25 minute piece but when we came to the practicalities of the album, the solo songs on the second side wouldn't have run so well, so we had to split it all up.* [95]

Tony may not have wanted the comparisons to 'Supper's Ready', but now that he's come out and said that, how could I do anything else? I'll have more to say about 'Supper's Ready' later on in this book, but for now let's just take an overly-simplified look at that song's structure. In a very broad sense it goes as follows: Intro, Powerful Section, Gentle Section, Rock Section, Epic Instrumental Section, Reprise of Intro, Reprise of Strong Section.

Now let's look at the big 'Duke' piece as originally conceptualised, through that same lens. That one ends up looking something like this: Intro, Powerful Section, Gentle Section, Rock Section, Epic Instrumental Section, Reprise of Gentle Section, Reprise of Intro.

Again, that's heavily oversimplified and doesn't account for the wide range of nuances, like how wildly different 'Lover's Leap' and 'Behind the Lines' are as Intro Sections, or how the Gentle Section of 'Supper's Ready' comprises multiple movements and a lot of time while 'Guide Vocal' is pretty brief by comparison. But in a very loose way, the skeleton of each of these things is almost completely the same. Why is that? Well, it's not because Genesis sat there attempting to rewrite 'Supper's Ready' - far from it! It's just that their songwriting sensibilities led them down a similar path: how to flow from quiet to loud, what to reprise and when to reprise it to neatly tie the whole package together, and so forth.

> **Tony:** *This album, I have to be honest...this is my favourite Genesis album really. It has such a sort of positive quality about it. I love the way it starts; I love 'Duchess', I think it works fantastically; and I love all the instrumental stuff towards the end, too, although I think [the album's conclusion] starts a little weak. But it just gets really good.* [3]

So within that established framework you have 'Duke's Travels' acting as a kind of analogue of the Apocalypse in 9/8 section of 'Supper's Ready', a segment that interestingly enough was written primarily by the combination of Tony, Mike, and Phil. That 'Duke's Travels' would carry a similar amount of water for its own musical suite therefore shouldn't come as much of a surprise. If anything, Phil was even more involved this time around.

> **Phil:** *My commitment to Genesis is much greater than it ever was before. I would fight for it more now than I would have done before because it's more me. That's what it comes down to. There's more of me in it. I've come a long way since And Then There Were Three, I really*

> *have...Duke for me isn't just another Genesis album. It's a whole period of growing up. A musical maturity if you like.* [95]

It's fitting for the song to be called "Travels", because this one's a ride. It opens with these warm cymbal waves, echoing guitar chords, and an almost tentative keyboard line. This all fades into nothing as Phil's drums take over with heavy intensity, followed by a more melodic and driving keyboard bit on top. Switch from the rapid hollow drums to some cymbals and back again. Then you get this big bit that sounds to my ears like an alternate soundtrack to Casino Night Zone. There's no melodic similarities there, but it's all about the feel; I can't help but picture Sonic the Hedgehog hurtling headlong into a slot machine, and this song predates that character by eleven years. It's like a brief glimpse into a bright, neon future. There are melodies, countermelodies, textures, with a masterclass in drumming underpinning the whole shebang.

> **Phil:** *There's definitely a side to us coming out which wasn't on the last album: the playing side.* [96]

Uhhh, yeah. Yeah, I'd say so. And now a pounding straight rhythm with some guitar/keyboard interplay, creating a whole lot of tension. Again, this is like the build in Apocalypse in 9/8 all over again, just with a somewhat different flavour. It's bigger, and bigger, and bigger, and then oh my goodness what IS that heavenly sound on top of these goosebump-laden chords?

> **Tony:** *The Arpeggiator was one of the things which I used on 'Duke's Travels', and what a marvellous effect that was! And it had a bass pedal on it and you had the polyphonic synthesizer on it so I could do all those other things as well. I have got two of them and there were only about a dozen of them [made], and I think the other ten only sold because I was using it! The company went bust after that or got taken over. It was a fun instrument.* [21]

The Arpeggiator sounds like the name of a supervillain, or at least a nickname a group of friends would bestow on one of their drinking buddies for reasons too wrapped up in a certain time and place for anyone outside the group to possibly understand. Here though? Here it's the hero of 'Duke's Travels', putting that sparkly shimmer in the sky above the song's most triumphant moment, making the whole thing dazzle in radiance while Mike's guitar finally soars out of the background and across the illuminated heavens. And to then have 'Guide Vocal' come back in the midst of it all? My, my, my. That's the "666 is no longer alone" shiver-down-the-spine moment of 'Duke's Travels', no question about it.

> **Tony:** *There's a strong emotional moment when it gets to the repeat of 'Guide Vocal' done within 'Duke's Travels', which is a very intense piece of singing. To me that's one of the strongest...one of the very strong moments in Genesis music.* [3]

And then the song gradually bleeds energy over the rest of the 'Guide Vocal' repeat, the emotion spent and the travels making their way home. A brief respite, a striking synth flute bit reminiscent of 'The Court of the Crimson King', and then the whole thing careens back into the Intro Reprise known as 'Duke's End'. I see a lot of people say things like "If Apocalypse in 9/8 were its own song, it would still be one of my favourite Genesis tunes." And I find that all those people also tend to really love 'Duke's Travels' because it is, essentially, Apocalypse in 9/8 carved out as its own track. The context of the larger piece makes it that much stronger, but it's perfectly capable of standing up under its own power as well.

The 2007 Turn It On Again Tour really brought this to light, I think. Selecting 'Duke's Travels' for inclusion in the set was a bold move, replacing 'The Colony of Slippermen' and 'In That Quiet Earth' as the middle leg of the big '~~In the Cage~~ Afterglow Medley'. Those are big shoes to fill, and it wasn't easy for anyone involved.

> **Tony:** *Before we did the last tour I spent quite a few months getting all the sounds together, whatever I thought I could, including some of the processes from the older ones like the Synclavier sounds and a few others, and tried to get everything as close as I could to being right. Even so, when we got out there I had to change quite a bit. I was pretty well prepared actually. Mike was well prepared. Daryl is ALWAYS well prepared! Phil was completely unprepared, so it took him about two weeks of just trying to get to play how he used to, which was tough. Especially on a piece like 'Duke's Travels', which was always a tough one.* [21]

And what about the audience? How would they react?

> **Tony:** *I think the set is more demanding as it combines so many instrumental bits from various eras, like the...'Duke's Travels' bits...It's also demanding for the audience. Some of them you*

will lose during the instrumental bits as they don't know them...The other thing is, we don't have anything to prove; we're just doing it. We're playing to fans who know they like us. We're not trying to convert them. Perhaps in the past we did that. [66]

I love this attitude. "We're going to play what moves us, and you'll either check out or come along on the journey." That attitude, that music...it's why in my opinion the 2007 version of the live medley is the best one they did. Something about that epic moment in 'Duke's Travels' just resonates, even when the arrangement changes so that the big vocal entrance is just an extension of Daryl Stuermer's guitar solo. You can totally see what Tony was talking about here: the crowd cheers wildly for the end of the 'Cinema Show' segment and even more wildly for the start of 'Afterglow' but generally stand around puzzled during 'Duke's Travels'. "Wait, what's this one? I don't recognise this one. Do you recognise this one?" And yet it's still the song that guides them home.

Strong as it was, the band couldn't quite manage to work 'Duke's Travels' into the set for 2021. Declining health had caused the dynamics to change too much.

Tony: *It'll be kind of different. Phil used to have some very dramatic moments on stage with Genesis. He'd never have the same kind of dramatic moments or intensity we used to have...sitting on a chair. Obviously, the effects can help things out a bit. So, you just say, "He's not going to do those the same way." We'd just do the songs. We've got plenty of good songs to do and it wouldn't be a problem. But I don't think we could have the extended keyboard solo we did on the last tour in 2007 which had a bit of everything in it. There wouldn't be much point, because the point of it was Mike, Phil, and I playing together, like we did on things such as 'Duke's Travels'. There would be a different intensity and a different kind of set list.* [18]

That's a real shame, because 'Duke's Travels' is a downright treat, especially in live form. I suppose we should be thankful we got what we did from it along the way.

But hey, speaking of live performances and context, what's the deal with these pieces anyway? The lyrics to the various individual songs in the 'Duke' piece don't have any immediately apparent connection, even the ones that remain linked together like 'Behind the Lines', 'Duchess', and 'Guide Vocal'. Is there some kind of meta-narrative happening here? Something where some duke of something or other is also a singer but betrayed...and then something about a TV? I'm really confused.

Thankfully, we have Phil Collins in concert during the Duke Tour to sort it all out for us.

Phil: *The story of a mate of ours whose name was Albert. Albert was a born loser. Nothing he did went right; he was one of life's failures. Written off, just like that. I'll give an example: Albert once fell in love with a lady.* [97]

Hmm, I guess 'Behind the Lines' could be about falling in love with a character in print, couldn't it? Reading the pages, feeling closer to someone, whether that be a fictional character or a celebrity in the news? Seems our old Albert was developing an infatuation!

Phil: *Beautiful lady she was, beautiful lady...a duchess. And the duchess was a very domineering lady. She was into S&M. Ah, but poor old Albert didn't speak Spanish or Mexican, so she kicked him out! And he went home that night and was very disappointed and dejected.* [97]

Ah, "duchess," like the title of the second track! I'm following this now, I think. Albert falls in love with this celebrity singer, who he doesn't really know except through print media. He encounters her in real life, but doesn't speak her native language, and his advances are rebuffed on that basis (and also because he's kind of a creep). So Albert gets upset and writes the whole thing off in a sulky bit called 'Guide Vocal' - dual meaning there, since a guide vocal is what you call the rough vocal track to line up the instrumentation before the real vocal is laid down. Albert thinks he's the reason the Duchess succeeded! This is getting good, now.

Phil: *So he sat down on the chair, and he turned on the television, and suddenly his whole life changed because he was back in love again! He fell in love! He fell in love with his television set. It was a really beautiful looking television set, square with sort of a glass bit in the middle. And it was a good conversational piece for his friends, but it was a bit of a one-sided affair for Albert. And in two days he was in hospital having the glass removed from his private parts.* [97]

Ouch! But yes, yes, we're seeing it now. "All I need is a TV show...down on my luck again..." This is Albert coping with the loss by finding a new medium for his romantic fantasies! I just hope that bit with the hospital is merely a joke...

> **Phil:** *So he went on a convalescing holiday abroad over there, where tragedy struck again. Because Albert fell in love. Again. This time, with his walking stick. We're not too sure about Albert; seems a bit of a weirdo. And I think you've guessed it: in two or three days time he was back in hospital having the walking stick removed from his private parts. So he came back from his convalescing holiday abroad over there, to England over here where we live, where he entered a home for unsuccessful young louts, called Duke's. But I can see you're getting very upset, but I don't want you to, because every cloud has a silver lining, and every silver lining has a cloud. Every bin has a liner. And it was in this bin that Albert wrote some fantastically boring books. He wrote such literary classics as Romeo & Albert and A Midsummer Night's Albert. Albert: A Space Odyssey. Albert Flew Over the Cuckoo's Nest. A horror film called Albert: Prince of Darkness. The Return of Albert. The Return of the Brides of Evil of Albert. And so it goes on. And the big change for him came when he started writing sex books. We have a very, very big one called Danish Albert on the Job; a big hit for him!* [97]

Wow, so 'Duke's Travels' is something literal! After some journeying around the world he entered a home called Duke's, so they were literally the Travels to Duke's! And saaaaay! That 'Guide Vocal' reprise with all its intensity is just Albert writing his books with an "I'll show you!" kind of attitude! This also explains the reprise of 'Behind the Lines', come to think of it! He's gone from "It's written in the book" to writing books himself by 'Duke's End'. It's a strange story, yes, but I think we've done it! I think we've cracked the code of this whole thing!

> **Phil:** *And now, to the music! Which has got nothing to do with Albert; I was deliberately wasting your time. This is some music from our album called Duke, and we call it - pretty cleverly - 'Music From Our Album Called Duke'. OK!* [97]

...Welp.

15 - Driving the Last Spike

from *We Can't Dance*, 1991

'Driving the Last Spike' is a marvellous case study on how three-piece Genesis wrote songs out of nothing. By this point they'd had two full albums of pure improvisation on top of another pair where they intentionally began turning the focus away from solo-written compositions. So even though *We Can't Dance* came five years after their last songwriting sessions together, by this point Genesis was something of a well-oiled songwriting machine. And I think this song provides the perfect window to see that in action.

For one thing, by *We Can't Dance* Phil Collins was so big it was a bit of a shock he'd even bother coming back. This was a guy who in late February of 1991 was on stage collecting the Record of the Year Grammy for 'Another Day in Paradise', and then a few weeks later was back at The Farm saying, "OK, what's next?" It's a weird juxtaposition, more surprising still because at this point Phil's buy-in had never been greater.

> **Phil:** *I was still very fully committed, and to me I was actually more involved in We Can't Dance than any other record.* [3]

So Phil's listening closer than ever when they whip out the drum machine and start cycling through different patterns they've programmed in, seeing if any catch their ear. This is the traditional start of how they put songs together by this time. And going through, they find one pattern that's been laying around a while, which now they feel they can finally get into. Enough so that instead of improvising around it for a couple hours or so like they sometimes do, they actually toy with it for multiple days, each time coming up with completely different ideas to lay on top of it.

> **Tony:** *There's an old drum machine pattern of Mike's, actually, that all the bits were originally written on. We had three or four different jam sessions on it, and different ideas emerged on different days. All the bits worked, so we thought it would be nice to find some way to stick them all together. So Phil wrote a rather more subtle part than what we originally had.* [82]

"All the bits worked." I want to emphasise that, because that's a really incredible statement in itself. I mean, these guys were really cooking at this point, weren't they? No wonder Phil bought in.

> **Phil:** *I love that song...Songs like that I really, really loved. And I was really proud of my work on We Can't Dance.* [1]

So now they've got a few different variations on the pattern, and Phil has simplified the pattern a little bit to let them all work together. At this point they know they're likely looking at a longer song, because all these sections are going to need to connect to one another. In the *Trespass* days they might've just shoved the bits up against one another and who cares about the rest? That's prog, man! During the latter Gabriel days they'd have smoothed the transitions with some links, but the overall philosophy would've been the same: do something complicated, because that's what makes better music. Not so by this era.

> **Phil:** *We still saw ourselves as a group of songwriters who were just as happy playing 'I Can't Dance' as we were with a twelve-minute song like 'Driving the Last Spike'.* [1]

Now crafty old experts with a wider portfolio, they've realised that length and complexity don't have to be locked in this eternal relationship of positive correlation; you could have a complex short song, or a long and simple song, and both expressions can be equally valid. In this instance they needed to simplify the drum pattern to help the various bits take shape, so keeping things simpler made a lot of sense, regardless of the song's eventual length.

> **Tony:** *There is a great difference between a ten-minute song like 'One For The Vine' and 'Driving The Last Spike', which musically is a much simpler song. [It] stays in its kind of feel for much longer, whereas 'One For The Vine' tends to chop and change around a bit more. I don't know really; there aren't any rules. I can't put my finger on it, but you just felt uncomfortable doing some of those things that were natural a long time ago. I don't think it is anything to do with age but there was never any kind of conscious decision to do things in a simpler way. It is all about what seems appropriate at the time.* [6]

So you know you're going simpler, and you've got the core musical thrust of each section, but like a hair stylist looking at a kid with one of those awful bowl cuts, you've still got to find a way to blend the layers together.

Tony: *Let's be honest: sometimes you know that you're going to have to add more bits, to build up to the chorus and all that.* [82]

And a big part of doing that is adding in the real drums. If you flip back earlier in this book to the entry on 'Tonight, Tonight, Tonight', you'll recall that I wrote about the way the live drums gradually "intruded" upon the drum machine, eventually supplanting the machine pattern entirely. That's a great transitional trick, especially for longer songs like this one, where they do it again.

Phil: *['Driving the Last Spike'] was basically written on the [E-mu SP-]1200. The same drum machine pattern worked at various stages of loudness throughout the whole song. Bit by bit, we took each section as it came once we put real drums on it, then started working on what to keep from the original drum machine. We replaced the machine cabasa with two live cabasas. It's nice to have certain elements of the drum machine in there but at the same time to make it human.* [82]

It's like creating a musical cyborg, isn't it? Sometimes you'll leave the pattern in, sometimes you'll replace it entirely, other times you'll have elements of both. When you're listening to 'Driving the Last Spike' you aren't typically thinking about the drums, and because you aren't, you're probably not noticing those individual components come and go. You hear a consistent beat from start to finish and the transformation of the sound doesn't register beyond the general feeling that the whole piece is getting steadily more powerful.

Tony: *The arrangement was almost there when the drums were put on...All we try to do is make the drums fit with what's already there.* [82]

And so now that you're going to accomplish these transitions through changes to the drum sounds, you know you're going to build the song up along the way. Which means arranging the improvised sections so the most powerful one comes at the end. You still want to "put a quiet bit next to a loud bit," as they say, so you'll reprise that gentle first section again after the heavier section that follows it, albeit with real drums added throughout so as not to lose any momentum. This is a trick itself reminiscent of 'Domino', so we're not talking about a one-off idea here. This is practiced, honed songcraft, building upon many years of experience. And then that final section works its way in.

Tony: *The real basis of the end section is the guitar riff. I just did this chord sequence that took it somewhere slightly different.* [82]

Mike: *That end section, that driving section is really basic. There's the keyboards, there's the drums, and there's the trashy guitars. There isn't much in there and I like that. It sounds like a band, which I think is good.* [98]

Phil: *We've done that stuff before. It's just that nobody's ever picked up on it. The feeling was Genesis are not in there; they're not hard rock.* [98]

Cool, the instrumentation is all there. Now you need a melody, but that's old hat for Phil at this point. Improvise away with your sing-song nonsense words!

Phil: *I love that song. I mean, I kind of sang the melodies to...the chords that Tony was playing.* [3]

It's just that simple, aspiring musicians! Listen to some chords and spit out a melody. What could be easier? So now the arrangement is pretty much done, you've got a ten minute song building from quiet to energetic to forceful (with a second spritz of quiet tossed in the back just to keep things interesting). All that remains is to decide what the thing's all about. Phil's been improvising melodies, but not many lyrics yet. The song's got a working title of 'Irish' just because of some sonic connection to one of the sections, but that doesn't really mean anything...does it?

> **Tony:** *'Driving the Last Spike' was a slightly interesting thing for us in a way, because it had always been, on previous albums - the previous three or four - the long songs: Tony writes the lyrics to the long songs, and all the rest of it. And on this one Phil said, "Well, let me have a go. I'd like to try a long song." So I said, "Well, here's ['Irish'], why not?"* [3]

A story, huh? What would make a good story that could stretch to fill ten minutes of music? Well, muses can be found in the unlikeliest of places, and it just so happened that Phil had trains on the brains.

> **Phil:** *After the Invisible Touch Tour, I decided to...that's when I started working on my train set, if I remember rightly. And then I did some film work. So I did Buster. So that took care of a fair amount of time: preparation, filming, shooting, editing, doing that soundtrack, or getting involved in that.* [3]

Model trains to relax before you make a movie about the Great Train Robbery? Hmmm...

> **Phil:** *I ended up being sent this book, actually, coincidentally around the same time [of the We Can't Dance writing sessions] called The Railway Navvies. And I read it, and I just...the idea of...the things you never think about. You know, like the railways. You know, you go through a tunnel on a long train, you don't think anything of it. Then you think of how that tunnel was built way back in the 1800s...* [3]

If you want to read in depth about the "navvies" I couldn't blame you; this kind of stuff is fascinating to me, too. But in short: these were gangs of generally poor manual laborers who built critical transportation infrastructure (for navigation, hence "navvy") under truly appalling working conditions. Phil describes his lyric writing for the song in the behind-the-scenes documentary filmed for *We Can't Dance*, *Genesis: No Admittance*. What jumped out at me watching the scene of him walking through the lyrical background was how emotional he became the longer he spoke. This had become personal to him.

> **Phil:** *The actual work that these guys did on the railway to make the English railways is a very touching story because they left their families. And some of them never went home again. Some of them died very young because of the amazing conditions they were living in and working in. And the accidents they had were pretty horrific. And if they did survive, you know, the strain on their backs, the physical strain of doing the job was just quite incredible. So I've written the words based on that. Based on one person's view of it, you know. Who leaves his family, not knowing if he's gonna go back. He goes to work on the railways and witnesses this horrendous accident. And the deceit. Because the people that were in charge of the railways didn't really care. Know what I mean? It was all hush-hush, all the deaths. If you weren't in that community you didn't know about it. And so there's that sort of shock of finding out that no one really cared about it. And then the fact that the guys really were sort of a breed unto themselves. Eventually he becomes hardened to the whole thing. So it's quite a lot; it's a ten minute song, so there's four pages of words.* [35]

Understand - and I don't mean this as cynically as it'll sound - that Phil Collins built a solo career almost entirely on the back of the agony of his first divorce. Go listen again to 'Please Don't Ask' from *Duke* where he cries "Oh, but I miss my boy!" Then imagine that man, with those emotions still a core part of his being, reading about other men who left their families behind to go suffer physical torture and possible death purely in the hopes that when...no. In the hopes that *if* they returned home, their families might be a little bit better off. Imagine how much Phil Collins must've sympathised with their need, their plight, their heartache.

> **Phil:** *How many people were killed making the tunnel when the tunnel collapsed, or the explosions to move [the rocks]? I just wrote this song about these people who just went off and left their families and maybe never came back. I mean, it wasn't war; this was just building a railway, you know?* [3]

That emotion comes straight through on the record. I can listen to any of the story songs of the Genesis prog heyday without the lyrics moving me too tremendously; myths and cryptic meanings are good fun and might make a person think, but I'm never really emotionally invested in Narcissus becoming a flower, you know? But 'Driving the Last Spike'? Man. This stuff gets me every time; it's a story, but it's *real* too. It matters.

> **Mike:** *There are words Phil writes that I'd never tackle. "Spades," for instance, on 'Driving the Last Spike'. It's a word I'd worry about putting down, but Phil wrote it and sings it great.* [98]

> **Phil:** *Well it was "shovels" originally, but it didn't scan.* [98]

It's that rare combination of words that mean something and yet, thanks to Phil's tremendous instincts, still scan well. My favourite lyrical motif, though, is the chorus of "Can you hear me," etc. Which sounds like a basic thing ("My favourite is the chorus!"), but the way I hear it, each of the four instances of this refrain has a different target. After the first two verses, the singer is coming to terms with the reality that he is little more than another blank face in the gang; a body more than a person. Disheartened, he finds his dignity again and asks of the foremen, the supervisors: "Can you hear me? Can you see?"

And then in a tumultuous section of music, the gang carves out a tunnel through the earth. The words "structural integrity" probably aren't even in the vocabulary of anyone involved, and there's a sudden cave-in. The singer is one of the lucky ones who didn't get trapped, but he's got friends on the other side of the rubble, and he calls to them in hopes they're still alive and can find their way back out: "Can you hear me? Can you see?"

The smoke clears and the dust settles, and all around are broken men. They have to come to terms not only with the loss of their friends and colleagues, but also the absolute disregard anyone seems to have for it all. They gather and mourn, and turn their watery eyes upward to a God who appears not to care: "Can you hear me? Can you see?"

But they harden. They know there is no safety net, nobody looking out for them. So they must become as firm as the steel they're pounding, inured to their circumstances and the toll of the work itself. Inured to the nightly thoughts of a wife and children who have no idea where their husband or father is, or even whether he's alive. Inured to danger, immune to fear. You and I, as listeners, as witnesses to their tale? We'll never see the likes of them again. "Can you hear me? Can you see?"

Yes...I see you, navvies.

> **Mike:** *I think 'Irish', which is now called 'Driving the Last Spike', is very strong. For me, I think it's one of Phil's best lyrics he's ever done in Genesis. I think it's extremely strong.* [35]

And now that you've got this extraordinarily compelling lyric, you can go back to the music and find ways to make them work together even more strongly.

> **Tony:** *And so he wrote the lyric, which I think from his point of view he really enjoyed doing, because he could stretch a little more and write more of a story, bring in other ideas. This is what you can do on a long song. And also the instrumental things kind of illustrate things, you know. He's got a nice sort of mechanical bit in the middle of that where sort of everything's going.* [3]

Tony's talking about the drum beat at 5:53 that kicks off the "We worked like the devil for our pay" section of the song. It's no accident that that sounds like a chugging train. That's a post-lyrical tweak. I don't have a clue what the drums sounded like in this section beforehand, but can you imagine anything more fitting than what's there now?

And so, you put these final touches on, record everything properly, and off your song goes. You've managed to put together something in the progressive vein that still sounds modern and accessible, you've provided a platform for a multitude of your musical ideas to see the light of day, and you've told a story with tremendous impact and worth along the way.

> **Tony:** *Although...We Can't Dance and Invisible Touch had strong poppy elements, they also had one or two significant long tracks. What we tend to find with Genesis albums is that people often buy them for the shorter tracks and then end up preferring the longer ones. I think one of the reasons why we've been around such a long time is because of the longer tracks, because it gives us strength and depth, and means we can be listened to repeatedly. You can't really do that with an album full of singles. Genesis albums tend to sound better after a lot of listens, and that's when the longer tracks come through. You've just got to convince people to listen to the album enough times.* [5]

I'll keep listening, Tony. 'Driving the Last Spike' is a marvellous ~~case-study on how three-piece Genesis wrote songs out of nothing~~.

14 - Undertow

from ...And Then There Were Three..., 1978

"Sometimes, you feel two feelings at the same time, and that's okay."

If you were a young child in the United States at any time between the years of 1968 and 2001, and you had access to a television, chances are pretty good you counted yourself part of Mister Rogers' Neighbourhood. A minister-turned puppeteer/composer/television host, Fred Rogers radiated kindness and patience, and perhaps because of that he also possessed a kind of quiet authority, on full display when he told a awards show crowd packed with self-absorbed TV stars to spend ten seconds in silence, literally timed them, and had many of them in tears as they found themselves unexpectedly reflecting on what it means to be truly and unconditionally loved and supported by the people who actually mattered in their lives.

If you have or had a young child in the United States at any time from 2012 to present-day (2021, as of the writing of this book), you're probably aware of the cartoon program Daniel Tiger's Neighbourhood, a sort of spiritual successor to that earlier staple of children's TV. It takes those same principles of patience, kindness, self-worth, and self-understanding and teaches them through a character that, apart from being a tiger, is more like the children he's trying to reach. My young son might respond well to a pleasant older gentleman encouraging him to express his feelings, but in Daniel Tiger he sees someone struggling with this emotional communication in the same way he does. And because of that, he can also relate to the way situations can improve once that communication is achieved.

There's one episode of this show that always stood out to me, called Daniel Feels Two Feelings. The gist of the episode is that Daniel finds himself in various situations where he has simultaneous yet conflicting feelings. We have a term for one such kind of blending: bittersweet. But that's not a word a young child might be expected to understand, and it doesn't help with other instances of emotional confusion, like when you're visiting a haunted house and feel both joy and fear together, or when you're confronted with a situation so absurd that it's every bit as amusing as it is rage-inducing. We don't have words for all these other nuances, so Daniel Tiger bundles them all up into a reassuring little sing-song statement: "Sometimes you feel two feelings at the same time, and that's okay." Emotional confusion is natural, the message seeks to assure children, and we all understand because we've all been there before.

But because we are verbal creatures, whose thoughts are defined by the parameters of language as much as anything else, the fact that we don't have easy words for all these different permutations of conflicting emotions means that often we still struggle to understand and express these feelings even as adults. Furthermore, expressing one's feelings too openly or too often - particularly if those feelings are themselves confused - sees one likely to begin receiving unwelcome inquiries into one's mental health. Whereas never expressing feelings at all leads to accusations (perhaps true ones) of keeping things too bottled up, creating a pressure valve situation that might burst with disastrous consequences down the line. Too much and you're a hopeless wreck; too little and you're a heartless robot. It's kind of a darned if you do, darned if you don't situation. Some people are simply no good at making clear sense of their own emotions, much less talking about them with others.

Tony Banks is one such individual, and though his deepest emotional thoughts have remained locked behind an impenetrable vault for at least as long as he's been in the public eye, he's made one heck of a career out of using music as an emotional conduit. The turbulence of opposing, simultaneous emotions? Well, that's basically the mission statement of 'Undertow': convey with music the "sound" of conflicting feelings, and thus trigger an empathetic reaction in the listeners so that they feel those emotions, too.

It works. Boy, does it work.

> **Tony:** *Musically I think that And Then There Were Three was probably one of my least favourite albums, although there are some songs on it which have great atmosphere, like...'Undertow'.* [6]

Much is made of the overarching sound on this album, that "Dave Hentschel thing" where the keyboards are big and blurry and warm. That's arguably never more true than on 'Undertow', with that hazy synth sound melting in near the end of each verse. Yet before it enters each verse is characterised by this combination of electric piano and organ, and the construction of the notes makes that same production quality sound downright frigid. I mean, there's a song on the record called 'Snowbound' and even it doesn't sound anywhere near this icy. It's a starkness they struggled to ever produce before because of the sheer quantity of instruments at work in the band - nobody likes sitting around twiddling their thumbs for an extended period of time, after all. But now with only three, they could get away with it.

> **Mike:** *It's a song of Tony's. He's got this Yamaha Grand piano which is the first decent amplified acoustic grand and we recorded it just the three of us. I think the guitar, piano, and drums...And we were thinking of arranging it more, but it sounded so good with the three of us that we kept it simple. We overdubbed a bit more, but the actual basic sound was so good with the piano that we didn't go to town on it.* [41]

> **Phil:** *If Tony wrote a song on the piano before we got this Yamaha piano it was nearly impossible to get an acoustic sounding track to sound good...But now it's a bit different, because we have got this acoustic piano which can be amplified and still sounds nice.* [41]

> **Tony:** *'Undertow'...I was kind of pleased...it was a slightly different way for me to write really. Slightly less chord dependent and a bit more dependent [on] the melody...the piano part has very much sort of got the melody and the chords all enveloped in it.* [3]

But then as soon as the song hits "Better think a while," the arrangement just sort of explodes, doesn't it? The drums come in with a big, heavy sound. Phil starts overdubbing in backing vocals. Mike's guitar comes more to the fore. Then the chorus comes with its bass pedals and massive vocal overdubs in the vein of "What if we used a Mellotron choir but Phil was actually the Mellotron?" It's the largest sound on the whole album, I daresay, and arguably a larger sound than most of the material even on albums past.

> **Phil:** *We make a big sound actually, the three of us.* [41]

Uhhh, yeah. So you've got the coldest, bleakest moments on *And Then There Were Three* stuck right up against the warmest, fullest ones. The two extreme ranges of the album are contained in the same song, which is almost unheard of. But within those competing textures there are individual battles being fought as well. The lyrics of the song lay these battles out plain to see.

Take that verse again. It feels distant, yes, but the first two words out of Phil's mouth are "Curtains are drawn; now the fire warms the room." This is a closing in, an intimacy building between two people. It's a rising heat in the air alongside the rising heat of passion. It's the flame in the fireplace and the igniting sparks of romance all in one. So why does the entire rest of the verse dwell on the poor souls outside? You can feel a gentle caress in the music, but it's bone-chilling, having much more in common with those for whom this may be their last night.

And then, as the music at last begins its attempt to match the warmth described in the room, and we expect that this guy is *finally* willing to enjoy this moment, he turns and asks his lover, "If this were the last day of your life, what would you do?" Gosh dang, man. Don't hit me with that deep stuff, I'm trying to get frisky over here! And yet we know this isn't coming from a place of disinterest, because the line "Better think a while or I may never think again" shows that this guy wants nothing more than to lose himself entirely in this moment. This is bliss, this is everything, and that's what makes it so incredibly dangerous to him. It's the titular undertow, threatening to carry him helplessly away. "I want this; I want you. But what about them? Is this right?" Love, lust, joy, guilt, fear, despair. Sometimes, you feel six feelings at the same time. Is that okay?

And then this triumphant sounding chorus, worded in the imperative tense like an anthem of commanding advice. Phrases that burst forth with inspiring sincerity like "Let me live again!" yet it's all set to the same kind of chord structure that makes up the ending of 'Afterglow', which I believe I previously described as sounding like "a waterfall of tears." Leaning into that is a command in the chorus to lay down and just sob until you have nothing left. None of this is consistent, yet somehow it's the most consistent thing of all. It's an alternating set of directives that attempt to describe everything about the human condition that is simply indescribable.

Be strong. Create your own destiny. Make your time count. Collapse under the weight of the world and scream out your grief. *Live.* Don't go quietly. Find comfort in the truth that *there will be an end* to all this suffering. Be weak. Be vulnerable. Don't be afraid to be afraid.

Sometimes, you feel two feelings at the same time, and that's okay.

> **Mike:** *I think this is one of my favourite tracks at the moment... I think Phil sings exceptionally well on this one, too.* [17]

Elsewhere, considering the second verse of the song illustrates a fear of the pitfalls of complacency, and therefore might implicitly be considered an encouragement to be bold and take risks, Genesis went surprisingly conservative with this track in a couple different ways. First there was the matter of its introduction.

> **Tony:** *I had written a long introduction to 'Undertow' on And Then There Were Three, but the others were keen not to use any introductions, and it had been dropped.* [1]

This rejected introduction pretty quickly got recycled into music for the soundtrack of the 1978 horror film The Shout, and then repurposed for 1979's Banks solo effort, *A Curious Feeling*, as the aptly named 'From the Undertow'. You can hear in the piano near the one minute mark a variation on the 'Undertow' chorus melody, so this was more than just a piano doodle that was going to be tacked on to the piece. But while Tony was obviously hoping to make an exception, Mike and Phil felt it didn't fit with their collective concept of *And Then There Were Three* as being an album of more concise tunes. I'm not sure 'From the Undertow' would've improved on 'Undertow' proper if the two pieces had ended up as the singular unit Tony envisioned, but I guess we'll never really know.

Beyond that was the live consideration, where again bold choices took a backseat to safe ones.

> **Tony:** *We tended to avoid including the slightly more subtle and softer songs, or at least we had to be more careful about using them. We never played, which I regret, songs like 'Blood on the Rooftops', 'Many Too Many', 'Mad Man Moon', or 'Undertow'. That was cowardice on our part, because we could have slipped the odd one in occasionally. And as time went on there was less room in any case.* [1]

It would be nice if they would've trusted in the material and the audience to respond to it, though I'm not sure this song would work quite as well without the extensive layering of sounds that come in the choruses. I guess we'll never find out.

13 - Second Home by the Sea

from *Genesis*, 1983

Previously in Play Me My Song!

"Oi, time to ride the ol' crime wave, eh? Say, 'at's a cosy lookin' cottage. Bound to have a few cohlectible trinkets! Up, up, up we go!"

Tony: *I thought, "Well, let's have a SPOOKY home by the sea!"* [3]

OOOOOooooOOOoooOOOOoooOOOO

Tony: *I had this idea of a burglar going into this house and suddenly finding out it was haunted. Which I thought was quite funny. And then sort of took that idea a bit further and sort of made it one of those kinds of songs looking back over people's lives, and those people kind of trapped in the past but there's nothing they can do about it.* [38]

"Uhhh nice ghosties...there there, let's play all nice-like. I'm uh, I'm only the cleanah, see?"

Genesis are the ghosts. The home by the sea is their catalogue. And we're the hapless burglars hoping to nab one more little ounce of pleasure from the music, only to find that the music has captured us for the rest of our lives.

SIT DOWN!

Will our burglar ever escape this torment?!

Will Genesis' ghosts ever release us as well?!

Just how DO you describe that drum rhythm, anyway?

Find out all that and more right now, in the exciting conclusion!

While we're at least temporarily ensnared by the spectral tendrils that make up the spirit of 'Second Home by the Sea', we might as well spend some time talking about Genesis and improvisation. I've said things like this before, and perhaps even many times before, but it bears repeating: *Genesis* was a pivotal record for the band in that it allowed them to not only rediscover the art of improvisation, but also learn new ways to employ that improvisation to make some truly stunning music.

The band had seen their collective songwriting philosophies shift frequently over the years, after all. When Tony and Mike started in Charterhouse school with Peter, Ant, and whatever drummer happened to be loitering around the cafeteria, they wrote predominantly in small teams. Pairs of writers would figure something out, bring it to the band, and they'd Frankenstein together a song from the individual bits. Once Steve and Phil joined, things became more collaborative in truth; while individual bits would still be brought in, they tended to be completed by band jamming rather than by other preconceived pieces. This attitude increased until Mike and Tony got upset at Peter for getting all the credit, at which point things slowly shifted to a more individualistic approach. That lasted right up to the moment when they both sort of said, "Wait, what are we doing here?" and slowly shifted back towards a renewed focus on collaboration.

Genesis is called *Genesis* because it's the first Genesis album written entirely by Genesis as a group effort. That sounds overly simplistic, but this was the album where the philosophy shifts stopped and the band finally - after eleven albums - locked in how they wanted to approach their songwriting. And so, though they'd done plenty of group songwriting in the years before, this was the first time it had been "codified," so to speak.

> **Tony:** *It was another new way of working, and something we couldn't have done without the comfort of our own studio.* [1]

> **Mike:** *We just go in and it's all improvised. In the old days, we started off that way. Then we went very much the other way. And Then There Were Three was very much a solo album by three different people. Which I didn't like. Oh, there were some nice moments. But it ends up a bit like, "You two play on my song, then I'll play on your song," and [then] why are we doing it?* [77]

There were highs and lows. Forcing themselves to not "pad" their improvisations with any prewritten individual bits, much less full songs, meant there was less material produced all around; there are no B-sides on *Genesis*, unless you want to count the later Mike + the Mechanics song 'A Call to Arms'. And that dearth of quantity made for what is generally agreed to be a comparatively weak second side to the album.

But when it worked, boy did it ever work. I've covered 'Mama' already in this book...well, I had the band cover 'Mama' I suppose, but tomayto tomahto, right? Anyway, great as that tune is, the highlight of *Genesis* for me is what happened when Phil found a really solid drum riff. How'd that go again, guys?

> **Tony:** *Phil had this sort of drum rhythm, you know, "bom buppa-bom-bom," like that.* [38]

> **Phil:** *'Home by the Sea', the boov-zh diddih-doov-doov chah...I sat down and played that pattern...* [3]

> **Tony:** *We were able to improvise. Phil had this riff: doon chigga-doon-doon.* [3]

Well, I'm glad we got that clear at least. Ghosts, am I right? They can never keep their stories straight. They can retell the tale for all eternity and it'll change a little bit every time. Regardless, the point was that they had this drum riff using snazzy new electronic drums, so they knew that sound was the core of what they wanted to do; particularly if Tony was already thinking about phantoms in the back of his head.

> **Phil:** *That album also was the first time we used electronic drums...that pattern on that sound with those pre-sets, it had such a lot of atmosphere, and everyone started playing along. It was a bit like, kind of comparable to 'Intruder' with Peter's thing, where you just sort of get a sound and you play with it, and suddenly that's a musical part, you know. And everybody jams along with it.* [3]

"Just keep doing that for a while, Phil!"

"Right, how long then?"

"Uhhhhhh..."

> **Tony:** *Mike and I just improvised on top of it. And we made up a couple 30 minute tapes of us just improvising on top of it.* [3]

> **Tony:** *Mike and I just played. We did about two or three hours worth of jamming on tape.* [38]

> **Tony:** *Mike and I were just playing over the top of that...we had two thirty minute tapes of it.* [6]

Tony: *Phil started playing this drum riff that Mike and I found attractive and we jammed on it for about two hours one day and an hour or two the next.* [23]

...Okay. More like "let us relive our *lies*," am I right? But hey, hey, hey, don't look at me like that, Tony. I'm still seated! Butt firmly planted on ground, OK? Just...just tell us what happened next...

Tony: *And then [we] went through it and just found the good bits and stuck 'em all together. And that's exactly what you've got on the piece.* [3]

Wow, just like that? That's incredible. He makes it sound so easy.

Tony: *We listened back to it and clocked the parts we liked, learnt what it was we'd played, and then re-pieced it back together.* [1]

Oh...so not just like that. A bit more time-intensive after all.

Tony: *A lot of it was sounding quite good but we couldn't sort of tie it down, so we actually listened to it, selected good moments of the jam, and then Mike and I relearned exactly what we played, even to the extent of counting, you know. So often the beats fall on a weird beat in the bar and stuff like that, because we were just fooling around.* [38]

So it took some effort, but they left the music exactly as it was by playing it over again. All right, I think I'm finally following.

Tony: *Mike and I just sat down and marked the best bits... the things we thought were good. We learned exactly what we played and if we changed the chord on the third beat of the bar, we did it [that way again]. I did exactly the notes I did on his things and then we just stuck it all together.* [4]

Yep, got it now. No changes whatsoever. Solid.

Tony: *One bit that sounded good we played twice...* [6]

...So just the one teensy change then...

Tony: *We learned exactly what we played down to the last detail. Of course, we worked on a few bits, extended some, changed others, just trying to get it into some cohesive form.* [23]

But he just said...

Tony: *It took us quite a while. Phil obviously adapted some of the things he was playing to suit what changes we'd made.* [23]

Hnnnnnnggggh. Before Tony sends me completely over the edge, I should point out that this is a song about reliving lives, and it was composed by literally reliving/recreating what had been previously produced spontaneously. The entire song of 'Second Home by the Sea' was written in the exact method as the stuff that it's all about. Life, lived spontaneously. Fleeting moments of clarity and blossoming creativity bursting out of the daily fog that characterises so much of our existence. A yearning for those moments, and memories that attempt to recreate them, with varying degrees of perfection. A focus on those memories until the fog might as well never have existed. And then the delivery of those manipulated memories to a captive audience. That's what 'Second Home by the Sea' is in its inherited lyrical concept, and it's also what it actually is in real life as a song.

Tony: *Again, we were trying to keep some of this spontaneous feel...It all sounds very natural on tape, so we knew it was a natural thing to go for...It's amazing to hear the original stuff that it came from. There's a lot of good stuff there, but we had to keep it down to about six minutes. It could easily have gone on for a lot longer.* [23]

I don't believe for a moment that Tony Banks could have easily gone on for a lot longer with an instrumental passage, except... *<checking notes>* ...yes, yes I can believe that.

Tony: *A real experiment as a sort of way of band writing...I think it produced a great result. It's one of my favourites of all our instrumental passages we've ever done, I think.* [38]

But if you don't abbreviate the jam, how could Phil ever come back in to spook us one final time? Well, one final time in a single play of the track, anyway. It's not like we're all sitting here in this supernatural shack of our metaphorical lives *not* getting haunted by this song, right? If nothing else, it's been an inescapable live staple since its release.

Mike: *On stage - people don't actually know this - but the parts of 'Home by the Sea' when Tony starts playing keyboard solos, I'm playing the chords. You wouldn't know it - you imagine one of his hands is playing chords, [but] in fact it's me on the guitar synth. A good example of Genesis when you can actually move around a bit. For that I use the Roland with the guitar that has the big, er...coat hanger.* [77]

Nice to know that even Ghost Mike is totally incoherent sometimes (it's the Roland G-707 for you guitar enthusiasts out there).

Mike: *'Home by the Sea' was a dark, moody, two-part, eleven-minute thing (the second part was called 'Second Home by the Sea'). It'd got size, it'd got grandeur, it'd got everything. We knew how to do pieces like this by now. It was like a classical piece, and when we played it live the automated Vari-Lite truss would break up into diamond-shaped pieces and descend on the stage, moving around and beaming down green light. This may not sound so special now that Vari-Lite lights are everywhere, but at the time it was one of our most iconic looks.* [14]

Tony: *The [on-stage] videos for 'Domino' and 'Home by the Sea' were even more spectacular [on the 2007 tour] because of the sheer scale of the screens.* [1]

Mike: *'Home By The Sea' [is challenging live] because the instrumental part changes moods so quickly. It was originally recorded in sections in which I assigned different sounds as I saw fit, but playing it live is very hard to do. One minute the sound will be very spacey and heavily echoed, with big flanging stuff and the next minute I'll need a very close-miked amp sound. The variety of sound over a four-minute passage was huge on the record, so trying to recreate that live is always a challenge.* [58]

Ironically, in the live shows the 'Second Home by the Sea' half of the song actually *does* change in a number of relatively-small-yet-still-noticeable ways from the studio track. They spent so much time meticulously recreating a given sound for the album. And then they went live with it and tried to meticulously recreate the recreation. And inevitably it evolved beyond all of that. Copies of copies of copies. Fallible memory retold again and again and again and again.

We're trapped in that loop, we fans. I don't think we can ever really escape. I don't know why we'd ever want to.

12 - The Brazilian

from *Invisible Touch*, 1986

Instrumental tracks are fun for me to write about, because they're kind of like blank canvases in a way. So much of any discussion around any song, Genesis or otherwise, naturally falls to considerations of the lyrics. Which isn't to say there's anything inherently wrong or bad about that; I've certainly done more than my fair share of lyrical analyses, and I daresay I'm not done yet, so I'm not throwing stones here. But in the same way that the lyrics of a song can dominate the music for in a listener's mind, subordinating everything else as "the background stuff," so too can they dominate discussions *about* the songs such as the ones I'm producing here.

Writing about a song's lyrics is fine, of course, and there are some lyrics that mean quite a bit to me so I want to do them justice. But there's always this underlying fear that I'm giving them too much weight. Why focus so long on this particular verbal phrase instead of this particular chord change? Or even in a much broader sense, if a song's lyrics are Important™, they can define what the track is all about, and therefore further define the entire way I write about said track. Often this is helpful if I'm looking for a muse, but there are times I feel a little restricted as well.

So it's always a breath of fresh air for me, both as a listener and a writer, when I come to an instrumental track. Be it as musicians making an album or as a writer penning a musical retrospective styled like a countdown, wordless songs are chances to breathe and be creative. "We can play whatever we want!" I can write whatever I want! Who's going to stop me? **Words?** I think not. So the only question facing both Genesis and myself is, "What to do with this blank canvas?" But before I really explore my newfound freedom, I suppose I should probably point out that in the case of 'The Brazilian', Genesis had to create the canvas itself in the first place. That is, they didn't set out initially with the intent of creating an instrumental thing.

> **Phil:** *It started to get moulded into an instrumental song as time went on. But it just started off as a little jam.* [3]

Yet this track has earlier beginnings than even the group's joint improvisation on it. It's a canvas born from Tony just fiddling around with his keyboards, as Tony is wont to do.

> **Tony:** *You can just stumble across things. With the [E-mu] Emulator [II keyboard] in particular, a lot of the sounds I use are ones I've stumbled across. I find the Emulator a useful tool for composition, too. What I often do is switch it on while we're improvising, and I get 17 seconds of everybody doing their thing and not even listening to each other. Then I play through it and sometimes there's something there. You edit out a few seconds and you've got something you can work with. On the new Genesis album there's a number called 'The Brazilian' that's got what sounds like a sequence pattern going through, which was done like that.* [85]

That low, echoing guitar sound? Those beat-agnostic little tings like muted triangles? Not a sequence but a sample. Just random noise in the rehearsal room that Tony captured and then toyed with until he could get it in a sort of rhythm that made sense. It's a showcase of his incredible ear and sense for what could be, given that the random noise he caught didn't even sound like it does on the track.

> **Tony:** *In the rehearsal room I'd often just switch on the machine, the Emulator, and just record whatever's happening in the room. And Mike was just playing along, and Phil was doing something, and I recorded it. And this thing was there, and I sort of slowed it down or something, or combined a couple of different notes to get an effect. Because what they played in there wasn't very interesting, I promise you. I put it together and it just produced this thing. And I looped it, and I thought, "Well that sounds really interesting."* [3]

Let's recap so we're clear. Tony records rehearsal room noise on a whim and gets a sound sample that is totally uninteresting in itself. Yet he somehow thinks, "Well, it COULD be interesting if I edited it down to this bit and stuck it onto this bit and altered the speed of it and then overlaid these two smaller parts together and then ran it into a loop so it's got a beat behind it." And then he just goes ahead and does that. As a former musician myself, I'm just continually amazed at Tony's musical instincts. He's a rare breed.

So anyway, then Tony goes back to the guys and plays them this looped sample, and then *that's* the blank canvas they use for their actual group improv session.

> **Tony:** *That little sound which it starts off with was just something I made out of a loop of stuff on the Emulator; extraneous noises in the room. Mike and Phil were fiddling about and I just took a twenty second sample of it and just stuck it in, and then wrote and played on top of it. Again, it was just trying to create some music out of nothing which sometimes acts as a catalyst and gets you going.* [6]

So what next? Well, Tony got to fool around a bit. Why not Phil?

> **Phil:** *'The Brazilian' was one of those sorts of things where we just started to fool around. Again, this was like with the Simmons [electronic drums] finding out what kind of different, odd sounds you could get programmed into one kit, you know. Obviously a drum kit's a drum kit. But this was like dikkigong go-dikkidun buh-bao chchchch. You know, you have these different kinds of sounds. I remember sort of just mucking about and getting a pattern, and Tony would start playing...* [3]

You can always count on Phil to give a great soundbite of imitating some kind of drum sound. Even when he doesn't have sticks in hands, he can't help but be percussive. So you combine this strange sample with these heavy electronic drums, and suddenly you're getting this big industrial rock vibe. Not that Genesis would even necessarily know what that is in 1986, although bands like Throbbing Gristle had been around for a while, putting out songs such as 'Still Walking', which were essentially just beat tracks similar in style to the one that forms the backbone of 'The Brazilian'. Heck, the frontman of that band was even named Genesis!

Nevertheless, industrial rock as a genre wouldn't really take off until the 90s with acts like Nine Inch Nails and Marilyn Manson. So even though 'The Brazilian' is a product of its time, it's still somehow ahead of its time. And not just by a few years into the 90s, but those big chorus hits to my ears really foreshadow even the likes of dubstep. Heavy accented bass that rapidly falls away, accompanied by an enormous cymbal crash? You can close your eyes and easily imagine a greasy, odorous male violently convulsing on a club's dance floor to this, right? It's clear as day to me, at least.

> **Phil:** *We were trying to be a little bit less pastoral. We were trying to sort of pull people along with what we thought was a slightly different kind of Genesis.* [3]

But even though the rhythm tracks look forward decades, those synths are still very much a product of the 80s.

> **Tony:** *The whole thing was quite quirky, so I just played a rather...what one review described as "the cheesiest synthesizer sound of all time," I think. And that was all kind of part of it for me. It was just kind of like, a bit strange. But I quite like things like that.* [3]

So they've got these pieces, and by now finally realise putting any vocals on top would ruin the whole feel, so they just don't add any. That's something you can more easily get away with when your lead singer is also your drummer; nobody feels left out. So a blank canvas, but one Tony had to make. Then heaps of sonic paint splashed on it haphazardly until something almost starts to form. That's true creative freedom there. And once it's been identified as an instrumental, let's add a guitar solo to the end! But let's make that sound really weird, too. It's like a cat trapped in a box wailing to be let out. And it works because why wouldn't it work? Who cares? Instrumental, baby, we're goin' to Rio!

> **Tony:** *Instrumental music is a very important ingredient in Genesis music. I think it's something that makes us distinctive. For those that know our records well, it's a lot of standout moments that have been that way...* [3]

The icing on the cake is that they actually made sure to play this one live, too. Granted, it was only on the album's supporting tour, but the sound was even better there. Sure, they lose a little bit of that oomph on the down beats of the instrumental chorus, but a lot more is gained along the way. It's just such a fun piece. Watch footage from the Wembley Stadium concert of the Invisible Touch Tour of the band playing this song. You'll see Daryl grinning uncontrollably in the background, as if he's thinking, "This song is so cool." Tony's into it too, bobbing his head emphatically, which for Tony might as well be the same as shouting his enthusiasm from a mountaintop. Meanwhile Phil can't even be bothered to look at his kit, he's so busy mugging at Chester across the stage. It must have felt so liberating: no pressure to sing, just banging out a song the audience probably doesn't even want to hear, doing what you want because you feel like it. Instrumental! No rules! Mike's gonna churn out a sick guitar solo on a guitar that may as well be a giant spatula (his Steinberger, to be specific), and that's fine too! What if Phil and Chester hit their cymbals with really exaggerated movements like a synchronised dance team? That sounds fun! Hey, speaking of synchronised dance...

> **Tony:** *There's always been a bit of a thing about these instrumental tracks...But Torvill and Dean danced to 'The Brazilian', so it can't be all bad.* [18]

Torvill and Dean the 1984 Olympic gold medal ice dancing team? *That* Torvill and Dean? So exciting! Or it would be, but...look, I hate to burst everyone's bubble, especially Tony's, but my research reveals that - alas! - Torvill and Dean never did perform a routine to 'The Brazilian'. They did, however, perform a routine to a Phil and Chester drum duet from the We Can't Dance Tour, so maybe that's what Tony's thinking of. Regardless, my point is that the blank canvas an instrumental tune presents is an opportunity for a whole lot of fun outside the norm. And now that I've established that, all that's left for me is to decide what to do with my *own* blank canvas here. I could take this entry anywhere I want!

> **Tony:** *The thing with instrumentals is that you either like them or you don't; they are kind of like interludes, if you like. And if you tuck one away at the end of an album you can take it off if you don't want to listen to it. But the real toss-up was whether to [include] 'The Brazilian' or 'Do The Neurotic', which sounded great to play. 'The Brazilian' won in the end because it had more of the quirkiness which I like.* [6]

Oh...end of the album, eh? Well shoot, I guess I'm out of time. But hey, not all is lost; there's still one instrumental to go! I'll get you yet, blank canvas. Just you wait...

11 - Duchess

from *Duke*, 1980

> **Tony:** *It wasn't just that he had started to write a bit more. It was more his voice. He suddenly was a singer. That was the first time I felt he was a universal singer.* [43]

Hello, world. Pleasure to meet you. My name is Phil Collins, and you're about to have to deal with me for a very, very long time. This song is called 'Duchess', and it's my coming out party.

> **Tony:** *For me it's the first album where he really sounds like a singer. I have to be honest about that. I mean, he did some lovely singing on the previous albums, but it's not as convincing as it is on this album I don't think. I just think some of the singing on it is really good. Not just on the songs he wrote, but 'Duchess', I think the singing on that is really tremendous.* [3]

Appreciate that, Tony. But let me back up a bit first. Some of you may know that I've actually been around for quite a while now. I've been playing with Genesis for oh, nine years now. Hickory 'fore that, though you may know them better these days as Flaming Youth. Been drumming with Brand X for five years or so as well. I'm a working kind of guy, you see. But people don't often notice the drummers, do they? I mean, musicians do. That's probably how I keep getting all this work! But you lot, the punters at home, maybe not so much. I started singin' with Genesis around, oh, 1976 I think? Did a few albums that way too. It was all right, or so they tell me anyway. Maybe you've even heard the hit single I sang on, 'Follow You Follow Me' from our previous album. But anyway this is something different now. I'm something different now, too. See,

> **[Phil:]** *We'd been to Japan in '78 for the first time, for a couple of weeks. They treated us like royalty, and Roland, which is a Japanese company or was then anyway - I don't know about now. But they gave us each one of these drum machines that were fresh off the production line. Programmable, slightly. Not quite cha-cha-cha waltz, you know. A little bit of that, but still original. And I said, "Oh, no thank you. Thank you very much, no thank you." Anyway, then of course I went back and I had this marriage stuff going on. Then I end up with my [in-home] studio and I say, "Can I have my drum machine please? I think I might be needing this." So I started to write what was to become Face Value, because 'In the Air Tonight' uses that. That drum machine is all over the place on that record.* [3]

Now, I know. *Face Value*? 'In the Air Tonight'? What are these things? Don't worry, you haven't heard them. Not yet, anyway. But give it a year or so. You will. The point though is that I've had quite a bit of time on my hands lately - pretty uncharacteristic of me, actually - and I think I've come around on this "drum machine" thing. I mean,

> **[Phil:]** *I think a lot of drummers have taboo feelings about it because most drum machines are there just to recreate drums, and that's when I lose interest in them. Because as soon as they begin to sound like the drums I have no real use for them, apart from as a writing tool. And I will always replace the drums if they sound like drums whereas these Roland things - Roland being one of the best in terms of sound - are percussion and odd noises so you can actually play drums with it. So they take a rather different territory. As soon as you hear a record with all that programmed bass drum and synth bass drum, I lose interest as well. I mean, I am the same as most other drummers in that respect, but I think if you use the percussion end of it I think it can be very usable as a tool.* [81]

I probably sound like a Roland salesman by now, don't I? I promise I don't mean to, but this has been something of a revelation to me, you know? And not me only, the guys thought the same! You know, I played them my solo demos in my bedroom,

> **[Phil:]** *And it was actually in the next room where we wrote 'Duchess'.* [3]

In fact, seeing as Tony and Mike are here with me, one of you want to weigh in?

Tony: *'Duchess' really developed more than anything out of the drum machine... That first time we ever used one was really exciting. The whole thing was kind of, it would carry on without you having to do anything. That was what was nice about it. So you could try something and if it didn't work, whereas a drummer always wants to do something fiddly. A drum machine just keeps on relentlessly doing the same thing. I had used it as an aid when I was writing on my first solo album, A Curious Feeling. I'd use the drum machine very much as a sort of basis to write against, but I didn't end up using any of it specifically on the album, which I slightly regret now. Whereas on [Duke] we did on that one track, and it gave it a very distinctive feel.* [3]

All that time fiddling away with that Roland CR-78 machine on my own paid off I guess, eh?

[Phil:] *I've used it on my demos, and after a year in my bedroom with it, I know what it can and can't do. It's incredibly limited, but it works really well on 'Duchess'.* [12]

Tony had some fun with the pattern too, as I recall, playing along with it.

Tony: *...A little drum machine sound I was trying to imitate on the keyboard...* [1]

Yeah, that actually made it onto the final track, which was great. Those little keys plinking along in the same rhythm really set the mood at the start of the thing, I think.

Tony: *We tried all sorts of things on that with heavy compression on the song, and simple chords.* [6]

[Phil:] *So it was a thing where people would play and this would keep time to it while I could sing. And all the fading in and fading out of things, it was good fun. But the drums played a big part of it, because you thought you had the sound and then suddenly the drums come in and then suddenly it goes CinemaScope.* [3]

Ah, sorry, CinemaScope. Ahh, you know, like the way a movie projector takes this tiny image and just kind of blows it up onto the screen larger than life? Well that's what I wanted to do with the rhythms here, and I think the real drums phasing in really accomplished that well. Then adding things like Mike's bass and Tony's syncopated piano chords on top of that droning sensation...it was really something, I think.

Mike: *We started writing again as a group, which used to bring all those magical moments. We hadn't really had those for a long time.* [10]

Not that it was quite so easy to tell until we got it all into the studio, though. With all the overlays and everything, we just sort of had to imagine how things might go and trust they would work out in the end.

[Phil:] *That was one of those things where you really did capture something that we kinda couldn't really do properly in rehearsal, 'cause it's got drums, drum machine, I'm singing, and it's all gotta be there. Couldn't do that justice in rehearsal. But in the studio it just came alive, and that was done very, very quickly.* [3]

I was really pleased with how it turned out, yeah. For me,

[Phil:] *I thought that for the first time...we had captured some of our live energy...* [1]

...ah, in the studio. I was thrilled. So I think that's what really made it special.

Tony: *I love the way the song comes out of nothing and goes back to nothing, a very simple approach to the career of a female rock star, called Duchess obviously. In the first verse she's up and coming, in the second verse she's made it, and by the third verse she's on the way downhill again. A very simple little tale, with simple emotions.* [1]

Yes, that's true. It's kind of a cautionary tale too, isn't it? "Hey Phil, don't get too complacent up there, the mob is waiting," you know.

Tony: *It was at that time that girl singers were becoming popular and that is where the idea came from. Also, seen from that perspective it would take it away from the group a bit because if it had been written about a man, people would have thought it was talking about the group, but talking about it that way gave it another dimension.* [6]

Right, but it *could* be about me, I suppose. I sort of had that thought a little bit when I was singing it, you know?

Tony: *I think listeners can relate to it in a lot of different ways. You don't have to be a singer to relate to the idea of a rise and fall in a person's career. Duchess was just a name for a female singer. It was a single-word name to represent her. The song talks about her starting off with a desire for success, then her achieving success, and then things going wrong for her at the end. It's a career arc if you will. I think a lot of careers have this kind of shape. The song could have just as easily been about Genesis itself. The one thing about a rock song - and it's why romantic songs are so successful, is that simple directness. If you get that right in a song, it's incredibly powerful. If you look at the lyrics for 'Duchess' on paper, they're nothing. But when you combine it with the music, it becomes something very, very strong. The song has a sort of flavour that's universal.* [18]

Yeah, that's very true. And I guess if you look at it that way, I'm starting the second verse here in my life. I feel as though I'm in that transitional phase between "up and coming" and "made it," I suppose. Well I hope I am anyway! Maybe I've already peaked! "Down with Collins! We've 'eard enough of that bugger!"

Tony: *I thought that it was at that point on the album, on that song, that Phil became the singer. He just got this edge to his voice and it took off from there really. He took a melody which I had written and gave it a different twist, which is what a singer should be able to do, really.* [6]

Well, thanks, that's kind to say. I guess if I think about it,

[Phil:] *I'd been through the process of a writer. I mean, I'd written all the Face Value stuff by the time we wrote Duke. So I kind of...I'd changed. I'd become a songwriter. And I'd become more of a singer because I was singing songs that I had written and emoting, if you like. And being kind of...putting things out there. So yes, it probably is true that Duke was the first album where I kind of felt more comfortable as a singer.* [3]

Tony: *I just think it's sort of, he also knew what to do a bit. When I wrote the lyric and melody to 'Duchess' on what we'd done as an improvisation, and I did a version of it. I sang it, made a tape of it, played it... All the elements are there. But when he sang it - and it's not just that he's got a better voice than me - it was the fact that all the little kind of embellishments and tails and things that happened on it just transformed it completely from being something like a sort of session guy might do to something that a singer does. And his own character is sort of right across it for that reason. The resultant effect is very, very strong.* [3]

Laying it on a little thick now, aren't you Tony? Not that I *mind* it, but anyway I really think the groove is the thing. That driving, pounding sensation it gets when the vocals come in, you know. The vocals obviously are part of that, but I think it's everything you guys do underneath it - well I'm playing drums too there, but you know - it's everything you guys are doing that really propel things forward.

Tony: *It is so simple and yet it seems to capture so much atmosphere.* [6]

Mike: *Phil's writing, writing stuff on his own, helped change the balance too, I think actually. Because he's always had a very good feel for writing songs that work, you know, in sort of four minutes. Which was never our forte. And that helped balance the album, too.* [3]

Well, 'Duchess' is a little bit longer than all that...six, seven minutes is it? But yeah, I get what you're saying. And I think that's why

[Phil:] *'Duchess' is one of my favourite songs.* [3]

And I think that's also why I'm hoping to have quite the long second verse here, luck willing. Drum machines, actual drums, rhythmic sense, production sense, songwriting immediacy, and now I daresay I've finally worked out this vocal thing too. I'm Phil Collins, the 1980s are just beginning, and I'm announcing our simultaneous arrival with this song called 'Duchess'. Are you ready?

Tony: *'Duchess'...still moves me and sends shivers down my spine. I hope [songs like that are] what we'll be remembered for.* [9]

No arguments to that one, Tony. After all,

[Phil:] *When I do go, I'd prefer my epitaph not be, "He Came, He Wrote 'Sussudio', He Left."* [12]

Sorry, you don't know what 'Sussudio' is, do you? Well hey, don't worry about that one just yet. It's just something that's been on my mind all the time lately. Maybe one day I'll do something with it. Anyway, I'll see you guys early next year. Should be fun. Can't wait!

Bonus Content! Let's Learn Some 'Duchess' Fun Facts with Tony Banks!

Tony: *I think one song that I was always sad wasn't a hit single was the song 'Duchess', because it's one of my favourite of our songs. Released as a single...sometime after 'Misunderstanding' and it didn't really take off anywhere. It was a much-liked song I think of ours, but it just didn't seem to work as a single. Which is a pity, because I think it's one of the strongest songs we've ever done.* [40]

And it's not just Tony who thinks that, but also the fans! I mean, it's sitting here as my 11th best Genesis song in the entire catalogue, so there's certainly something to be said for it. Now I know, I'm just one guy with a bevy of questionable opinions. But hey, even some celebrities came out in support of 'Duchess'!

Tony: *Another lyric I wrote. I've often said it's my favourite Genesis song. It's been resurrected a few times over the years. Rosanna Arquette told me it was her favourite song.* [40]

Super random, but we'll take it! But perhaps my favourite 'Duchess' fun fact is that it almost wasn't even called 'Duchess'. No, the song's ultra-successful diva might've had a different mononym altogether.

Tony: *'Duchess' is one of my favourite tracks we've ever done. Very simple, and a lyric that's very easy to relate to in the sense of the rise and fall of a female rock star, really, [who] is called Duchess. We could've called it 'Madonna'. We sort of thought about it. Because Madonna hadn't been created by that point, but it would've been more interesting, wouldn't it?* [3]

'Duchess' is a terrific title and I don't wish it were changed, but on the other hand how crazy would it have been for Genesis to make a song called 'Madonna' about the rise and fall of a female pop star and then have 'Holiday' come out in the fall of '83, kickstarting Madonna's career as it did in the real world? Would people have drawn parallels to the song? Would people have accused Madonna of ripping off Genesis for her stage name (they'd be wrong, of course; Madonna is her actual given name from birth)? Would 'Duchess' itself then have gotten more retroactive traction because of association with her? I guess we'll never know. Fun to think about, though!

10 - Los Endos

from *A Trick of the Tail*, 1976

Around Christmas of 1974, Phil Collins gets a call from the head of Artists & Repertoire at Island Records. This was a man with whom Phil was loosely familiar, as the record exec had formerly been a writer for Melody Maker, which had covered Genesis somewhat extensively. Island Records had just signed a new band, and they needed a drummer. Would Phil come and rehearse with them a bit? Genesis are in the midst of The Lamb Lies Down on Broadway Tour but have a few weeks' holiday, so Phil figures, "Why not?"

> **Phil:** *I join them for rehearsals, and we have some fun... They have a singer, but for much of the time there's nothing for him to do... Nonetheless, I like these guys, and I like the freedom they offer, so I agree to join Brand X on a part-time basis, even though I don't really know what I'm joining. There are no gigs and only distant rumours of a record.* [12]

Somehow in that brief time during the winter, those distant rumours quickly crystallise and they manage to actually record an album. They send it off to Island Records, and the exec comes right back: "This is no good. Lose the vocals. Write new stuff." A blow to egos, perhaps, and then Phil runs off to finish touring The Lamb. By April 1975, The Lamb Tour is back in England and Phil reconnects with the Brand X crew, now having lost a pair of members - including that pesky singer. By May the Genesis tour is over and that band takes a month off before hunkering down to write for their next album. So Phil, ever bored and thus ever busy, dives into Brand X completely.

> **Phil:** *When the four of us instrumentalists start playing, Brand X become a whole different thing. These are the days of fusion and jazz-rock, some of which is definitely too noodly and self-indulgent for me. But we will make a few interesting records...* [12]

Phil spends the next few months bouncing back and forth between Genesis and Brand X, writing with each band. In fact, the Brand X debut album *Unorthodox Behaviour* is recorded about a month before Genesis goes into the studio to lay down *A Trick of the Tail*. So it's no surprise at all that Phil finds himself in that kind of musical mindset during the Genesis writing sessions; hard to keep those two projects musically distinct in his head, I'd imagine. Especially since Genesis at this time has him being reluctantly pressed into the spotlight as a singer, when all he really wants to do is bang away at his kit some more.

> **Phil:** *I'm happy at the back...I'd rather be in an instrumental band than take over the microphone... At least we've written some strong material...* [12]

Ah, an instrumental band. That would be the life, wouldn't it? Phil had even championed the idea more than once to his Genesis bandmates, hoping that it might catch on with them.

> **Phil:** *Although I loved Pete and still do, my feeling [was], "Well, we'll just carry on as a four-piece! Forget the vocals, we'll just carry on as an instrumental four-piece!" It was no slight on him; it was just meant to be the fact that I thought we could just carry on and still do it. And in fact, in doing it, prove to people that we weren't "Pete's band."* [3]

There was a *bit* of traction...

> **Mike:** *I remember Trick of the Tail, we had a brief. We said, "Let's try and be a bit more instrumental." Because we thought, you know, some of our strongest passages in the past without Pete were instrumental moments.* [3]

...but not enough.

> **Mike:** *But of course, as always, you have no control and it's a heavily vocal album!* [3]

But Phil can't quite shake that bug. Doesn't help that in his spare time he's listening to even more jazz fusion type of stuff.

Phil: *It was about ideas and arrangements. I'd heard the Santana album Borboletta, and there's a tune on it called 'Promise Of A Fisherman'. If you've got it...have a listen and think of 'Los Endos'. That's where it came from – I was more involved in that.* ⁹⁹

So they're all in there, working up material, and several songs start to emerge.

Mike: *A fair amount of the album was from scratch. '[Dance on a] Volcano' was just a jam that started, 'Squonk' just sort of came on the day, I think… So it was quite sort of live and jamming at that stage.* ³

There's also a track which will eventually get cut from the final album: an emotional vocal piece followed by an Eastern-inspired instrumental jam called 'It's Yourself'. So with these group efforts all coming out and the album's space beginning to be allocated, Phil can't resist the urge anymore: for possibly the first time in his Genesis career, he takes charge of a song.

Tony: *'Los Endos', which was a development of 'Squonk' and all the other pieces, was an idea which came more from Phil because he was very into jazz/rock...* ¹

He goes wild on the percussion, just as he'd heard in that Santana tune, and decides to use the three-chord progression from 'It's Yourself' as the basis to play around a bit with everything.

Mike: *The three chords it's based around were part of a soft thing which didn't make the album.* ³¹

Phil: *It was kind of more my baby than anybody else's. I mean, obviously melodically I'd say, "Go [like this:] dowwww-dowwww-dowww then down-down…" and Tony would sort of make sense of the kind of the humming it.* ³

Steve: *The main melody for 'Los Endos' was mine. Phil came up with the furious rhythm to propel it beyond my dream. I've always loved the combination of slow, memorable melodies with fast rhythms and this track caught fire from the word go.* ⁷⁰

It's a fun image, picturing "Staff Sergeant Hackett" and "Lt. Junior Grade Collins" dictating melodies to Tony and pushing everyone to build around this core concept. Isn't this drummer guy supposed to be the affable chap who simply does whatever we tell him to? Who made him the boss? But hey, it's a feel-good sort of time in Genesis.

Tony: *I think we were very confident we could write material that was strong enough.* ³

Steve: *It is a very 'up' album isn't it? Well, again I was essentially happy and that translates… We were rehearsing [and] as far as I can remember it was summer, and these things do make a difference… If you see any photographs of that time we are all laughing and you can see it is becoming a happy band again.* ³⁰

So they open the song with the bit from 'It's Yourself' - which to Steve's point there was originally called 'Beloved Summer' - and base the main thrust of the piece on that same progression; a touch that's pretty much lost to modernity since they left that song off the album, but oh well. And Phil just tells them, "Hey, go wild!" It's all about experimenting around this riff, so throw some heat on the fire and really go for it. Mike's enthused but this isn't really in his wheelhouse. Tony and Steve though? Completely on board.

Tony: *On tracks like 'Los Endos' [Steve] and I had been swapping licks and I loved that. It was great to have someone who could come up with ideas and play in harmony and unison.* ¹

Steve: *We all kicked up a storm together with the creation of 'Los Endos'!* ³⁹

But instead of just rolling along in the speedy vein, how about a variation? The bottom drops out and Tony plays an unhurried top line that's vaguely reminiscent of the chorus line for 'Robbery, Assault and Battery'. When Phil sings the word "battery" in that song, the notes he hits are F, G, and C. Meanwhile, the ascending notes on Tony's melody in this "breakdown" bit of 'Los Endos' are E♭, G, and C. So it's not *exactly* the same thing, and can't even properly be called a reprise, but hearing even two notes of an earlier chorus melody repeated prominently here brings the mind back to that point. It's sort of an unintentional reprise-lite, if you will. That said, this keyboard line also happens to be an *actual* reprise, if rearranged, of 'Dance on a Volcano'. It's the guitar line of that song's chorus, now switched to Tony's keyboard, slurring away. Sneaky stuff, huh?

Then the drums come back, Mike plays some funky stuff that Phil probably told him to, and we're off again into congatown. Then another Tony pit stop to dance around three notes where oddly enough I'm *also* reminded me of 'Robbery, Assault and Battery'. There's not any clear connection anymore based on pitch or melody, but it's more a rhythmic thing; the rhythm of Tony's repeated keyboard phrase is identical to the rhythm of the word "robbery" in the chorus of that earlier album tune. So again, not a full-on reprise by any means, but it keeps that earlier tune indirectly in the consciousness and weaves more of the thread that binds the album together.

Now more rapid-fire percussion and more trading licks until it all winds down in a controlled slump. And now, here's a thought. We've already got a whole bunch of improv stuff built around 'It's Yourself', we've done a sneaky reprise of 'Dance on a Volcano', and whether we meant to or not we're calling back spiritually to 'Robbery, Assault and Battery' as well. Why not just go all the way with this?

> **Tony:** *[Phil had] this idea of using all the melodies we had throughout the album and placing them into a slightly different feel to produce a song on its own.* [1]

Come on back, 'Dance on a Volcano'! We're reprising you for *real* this time, proper instrumentation and all! But hey Mike, while Steve's playing that riff, why don't you throw on some bass pedals? And Tony, maybe a Mellotron choir or something? Let's really get this full sound thing happening on it this time. And then Steve can play his guitar like it's a washboard while we change the tonality of the three-note pattern so it sounds all dark and threatening! And then and then and then...uh...

> **Phil:** *And then we reprised 'Squonk' at the end of it because that kind of gave the album a bit of a bookends feel.* [3]

Yeah, let's do 'Squonk'! Just the whole bloody main part of it! Why not? We can all embellish the heck out of the thing, make it even stronger sounding than it was before!

Back in my entry for 'Squonk' I made the point that starting a track with that much power gave it nowhere to go, and so the rest of the song became an exercise in trying to sustain that oomph. It performs that task about as admirably as anyone could hope for, but nevertheless still feels a little burdened by that weight of expectation. That's not a problem on 'Los Endos', where the 'Squonk' bit gets to close the song; now the rest of the piece can build up to it, and nothing comes after to detract. Tony and Mike wrote 'Squonk' together, but it was Phil who ultimately sussed out the best way to use it.

> **Phil:** *It's more milestones than favourites. Personally I prefer '[Wot] Gorilla', which is the same kind of thing, but 'Los Endos' was the first time we did it. I see it as our little excursion into the world of...I don't call it jazz-rock.* [31]

> **Phil:** *It was the first time I thought Genesis played the type of music they'd never played before - American music vaguely in the mould of Weather Report. It stemmed from this rhythmic idea I had. We also worked in some reprises because it was the end of the album, including the reprise of 'Squonk' at the end. It was the first time we hit on...I say jazz, but I think we were playing a different type of music on that track. It was still tight. It wasn't a blowing tune, but it was the first time we'd tried anything in that vein. To me, it was great to do that kind of thing with Genesis rather than playing it with Brand X.* [31]

If 'Dance on a Volcano' was the band starting life after Peter and realising they'd probably be OK, 'Los Endos' is the definitive stamp on the album, the band confidently asserting, "In fact, we'll be even better." Phil even throws in an homage to his departed buddy, calling over the strains of 'Squonk' with "There's an angel standing in the sun, freed to get back home!" It's one final throwback: a lovely goodbye, a mini-reprise of 'Supper's Ready', a well-wishing for a dude eager to spend some time just being a dad and tending a garden. And yet it's also a declaration of independence. "Farewell friend; we need you no longer."

> **Mike:** *I think with A Trick of the Tail we were definitely worried about what came next. We definitely thought, "Will it work?" So we did what we always do, is we said, "Let's go in and try a bit of writing. See what happens."* [3]

Old singer gone, drummer promoted (or demoted, if you'd asked Phil at the time), and now he's rallying the troops to make what will become arguably the band's most important live number ever.

> **Tony:** *You knew that the first time you played a piece on stage everyone would want to hear the old songs, as they called them, which was the material from the previous album which they hadn't wanted to hear at all on that album's tour. But you could introduce the new songs in a way that made them very palatable; you didn't necessarily have to play a whole string of them one after the other. On the first tour we did after Trick of the Tail we even used 'Los Endos' as the end song on that tour, even though it was a new song, and it worked really well.* [1]

The crowds in 1976 might not have gone in wanting or expecting to hear 'Los Endos' as a closer, but they sure weren't complaining when all was said and done. How could you *not* put this song in that role? If you're playing the main songs of the album anyway, then in concert 'Los Endos' serves the exact same purpose; you basically get to relive the whole show within that seven minute span of time and go out on the highest of highs.

> **Mike:** *'Los Endos' was a thrilling finale. It was so impressive that I didn't realise there wasn't anyone singing until a few years later, when Elton John pointed it out: "I can't believe you end the show on an instrumental: what a great idea!" I had to think about it - did we really end on a song with no one singing, no one out front on stage? It sounded suicidal if you put it like that.* [14]

When Elton John essentially says "Look at the balls on you guys!", well. You're probably doing something right.

> **Tony:** *I felt A Trick of the Tail produced three exceptional live numbers in 'Volcano', 'Squonk', and 'Los Endos'. That was something we really needed.* [10]

There's a great concert video of the Trick of the Tail Tour out there. Try to find it if you can. What you'll see is Phil, back on the kit where he belongs, feeling like he successfully duped the band into letting him drum a little while longer. Dude's arms are like machine guns.

> **Mike:** *My only regret [with Phil taking over as singer] was that I would never again play a whole show with Phil on drums. No one could play drums like Phil - he'd play for the song, not for himself - and I missed that to the end. From the drumming point of view, it was never quite the same again live.* [14]

And then over on the percussion side you've got Bill Bruford (BROOOOOOOF!) firing off bullets as well. You go to a Genesis show and see *this* spectacle? Yeah, you're getting your money's worth. It was so strong that they basically had to leave it in the set forever. It vanished during the 90s, but came back in 2007, only departing again in 2021 because Phil was no longer physically capable of playing it. To date 'Los Endos' has been played upwards of 650 times by Genesis in concert, more than any other song we have statistics for. And it deserves every bit of it.

> **Phil:** *It's become over the years one of the long-lasting songs from that album, because it was a great stage song… So that's always been one of my favourite things on the record, 'Los Endos'.* [3]

> **Tony:** *Well 'Los Endos' I think works very well. I mean, it certainly turned into a great live piece. It was great fun to play, and I felt it really rounded off the album well.* [3]

> **Mike:** *I think 'Los Endos' in a way is quite a special track. It's becoming more and more special in my mind as time goes on, actually. Because not many bands do a sort of seven minute instrumental with a sort of jazzy feel. And we're still playing it!* [3]

Even Steve is still playing it, and he's not even in Genesis anymore! His Seconds Out and More Tour goes on through 2022, ensuring 'Los Endos' will continue to endure on stage in one form another.

For a last thought, consider this: in May of 2007, a month before the start of the Turn It On Again Tour, Genesis was one of four acts honoured at the Second Annual VH1 Rock Honours show (and there would only be three before the show ceased to be). The format was that the honoured artist would be introduced, then another band would play a song in tribute, and then the band itself would come out and play a few songs. Genesis were the third honoured act of the night, following ZZ Top and Heart. After Keane played 'That's All' in tribute, Genesis themselves took the stage and played 'Turn It On Again', followed by 'No Son of Mine'. At which point Phil went back to his drum kit for a brief duet with Chester, leading into, you guessed it, 'Los Endos'.

I found an online blog post from someone who was asked by VH1 to be a "seat filler" for the evening; I guess that's part of why they cancelled the event a year later, if they simply weren't able to sell enough tickets in the first place. Anyway, here's what this individual had to say about the Genesis portion of the show: "Genesis starts off with 'Turn Me on Again' and then they did 'No Son of Mine'. From there they did an instrumental that I have no idea what it was – again I thought it strange since they have so many other hits..." [100]

This guy's site is all about heavy metal, and indeed, in the audience during this event you can see a lot of metalheads who were clearly there for the fourth honouree of the night, Ozzy Osbourne. On a night where you get three songs and people just expect you to play your hits then go away, Genesis put a thumb in everyone's eyes. "No, *this* is what we're all about." They spent seven minutes on an instrumental. Phil played through tremendous, visible pain to pull it off. The crowd had no idea what they were hearing. Their faces were stoic, bored, and unamused. They started clapping in the middle of the song, hoping it was over early. VH1 cut the entire song from the TV broadcast, content to pretend it never happened. And Genesis just didn't care. They played 'Los Endos' because *that's* what Genesis is all about.

And yet! By the heart of that 'Squonk' reprise, with Daryl shredding his guitar over that near-flawless groove, there's a shot of the crowd again. You can see smiles forming on their faces. You can see heads bobbing with the rhythms. You can see a couple friends turn towards one another with expressions that say, "I didn't know Genesis could do *this!*" And as Phil hits the final cymbal crash and steps away from the kit in agony, the crowd erupts. Welcome to Genesis, friends. Now you know.

9 - The Cinema Show

from *Selling England by the Pound*, 1973

"Have you ever heard of the Boat of Tiresias?" That was the question posed to the class by one of my college philosophy professors. Nobody raised their hands; though I had heard of Tiresias in another context, I wasn't aware of any particular association with a boat. The professor went on to explain that the Boat presented a question of metaphysical identity. He posed the thought problem to us thusly:

> Tiresias had a boat that was of such cultural/historical importance that it was preserved in Athens, but, as the boat was constructed of wood, it slowly began to rot away, one board at a time. And so, being good caretakers, those tasked with the boat's preservation would remove the rotting piece of wood and replace it with a fresh wooden board of equal dimensions. Piece by piece the boat was restored and replaced in this manner until after many decades no wood from the original boat remained. Was this, then, the same boat as the one that entered their care? Or was it now a different boat entirely? And if it were a different boat entirely, at what point did the identity of the boat change? After one plank? After every plank? Somewhere in between?

This is deep, thought-provoking stuff. So the idea that Genesis wrote a song heavily featuring Tiresias? Must be pretty heady material indeed!

Peter: *We seem to have lost the adolescent preoccupation with sex and death, and what we have now are certain kinds of unrelated lyrical ideas.* [101]

So one just looks at the lyrics and...wait a minute here. Romeo? Juliet? An extended metaphor about earth and sea as pertaining to erotic pleasure? ...This song's about sex, isn't it? Peter lied to me. Come on, man! Where are my metaphysics? Where's this boat I've heard so much about? There must be some misunderstanding! There must be some kind of mistake!

Oh, what's that? It's the *Ship* of *Theseus*? It's not even a boat?! My professor of Greek philosophy just had his classical Greek figures confused the entire time?! Well, that's just great. There's modern education for you. <sigh> All right then...I suppose sex it is!

Steve: *It's a very beautiful song, very romantic...* [13]

<deep breath> OK. Let's talk about this *romantic* song, shall we? It's a lovely little opening here with the tinkling 12-string sound. It gives similar vibes to 'The Musical Box' a couple albums earlier, though the notes and structures are very different. But it almost wasn't to be.

Steve: *When it was originally put together it was linked to 'Dancing with the Moonlit Knight'. We had a very sort of contentious meeting about this at the time. I remember Phil saying, "Well, if there's a 12-string passage in something, does it mean that every long song has to have a 12-string passage in it?" There were some crestfallen faces. So we started to do some long songs that didn't have 12-string passages in them.* [13]

You can almost see Mike's face getting even longer than usual at an exasperated Phil saying "Enough with the 12-strings already!" And indeed, while the 12-string wouldn't exactly go away until the three-piece era, after this album it did become slightly less ubiquitous. But by golly, 'The Cinema Show' is a romantic song, and romance means 12-string guitar!

Mike: *Another good example of when I tuned my 12-strings. Normally you've got twelve strings and they're paired up, and you tune each pair to the same note. I started tuning each pair to harmony notes. Which is how the song starts with that little rundown. Now what the hell that tuning is, I haven't got a clue. Because [in 2007] in New York they were saying, "Let's do the first half of 'Cinema Show' maybe." And I said, "Well, I have no idea how I played it. We'd have to work a compromised version out."* [3]

Spoiler alert: they never did work a compromised tuning out, so if you're disappointed that you never got to hear 'The Cinema Show' in its entirety in the 21st century, it's all Mike's fault. Anyway, there are a *lot* of guitar strings tinkling around in this one.

> **Steve:** *I was influenced by the flute work of Ian McDonald working with King Crimson, so I tried to play very pastoral phrases. I developed it a bit more when we did it live, doing percussion noises and what-have-you. But in some ways it typifies the Genesis sound because you've got almost a plethora of 12-strings going: sometimes two 12-strings, sometimes three. And an electric 6-string as well. And this jangly sound where you can't tell: it sounds almost...is that a keyboard? Is that a guitar? What is that sound?* [3]

And then we get the story, or really more like a snapshot, of this busy young woman trying to tidy up her place and herself before going to catch a movie with her date. I confess when I first heard the lyric that she "clears her morning meal" I thought it meant she was having some gastrointestinal difficulties, if you catch my drift. Decidedly *un*romantic, that. But I wouldn't have put something like that past Peter. Was it Peter? Who did the lyrics to this one, anyway?

> **Phil:** *'Cinema Show' was lyrically I think Tony and Peter. I think. Either Tony and Peter or Mike and Peter.* [3]

Was it you or was it me? Ah well. In any case, from Juliet we go straight to Romeo, who is basically just looking to get laid. It's a classic story: boy meets girl, boy lusts after girl, girl agrees to a pleasant night at the cinema, boy gives girl chocolates, girl thinks boy is nice, boy propositions girl, girl becomes disillusioned, the night ends with everyone a little bit disappointed. Tale as old as time, that one. And it's from there that Tiresias makes his appearance, where his *actual* background is relayed. There are variations on the classical myth, but Genesis lands on one of them in particular.

Tiresias, as the story goes, was hiking up a mountain and saw a pair of snakes, um, "getting nasty," as I think they called it back then. He used his walking stick to "break that mess up," I think was the historical parlance, which incurred the wrath of the goddess queen Hera, who was aspected to things like fertility. Hera was a capricious and impulsive goddess, and so she immediately decided that interrupting a pair of fornicating snakes ought to be punishable by forced sex change. Thus, she transformed Tiresias into a woman and made Tiresias one of her priestesses so (s)he could atone. Tiresias was surprisingly not much put out by this turn of events, being something of a laid back soul, and before long found a nice man to settle down and have kids with. After some years, Now-Mother Tiresias found some more snakes doin' the deed, and wisely left them alone. A satisfied Hera then turned Tiresias back into a man since he'd seemed to learn his lesson, which meant that in a very strange twist of fate, his kids now had two biological dads; I imagine the family dynamics probably got a little awkward after that.

Later, Hera and her husband Zeus found themselves in an argument over who derived more pleasure from sex - men or women. Being exceedingly petty gods with victim complexes, each one wanted the *other* sex to be the "winner." That is, Hera argued that men enjoyed sex more, and Zeus the opposite. At an impasse, Hera summoned Tiresias on the basis that he was the only person - mortal or god - who had experienced sex from both sides of the equation. They posed the question to him, and though he was a priest(ess?) of Hera, he felt compelled to answer truthfully: women get *way* more out of it than men do. Genesis translate this reply thusly: "Once a man, like the sea I raged. Once a woman, like the earth I gave. But there is, in fact, more earth than sea." A furious Hera struck him blind on the spot for embarrassing her, but a very pleased Zeus tried to make up for it by giving him foresight instead. Thus, Tiresias became known as a blind seer, one more expression of duality wrapped up in the same individual.

So, in summary, 'The Cinema Show' isn't an adolescent fixation on sex. No, it's an adolescent fixation on sex *combined* with classical Greek mythology. See? All grown up now! In fairness though, musically that maturation is *very* clear. After our first dalliance with Tiresias, we go into a veritable forest of guitar strings once again, featuring oboe and flute solos. I've only ever heard one other song that sounds anything like it, and that's 'The Dreaming Tree' by Dave Matthews Band, which came out 24 years later and may well have been influenced significantly by this song in the first place. It's such a unique atmosphere. As much as I love the live versions of this song, listening to this section on *Seconds Out* you can't help but feel like an entire audio channel is missing. Those jazzy, improv style woodwind lines have an impact that to me can't be overstated.

Then we get some really delightful vocal interplay on simple "la la la" stuff before one last little trip back with Father Tiresias, and one last declaration that there's more earth than sea as Steve's electric guitar gets a little solo to bring us home. Or is that a keyboard? Dangit guys, you've got me all confused again.

> **Steve:** *It's a very beautiful combination I think of 12-strings and keyboards.* [13]

Tony: *The other song on this album I suppose that kind of was a big development for us again was 'The Cinema Show'. Which was another one of those things which starts off with a sort of quiet, acoustic beginning and then ends up doing something else at the end.* [3]

Mike: *Bloody hard to write [the album]... The funny thing was we thought we had the bulk of it written. 'Cinema Show' was put on at the end, and that became one of the best things - one example that you shouldn't force writing.* [10]

Phil: *I'd like Genesis to get a bit looser, while keeping the arranged things. I want to get more into different time signatures. I think my playing has improved a lot...* [102]

Tony: *Mike had this riff which was in seven, just going dun dun dun g-jun-dun, like that. And he was playing along and you know, then I just sort of started fiddling around on top of it.* [3]

Phil: *A guitar riff [and] a 7/8 drum riff. And then Tony just had sort of lots of bits on top, and eventually that became "the thing." Which was very strong, I think.* [3]

Mike: *The rhythm was 7/8, which feels different but doesn't sound clever-clever.* [14]

Tony: *There is a tendency to avoid rhythms like seven [in later Genesis music], because at this point in time they sound a little bit dated. Like the seven we used in 'Cinema Show'. You can go into the studio, tap out a rhythm in seven, and almost say it's 'Cinema Show' because it's so identifiable.* [23]

Huh, that's weird. I've listened to this thing a number of times and I don't hear anything in seven, much less in such an iconic way that it should prevent the band from doing much else in seven going forward. Wonder what they're talking ab-

dun dun dun d-d-dun dun dun

...Did you hear that? That was pretty we-

d-d-dun dun dun d-d-dun dun dun

There it is again! What in the wor-

d-d-dun dun dun d-d-dun dun dun

dun dun dun d-d-dun dun dun d-d-dun dun dun d-d-dun dun dun d-d-dun dun dun

Whoooooa there. There is something else *entirely* happening here. What is going on?

Tony: *'The Cinema Show', again like 'The Musical Box' or 'Supper's Ready', had started off with an acoustic idea. But this time once we went off into the instrumental section at the end we didn't come back; it developed its own life. When we played that song to Tony Stratton-Smith, who was obviously a big fan of ours, he didn't like it. He felt we were trying to move into the area of ELP and that we were drifting away from what we did best. My feeling was that you can't stay doing the same thing forever and that particularly with 'Firth of Fifth' and 'The Cinema Show' we were trying out things we hadn't done on the previous albums.* [1]

Man, Tony's doing some *work* on this. What even...

Mike: *Selling England wasn't my favourite album but 'The Cinema Show' was a real standout moment. The second half of the song was the start of a new phase between me and Tony... I'm moving around chords, Tony's reacting and improvising over them, and between the two of us we're coming up with something that would go on to be the essence of the Genesis sound for the next twenty years. And the drumming's great, too.* [14]

Gracious, the drumming! How did I miss that? Just listen to that cymbal work! That's incredible! How the...

Tony: *And then we thought this could be really good, so again Phil, Mike, and I just went off really, and put this all together and worked on all of those bits. And I just improvised for hours and got these little bits and pieces going, and Mike would change the chords, and we ended up with this piece. And you know, it was such a strong rhythm in the first place. A lot of things you play on it could be really good. But I got one or two quite good melodies on top of it...* [3]

I guess you mean this wonderful melody here? This splendid little dance around the A-major scale? What a delight!

Steve: *The famous melody. Of course in a way it always deserved to be heard live to get the full impact of this. Last time I did it with my band, it virtually raised the roof. I'd never heard anything so loud in my life. The bass pedals were enough to bring the ceiling down. And those famous Mellotron voices of course. ...I think the cinematic effect, the soundtrack effect, really comes from the instrumental stuff and Tony's extraordinary keyboard work on this.* [13]

Raise the roof? Bass pedals? What are you talking about St- **OH MY WORD**

Tony: *The solo on 'Cinema Show' was very much the thing... Obviously, 'Cinema Show' went on to become a live classic.* [6]

WHAT WAS THAT SOUND? AND WHERE DID MY BODY GO?

Steve: *We'd just acquired the Mellotron voices. I pushed the band into getting a Mellotron way back in the day, and of course we bought our original one off of King Crimson. But the Mellotron voices hadn't really been invented at that point. I remember Mellotronics said to us, "Ooh, there's some very interesting stuff. You might like to come down and hear." And Tony Banks and I went down to listen to their latest stuff and it was male and female voices mixed, and you could get them separately if you wanted. So, you know, we opted to have the full whack of them all together.* [13]

Male and female mashed together, huh? Clever-clever, Steve! I see what you did there!

Mike: *But the second part, once again it seems to me we'd started this movement I think with myself, Phil, and Tony... playing, jamming, getting instrumental moments like the...9/8 in 'Supper's Ready', this one [in 'Cinema Show']...which became a large part of our trademark, really. The instrumental part was a huge sort of crowd pleaser. Very "live" song.* [3]

"Crowd pleaser..." ya think? Man, gonna take a bit to come down from that...wait, why isn't it coming down? WHY ISN'T IT COMING DOWN? Good gravy Tony, aren't your fingers tired yet?! HOW IS THIS STILL HAPPENING?

Peter: *The solos are longer on this one and we've played our things to their natural length. In the past we rather nervously tended to cut things short. The new [album] has longer solos - at the risk of being boring. We hope the fans will stay with us at any rate.* [86]

STILL HERE, PETE OL' CHAP!

Mike: *When we played the song live, Pete and Steve would leave the stage at the end so it was just me, Tony, and Phil. It was so strong and it was just the three of us. Although I wasn't conscious of it at the time, I think that must have been something I stored away in my memory: the knowledge of what the three of us could do.* [14]

Oh, poor Steve. Must've been a little dull for him there. I feel really bad for the guy.

Steve: *For me the most creative album the band did is Selling England by the Pound. I think that showcased both the song aspect that the band had, I think it showcased some of the playing talent...like, you know, occasionally the instruments were allowed to breathe. I mean, you know, unaccompanied things. Not very long, but, you know, occasionally. I think the odd solo was too long. I think 'Cinema Show'", I mean that keyboard solo which went on*

> *interminably on one chord in 7/8 for God knows how long. I think that was pretty damn long. Apart from that I think it showcased the individual abilities pretty nicely.* [103]

Don't you dare edit this down.

> **Tony:** *The things I get bored with [playing], I cut out [live]. Like lots of parts of 'Cinema Show' I couldn't stand playing anymore. So we only do the three best parts of it.* [23]

Son of a...OK, you know what? Forget it. I'm in too good a mood to let this get me down, you know? Let's gooooooo!

> **Tony:** *I think the instrumental at the end of this was probably the best of the ones we did - at this stage of our careers, anyhow. ...and it again built up to a very nice sort of climax I think. Probably better on stage than it was on the album in many ways, because on the album it sort of fades out into the next bit, which I'm not too sure is quite so good. But it was an exciting thing to have created at the time. We were very pleased with it.* [3]

Ooh, on stage, yeah yeah yeah! I can only imagine hearing this part live. Got to change the dynamics of the thing a little bit, right?

> **Tony:** *Although Chester [Thompson] came from a slightly different area of music, he was very able to adapt to what we were doing, and he added to our very English kind of music a hint of something which I really liked. A song like 'The Cinema Show' really developed and came alive with the double drumming between Chester and Phil - which we had first tried out with Bill Bruford.* [103]

Double drummin', gimme gimme! I can't get enough of this thing man. This song is pure fire in keyboard form. Unimpeachable. Magnificent.

> **Phil:** *'Cinema Show' is a huge tour-de-force. [The album's] certainly got a lot of things we still play. Huge stage classics on it. I like 'Cinema Show' in particular. The first half is great as well.* [3]

Wait, what first half?

8 - The Musical Box

from *Nursery Cryme*, 1971

And all this time that passed me by…

Phil Collins finishes his caress of an imaginary young lady and puts on his most threateningly cruel face. He hunches over, sweat dripping from every pore in his face, and demands to be touched. For emphasis, he says the imperative "now" 24 times in succession to the rapt attention of the 1992 audience in Wolverhampton. It is the last time Genesis will ever perform any part of this piece, and here, as before, they are only performing its closing section, which flows from 'The Lamb Lies Down on Broadway', just as it had 15 years previously. The snippet is merely one-eighth of a longer jaunt through the band's back catalogue: a collage that would later be known simply as 'Old Medley'. Yet this section remains one of the highlights of that medley and indeed the entire show. After all, they've had over two decades to hone the thing.

> **Mike:** *The studio version doesn't have the bite on the powerful sections that the song did live.* [31]

She's a lady, or at least a lady of the night; The Mama Tour is in full groove by the middle of January, 1984. The set has been working, but nevertheless the band decides to shake things up a bit heading into Arizona, adding an old classic into the line-up as part of a medley after 'Mama'. Phil does his best Peter impersonation to try to recreate the classic feel on the line "You stand there with your fixed expression…" It's a crowd favourite, but in the age of VHS, recording space is limited; the medley is dropped from the eventual video release.

> **Tony:** *I think it created that sort of fantasy, the lyric relating to all this sort of…the old Victorian kind of quality it has, and the album cover which related obviously to that as well.* [3]

Peter Gabriel needs help. His WOMAD project is a financial disaster and it's threatening to bring him down with it. Launched two years earlier, by 1982 both WOMAD and Gabriel's funding company are facing utter ruin unless they can make an awful lot of money in a very small amount of time. Gabriel's manager Tony Smith, who is also the manager of Genesis, suggests a one-off reunion concert they'll call Six of the Best. After a few songs, Peter addresses the crowd. "Croquet is a particularly vicious British sport." He proceeds to relay the story of Henry and Cynthia in words and in music, as Genesis plays 'The Musical Box' in its entirety for the final time.

> **Peter:** *A lot of it is based on fantasies, without them taking over from the music. There is a lot of freedom in the music. Nobody has to compromise too much. In our writing we are trying to do something that hasn't been done before, and that is to write a combination of sections that match. We have a number called 'The Musical Box' that is composed in this way. It's quite a complicated story - about a spirit that returns to bodily form and meets a Victorian girl. He has the appearance of an old man and the relations with the young lady are somewhat perverted, so he gets bumped off into the never-never.* [89]

> **Mike:** *Peter's performance was half trying to explain what the song was about. That's how it started, really. Genesis music has always had a fair amount of drama in it. And so the more… you can add to the drama, the better, really.* [43]

The City of Brotherly Love demands an encore. Again. There's something the band has tucked away in the arsenal, though it's been a while since they've used it. Certainly it hasn't come up so far in the Duke Tour during this year of 1980, but nine minutes or so is a big ask for a second encore, and they haven't put in the rehearsal time to make the full song work. So they opt for just the end section, same as most of the audience heard on the previous live album, same as they've been doing for years. It's the most powerful bit anyway, right? Who's going to complain?

> **Tony:** *I think the real strength of the song comes towards the end really, with this little bit that starts "She's a lady." And the organ comes in playing this little sort of fugue-y type thing… On*

> *stage once we started playing this, I realised just how strong that was...it was a real standout moment on stage, I think.* [3]

Genesis has been adapting to life as a trio, spending a third of their set on material from the newest album, with another third coming from the next most recent pair of albums they've done. But there's still a desire to play a few of the old favourites, and here in Vienna in 1978, they decide to change things up slightly and dust off a bit that's older than anything else they're playing on the tour - older even than 'The Fountain of Salmacis', which is a regular in the setlist. Once again they tie this end section of 'The Musical Box' together with 'The Lamb Lies Down on Broadway', but now position the pair as an encore; a little hat tip to an appreciative crowd who don't realise they're hearing something particularly rare.

> **Tony:** *I think two songs on [Nursery Cryme], 'The Musical Box' and 'The Fountain of Salmacis', are exceptional.* [10]

The band is mixing *Seconds Out* when Steve Hackett finally bites the bullet and leaves the band, leaving this live album as his final playing legacy. The music on the 1977 album is meant to serve as a time capsule for that year's Wind & Wuthering tour, where the band decided to bring back old favourite 'The Musical Box' in an abridged form, attaching it to 'The Lamb Lies Down on Broadway' and playing only the song's most powerful section. Tony jokes that Genesis mixed Steve out of *Seconds Out* once he quit; apparently they also mixed him out of the accompanying promo video that was created using the song.

> **Steve:** *I think it's that thing about Genesis where you get a very long song that builds and builds and builds - you get these sort of Sousa crescendos - finally hitting with this bit that we did on Seconds Out, of course. The most memorable bit perhaps of the song but there's so much more to it. Very English, but... insistent and urgent, you know? There's something about this... It's something that...that music...it really speaks for itself, doesn't it? That feeling of the crescendoed peak of the song with something that is quintessentially English, but at the same time you've got haunted nurseries and this kind of Victoriana and eroticism all kind of mixed in together in that very impressionistic, rambling way that Genesis did at that time. But I still love the track. I get to play it as many times as I can live. I still love it.* [13]

Genesis are asking a lot of their audiences. Here in late 1974, they're about to go on the road to play their concept double album, *The Lamb Lies Down on Broadway*, in its entirety. In most cases, the people they're playing to won't have heard any of the music for the entire show. But with over a hundred minutes in the set already and a self-contained story to tell, there's no room to slip the fan favourites in between. So a compromise of sorts is reached that they'll play one beloved tune as an encore when the audiences are receptive to the elaborate stage show that is The Lamb. 'The Musical Box', a consistent live staple for the past four years, is chosen to be that song.

> **Tony:** *The music we were never going to compromise in any way with anything we did on the records. But when it came to the stage show and what you could do for publicity, I mean we were pretty open really. And I think it helped Pete, because he's not a natural on stage really. It gave him something to hide behind. It gave him something to work with. And so once he'd done that, the idea of costumes and masks and sort of in a sense acting out characters all the time came very naturally to him.* [43]

> **Mike:** *We were starting to create an atmosphere about the band. As a perception. Slightly quirky, people seeing this artwork, hearing the songs, Pete's performance...I felt were starting to become something that was a little unique in the music business in England. And that was a good thing, I think.* [3]

> **Steve:** *Brian [May]...said to me, he was aware of the early Genesis material, in particular, 'Musical Box'... And I played there a harmony guitar solo on the end of that, and he said to me that I had influenced him. I was completely out of way with this because I always thought that his harmony guitar style was something which he really came up with and pioneered.* [104]

Genesis are becoming established in the live scene. 1973 is proving to be a pretty good year for their reputation, on the back of their album *Foxtrot* and with its follow-up providing even more great material. But 'The Musical Box' remains the crowd favourite. Around this early era, an enterprising Mike Rutherford figures he can probably accomplish more playing live if he attaches a guitar to a bass guitar, and so begins to be seen playing the "double neck" in concert from time to time.

> **Mike:** *Double-necks have their downside... They're heavy brutes to play and they unbalance you, although I only ever fell off stage once. It was during rehearsals somewhere in the*

> *American Midwest and no one realised I was no longer there. I could have killed myself and they would have just carried on playing. 'The Musical Box' had no bass until the pedals at the very end - the middle section was just the low strings of the guitar, filling the bass area in. But as I was lying there flat on my back, pinned to the floor, slightly concussed, I can remember thinking that it would have been nice to have been missed.* [14]

> **Tony:** *'Musical Box' is part of a series of songs that built up to 'Supper's Ready', which was the best of that kind of song - long, acoustic-based numbers that told a story.* [31]

A young, earnest Steve Hackett has his ad in Melody Maker answered and soon finds himself part of a group called Genesis, who have just fired their previous guitarist after a brief probationary period. He's run through the ringer of learning the band's back catalogue, and after a few months of trial by fire on stage, he retreats with them to write what will become *Nursery Cryme*. He's happy to be involved in the material, but there's one song on the album that's already essentially completed by early 1971 when he joins them: something called 'The Musical Box'. He dutifully learns the piece along with the other material, but finds a place to put his own stamp on it before the album is officially recorded.

> **Steve:** *'The Musical Box' was the only song that I think was written before I joined. Although the song was written, there was still a lot of room to make improvements. No one was making the sound of a musical box...so I felt well here's me for a start!* [29]

> **Steve:** *Here I used vari-speed, recording guitar at half speed to make it sound like a musical box. Working with sound colour was important to the band. Genesis' approach was often like an orchestra, at times very subtle but with the ensemble approach we could sound incredibly strong.* [70]

It's clear in late 1970 that playing with only four people isn't going to work out for the long term, so a new guitarist by the name of Mick Barnard is brought on board. His playing talent isn't terrible, although he seems to be a bit useless in the writing room. It soon becomes clear that Mick isn't the answer, but as they're about to begin auditioning other guitarists behind his back, he comes up with an electric guitar solo at the end of the piece called 'The Musical Box' which really adds a lot of power and character to the song. They wonder where this has been all along, even as they spot an intriguing ad in Melody Maker.

> **Tony:** *Steve was in the band a very short time when we recorded Nursery Cryme. All the guitar parts on 'Musical Box' were actually written by Mick; Steve tended to play pretty much what Mick had played 'cause there wasn't much time to learn new parts. Most of the guitar on it is Mike anyhow - all the rhythm guitar, it always was. There wasn't that much lead guitar on it.* [10]

> **Tony:** *The melody line at the end of the song was actually written at the time that Mick Barnard was with the group, so that was his contribution to the song.* [6]

> **Tony:** *Mick Barnard...was actually good! But he just probably wasn't assertive enough, you know? And while that really wasn't working, we then auditioned Steve.* [3]

With Mike rejecting every guitarist out there, the band is stuck at four. They can't afford to stop gigging, so they rearrange some parts. Tony will play lead guitar through a fuzzbox on his organ, while Mike will play rhythm guitar and invest in some bass pedals so they don't lose the bottom registers of the songs. It's difficult, and some songs don't work at all, but one of them - 'The Musical Box' - actually comes together pretty well.

> **Tony:** *Although it was probably never great, the four-piece thing, we did get it so it wasn't too bad. And we started writing this piece which became 'The Musical Box'...and we knew this was really good; we used to play it on stage and stuff as a four-piece, it was good.* [3]

> **Mike:** *It's interesting because in a sense we were trying to work as a four-piece and it wasn't really working. Tony doing all the lead parts on fuzz piano, you know. But actually funny enough, this song was the first I felt that did work as a four-piece. The sound we made - I'm playing pedals at the end, Tony's playing keyboards - I mean, had we gone the four-piece route, this song might have been where we might've gone. I'm glad we didn't. But in a sense this song worked well on stage as a four-piece.* [3]

> **Steve:** *They did a few gigs without a guitarist before they had Mick and Tony said he was trying to play in a guitaristic kind of manner with his keyboards. So he had a Hohner Pianette going through a fuzz box, not a synthesizer; this was way before all of that stuff, and I thought, "That's interesting, here is a keyboard player trying to sound like a guitarist," and so some of the lines I came up with on that song I wanted to sound like a keyboard... That was what was*

> *interesting about the band, the fact that what am I hearing here? Am I hearing a guitar or a keyboard?* [29]
>
> **Mike:** *See, there we are, we're kind of going acoustic, but going more electric. You know, it starts soft and it builds and builds and builds. By the end it's just, everything's going, you know. It's as big as any song we've ever done really, I think. And I guess probably this must be the first time with the bass pedals. Because Trespass was a five-piece so you didn't need bass pedals, but we've gone to that four-piece scenario with Tony playing the lead parts and me trying to play rhythm guitar parts and bass pedals at the same time. So it's funny how things happen. You get stretched and forced into doing something. I'm sure if we'd never have been a four-piece I'd never have bothered to pick up any bass pedals.* [3]

Tony Banks comes up with an exciting ending for the work-in-progress 'Musical Box' song, a big organ chord run over Mike's playing that really ratchets up the drama of the piece, providing it with a suitably epic conclusion. Peter Gabriel, both inspired by the sound he's hearing and annoyed at what he perceives as Tony's lack of common sense, writes some lyrics to go over top of it and sings them in rehearsal.

> **Tony:** *The part I was most happy with on that particular song was the final section, where Mike had this little chord sequence and I started playing these very simple major chords on top of it so that it became almost like a fugue, quite quietly, before developing into something that was really, really exciting. I remember a bit of an argument at the time about whether there should be vocals on it or not. I felt there shouldn't [be] because I thought, "It's such a great piece of organ playing!" But Pete started singing and although I initially felt, "Oh no, no, shut up," then I stopped myself: "Hang on, this sounds really good." The combination moved it onto another level, a big high...* [1]
>
> **Peter:** *This was one of the regular battlegrounds. Because Tony would [be] blissfully unaware of an audience and want to stretch things out for ten or twenty minutes for big keyboard instrumental things. And I would be thinking, "Well we're trying to tell a story here, too. We need to re-plug in back with some vocals." So I think there were a lot of arguments about those type of issues... And it was an important part, because you didn't want all the "up" moments to be instrumental only, and all the "down" moments to be the vocal bits. I certainly didn't!* [3]
>
> **Mike:** *'Musical Box'...to me was 'Stagnation' one stage on. It was a quirky, fantasy fairy tale story that started quietly, built up and, at the end, had a huge dramatic finish that would be one of our best bits for a long time to come. Even today, when I hear Pete sing, "Now, now, now, now, now" it raises the hairs on the back of my neck. It's almost annoying: as I'm not a singer, I could never do something so simple that would sound so emotional.* [14]

New Genesis drummer Phil Collins is, from his first day in the fold, the most accomplished musician in the band. He's no songwriter, of course, but he's more a master of his instrument than any of the others here. So when they're looking for a little bit of a harder edge for the up-tempo bits of 'The Musical Box', he shrugs his shoulders and offers a sample of what he can do. The band is quite enthused.

> **Phil:** *I never saw Family, the group Family, but there was a thing they used to do called ['The Weaver's Answer']. Which was like...kind of a rolling thing. And I had a pretty good foot, you know. So I could [do it too]. And they kinda liked that. So I put that with their rhythm and suddenly it was like "Whoa, hey, we're off!"* [3]

Developments have been promising on 'Manipulation' and it seems like it's going to become a proper Genesis song. Peter has been writing lyrics that work as a natural extension of his creative storytelling skills, inspired by sights from his youth, flights of fancy, and good old fashioned young male lust. The story he creates will end up lending the song its final title: 'The Musical Box'.

> **Peter:** *I think my head at the time also was in this Victoriana world which I pictured around the house my dad had grown up in. So this sort of controlled English mental landscape under which festered violence and sex was the sort of flavour that I was trying to bring into the lyrics and vocals.* [10]

Anthony Phillips leaves Genesis for personal reasons, taking with him the hopes for pieces like 'Let Us Now Make Love', 'Silver Song', and others. The promising tune 'F' however - known now as 'Manipulation' thanks to the television special - survives the jump and continues to be developed by the remaining three members of the band; three, because *Trespass* drummer John Mayhew is fired in the wake of Phillips' departure. The BBC special will never air.

> **Mike:** *Parts of it were around when John Mayhew was still with the band... A long time ago we did some music to go with this guy's paintings for the BBC which never in fact got shown. But we recorded it and 'Musical Box' was one of the sections on it - a fairly short bit, but that was the basis of it. It went through a couple of drafts.* [31]

Genesis, working diligently to continue building upon *Trespass*, see 'F' as being another "journey song" in the 'Stagnation' mould; an acoustic piece that will go between different ideas and moods without ever returning to any of them along the way. Peter, wary of the song remaining stuck in a gentle folk rut, lobbies for at least one section of harder playing for the sake of contrast. The band also get a gig with the BBC, allowing them to record four work-in-progress songs to be used as soundtracks to a series of paintings. The show's production crew assigns each song to a named painting, which effectively gives each of those songs a new working title. 'F' is selected by the band to be one of the four songs.

> **Tony:** *It was a very atmospheric piece. And it was musically interesting. And it went through all these changes and other stuff. It was a sort of precursor perhaps of what was to come later. You know, we have the little bits and lack of repetition in the song. You start off with one bit, which is a really strong section, that opening part, but it never comes back again, you know? And we used to quite like doing that. Like using a bit once and then going to a very loud bit, and a very quiet bit, and another loud bit, then a sort of serene bit. I think it's a song with a lot of contrasts in it, which for some people is very appealing. But some people just find [it] irritating, because it never centres into a groove, you know. You're doing one thing, "This is great," then "Ohh, it's stopped again," a time change and everything. So it is a very sort of typical Genesis song. Followed on from 'Stagnation' I suppose, you know that same kind of thing, but perhaps a little bit more dramatic.* [3]

> **Peter:** *Mike started off with the first [chords] and I was a big fan of The Who, too. And I really wanted to try and persuade Mike to find something like a little Townshend arm-waving, ballsy attacking section that we could add in there. And I think I was pushing really hard for that... And it was I think exciting when that sort of first came to gel as a piece.* [10]

Excited by what his writing partner has come up with, Ant goes to work on 'F', dressing up the rudimentary guitar parts with ones that sounded a bit more robust and interesting. As they have many times before, Mike and Ant play their 12-string guitars together to really enrich the sound and begin developing the piece out a little bit, unsure whether anything might come of their efforts.

> **Tony:** *It...developed right from the early days out of playing with Ant and Mike. And so it had that sort of two guitar thing. And I played guitar on it as well. The first part of it is all guitar. A few ideas came out of that.* [89]

> **Tony:** *It always was more Mike's thing... Ant certainly embellished those parts and I always felt that Ant should have got a credit on that song as part of the writing team. We then took it somewhere else...That track has the influence of three guitarists on it.* [6]

Mike experiments with some guitar tunings, looking for songwriting inspiration in strange places, hoping something might just click into place. As a lark, he tunes the top three strings of his 12-string guitar to the same note and plays a few chords. Anthony Phillips likes what he hears and they decide the little bit of playing is good enough to warrant learning and giving a working title. The name 'F' is settled upon: the note that three strings are all tuned to.

> **Mike:** *It started with Ant, actually. Ant and I, I think. I'm sure it did. Playing 12-string stuff together. And I had this Rickenbacker guitar, I tuned the strings...I had started to do weird tunings. And this is a very bizarre tuning. All the top three strings are tuned to F. Which is just mad. But it made that jangly sound. And it meant that that big chord when we go "bom bom" had this lovely open string feeling.* [3]

Play me my song...

---

7 - Heathaze

from *Duke*, 1980

It's a pretty commonly held maxim among film critics and moviegoers that the sequel to any given flick will inevitably be worse than its predecessor. In fact, the more sequels are made to a given film, the worse they tend to get. It's not terribly surprising; you've got a lot of people involved in the production machine and the whole point of the sequel from a business point of view is to capitalise on the success of the original. What better way to do that than to attempt to produce more of what made the first movie resonate with audiences? So you end up with this phenomenon known in the tropes world as Sequel Escalation: give us the same thing, but more of it. And more. And more. Until we're all just kind of numb to it all, and suddenly by Transformers 17: Death of Explosions any magic we initially had is gone.

There are exceptions, of course. Terminator 2: Judgment Day holds up magnificently to the first film. My wife swears by National Lampoon's Christmas Vacation. The common thread there is that these sequels aren't content to just do more of the same, but instead try to change the nature of the thing along the way. Yes, we'll have more robots with shotguns, and so those action sequences will be even more compelling, but we're also going to tell a different kind of story, with different kinds of characters and different dynamics. Yes, we'll have more semi-slapstick family comedy, but now it's at Christmas instead of on a road trip. More of what you liked, but different context and delivery. The same, but fresh.

Video games and books all have similar problems and their own potential solutions to "the sequel issue," but music is a realm where this doesn't typically ever come up. Sure, you can have songs that act as continuations or movements, like Moon Safari's series of 'Lover's End' tracks, but these aren't really sequels in any real sense, any more than you might consider John Williams' score for The Empire Strikes Back to be a musical sequel to his score from Star Wars. The very concept of a musical sequel is so alien that it creates humour in itself; we're still waiting on Peter Gabriel to release 'Big Time 2', for example, and likely will be for the rest of human existence. There's something inherently amusing about taking a song and saying "do that, but more, and bigger, and better, and number it."

And yet, that doesn't stop everyone, does it? Metallica in 1991 put out a song called 'The Unforgiven', followed by 'The Unforgiven II' in 1998 and 'The Unforgiven III' in 2008. Against all presupposition, it seems that musical sequels can exist after all, which I still can't quite wrap my head around. How is it that a songwriter can pen a piece of music with the thought of "This is going to be like this earlier piece" in the same way a filmmaker might look at a big box office follow-up? What would it take to get to that point?

I'd like to rewind time to 1978 and Tony's song 'Undertow' from *And Then There Were Three*. You can flip back several pages to get my full thoughts on that one, but in summary it's a song with bleak, spare verses and giant, warm choruses. It's a song that plays with emotions, intermingling hope, longing, grief, and confusion all into one package. It's got lyrics that play up all these mixed feelings, coming from the perspective of a distracted lover unable to commit to a single moment in time because the weight of the world is too big, and the icy death outside is too much to bear. It's a terrific and strong piece; the biggest highlight of the album for me.

A year later, Mike and Tony had some time to burn while Phil was tending to his failing marriage, and they released solo albums. Here Tony could finally put out his previously discarded piano intro for 'Undertow', yes, but other ideas came forward as well. Yet even more than the individual ideas themselves, what *A Curious Feeling* brought was a feeling of true artistic freedom.

> **Tony:** *There were things I wanted to do but couldn't within Genesis… Obviously I can't help sounding a bit like Genesis on everything I do, but I wanted to take certain things further…* [96]

Consider that 'Undertow' is a song credited to Tony only, and yet the band environment still saw concessions being made (the aforementioned cut intro). Now he got a chance to put forward his visions in an uncompromised form, and his prevailing thought was to "take certain things further" than he had with the band. "I want to do this, but *more*." Tony recorded A Curious Feeling in the middle of 1979, and then more or less moved into Phil Collins' apartment for the *Duke* writing sessions right after. The band all did their jamming on the pieces that would comprise the 'Duke Suite' of course, but they also got to bring in two solo songs apiece to fill out the album. That's where 'Heathaze' comes in.

Duke was produced by Dave Hentschel, same as *And Then There Were Three* and a couple previous albums before that. Yet each album has its own distinct kind of feel to it, with *Three* especially having its own unique kind of flavour that doesn't quite come through on any other Genesis album. By contrast, when I think of *Duke* I'm not thinking of lush, blurry keyboards and purple skies; I'm thinking of driving beats with powerful vocals. It's still a full sound, but it's not quite as pervasive. It's a more controlled fullness, if that makes sense, which allows the songs some additional clarity of rhythm and content. In a nutshell, it's a less muddy, "cleaner" kind of sound that dominates this album.

'Heathaze' isn't that at all. As a *Duke* listener you've just finished 'Misunderstanding', a pop rock song built around a slick, tight groove, and you're on your way to 'Turn It On Again', another pulsing rocker that shows off the remarkable level of polish that the Genesis trio has managed to achieve on their sophomore effort as a three-piece. But wedged in the middle is something else entirely. From two seconds into 'Heathaze' there's an uncanny feeling that you've been down this road before. That liquid piano sound, that wistful atmosphere, and then that completely unmelodic vocal melody floating lightly above it all. It's not merely a sound straight out of *And Then There Were Three*; it's 'Undertow' resurrected specifically.

This time the guitar comes in a bit earlier, texturing the piano playing a bit more, but it's readily apparent there's the same kind of musical idea here. The notes are different, the chords are different, the semi-melodies are different, but this is still unmistakably 'Undertow 2'. Then here comes the pre-chorus vocal line and yep, there are the drums making their entrance into the piece. But now here's a change: this pre-chorus vocal bit doesn't segue straight into the chorus. Now there's a little interlude that builds drama on its own, adding synth lines and a big swell into that first bombastic beat. That's new, and another learned behaviour along the way for Tony.

> **Tony:** *We all like thick sounds, a very textured sound - we enjoy building up, orchestrating our music. It's just a question of the instrumentation you use; you can use synthesizers to build up different kinds of sounds.* [105]

But this is a sequel, right? We can't just do the same thing. We've got to do it *bigger*. To that end, 'Undertow' has Phil kicking his bass drum on the 1 beat and firing off a snare on the 3 beat, with only lighter cymbal work in between. This creates a kind of deliberate, almost-but-not-quite-plodding feel to the whole thing. It's a kind of heaviness designed to make you really feel the weight of what's being sung. By contrast, in 'Heathaze' Tony has Phil doing the *exact same thing* right down to the individual beats, only this time he's kicking that bass drum in conjunction with the snare hit, making the third beat of each measure just BOOM out from the sound. The drums themselves are also mixed to be louder/more powerful this time around, so now these choruses sound even more heavy than the ones from the earlier track.

Going along with that, in 'Undertow' you get Mike playing this up-and-down kind of guitar line in the chorus, which gives it some momentum so that Tony can just roll out giant chords without needing to hold down a particular rhythm. In 'Heathaze' those lines shift to the bass guitar instead, which is both much more dynamic in the notes it plays, and crucial to giving the song some extra gravity. Additionally, instead of those up-and-down phrases coming as a kind of countermelody to the vocals, here they are most prominently in unison to them. Listen on the line "the same wind but whereas" and you'll notice that the instrumental movement runs an octave under the lead vocal line, except for two notes in harmony. Here are the notes side-by-side (well, top-by-bottom) for comparison:

F# - F - F# - G# - C# - C# ... Vocal Line

F# - F - F# - F - F# - C# ... Instrumentation

It's essentially a backing vocal harmony part, flowing in and out: three unified octave harmonies, then a major chord (the third and fifth without the root), inverted major fourth, and finally back to the octave. Of course, those chord identities are a little fluid as the underlying chords themselves keep changing, but my point is that this construction is the sort of thing a singer would do. Instead though, Tony's got it all arranged elsewhere; Phil's lead vocal will stand alone as the only voice on the entire track. Doesn't seem like that'd actually make things "bigger" in that sequel kind of style, right?

Wrong.

Wrong because on 'Undertow' Phil was still trapped in his gentle choirboy voice. He delivered those lyrics with passion, yes, and they worked wonderfully for the material, but two years later Phil's voice was something new and fierce. Mike calls it the "crunchy voice," but man oh man what a difference a little time, heartache, and substance abuse can make. Tony picked up on this and wisely decided he needed to get out of the way and let this man belt. 'Undertow', but more. Same general style, but no more uncertainty; where 'Undertow' flights, 'Heathaze' fights. Listen to that delivery of "Beware the fisherman". That kind of jagged dagger of a vocal simply wasn't possible in 1978. But this is the sequel. We're going big.

And that takes me to the lyrics, which are themselves built upon what came before. Again, 'Undertow' is a song about struggling to deal with feelings, and situations, and making sense of this mad world we live in. It's equal parts hope and anguish, and for that reason really resonates strongly with anyone feeling either (or both!) emotions when they listen to the track. Well, 'Heathaze' is that, too, except all grown up. One can even pretty easily imagine the singer to be the exact same person from 'Undertow' now a bit older and more jaded.

Listen, I don't know how much it comes through in these ramblings, but for better or worse I am at my core a very cynical person. I try to tone that down a bit where I can; it's a big part of why, outside of the very lowest rated entries in this book I've gone out of my way to avoid criticism and instead focused just on what I perceive to be the songs' strengths. Negativity in small, focused doses can provide good contrast and even at times be pretty amusing, but consistent pessimism is just a massive drain on everyone involved. That's not a place I really want to go, but it is ironically closer to the way I'm naturally inclined to see the world in my everyday life. And I think that's why I connect so well with 'Heathaze' on a lyrical level.

The singer of 'Heathaze' is a man who's just had enough. He's gone from the feeling of "Why do a single thing today?" all the way to scorning those who feel that "nothing must be done." From pondering the fate of those stuck in the cold to scoffing at those in the heat who "do all those things they feel give life some meaning." No longer the intoxicating smell of perfume lingering here and there, but instead "betrayed" by the aftertaste of "perfumed poison." This man has loved, lost, and he's done with it all. Look at this sap trying to fish in a dry pond. He doesn't even know it's a waste of time! But don't try to tell him that 'cos he won't believe you. You shouldn't suffer fools, because they won't suffer you. They are fools, after all. Not like me. They haven't seen what I've seen.

'Undertow' is water, threatening to pull you under and sweep you away. 'Heathaze' is fire, orange lights and smoke razing everything to the ground. It's a lashing out of rage, and yet under all of that there's real hurt. The trees and I both have withered leaves, and the winds of change strike us both. The trees' withered leaves fall away, allowing rebirth and new growth, but mine? I'm still clutching mine tightly. I want them gone, but I can't let them go. This pain, it's a part of me now. I don't want it, but how can I live without it? All these people all around, so carefree and happy? *They're* the fools, not me! NOT. ME. I feel like an alien trapped among them.

Cooled by gentle breeze? No...only hot winds here. Shout it out, Phil. Blast those choruses, Tony. 'Undertow' has lost its innocence, and it's got a bone to pick with all of us. Most sequels can't measure up to the originals, but every now and then something special happens. Someone takes an idea, ratchets up the intensity, then turns the whole thing on its head and creates something remarkable. 'Undertow' created a brilliant formula, yes. But it was 'Heathaze' that perfected it.

6 - Entangled

from *A Trick of the Tail*, 1976

I have sleep apnoea. If you haven't heard of this condition, it essentially means your body occasionally stops breathing altogether during sleep, causing you to "wake up" so you can begin breathing again. These stops and starts usually aren't noticed consciously, but can be characterised by things like tossing and turning, and of course snoring. My case began relatively mildly as these things go, but steadily increased in severity over the years to where it's become a real health concern. This isn't mere assumption either; I've actually done a sleep study at a centre and been officially diagnosed, and then a second home sleep study more recently that confirmed the more advanced diagnosis.

That inpatient sleep study was a particularly strange event, as I recall. For one thing, it was the first night I'd ever spent away from my wife since we had been wed a couple years earlier: a sweet but disappointing footnote in our marital history. But mainly it was the fact that my face had to be covered in sensors, which were affixed with a kind of thick paste substance. I had wires and goop all over, was laid down on a fairly spartan cot with a pillow of questionable make, surrounded by lights turned low but not all the way off, with a live camera watching every movement and listening to every sound I made. I always sleep on my side; they told me I had to lay on my back, lest the sensors not work properly.

"What if I have to go to the bathroom?"

"Well, you'll need to unplug all these wires, take these monitors with you, do what you need to do, then come back in and we'll hook you up again."

I was fairly confident I suffered from sleep apnoea going into that study, but was there ever any doubt I'd come out of it with a firm diagnosis? How could *anyone* get their best sleep under conditions like that? I probably managed a combined three hours that night, which was enough for them to tell me I officially had a problem. They recommended I order a CPAP (continuous positive airway pressure) machine, which is a device that you hook onto your face before bed every night that blows air into your throat so you don't wake up due to temporary airway collapse. It is not a cure; it is a solution that only works if you are actively using it, and therefore a chronic sufferer of sleep apnoea who opts for this treatment method must use it every night for the rest of his or her life. If you think this sounds uncomfortable and onerous, you're not alone: half of all CPAP users quit within the first year of using the device because for them the solution to the apnoea proves worse than the apnoea itself.

I counted myself among those sufferers who were less than keen on sticking a reversed vacuum onto my face every night, so I talked to my dentist, who recommended a certain oral appliance that he was confident would be effective for a condition as mild as mine was at the time. But then we hit a snag of insurance coverage, and that dragged on, and eventually the matter was forgotten entirely. It took years for me to finally follow up again on any of this; long enough that I had to have that second in-home sleep study done to confirm I still had a problem. Thankfully, that test was a bit more reasonable: a Darth Vader style chest box strapped around the torso, tubes in the nostrils and taped to the face, and a finger sensor for pulse readings.

Why did it take me so long to try to proceed with treatment? Well, in my mind, my reality just kind of was what it was, you know what I mean? I am *always* tired. Like anyone, a particularly bad night can send me into deeper fatigue, but I don't have a "well-rested" baseline. Not really. It's just varying levels of functional. But see, that's all I know. It's all I've ever known. I can't remember ever feeling one hundred percent, fully energised in a healthy way like some people talk about, so I can't miss it. My body's adapted to these reduced energy levels on a permanent basis; I'll yawn all day but I'll make it through, no worries.

But it does mean that when I get exhausted, I get *really* exhausted. Some nights I just crash hard, no matter what I'd rather be doing. I'm always tired, but if I *tell* you I'm feeling tired, I'm probably almost gone. And there are activities that prove especially draining. Not physical ones, surprisingly; exercise doesn't wear me down that much. It's the mental side of things that gets me. A day at the office juggling five different meetings for five different clients on five different subjects? That kind of rapid gear switching is a recipe for complete burnout when I finish the day. Writing an essay about a Genesis song for a book? Man, that's exhausting work. Coming back to the computer a few hours later to write another one on the same day? Forget about it. I don't know how I can summon the mental energy to pull that off.

So I get what Steve Hackett means when he says that after writing and recording his first solo album *Voyage of the Acolyte*, he was totally spent.

Steve: *My first memory [of the Trick of the Tail writing sessions] was of day one of rehearsal, of being very tired. As if I'd just given birth once and I was required to come up with another baby very quickly!* [30]

Creating things is *hard*, man. Whatever your art, whatever your method, it's never easy to make something out of nothing. Sometimes you're flush with ideas, but even then you've got to deal with refining them, assembling them, filling in any gaps, and so forth. That's why when you hear songwriters talking about how easy a song was to write, it's almost always a surprise to them. They know their own talent and expertise, so why should they be shocked that this song came together so well? Because that's not normal. Usually the ideas are more scattered and take a lot of time and effort to fully form.

Steve: *What I used to do was probably throw in a few riffs and licks rather than whole songs. Although there was 'Entangled' and there was 'Los Endos' and the outro of 'Dance on a Volcano', those sort of things, you know. Sort of kick in with those ideas.* [3]

This is even true for Tony Banks, who was working just as hard at writing songs as Steve, but didn't have the creative outlet of a solo album siphoning them off.

Tony: *I came in [to the Trick of the Tail sessions] perhaps with the most complete songs. Mike came in with sections, as did Steve, and as it happened the bits we used to sort of finish them off were my bits, so I ended up being credited on every track on this album. Which was sort of quite funny.* [3]

So there's Steve, mentally and creatively fatigued, doing his best to chip in with little fragments that the band might be able to make something out of. Or really anything that might come to mind at all. Perhaps drawing on this kind of lethargy, he conjures up an acoustic bit in F minor. It's just a riff, played at a very languid speed. I doubt he was sitting there with a metronome, but if he were he'd find that his riff clocked in at about 75 beats per minute, or BPM. This happens to fall right in the normal range for resting - or even sleeping - heart rates for human adults. Breathe in, breathe out. Drift a little, riff a little. It was tranquil, it was lovely, and it caught Tony's ears.

Tony: *Steve had come in with this really nice sort of guitar bit, and it happened to be in 3/4. And I had this chorus that I had that was sort of hanging around; I hadn't got any home for it. Which was in 3/4 as well. So we tried the two together and it worked really well.* [3]

See, Steve's bit, though very pretty, didn't really do much of anything. He'd kind of loop the riff, chime a little around the scale, and...then what? The creative juices were spent. But that's the beauty of being in a band setting with multiple writers; others can pick up the slack.

Tony: *What Steve had written didn't really have a chorus. It needed something to kind of lead you to it. So this sort of "If we can help you we will," that bit, I had this sort of bit I had originally written on the piano in fact, and then transferred it to guitar. And with the voice then singing what the piano used to play, which was kind of like where the chords change. It produced quite a nice little harmony piece I think.* [3]

"Yeah Steve, let's mash this thing up against my bit like the good ol' *Trespass* days...well, trust me, they were the good ol' days. Oh, and, pick it up a little will you? You sound half asleep over there."

Steve: *Sped up guitar on the introduction; I was playing at half speed. And then it gets joined by Mike and Tony. Very sort of typical Genesis feel on this one. Guitars chiming away.* [13]

Now running a much brisker 150 BPM after doubling the tempo, the song maintains its sleepy feel but gains an all-important lilt that will allow its melodies to really come alive. It's Steve and Tony, just duct taping their ideas together. Hey, it worked for 'Hairless Heart', right? Let's give it the ol' fusion dance one more time. But wait a minute, this one has voice in the arrangement. That means lyrics, right? Who's going to take those? Steve, got any ideas? Steve? Steve, wake up. I need to know if you STEVE, wake up please. Do you have any ideas for the lyrics?

Steve: *"Freudian slumber"...I was thinking about a psychiatrist at the time hypnotizing a patient and taking him back into a world of troubling dreams. Phil Collins at the time, I think with the "over the rooftops and houses" thing, he said he thought it had a Mary Poppins feel, maybe a sort of chim-chimney-cheroo thing. But I think it was dealing with sort of deeper issues than that. The lyrics [are] basically mine. What sounds like the chorus is really Tony Banks' [music], but nonetheless it's my lyric that wraps the whole thing together.* [13]

Hypnotic music this is, so why not try to actually hypnotise someone in the words? Calm, soothing descriptions of dreamy visions, all unclear but not unpleasant. Images to replace the unwanted subconscious intrusions that plague him when his eyes are closed. Fading awareness melting into the light "ahs" of multi-tracked Phil, sending you off to rest your weary bones. Then a turn in the chorus from minor to major; a conversation with the professionals who will solve all your sleep problems. Don't worry, we do this all the time. Just try to sleep in this quiet room; we'll play some light music to help you. Let yourself drift away.

> **Steve:** *Tony and I enjoyed writing 'Entangled', exploring the other-worldly atmosphere of the mind floating free beyond the world of harsh reality.* [39]

> **Tony:** *I think 'Entangled' is one of my favourite songs on the album. It makes for a very strong combination with the lyric written by Steve, which I think works really well as well.* [3]

> **Steve:** *I thought Phil sounded spectacular on it and he delivered a great three-part harmony.* [70]

If 'Entangled' stopped there, after two verses and two choruses, it would be a great song. It's a song about sleep and dreams - more so even than the later effort literally titled 'Dreaming While You Sleep' - and it *sounds* sleepy and dreamy through and through. But it doesn't stop there. Not at all.

> **Steve:** *And then, you know, it floats off into something much bigger toward the end.* [13]

> **Tony:** *'Entangled' was more just a chord sequence that I was playing and that end bit was Mike's actually, and we just used it. We were blues-ing on it and playing chords against the chords and seeing what I could get away with, which was something I have always liked to do.* [21]

This is an interesting admission here, since Mike doesn't have a writing credit on the song. I can only guess that Tony was improvising with Mike, heard him play something, then said "Yeah, do that, in this way," so that Mike was more the inspiration rather than a full writer. But it is curious. Regardless, after this serene song about trying to get rid of troubling dreams, the song ends with a pair of jokes. The first, of course, is the line about being presented the bill. Just a playful little wide-eyed moment for the patient just before the end. That's the obvious one. But the bigger joke is the precursor phrase to that, "You'll have no trouble..." This guy goes into a clinic to get hypnotised so his troubling dreams can be dismissed away, then goes to sleep in the end and we get this swirling, churning combination of keyboard, guitar, bass pedals, and Mellotron choir. In other words, troubling dreams. It didn't work! The doctor was a quack all along!

> **Tony:** *Probably my favourite track on that album, ending with a great cathedral-type feeling. The ARP Pro Solo[ist] synthesizer I was using had a touch sensitive keyboard and if you pressed a key hard you got this vibrato and could produce this marvellous high note that sounded like some wild cartoon soprano female.* [1]

Take it from me: a sterile sleep clinic is basically the worst place on earth to sleep. And I'd imagine that planting images into the head of a patient struggling to expel his or her own images is basically the worst way to treat insomnia. I'd say these are nuggets of wisdom that 'Entangled' taught me, but I know these truths viscerally through my own life experience. It seems that perhaps Steve Hackett knew them too.

> **Steve:** *Psychiatrists and couches and a guy being hypnotised. Many years later, after I'd been playing thousands of shows, I hit a reef and I started to get stage fright after I'd played with an orchestra live. And I saw a psychiatrist myself, who gave me some hypnotherapy. And I didn't realise that I was actually very successfully hypnotised, and the more this guy talked about positives, and about how good I was at what I was doing, I started weeping openly in front of [him]. And I said, "Well that must be very unusual." And he said, "Actually, it's very common. It's because when you're hypnotised, you don't have the usual emotional blocks." Because I don't normally burst into tears in front of complete strangers. But I remember Terry Jones of Monty Python doing exactly the same when he was hypnotised on TV. Anyway, I hope you still love the song; I do.* [13]

'Entangled' is the perfect song to get lost in. It's the blissful union of two tremendously progressive songwriters, of words to music, and of conveyed mood to receptive listener. Have you ever just closed your eyes, laid down, and listened to this track? Whenever I do, I inevitably feel myself beginning to float away. Without fail the song ends before I fully fall asleep, being only six and a half minutes long, but the effect remains profound. It's a soporific of synths, a sedative of strings, an anaesthetic of auditory pleasure. Genesis may have other songs that are more complex and involved compositionally, but for my money they don't have any that are more atmospheric.

Now if you'll excuse me, I need to get to bed.

5 - One for the Vine

from *Wind & Wuthering*, 1976

Well here we are into my personal top five Genesis songs. Congratulations and a big thank you for making it this far! But in all honesty, I've gotta say, these entries have gotten WAY out of hand, haven't they? As the amount of source material increasingly piles up I feel a kind of compulsion to include it all, which is something of a double-edged sword. On the positive side it gives me a kind of guidance: seeing what the band has to say about the song might encourage me to think about something in a different way and provide an angle or direction to write about the song on the whole. When those roads are especially easy to see, I usually end up just going with the flow on them. Why fight it? But the downside is that when I let the material dictate where I'm going to go, I lose a bit of stylistic and topical flexibility.

I've tried over the course of this book to mix things up from time to time. Never enough to lose all sense of coherence, naturally, but experimenting with different styles has been one of my favourite parts of writing all of these individual song entries, and frankly a little necessary to keep myself sane with the workload. Yet if you flip back and look at my wildest departures in style, they tend to happen most when I have limited research material (i.e. band quotes) to draw from. It's creativity out of necessity in a way; how can I say something in an interesting way when nobody else is saying anything interesting to begin with? I like to refer to these diversions as "creative left turns," and I cherish them.

Now approaching the end of this ranking process and with plenty of source material to go around, I feel that this embarrassment of riches is trying to lead me towards a more or less straightforward song analysis with a smattering of well-interspersed quotes providing historical context. That is, after all, the bread and butter, the dominant archetype, the "main thing" of this whole endeavour. But I've done that. Many, many times have I done that. And so now I just feel this urge to take the creative left turn, abandon the research, and just write what I feel is right. I'm going to look at this song on my own terms, and instead talk about what really moves me. Straightforward analysis, I'm done with you.

So what is 'One for the Vine' to me? Well, it's fantasy literature, basically, except in song form. I'm an avid sci-fi/fantasy reader - whether that will surprise anyone at all by this point I have no idea - but it's by far my favourite genre. I'll read all kinds of other things too, of course. Always happy to sit down with a well-written biography of an interesting individual, or some historical fiction, or whatever else might sound good at the time. But I always come back to fantasy, I think because fantasy can tell us very real things about the human condition even as it provides a temporary escape from that condition.

Take the novel The Eternal Champion by Michael Moorcock, for example. In this story a man is spiritually transported into the personage of an ancient hero, summoned to save humanity by defeating a race of invaders. But inside he knows that this isn't his body, his world, or his fight. Is it really morally justifiable for him to even get involved? Does he owe humanity his protection solely on the basis that he is also human? How does one even know what "right" is in this kind of confused situation? In the follow-up to this particular story, the poor sod is flung again into a different world, this time suddenly finding himself doing manual labour on a glacier. How do we, as people, deal with sudden changes to our routine? What does that say about us?

> **Tony:** *This guy suddenly finds himself in a snowy landscape and there's a bit of that in ['One for the Vine']. I've always liked science fantasy and fiction stuff and it's got a bit of that in it.* [27]

See? It's not just me. Fantasy asks those big questions - good fantasy does, at any rate - even when it disguises them with magic and monsters and heroes and villains. And 'One for the Vine' does this better than most fantasy tales out there. It's just a song (albeit a ten minute song), but it's one of my favourite fantasy stories of all time. Let's take a detailed look, because if any set of Genesis lyrics are worth the extended time, it's these.

The protagonist of this story is a soldier in the army of a god-king, who is marching his army aggressively on his enemies. The soldier seems to respect the god-king's strange humility ("though he never voiced [his claim to the throne] loud") but in the wake of the slaughter of thousands stops believing in his ruler's divinity and has a crisis of morality, which causes him to flee up a mountain.

Near the summit, the disillusioned soldier slips and, eh, rides the scree down the opposite side of the mountain to find himself in an icy wasteland. He's discovered by a relatively simple culture who, because this man apparently fell from the sky and looks very strange, assume he is a god sent to them to help them prosper and conquer their enemies. The bewildered former soldier, merely wanting to get home, decides it would be dangerous to risk the wrath of these people by telling them he's not their god, and figures that if he goes along with the charade he might have a better chance of getting away ("I'll play the game you want me until I find a way back home").

Before long the realisation strikes him that he is becoming the very thing he fled in the first place: a false god-king who serves as a focus and amplifier of a people's bloodlust. Finding himself once again in a crisis of conscience, he asks his servants (he has servants!) to leave him alone ("let me rest for a while") so he can figure out how to extricate himself from this madness. As he thinks on it, he realises that he's now, eh, in too deep to escape. If he refuses to lead the people - his people? - into battle, they'll execute him for falsely claiming to be their god. If he agrees, he'll be sentencing untold numbers of people to death for (in his mind) no good reason at all. He turns to wine to try to find his nerve ("and then [talked] with the vine"). Ultimately his mettle is revealed: he is a coward, too afraid to tell these people the truth, and so convinces himself that he has been given no choice at all. Thus he resolves to continue playing out his role and lead these people to their deaths.

So off they all go across the frozen wastes to confront their so-called enemies, with the "god-king" fighting his own internal battle against guilt, despite continuing to quietly assert his claim to his position. Which is when he sees a warrior from his army abandon the march and flee up a mountain. He "thought he recognised him" by the actions that mirrored the king's own at the beginning of the song. Is this another individual about to embark on the same ill-fated journey? Is this some sort of strange time loop where the ruler from the start of the song and the protagonist were always the same person?

Or is it just a hallucination? A reflection of a man, projected out from his own mind? A musing on how even the most powerful man on the planet might be utterly trapped by his circumstances? Perhaps it's the breaking of a spirit as it takes a step over the ledge into that which cannot be undone, reliving the choices that brought him to this point, seeing ghosts of himself through the tears.

> **Tony:** *The lyrical idea I got after I'd written all the melody. It tells the story of a guy who's been tricked by fate into being the god he didn't believe in [during] the first half of the song. It can have a very wide application to anyone who finds themselves doing something they didn't believe in before.* [31]

In essence, you have what appears to be a good character taking a stand against something bad, and then there's this compelling "fish out of water" sequence that sees him slowly becoming that same kind of "bad" thing he rebelled against. Self-awareness starts to creep in a bit, but by then the wheels are in motion and he can't stop it, eventually coming full-circle to the same situation as the beginning of the song, but now from a different vantage point. It's the cyclical nature of the story that's so engrossing to me.

> **Tony:** *It's about a person who becomes the thing he originally despised—a sort of messiah-like figure. At the end, he's disillusioned with it, which is probably quite true in a lot of walks of life, particularly politics.* [18]

Tony's lyrics read more like prose than poetry here. This is more ammunition for the "Tony will never be able to write a hit single" camp as well as the "Tony lyrics just don't flow well in general" camp, but here we don't need a hit and we don't need catchy phrases. We don't even need to use big, impressive words. We need the story to be clear and easy to follow, because the profundity comes not from any particular line of it but rather from the story in its entirety. Tony delivers on that masterfully here. But what *really* makes the story work so well is the way the music parallels the story itself.

Now, as Tony mentioned, the lyrics here were written after the music. But they nevertheless share the same spirit.

> **Tony:** *I've always liked writing music that doesn't go where you think it will. Key changes and chords that you are not expecting in pop songs, without trying to make it too awkward. I'm a big fan of Brian Wilson who has always been able to use strange harmonies without realising he's doing it... We were trying to tell a story and never quite go back, only to that main starting point. I liked the cyclical nature of the story: the person in the end becomes the prophet he didn't believe in and becomes disillusioned.* [27]

Exciting, right? Follow me through the song, if you will. Think about how the song starts and then about how it ends. You've got this piano/guitar call, followed by a piano-driven verse, and into a...well it's not a chorus. It's not even a pre-chorus. But it's also clearly no longer the verse. Kind of just a section A, then section B. Then A again, then B again, then this really jolly middle section after them. I guess that's C. Which abruptly ends with a cry of "No, no, no!" as we hit a section D, characterised by sombre piano. Here we talk with the water and then with the vine: a moment of peace before the turmoil to come. The eye of the storm, you might say, of 'One for the Vine'. And then that call again. It hearkens back to the beginning, because this is where the decision is made to relive the events that led *to* the beginning, even if that decision was made while drowning sorrows in wine. And then the imaginary mustering and horseback riding of the instrumental section E that follows: "If I go through with this, here's what's coming." To arms, men! A full embrace of the role in a brief section F spelled by a variation on that signature call we've heard twice so far. And then there it is again. The turn of fate, fifty thousand fates sealed. And after traveling through so many sections, we land right back at A, and into B, as the snake begins to eat its own tail and the circle is closed. A section G to wrap a brilliant concluding bow on proceedings, and here's that call, one last time. Only now it's the piano by itself. No edge of guitar, no glint of steel. Just a claim, voiced quietly, for all to hear.

> **Mike:** *'One for the Vine'...features Tony on piano. We'd tried it quite a few different ways in the studio until we settled on a ten minute piece based on acoustic piano. There are electric sections but it always comes back to the piano.* [36]

> **Tony:** *To me it's the best thing I've written; certainly instrumentally it's the most adventurous thing I've done. It's an idea I've wanted to do for a long time of using a lot of instrumental ideas which flow from one [to] the other without repeating themselves. I went through all these series of ideas which climaxed in this triumphant kind of march. And a lyric to carry that mood with it.* [31]

> **Steve:** *It works very well.* [27]

Big understatement from Steve there, but it occurs to me that this entry is beginning to take a turn from lyrical towards musical analysis, which is specifically what I wanted to avoid. I wanted to just focus on the story of the thing and how powerful that is to me, but it feels like a story that can't be told *without* the music, you know? I just wish I could think of another way to take this. My creative left turn is bending back to the right, frustratingly. I guess I need to brainstorm a little. How can I get my point across without resorting to the ho-hum standard yet again?

Maybe I can do a fake dialog? Or tell a personal tale of mine? Or even write a lyrical parody of some sort? No, no, no, I've done all that before, too. Maybe I can write a short story that serves as a stand-in for the song somehow, so that people reading the short story will really get what I'm trying to say about the song too? Like a piece of independent fiction, except that it ties back to this with hidden meanings. Hmm. Gives me a chance to really branch out with characters, plot, whatever else, but say something insightful about this other medium, too. That could be interesting. But man, it would take a long time. Longer than I think I have to get this done. And it'd be quite a stretch too; who would even gather that whatever random story is actually an analysis of a song from a 1976 Genesis album? What would even be the point?

And how do I talk about that up-tempo instrumental section adequately with any of those ideas? Because I almost *have* to say something about that one. Who decides to start a powerful instrumental bit with cowbells and a quacking duck? Why does it actually work exceedingly well? Why are these driving piano rock chord melodies so dang hot? Why is the groove at 5:26 so flawless? Are those tambourines sitting on vibrating hotel beds? If you told me Phil Collins was playing a rattlesnake on this section, I'd believe you.

Well...I guess it is what it is now. Come on guys, get in here. For better or worse, we're talking music.

> **Mike:** *I think Wind & Wuthering is probably very much Tony's album favourite. He was very much I think involved in the sound of that one. Probably the album he had the most influence in, actually. 'One for the Vine', 'Afterglow'...* [3]

> **Phil:** *Pete and Tony were [combative with one another]. I mean, best of friends, but [combative]. And possibly with Peter having long gone by this point, Tony realising that possibly...you know, he was able to sort of like mercury kind of spread out a little bit and get much more of him out.* [3]

> **Tony:** *Overall for me it is one of my favourite albums. I think that obviously 'One For The Vine' and 'Afterglow' for me are crucial moments in my own writing and they were realised quite well on that record... It was the most extreme album in many ways; the most difficult of our albums, if you like. But I don't really think it has a weak point on it for me. Some of the songs I like more than others, like taking the riff I had for 'One For The Vine' and making something quite different of it. That was quite fun and I had never tried that before.* [6]

When you think about how expertly this song was crafted, how every section works magically within itself; how they all also work as part of a larger whole; how the sections themselves aren't obviously musically related despite this; how they're all arranged to create a compelling cyclical story...it's pretty incredible. Fittingly, it took Tony quite a bit of time to work on.

> **Tony:** *That song had really taken me since A Trick of the Tail I'd sort of been working on that and honing it, and trying to get it right.* [3]

Recording for *A Trick of the Tail* wrapped in November 1975 and writing for *Wind & Wuthering* began in mid-1976, so we're talking what, six or seven months of grinding away at 'One for the Vine' until it was ten minutes of near perfection?

> **Tony:** *A piece like that is not to everybody's taste. It is very structured music and requires every beat to be in the right place.* [1]

And then Tony shows up to the writing sessions with no idea what anyone else has to offer, but just *knowing* he's got the best of the lot regardless.

> **Tony:** *When I played 'One for the Vine' to the guys, it was kinda like, I just played the whole thing through with me sort of warbling on top, you know. And I don't know what they thought at the end of that. I think they thought, "If we don't do it, he'll get so irritable [and] start throwing things that we'll have to have a go at it." So we just put it down in the studio. I just put the whole thing down with a piano and drums really. And then we sort of overdubbed everything else on top of it. And it was just faith, really at the end, that they stuck with me I think. Because I think it turned out good actually, and I think the contribution of all the others is really good as well. So I was quite pleased with that.* [3]

Temper tantrums or not, Tony was right to be unwilling to take no for an answer on this one. And he's right to praise the other members' contributions as well: it's Tony's song, but everyone shines. That's probably why, unlike a number of other solo-Tony contributions, they didn't offer much objection to playing it live. Which is a bit of surprise given just how dense the instrumentation is on the studio track.

> **Tony:** *We laid the whole thing down with piano, drums, and a simple bass part, and added everything else as overdubs. That was fun for me because it's got loads and loads of keyboard overdubs, a whole orchestration of synthesizers and Mellotrons.* [1]

Keyboards on top of keyboards on top of keyboards on top of everyone else on top of everyone else. I don't know how many sound channels they had available in the studio mixer, but I'm guessing they used them all. So doing it live inevitably meant some level of scaling down, but the live sound on something like *Three Sides Live* is still really, really good. So who knows. Maybe it's just a little bit of fantasy magic.

> **Tony:** *This was during the stage in which I'd just play a whole song to the other guys as they were working on it. What we'd do is first put it down in the studio with just me and Phil. I'd sit down on the piano and Phil would be on drums. And then we'd do all the overdubbing on it. I think it turned out pretty good and it got better live. It would have been nice if we could have rehearsed it a bit more before recording it. But the way we did it gave everyone a chance to be a bit quirky, particularly with Phil's drumming and Steve's imaginative playing. I think Steve sounds really good doing all the little bits and pieces he does on it. The song was a bit like a mini-suite at 10 minutes with quite a strong, dramatic ending.* [18]

Well...this entry certainly didn't go the way I intended it to, but I suppose it went the way it always had to go in the end. And you know, that reminds me of something, I think...if only I could put my finger on what it was.

4 - The Lamia

from *The Lamb Lies Down on Broadway*, 1974

Let's talk about perspective, shall we? Point of view. Narrative reference. These are literary ideas, and so might seem a strange thing to discuss when talking about music. But then, *The Lamb Lies Down on Broadway* is a strange album, isn't it? Running north of 94 minutes and revolving around a concept that is real, Rael, and everything in between, this isn't your average listening experience. If any album might be ripe for analysis in literary terms, this is probably the one.

And so, perspective. Within the storytelling world there are various forms of viewpoints an author might choose. First-person is when we see the story through the eyes of one or more of its characters, as though they themselves were sharing the tale with us. This is where we find pronouns like "I", "me", "we", and so forth. Second-person view is much less common, involving the audience directly as a kind of character-by-proxy. It invites us to feel like we're taking a more active role in the story, as characters might speak to us knowingly (called "breaking the fourth wall" in certain contexts). Fittingly then, the pronouns involved here tend to be, simply, "you" or its variations.

Third-person view is by far the most common narrative device out there, incorporating in its style a sense of distance from the subjects. The story is being told by someone who is not part of it, which opens up some flexibility. As a result, third-person perspective can itself be divided into two forms: omniscient and limited. In the omniscient variant, the narrator knows all and relays all the important elements to the audience, who therefore become privy to details some of the characters within the story may not even know. In the limited variant, the narrator only relays information pertaining to a single mind, or location, or some other fixed target, which ends up making this style feel more like an expansion of the first-person perspective as opposed to its own unique thing.

Each of these styles has its own advantages and disadvantages, its own method of shaping the way we receive and think about the story it communicates. Deciding on which type of perspective to use for a work is one of the most important artistic choices any writer faces. It's a decision that has to be informed by a deep understanding of the kind of story that's being told, how the drama of that story should unfold, how intimately the audience should know the story's characters, etc. What point of view a piece of writing uses - first-person, second-person, or third-person - tells you an awful lot about it before you've even read a word.

The Lamb Lies Down on Broadway uses all three.

Let's put that second-person viewpoint aside for a moment, as it's rare even in this context, and focus for simplicity's sake on the first- and third-person perspectives. To aid me, I've made a handy chart illustrating the way these perspectives break down on a song-by-song basis over the course of the album. To get these figures, I worked through the lyrics and tallied every time I found a line written distinctly in first-person from Rael's viewpoint (e.g. "**I'm** counting out time" or "This is the one for **me**") as well as every time I found one written from the third-person style (e.g. "**Rael** imperial aerosol kid" or "**he** knows **he** must be near"). Then I just totalled the tallies and divided to get the percentage of each song's lyrics in one style or the other. The results are, well, pretty striking.

The Lamb in Perspective

If you notice some tracks missing from this chart, don't fret; I didn't forget them. Of the six missing songs, four are fully instrumental, while the other two ('Broadway Melody of 1974' and 'Here Comes the Supernatural Anaesthetist') solely describe things other than Rael, and so can't be said to clearly fall in one bucket or the other. But I'm sure it only took a slight glance at the diagram to catch onto the anomaly here. 'The Lamb Lies Down on Broadway', 'The Lamia', 'The Light Dies Down on Broadway'... Why are these three songs - and *only* these three - sitting at less than 100%? Why do they contain the only instances in the album of the story going "off perspective" and shifting into the third-person? Is there something special or meaningful about these tracks that warrants such treatment? Or was it just an accident - an "oopsies" on an otherwise meticulously crafted effort? What's really going on here?

Let's zoom out a little to the writing of the album in general. Due to severe time constraints as well as *The Lamb* being positioned as a concept album, it was (begrudgingly) decided that there should only be one lyricist for the entire double LP: Peter. His main point was that a concept album needed a coherent story (ha!) and that in order to create that coherence, a single lyricist was the only reasonable solution. Thus, the expectation might be that Peter would pick a point of view and stick with it for the sake of consistency. And indeed, for roughly three quarters of the album, that's exactly what you get: Rael's journey told through Rael's eyes.

But Peter did something else with this album too. He knew that no matter how well he maintained his lyrical flow-through, there would be little gaps and jumps between songs. He also knew that the more bizarre and surreal his imagery and details became, the harder it would be to actually follow the plot of the story at all. To that end, he wrote additional non-lyrical story snippets; extra narration that would explain what happens before, after, and frequently during the actual songs. This story would be printed in the booklet, or liner notes of the album, and was meant to be a companion to the listening experience. And right at the outset of this additional material, Pete employs a particular narrative device to act almost as a kind of disclaimer on the whole thing: he sets up *The Lamb* as a frame story.

> *While I write I like to glance at the butterflies in glass that are all around the walls. The people in memory are pinned to events I can't recall too well, but I'm putting one down to watch him break up, decompose, and feed another sort of life. The one in question is all fully biodegradable material and categorised as 'Rael'. Rael hates me, I like Rael, - yes, even ostriches have feelings, but our relationship is something both of us are learning to live with. Rael likes a good time, I like a good rhyme, but you won't see me directly anymore - he hates my being around. So if his story doesn't stand, I might lend a hand, you understand? (i.e. the rhyme is planned, dummies).* [57]

To loosely translate: "I am the narrator and I am going to tell you the story of Rael. I like rhymes and poetry, so I'm going to tell you his story in song form, kind of like an opera. This does mean that sometimes I'm going to say things in an unclear manner in order to preserve the musical aspect of the thing, but when that happens you can refer to this more straightforward narration for guidance."

And so the album opens with 'The Lamb Lies Down on Broadway', the album's title track. Look at the verses of that song and what you find is that they are purely descriptive. Again, it's like an author adding lots of little details to bring a scene to life. But in context, in a very literary sense, this is *setting*. It's the narrator telling us how and where the story starts. When Rael is introduced, it's in the third-person: "Rael Imperial Aerosol Kid." I've been comparing this to literature proper, but what we soon realise is that this isn't a novel but *a play*. The third-person narration is telling us what the backdrop looks like, and then it's "Enter Rael, stage left." The final verse of the song then shifts; now that Rael is fully on stage and properly introduced, he can tell his own story. The third-person narration won't return until the end of the album's third side. It's all eyes on stage, now. We who've read the liner notes know that this is all really just the same presenter speaking in a character voice like you might hear on an audio book, but the effect is the same. *The Lamb* is configured as one narrator effectively reading us a script. Layers of style.

Meanwhile back in the real world, other members of Genesis are bristling a bit at not getting to put words onto their songs.

> **Peter:** *To try and keep everybody happy, there would be parts of it where we'd be discussing lyrics and throwing some of the words around for different bits. And so 'The Lamia', which was sort of Tony's musical piece, or 'Supernatural Anaesthetist' which Steve had brought in...they would discuss some of the lyrical stuff with me because they'd sort of got the writer's ticket.* [3]

> **Tony:** *I think the lyrics [on the album], although they're good lyrics...no song really kinda stands out on its own. You know, what could have been some really pretty song like 'The Lamia' for example. I mean, if you start singing that out of context it makes no sense at all. You know, sort of about snakes and stuff. So I slightly resent that aspect of it, I suppose.* [3]

On top of that, there were still the aforementioned time constraints, where Pete was having to absorb the music the other four guys were writing, figure out what part of the story he wanted to tell over them, and then come up with lyrics that would sing well, flow well, relay the story well, and so on. It's exhausting work. And though he didn't want to concede any kind of creative control, pressures from time and peers closed in on him.

> **Peter:** *There was the odd argument about having to do [the story] democratically, so I conceded on sharing some of the lyrics.* [1]

By "some" Peter means "one song." And by "concede" he means "I gave Mike and Tony a plot outline and made sure that what they wrote followed it." The result was 'The Light Dies Down on Broadway', which is, if you'll recall, another of the tracks featuring a hybrid first- and third-person viewpoint. Now, we're entering the Unsupported By Direct Evidence Theory Zone (brought to you by Dr. Pepper) so bear with me, but I think it's got a hybrid perspective precisely *because* it wasn't Peter who penned the words. Musically, as is obvious from the title of the song, the band here was reprising the album's title track. Mike and Tony had to write lyrics and follow a plot thread while also calling back to that earlier piece with the lyrics. So what do you think they did? Did they just cross their fingers and hope it all worked out, or did they look at the lyrics Pete had written for 'The Lamb Lies Down on Broadway' and try to imitate that style? I think the latter is far more likely, and they would've seen in those lyrics this hybrid POV at work. And of course, at the time *they* didn't have the benefit we do of seeing Peter's companion prose, and thus wouldn't have any reason to know that this was a frame story configured like a play. Without all that context, it feels like the song just switches from third- to first-person on a whim as suits the flow of the melody, and I believe that's exactly what Mike and Tony did.

That said, Mike and Tony had another major reference point for their lyrical effort as well: 'The Lamia'. As mentioned earlier in my entry for 'The Light Dies Down on Broadway', that song reprises not only the album's title track but also the primary chorus melody of 'The Lamia' in its verses. It does wonders for the album's musical cohesion and is also likely why I enjoy 'Light Dies Down' even more than 'Lamb Lies Down' in general - but more on that to come below. For now, consider the chronology of the album's writing, which took place from June to August 1974, with the recording stretching into October. Consider that Mike and Tony wrote lyrics for 'Light Dies Down' because of time concerns, which means it must have happened late in the process. And then consider what Tony has to say about the timing of the lyrics for 'The Lamia'.

> **Tony:** *'The Lamia'...was quite fun as Pete had written all these lyrics over Christmas 1973. I took them all back with me [and] just fitted them on top of this basis that we had for 'The Lamia'.*

> *I just weeded it down and used just one word in five. We didn't have the melody line but we had the piece written, and Pete had all these lyrics which were like poetry. I tried to get them to fit the melody and essence of the song, which was fun to do. I enjoyed that.* [6]

This is Tony getting that "writer's ticket" and feeling like he's got some kind of control, which was critical to keep the peace. But at the same time, he's just editing down from what Peter already wrote, and what Peter wrote was something that again had a hybrid POV style about it - perhaps in part because he hadn't yet committed to one style or the other for the album, it being so early in the process. Thus, until partway through the second set of verses, everything in this song is told from that third-person perspective. Then it shifts as Rael enters the pool; his body begins to transform at the same time the POV itself transforms, returning to the first-person viewpoint of the rest of the album. As a capstone, the final line of 'The Lamia' says "the stage is set," explicitly reaffirming the album's "narrated play" style of delivery.

It could be that if Peter had had more time to review everything, he may have shifted the first half of 'The Lamia' into first-person as well for consistency's sake. But the benefit of retaining that hybrid viewpoint is clear: now anyone listening to 'The Light Dies Down on Broadway' doesn't need to be confused. The lyrical perspective of that song isn't shifting randomly, but rather it's part and parcel of that 'Lamia' reprise. Even as the musical melodies return, so too does the rare third-person POV. It's a reminder once again that we are watching an opera, or at least listening to the retelling of one. What could've been a clunky fumble caused by bringing in not one but two additional lyricists is deftly morphed into a tasteful reference, strengthening the album's cohesion even further.

As for that second-person point of view? It comes up two times over the experience of *The Lamb*, both in very similar ways. The first is that last line of 'The Lamia' again. It's not just that the stage is set, but "the stage is set for *you*." We have been taking this journey alongside Rael and for the first time we are invited directly to share his experiences. This makes 'The Lamia' significant in that it actually contains *all three* POV styles within a single song; that it does so tastefully and effectively makes it an exquisite lyrical accomplishment, snakes or no.

> **Steve:** *To my mind this is the most poetic song on The Lamb... It expresses...magic amidst the urban sprawl of Rael's tale. It's a song that speaks to women as much as men.* [106]

The second and final "you" of the album comes again at an ending - this time of the accompanying story in the album's sleeve. As '*it.*' dissolves into a purple haze, the ball moves into the listener's court: "*It's* over to you." It's the storyteller's goodbye, turning the story over to our care to make of it what we will. Notably in the liner notes themselves, after some legal credits the story then starts over again from the very beginning until the page runs out of space. Perhaps that's us becoming the narrator, telling this story again to the next audience, following a grand oral tradition and ensuring *The Lamb* always lives on.

When you think of it that way, it kind of puts the album in a different perspective, doesn't it?

Regarding my personal opinions on 'The Lamia' as a piece of music, the obvious thing is that it's in my top five Genesis songs of all time, so I think it's fair to say I believe this song is doing something right. I actually generally agree with Tony about the lyrics, too: they don't work out of context from the story and therefore the song has a lot of trouble standing apart from *The Lamb* as an independent work fo art. And given that I also agree with Tony about not being overly fond of the story of *The Lamb* itself, it seems like this one would be something I might quickly write off as "that one snake song where Pete stands in a blue cone on stage."

> **Phil:** *One [song where the visuals got in the way] was 'The Lamia', where this thing came down and Peter was in the middle of it. And sometimes the microphone cord would get caught up at the top or the bottom of it. And so either it didn't move or he had to move with it.* [3]

> **Peter:** *In this post-MTV world it's very hard for people to imagine how strong being bombarded with different visual images in parallel with the music was for audiences at the time. Film had always been my passion and that was really the only place audiences had seen great images and music working extremely well together. We didn't get there always, but I think we got there more than most at the time.* [1]

Nevertheless, even if I'm not a particular fan of *what* the lyrics are describing, I'm a huge fan of *how* they craft those descriptions. Pete's words have a fantastic poetic quality to them, here more than almost anywhere else on *The Lamb* or indeed in his time with Genesis as a whole. And Tony did a bang-up job of selecting the right phrases to go over the melodies so that it all just flows gorgeously out.

> **Steve:** *It's funny, you know...The Lamb Lies Down on Broadway, you have this New York City, and of course it's also, the contradiction is it's a mythological journey for Rael, the imagined character. And you have this song that is I think the most romantic part of The Lamb. Although it's in New York City, you have this idea of the character wandering into this realm of female temptresses, the Greek idea of the Lamia. Subject matter that wasn't unknown to the Pre-Raphaelite artists, who were very fond of this kind of image of these girl-women that look very innocent [and] sweet on the surface but underneath... The underlying idea is of course that they are potentially lethal. So in a way it's that kind of poetic contradiction of the two. And it's part of Rael's journey. But in a way I personally was very drawn to this. In the midst of the urban angst that was driving Rael - and the band at that time - I think there were two types of Genesis. There was this forward motion thing, but then there was always the nostalgic looking backwards that characterised so much of the band's work. And I think this song embodies those contradictions. You get these very whimsical, impressionistic moments: "only a magic that a name would stain." Beautiful, beautiful lyrics from Pete. Absolutely gorgeous. Still love it.* [13]

Speaking of melodies, that's what does it for me with this song. I've said before in this book that I'm a melody kind of guy, and let me tell you: in my opinion, 'The Lamia' is the greatest melody Genesis have ever done. Period. It's a haunting track, but not the overt ghostly kind of haunting like a 'Home by the Sea'. It's the kind of haunting that stays with you, just out of your conscious awareness, but always lurking around in your mind.

> **Steve:** *There are certainly haunting moments in The Lamb as in 'The Lamia'...influenced by the bleak, melancholic atmosphere of [Headley] Grange.* [70]

Once I was logging into a voice chat for an online game, and had this song playing in the background while I was the only person in the channel. One of my friends, who is not a Genesis fan, logged in and was immediately intrigued: "What is that? That sounds really nice." I told him it was a Genesis song called 'The Lamia', and he didn't really care, as I wouldn't have expected him to. But perhaps two hours later, in an idle moment, he began humming the song's chorus melody to himself. He'd heard it once and didn't even register it as anything more than "hey, that's kinda pretty," but it had already snared him. He caught himself doing this and, surprised, announced, "Wow, that song is actually really good, I'm going to have to look it up."

> **Tony:** *What I can say is my whole experience of music is very pure. I hear music as music. I don't hear it in any other way. So, I try not to analyse it. If I do, then it becomes something else. When I don't analyse music, there's something going on in my brain that is completely unrelated to anything physical. It's something totally outside of that.* [18]

That's the unrelenting, unconscious power of 'The Lamia'. It gets everything right. The grand piano on the verses? Perfect. The mini solo that could almost be a flute thing but for some reason isn't? Still perfect. Making Steve and Phil and Mike sit on their hands until the chorus? Perfect. Because that means their tasteful restraint upon entry in the chorus can be perfect too. Phil's backing vocals and drum fills near the chorus' end? Perfect. The Mellotron choir, Steve's guitar synth, the build to bring the chorus to a climax? Perfect. The transition returning down into the spareness of the verse? Perfect. The addition of ethereal backing vocals on the back half of the second verse? Perfect. The intensity of the final section where Pete sets the stage for us? That guitar solo???

> **Steve:** *I was proud of my guitar on...'The Lamia'...* [39]

Perfect. And it's spelled with a taste of that very flute we were denied earlier in the song, as though it was being saved just for this moment. In a song about the dangers of giving into blind temptation, we're shown by the music the value of delayed gratification. It's marvellous.

So don't fret, lyrics. You don't need to be about something other than snake people. You don't really need to be about anything at all. Because everything around you is very nearly as good as it gets. And maybe, just this once, we should take a cue from Rael and jump in blind ourselves. Just turn off our brains and see what happens when we let this rose-water music wash over us. Who knows? Maybe we'll find some magic.

3 - Fading Lights

from *We Can't Dance*, 1991

When you think about it, it should be no surprise at all that 'Fading Lights' is a personal "Top 3 Genesis Song" for me. After all, this book is all about looking back on the music of Genesis, and what is 'Fading Lights' if not the musical rendition of that very "looking back" concept?

> **Tony:** *[My favourite lyrics on We Can't Dance are]...'Fading Lights', which I wrote quite quickly, in fact. [Producer] Nick [Davis] calls it one of my "terminal songs." It's sort of...perhaps as you get older really, you find yourself looking back sometimes and thinking about things that can't be anymore. And you don't quite know what's going to happen in the future, so you don't know quite what is a final thing. When you're actually experiencing the last time you ever do something, you don't know that it is the last time you'll ever do it. Which is an interesting thought, I thought. So I kinda wrote a song about that. Sort of just generally looking back. It's a nostalgic sort of song. I mean, you know, it could be corny, but I think I was quite pleased with some of the lines.* [35]

And if you don't like that, well, I suppose you can always just close the book right now.

> **Tony:** *We put ['Fading Lights'] right at the end of the album so that if [people] don't want to hear it they don't have to listen to it - well, that's kind of my attitude a bit... The lyric is very reflective; it looks back on the past. It doesn't necessarily apply to the group although it obviously can, but I think when you get to a certain age in life you find yourself looking backwards a lot and this song is very reflective. Also, I thought it would be a very nice last word for an album too: "remember."* [81]

We start our own look back at this track as Phil Collins winds down his latest solo tour, checks his schedule, sees a Genesis album commitment, and realises he's forgotten what that really means.

> **Phil:** *I approached this album with a little bit of trepidation. I didn't know. I'd been on the road with my band for ten months playing my music and I loved it. I really had a great time. I did But Seriously... You know, solo albums are great fun to do. And I thought, "A Genesis album...Well we'll do it, but I wonder what it's gonna be like? Because I don't know..." I genuinely didn't know. And after a couple of days when you see the kind of material that's coming out from just the three of us being in the room, you think, "Yes, this IS good fun. I AM enjoying it." And so it's almost, when I say at the end of it, "It's great, I'm really proud of it!" it's actually more surprise, you know? That I'm surprised it actually turned out as good as it did.* [92]

Here's the thing with memory: it's not versatile. It's a thing of strengths and weaknesses, even if the mind is in flawless health. Think about things you most strongly remember, and then how you'd define those memories. Chances are most of you are thinking about significant experiences in your lives that helped shape you into who you are today; vivid recollections of your most meaningful moments. And you'd be wrong. Because those aren't the things you remember most precisely.

No, what you remember most of all are *facts*. Data. Knowledge. 2+2=4 is something so obvious that we don't even have to think about it. And while yes, we can pretend to forget this mathematical truth and arrive at it anew with logic and reason, we don't need to; all of us simply know it by rote. Just as we know our own names, or phone numbers, or the roads we need to take to get home from the office. *These* are our clearest memories, so untarnished we don't even typically consider them to be memories at all.

Next come our experiences, themselves a more complicated form of data, themselves varying in strength of recall. The most vivid of these memories is still incomplete; the most hazy is almost entirely unreliable. And then there's everything in between. "How did that conversation go again?" "What colour was that car that cut me off earlier?" "What was she wearing that night?" We remember events, but often not details; not unless those details are critical to forming the memories in the first place, at any rate. But usually we form these memorial links to events because they trigger in us some kind of powerful emotion. Images of sorrow, pictures of delight, you know...the things that go to make up a life.

Ironic, then, that emotion is where memory fails us the most. Emotion is so volatile, so inextricably bonded to the here and now, that it's all but impossible to remember. Take a moment and go to your "happy place" - try to summon the most joyful memory you have. You can remember on a factual level that you *felt* joy in that moment, but you can't remember the *feeling* of joy itself, because emotion isn't subject to that kind of temporal recall. The best you can hope for is that, in the act of recalling, the memory itself allows you to feel *new* joy as a kind of echo of what came before. Emotions aren't data; they can't be pulled up at will.

This was a long detour, but my point is that Phil Collins in early 1991 could think back to making *Invisible Touch* and all the albums prior, and he could remember that "I seemed to have fun," but he *couldn't remember the feeling of fun itself*. He could remember that he had great chemistry with the guys, and he could remember as a kind of bullet point that the songs flowed easily and excited them all, but he couldn't remember the actual feeling of being in that moment. And because he couldn't remember that, he didn't trust it, and so went into the process worried that they were going to waste their time creating something lacklustre together.

He needn't have fretted, of course. While the memory of creative chemistry withered, the chemistry itself never left.

> **Mike:** *In the writing process for us, so often we find things by mistakes. Someone hits the wrong note. And it sets you off in a direction that you hadn't even thought about going. When we're writing, Tony and I don't know what key the other of us is playing in. And sometimes we come to record songs and I'll say to him, "Is that what you played? Because it didn't sound like that to me!" And when you combine the two parts it makes up a nice sound. But individually they're often quite different. And vice versa; he'll say, "You didn't play that, did you?" And it's just, he hadn't heard it that way until he isolated my part. And that's the kind of chemistry that I think is what is good about Genesis.* [35]

And though one can't perfectly recall the exhilaration of improvising strong material, once in that groove, you don't really want to leave it again. How convenient, then, that compact discs had emerged in the five years since *Invisible Touch* as an increasingly dominant format for musical albums.

> **Tony:** *The great thing about the CD - you've got 70 minutes of music on the We Can't Dance album - and therefore you feel you can stretch out a bit more. I think we felt with Invisible Touch we had our hands tied a little bit more, and we didn't want to put on too much of that kind of thing. This time, a lot of good instrumental music was coming up, so we decided we would get them on the record... As I said, that's the great thing about CD: you've got more time to play with.* [107]

> **Phil:** *We weren't going to be shy of anything, including doing long tracks.* [108]

> **Tony:** *Historically, our strength has always lain in being able to give ourselves a bit of room to breathe. We work well in long songs; it gives us a chance to do more instrumental work, and a chance to tell more of a story with the lyrics.* [108]

So with this freedom in mind, they spin up the drum machine to see what might happen. And here on this song, that machine pattern conjures up a sense of distance. It's sombre and restrained. Something difficult to see on the horizon, but still somehow within reach, as though a bit of squinting might enable you to make it out.

> **Phil:** *If the part is more percussive than usual, and not just a simulation of real drums, we usually end up keeping the drum machine part and overdubbing drums to the percussion part, which is really important to the mood of the song. But when the drum sounds are regular snare and regular bass drum, you usually need real drums. It also depends how intrinsic the drum sound is to the mood of the song. On something like 'Fading Lights', the atmosphere is set up by the drum machine.* [82]

Then Tony plays some chords which bring that mood to life and end up giving the song its working title: 'Nile'.

> **Mike:** *It kind of sounds like, you know, the boat going up the Nile, slow moving ship in the water, that kind of thing.* [35]

This is already a throwback of sorts; in 1974 Genesis wrote a song called 'Fly on a Windshield', which had the working title of 'Pharaohs' and was conjured by Mike suggesting they play something that sounded like "pharaohs going down the Nile." Maybe this is a fixation of Mike's, but it's fitting that here in the trio's swan song they find themselves unwittingly retracing the steps of one of their earliest improvisations.

More reminiscing in the melody: the chorus line of "Far away, away" hits five notes, four of which are identical to the notes of "Sail away, away" in the chorus melody of 'Ripples', if you were to transpose 'Ripples' down a mere half-step. That one changed note (the second syllable of the first "away") is meaningful, too: the 'Fading Lights' note is a whole step lower than the 'Ripples' one, giving the phrase a more melancholy feel this time around. I don't even know if Genesis were aware they were doing this; bear in mind the lyrics weren't written when the melody was established. But the chorus of this wistful piece about things that once were is itself a yearning recall for a song that used to be.

Lyrics or no, they know they've got three verses and three chorus runs with this drum machine. They're sounding good and have a great mood, though on their own they're not quite enough to carry the piece. But it's the CD era now. There's more time to explore.

> **Tony:** *We wrote together the longer, more traditional Genesis pieces, and I think we decided that we were going for compact disc length. And so we thought obviously it would be nice to get back to a solo or two, and so we had this really strong instrumental part to 'Fading Lights', and we just thought, "We've got to use that."* [6]

Phil Collins? Still in that groove and completely on board.

> **Phil:** *I think though the middle part could be called traditional Genesis instrumentally, the actual song part is very untraditional. I mean, I think that it's very rare that we hang on a couple of chords...well, four or maybe five chords on a very simple drum machine and a vocal. It's rare that we do that and in some respects it has both ends that Genesis do.* [81]

Crashing cymbals from Phil, heavy chords from Mike, then a big keyboard riff from Tony announcing to the world: "Genesis is back." Now a proper keyboard solo: "Genesis never left." Another riff. Another solo. Funky synth sounds never possible in the 70s, even as this extended keyboard exploration summons up its own memories of Cinema Shows long gone by.

> **Tony:** *That's a modification of a Wavestation sound. I liked it because I could play very aggressively on it. Those sounds are great for leads; they automatically attract attention to themselves. Two or three different sounds are actually used on that lead at different times.* [82]

More and more grand soloing. It's the age of the compact disc. We have the time.

> **Tony:** *With those kinds of things, it's a question of trying to condense it down to a reasonable length. I mean, 'Fading Lights', we've had improvisations of about 3 or 4 hours on that one riff, you know? Which was sort of fun to do! We have no problem coming up with those kinds of things... And I think in many ways 'Fading Lights', the way it works, it's a very strong piece of music...because of that instrumental section in the middle.* [107]

We have to condense it down. We don't have enough time. There's never enough time, is there? That keyboard riff again. That bang of the gong. That scaling down. "Genesis is leaving. Farewell, friends. What a run we've had."

> **Tony:** *I often see solos as a little bit like stories and things like that. You know, when I'm doing something like the 'Fading Lights' thing, the reason I wrote the lyric the way that I did in the end was because I thought the idea of the solo being a sort of example of a kind of life, you know? Ups, downs, things going right and wrong...it's quite a nice way of doing it. Because the way I write solos is they have a lot of variety in them. They're not going to stay in one mood all the time, so you tend to get the different flavours coming in and out.* [35]

It's enough. Phil Collins, entering with such worry, comes away feeling as though he's helped create something magical. He emerges from the studio, his passion for Genesis higher than it's ever been before.

> **Phil:** *As long as I'm proud of what Genesis does, that's good enough for me. It's an extraordinary situation... This isn't the last Genesis album, as far as I'm concerned.* [108]

They take the album on the road. They play an 'Old Medley' walking through the span of their careers together. By the end of the tour, they immediately follow that medley in the setlist with 'Fading Lights'. Daryl Stuermer and Chester Thompson leave the stage. They're beloved, but they're not needed here...and then there were three. They play the entire song with only the three of them present, relishing the moment, feeling things they don't even realise they won't remember in the years to come. Mike extends his guitar solo near the end; this is for all of them.

> **Phil:** *From the start of that global run of Genesis' biggest-ever shows, there was a sense of nostalgia, a sense of "look how far we've come." This was most apparent in the footage we showed on the screens during 'I Know What I Like' (in the 'Old Medley'): lots of archive film, stretching back through the Peter era. It was moving stuff.* [12]

But all things must pass. The tour ends, and they all part ways once again, off to engage in their various solo efforts. And during that time, Phil endures a divorce and unwanted press attention, even as he makes an album that he feels deeply connected to. And in light of those emotions, those things he has going on in the here and now, he does something very human: he forgets. Just as it had through the end of the 80s, the magic of Genesis becomes hazy and abstract, more a burden in his mind than a blessing. And in that forgetting, he makes a choice based on the only feelings he knows: the ones he can feel right now. Phil Collins decides it's finally time to move on.

> **Phil:** *These are my oldest musical friends. Two of my oldest friends, full stop. And I'm about to formally say goodbye to them… We give each other a hug, wish each other well, and say goodbye. We know that we'll see each other again, but not in the same light.* [12]

> **Mike:** *Phil would still make us laugh, but there had been a transformation from the laid back, beer-drinking hippy he'd been in the early years into someone who had gradually become more serious… He'd become very meticulous… I'm sure it was a coping mechanism - he would try to keep his own life in order in an attempt to help him handle the workload, the pressure, and the fame. Looking back now, I see how strange it was for him to have gone from being the drummer to the singer. He did it so effortlessly that I don't think Tony or I ever thought much about it at the time, but it had never been part of his plan. All of this meant that when…Phil said, "I think I'm going to call it a day," it wasn't really a surprise.* [14]

> **Tony:** *I had thought that We Can't Dance might well be the last album we did with Phil, so when I wrote the lyric to 'Fading Lights', I had the idea of ending the song with the word "remember." And it is very poignant in that context, because it marked the end of a large part of our career.* [1]

Eleven years later, Phil would meet up with his friends again. And though they wouldn't do any writing, as they enjoyed one another's company in rehearsals and on stage, there was an experience they all shared: they remembered. Thirteen years after that, they remembered once again, and went on the road to share those memories with the world one more time, playing the first section of 'Fading Lights' to eager crowds along the way. Perhaps that was the last time, and perhaps they knew that going in. But for now, at least, we can imagine that there is always one more day to go.

> **Phil Collins, 1973:** *I think Mike and I work together really well, and with Tony… I think some sparks are going to fly!* [109]

They did, old friend. They sure did.

2 - Supper's Ready

from *Foxtrot*, 1972

I. Lover's Leap

In which two lovers are lost in each other's eyes and found again, transformed into the bodies of another male and female. [110]

> And when he had opened the seventh seal, there was silence in heaven about the space of half an hour.
> And I saw the seven angels which stood before God; and to them were given seven trumpets.
> *Revelation 8:1-2*

Quick, listen to this acoustic guitar bit with its high-to-low-to-high kind of pattern and tell me who wrote it. Was it Steve, the active guitarist of Genesis? That seems a pretty good guess, especially hearing this song flowing right after his own acoustic 'Horizons'. But it's not the *correct* guess. Is it then Mike, the band's steady rhythm guitarist and long-time 12-string guru of sorts? Sure sounds like something he'd play! But no - while Mike is *playing* the guitar pattern here, he didn't actually *write* it. So it must then be a holdover from Anthony Phillips, right? That makes sense, given how much he and Mike played their 12-strings together and found interesting sounds and patterns therein. If it's not Steve or Mike, gotta be Ant, yes? Except...no. No, that's still not right. So uh...is it...uh...Mick...Bar...nard...?

No, no, and no again. This one belongs, surprisingly, to Tony Banks.

> **Mike:** *The intro was Tony's, who had come up with it while we were waiting to play a gig... We were in a gym with a lovely big echo when Tony picked up a guitar, and suddenly, there it was. "God! Tony, that's fantastic!" "What? What did I do?" ...It was probably because Tony doesn't normally write on guitar that he found the chords in the first place. It was just three notes and not a shape that a guitarist would ever play.* [14]

> **Tony:** *I'd written a descending chord sequence on the guitar, and...I was in the changing room tuning the guitar and playing these chords. The room had a fantastic acoustic which made this particular chord sequence sound wonderful; Mike walked in and said, "That sounds great, what's that?" So he learnt the part and we played it together, and then we got the others in and played this sequence to them. I didn't know what we were going to do with it, but it was obviously something we could use as a starting point.* [1]

Even though Tony wrote it, getting someone else to play the guitar part was important, because so much of this section's atmosphere comes from the simple chords being played under the plucking strings. With no drums, the guitar playing serves the momentum of the piece, as well as its melodic feel. But the overall atmosphere? That's in the keys. And then even more so in the "ahhh"ing vocals after the primary verse. It's notable that this section runs nearly four minutes, but the lyrical part of it is finished in less than two, after which it's a gentle yet tense kind of keyboard solo for the whole rest of the run. It's kind of like 'The Cinema Show' in microcosm, and one wonders whether Lover's Leap was in the back of Tony's mind when they began spinning up that song one album later into the progressive epic it became. At any rate, they knew from the start with Lover's Leap that this was going to be something bigger than anything they'd attempted thus far in their careers.

> **Tony:** *We decided we were really gonna go for the long one this time, because we'd done 'Musical Box' and 'Stagnation' and things, and we said, "Well let's just go for one whole side of an album...and see what we can do." And we got these ideas; we actually sort of put bits and pieces in the thing. I mean, this song started off just like 'Stagnation' really in a way. I had this guitar piece I'd written, which I thought was a really strong opening part. The first two or three minutes of the song was based on this part.* [3]

> **Steve:** *I was particularly keen for us to do something of that length - a real opus and challenge for all of us writers! Everyone was involved...* [70]

> **Peter:** *I think we were confident in a way that we hadn't been before, and so that gave us the mental platform on which to build something like 'Supper's Ready'...* ³

Lyrically, I love the imagery here. The idea that The End can come at any moment, with a warning so small as a vision of monks shuffling across the lawn, or even with no warning at all. The idea that two people can share a bond that goes beyond the mere physical, such that they might be whisked away on this spiritual journey together. Such a simple thing, "It's good to feel you again." So pure and vulnerable. Where did Peter generate this concept, I wonder?

> **Peter:** *I think it was a sort of personal journey which ends up walking through scenes from Revelations [sic] in the Bible. I'll leave it at that.* ¹¹¹

Well come now Peter, that's unsatisfying. Inquiring minds want to know! Digging up yields conflicting theories, or perhaps it's just a bit of misinformation to throw people off the trail. Sometimes it's attributed to Peter sitting with his wife Jill when suddenly she began speaking in tongues as though possessed by someone or something. Some might call this a deeply religious experience. Others, a mild stroke. Perhaps both, or neither. A different account has Peter and Jill still together, but also joined by *Trespass* and *Nursery Cryme* producer John Anthony - what's he doing there? That version of the story goes that Peter's wife slept in a room with purple walls, and that the colours reacted to her spiritual energy, putting her into hysterics. Yet another account features Peter at his in-laws' place, looking out the window but convinced he was seeing someone else's front lawn, complete with seven shuffling monks. Whatever the tale, the common thread is an insistence that this was a real spiritual event of some sort. But not everyone was convinced.

> **Steve:** *I believe there'd been some drug taking going on. I believe [Peter's wife] was having a bad trip at one point, and that Pete and a friend managed to talk her round and get her out of the horrors or whatever it was. So that's a part of what the song was about, but in a way there's a kind of redemption implication that goes with that.* ¹¹²

Peter denied drugs played a part at the time, but then any good husband would want to avoid saying "Yeah, my wife was lit and acting totally nuts," so it's hard to know how the events (if any!) actually unfolded. But it also doesn't entirely matter what the true inspiration was, because what it produced can't really be denied. And as Steve says, even something as simple as "She's having a bad reaction to these substances and I need to help her" has a kind of romance about it. "I'm here. It's all right. Hey, my baby, don't you know our love is true?" Strong stuff there, and it really helps paint the keyboard work after it in a different light. This isn't just a musical and spiritual journey; it's a musical and spiritual journey being taken *together*, and that means something a little more.

Note as well that already the song touches on its primary theme of transformation. The lovers peer into one another's eyes and find themselves not simply lost in the moment, but actually metaphysically transported into different bodies. Whether these are their own bodies in an altered state, newly created bodies made just for them to inhabit, or the bodies of other individuals altogether in a different place is never made quite clear. Regardless, though together, the two are already finding themselves swept up in the transformative energy that surrounds this end-times event.

II. The Guaranteed Eternal Sanctuary Man

The lovers come across a town dominated by two characters: one a benevolent farmer and the other a head of a highly disciplined scientific religion. The latter likes to be known as "The Guaranteed Eternal Sanctuary Man" and claims to contain a secret new ingredient capable of fighting fire. This is a falsehood, an untruth, a whopper, and a taradiddle; or, to put it in clearer terms, a lie. ¹¹⁰

> And he causeth all, both small and great, rich and poor, free and bond, to receive a mark in their right hand, or in their foreheads: And that no man might buy or sell, save he that had the mark, or the name of the beast, or the number of his name.
> *Revelation 13:16-17*

From Lover's Leap the band knew they wanted to do something bold and big, but of course they didn't have a clear idea at the time what that might look like. The song certainly couldn't stay treading water in this form for another sixteen minutes.

Tony: *We'd say, "Why have you got to go verse-chorus-verse-chorus, etc.?" [That's] fine for some, but it's nice if you can go somewhere else. And you can tell more of a story that way, without the repetition.* [113]

Peter: *We are learning all the time, and on the whole in this business, it is the easiest field in which to be highly successful and mediocre at the same time. One should be constantly maintaining higher aims.* [109]

Tony: *We wanted to go further. We'd all been wanting to push away from the regular structures. It turned out better than we'd thought.* [113]

Peter: *We were then trying, consciously, to break out of tradition. We were tossing together different ideas and influences to see if there was a fresh way of putting them all together.* [113]

Luckily, by this time they had some experience pushing away from the norm, creating longer-form songs that did interesting things. In fact, there was an attitude that maybe they had it down to something of a science.

Mike: *As a band we'd found a formula for writing music: short pieces that we'd join together into a single song, the length of which would allow us to do something brave and interesting. 'Supper's Ready'...was a great example.* [14]

Peter: *I think we were beginning to know who we were as writers, and also know how to deliver it as performers. So it's a coming of age piece, I think, in lots of ways.* [3]

Steve: *It was about creating a film for the ear rather than the eye.* [113]

Tony: *It was a very important piece. It justified its length, which is quite difficult to do sometimes... There are one or two parts that in reality we shouldn't have stuck with if we had the chance to review it, but all the parts stand up pretty much. They flow nicely from one to the other.* [6]

All well and good, but in order to join all the shorter pieces together and create that kind of flow, you've got to have shorter pieces laying around in the first place. We've got our intro in Lover's Leap. So, uh...who's got next?

Tony: *I tend to remember on this album you'd come in with ideas: a riff or something like that. I mentioned the beginning of 'Supper's Ready' but it also applies to [The Guaranteed Eternal Sanctuary Man], which is another thing I'd written. In fact I'd written on guitar at university I think... So you had these kind of quite specific bits...and we had these quite big chunks that were all written by people... And then the individual bits that came in, we just developed them. I was very free with them.* [3]

Tony again, eh? And with another guitar-centric bit no less? Well this is starting to get very interesting indeed.

Tony: *[The section] has simple chords but they sound nice on guitar... There are just lots of little bits that came together.* [6]

Tony may have written this on guitar, but the arrangement the section eventually received elevated it a cut above. Bass pedals, prancing keyboards, the soaring guitar figures...

Steve: *Before we had the synth, my guitar playing was the only way to bend a note, and I'd also make the sound of a trumpet on guitar. You hear that particularly on the weird and wonderful 'Supper's Ready'...* [70]

...and of course, this section also marks the arrival of Phil's drum kit, announcing itself with some tasteful and immersive cymbal work before diving in with a drum roll and one of his signature fills. The result is a sound that is heroic and grand, especially when compared to what came before. Another classic Genesis trick, that.

> **Tony:** *We've always worried a lot about pacing, perhaps more than most groups do. I mean, to us it's very important. We spend a lot of time thinking about what order the tracks go in. We've always felt, and this was true of our long songs in the old days, that you can make a piece sound stronger by its position. I mean, we used to do like a loud piece against a quiet piece, or a slow piece against a fast piece. Some things are less obvious than that. Sometimes you are trying to increase the pace: you do a slow piece, followed by a slightly quicker one, followed by a very quick one. And you can manipulate people. A song like 'Supper's Ready'...was a series of sections, all of which I think felt stronger because of the bit that came on either side of it.* [73]

And why shouldn't it be a grand, heroic entrance? This is, after all, the fanfare of The Guaranteed Eternal Sanctuary Man. He's offering, well, guaranteed eternal sanctuary! What could be grander? What could be more heroic? When you hear the strength of this musical entry, it's easy to get swept up in the majesty of it all. "I know a fireman who looks after the fire" is a good line, but an even better delivery. It has a kind of gravitational pull about it that earns your buy-in right from the outset.

It's significant enough that the farmer only gets a pair of lines, both essentially the same, before he's brushed aside musically and lyrically for the rest of the song: "Can't you see he's fooled you all?" And I think the point is that no: no we can't. Lover's Leap was entrancing and romantic; this section is intoxicating and powerful. It feels *right*, like the culmination that was always meant to come. It's enough that the sheer ridiculousness of the things this man is saying (e.g. "Look into my mouth!") don't really faze. We're told he's a trickster, but we don't really care, because his theme music - his *presentation*, if you will - is too dang good. He's even got a contingent of daggone backup singers! The charisma is undeniable. Where do I sign that lease again? Because I'm so there.

> **Steve:** *There's more cynicism in the lyrics than people give credit for. People tend to take them so seriously.* [31]

> **Tony:** *It's quite complex. It's an excuse for a lot of fun with lyrics. It's loosely based on the idea of a Second Coming, but it's all a bit tongue in cheek.* [31]

Oh, the children! Look at the lost little children flocking to this guy! He must be the kindest of souls, him.

Speaking of children, it seems Genesis ended up having to do a little Guaranteed Eternal Sanctuary Manning themselves to get this thing on record the way it ended up. Hear those little street urchins on record? Always ones to endeavour for authenticity, Genesis went out and got *actual street urchins* to sing about keeping a little snake sad and warm. As reported in a contemporary interview...

> *For one sequence of 'Supper's Ready' they sent out for eight children off the streets...to sing a choral part, and paid them ten bob each for the privilege.* [114]

"Bob" in this case is slang for "shilling," and ten shillings made half a pound. At least, that was the case before February 15th, 1971, the so-called Decimal Day, when the shilling was officially replaced with a "five pence" or "5p" coin. The slang term "bob" stuck around, however, so even with the change in coinage these kids each got half a pound in wages to sing-threaten a snake. Half a British pound in 1972 could net you twenty candy bars, if my inflationary maths is correct, so while I'm sure these kids felt like Genesis had done them right, it's a bit of a sketchy lookback. Phil Collins, who played the Artful Dodger in two West End runs of the musical *Oliver!* should've known better, if nobody else. Ah well. When a gang of supersonic scientists come flashing fifty pence, what little tyke could say no?

III. Ikhnaton and Itsacon and Their Band of Merry Men

Who the lovers see clad in greys and purples, awaiting to be summoned out of the ground. At the G.E.S.M.'s command they put forth from the bowels of the earth, to attack all those without an up-to-date "Eternal Life License", which were obtainable at the head office of the G.E.S.M.'s religion. [110]

> And there came out of the smoke locusts upon the earth: and unto them was given power, as the scorpions of the earth have power. And it was commanded them that they should not hurt the grass of

the earth, neither any green thing, neither any tree; but only those men which have not the seal of God in their foreheads.
Revelation 9:3-4

Ikhnaton, or Akhenaten, was an ancient Egyptian pharaoh who turned his back on the traditional Egyptian pantheon, altering (temporarily) his people's culture from a polytheistic society to a monotheistic one, with the singular focus of worship here being the sun itself. So in the title of this section alone, we see a continuation of the theme of transformation that permeates this epic piece; invoking the name of this particular king of a bygone age signifies that the transformative power is entering an active rather than a passive state. This shouldn't be *too* surprising, given that the Guaranteed Eternal Sanctuary Man just made a name for himself by promising a kind of trans*port*ation: that of the soul to the promised eternal sanctuary.

He's joined by Itsacon, who is himself not an actual historical figure, but another warning in disguise: "It's-a-con." Not that anyone might actually be in sufficient frame of mind to smell all this out when these two are spilling violently out of the earth to annihilate anyone who doesn't get with the program. Of course, our lovers aren't aware that any of this is in the works when the section begins, which is why it's able to open so gently and pensively. That flute melody, a reprise of Lover's Leap, is meant to reconnect the lovers to one another ("Did you see that, dear? What was all THAT about?") but also to reflect on the merits of what they've heard. It's them wrestling with whether to believe in the G.E.S.M., or the farmer whose warnings were quickly drowned out, or perhaps neither; they could still theoretically go their own way and ignore all of this.

In a way, the characters here are a mirror to Genesis with 'Supper's Ready' itself. This piece was anything but a sure thing, and they were still essentially finding tiny bits of music and mashing them up against one another, hoping for the best. So far so good, but there's that constant nagging worry: will whatever's next measure up?

Mike: *We always started each album - I did - with a degree of trepidation. Excitement. A bit like, "Well, this is a new one, let's see what we've got here." But like, will it be good? Will it work?* [3]

Tony: *This was the culmination of something... The strength of some of these songs is their length... If you do it right, you can tell a story within a song like that, and use the contrasts in the music. 'Supper's Ready' was lots of bits.* [10]

Ah, contrasts. That's the ticket. We opened with a gentle if somewhat intense section, followed that with a happy, "up" kind of strong section, now a flute reprise of that initial gentle section again. So I guess...go heavy again? Heavier than the last one? Let's try it!

"WAITING FOR BATTLE!"

Tony: *We felt that we were underway, that we were heading somewhere different. Foxtrot was where we started, in my opinion, to become significant.* [113]

Listen to Phil's drum part here. It's a variation on the standard 2-4 snare beat pattern I've talked about repeatedly before, but the variation itself is significant. Here he snaps in before each beat, playing "and 2...and 4" in sequence under the words. The result is that the beat is maintained, but feels almost like it's stumbling forward, about to fall down and fall apart at any moment. Now put with that feeling the imagery of a swarm of monstrous beings (perhaps human, but if so their actions make them monstrous all the same) pouring out of tunnels and other underground passages. Flooding into city streets. So many, and moving so rapidly, that they can't help but trip over one another in their bloodlust.

It's terrifying imagery, but the imagery itself isn't the most terrifying part of this section. The real scare is that the music is so *buoyant* as all this is going on. "Bang bang bang" as bodies fall, but "I'm feeling good" all the same. This isn't just a lyrical play; this is indeed a "feel-good" kind of section of music. Isn't that just a little distressing? Tony Banks in 1986 would write lyrics for 'Domino' calling out the way mankind revels in the horrific; Peter Gabriel covered that ground fourteen years earlier. It was just buried in the fantasy of a song with an awful lot of things going on, so it was easy to miss. Especially when the section also has a big guitar solo featuring some of Steve Hackett's best tapping work.

Steve: *On stage I tend not to use the guitar as a guitar, but rather as a voice in the oneness of sound. A lot of the time people say, "Where's the guitar? I can't hear it." It's more of a special effects department.* [109]

Once again, it's a transformation at work: watch as the otherwise normal, generally moral human beings celebrate slaughter. The warlord who has just ordered something bordering on genocide now orders rejoicing and dancing in equal measure. Nobody seems to have any problem with this juxtaposition. Indeed, it again seems happy and right. It's only when we contrast back to something more slow, quiet, and restrained that the weight of it all begins to sink in.

> **Mike:** *It's funny looking back. The way it happened, it was never like you knew what you were doing, you know what I mean? We had a whole lot of bits, then we started sort of stringing them together... So it shows a bit more freedom. Because we tend to write songs much more compact. Lots of bits in it. Whereas this is a bit freer. You stay on a section for a bit longer and let things happen.* [3]

> **Phil:** *The music and imagery worked so strongly together.* [113]

IV. How Dare I Be So Beautiful?

In which our intrepid heroes investigate the aftermath of the battle and discover a solitary figure, obsessed by his own image. They witness an unusual transmutation, and are pulled into their own reflections in the water. [110]

> And when they shall have finished their testimony, the beast that ascendeth out of the bottomless pit shall make war against them, and shall overcome them, and kill them. And their dead bodies shall lie in the street of the great city, which spiritually is called Sodom and Egypt, where also our Lord was crucified. And they of the people and kindreds and tongues and nations shall see their dead bodies three days and an half, and shall not suffer their dead bodies to be put in graves.
> *Revelation 11:7-9*

If the title of this section seems to be in startling contradiction with the imagery it contains, well, that's no mistake. This is the big ol' "Oh no" moment of it all. Note that the "intrepid heroes," the two lovers we met in the very first seconds of the song, have not been corrupted. They are witnesses to the battle and the ruin it's left behind, but were not active participants on either side. Unfortunately, we listeners are not afforded the same luxury of being bystanders; Gabriel makes that all too clear when he tells us that the poor soul stamped "Human Bacon" is "you," which is to say, us.

It's not clear what "side" of the conflict this young figure was on, if any at all. It hardly seems to matter now, anyway. This is a conflict with no winners, it would seem. Just death and destruction on a massive scale, with no end in sight. Or, perhaps, with only The End in sight, bringing doom to all peoples. Rejoicing and dancing this ain't.

So it's important to talk here about the impact the audio engineering had on this piece. For starters, the guys in the band didn't even register that they could "cheat" when they'd record the song until *Foxtrot* producer David Hitchcock clued them in.

> **Dave Hitchcock:** *[My value was in] explaining they didn't need to play it all the way through to record it; that we could do it section by section, with crossfades and edits, then put it all together later. That allowed them to concentrate for the three or four minutes of each section and get the best possible performance, while also allowing them to bring in different sounds for each section, rather than playing it straight through with one long, homogenous sound.* [112]

This was hugely advantageous; a revelation in music recording for them. But it came with its share of drawbacks, too. For one, 'Supper's Ready' had no sense of cohesion in their minds. They could map out conceptually where it was going and try to imagine the various bits and pieces running up into one another, but rehearsing and playing it in fragmented form made all of that easier said than done.

> **Mike:** *I remember writing it and at the time we weren't really paying that much attention to it. We were working on the Foxtrot album and we were worrying more about other tracks. We didn't realise quite what we'd got. 'Supper's Ready' is very difficult to play all the way through. We pieced it together in the studio and slowly we became aware of what we had, and started recording it. We had no idea how long it was. We thought it was only 15 minutes long.* [31]

Tony: *I think what I liked most about this song was that after writing it and sticking it all together we weren't too sure, because all the elements had been done very piecemeal and the first half of the song had been a bit traumatic, because that was when we'd changed the producer and engineer. We finally heard the whole piece back and thought, "This is fantastic."* [1]

Yes, see, that's the other part of this equation. *Foxtrot* had a difficult production cycle, with *Nursery Cryme* producer John Anthony proving too expensive for another go, and replacement producer Bob Potter not actually liking the band's music. So they fired Potter, kept on his audio engineer, and brought in a guy named Tony Platt to produce...who was soon also fired for not getting along with the band. Finally Dave Hitchcock came in, who Tony didn't care for but *someone* had to produce the dang thing. And then they decided they'd had enough of the old Potter engineer and sacked him, too.

Tony: *We recorded the first half of 'Supper's Ready' with this other engineer, [Bob Johnston]. And then we got this other guy; John Burns came in as the next engineer and we finished off the song with him, and did the rest of the album with him.* [3]

Transformations on top of transformations. Not that even this happened smoothly; the switch in engineers occurred in conjunction with the band having to abandon the recording process entirely in order to go play some shows in Italy.

Tony: *The latter stages of 'Supper's Ready' we pretty much produced ourselves with [engineer] John Burns. David Hitchcock was there but he wasn't very important. That's why we didn't use him again after that. The album was very fragmented anyhow. We did an Italian tour in the middle of making it.* [10]

Steve: *I remember flying back from Italy to be [at the studio] a day or two ahead of the others, who were travelling by road, just to finish off my guitar parts over the end of 'Supper's Ready'.* [113]

Tony hates flying, you see.

In any case, you've got what is by now an eleven-minute song - longer already than both spiritual predecessors 'Stagnation' and 'The Musical Box' - and though it's had some good contrasts, it also hasn't totally gone anywhere. Not anywhere that would produce a satisfying climax, that is. I guess that means it's time for the grand ending to be developed, right? Some big organ bits like on those other two tracks, big major key things, round this thing off by the 13-minute mark maybe, yeah? That sounds good. And also remarkably familiar...

Tony: *It was sounding really good, and we were carrying on. And it was developing, doing little tinkly bits after that and all the rest of it, a few vocal bits. And I thought, "If we do this, it could just be ending up sounding exactly like 'Musical Box' if we're not careful." So I said, "Well let's just stop the song..." - we had a really romantic bit - "Let's just stop the song now and go straight into this other piece we have,"...this thing that Peter had written. I said, "Let's just go in there. You've got this really pretty bit, this really ugly chord sequence suddenly coming in after that...should sound great!" And so we did that.* [3]

That's a pretty brave move. You have something going and you admit it's building nicely, but even though you're feeling good, something tells you you'd better activate your other song? So instead of developing or even rewriting any of what you have, you're going to simply leave it where it is, cut it off completely, and go into something completely different? Are you sure?

Steve: *I can't remember whose idea it was, but we came to the conclusion that you could join any two bits of music together, no matter how disparate the styles, provided the bridge or atmospheric link was strong enough. It creates for the listener an adventure, an odyssey. You've got the stuff of concertos and symphonies, which nod to the past, but it was also futuristic at that point. Bands just weren't creating pieces of music like that. I think it was then the longest piece that any rock band had ever played live.* [113]

Tony: *'Supper's Ready' was sounding quite pretty so I made a suggestion: "Why don't we stop the song there, and just whang into Willow Farm to see what it sounds like?" Because I always like contrast. We all decided that sounded good and when it came to doing the vocals and lyric on it Pete, in the gap, said, "A flower?" Which was great, because it set up the contrast between* *what had been an ultra-romantic moment and what was about to come up, which was anything but. It's a key little moment.* [1]

Eh?
A flower?

V. Willow Farm

Climbing out of the pool, they are once again in a different existence. They're right in the middle of a myriad of bright colours, filled with all manner of objects, plants, animals, and humans. Life flows freely and everything is mindlessly busy. At random, a whistle blows and every single thing is instantly changed to another. [110]

> And another angel came out of the temple, crying with a loud voice to him that sat on the cloud, Thrust in thy sickle, and reap: for the time is come for thee to reap; for the harvest of the earth is ripe. And he that sat on the cloud thrust in his sickle on the earth; and the earth was reaped.
> *Revelation 14:15-16*

This is where it all started, you know. Lyrically, I mean. Willow Farm is a very silly place, and Peter Gabriel is a very silly person. Sometimes. And so, given a piano and a moment to play it without Anthony George Freaking Banks tsk-ing over his shoulder, Peter Gabriel found himself in the position to write a very silly song.

> **Peter:** *One of the great troubles with the mind is that it's always lost between two extremes. That's partly what Willow Farm is about. Wherever you are and whatever you do, there's always a left and right, an up and down, a good and bad.* [113]

Whatever you do, there's always something done, and wherever you go, there you are.

> **Steve:** *I don't think it's crazy... I wouldn't say it's particularly misunderstood, either. Though it is hugely open to interpretation.* [112]

Was this song a loon or simply a tune? Was it profound, out of bounds, or underground? Or was it he or she? Who sung it?

> **Steve:** *[Willow Farm is] part 'Teddy Bears' Picnic', part 'I Am The Walrus'.* [112]

Ah yes, pigs from a gun, we've had that I suppose. Cornflakes still to come, don't you worry about that. Well. Now that we're here and gorgeous as geese (they'll make a comeback too, mark my words!) I suppose we ought to look for some hidden doors, eh? Like maybe this whole jumbling jambalaya jamboree has a secretive little nook of its own, oi? The shift is the thing, know what I ming? You gotta get in to get out - the egg was a bird and the bird, bird, bird, bird is the word, and the Word was made flesh, ya dig? What am I saying, of course ya dig; you're under the soil.

> **Tony:** *We got to the end of the [previous] section and had this idea to stop and do Willow Farm, a complete song written by Peter that had nothing to do with anything else - just to put two completely different things next to each other to see what the effect was. Once we'd done that, what came after was obvious and the whole song developed from there... Since Peter had written a lyric for Willow Farm as a complete song, he wrote the lyrics for the rest around it. The way it turns out gathers momentum and has a very strong overall mood, which makes it our most successful song from those early days.* [10]

Yes, the path is clear, though no eyes can see; hmm. Probably best then that we tidy the floors. Just a bit.

> **Tony:** *We had this completely distinct song that Peter had written on piano called Willow Farm. I took the left-hand part and played it on the Mellotron brass, and played the right-hand part*

> on the organ, which created this rather ugly sound, and the first run-down had a very strange note in it that made you sit up. [1]

> **Tony:** And that suddenly took the whole song to another dimension, you know? Suddenly the drums were in, everything was going, and the second half of the song becomes very electric. [3]

Ah yes, much better, wonderfully clean in the morning. And now, if you please, I think I might like some more applause.

> **Steve:** It also gave Pete the opportunity to depict the action of the songs, helping to bring them to life and adding to the magic. [Having] a lead singer who was prepared to dress up in anything, including a fox's head with his wife's clothes or whatever the occasion demanded and not be shy about it was all to the good. [70]

> **Tony:** Well Peter had started trying to find things to do on stage, which developed into wearing these kinds of masks and everything, which on 'Supper's Ready' worked really well. I mean the flower idea at the time seemed very crass, but it just worked so well. At that point in 'Supper's Ready'...the music went from pretty to silly, and he just suddenly said, "A flower" and stuck this thing on his face. And it was a great musical moment. [3]

> **Steve:** I like to think we conjure up mental pictures for people and create moods. When Peter wears a flower on his head or shouts "All change!" it could mean nothing. But within the context of the music, it can help get the number across. We all relate to fantasy… [109]

> **Peter:** I want to create a fantasy situation. The flower head should be hamming it up. It's consciously supposed to be unreal. I don't specifically want to frighten… In fact the flower walk was probably more influenced by Shirley Temple… [109]

And time! Time, time, time, never enough time. We've been here all the time, but need to be here more. Wait, is that how it goes? Or is that here needs to time there longer? Can't recall...bears further study.

> **Tony:** When I write a lyric, I try to think of Peter, who has to sing them. Peter's own lyrics tend to be more abstract and I tend to have reservations about obscurity. I think he wrote 'Supper's Ready' too hurriedly. [109]

> **Phil:** 'Supper's Ready' was left till last, really. Peter was rushing through the lyrics while we were putting down the backing tracks. Perhaps more time would have made it better. [115]

> **Tony:** I was never really happy with the title… I wanted it to sound more epic, I suppose. [43]

Ah well. We all fit in our places, don't we? Yes, I'm sure it'll work out all right. In the end you'll simply have to like what you've got.

> **Mike:** One of the things I've always loved about this business as a writer, and you learn it as you go along, is luck. I mean luck does come into it. And things that seem quite effortless, as this was, are always good. You know, we weren't aware when we put it all together that we had a really strong thing. We thought it was good, but the things that happen without feeling you're trying are often the best things, I think. And I think 'Supper's Ready' had that sort of feeling about it. [3]

ALL CHANGE!

> **Tony:** It's a number of contrasts. It's the loud against the soft and the very romantic against the incredibly stupid. And by doing that you make the romantic more romantic, and the stupid more stupid. [31]

Awright, 'at's enuff changin' fer now. 'Owzabout a flute solo?

V½. Interlude

Tony: *We kinda put [our individual bits] all in the same song, and then it was the kind of filling out stuff that almost ended up being the strongest stuff though… So yes, I think we were writing well together.* [3]

Steve: *We'd gone out on a limb. It was labyrinthine. It was like when The Beatles released Sgt. Pepper's Lonely Hearts Club Band and then they worried whether they'd gone too far and might get the thumbs-down. Except we didn't have their number of fans!* [113]

Mmm...melancholy, reflective, sombre, transformed seeds scattered like dust into the world they call home.
Let's burn it down.

VI. Apocalypse in 9/8 (Co-Starring the Delicious Talents of Gabble Ratchet)

At one whistle the lovers become seeds in the soil, where they recognise other seeds to be people from the world from which they had originated. While they wait for Spring, they are returned to their old world to see the Apocalypse of St. John in full progress. The seven trumpeteers cause a sensation, the fox keeps throwing sixes, and Pythagoras (a Greek extra) is deliriously happy as he manages to put exactly the right amount of milk and honey on his corn flakes. [110]

> And when the thousand years are expired, Satan shall be loosed out of his prison, And shall go out to deceive the nations which are in the four quarters of the earth, Gog and Magog, to gather them together to battle: the number of whom is as the sand of the sea.
> *Revelation 20:7-8*

First things first: who is Gabble Ratchet?

Tony: *Fictitious, I'm afraid. [It would be] nice to give some sort of different answer to that, but that's the way it goes.* [107]

LIES! Everyone lies! "Gabble ratchet" is a British colloquialism referring to either a flock of ominous birds, or else the cry they emit as they go about their death heralding. In other circles "Gabble Ratchet" is also known as "Gabriel's Hounds," (referring to the *angel* Gabriel, but you know what you're doing, Pete) which are sometimes called the Hounds of Hell. But even then those hellhounds are sometimes depicted as wild geese, because it's just that kind of world. And indeed, if you listen to the studio version of the song closely just before the section's big climactic moment, aye...thar do indeed be some geese-a-honkin'. So despite what BIG LIAR Tony Banks has to say about it, Apocalypse in 9/8 actually does, in fact, co-star the delicious talents of Gabriel's Wild Geese, and is all the better for it.

Now that we've rectified that grave injustice, let's talk jams. A musical jam is where you kind of just sit there and make it up as you go along. That resonates with me because that's exactly how I write most of the time and exactly what I'm doing right now as I compose this initial draft, in fact. There are multiple kids downstairs screaming (in glee, pain, and everything in between), it's hard to hear myself think, I'm stressing out about running out of time, and I've got no real plan. What better mindset is there for writing about Apocalypse in 9/8?

Tony: *The main bit I think we wrote sort of on the spot really was bit that was called Apocalypse in 9/8. Mike had this idea of just alternating between bass pedals and his guitar...but [in] very random fashion. He wasn't doing anything particular at all. And then Phil had the idea of sort of trying to tie it down to a riff.* [43]

Oh, so Phil was there too?

Phil: *I am absent...for a few hours one day, and when I return Tony, Mike, and Steve have messed around with a riff in 9/8.* [12]

Oh OK, so it wasn't Phil with the riff, it was Steve.

Mike: *The Apocalypse in 9/8... Peter wasn't there, so Phil, Tony, and I started working on it; Steve didn't have much to do at that point. And it marked a start of what was later going to be the three-piece unit. And in a sense the piece was less written; the chords were set up and the mood was there. It was more like a group composition in that sense because the music was in place and Peter came in with the vocals afterwards.* [1]

Oh OK, so Steve and Phil were actually both there, but Steve was just kind of watching it all unfold.

Phil: *[Apocalypse in 9/8 is] the best thing we've done. It started off as a jam. Steve and Peter were away for some reason and Mike started playing this movement on bass pedals - totally abstract with no time signature at all. Then we tied it down and we worked it out to a two-bar riff. I just knocked a beat out and it became a bar of nine. That's the way things are often done in the band and that's the sort of thing I'd like to work more to, because I personally like playing in [unusual] time signatures.* [115]

Oh OK, so Steve wasn't actually there at all, but Phil was there and did help tie it down to a riff.

Mike: *The first time it happened like this - the second half, you know, keyboard solo to the end - it showed a bit more freedom. You know what I mean? The keyboard solo was just really myself, Phil, and Tony and Steve just sort of jamming. Tony writing stuff over that riff that's playing all the time on the bottom.* [3]

Oh OK, so Steve actually was there and he was part of the jam too, so it was actually all four of them.

Phil: *The big stuff on 'Supper's Ready', like the big instrumental stuff, I remember we were rehearsing it...and I had something to do in the afternoon. And I came back, and Mike and Tony had written basically the Apocalypse in 9/8. That's what it ended up being called. This was just this riff...and I said, "Oh, that sounds good!" And Tony had written - not thinking about the time signature - he'd sort of written this keyboard thing and actually the thing was in 9/8. So I maybe played it once or twice but never really thought about it too much.* [3]

Oh OK, so Phil wasn't actually there and Mike and Tony did all the work while Schrödinger's Steve either was or wasn't there.
Glad we got that sorted.
I've got to say, this keyboard solo is phenomenal, yet if you asked me to talk about epic keyboard solos it would take a long time for this one to pop into mind. I think it's because it's all so tied into the rhythm and the momentum of the larger piece. This isn't a keyboard solo where Tony just shows off his fancy finger moves to the oohs and ahhs of the evening crowd at the local lounge. This is a solo moving like fine brush strokes, painting a picture.

Tony: *The organ solo started out as a very tongue in cheek thing. I thought I would play like Keith Emerson to see what it sounds like. There were little phrases in there that were supposed to be almost humorous in a way.* [6]

At first it's exciting, especially after the raw weirdness of Willow Farm: oh boy, a fun keyboard solo! But the fun fades and the stakes rise, and soon you're not even listening to a keyboard solo at all; you're listening to the relentless march of the armies of Hell as they scour all life from the Earth.
This only works because Tony - meandering, long-form Tony - had the sense to tell Mike to limit himself as he played. Mike listened, and Tony crafted a masterpiece of menacing mood atop the backdrop of otherworldly rhythm.

Tony: *The section of 'Supper's Ready' called Apocalypse in 9/8 was the best instrumental piece we'd created up to that point. Mike had a way of playing bass pedals and then putting guitar chords across it, which just sounded great. And I said, "If you can tie it down so you're playing an E on the bass, and then just play an F and B at the top, don't play any other notes.*

> *Then I can play any chord I like on top of that which will give me great freedom to write a solo on top of that." Mike and Phil created a 9/8 riff, but I didn't want to be tied to the time signature so I just took it as a 4/4 thing and played right against their riff, starting off with cheeky little major tunes, almost a pastiche, and then slowly making it more and more sinister and unsettling, so you're not quite sure where it's going to go.* [1]

> **Mike:** *There's no movement [in the bass riff], so he can move around the chords a lot.* [3]

> **Tony:** *The idea of that part was to use a riff and not give myself any boundary with the chords, just virtually using any chord in it. The way you can change the character of a riff just by putting different chords with it is amazing. It's something which has always interested me. I was very pleased with the way it turned out. It was all done on organ - before the synthesizer days.* [31]

It's the drumming, that's what it is.

> **Phil:** *Some of my best playing is on the 9/8 things on 'Supper's Ready'. It's interesting to play.* [109]

Interesting to play, because he has no idea what he's even doing. Just pick up the sticks, point them at the drums, and pray.

> **Phil:** *I haven't a clue what is happening, and just start to play. At some points I play with the riff, at others I join Tony. I'm still immensely proud of the final recorded performance of the piece which became Apocalypse in 9/8, which captures me making it up as I go along.* [12]

That's the thing that's so gripping about this. You expect the drummer to hold down the groove, especially if the keyboardist admits he's going rogue and just doing any old thing. And much of the time, he does. He's keeping that 9/8 beat with Mike, but then instead of random flairs and fills, he just goes off script and follows his wayward keyboardist. Shoot, sometimes he does a third, unrelated thing instead! So you get one rhythm in the low register: constant, cold, cruel, the demonic legions spilling forth. Up top you have what seems like it might be a second rhythmic pattern but is really just a wild man with crazy eyes raving about the end times - and unfortunately this particular doomsayer happens to actually be correct. And then in between them you get the panicked throng running with percussive footsteps between them, or else off in random directions in search of non-existent safety. It's *intense*, man.

> **Phil:** *Of course, we went in to record it, still not really knowing what it was. But it was just like one of those moments where the tape was playing, and you're recording, and it was just captured. That's one of our best spontaneous moments. I still listen to that and can't quite work out how it just all happened at the right time.* [3]

It all makes for a natural build until a high organ note starts oscillating, wild geese take off in flight, and you just know something has to give. The intensity is like a dam about to burst...but into what?

> **Tony:** *And then I brought in the really big chords again, finally going back out of the minor key to an E major chord, which created this very serene, simple chord sequence; a strong, uplifting moment. It's like the angels have arrived, the heavens have opened. And it had taken about twenty minutes to reach this point: that was what was so great about it, and people don't often understand that. You have to have twenty minutes of build-up, and then you get to that moment and wow, it really gives it to you. I like those moments which can send a shiver up the spine.* [1]

Tony's choice of words there is interesting. Is he saying it's like the angels have arrived because that's how he always envisioned it even when the whole song was just an instrumental thing? Or is he saying that because of what Peter transformed it all into?

> **Tony:** *It was a coincidence to some extent what happened there. Again, it was another one of those places where I had this keyboard solo and it ended on these big chords, and I thought, "Yeah, big chords!" you know? I had this idea of just vocal harmonies going "Ahhhhhhh," you know? And then again Peter started singing on top of it, you know? And I thought, "Ah shit, here he goes again!"* [3]

> **Mike:** *But the moment when we built to that "666" bit, it was one of those few moments in your career where you actually got a great sounding thing, and Pete came in with a vocal line we hadn't sung together. He laid it on top. He hadn't been rehearsing it that way. He just came in...it just sounded fantastic...Laid this vocal down and it's like, "FANTASTIC." So strong.* [3]

> **Tony:** *When I brought in this big sequence at the top of the solo, I'd assumed that there would be no lead vocal… But I have to say, this time it only took me about ten seconds to think, "This sounds fantastic; it's so strong," even though that hadn't been my plan. That taught me another lesson, that however much you can climax a keyboard solo, if you have a vocal or even a guitar to finish it off, it takes it onto another level.* [1]

> **Peter:** *I felt like I was singing from my soul - almost like singing for my life.* [116]

You wouldn't expect a line that starts "Six-six-six" to be the most hopeful, brightest moment of the song, but that's what Genesis achieves here. It's one more transformation: dark to light. "666 is no longer alone." Who? Who has joined him?

The Hosts of Heaven, that's who.

It's a piercing ray of light shattering through the cloud cover. Shivers up the spine, marrow from your backbone. The seven trumpets sound salvation; God has said "No more." When this bit plays, and the powerful vocal-less chords that come after it, I can see the imagery play out in my head. When people think of the denizens of Heaven, they tend to picture what essentially look like humans with kind faces, long hair, white robes, and feathery wings. Maybe toss a golden halo on there. We've associated the image of the angel with cherubic babies, Cupid, the tops of fir trees in the holiday season. We like to think of heavenly beings as sweet, peaceful, gentle souls.

We are wrong.

The heavenly host are the soldiers of God. They are armed and extraordinarily dangerous. They may be beautiful to behold, but only in an awe-filled, raw terror kind of way. They will eradicate, without mercy. And God has turned them loose on the demonic hordes. Listen to these bright chords over this dastardly beat and see in your mind's eye the scores of glowing beings rocketing down through a hole in the sky. See their streaks of gold violently slash across the legions of darkness, blades of holy fire cutting down all shadow until only light remains. This isn't a battle, it's a massacre. It's a purging of all evil on Earth, forever. "666 is no longer alone." Now, neither are we.

> **Tony:** *The concept of the lyric was good in the sense that it was completely over the top: a fight between good and evil. I think that on most levels it worked very well, although it was perhaps something of a fluke - I have to say that.* [6]

Now we find ourselves safe but in shock, unsure of our places in this new, holy world. What's next?

VII. As Sure As Eggs Is Eggs (Aching Men's Feet)

Above all else an egg is an egg. "And did those feet…" making ends meet. [110]

> And he hath on his vesture and on his thigh a name written, KING OF KINGS, AND LORD OF LORDS. And I saw an angel standing in the sun; and he cried with a loud voice, saying to all the fowls that fly in the midst of heaven, Come and gather yourselves together unto the supper of the great God.
> *Revelation 19:16-17*

Ohhhh, those tubular bells. Is there a more victorious sound in all of music than these three chimes to open this final section? It's, well, divine.

> **Peter:** *It does feel like we captured some emotion there, particularly at the climax. For my part, it was influenced by John Bunyan's The Pilgrim's Progress, as, later, was The Lamb Lies Down On Broadway. It was that idea of a journey… I still enjoy it now; I'm still attracted to it.* [113]

The lovers, with whom we've taken this massive journey, are restored to their proper bodies, and united at last. Simultaneously comes the "marriage of the Lamb," where Jesus Christ is restored to the bride, which is the church. And so this reprise takes on the weight of two romances: one between the song's lyrical couple, their bond now made unbreakable by the experience they've shared; and one between God and His people. "I've been so far from here...but now I'm back again, and babe it's gonna work out fine." This line is so powerful because it's coming from *both* sources.

> **Peter:** *There's a line in Revelations [sic] which says, "This is the supper of the mighty one"...Anyway, there are very straightforward levels at which you can take the lyrics if you want.* [114]

And then as the warmth of all of that floods over us and the drum fill brings some rhythm back in, we hit my personal favourite moment of the entire thing.

> **Tony:** *The reprise of The Guaranteed Eternal Sanctuary Man at the end was good...The idea of doing it at the end of the song with the Mellotron was something that never occurred to me, but it sounded great. There is some lovely guitar at the end there too. There are just lots of little bits that came together.* [6]

Think all the way back to the first time we heard the section known as The Guaranteed Eternal Sanctuary Man. "Can't you see he's fooled you all?" That's the melody line. It's a warning about this guy, but the music doesn't *feel* like a warning at all. It feels strong, powerful, *really good*. We know on an intellectual level that this section is bad news a-brewin' but we sort of don't care, because it sounds so triumphant.

Here the same melody kicks in on the line "Can't you feel our souls ignite?" instead and the difference in atmosphere is *palpable*. There's a night and day contrast between the first time we hear that melody and its reprise. *This* is strength. *This* is power. *This* is truth. It's so immediately and utterly convincing that we almost look back and wonder why we thought that previous section was so strong to begin with. And the answer is because The Guaranteed Eternal Sanctuary Man was the false prophet. He was selling a lie based on a distortion of the truth, and it sounded good only because we didn't have the *actual* truth in front of us. Once you're experiencing real eternal sanctuary, you become immune to attempts to convince you about false ones. He's returned to lead His children home, and there's no need to sell when you're homeward bound. It's a lyrical and conceptual master stroke; the words elevate the music and the music elevates the words. It's awesome, in the most literal sense of the word.

> **Peter:** *I think 'Supper's Ready' was again one of these journey songs where we were really trying to take people along this dream journey. When it worked, and we got to the sort of New Jerusalem stuff at the end, you could really feel you were touching people in quite a deep way. There was a guy who...when he heard 'Supper's Ready' for the first time he invited us to perform it at his church in Normandy. And this was a guy who didn't normally relate to rock music... And there were things like that that were sort of growing in the music, that sometimes you'd get a feeling and get an area that you could harvest in different ways. And I think capture people's imagination.* [3]

> **Tony:** *It just worked well. The ending was sort of like a nice, relaxing, quite triumphant sort of bit.* [43]

> **Phil:** *The last bit, you know, New Jerusalem. I think that's fantastic. So that's probably my favourite song on that [album].* [3]

> **Steve:** *Many people's favourite moment. This is Pete really giving his all on vocals here.* [13]

> **Mike:** *That end section happened effortlessly, as good music often does. The act of doing 'Supper's Ready' seemed quite easy. If things take too long, it's a bad sign... The game got raised.* [113]

> *[Jerusalem=place of peace.]* [110]

And God shall wipe away all tears from their eyes; and there shall be no more death, neither sorrow, nor crying, neither shall there be any more pain: for the former things are passed away.
Revelation 21:4

Amen.

Epilogue I: Fresh from the Oven

One thing repeated a couple times by the band in the quotes above really stuck out to me: the notion that they "didn't know what they'd got" with 'Supper's Ready' really until the whole thing was done. That's incredible to me, even as it makes total sense. A song so ambitious and sprawling, comprised of so many smaller bits, recorded in chunks rather than all at once...of course it would be impossible to see the big picture until it was right in front of you. And yet, without that big picture, how does everything click into place so well? It's like doing a jigsaw puzzle blindfolded and getting it right on the first go. You can feel the shapes of the individual pieces and make good guesses as to what will fit with what, but you certainly can't reasonably hope to complete the whole puzzle that way, can you?

> **Tony:** *When we first heard it back, having written and recorded it - we hadn't heard it all back! We actually stuck it together with Mike and I going to another studio, because we'd actually run out of studio time. And actually sticking these two parts together, which incidentally was slightly out of tune, so we had to slow down the track in order to make it work, which we were able to rectify on the remixes obviously. And just hearing it back all as one thing, I thought, "Well this is fantastic. This is so much the best thing we've ever done. I'm really excited by this." So it was a very strong moment.* [3]

> **Phil:** *I have very fond memories [of recording the album]... Hearing those things, and hearing 'Supper's Ready' put together, it was very strong. We were actually getting somewhere.* [3]

> **Mike:** *Obviously 'Supper's Ready' is a huge piece...one of our best moments.* [3]

Nobody in the band knew it was great while making it; everyone knew it was great once it was made. But what would the fans think? You've got five excited young men eagerly telling their listeners to spend twenty-three minutes and change on a spiritual journey through the end of days. Feels like a pretty hard ask, doesn't it?

> **Steve:** *I thought, "No one's gonna buy this, because it's too long. The references are too far-flung. It's totally ambiguous." I thought the first time [Charisma Records head] Tony Stratton-Smith heard it he was gonna say, "Sorry boys, game's up, contract's cancelled; you'll be hearing from our lawyers."* [112]

> **Phil:** *Most of all, credit must go to Tony, Mike, and Peter for seeing that all those parts could fit and be more than just five songs strung together over twenty-three minutes... Genesis are literally pushing the boundaries of what bands can do on an album.* [12]

> **Tony:** *Well Foxtrot was the first album I think where we sounded convincing to the outside world. I think we sort of convinced ourselves with the [previous] two albums, and convinced maybe our fans. I think doing 'Supper's Ready' just took it on slightly another level. People could hear this album who had never heard Genesis before and be interested in it. I think that was a significant moment.* [3]

> **Steve:** *When we finished 'Supper's Ready' I wasn't sure whether anyone would like such a great long piece of music. The word Elgar comes to mind for some reason, Elgar on acid perhaps. We weren't on acid, we weren't on drugs: we were on beer and wine and Earl Grey. I thought the game was up, no one was going to like it, the record company were going to sack us, and we would disappear into a black hole. I was proved so wrong and I've never been so happy to be proved so wrong: it ended up becoming the band's anthem.* [1]

Epilogue II: Meals on Wheels

Deciding to release 'Supper's Ready' on *Foxtrot* and trust that the fans would "get it" is a brave move. Performing it on stage, though?

Tony: *We were always tempted to try and do it on stage, but it is 26 minutes of a show, and that's an awful lot to give over to one piece...* [3]

From a pure setlist configuration standpoint that's a bit of a nightmare already. But even beyond that, how are you going to hold an audience's attention through a single piece of that length? Tony spoke before about how the twenty minutes of build-up were necessary in order to get the big payoff at the end of Apocalypse in 9/8. He was right, of course, but there's a big difference between sitting in a room with a record player for that length of time and standing in a theatre watching this rock band sitting in place trying to get twenty minutes of notes right. Something had to give.

Steve: *You know, if you really want to truly inhabit the fairy tale regions, then we needed as wide a canvas as possible. I remember being against doing 'Supper's Ready' live before we had all these [additional] things, because I felt it wouldn't work. I remember it was me and Pete and the two of us were saying, "We shouldn't do it unless we've got all the sound effects: of the train doors slamming, and Uncle Tom Cobley, and all," because we had performed a number of these type of things live and people just wandered off to the bar. We wondered, "Why?" It wasn't because the sound wasn't enough, and so we really had to get the whole production together before things started clicking [live] with Genesis in those days.* [30]

Phil: *Performing 'Supper's Ready' [live] brings its own challenges. The first dozen or so times we do it...the five of us are constantly trying to catch up with each other, such is the concentration needed to perform a long piece of music. However, from the off, it's a hit with our audiences, and we always breathe a sigh of relief when we reach the end. Especially if we reach the end at the same time.* [12]

Genesis were blessed to have such loyal fans, but then again, terrific foresight to understand that a piece like 'Supper's Ready' needed that little bit extra to push it over the edge with them.

Steve: *Both Pete and I insisted that 'Supper's Ready' needed all the bells and whistles to do it justice live...a light show, the Mellotron, sound effects like slamming doors, the cry of "All Change!", Pete's costumes such as the flower headgear...everything that excited audiences. It helped the band to move into a whole new gear. The more risks taken, the better.* [70]

Which isn't to say that they always got it right, mind you. If the fox head in the red dress was the start of the Genesis on-stage theatre, and the tour for The Lamb was theatre in excess, with 'Supper's Ready' we can sort of trace the trail from Point A to Point B.

Peter: *At the end of 'Supper's Ready', I had this 666 character in a big, heavy cloak with a fluorescent six-sided headpiece which would drop away to reveal a hammy but light lamé costume, a white out of black moment, the moment of ascent to heaven. It was supposed to be partly humorous but I think it ended up, in that great tradition of Spinal Tap, a little more humorous than I'd intended. In London you only needed one guy to operate the fly wire but in America there were about four to do the same job. This nearly ended up killing me because the person operating the wire was out of sight of the person giving the cue and they lifted me up before I was ready. I'd got a wire for the harness twisted around my neck in putting this mask on, which was serious because there was enough weight there to hang me. The clock was ticking and I had to get this wire off my neck. I didn't really want to take the mask off because it would blow the visual moment but in the end I hid behind a piece of stage prop while I readjusted my hoisting wires and survived to live another day. But it was scary at the time.* [1]

Steve: *I guess it's Genesis at its most adult, with all these kind of philosophical themes. So many things. I think it marks the beginning of the band moving into what was known by the Americans as theatrical rock. I think it's because we were presenting the band with a light show, with a singer who was depicting the action, [using] a white muslin backdrop and ultraviolet lights. So you got the full whack of it. I know that Peter Gabriel and I were very keen on, if we were going to do something the length of 'Supper's Ready' in front of new audiences, it really had to engage visually as well as musically. So I think it marks a change with the band taking a leap into the unknown. I remember doing this for the first time in London at the Rainbow Theatre, and when the concert started there was a guy in the audience started out over the strains of the keyboards that kicked off. He shouted out, "Genesis is the best band in the world!"... And for that moment in time, the band WAS the best band in the world. I certainly felt I was playing guitar with the world's best band at that time.* [13]

For myself, I must admit: as good as the studio track is, whenever I want to listen to 'Supper's Ready' I find myself almost exclusively choosing the *Seconds Out* version of the track. No knock against Peter, naturally, and there are moments where he's missed, but all around it just feels like a much stronger performance, and it's through that version of the song that I was drawn to the track in the first place. And that version is a minute and a half longer!

> **Tony:** *The one big advantage to [Seconds Out] was that we hadn't included 'Supper's Ready' on Genesis Live and we were playing it so much better now. That's such a strong song from our past; on Foxtrot the final parts sound great but the early parts are a bit rough. Seconds Out was a chance to do the whole thing with some flow to it, which it didn't have before.* [10]

Epilogue III: In Digestion

From being nervous that the fans would hate it, to putting on a deeply involved stage performance to convince them to tolerate it, all the way to the incredible enthusiasm the Genesis faithful showed to the track then and now: the legacy of 'Supper's Ready' is really something special, even if it doesn't have quite the exposure it would need to bring in a steady stream of new fans.

> **Tony:** *It's funny, because it's not kind of quoted as much as it used to be. Back in the 70s I remember they used to have these sort of polls on...radio. And the 1 sort of rock track of all time was 'Stairway to Heaven'. Inevitably, I suppose. But 2 was 'Supper's Ready'. Well, that wouldn't happen now. One of the reasons for that I think is because 'Supper's Ready' never gets played, because it's too long. No radio station is going to play a song that's [that] long. And that applies even in England. So it's not really known about much apart from people who know the group and like the group. Who bought the album, I suppose, and the live shows... So it's a little bit forgotten, but I think it's a very strong moment.* [3]

Tony's looking at the song there through the lens of someone who had experienced (by 2007 when the interview was conducted) enormous mainstream success. By that metric, sure: 'Supper's Ready' is something of a "forgotten" track. But then again, he helped write it, didn't he? It's been my experience that creators - good ones, anyway - tend to be a little more "down" on their work than the people who consume it. This isn't a bad thing.

> **Steve:** *Sometimes you get a great crystallization. You may not fully recognise it at the time - as musicians you may still be searching. But the audience, the true owners, will see it as a Mona Lisa. They'll say, "Look no further, we've found it."* [113]

That audience buy-in is the important bit, and it's impossible to underestimate just how critical 'Supper's Ready' was for everything that came after. Without 'Supper's Ready', what does *Selling England by the Pound* look like? Are they willing to do something as ambitious as *The Lamb Lies Down on Broadway*? Does the so-called 'Duke Suite' remain a coherent side-long whole because there's no previous side-long effort to which it can compare? Or does that album take on a different colour entirely because they never consider doing a side-long piece in the first place?

> **Steve:** *The fact that audiences responded so readily to it gave us a kind of go-ahead to start doing things of endless complexity. It's very strange that that is our most successful song because it's really quite difficult to listen to. It does go through so many changes. And so in a way it meant that all things are possible, really.* [31]

That's the meat of it right there. 'Supper's Ready' is here, it's successful, and the shackles have been removed. All things are possible. Genesis can be whatever it wants to be, walking whatever paths it wants to walk, and blazing new ones all along the way.

> **Peter:** *Either 'Supper's Ready' or something from The Lamb Lies Down on Broadway...I think those two areas are my favourite from Genesis material.* [111]

> **Phil:** *A lot of Genesis "heads" regard it as our magnum opus, and I'd go along with that. It's greater than the sum of its parts, though some of those parts are brilliant; notably Apocalypse in 9/8 and As Sure As Eggs Is Eggs.* [12]

Often imitated but never duplicated; 'Supper's Ready' is the single most important piece of music Genesis ever created.

1 - Firth of Fifth

from *Selling England by the Pound*, 1973

Here at the end, it feels only appropriate that we go back to the beginning. Well, *a* beginning, at any rate. You see, streaming internet radio was a relatively new service during my college years. I'm not talking about simply pulling up a local radio station's website and streaming its actual live radio feed, mind you, but the idea of subscription-based, curated music; radio stations made especially for an individual. We tend to take that sort of thing for granted now, and there are presently a number of options available, but for a student in the mid-2000s, it was a novel, exciting idea. I don't recall exactly how I heard about the particular service I used, but I made a free account and decided to try it out.

I don't know exactly what I expected. I imagine that I didn't expect much at all, frankly. The idea of "you say you like this one song so we'll give you other songs you like" felt a little like "yeah, right" to me. But modern live radio wasn't proving interesting to me anymore, and I liked the idea of being exposed to new things, so I figured why not? The first thing I was asked after confirming my new account was to "create a station," and to do that I had to select a song or artist I enjoyed so it could find more things like that. That was a really interesting question I hadn't quite been prepared to answer. What *do* I want to hear more of? I like Journey, but do I want a radio station dedicated to arena anthems? I like The Beatles, but will a 60s rock station have any staying power for me? I like a bit of 80s and 90s pop, but will that actually expose me to much of anything new?

In the end, I made what in hindsight was one of the most important musical decisions of my life. I told the service to build me a station around the song 'Funeral for a Friend / Love Lies Bleeding' by Elton John. My parents both liked Elton John and I'd heard a fair bit of his music, liking almost all of it. Great piano rock stuff. Yet this song had captured me in a different, deeper way. For one thing, it's eleven minutes long, and the first half of it is entirely instrumental. It runs through multiple moods with an arrangement covering a lot of different sounds...it is, in a word, "progressive," though that wasn't really a word in my musical vocabulary at the time. And then the second half was this exquisitely-arranged *jam* of a song; thumping piano rock, melodic guitar solos, intricate bass work, outstanding vocal harmonies, and again a range of sounds and moods. In my mind, this was a totally unique thing in the world of music, utterly captivating start to finish. "Give me more songs like *that*. Do any even exist?"

It took a bit of time. Through selectively "liking" or "disliking" tracks, I was refining the station's perception of my musical taste and driving it towards discovery of other music in this vein, though I got a wide variety of other great stuff along the way as well. My routine at the time was that I'd boot up World of Warcraft, mute the game, turn on this station, and do some mindless in-game tasks so I could just enjoy the music. At one point, a song came on that I didn't recognise, though I knew Phil Collins' voice instantly. The station listed it as 'Old Medley (Live)' from Genesis. I wasn't too keen on hearing live versions of familiar songs on this station, given that I traditionally preferred studio renditions unless I was physically at the concert myself, but this was new and unique, and I'd always liked Genesis growing up. By this point in my life I knew all their hits and could recognise a few album cuts as well here or there, so I figured eh, I'll leave it on. At nearly twenty minutes long, something interesting was bound to happen, right?

The opening bit (what I'd later learn was called 'Dance on a Volcano') felt was pretty good even though it didn't leave a tremendous impression on me right away, but then came 'The Lamb Lies Down on Broadway', and hey, I knew that one! Then another bit I didn't recognise (the end section of 'The Musical Box'), though it sounded pretty strong, with a big "Wow" moment at the end. Then off into a keyboard solo...that's pretty good I guess, cool drumming too. And that's when my musical life really changed. Because after that keyboard solo wound down, I heard a guitar solo that made me stop everything else I was doing and just kind of go, "Whoa...." for a while. The medley then proceeded on without me, into some other riff-focused bit I didn't recognise, touching lightly as well upon a number of other songs with which I was half-familiar. Yet I was left behind, still running that guitar solo over in my head. I had to know what in the world I'd just heard. So I pulled up a browser and searched for this 'Old Medley' to find its component parts, eventually learning that both the guitar section and the preceding keyboard solo were from an early 70s tune called 'Firth of Fifth'.

"Well that's a ridiculous name."

> **Tony:** *There's a river in Scotland called the Forth, and the word for a delta or inlet in Scotland is a "firth." So, it's known as the Firth of Forth. It's sort of north of Edinburgh. So, I thought, forth, fifth, you know, 'Firth of Fifth'. We're talking about the early '70s here, so it was a little bit pretentious, in a way. But it's quite a fun title. It's totally untranslatable, of course, so I'm always getting these questions from Germans and French people asking, "What does it mean?" It*

sounds more profound than it is because it was supposed to be just a slight joke, really, as a title. [117]

So I hunted for the song. Back then YouTube wasn't replete with music and I didn't really have any ability to pull it up on-demand anywhere, but perseverance tinged with a dash of piracy was a powerful combination back in the lawless Double-Naughts. Somehow I managed to locate this track, download it, and eagerly play it in its entirety. And man, even with that taste from the 'Old Medley', I had no idea what I was getting myself into.

Listen to that classical piano intro and try to work out the time signature. See if you can count a consistent beat throughout. Then after you've failed miserably, come back here.

Back? Great. It was, of course, a trick: you can't count the 'Firth of Fifth' intro. It's a monstrosity of different time signatures all cobbled together, just waiting for Tony's jolt of lightning and shout of "IT'S ALIVE!" to begin lumbering around the castle dungeon. It's 2/4 that goes into a 4/4 that's actually functionally more like a 16/16, then back to 2/4 only to transition into 13/16 followed by some 15/16 stuff as well. And if you, like me, had a bit of trouble following that in prose, imagine doing so on stage with an instrument. I mean, I'd heard this stuff in the synth solo in the 'Old Medley', but with the full band playing it didn't really register for me how enormously complex it was. Now, hearing this stuff played on an unaccompanied grand piano in the song's intro, I was just overwhelmed by this indescribable feeling: "WHAT?!"

> **Tony:** *I just played it on a piano. It was kind of difficult at the time. I remember in the studio we were in, it was very difficult to get the noise of the pedal out of the way, so I tried to play it without the pedal, which was a bit difficult to do because it's not the easiest thing to play. But it was something I'd written and developed. I had this sort of arpeggio idea that I was working with. I'd written another piece which used a similar feel, which we never ended up using, and I just had this section of it, which I then developed and made this piece of. I thought it worked really well as a piano piece on its own, and then it worked well with an arrangement, as well. So, it's just one of those things. With Genesis, we just did what appealed to us, really. We didn't worry too much how other people were going to respond to it. It was a fun thing to do. It's a difficult thing to play live because, at the time, I didn't have a real piano. I tried to play it on the electric piano and that was quite difficult. I don't think it ever really sounded very good, but it was fun to try.* [117]

It's a shame that a mix of sound quality concerns and logistic issues prevented this intro from being played live until it was too late in their careers to do the song in full anyway, because that piano intro carries a LOT of water for setting the stage for everything to come. At this point in my initial listen to the full studio track I knew that I'd likely hear this absurdly complex melody again in synth form, and I knew that juicy guitar bit was going to show up later, but I had no idea how I'd get there. Yet I had a sense from hearing this piano intro that the rest of the song was going to measure up just fine.

The piano intro concluded, but by "concluded" I really mean "the band exploded in on a huge chord" as Peter began singing the opening lines. "Oh, that's right, Peter Gabriel was in this band, wasn't he?" The lyrics he was singing didn't seem to mean much to me. Some decent turns of phrase like "And so with gods and men // the sheep remain inside their pen // though many times they've seen the way to leave." That's a good bit! What it means I couldn't really tell you, but it certainly sounded profound at the time! And these words were being well-delivered by a voice with an unusual quality to it that made the whole thing somehow more mysterious. Even so, there didn't seem to be much conceptually tying these various phrases together. And...did he just say "cancer?"

> **Tony:** *We were a bit stuck for an idea for a lyric. We started off writing very simply about a river, then the river became a bit more...a river of life. You know, it's quite allegorical and I don't think it's our most successful lyric. I've always been a bit disappointed with the lyric on that. It's a great piece of music but it's a pity we didn't get a better lyric. I don't think it says very much. We tried a bit too hard. It just didn't come, whereas the other one we wrote on the album, 'Cinema Show', we were much more pleased with. There we had a specific idea to aim for.* [31]

Nevertheless, it's all pretty compelling, and oooh, "undinal" is a fun word. Sirens' cry? So is this song actually nautically themed then? I think I can dig that. Oh hey, a flute! That was unexpected. This is really good, really haunting. Pretty and understated but totally entrancing. Ohhhhh like a siren! I get it now!

Tony: *With 'Firth of Fifth' I was pretty pleased with that at the time, I have to say. Because you had lots of bits in it... My favourite bit really is what was a flute solo. And I'd really just seen it done like that, just flute and piano.* [43]

Steve: *As the melody starts to move and it starts to weave upwards and duck downwards...it's got lots of bendy notes in it. Slightly oriental sounding, slightly sort of French-impressionist-Erik-Satie-type melody stuff. Originally Tony played it on piano and I thought, "It's a very interesting sketch, but we need to flesh this out." When you first hear that melody, Peter Gabriel plays it on flute along with the piano... I think there's something very poignant about the melody. I don't know...it seems to touch people. In fact my mother, whenever she comes to a gig, she says, "It always makes me cry, that thing."* [45]

Then this piano bit again picking up tempo - man, this is really getting going now! And then, ahhhhh I know this! It's that synth solo from the live medley! But wow, I hadn't heard just how crazy that drumming is before, or picked up at all on those oscillating guitar sounds. This is really something else!

Steve: *And then you get a recapitulation of the solo piano thing that starts the thing out; it becomes a synth solo. Fast and furious drum and bass happening from Mike and Phil.* [45]

Tony: *[This album was] the first time I ever used a synthesizer as well. So it was quite a big move for me to have this instrument, this ARP Pro Soloist thing, which was quite a simple monophonic synthesizer, but it had quite a nice little range of tones on it. And it was one you didn't have to do any programming; just pre-set sounds, which was nice for me. Obviously 'The Cinema Show' is very much based on that, but I used it throughout the album on little bits and pieces and it was a really interesting addition to the armoury. In these days it was organ, piano, and Mellotron. To have something alternative to play lead on like this opened up possibilities for me... When the synthesizers came in it just opened up the keyboard world so much.* [3]

But oooh, hearing all this crazy synth solo stuff means that guitar solo has got to be coming up next, right? Right???

Tony: *I think it's the most successful all-round song on Selling England by the Pound. It's a very romantic song. It builds to a climax with the guitar solo - which recalls an earlier flute theme - with masses of Mellotron.* [31]

Peter: *Steve definitely I think gained in confidence and 'Firth of Fifth' is very much a Tony piece, in terms of how it started and how it built. But Steve did let loose in I think probably the best way up to that point, at the end.* [3]

Steve: *I tend to come alive when I think of Selling England... I think I was able to infuse that album with the enthusiasm of a player and as an interpreter on, for instance 'Firth Of Fifth'. Basically the whole song was Tony's baby from beginning to end, apart from the lyric which he co-wrote with Mike. [Yet] the thing that people mentioned about that song was the guitar solo, which is my most well known solo really, and really that interpretation of that melody played legato with all that anguish.* [30]

To my great surprise, the guitar sounded...different somehow. It wasn't just the fact that there were twenty or so years between the recordings, either. No, the version I'd heard in that medley was a dazzling technical display, flooring me with its great melody but also the pyrotechnics of the player. This? This wasn't that.

Steve: *I play it at a deathly slow speed. Funereal speed. As a colonial guitarist it's different for Daryl. Seriously, to play someone else's part is almost impossible. I understand his need to play it differently. It is very difficult to play exactly the same notes as someone else... I think these things for musicians are not sacred. Somebody has always to give something of themselves.* [42]

And yet that realisation didn't bring with it a sense of disappointment. I may have missed a couple small embellishments, sure, but the passage nevertheless gave me the same goosebumps as before. I was still completely enthralled by what I was hearing. A little confused, I suppose, but enthralled nonetheless. I did a bit more digging on it later; ah, this was a fellow named Steve Hackett who used to play with the band but had left, meaning the 'Old Medley' recording featured a different player. That did explain things satisfactorily.

My excitement didn't abate there though with the first hearing of the Hackett version of the solo; I still had a whole minute of song left! And...it's another verse, eh? Yeah, that works. Sounds good, sort of repeats that line about gods and men and sheep I liked. "The sands of time were eroded by the river of constant change." Oh now that *is* good. Maybe all these words did actually mean something more and I just need to listen to them better, or perhaps have the lyrics beside me next time I play the song. Mental note created.

And then a grand piano outro, fading out gently. What a pleasant little bow to put on this terrific musical package.

> **Phil:** *It came to life on the [Trick of the Tail] tour. It really got a great audience reaction whereas before…'Cause the ending is quiet and people would sit around waiting for somebody else to clap. Maybe it was because everybody knew it by the time of the last tour...And with two drummers it just seemed to happen.* [31]

Alone with my thoughts at the conclusion of the song, I could only think one thing. "Man...that guitar solo though. This song was nice, but that guitar solo..."

> **Steve:** *Many have always found this solo hugely moving and I feel that playing slowly over strong bass and drums can be very powerful.* [70]

"...I'm a play it again."

I found myself deeply impressed once again by how intricate the piano work was. I paid closer attention to the lyrics; did the verses make more sense now? Hang on, who is the "he" who's riding majestic? What scene of death are they talking about? Oh, not a mishearing: they really did say "cancer growth." Gross.

> **Tony:** *Mike and I wrote the lyric together, although it was mainly me - I won't put too much of the blame on Mike. I don't know really. It was just following the idea of a river and then I got a bit caught up in the cosmos and I don't quite know where I ended up, actually. But, it just about stands up, I think, for the song. For me, musically, it's got two or three really strong moments in it and fortunately they really carried us along. It's become one of the Genesis classics and I'm very happy for that.* [117]

OK, I'll just set that minor wave of disgust aside and focus on the upcoming instrumental middle again...oh! That's a guitar or something doing an actual siren wail! I didn't even catch that before. That's really cool! Super clever touch.

> **Tony:** *Steve I think was really starting to find his feet a bit more as a player, and live and everything. And also he always contributed…A lot of Genesis music obviously required a sort of guitar, acoustic guitar picking and stuff, but people notice it less, I think. People tend to notice lead playing a little bit more.* [3]

> **Steve:** *With the show I am doing at the moment [my solo band] decided to do a full-length version...of 'Firth of Fifth' rather than just the guitar solo. It is arguably Genesis' best-known guitar tune, and it is a damn good song there that isn't heard. I don't think even Genesis do that anymore, and maybe they never will. I do enjoy a lot of these songs in their entirety. The fact that I left the band doesn't mean to say that I am not, in spirit at least, one with many of those tunes. I still love them, for what it's worth.* [42]

Hey, wait a second! That flute melody is the same as that guitar solo melody! That's fantastic! This song is like three distinct sections but they all get done in different ways! What a brilliant approach to the music! How did they even figure out that they should combine them all like this?

> **Tony:** *I had these three bits I'd written, which I originally assumed would go into three different songs. But I think, probably because the others wanted my stuff sort of [shoved into] a kind of Banks ghetto, they all ended up in the same song, which ended up being 'Firth of Fifth'. I really just strung the three bits together; well, made sense of them in a way to make them good.* [3]

Phil: *'Firth of Fifth' was one of those things where Tony just sort of, you know...we'd all get together to play each other our bits, of which he had hundreds. Mike had quite a few and Peter had a few. And we'd be steamrollered into playing 'Firth of Fifth'.* [3]

Tony: *It was pieced together with the whole group around so it was one of those things where the group arrangement is quite important. There were three separate sections and it was Mike's idea to put them together. I was thinking of keeping them separate, but they worked very nicely together. I'd offered some of it at the time of Foxtrot and Phil found it very difficult to play on it - this one part of it - so we dropped the idea. I'm glad we did 'cause I developed it a lot better. I think it was great to be told "no" at that point and produce something a lot better as a result of it.* [31]

This thing works really, really well as a flute melody too. I guess they probably came up with this wicked guitar solo and some genius figured out "it could probably work scaled down on flute, too," and then they actually did that! So cool.

Tony: *The way the guitar solo evolved was quite interesting really. Because I'd written the three bits, and the second bit I'd written was just really a flute and piano melody. I'd just seen it as that. We played it a few times and it sounded really nice. And then one time Steve started playing it, you know. Started playing it [big] like this. I thought, "Well, great! Let's put the Mellotron in, big chords!" It was almost like a joke. We were kinda doing this sort of "a la King Crimson" is how we saw it. Just this overblown thing. And I thought, "That actually sounds really good, this!" So for the reprise of that melody when it came in the second half of the song, we said, "Well, let's do it this big way. See how it works." And it worked really well. It gave a chance for Steve to actually do a sort of proper guitar solo.* [3]

Steve: *On keyboard I thought it sounded a bit sketchy, but I felt its potential and tried it on my trusty Gold Top Les Paul... I altered the melody and bent notes to give extra emotional resonance, which had the effect of sounding slightly Eastern, bringing out the epic nature of the melody again with an orchestral feel.* [70]

Tony: *And so we used that as the sort of peak for the song, and stuck all the other bits in with it. It's just an example of how...If I'd written the song on my own and it had just been credited to me, it would never have done that probably. It needed the whole band there to do the other thing with it. And that's the sort of thing you get out of a group. I think it just leads you places you weren't perhaps otherwise gonna go.* [43]

Well hello again, guitar solo. You're looking lovely this evening. You know, it's OK if it doesn't sound quite as technically impressive as that live rendition. This is actually way more artistic I think. Sounds a lot more like it's "supposed" to sound, if that makes sense. And good grief, he's holding that one note out forever!

Steve: *I was bending all the notes... I remember one or two people said, "It sounds a little bit Indian, almost like a sitar." There was a note that I was able to sustain that would work nine times out of ten. At the top I'd do a high F, and just with proximity to the speaker cabinets, it fed back. So it sounded like I had perfect sustain on every note; I didn't. But I was able to fade in the notes on the beginning of it and sort of wait for it, wait for it, wait for it. Coast over, sort of atmospheric section.* [3]

Ooooof, I'm melting into this sound. Those big chords on the guitar's second run through the main melody. That deep bass. It's a guitar solo, but the guitar isn't even what makes it so strong! It's everything else. That guitar is just riding on top of it. *Perfectly*.

Steve: *So you have that idea of the song, the whole sort of idea of water; the sea and rivers and all of that. Very Genesis kind of tone poem type stuff. And I was trying to create the idea of a bird in flight. So I held it and made it sustain, and I thought, "Well, this could be a little bit like a seagull over a calm sea." And then it becomes more turbulent... It's just one of those gorgeous melodies.* [45]

So daggone good. Did they play it live in full? I bet they played it live. Probably no fade-out ending there either. I'm a find a live version. Oh, here's one, on some live album called *Seconds Out*. Interesting name, interesting album cover. Let's see what we've got.

> **Tony:** *We're doing 'Firth of Fifth'...and musically it stands up very well... It's a sort of period piece... We're not trying to change the old songs. It's nice in some ways to recreate the era. Because you're playing in a way you don't play now but did play then. It also means that the songs stand up for themselves, the old and the new. But we've always done that you know.* [34]

Aww, no piano intro here. No flute either! Phil Collins singing instead of Peter Gabriel too, but that's fine, I love Phil. Doesn't matter anyway; this still sounds really good! That bass comes through beautifully during the guitar solo. And hey, my embellishments! They're back (or perhaps since this came earlier I ought to say "they're finally here"), but still done really tastefully! It's got that artistic sound and restraint but a bit more technical oomph to go with it. I guess this is actually the best of both worlds! THOSE BIG CHORDS. And man, I didn't notice before, but this thing just rolls on longer than guitar solos typically ever have a right to, doesn't it?

> **Mike:** *Once again it's a nice section. You know, it's about more space. We're taking the main theme from the song and just letting it run for about four minutes, with a lovely guitar solo playing the melody and some lines in between. So we're starting to give sections more space, and more time to sit in one mood rather than move on too fast.* [3]

> **Steve:** *It's kind of become Genesis' most well-known guitar solo. So yeah, I was allowed to play - forever, it seems - this great long guitar solo in the middle of something written by Tony.* [3]

Ooh, the outro! Is it gonna fade out? They can't fade it out live, can they? Yep, nope, they didn't! Oh, that's exquisite. That gentle slowing of the tempo into a final note? Shoot, can we retroactively add that to the studio take?

...I'm a listen to it again.

Come back to me, oh marvellous solo. I shall earn your company by listening to the rest of this music as well, but then with me you shall stay, forever and ever.

> **Tony:** *I suppose on this it was more of a genuine guitar solo. Some of the others were a bit tricksy; he was kind of thinking very hard about every note he played, and so it didn't sort of soar in quite the way that this does. Where I think he allowed himself to have a bit more freedom with it, particularly before the main melody starts; just some really nice little phrases and stuff. So he sounds more like a real guitarist.* [3]

> **Steve:** *Iconic instrumental stuff... It aspires to symphonic rock at its best. I think without the Mellotron, that wouldn't have happened. This is three guitar takes all played back together for the last time around that favourite melody. John Burns, who was engineering at the time, said, "Why don't we just play them all back together?" So I was able to get away with something that's nearly a three minute guitar solo. Unheard of for Genesis back in those days, but I think the whole song is absolutely beautiful. Of course, it's also I think memorable for keyboard players as well. But being a guitarist of course, I have favored the famous guitar moment!* [13]

...Friends, I never did stop hitting that replay button. 'Firth of Fifth' is not only my favourite Genesis song, and not only one of my favourite songs period, but it's the song that broadened my musical horizons. It's the song that taught me what "progressive" means. It's the song that sent me spiraling down into what then felt like a dark, bottomless pit of Genesis material to explore. Well, I've explored that shadowy pit now. I've mustered enough light to identify one hundred ninety-seven individual works of art down here, and I've assembled them into a big pile so I can climb back out. And here, at the peak, is the song that got me into this mess in the first place. I always "liked" Genesis for about as long as I can remember, but 'Firth of Fifth' made me a Genesis fan in earnest.

> **Steve:** *When I play guitar on 'Firth of Fifth' to this day it still feels like flying over a beautiful ocean.* [39]

I'm soaring right beside you, Steve. Every time.

> **Phil:** *'Firth of Fifth' was a big tour-de-force.* [3]

Tony: *This album I think we came together much more as players. We sound convincing as players to a greater extent... There's a bit more technique in there. I always like to think that technique is just another sort of paintbrush, in a way. It's something you can use, and it can be very effective at times. It should never take over. I think with some groups it takes over; it becomes "the technique's the thing." You know, you've got a guitarist who can play so fast that he can't stop doing it. And we're very happy...I'm very happy to just sort of sit down and hold down chords, which I do a lot of the time. And other times, you'd go mad. The contrast works and you just use it [to] illustrate something you want to try to illustrate with a piece of music you're writing. That's the thing. And I think Steve's playing on this was really good. Obviously the 'Firth' solo was a standout moment for his time with us.* [3]

Steve: *The song had an aspect of blues, an aspect of gospel about it. It had something of English church music, but it also had an aspect of something Oriental or Indian, almost. So, it was a fusion of influences. But at the time, we weren't using the word fusion - and we weren't using the word progressive. It would eventually be described as progressive, which was a catch-all phase covering an awful lot of bases. I think it can support [its length] because it's thematic. Basically, it's the same melody played three times with minimal variation. It's done like jazz, with the statement of the theme then you go off and improvise, and then return to the theme. On 'Firth of Fifth', when it comes back it's a larger arrangement. It's the tune as written, then "let's take this to the mountains," to a certain extent.* [79]

The construction is so compelling. 'Firth of Fifth' might be the "Banks ghetto," but it's the interweaving of those three main ideas that make the song as powerful as it is. You've got your intro in Section A, then a verse we can call Section B, followed by a development of B that heads into the third distinct bit, Section C (the flute solo). Then A comes back in a more heavily arranged form, followed by a new flavour of C (melody exploration) rearranged to the guitar, then a proper reprise of C on guitar. C then develops a little bit more, reprises once more, and then finally gives way to another verse, B. Which then itself gives way to the outro, itself another call-back to A. All in all, here's the pattern:

A-B-B-B'-C-A-C'-C-C"-C-B-A

One can very reasonably simplify this, however, by identifying only the changes between the distinct bits themselves, disregarding repeats or developments as separate entities. In which case the construction ends up looking like this:

A-B-C-A-C-B-A

It's a palindrome, you see. Why does 'Firth of Fifth' work so well? It's symmetry in musical form. The first time I heard the song I felt the re-entry of the vocals on another verse after the guitar solo just innately made sense. I felt that way about the piano outro, too. That's not a coincidence; it's pattern recognition. It's one thing to say "here's three pieces of music and we're gonna mash 'em together," but they way they all seamlessly interlock is magnificent. Who knows what may have happened if Tony had been allowed to take the three bits and develop them all out individually as their own songs. Perhaps we might have had triple the progressive rock goodness to enjoy, but somehow I don't think so. It feels like this is the form the music was always meant to take. It feels *right*.

Peter: *Most of our stuff took time, took a few plays to sort of open up to a listener. But if they got it, it would stick around for quite a long time.* [3]

The sands of time may erode, but 'Firth of Fifth' has become a constant in my life. It took me many listens to understand the magic, but only one to be captured by it forever. I hope the magic finds you, as well.

Part II: The Albums

*Overviews of every Genesis studio album,
ranked by personal enjoyment*

15 - From Genesis to Revelation

March 7, 1969

The Art

Perhaps the most famous thing about *From Genesis to Revelation* is its album art. That's a problem, because the only historically notable thing about this cover is the fact that it's so confusingly lousy that record stores filed the album under the religious section where it "died a horrible death," as Peter Gabriel sometimes likes to say. There's a reason reissues went a completely different direction from the original release, displaying early band pictures and such; there's simply nothing here on the initial cover. One imagines that, just as the over-the-top visuals of The Lamb tour inspired the Spinal Tap stage show, the cover of *From Genesis to Revelation* may well have been the inspiration for the iconic scene of that pseudo-band seeing for the first time the censored cover of their album, *Smell the Glove*. It's like, how much more black can this be? And the answer is none. None more black.

The Review

It's a debut so underwhelming that the band doesn't truly consider it their debut at all. Ask any one of Tony, Mike, or Pete about Genesis' first album and they're likely to start talking about *Trespass* before they realise what you meant. Part of that is a stylistic thing; "Genesis music" began in earnest on that second album when they broke out of the shackles of Jonathan King's influence and moved into more adventurous territory. But part of it is a quality thing, too.

I don't think the Genesis lads are particularly proud of *From Genesis to Revelation*, which is something of a shame, because it's still quite the accomplishment in context. Here are thirteen tracks written by teenagers and released on an actual record label. That the record itself could only manage to sell copies at church yard sales isn't the point. Many years ago I was in a small band and we got as far as recording our own debut album. Considering all the costs related to the album's production came straight out of the bandleader's pocket, and people in their early twenties are not typically the wealthiest of folk, budget constraints meant that we ended up having to record in some guy's basement. Granted, this guy had converted his basement into a very functional recording space, and we could have done far worse, but this was not the glam and glitz of heading into a proper recording studio to lay down some tracks, you know?

Even beyond the space constraints, we were on a tight schedule, too. About two days total to record the entire thing; just one day for me, as a vocalist, to get my parts down. No pressure, right? In the end I'd estimate we made about two hundred copies of the album and probably sold a mere thirty. So my point is that for these Genesis guys - younger than I was when I had my own ill-fated recording experience - to have a label behind you, actual studio production, and to be able to get the record into retail storefronts at all is already a tremendous accomplishment. That's more than most aspiring musicians can even dream.

Now, all that said, from a listening point of view, I'm quite a bit less impressed. It's not that I dislike baroque pop, I don't think. Though I suppose I don't have a great way to gauge that claim since I can't say I've made a point to go out and listen to any other examples of the genre. It's just that *From Genesis to Revelation* doesn't quite get there for me. Probably doesn't help that what I view as the album's highlights are the things the band didn't even want in there; I actually tend to like the strings on this album more than anyone in Genesis does, and I think the music starts to shine a bit more when it's at its gentlest and most vulnerable. The album has a number of moments like that which really shine a pleasant light on the proceedings, I think. But there are two sides to the Genesis coin, and while they get the soft stuff mostly right on this album, the hard stuff just doesn't manage to connect with me. That's an unusual opinion among fans, I think; 'In the Beginning' and 'The Serpent' are two tracks I often see cited as the highlights of *From Genesis to Revelation*, but I think they're two of the least successful songs the album has to offer.

All in all, this one has a few soft pieces I genuinely like, a few heavier ones I genuinely don't, and a whole lot of ho-hum in between. I don't ever spin up *From Genesis to Revelation* for the sake of pure listening enjoyment (and I doubt I ever will), but it deserves to be recognised all the same for the achievement that it was at the time, and it deserves to be appreciated for giving Genesis the springboard to do much, much better things afterward.

14 - Abacab

September 18, 1981

The Art

Ah yes, non-descript splashes of colour, that's the ticket. If Genesis had gone the Peter Gabriel route and started self-titling all their albums, it's fair to say they would have gone back to back with records known as *Colours* and *Shapes*. Toss some *Numbers* and *Letters* in there somewhere and you've got a preschool classroom on your hands. Shoot, they even put out multiple versions of the album cover with different colour configurations on each, and you know kids like collecting stuff. Baseball cards, Pogs (remember Pogs?), heck I even collected rocks. *Abacab* might as well be Pokémon: The Album.

That aside, the abstract nature of the cover is actually a perfect match with the album's content; the benefit of a cover that doesn't mean anything is that the album's music is free to imprint its own meaning onto the image without interference. One imagines that's why it was selected, giving cover designer Bill Smith the easiest payday of his life.

> **Bill Smith:** *These boys were quite difficult to design for; they only ever knew what they didn't like. Anyway, Mike Rutherford saw these bits of torn Pantone swatch book colours in my sketchbook… He just said, "I love that"… Ah, those were the days.* [118]

You can't dissect the *Abacab* cover. You can't really consider it as an independent bit of art as you could with some of the band's earlier covers. You just see this image and instantly think of the music, and I suppose that's the point. Not my favourite cover per se, but in that sense it's certainly a successful one.

The Review

Welcome to *Abacab*, the album where everything's made up and the songs don't matter. I'm going to admit here that I've never gotten "into" *Abacab* as a full album listening experience. It just doesn't quite work for me. Interestingly enough, I think that's a symptom or side effect of the album doing exactly what it sets out to do. This is Genesis at their most experimental, pumping out songs that sound foreign, strange, "un-Genesis-like," one after another. This makes each song a kind of adventure in itself; what kooky idea will Genesis come up with next? But to get there the album necessarily sacrifices some conceptual flow-through that would make the whole thing cohere a bit more.

Most Genesis albums are more than the sum of their parts because of this. How many times have we seen or heard someone slag off some song or another out of context only to receive a retort of "Well, you need to listen to it in context of the album"? *Abacab* defies that a little bit; I actually think the songs are better on their own here than they are in sequence. The title track has its own funky synth jazz sort of feel, which works fairly well going into 'No Reply At All' with its initial trumpet punch. But then the piano journey into insanity that is 'Me and Sarah Jane' doesn't *quite* flow from what came before, and the weirdness of 'Keep It Dark' is really something all on its own. 'Dodo/Lurker' is a really strong side opener, but gutting 'Submarine' and 'Naminanu' from it to roll instead into 'Who Dunnit?' Not great! I really like 'Man on the Corner', but what is it doing *here*? And then the last two pieces don't gel much for me either, as individual tunes or as album closers.

So it's an album where Genesis dared to be different, and they managed to do that swimmingly. I don't think *Abacab* is an *unsuccessful* album by any means. It certainly lives up to its mission statement. But between 60% of its second side being bottom roughly bottom quartile Genesis fare for me and the fact that the album doesn't have a flow that I find I can get into, it's not a record I find myself gravitating towards. I'm pretty likely to pop on a song from *Abacab* here and there on its own, but I almost never play through the album in full. More often than not, I'll just put another record on.

13 - Wind & Wuthering

December 17, 1976

The Art

Another triumph of matching musical mood to image, the cover of *Wind & Wuthering* is a bleak thing to look upon. That works well, since everything surrounding the music is bleak, too. 'Eleventh Earl of Mar' about military failure and containing a passage evoking bitter winds; 'One for the Vine' and its doomed battles over frozen wastelands; 'Your Own Special Way' being a wince of a love song; 'Wot Gorilla?' making Steve take his toys and leave; 'All in a Mouse's Night'...poor Tom; 'Blood on the Rooftops' literally opening with the words "dark and grey"; the instrumentals near the end taking their titles from a line in Wuthering Heights about the dead; and then 'Afterglow' where a guy lost his love to a nuclear bomb.

You know, just a little light-hearted sort of thing.

Anyway, if the goal of the album is to put the listener in a melancholy mood, nobody could go to the record shop in the middle of December, see this cover, and not know what they were getting into. Artist Colin Elgie nailed it with his watercolour design.

> **Colin Elgie:** *I thought [Wind & Wuthering] was a great, visual title. Images immediately sprang to mind - Heathcliff, the moors. Around that time, I'd seen a movie on TV called The War Lord with Charlton Heston. Set in medieval England and northern France, it had a scene in it where Heston is by a tree and the birds take flight: that's where the idea came from… I wish I'd done it...with a hint more colour, less monochromatic.* [27]

With respect to Elgie, I disagree that this cover needed more colour. It's a blustery, depressing landscape for a blustery, depressing album. If Bob Ross had been the one to paint this cover, even he wouldn't refer to that little tree as "happy." Though I'm less sure about the band logo/lettering in the top left corner, I think this is a great album cover all the same.

The Review

This is an album of extremes for me, bouncing between ups and downs. But it's got such an intangible restraint about it that the jostling isn't violent. It's less a mechanical bull and more like one of those little toddler horses that you put a penny into. Peaks and valleys undulating gently until the ride comes to a complete stop. Unfortunately, just like those kiddie rides, the most exciting part is the very beginning when the thing first goes into motion, because it hasn't had a chance to disappoint you yet.

The intro to 'Eleventh Earl of Mar' sets up expectations that the rest of the song and indeed the rest of the album itself can't quite deliver on. And yet right after 'Earl' concludes with echoes of "DADDDYYYYYY" still lingering in your ear, you get 'One for the Vine', which is one of the best things Genesis has ever done. Expectations rise once more, only for 'Your Own Special Way' and 'Wot Gorilla?' to dash them against the stony ground of muddled mediocrity. 'All in a Mouse's Night' is almost fun, but then 'Blood on the Rooftops' comes to take your breath away before the end sequence. That sequence is interesting, engaging, and also only worthwhile in the context of 'Afterglow'. Unfortunately, the studio version of 'Afterglow' is blown out of the water by virtually any medley-ending live rendition of the song, so it's hard now for me to go back to *Wind & Wuthering* and not wish I was hearing a different version of the song instead.

> **Tony:** *There was quite a lot of music written beforehand on this album, and I think when we had finished the album, the only thing that worried me a little bit was perhaps the album was...really quite a heavy album. A quite difficult album. But I mean, I like that, you see. I like an album to be challenging. It wasn't an album that was gonna be liked the first time. Apart from possibly 'Your Own Special Way', virtually every other track requires quite a bit of listening to get into. But at that time I think we had people who were prepared to give us the time.* [3]

Tony's point about *Wind & Wuthering* being a very difficult but rewarding album gets a lot of support among Genesis fans, I think. And Steve, too, for what that's worth.

> **Steve:** *Wind & Wuthering was four young guys and all their attendant capabilities at the time and technological limitations – it's magic for the converted listener. It's one of my wife's favourites: it was the first album she heard by Genesis and one of the ones she likes best of all. It got her at the right time – she was 15. She said that this was a band that was able to take you to different worlds and when you're a young listener, you have time to be transported. When you're in it, you don't always understand it – the true owners are not the creators; it's the listener. They hear everything that's working.* [27]

There are many more out there like Steve and his wife, to be sure. But me? I think I'm much more solidly in the Rutherford camp this time around.

> **Mike:** *I get my kicks out of this album, really. There's no central theme to it…* [36]

Wait, no, not that quote. That's something he said while he was making it and thought "no central theme" was actually somehow a positive.

> **Mike:** *It's Tony and Steve's favourite. I'm never as strong on this album. If it's two of the band's favourite album, it probably means that it's not mine. I like it, and the good bits are good, but I think some of the tracks are weak.* [27]

Yeah, there we go. Mike thought this thing was the bee's knees until it was finished, and then in retrospect there's a "Why did we go for that?" kind of mentality. See, for me (and I daresay for Mike as well) the "difficulty" of the album doesn't lie in the complexity of the music, which I can follow well enough, but in the fact that a lot of it just doesn't really speak to me on a deep level. "Some of the tracks are weak." Then on top of that, "there's no central theme to it," so the album doesn't flow very well either. Thus, despite taking the time to "get it" on a musical level, I don't feel particularly rewarded by *Wind & Wuthering*.

Still, it's effective in setting its mood, and does feature a few of the band's greatest songs, so it wouldn't be fair to say I dislike the thing. It's just kind of there, a less desirable listening option by comparison, even if it's not so bad in its own right.

12 - Foxtrot

October 6, 1972

The Art

The cover of *Foxtrot* is an iconic one, I think as a result of two different things: first, the music on the record is very highly regarded among progressive rock fans, and secondly, Peter Gabriel did everything he could to make the cover make any sense at all.

See, it can be easy to get the order of events twisted and believe that *Foxtrot* features an image of a fox lady in a red dress because Pete was donning his wife's dress and a fox's head on stage. The thinking is that the album art is a reference to Genesis' live shows of the era. Thanks to Peter's efforts, that's what it effectively became, but it actually started the other way 'round.

> **Peter:** *On the Foxtrot tour, I had a conversation with Paul Conroy, who was booking gigs for us; he was suggesting that we employ a person to walk around wearing a costume of the character Paul Whitehead had drawn for the album cover, the fox in the red dress, as an extension of the illustration. But then I thought, "Right, I'll try putting that on, I'll see if I can get a fox's head made," because I thought I should be the person dressing up rather than a stunt person.* [1]

Why is this important? Well, because the album art on its own is just needlessly strange. I'm guessing Whitehead heard the line "fox on the rocks" in 'Supper's Ready' and decided that should be the visual focus of the album, which is an utterly bizarre choice given the relatively throwaway nature of that lyric as opposed to all the other strong imagery on the album. Then you put it in the shallows of the ocean on a slab of floating ice? I guess that's a thin reference to 'Can-Utility and the Coastliners', maybe, but then what's up with that tiny whale? The back of the sleeve has an apartment building off in the distance; I suppose that's the reference to 'Get 'Em Out By Friday'. There's four men riding horses, which I think is another loose 'Supper's Ready' reference in being the Four Horsemen of the Apocalypse, but of course the horsemen aren't even mentioned in the song itself. One of those horsemen appears to be an alien: the 'Watcher of the Skies', one might presume. And then, even in the world of the painting, nobody's got any time for 'Time Table'.

So you can see where he was going with all of this and how the album cover is ostensibly an illustration of all its music...but it just doesn't work at all. The art all *references* the music, but none of the art actually *understands* the music, and the result is this array of totally unrelated, meaningless images that ultimately tells you nothing about the music contained within.

It's a pretty drawing, sure, but as an album cover it's frankly just not very effective. If Pete hadn't salvaged some kind of thematic connection by dressing up like this randomly conceived fox lady (note that the art was done before the album was even titled!), it would likely be widely considered one of the band's worst covers.

> **Paul Whitehead:** *Well, the reason [they didn't hire me for Selling England by the Pound] was because I moved to The States. In those days...there wasn't any FedEx, there wasn't any email, we didn't have a lot of the things we have now. Long distance telephone calls were very expensive... So, moving 8,000 miles to California kind of made it very hard to work together.* [119]

Oh, Paul. Paul, Paul, Paul. It wasn't about you moving to California. It was about the fact that this cover is a conceptual mess. Don't believe me? Take it from the band themselves.

> **Peter:** *I was less happy with this sleeve than I was with the first two [by Whitehead]. I think the style was losing some of its appeal to me, even though the fox character I think worked.* [3]

> **Steve:** *When I first saw it I wasn't sure about it, to be honest. If I'm honest, it looked rather like a kind of collage of unlikely things. It looked like a number of cut-outs. Since then I've come to understand the concept of collage a little more, and I think it works. But at the time I thought, "This is just strange," and "Does it work?" And it had this sort of flat, one-dimensional sort of look because it was collage, I suspect.* [3]

Tony: *Well I thought this was the weakest of the album covers he did, certainly at the time. I mean, you come back to it now, it's rather difficult to view it objectively. The mockery of the hunt sort of thing seemed a bit of a cliché and everything. And it was his idea to do what he did, and it doesn't really relate to anything on the album. So it was all a bit of a thing. But we managed to kind of make it make sense by giving the album the title Foxtrot. Helped to kind of rationalise it a little bit. But I think we weren't terribly happy with it, to be honest. It was just one of those things that as a group we weren't that happy with. I know a lot of people think it's good, but not so much for me.* [3]

Mike: *It was OK, but he just put together a bunch of images that were in the lyrics, in a sense. Didn't do it for me. It was a bit weak. And I guess that's why we changed the [artist for] the next one, actually. Trying to move on, in a sense.* [3]

Phil: *For me it was like, getting a little bit busy. I guess that was one of the reasons why...that was the last one that Paul did for us. I just felt, you know, Trespass did have an elegance about it, and Nursery Cryme had more butch, but this was just a bit busy. It didn't look professional, for some reason. The fox's head lady on a bit of ice was it? In the water? It's all a bit dated now. But I mean, it does sum up the album, the period. Straightaway you're there. But what do I think? What DID I think of it? I thought it was OK, but not particularly special.* [3]

That's a unanimous decision: five outta five members of Genesis all agreed. So I'm sorry, Mr. Whitehead, but I'm afraid it's time for you to leave. But if you need to tell yourself it was your move to the United States that did the partnership in, hey: I understand.

The Review

Let's get the obvious out of the way here: *Foxtrot* is typically regarded as one of the band's absolute best albums and a pinnacle of progressive rock in general. That I have it ranked a mere 12th out of their 15 albums (behind *Calling All Stations*, HARUMPH HARUMPH!) probably merits some kind of severe flogging in a lot of people's eyes. I'm way lower on this album than almost any other Genesis fan I've met. Why is that?

I think it's because there's just a lot going on with nearly every song. Tony said *Wind & Wuthering* was one of their most difficult albums, but I think *Foxtrot* might be even more so (Tony Banks is, at least, a consistent fellow and cites *Foxtrot* as his favourite of the early albums). You've got the big, grand opening of 'Watcher of the Skies' which I adore, but that then goes into a complex rhythm pattern with a melody that jolts like a car on a bumpy road with no shock absorbers. 'Time Table' is nice but even at under five minutes goes to a few different places, so it's not quite a palate cleanser; it still demands some listening attention. From there into 'Get 'Em Out by Friday', a script-like dialog where Pete rapidly shouts lines at the listener, changing characters all along the way. 'Can-Utility and the Coastliners', like 'Time Table', is *almost* a respite but still does enough to demand attention.

It's not until you flip the album over to its second side that you get anything like a breather in 'Horizons', which is lovely and wonderful and lasts for under two minutes before you're tossed into the twenty-three minute apocalyptic fires of 'Supper's Ready'. *Foxtrot* demands a *lot* from its listeners, and while there are times I'm happy to give it - this album does get semi-regular play from me - usually I just find myself feeling that it's, well, "a bit too busy."

What really doesn't help its case is the availability of other, better versions of the tracks. 'Watcher' I vastly prefer in its non-vocal form on *Three Sides Live*, where it sits as the rousing finale to a show. 'Supper's Ready' I greatly prefer from *Seconds Out* where they've had time to refine their playing to near-perfection. If I actually liked 'Get 'Em Out By Friday' I could listen to that on *Genesis Live*. So that leaves 'Time Table', which I enjoy but won't ever go out of my way to hear, the solid 'Can-Utility', and the beauty of 'Horizons' as my main reasons to spin up *Foxtrot* proper. And I suppose those reasons just aren't quite as compelling for me as they are to most others.

In the end, I don't dislike the album, but it's this non-stop barrage of complicated music with only middling audio quality, and that can make it a chore to get through. Sometimes I'm all too happy to take that task on; often I'd rather go a different direction instead.

11 - Genesis

October 3, 1983

The Art

The self-titled album is a tricky thing to illustrate, isn't it? Maybe you go with a picture of yourselves in order to show the world who you are. Maybe instead you opt for a visual rendition of your band name to accomplish the same thing. Maybe sometimes the band name is the announcement in itself and you can get away with any old art you want to put on there. Or maybe you just go for a sea serpent because that's universally cool.

Regardless, self-titled albums tend to have one thing in common; they're almost always debuts, or at least come very early in a band or artist's career. This helps a lot with shorthand, because when we talk about albums it gets verbally confusing to constantly differentiate between a band and the album of the same name *by* that band. Kicking off a career with a self-titled effort simultaneously announces your existence to the buying public, and also gives everyone an easy means to talk about you: until you release a second album, that initial one is just "the" album, and afterward it's forever appellated "the debut." Clean, simple, effective.

But what if the self-titled album comes later in the career? What if it happens well after everybody already knows who you are? Well now that's just boundlessly confusing, isn't it? What is a fandom to do? The answer, of course, is to look at the art and make up a name based on that. Come on down, The White Album. A fine how-do-you-do, The Wedding Album (Duran Duran). So glad you could make it, Melt (Peter Gabriel). These are interesting, compelling images that convey something about the artist and/or the music contained within the album itself - yes, even a purely white album speaks volumes about The Beatles' state of mind at the time. They're statements of "This is who we are at this point in time, and we stand behind this music, and it matters to us." It's album art that has something to say that transcends a title.

And then, over here, we've got Genesis playing with Shape-O, the toddler toy from everyone's favourite thinly-veiled pyramid scheme, Tupperware. Other than giving the album its colloquial alternate title in the States (my understanding is that most fans in the UK refer to it instead as "*The Mama Album*" in recognition of its opening track), the cover art for "*Shapes*" doesn't provide its album with anything valuable whatsoever. There is no common thread being tugged between the art and the music. The shapes themselves are meaningless. You could attempt to draw a giant metaphor between the band writing every song as a trio for the first time and thus being a situation where their "individual shapes" all join together at last, but you'd be wrong for doing so.

Distance yourself, if you can, from the associations the art makes in your mind with your opinions of the songs themselves, and I'm sure you'll agree: this is a pretty rotten cover.

> **Mike:** *The Genesis cover was, I think, probably our worst cover. That was well dodgy, actually, I think...the kids' bricks. I remember that one really, it was a moment like "The album's gotta come out, we've got a tour coming up, here are the choices. Which one do you dislike the least?" And that was it. Not a great cover.* [3]

> **Tony:** *The inspiration was very lacking, I think, on this thing. I don't know, we used the guy Bill Smith who had done the previous album, the Abacab album, which we thought was a great cover. We really liked that a lot. And this one, it was just...we were a bit stuck for ideas. And he'd got this photo we looked at, and in a lot of ways it was quite interesting, but then when we actually put it on the album we thought, "Oh, we don't think this is very good." And we always tried to do a last-minute sort of change of the cover. But in the end it's just become...it's just a cover, I suppose. But it's not a classic one. The idea seemed better than the result. Put it like that.* [3]

The Review

The classic complaint about this album is that it's a tale of two sides. You've got the epic, immense quality of Side A on the one hand, and then a Side B that sounds like they were running thin on ideas and just going with whatever they could to fill space. I don't exactly agree with that assessment, but I can pretty easily understand where it's coming from. Side A is four songs that really ought to be three songs, once the two 'Homes by the Sea' get properly merged into a single track. It's a journey that embarks from the otherworldly pop/rock/prog of 'Mama', into the impeccable piano pop of 'That's All', into the masterful rock/prog jam of 'Home by the Sea'. If you're putting this on in 1983 not sure what you're going to get from your favourite band, this Side A was pretty much your best case scenario.

And then a cheesy song about immigration concerns in the United States? Nevermind that its lyrical content is irredeemable in this day and age; even at the time when it was considered just a goofy bit of fun, 'Illegal Alien' felt a little out of place with the tone the album's first side had established. 'Taking It All Too Hard' gets back to the solid 'That's All' mode for a little bit, so it feels like it fits a bit more, but then 'Just a Job to Do' is a straight-up 80s rock song. I like it quite a bit, but on this album instead of, say, *No Jacket Required*? I'm not so sure. 'Silver Rainbow' wanders back into a heavy kind of feel, and then 'It's Gonna Get Better' ends things on something of a whimper for me.

I don't think it's fair to say Side B of *Genesis* doesn't have any good music on it, but I do think it's fair to say it doesn't deliver quite as strongly as Side A, and as a result the album can sometimes feel like it should've been called *Diminishing Returns*. It sort of bounces back and forth between gritty urban sprawls and whimsical fare, and while at first it seems like that'll be able to work, by the end it's clear that it didn't quite manage. I think it needed to go all-in on one or the other mood, probably with additional material to flesh out any gaps, and leave the other for a quick follow-up album or perhaps EP. That would've allowed things to fully coalesce, but alas - Phil had hits to go write.

10 - Calling All Stations

September 1, 1997

The Art

You know, first impressions are strong forces, and so are the connections we form between the things we hear and the things we see. This is why music videos became so big and influential. Once the first few were out the door, everyone else began pouring their time, money, and attention into them as well. It was the single most effective way to get a song permanently ingrained into a customer's consciousness. I'll give you an example: go play the audio for Devo's 'Whip It' and try not to think about red pyramid hats and strange men in black tank tops on a dude ranch. It's all but impossible, despite the fact that the song's lyrics have absolutely nothing to do with any of that. Once we have a visual, we latch onto it and associate a piece of music to it for the rest of our days. We can't help it.

Album covers do the same thing, albeit on a somewhat smaller scale. Go into a record shop and you might have an idea of the *kind* of thing you want, but it might well be the album cover that jumps out and speaks to you that earns your purchase. You could pick up an LP (or cassette/CD) and already you'd be forming ideas of how this album might sound. That could be an exciting, "I've *got* to hear this!" kind of impression; it could also be a "This looks like a total waste of time" impression.

Which takes us to *Calling All Stations* and its Windows 95, Microsoft Word clip art image of a man peeing into a dark pool. Look, I get the intent here. This is a guy, all by his lonesome, trying to get a signal out to anyone who might hear it. He's wearing a coat and he's got his hands in his pockets and his head down, because it's cold out there when you've no one else in sight. The blue circles are emanating from him directly, as he's the one who is "calling all stations" with his desperate broadcast. Then you've got the album title surrounded by ellipses and shrinking into the distance, like the pulses of a radio signal. The cover figure is essentially the radio antenna. It's a pretty good idea, honestly, and it lines up well with the lyrics of the album's title track.

And yet... the cover itself just doesn't work in the slightest, does it? The solid black background is meant to highlight isolation, but instead just looks lazy. The primary figure and his blue circles similarly look like they were created with minimal effort, and though you can get the intent if you think about it, it's not an obvious thing. Add to that the orange band name with its distorted and stretched letters - what's that supposed to represent, if anything? - and things really fall apart. Look, blue and black are the primary colours you're going for on this cover, in an effort to visualise loneliness. *Lean into that* and make the "Genesis" logo blue, too! Does that single colour change make it a *good* album cover? No, not at all. But it does give it a consistent mood, which is itself consistent with the album's themes. So it's a *better* cover. The orange text might pop off the label more, sure, but it muddies the message.

Anyway, this cover stinks. The album itself though?

The Review

Calling All Stations sits in a sort of compressed range for me. It's got a higher floor than most Genesis albums: what I consider its worst song still resides in the decent-to-good area for me. But it's also got a lower ceiling: my favourite song I'd only consider "great," as opposed to the larger superlatives that could be heaped upon the truly best-of-the-best in Genesis canon. Thus, pretty much the entire album I tend to regard as having pretty good quality. That in itself is almost a sin among some fans to say; even considering the entirety of my wide array of unusual/unpopular opinions about this band's catalogue, nothing in my experience has resulted in more incredulous pushback than the fact that I actually dig a lot of the songs from this late 90s effort. Should it really be that shocking? I wonder if it's just a matter of how we receive the information.

If I met a typical Genesis fan on the street and told him or her that I actually liked *Calling All Stations*, the response might be one of mild surprise, but probably also ready acceptance. If I said to someone, "I like *Calling All Stations*, but there are at least thirty Genesis songs I like better than even my favourite song from that album," I expect the response would go something like this: "...Yeah." But of course, if you change the presentation in such a way as to say "I think the worst song from *Calling All Stations* is still better than 'The Return of the Giant Hogweed'," you're liable to see a fight break out. That's a shame, because *Calling All Stations* does have a lot to offer, even though it's far from perfect.

Ultimately I've already written quite a bit about *Calling All Stations* as an actual album back in the previous section of this book, and especially in the entry for 'The Dividing Line'. To sum up my contention from that essay, I see *Calling All Stations* as a kind of loose "theme" album (not quite at the "concept" level), built around thoughts of unwilling solitude, inner turmoil, and an overarching radio metaphor tying it all together. And then I also believe the track listing is totally out of order because Mike and Tony were too timid to follow through on the vision of escalating the album's power track by track, dialling up the amp from 1 to 11, as it were. I still find *Calling All Stations* to be completely listenable and enjoyable in its official form - rare in itself perhaps - but I think the album that it was meant to be is stronger than the album it became.

Regardless, I find the bottom half the album to be "better than bad" and the other half to be "very strong," so it lands just inside my top ten Genesis albums even despite my issues with the track order. Any album with zero clunkers earns that right. Naturally, I say that knowing many of you will disagree that it has zero clunkers, but ah well. You can't please everyone. And speaking of not pleasing everyone...

> **Mike:** *Ray Wilson did a good job as the vocalist but he wasn't a writer. Without a third writer, there was no one to glue Tony and me together; we didn't have anyone to pull us back into the middle ground, the centre of the musical Venn diagram. I'd never been aware before of quite how far apart Tony and I were musically until this album. It only hit me then that Phil was the one who had reined us both in, took what we did best and found a setting for it...Tony and Ray were keen to carry on but I knew we'd have had to bring in another writer. To me it felt right to just stop there - no real harm done.* [14]

This bit of reasoning is just so sad to me. With an extensive post-Genesis solo career, it feels pretty evident that Ray *was* a writer. The problem was that he didn't get hired on until after virtually all the writing was done, so to hold his lack of writing credits on *Calling All Stations* against the guy is a bit ridiculous. Could Ray have been that bridge Mike and Tony needed in the writing room? Maybe not, but he didn't even get a chance, in large part because Mike was too afraid of failure to give him one. What a bummer!

9 - ...And Then There Were Three...

March 31, 1978

The Art

Often cited as not only one of the worst Genesis album covers but also one of the worst covers designed by renowned firm Hipgnosis for any band, the art for *And Then There Were Three* is a mishmash of ideas and images that don't really seem to ever make any sense. Sleeve designer and all-time metal name Storm Thorgerson explains the attempt.

> **Storm Thorgerson:** *That [cover]'s a failure. We were trying to tell a story by the traces left by the light trails. It was a torch, a car, and a man with a cigarette. The band was losing members and there were only three of them left. The lyrics of the songs were about comings and goings and we tried to describe this in photographic terms by using time-lapse. So there's a car going off to one side and then the guy gets out of the car, walks over to the front of it, and lights a cigarette. But as he walks he uses a torch and the car he was in leaves. There's a trail left by the car, a trail left by him as he's walking and then he lights a cigarette, which on the cover is where there's a flash of his face.* [120]

Time-lapse to reflect comings and goings, and especially to highlight the reduction of the band's size while referencing the album's title...these are all actually pretty good ideas. Where did it go wrong? For one thing, the positioning is all out of order. You've got the guy driving a car happening first, but that's on the far right side, the opposite of the natural reading direction for Westerners. Then the second thing is the guy walking with a flashlight (torch), but that's happening on the far left, so even if we start in the correct place we still can't track this thing in a straight line. Finally, the guy lights a cigarette for some reason, and that happens in the centre. Add in the time lapse effects and now, especially because of the way the images are sequenced, it looks like three different guys: one is driving away, one is smoking, and one is casting Fire2 on a party of enemy sahuagin.

Now add to that the utter strangeness of the logo. Consider that Genesis had been cycling through band logo fonts on a per album basis after the dismissal of Paul Whitehead following *Foxtrot*. They went straight font for *Selling England by the Pound*, angular stretch font for *The Lamb Lies Down on Broadway*, "thick-and-thin" classical font for *A Trick of the Tail*, and then a similar "thick-and-thin" for *Wind & Wuthering*, albeit in vertical orientation in a cross pattern over the album title. So what's the new style for *And Then There Were Three*?

"Well, you see, it's the same font we used on *The Lamb*, except this time it's getting eaten by green slime."

Look, I can't defend these things, and I won't try. What I will say is what I've said before in the previous section of this book: when you ignore the lettering and you ignore the bottom half of the sleeve with the failed time lapse experiment, you're left with an image of a tumultuous sky, purple and orange, roiling with dark clouds. And I can't think of any visual that better matches the actual sound of this album than that.

> **Tony:** *Well I think for one reason or another we weren't very happy with the And Then There Were Three cover. We just felt it didn't really do much. It was a bit nebulous and everything. We were a bit stuck for ideas, and I don't think Hipgnosis came up with their best idea for that, really. It sort of has a character to it because you relate it to the album now, really. But the album was a bit more straightforward and quite fresh. It's got a very gloomy, dark cover. I think you could've had something a bit more "up."* [3]

The Review

A successful album is about much more than simply the quality of its individual songs, though that's obviously a critical factor. No, a successful album finds a certain kind of mood, or flavour. It takes you on a journey through its songs like a scenic train ride in a lush musical landscape. It flows naturally from piece to piece from beginning to end, so that the real "piece" was the album itself all along. That's what the best albums do.

And Then There Were Three isn't one of the best albums. Not in my opinion, at any rate. But it does do something none of my previously ranked albums have managed: it finds a coherent and consistent sound. Some people love that sound. Some people can't stand it. I'm somewhere in between, though leaning more towards "love" than "hate." When I turn on this album, I know I'm getting into sweeping, smeary synth tracks and a loud, hazy kind of feel. That's this record's niche, and it delivers on that promise track after track. There's no other Genesis album that sounds quite like *And Then There Were Three*, though an individual song here or there might borrow its mission statement from time to time. It's a uniquely enjoyable experience, if you like that sort of thing and/or find yourself in the right kind of headspace.

So then why do I rate it only ninth among Genesis albums? Well, for me, it's the song flow. Not that the tracks need to be reordered or anything, but rather that a couple of these tracks simply don't work at all in the first place. 'Ballad of Big' is an awful song in my book, and despite the fact that 'Undertow' and 'Snowbound' would work perfectly going one right into the other, 'Ballad of Big' is sitting right there in between them sticking its tongue out at the listener, making sure there's no chance of getting properly lost in the music along the way. It's almost infuriating. I'm not a huge fan of 'Scenes from a Night's Dream' either, but at least that song *sounds* like it belongs on the record, you know?

'Say It's Alright Joe' similarly pulls me out of the overall mood of things, and I'm also not terribly fond of that one, but by that point in the album I've begun to lose my investment in it anyway. It's a real shame, because 'The Lady Lies' swings right back into what *Three* is all about, and 'Follow You Follow Me' ends things with a lovely little beauty of a song, even if its flanged guitar basis feels almost-but-not- quite foreign to the album's sound itself. At 53+ minutes, *And Then There Were Three* isn't egregiously long, but nevertheless I think it really could've used some addition by subtraction.

8 - Invisible Touch

June 6, 1986

The Art

Let's talk about that hand, shall we? I think it's pretty safe to say that the hand itself is meant to represent the titular concept of an invisible touch. Right?

> **Mike:** *I remember thinking the album cover was a bit dodgy, actually. I wasn't convinced by it. I'm still not, really. I mean, the hand works OK with the title Invisible Touch and the hand...just about gets away with it. But looking back it's not a great album cover.* [3]

> **Tony:** *I always liked the idea of the invisible touch. Obviously in the [song] it's all about a girl, but "invisible touch" is also quite a nice way to describe music. So you've got this hand on the front which is coming out to touch you. I think we all thought that was quite an effective thing. The resultant effect I don't think is particularly beautiful, but it's quite distinctive. If you saw it in a shop you'd go, "Oh, it's there!" You know, instantly recognisable. And again, it works pretty well in the CD format, because it's small and distinctive. So it's one of those examples of a good piece of graphic art without being particularly beautiful.* [3]

All right, so yes: the band felt good about the idea of a hand emerging from the album to touch the listener and the metaphor that represents. And indeed, I've seen altered images people have made of this cover, inspired by that concept, showing this hand in more detail. But here's the issue: look at which side that thumb is on. If the hand is emerging out of the album toward you, the person holding it, then must be someone's right hand, yeah?

OK, now look at the wrist and the little bit of forearm beyond it. A right hand, open with palm facing you, cannot possibly have a wrist/arm at that angle unless its poor owner has been badly mangled. The only way that arm angle makes sense is for the hand to actually be a *left* hand, facing *inward* as though someone was laying their hand upon the album itself. And if that's the case, then what's even the point of this deep metaphor? Nothing is coming out to touch us at all! It's just a hand!

So it's important at this point to note the other element of the album art that I somehow never managed to parse for multiple decades until very recently: within that green patterned background (purple through the hand's own translucence) is a grey shape or two. And honestly, at a glance? They looked like guns to me. Maybe a James Bond style silenced pistol on the left, maybe a Princess Leia style Star Wars blaster on the right. And I always thought, "Well that's a bit strange." Maybe it would've made sense with 'Just a Job to Do' an album ago, but why are there guns on the *Invisible Touch* cover? Is it an oblique reference to 'Domino'? That seems unlikely.

So then you need to look even closer at the negative space in white left by those grey patterns, while ignoring all the distracting green stuff in the mix. And once you do that, and look at the bigger picture, you see that this is actually a silhouetted family of four: father, mother, son, daughter. And you see that, though they're contained within that square of vaguely fingerprint-patterned green stuff, the hand itself extends beyond it. And then you realise that this isn't a hand coming out of the album to you, the person holding it, but the idea of a hand coming out the album to *them*, a family buying at the record shop or wherever. The album cover itself is like a window and we're seeing this hand - this decidedly left hand - move toward that window to reach the listeners.

So in the end, I think it works, and it ends up being a pretty good metaphor after all. The fact that it took me 34 years to understand it, though? Well that means that it's either too opaque and ugly a design to get its message across effectively, or that I'm just a big dummy.

Eh...why not both?

The Review

Nobody ever goes out and buys a band's or artist's greatest hits album and expects anything like a meaningful, overarching concept. It's a greatest hits album. The concept is that these are hits and you like them. You don't need anything else, right? And yet song flow is still a key concept when putting these things together. Take, for example, Duran Duran's *Decade*. Released at the end of 1989, this was a greatest hits album conceived as a chronological journey through the band's hit catalogue. The idea was to hear the album and listen to the band slowly evolve over time, even if you were still just listening to the hits out of their original album context.

But in 1998, after more studio albums and (surprisingly) more hit singles, Duran Duran put out another greatest hits album, the aptly titled *Greatest*. Despite containing all 14 tracks from the previous release, the chronological concept was completely eschewed this time around, and the tracks were arranged in what appears to be a random order. Yet listen to *Greatest* and the songs just flow brilliantly from one to the next, as though this were the order in which they were always meant to be heard. 'A View to a Kill' came out in 1985 and 'Ordinary World' came out in 1992, but I'll be danged if their transition doesn't feel downright flawless. So even on a compilation album, it's important to never underestimate what a lift good album flow can bring.

Now why am I talking so much about hits and compilation albums here? Because, in a sense, *Invisible Touch* is Genesis' first greatest hits album. Not that this was by design or even an actual compilation album, but, well, the results pretty much speak for themselves:

- 'Invisible Touch' - UK 15, **US 1**
- 'In Too Deep' - UK 19, **US 3**
- 'Land of Confusion' - UK 14, **US 4**
- 'Tonight, Tonight, Tonight' - UK 18, **US 3**
- 'Throwing It All Away' - UK 22, **US 4**

That's 67.5% of the album landing as top 5 US singles, which is absolutely ludicrous. The entire Side 1 of *Invisible Touch* can be very readily argued as amounting to little more than a compilation of the top American hits in the Genesis catalogue. Then jump to Side 2, where 'Anything She Does' never got a single release, but nevertheless still had a music video (primarily used as an intro for the Invisible Touch Tour). Then 'Domino' got split in half and each half appeared as a B-side to one of the aforementioned top five singles, putting that song squarely into people's pockets via single releases as well. 'Throwing It All Away' itself one of those top 5 hits, and then closing with 'The Brazilian'. That song also didn't make it onto a single, but that doesn't mean it was out of the public eye; it received copious TV usage during the 1987 World Championships in Athletics. Oh yeah, and it also garnered a freakin' Grammy nomination.

Folks, it's fair to say *Invisible Touch* was something of a success.

Now, that success is something of a double-edged sword for me. With the exception of 'Anything She Does', which I've never particularly cared for, every song on this record deserves all the love it gets. They're all musical achievements, some brilliantly so. I can cruise through this album and thoroughly enjoy seven of the eight stops along the way. That's tremendous. But at the same time I never quite feel like I'm listening to an *actual* Genesis album, you know? Between the cavalcade of hits and the ultra-crisp production, *Invisible Touch* feels more like a collection of songs than a true album journey to me. That the songs are so good saves the experience, but when I'm in the mood to listen to an album, I want one that's going to take me somewhere - somewhere I can't go simply by turning on a generic 80s radio station and jamming with the hits.

And so we're back to that idea of song flow, where *Invisible Touch* just doesn't quite pull things off for me. I think if something like 'Do the Neurotic' had been worked in and at least one of the shorter big hits ('In Too Deep', maybe) had been moved to a standalone single, maybe things would have felt a bit more "album-like" to me. As it stands, I can't hear the first side without getting that "this might as well just be the radio" feeling, and then I don't like the kick-off of the second side. The 'Domino'/'Throwing It All Away'/'The Brazilian' stretch lets *Invisible Touch* finally begin to feel like an album proper to me, but by then of course it's all over.

It's hard to fault Genesis for being too good at making hit music, but I think *Invisible Touch* will, for better or worse, always be in that "great but not immersive" territory for me. Good problem to have if you're the band, I'd say, but it does mean I ultimately rate the album squarely in the middle of the band's LP efforts.

7 - Trespass

October 23, 1970

The Art

The first Paul Whitehead album cover also was the most exemplary of his style with Genesis: create something fanciful while trying to make references to all the songs on the album. You've got a pair of people gazing out an archway, perhaps 'Looking for Someone' in the distance, where there is peace amongst the hills as in 'Stagnation', and a prominent 'White Mountain' to be seen...or a mountain capped in white, at any rate. There are 'Visions of Angels' in the form of a cherub, and the scent of flowers coming from the dark areas as a call to 'Dusk'. Finally, as 'The Knife' got added to the album after Whitehead had already finished the cover, the band insisted on a redesign that incorporated it. With Whitehead understandably reluctant to waste a perfectly good cover, the band came up with a compromise: keep the existing cover, but take an actual knife and just slice through the art itself. The end result works surprisingly well as a parallel to the way 'The Knife' contrasts the rest of the album at the end.

Ultimately though, the art itself doesn't mean much to me, and its connections to the music are tenuous - clearly the work of someone who was just looking at some lyrics without bothering to try to understand what they really meant. That's fine, but eh. Like his *Foxtrot* cover, *Trespass* to me just ends up feeling like a jumbled collage of unrelated images. There's nothing deeper that draws me into it, although I have to admit that I find the larger notion of the cover being not a painting but actually a photograph *of* a painting with a knife sticking out of it pretty compelling. It's very much a "things are not always what they seem" kind of idea, especially because the "truth" isn't clear until flipping the cover around and seeing that knife on its backside.

And yet, what the *Trespass* art does terrifically is reflect the *musical* texture of the album. The individual images do nothing for me, no, but when I look at that tranquil shade of blue spelled by those black and white sketches, "gentle prog folk" springs effortlessly to mind. The creepy face in the top corner and the knife slash remind that there is more than that, too, but Genesis would continue to do some harder stuff and they'd continue to do some of the longer, more epic stuff. They would not continue to do the folkier stuff, so that's the flavour this album inevitably has for me, and the art - relatively haphazard though I think it might be - captures that very well.

> **Mike:** *In those days - the first two or three albums - we had Paul Whitehead, who was a good artist who at the time was involved in doing album covers and stuff... So you kind of let him go. You let someone go away and do something that excites them, and then see what you've got. And it looked great with the big sort of knife slash across, I thought.* [3]

> **Tony:** *Well I thought it was quite a nice idea. We saw the music we'd done, and a lot of it was sort of pretty and romantic music. We had this one song, 'The Knife', which was anything but. A sort of violent song. So we just pictorially did that. We said to this guy, "Just draw a fairy drawing," and then [after adding 'The Knife' to the track list], "Knife slash through the middle with a knife sticking out the end of it." I think it's quite good really, because it's deceptive, Genesis sometimes. You see them as one thing, but in fact there's this other thing going on... We've always had those two sides to us...the romantic side and the more aggressive side. It's a very important part of what we do. So I thought that particular cover was really good, because it was supposed to be a sort of cliched, kind of fairy-like cover, and then with this knife on it, which did something special, I think. Best of the early covers. Well, best of the first three covers, anyhow.* [3]

> **Peter:** *We talked to Paul [Whitehead] at some length, and he heard some of the folky stuff, and mythical bits. And I just felt it was getting too twee, so I suggested that we get a big knife and slash it, which fortunately...they went for it. I was going to go for a quite crude knife, but Paul in the end chose this more elegant dagger, which wasn't quite what I'd had in mind, but I think it did [its] job. For fans it had its own personality, which I think is what we wanted.* [3]

> **Ant:** *I think it seemed to be a pretty good compromise between the kind of folky sort of tendency, these slightly medieval echoes...and then there's the sort of harder-edge stuff. So you want to draw someone's attention as well. So a great way of combining it is you've got one*

thing, which is a sort of...characters, plus this knife slash, which might look a bit [over-the-top] and grotesque to some people, but it seems to me to be a pretty good reflection. And you can see commercially why that was a good move. [3]

The Review

Earlier in this albums countdown I mentioned *Calling All Stations* as a kind of "quality compression" of an album, with no truly bad songs but also no truly incredible ones. Well, *Trespass* is right there beside it, perhaps even more compressed in its way. Of its six tracks, I think three are great but not jaw-dropping, two are solid, and one is only "pretty good." That's not a bad collection at all, so already this album gets a leg up on some of the ones that are marred by their inclusion of (to my ears) weaker songs.

But as stated multiple times before, what's more important than the songs themselves to me is the way they flow together. 'Looking for Someone' is a tremendous choice for the opener here, starting as it does with just voice and organ. It's gripping right from the get-go. Its final chord into 'White Mountain' is also a fantastic transition, creating a very strong 1-2 punch to kick off the album. From there, 'Visions of Angels' is a functional link if not an inspired one; it at least retains some of that same acoustic feel as a through-line to finish out the first side.

Then, even if the beginning of 'Visions of Angels' doesn't precisely match the feel of the end of 'White Mountain', its end does align really well with the start of 'Stagnation'. Which of course goes on its own winding journey to its own grand ending. Unfortunately, as much as I like 'Dusk', its entrance is a little bit jarring after 'Stagnation' and doesn't quite work for me in that regard. Once it gets going though, it does feel of a mind with sections of 'White Mountain', which means it's in a weird position of helping glue the album together even as it fails to fit squarely in its slot.

Similarly, 'The Knife' doesn't strictly work after 'Dusk', either. That dancing, tense organ isn't quite a shock to the system, but it does sound initially out of place when it comes in. Here's the thing though: that's kind of the point. Just as the album art was completed before Whitehead came and slashed a knife through the canvas, so 'The Knife' slashes through the musical canvas of *Trespass*, disrupting its serene folk vibes with a hard, angry riot of a song. Its lyrics are rooted more in realism than the general sense of fantasy that pervades the rest of the album as well. It's a song designed to unbalance the listener and it's situated as the closer so it can do that job unimpeded. Unfortunately this does mean that it can sometimes overshadow the rest of the album, but there's nowhere else on *Trespass* the song can reasonably sit.

I tend to like the more acoustic stuff on this album than the bigger, longer, harder pieces, though all of it is "good" at worst. I think I'm a fan of *Trespass* because it's got stuff you simply can't hear anywhere else in the Genesis catalogue. It doesn't flow quite as well as I'd like it to, but it does a respectable enough job that it's a nice listen any time I'm in that kind of quiet mood.

6 - Nursery Cryme

November, 1971

The Art

The middle child of the Paul Whitehead trio of covers, this one is definitely my favourite of the bunch. Look at that little croquet coquette there. She's flirting with us with that gentle smile as though she hasn't just finished the backswing of her decapitating stroke. The heads are right there! We can see them! You know what you did, Cynthia.

The key here is that Whitehead didn't go for the "let me get a bunch of images relating to everything on the album that I possibly can" method, which is what he did on *Foxtrot* and (to a lesser extent) *Trespass*. Here it's just that one image from 'The Musical Box', which is itself the "nursery crime" of the album's title, and it's carrying the weight of the whole set of songs beautifully. I mean, OK, if you want to be a certain kind of way about it, the back of the sleeve does throw some extra references in there: a classical Venus statue vaguely referencing 'The Fountain of Salmacis' with its mythological tones, a hogweed growing in the foreground...but these aren't intrusive things and they don't distract from the primary scene in the way of a cover like *Foxtrot* where there really is no primary scene at all, and none of the elements work together in any way. Here even the colour of the lawn works brilliantly: instead of a simple green, the alternating stripes of yellow evoke a kind of pastoral flavour, which shines through on the album in pieces like 'For Absent Friends' and 'Harlequin'.

It's so strong a bit of artwork that even the folks at Charisma Records wanted a piece of the action, apparently.

> **Paul Whitehead:** *The originals were stolen from Charisma. When Charisma was sold to Virgin [Records], and the staff at Charisma got wind of the sale coming down, they just looted the place. So, no one knows where the originals are. They just disappeared.* [119]

They say imitation is the sincerest form of flattery, but I think robbing your artwork as you're heading out the door has got to be a pretty close second, right? Anyway, while I don't think I'd call *Nursery Cryme* my absolute favourite Genesis cover, it's right up there. Top 3 for me, probably.

> **Peter:** *Your taste changes over the years with all sorts of things, but there was a mood which Paul nailed, I think. Which, although an external scene because of the croquet game and the sort of suppressed violence, was I think accurate for the vibe that we were trying to portray at the time.* [3]

> **Steve:** *It's certainly weird. It's as crazy as any wallpaper that was around at the time. But you've got to remember that the 60s had just passed. Only just. So I think it very much reflects its time.* [3]

> **Tony:** *I almost prefer this cover coming back to it [more] than I did at the time, in a funny way looking at it. It's a bit difficult for me; it's so much a part of my past and youth, and I've signed so many copies of these things that I sort of see them all the time now. So it's rather difficult to have an objective viewpoint. But I think it's a strong image, with the lawn stripes and everything. It gives a very strong feeling. And it fits well with the idea of the title and that association with 'The Musical Box'.* [3]

> **Phil:** *I remember at the time Paul Whitehead coming in with the idea, and obviously he had worked with Peter on a couple of ideas on the phone, I would imagine. You know, it was before the days of email, so if you wanted to see something you had to actually get together in a room and look at it. And the thing with the croquet with the heads, that was all very, kind of off-the wall. I mean, fortunately it wasn't as romantic and feminine as Trespass, which was good because it showed that there was a little bit of an unusual side. You know, not just a wistful side to the band. Because I think Trespass, the music and the cover looked a bit wistful, even though there's a knife on it. But you know, it doesn't feel quite as butch as Nursery Cryme.* [3]

> **Mike:** *I thought the cover was good. I like the cover, actually. Quite strong image of the little girl, the croquet lawn, and the head.* [3]

The Review

We're getting closer and closer to the top, and that means there's less and less tolerance for songs that don't quite make the grade. *Nursery Cryme* is one of three Genesis albums that is "marred in the middle" for me with one single track near the centre that attempts to derail the whole thing. The others are *Selling England by the Pound* and *A Trick of the Tail*, but each of their "skippables" strikes me as being better than this one. Most of the time I'll even let them play through, but this? I'm afraid this one's simply got to go.

I'm talking, of course, about 'The Return of the Giant Hogweed', but I'm not going to dwell on my feelings about that track here. Suffice it to say that I find that song to be a major outlier on an album that otherwise delivers pretty strongly across the board. And ultimately that delivery is more important, because the main focus for me with these album rankings is on sonic cohesion. The songs on *Nursery Cryme* don't all sound the *same*, but they do all sound like they belong here.

The blending of acoustic and electric on 'The Musical Box' is an announcement that the band is "Like *Trespass* but with more balls now," and then that fierceness is immediately pulled away on 'For Absent Friends', which is gentle without ever feeling impotent. For better or worse, 'Hogweed' does what it does, and then 'Seven Stones' provides a big organ showcase with gorgeous vocal work performed seemingly by the whole band, again connected by a sense of overarching mood. 'Harold the Barrel' is a silly but meaningful addition, in that it takes the rougher edges of the earlier pieces and plays around with them to make them something fun. Finally, the oft underrated 'Harlequin' is pure pastoral atmosphere (those yellows from the cover once again) before 'The Fountain of Salmacis' concludes things with an ebbing and flowing organ showstopper that nevertheless doesn't ever step outside the boundaries the rest of the record has created.

I think *Nursery Cryme* has an awful lot going for it, where even the "middling" songs excel in context and help guide the listener on this semi-romantic, semi-lethal journey through the British countryside. One big black stain might be enough to keep it out of my top five, but it's not enough to ruin the album altogether. I find myself coming back to this one with a fair bit of frequency, and I seldom come away disappointed.

5 - We Can't Dance

October 28, 1991

The Art

Sometimes album art tells a story. Maybe that's as a unique story in and of itself, or maybe that's as a reflection of a story being told by some (or all) of the music contained within the album sitting underneath. Sometimes album art paints a picture. Maybe that's a picture of a single striking image described somewhere within the labyrinth of lyrics, or maybe that's a picture of something more abstract, like trying to capture a mood in colour and form. Sometimes album art commands attention. Maybe that's accomplished by using bright colours and sharp angles to make the sleeve stand out from its competitors on the shelves, or maybe that's accomplished by crafting a sight so unique that its impression leaves an indelible mark on the viewer, who will immediately and forever associate that sight with this particular musical effort.

Sometimes, though, album art is just a high school kid with an ugly half-growing moustache line, trying to look cool and blend in with actual adults, asking to bum a cig even though he doesn't want anything to do with the act of smoking. That's the art of *We Can't Dance*. It's there, it's inoffensive in itself, and maybe kinda cool if you get to know it, but it's trying to fit in somewhere it's got no business being. Everyone knows it, everyone's made a little uncomfortable by it, but nobody wants to say anything because, well, it's just a little bit awkward, you know?

This is an image of a father and son. The father is holding something; I have no idea what. They're on top of a hill, staring at the sky. The sky is vaguely divided into blue and orangeish hues, as though it's a sunrise or perhaps a sunset. I've seen interpretations that this is the dad essentially reciting the lyrics of 'Way of the World' as wisdom to his son ("why's the blue sky..."), and I like that idea if only because it's the only way this image ties into anything on the album at all. The picture takes up about 50% of the cover real estate, doesn't "sound" like the album to me, and doesn't mesh even slightly with the title. About the only thing that "works" in terms of marrying the cover with the material is the new band logo, and that's probably only because I'm so used to seeing it now.

Look, don't get me wrong. I like the picture. And I think the art inside the album's lyric booklet in the same style works well for the individual songs. As an image representing the whole of *We Can't Dance* though? I've got to regard this one as a failure. But the band, as it turns out, have much more positive opinions...

> **Mike:** *The We Can't Dance album was a good album cover. Some of our best work comes from when you find something that was already out there and adapt it. It's quite hard commissioning sometimes, because they come back and you kinda go, "Well I don't actually like it," you know? So I think it was just a nice...little men on the moon...it reminded me of that book, The Little Prince. Petit Prince by Saint-Exupéry had that same look: a little man on that planet. And I think our stuff often works quite well slightly animated.* [3]

> **Tony:** *The We Can't Dance album cover I thought was a nice return to form. I thought it was the best album cover we'd had certainly since Duke. Again, kind of similar to Duke in a way: a very simple sort of cartoon-type picture, almost. Strong atmosphere, I think, and just the feel about it suggested that the album had a little more romance in it perhaps than the previous one. I think it worked nicely. And a great logo too, which of course we've ended up using ever since then. The E's the wrong way 'round, you know. Just seems to still fit.* [3]

I'm glad they like it and again: I do appreciate the art for what it is as well. It would be a lovely wall piece in the right kind of room, you know? But as an off-centre panel on a tan square, underneath a big purple logo that looks like it was drawn by a 5-year-old? With a straight font album title encroaching into its space as well? Just doesn't work for me.

The Review

It would be a huge overstatement to say that *We Can't Dance* defined my childhood or even that it was a kind of soundtrack to it. Nevertheless, this was the Genesis album that was most significant during those formative years; the one of which I have the clearest and fondest memories. Which isn't to say I could've even told you its track list back then, because I wasn't anywhere near that engaged. But working through this project and listening intently to every song on every album, coming back to *We Can't Dance* was like snuggling into a warm bed at the end of a long day. Even its filler tracks are pretty good, 'Tell Me Why' notwithstanding.

I've heard all kinds of opinions on *We Can't Dance* over the years. It seems that most Genesis fans agree it's at or near the bottom of the barrel, but they can't ever seem to agree on why. One group claims it's because *We Can't Dance* marks the ultimate devolution of the band into pop dreck, when all prog had left them. This group is also known as "people who didn't actually listen to the album," because songs like 'Driving the Last Spike' and 'Fading Lights' are progressive-style epics, while 'Dreaming While You Sleep', 'Living Forever', and even 'No Son of Mine' all draw from that same well. Another group claims the music is mostly good, but the album fares poorly because of its runtime. This has some merit; *We Can't Dance* runs pretty long for a non-double-album, and trimming some of the fat like the aforementioned 'Tell Me Why' or one of the other oft-cited least favourite tracks would certainly help to streamline things.

I've heard people say the pop stuff is great but the prog stuff falls short. I've heard people say the prog stuff is great but the pop stuff is a waste of time. I've heard people say all of it is terrible because it wasn't made in 1974. My opinion? It's all really, really solid.

With an album this long and no overriding concept, it would be a tricky proposition to have every song flow perfectly into every other one, and indeed there are a couple minor missteps in this vein. But by and large *We Can't Dance* gets that job done. The marriage of all the tracks here is less about notes or lyrical themes and more about the production quality of the thing. *We Can't Dance* is pristine but manages to be so without sounding like a relic of its era in the *Invisible Touch* vein. That one had crisp, clean production that sounds almost over-sterilised, but that sound worked brilliantly for 1986. With *We Can't Dance* producer Nick Davis adds some mud back in the mix, but not in that Dave Hentschel *And Then There Were Three* kind of way. This is highly controlled levels of sonic dirt, helping things feel a little more natural even if you can tell it's anything but. It's a strange paradox, but it creates a consistency in the sound of the album that the songs themselves lack.

Which means that *We Can't Dance* is an album that sounds like a cohesive thing yet one that contains incredible variety. You've got the effortless pop hooks of 'Way of the World' going into the bombastic, justified overwroughtness of 'Since I Lost You', and then that's followed by the extended 'Cinema Show'-lite keyboard solo work of 'Fading Lights'. Those are consecutive tracks! And the transition between them never even feels "off" in any way! What an achievement.

People often talk about the late era of Genesis and point to *We Can't Dance* as emblematic of what that means. In some ways, like the production quality, I agree with that label. But for me *We Can't Dance* isn't "late-era" Genesis. It's a synthesis of *every* era of Genesis, delivered in one mostly-coherent package. That's a pretty strong product in my book, worthy of much greater praise than I see this album typically receive.

4 - The Lamb Lies Down on Broadway

November 18, 1974

The Art

If you're working through the Genesis album covers chronologically, you find a running theme. Except for the debut (which might as well not have had a cover at all), the Genesis album cover catalogue through 1973 was defined by paintings: hand-drawn artwork, reflecting a sense of fantasy within the music. There's the castle and countryside of *Trespass*, the Victorian lawn of *Nursery Cryme*, and the seaside scene of miscellany of *Foxtrot*. Even once Paul Whitehead was dismissed, *Selling England by the Pound* featured yet another painting. This one had a little less of the fantasy in it, but still plenty of whimsy to spare. To any Genesis fan at all, this cover art *was* Genesis.

And then comes the sleeve of *The Lamb Lies Down on Broadway*, arresting in its rawness and sense of reality. Here's an actual person, not a stylised painting. He's in a variety of scenes which are created by modifying photographs, not through someone's work on a canvas. He's wracked with pain in the centre of the cover, yelling in another panel, and on the back of the sleeve he's even leaping through a pane of glass. This isn't fairies and fun at all. This is rage, and fear, and anguish, and confusion. Another rear panel has the figure with no mouth at all, even as ten terrifying faces behind him are caught mid-speech. Two of the six panels across the front and back covers display endless corridors of some sort, while in one of those the character has stepped out of the artwork entirely and wandered off to view himself elsewhere.

So all at once you have this feeling that this album is more anchored to reality than any that have come before, and yet there is some *weird* stuff happening. More gritty than romantic, more solid than airy, yet perhaps the strangest and most subversive they've ever done to this point. That's an accurate description of *The Lamb* from a musical perspective, and you get all that from the album cover immediately. The band logo here is just the icing on the cake. The word "Genesis", when displayed in all uppercase font, contains three letters with ample curvature: one G and two instances of S. Yet *The Lamb Lies Down on Broadway* features a "Genesis" logo with no curves at all. Everything is angular, sharper, edgier than before. And it's all being reflected out on a glossy panel, because this is Broadway, baby.

If you want to dissect the individual scenes and try to make sense of them as pure snapshots in the story, then maybe this cover won't make the grade as much for you. But in terms of communicating to a prospective buyer what they might expect from this album, especially as it relates to any preconceived notions they might have as a result of the band's earlier work? This cover is about as good as it gets.

Tony: *I think it works pretty well. Obviously the idea is it's showing images from the story and everything, and it has a sort of graphic novel kind of quality about it, which I quite like, because I'm a bit of a graphic novel fan. That's why I quite like the sort of dark, dark thing about it. But I think it was a question of how we used it: whether we used it bigger over the whole album, or we'd just use that sort of band of stuff, I think. And I think it works pretty well. I mean, it's a lot of character. And also the writing, that sort of Greek lettering we used, which we've obviously come back to a few times in our career, looks very strong on it. I think it was good because whereas all the previous albums were all a bit more romantic, this was a lot less romantic, this album. And having a stark black-and-white cover like that, I think it made you aware that this wasn't going to be quite as cuddly perhaps as some of the previous stuff.* [3]

Peter: *I really like (Hipgnosis founder) Storm (Thorgerson), who's a wonderful character. Very dry, cynical, sardonic, and very talented. He was just a lot of fun to interact with. He was always rude to everybody, but when you're riffing ideas, it's a lot of fun. He also has this bag of the unused Hipgnosis ideas that he tries to palm off on everyone as "new and fresh," but here there was a story and some strong ideas for pictures. I had a sort of Puerto Rican figure in my head - perhaps West Side Story was maybe another influence as well as El Topo - but the faces they were able to find in the UK didn't seem anything like what I had in my head. We had, I remember, a big search to try and find someone acceptable as Rael, because I thought the face has to be right. And I think we got pretty close. Like 8.5 out of 10.* [3]

Steve: *Hipgnosis for years had been trying to get us to use a photographic cover. They always wanted everything to be edgy realism and the band always wanted something much more - to* *their minds - what Hipgnosis considered to be airy-fairy, "Ah yes, you want all this romantic stuff. You know, why can't you have something that's contemporary, photographic, literal, perspective-driven…" You know, just like all their other covers! The cover? I don't think it's the greatest cover ever. I think that Hipgnosis did do great covers occasionally for Led Zeppelin, who I think were perhaps more open to some of their ideas. Like I remember them saying, "What about if we have a family sitting around and they're staring at something in the middle of the table, and no one really knows what it is?" And everyone said, "Nope! Don't like that." But everyone was sure that they DIDN'T want their photograph on the front. No one wanted their own face to be on the front of the album.* ³

Phil: *Yeah, I feel it's a little bit as confused as the story. It's a distinct package… But again, it's different. When someone plunks an album in front of you to sign, what you're signing, very quickly…the filing cabinet in your head goes back to all the things. So every album cover has straightaway - even though you're signing your name to something that's thirty years old plus - it has those sort of emotional attachments. Some good, some not so good, but it at least evokes something.* ³

The Review

All right, let's get something clear up front here. I don't really like the story behind *The Lamb Lies Down on Broadway*. I'm firmly in the Tony Banks camp on that one. It's weird, it's grotesque, it doesn't hold together over the album's duration, and it fails to yield anything like a satisfying ending; I think '*it.*' is little more than a narrative cop-out (and it doesn't do a lot for me musically, either). It feels like every time over the course of *The Lamb*'s 94 minutes that I start to allow myself to be pulled into the story, something happens to push me straight back out again. I can appreciate the intent behind it and I can appreciate the artistry/poetry of much of the record's lyrics, as well as the imagery and clever metaphor those lyrics create, but the concept on the whole? That can get right on out. It's a big nothing for me.

Perhaps that's why I have *The Lamb* rated as "only" my personal fourth favourite Genesis album, but at the same time, if you compare against the individual song rankings and reactions from the previous section, it becomes pretty clear that I feel better about this album as a whole than the mere sum of its musical parts would indicate. That's because while the narrative concept behind *The Lamb* doesn't work for me, the *musical* connections work marvellously. As stated in the individual entry for the song, my first "intentional" exposure to this album was when a college friend played me 'The Waiting Room' during a car ride, and I loathed it. No context, you see. When I went back on my own some years later and listened to the album in full though? Despite dreading 'The Waiting Room' and indeed still not particularly caring for it, I *did* at least begin to "get it." And that made a world of difference. Now? Now I…still am not incredibly fond of the song, and would never listen to it in isolation, but I don't shudder as it nears. So that's something!

No Genesis album does musical context quite like *The Lamb*. I devoted two essays ('Back in N.Y.C.' and 'The Lamia') during the previous section to analyses of this album structure, and I feel like there's potentially a lot more I could've said, or additional angles I could've taken to look at the album as a whole. Everything just *flows* extremely well for three full sides of music. The fourth side - which as a unit I don't get very jazzed about - may not connect all that well to the other three in my opinion, but it does nevertheless cohere musically within *itself* very tightly. It's kind of like having a big ball of orange Play-Doh as one homogenous mass, and then a ball of purple Play-Doh, equally homogenous but a third the size. You can smush them together and blend the edge so that they're all one *substance*, but the *colours* are still different, you know what I mean?

Anyway, that's a small nitpick in the grand scheme of things here. The fact is that this album strings together 17 tracks about as well as I could ever hope for, and then strings together 5 more on the back end for good measure. And then closes with '*it.*', which doesn't mesh with anything else the album is doing whatsoever, but that's beside the point too. I'll listen to songs in isolation from this album, as indeed I had to in order to perform the entire exercise that started this whole shebang. And the band will pull out songs in isolation (or medley form) as well, and those can all work. But if there's one single Genesis album that demands to be appreciated in full rather than piecemeal, this is it. It's not quite perfect, but it's a true masterwork nonetheless.

3 - Selling England by the Pound

October 13, 1973

The Art

See ya, Paul! After the confusion of the *Foxtrot* cover, the band decided to go a different direction for *Selling England by the Pound*. For starters, they didn't want to bother with the idea of commissioning a piece of artwork and then hoping they liked whatever they got in return. And so they happened upon a painting by English artist Betty Swanwick called *The Dream*. It featured a character sleeping on a bench against a perspective-driven hedge lawn lined with people out and about, enjoying the weather. It was cheery, quaint, pleasant...in other words, it was English, through and through. And it was *almost* perfect for what Genesis wanted. They asked Swanwick if they could commission her to do something like this, except more referential of the music. Swanwick didn't have time to conjure up something brand new, so she offered a compromise: she'd repaint *The Dream* but add in a lawnmower next to the bench, solidifying that foreground figure as the singer from 'I Know What I Like'. And they were sold.

> **Peter:** *So Betty Swanwick was a wonderful woman. She was a little bit like Miss Marple, or an Agatha Christie character: full of life, very smart, and mischievous.* [3]

> **Tony:** *We had tea on her lawn. But what was great was the table was on the lawn [slanted on a hill], and she put the tea on that, and everything was sort of sliding, sliding down the thing. Very strange. And the whole time we were there, there was this parrot that sat on Peter's shoulder, sort of nibbling his collar. It was kind of a somewhat surreal moment, anyhow.* [3]

> **Peter:** *She seemed to have a good combination of Englishness and yet exposing the underbelly. And I went down to see her...and she was a wonderful character. She had a parrot, and she kept on talking to the parrot in the middle of the conversation. You weren't quite sure if you were being addressed or the parrot.* [3]

> **Tony:** *She said she'd love to do [the cover], but she couldn't do it from scratch in a month, which was what we needed. So we said, "Well can you modify the picture that you've got?" Which is what she did. She just took the picture she had and she added a lawnmower to it, so it fitted with the lyrics to 'I Know What I Like'...and it worked really well. I mean, in many ways it's the best piece of art we've ever had on the front cover. Whether it's the best cover I don't know, but it's the best piece of art on a cover.* [3]

> **Mike:** *She was a great old lady. Nice seeing someone from the other world, you know, not just the music world but someone in the art world, who was up for sort of trying something.* [3]

I think *Selling England by the Pound* is a terrific cover. It's got that same striped lawn effect as *Nursery Cryme*, very strong in generating a certain kind of mood of English restraint. The characters are human but slightly deformed. Not to the point of monstrosity, but it creates this aura of light fantasy around the whole thing: this music will be grounded yet fanciful at the same time. Then putting that in a box surrounded by a muted yellow? This is essentially *Nursery Cryme Vol. 2* from an artwork perspective, and it's brilliant. I even love the font choice, to have simple lettering for both the band name and album title in a typeface with no serifs (serifs are the little embellishments on the edges of certain letters that are a hallmark of Times New Roman font, among many others). It's clean, it's elegant, it's Englishness in a nutshell. And that's a perfect marriage to the music on the album itself, as well.

Definitely a top tier cover in my book.

> **Tony:** *In many ways it's the best piece of art we've ever had on the front cover. Whether it's the best cover I don't know, but it's the best piece of art on a cover.* [3]

Steve: *I thought the cover was absolutely brilliant. Betty Swanwick, the fact that she'd done that picture, she was a member of the Royal Academy, and I think it was the front cover of the catalogue advertising the summer exhibition.* [3]

Phil: *For me, the cover was a great cover... That showed that there had been a change of sorts from that almost sort of schoolboy graphic stuff, which was Foxtrot and Nursery Cryme. In the way [they] were done, I sort of felt it was a little bit schoolboy-ish. This was something that was kind of elegant, the Betty Swanwick characters. And that stayed with us as well. It's a good album [cover].* [3]

The Review

This is the purest case of potential addition by subtraction for me across the Genesis catalogue. If you simply remove 'The Battle of Epping Forest' from the album entirely, this would probably be my overall favourite Genesis album. That's despite considering the fact that I'm lukewarm on 'I Know What I Like (In Your Wardrobe)'! That comes in part from having heard it too many times, but even accounting for my fatigue with that track, *Selling England* is a through and through perfect album...or would be, if not for that daggone 'Epping Forest' sitting right smack in the middle of it.

And yet. And yet! I can't deny that 'The Battle of Epping Forest' simply overflows with personality and the quintessential Englishness that permeates the themes of the album. I wouldn't go nearly so far as to say it's the glue that holds the album together, but nevertheless I can't deny that it truly does belong here. Why, there are times when I'm listening to *Selling England* that I don't even bother to skip it! So even though my general dissatisfaction with the track causes the album as a whole to drop a spot or two in my mind, I've got to admit that it's a strong contributing factor to what makes the album ultimately work so well.

Outside of that track, the bookending of 'Dancing with the Moonlit Knight' and the perennially underrated 'Aisle of Plenty' is divine, to say nothing of twin epics 'Firth of Fifth' and 'The Cinema Show': both top ten songs for me across the entire Genesis catalogue. And then on either side of 'Epping' there's the charming 'More Fool Me' and the warm relief of 'After the Ordeal'. The icing on the cake is that they all flow together swimmingly from song to song as well, and I include 'The Battle for Epping Forest' in that statement. *Selling England by the Pound* never feels as though it's got to try too hard to weave its songs together. Rather, they cascade seamlessly one into the next, like following a gentle stream as it winds its way through the English countryside.

I love this album from beginning to end, even if I need to occasionally avert my eyes from the big ol' wart in the centre of it. Easily one of my most played among their catalogue, and likely will be for decades to come.

2 - A Trick of the Tail

February 13, 1976

The Art

I had no idea this was a Hipgnosis cover until I looked it up, because it's just so unlike their typical edgy kind of style. This isn't a photograph with surreal undertones and visual effects. It's not a splash of unique, angular graphic art. It doesn't look like Led Zeppelin or Pink Floyd or even Peter Gabriel's solo career. This is hand-drawn artwork in what amounts to the sepia-tone version of monochrome, covering only half or less of the record sleeve's real estate. And it's essentially perfect.

Paul Whitehead tried repeatedly to nail the art of collage and ended up with a confusing mess of (reasonably pretty) imagery that ultimately got him fired. Hipgnosis themselves had tried a bit of collage with *The Lamb Lies Down on Broadway*, and that worked really well because of the way the exceedingly strange, exotic nature of that effort tied in with the strange, exotic nature of the album's story itself. But *A Trick of the Tail* has no unifying story. It's got no overriding theme that can serve as a visual focus point to tie everything together, as Rael did one album prior. So illustrator Colin Elgie over at Hipgnosis had to figure out a different way to connect everything.

> **Colin Elgie:** *A Trick Of The Tail was the first project I did with the group. I didn't know that much about them, so I didn't have a lot of baggage. I knew Peter Gabriel had left and they'd done the Betty Swanwick cover [for Selling England By The Pound], which was more like my stuff. There was no music to listen to, but we had typed-out lyrics – very low-tech. [Hipgnosis boss Storm Thorgerson] had suggested that I illustrate the characters as if from a play. I loved the Victorian engraving style, and the characters seem to suit that approach. I got some old parchment and did the artworks separately and dropped them in on the background. I hand-lettered the Genesis logo that was used on that and Wind & Wuthering. I knew they liked it as I did a whole bunch of stationery for them based on the imagery from A Trick Of The Tail.* [27]

Ultimately he went with style. *A Trick of the Tail* is an album that, despite lacking a unifying theme, still does have a kind of unified sound. More on that to come soon, but Elgie must have picked up on the notion; if you ask me what *A Trick of the Tail* sounds like, sepia-tone figures out of a 19th century comic book is pretty much where I'd land. The sketchwork quality of it, the brown hue like it was inked on a scroll of parchment, the elegant script of the album's title? Just fantastic all around. So good.

And the collage aspect is dead-on here, too. You've got the old lady looking wistfully at her younger reflection to represent 'Ripples…'. You've got a robber and a cop and a dead body for 'Robbery, Assault and Battery'. You've got the circus ringmaster collaring the beast of 'A Trick of the Tail', and you've got birds flying overhead subtly representing 'Mad Man Moon'. That's just the front. The back has the hunter and his captured 'Squonk', the nurse/assistant at the sleep clinic for 'Entangled', silhouettes in the background lugging a cross - guessing that's 'Dance on a Volcano' there, and finally some street urchins getting sprinkled in fairy dust while a stern schoolmaster looks on with disapproval.

Gotta be honest, I don't have a clue what that one's all about. Best guess is that they're two separate illustrations and the schoolmaster looking guy is actually a judge from 'Robbery', but that still leaves the mystery of the kids. "Mesmerised children are playing" in the 'Entangled' lyrics, and perhaps the fairy figure is the Sandman of 'Mad Man Moon' who puts children to sleep? It's all rather confusing, but by golly it all fits anyway! Even the band name font is a blending of thick and thin that feels juuuuust right, like I'm the Goldilocks of album art consumption and *A Trick of the Tail* belongs to Baby Bear. It's great, man. All of it. Best album cover in the catalogue for my money. No question about it.

> **Mike:** *I would say that the cover for A Trick of the Tail was out of character actually with Hipgnosis, given what they normally do and what we know them for. The Floyd covers and some Zeppelin, and 10cc, and our other ones…They didn't kind of do this rather slightly romantic, softer drawing style.* [3]

> **Tony:** *Album covers can give a very strong identity to an album. A Trick of the Tail is one where that's the case, really. You get this idea of a sort of storybook feel out of it, and the songs are quite distinct, and a lot of the songs do have a kind of story to them. I think that*

makes it very strong. Slightly sort of Dickensian sort of look, I think, which worked just so nicely, the brown on that kind of parchment-like paper. [3]

The Review

Kind of like a less extreme version of the issue I had with *Selling England by the Pound*, *A Trick of the Tail* is an album with one single song that acts as a mostly-unwelcome interruption to the groove the album otherwise creates. I say less extreme because in this case, I am far fonder of 'Robbery, Assault and Battery' than I am of 'The Battle of Epping Forest', glaring lack of Oxford comma notwithstanding. Which is to say I find it mostly tolerable as opposed to mostly tedious; I still wouldn't go so far as to say I deeply like the song through and through.

But again, like 'Epping' with *Selling England*, 'Robbery' perfectly aligns with the overall tone and feel of this album. It's not my favourite by a long shot, but I can also recognise that it's exactly where it needs to be. At the very least I'm a good bit less likely to skip it on a playthrough - though my smile may find itself rather muted for about six minutes time until it blossoms once more when the album resumes with the sublime 'Ripples…'. And like that previous album, everything on *Trick* flows brilliantly from one song into the next, creating a whole arguably more coherent than even *The Lamb Lies Down on Broadway*, which of course was a concept album.

> **Mike:** *I think compared to some albums A Trick of the Tail is very consistent. And because of its very high standard it's difficult picking out any one track [as a favourite].* [31]

You've got the final chord of 'Dance on a Volcano' teeing up 'Entangled' magnificently, and then the drop from that song into 'Squonk'? That's too good to even be real. Then 'Squonk' fades out setting up 'Mad Man Moon' elegantly, even if 'It's Yourself' was cut from the album and may have originally played that role. Then 'Robbery, Assault and Battery' is there, kind of intrusive, but forgivably so as it's the start of a new side. 'Ripples…' comes from it, again not perfectly linked but again forgiven because this is brilliant stuff once more, and then the jaunty title track and a little ditty called 'Los Endos' to tie the whole room together. Near-flawless stuff.

Ironically since I've only got it in second place here, I think this is probably my most frequently played Genesis album. There's just something about its sound that transports me to another place. One that's filled with sand and sorrow, perhaps, but also with blue girls and cryptids and wonders to behold. Just give me the live ending to 'Los Endos' instead of the studio album's early fade out and man, I'm happy as can be.

1 - Duke

March 28, 1980

The Art

OK. This cover... Man, this cover. I just don't know about this cover, friend. I can't suss out how I actually feel about it. Let me explain.

First, the good: the colours work terrifically. The stark white background was previously used for *The Lamb Lies Down on Broadway*, but there it was offset by colourless photographs filling much of that open white space. Here it's just a window within the white. A window with shutters of pink and grey, opening to reveal a night time sky of blue, highlighted by a yellow moon. And all of it being viewed by a man in green, while the playful font of the album and band names run a yellow-to-green gradient. The various colours might seem like they should clash, but they don't. Instead they pop against that white background, making this cover look even more vivid than that of its follow-up, *Abacab*: an album cover essentially defined by colours themselves. It's a great effect and it creates a kind of allure and mystique about the album to come.

It helps as well that the primary colour one reads when glancing at this cover is that green, both from the man at the window and in the text. *Duke* is a very "green" kind of album, full of jealous splits and the pains of loss, yet also very vibrant and alive. It's a solid marriage of colour to feel.

And yet. And yet. I just struggle a lot with the style of it all, you know? This artwork wasn't commissioned, but came from a French children's book by Lionel Koechlin called L'alphabet d'Albert, from which the "Albert" character also takes his name. As any parent knows, children's illustrations are very hit-or-miss kinds of things. The genre is flush with unique takes on the human form, art that seeks to stand out and be different while still retaining the ability to connect with children and allow them to relate to the books' subjects. Sometimes these are great successes, but just as often you'll look at one of these and think, "Nope, don't care for that one bit."

L'alphabet d'Albert, and therefore *Duke* by extension, is one of those latter ones for me. The giant body with the grotesquely shrunken head and extremities? I can't get behind that. It's downright unsettling, far from the "fun and whimsical" it's supposed to be. I mean, take for example the 'Duchess' single cover art with that tiny head with Bart Simpson-esque hair spikes. Those tiny hands and tiny feet. Some people may love it, but for me that's borderline nightmare fuel. I can't do it.

So that's the art of *Duke* in a nutshell for me. Outstanding use of colour, fantastic core conceptual design, horrifying "must look away at all costs" primary focal point. I have no idea where that all averages out to place my opinion of the thing.

> **Tony:** *With Duke we just thought, "Well, we want something different," so we looked in a different area for a designer. And he actually came down with various suggestions of possibilities, and one thing he came down with was this ABC book by this French guy, which had this character on it. And we looked through; we really liked this style. "This is great!" We looked through the book and we got to Q, and had what is actually the album cover. It had a question mark above it [for Q]! It was just a simple alphabet book, you know. We took the question mark out and used it.* [3]

> **Mike:** *If you can find something you like, and see it... Commissioning an album cover's always hard, because you think: produce it, having shot it and spent money and gone somewhere with a photograph, then come back and see it and you don't like it. You always feel a little bit obliged to sort of work with it. Whereas this you can see it and knew his style, what he did. And it's a great cover, actually... We've always been very keen, I think Genesis, on quite simple images. Graphic ones, rather than a mishmash of lots of ideas. I think Duke kind of embodies that. It's a really simple, strong, quirky style image.* [3]

> **Phil:** *It was just nice. I mean, we're calling the album Duke, and there was this guy. This fat guy! It was just...he wasn't Duke, but he could be! You know. It was a nice, strong piece of artwork.* [3]

The Review

How good is *Duke*? Consider for a moment that when I first consciously decided this was my favourite Genesis album, I owned CD copies of ten different Genesis albums so I could listen to them in rotation in my car, and *Duke* was not one of those ten. Now, since then I've rectified this issue and have *Duke* ready to go at a moment's notice, but the point was that the album became so strongly embedded in my consciousness that I didn't really need it at the ready in order to place it at the top of the mountain.

Oddly enough, I think the album's strength comes from what it *doesn't* do. As I wrote about seemingly ad nauseam in the individual song entries during the main part of this book, the initial conception of the album was to dedicate an entire side to an epic piece under the working title 'Duke'. Not wanting the inevitable comparisons to 'Supper's Ready', Genesis abandoned that plan and instead split 'Duke' into its six component songs: 'Behind the Lines', 'Duchess', 'Guide Vocal', 'Turn It On Again', 'Duke's Travels', and 'Duke's End'. Then to maintain some of the cohesion they had when the piece was all one big thing, they stuck the first three of those pieces at the beginning of the album and the last two at the end. 'Turn It On Again' would then land squarely in the middle, sitting at track 7 out of the album's 12.

What this does is create a really strong skeletal structure for the album. It's going to end in a manner consistent with the way it starts, and it's got a built-in "reminder" at the halfway point. As long as the "filler" tracks don't veer too wildly off course, things should work out. I want to caution that here I'm not using "filler" in the derogatory, "this song is just there to pad time but isn't very good" sense; more in the matter-of-fact "this is the stuff between the pieces that comprise the core of the album" sense.

And so we look at these "filler" pieces and what do we find? First there's 'Man of Our Times', bombastic on a level with the fanfare of 'Behind the Lines' but with an almost mantra-like quality to it. It fits in perfectly with the atmosphere of the 'Duke Suite' even though it's not part of it. The next "filler track" is 'Misunderstanding', which almost foreshadows 'Turn It On Again' by being a well-crafted, radio-friendly, upbeat tune. It's not like what came before, but it still fits like a well-worn glove into the overall texture. That's followed by 'Heathaze', a plunge back into the deep synth that defined both the previous album and 'Behind the Lines'/'Man of Our Times' on this one.

After 'Turn It On Again', 'Alone Tonight' works as a kind of bridge between 'Misunderstanding' and 'Please Don't Ask': it's got that pop ballad kind of feel, enough that the record company wanted to release it as a single until the band overruled them. Then 'Cul-de-sac' is arguably the most regal-sounding piece on the album, more deserving of the name 'Duke' than perhaps even the 'Duke Suite' itself. And then there's the aforementioned 'Please Don't Ask', raw and vulnerable; not poppy enough to be a single, but still very accessible. And then it's back to the 'Duke Suite' for the final stretches.

So really, *Duke* to me consists of three key groupings of songs: first there's the 'Duke Suite' and its six pieces; then three pieces in 'Man of Our Times', 'Heathaze', and 'Cul-de-sac' that blend seamlessly into the suite's atmosphere if not its melodies and motifs; and lastly a separate three-song string of more immediate tunes in 'Misunderstanding', 'Alone Tonight', and 'Please Don't Ask' joined by their shared themes of heartbreak and loneliness. Like the component strands of a rope, these three groups of songs interweave over the course of the album, all reinforcing one another to create an end product that is incredibly strong.

I've called out other albums in the catalogue as being nearly perfect give or take a song here or there, but while I'm naturally fonder of some songs on *Duke* more than others, I'm not really ever tempted to skip anything when I play it. Every song works, top to bottom. I know there are those who prefer the B-sides 'Open Door' or 'Evidence of Autumn' from these same sessions, but for me this album is about as flawless as can be, and I don't think I'd change a thing.

Part III: The Band

A look at moments of intersection in their solo careers

ANTHONY PHILLIPS	445
STEVE HACKETT	449
PETER GABRIEL	454
PHIL COLLINS	458
MIKE RUTHERFORD	461
TONY BANKS	465

Anthony Phillips

1974 - *[redacted]*

'Silver Song' and the Case of the Phantom Single

History doesn't have much time to spare for the story of John Silver, second drummer of Genesis. To be fair to history, I suppose it's not really much of a story to begin with. Genesis' first drummer, Chris Stewart, was fired after the failure of the band's early singles, and Peter Gabriel knew a guy from school named John Silver who was also familiar with the ol' sticks. Genesis in 1968 were in no position to actually audition anybody, so "This is my friend John, he's nice and plays drums" was basically all it took to get Silver in the band.

John Silver had a jazz drumming background, which meant he was probably a poor fit for the baroque pop stuff that teenage Genesis was going for on *From Genesis to Revelation*, but he was more competent than Stewart, and fit in well socially with the other guys. That was enough for everyone, really. That is, everyone except John Silver himself. Feeling pressure from his family to stop screwing around and do something serious with his life, Silver semi-reluctantly left Genesis a few months after the release of their first album.

> **John:** *I had no real interest in studying management but I did fancy the idea of going to university in the States. I went there absolutely sure that Peter would phone me at any moment to say…"Get back over here now." That is what I really wanted to happen, no doubt about it…I waited to get the call. But it never came.* [1]

And indeed, the universal reaction to his departure amongst the band was one of sadness. To a person, nobody wanted to see John leave; he certainly wasn't fired or forced out.

> **Mike:** *Jonathan Silver had left. He had decided to go to Cornell University to study…it was his own decision.* [1]

> **Tony:** *We would never have kicked John out…we were sad to lose him, he was a nice chap. We're still friends.* [1]

> **Peter:** *He was a real enthusiast and a great source of energy.* [1]

From a songwriting perspective, Silver's brief time with the band was pretty much the Peter and Tony show. Ant and Mike considered themselves a writing team in their own right, and Ant did have a few bits, but by their own admission, their contributions weren't really on equal footing.

> **Mike:** *Although all the songs were credited to us as a band, the truth was we were more like two gangs of friends; Ant and I, and Tony and Peter. Neither Ant nor I had really got going as songwriters at this point. Our attitude was always "one for all and all for one," but From Genesis to Revelation was mostly Peter and Tony.* [14]

> **Ant:** *Peter and Tony were way out front on the first album, no doubt about it. Mike and I were playing catch up.* [1]

So it was that in 1969, well after the debut album had actually been recorded, Ant and Mike decided to play catch up in earnest, hunkering down together to write as many songs as they could. It was during this push for material that John Silver announced his departure. Thus, while everyone in Genesis was disappointed at the turn of events, it was Ant (with Mike's help) who channelled this wistful emotion into an actual piece of music, which he appropriately titled 'Silver Song'.

> **Ant:** *There was an abundance of material which Mike and I recorded during the summer of 1969 the period when the group were switching from the From Genesis To Revelation period to 'The Knife' and 'Looking For Someone', and doing the heavy electric guitar stuff. Some of*

> *the stuff that we recorded...were things like...'Silver Song'...it was from that same era. Most of it never ended up going through Genesis.* [121]

Genesis indeed went on to make *Trespass*, which did feature a previously unused early Ant piece in 'Visions of Angels', but the emergence of true group efforts ('Looking for Someone', 'Stagnation', and 'The Knife') and the maturation of Ant and Mike's own tandem writing ('White Mountain' and 'Dusk') meant that 'Silver Song' got lost deep in the shuffle along with the other Ant/Mike material from that burst of writing in the summer of '69. And then, of course, Anthony Phillips left Genesis.

This isn't a tale of the reasons for Ant's departure, so I'll skip ahead here a couple years to 1972, around the time of *Foxtrot*. Ant had been studying classical music and musical theory, and was in the middle of these studies when he got together with Mike Rutherford again. Not in any formal kind of way; it was just two old friends hanging out, as two old friends do. But soon enough one thing led to another and before they knew it they were both noodling away.

> **Ant:** *There was a twelve-string guitar sitting in the kitchen, and Mike came in and started improvising on the guitar. Shortly afterwards I also went into the kitchen and played some improvisations. Somebody who heard both of us said later that they were absolutely amazed by the similarity of what we were both playing.* [1]

The idea began to form that maybe they could record something together for old time's sake. You know, maybe repurpose some of the older stuff that hadn't yet seen the light of day. But there was also a new idea in that batch: that they should write a modern hymn. This was back to the kind of core of what Genesis was originally supposed to be about: songwriters writing songs for other groups to sing and perform. In this case, those "others" would be a church choir, and there was something poetic about the notion of members of the band called Genesis - whose first album was erroneously displayed in record stores in the religious music section - creating a piece of actual worship music intended for use in churches. This song, 'Take This Heart', would end up being recorded by the Charterhouse Choral Society and stuck on a 1975 Charisma sampler disc called *Beyond an Empty Dream*, but would resurface decades later on a deluxe edition of Ant's joint effort solo album with Andrew Skeet, *Seventh Heaven*.

Back to the summer of 1973 though, in the midst of the writing sessions for *Selling England by the Pound*, and Ant and Mike's modern hymn still needed to be demoed just like any other proto-recording would. Mike figures, why not call Phil Collins over to help out for a day?

> **Ant:** *Mike and I began to play again together in 1972/73 and Phil came down...to help with the demo of our modern hymn 'Take This Heart' around that time. We all got on very well and somewhere along the line we must have played him 'Silver Song'. Phil had bags of energy, enthusiasm - aside from copious talent! - and was very positive about it. So we did a demo. Charisma loved it...* [122]

Phil Collins of course by this time had already sang 'For Absent Friends' with Genesis, but this experience may well have been a strong catalyst for why Mike decided to use him as lead vocalist for his own song 'More Fool Me' on the then-upcoming Genesis album. But unlike those other songs, 'Silver Song' was something fun and upbeat, with a repeating, sing-along chorus. In other words, a potential single. And who knew the drummer from Genesis could pull that off? Again, other than 'For Absent Friends', Phil's lead vocal catalogue was basically squat at the time.

> **Ant:** *He was already doing some really good backing vocals for [Genesis]. Mike used him on 'More Fool Me', didn't he, which I think they recorded in 1973, for Selling England [By The Pound]...So I don't think I was the one that discovered him, but Mike and I were probably the ones who tried solo stuff with him before he did any solo stuff later.* [123]

Charisma, loving the demo and keen to print some money, managed to book some studio time in the middle of the *Selling England* tour for Phil and Mike to go meet Ant and get this recording of 'Silver Song' done properly, including sticking Phil on drums to really liven up the rhythm section. Here's the account from Ant's own website:

> In October 1973 it was arranged for the recording to take place at Island Studios in London on one free day in the busy Genesis touring schedule. Ant, Mike, and Phil recorded 'Silver Song' and another track, 'Only Your Love' during this session, with a view to Charisma releasing the two tracks as a single. Genesis then carried on with their touring schedule until the summer of 1974 when it was anticipated that the 'Silver Song' single would be released. To tie in with this,

Phil gave an interview on BBC Radio One in June 1974 where he talked about the background to the single being recorded and a tape of the completed version of 'Silver Song' was played at the end of the interview. [124]

Understandable that Charisma would want to wait for a Genesis tour to conclude before marketing a single with three current or former Genesis members on it, but it's very clear that the song was definitely going to be released in 1974. And why wouldn't they be excited about it? Just listen to how happy and energetic this thing is. The moment Phil jumps in I get major Mumford & Sons vibes, to give a twenty-first century parallel, and their song 'I Will Wait' blew up the charts in an era where folk rock was already long buried. This song, where the entire second half is just an endless chorus dance radiating life? In an era where folk rock actually had something of a market? That's basically an automatic hit. You can't pass that kind of thing up.

And Phil didn't merely give one radio interview to market the thing, but was happy to tell anyone and everyone about it, anytime he could.

> **Phil:** *I'm also cutting a single which came about when I demoed some songs for Mike and Ant Phillips, who used to be in the band. I was just demoing the songs for them but [Charisma boss Tony] Strat[ton-Smith] liked what he heard and decided to put it out as a single, though I don't yet know what name it'll go out under.* [125]

And elsewhere…

> **Phil:** *I don't see any great success for [the single], but if it gets some nice reviews I might do an album of my own.* [126]

Is this where it all went awry? After getting so fired up about this song and letting Phil Collins go hype it up to the press, Charisma simply never bothered to release it. Did Stratton-Smith simply change his mind and decide the song ultimately wasn't very good after all? Or was there something else happening behind the scenes?

> **Ant:** *The rest could have been history! The [single] master, though Phil is brilliant on it, felt a little cold and anodyne after the loose, throwaway country feel of the demo. Charisma lost interest - or perhaps there were other more complex reasons for it's failure to be released…* [122]

Complex reasons like…"what if this is TOO successful?" Here's Ant's website again:

> For reasons that remain unknown to this day, the 'Silver Song' single release never appeared. It is reasonable to suggest that Charisma Records may have felt it was too early in their career for Genesis to have breakaway projects, but there was no one definite reason that Ant is aware of as to why the single was not released. [124]

With Genesis about to sequester away at Headley Grange to write what would become *The Lamb Lies Down on Broadway*, Charisma couldn't very well afford their star drummer getting bigger than the band, much less thinking about a solo album of his own. This attitude would continue to prevail for Ant's debut solo album, *The Geese & The Ghost*; upon initial completion in 1976, Ant submitted the album to Charisma Records who - perhaps also feeling they made a mistake allowing Steve Hackett to put out 1975's *Voyage of the Acolyte* - refused to release it. Ant then struggled to find a label, eventually causing Genesis manager Tony Smith to create his own: Hit and Run Music Publishing. *The Geese & The Ghost,* comprised in part of songs written in 1969, would finally release in early 1977.

Yet the album notably did *not* include 'Silver Song', because Ant was still determined to make it work as a single.

> **Ant:** *With 'Silver Song', I did a number of versions of the track over the years. There was an attempted single version done under the auspices of Arista which was done during an all-night session with Rupert Hine, John Perry, and Trevor Morais. The strange thing with that track is that often the punters like it but the musicians don't. The only result of that session was wasting the record company's money! Every time a project came up it was a case of trying to get 'Silver Song' in there somewhere…* [127]

But it was never to be. A 1978 band version of the song never appeared. A 1981 version with a Caribbean feel disappeared without a trace. A reworked version for a 1986 Eric Clapton project was cast aside. That alternate 1986 demo, at least, would eventually show up on the 2010 CD release of Ant's archive collection, *Private Parts & Pieces*. But every one of these potential iterations of 'Silver Song' vanished into the ether about as quickly as they formed, and the original Collins single remained nowhere to be found. It's a great "what if" story. A poppy folk rock song, composed by the Ant/Mike writing team that proved so effective on *Trespass*, bolstered by the singing and drumming of Phil Collins. It's like a kind of miniature side-Genesis, a brief glimpse into a world where the three of them might have co-existed in the same band.

Some time after the initial disappearance of the single, when Peter Gabriel wanted to get some demos down of the material for his own first solo album, he invited over musicians he knew and felt he could trust. Specifically, he called on Mike Rutherford, Phil Collins, and Anthony Phillips (along with Phil's Brand X bandmate John Goodsall).

Ant: *It was the only time I've ever played with Mike and Phil together as a proper bass and drums rhythm section - on the earlier occasion Mike and I had both been playing acoustic guitars. That was another moment that made me think, "What have I missed here?" because Phil and Mike were so solid and yet so relaxed together, the kind of relaxation that only comes from confidence and empathy and years of understanding. It was an absolute dream, in fact. I just played a few chords and sat and listened to the two of them. They were so good.* [1]

In 2015, 46 years after its writing and 41 years after it was originally slated for release, the single version 'Silver Song' finally saw the official light of day as a bonus track on the CD reissue of *The Geese & The Ghost*.

Steve Hackett

1975 - *Voyage of the Acolyte*

'Shadow of the Hierophant' and the "Lost Genesis Album"

As the above title suggests, a lot of fans refer to Steve Hackett's debut solo album, *Voyage of the Acolyte*, as sort of a "lost" or "hidden" Genesis album. It's an understandable sentiment, and one that has a few really strong reasons for existing. The first and perhaps most important element is that the album sounds to some listeners like, well, Genesis.

> **Steve:** *I don't feel happy making background music. I hope people will listen to my album at least once, really listen. You couldn't hold an unbroken conversation while it's playing. Neither could you to a Genesis album. We require more from an audience point of view...* [128]

As Steve Hackett was a member of Genesis so this is perhaps unsurprising. Well, I say "was," but the fact is that this album came out in 1975 while Genesis were auditioning singers to replace Peter Gabriel. Which is to say that at this point, Steve Hackett *is* a member of Genesis. He's still very much in that Genesis musical mindset. But the most obvious checkbox of all for the "This is basically Genesis" crowd is the personnel, which includes a couple of recognisable names, courtesy of Steve's apprehensions.

> **Steve:** *The thing I was most worried about was getting the rhythm tracks sorted out. If they didn't make it...well, I had Phil and Mike to help me and they did a marvellous job.* [129]

That's right, as of the time of the release of *Voyage of the Acolyte*, 75% of Genesis were credited as players on it. That's, uh, significant. But I'm not sure it's quite significant enough for me to really consider a "hidden band effort," because for the most part Phil and Mike were acting as essentially session performers on material they didn't have a hand in writing. That's not at all an uncommon thing, and in itself it's maybe not that worthy of note. In fact, I probably wouldn't be writing this retrospective at all, if not for the album's closing track, 'Shadow of the Hierophant'. This piece has a slightly different history from the rest of the album; a history that dates back to 1972.

> **Steve:** *Genesis were famous for keeping things on the backburner for the next album, or the next album; we had material coming out of our ears...The last track [on my album], '[Shadow of the] Hierophant', was something that was rehearsed during the Foxtrot sessions three years earlier. And I thought, "The band's never going to do this," and I asked Mike if he would be up for me doing a version of that with him, so we did a co-write on that tune. I think I did it slightly faster. I think he imagined it was going to be half that speed, which is probably why it didn't work with the band. Because it's already slow, pondering. But it's kind of mighty...I remember it making waves at the time, and I remember Tony saying, "Oh, we could've used that with Genesis," but I thought, "Well [when's] that gonna happen? It's three years later, we've got this magnificent thing, [and you're] suggesting that we do it but [we] never did." So obviously he liked it. The guys were complimentary at the time, and I had the cooperation of so many of them to make it.* [130]

At first blush this seems bizarre to think about, doesn't it? Steve has a bit he brings into Genesis, and they like it, but not enough to really finish developing it or get it on record. But Mike is keen enough that he agrees to work with Steve to get it fully written. Genesis still aren't using it, so Steve takes it as his album closer, which causes Tony to get upset. But everyone plays on the song (and album) *except* for Tony, which naturally leads me to conclude that he (and/or Peter, I suppose) was the roadblock to getting it done in the first place. Then he later criticises Steve for putting out a solo album full of material Genesis could've used? The band politics here are a bit of a tangled mess.

From a musical perspective, though, it's a bit easier to see why 'Shadow of the Hierophant' landed on the permanent backburner. Consider *Foxtrot*, where the end section of the song was rehearsed. It hadn't yet coalesced into a full song, and with the abundance of other material on hand - to say nothing of 'Supper's Ready' itself taking up virtually an entire side of the record - there simply wasn't any room. Then comes *Selling England by the Pound*, a quintessentially English album designed to sound quintessentially English.

Which is to say that a song built around a giant, repeating, ominous crescendo wouldn't really find a home. Next came *The Lamb Lies Down on Broadway*, where there's more of a sonic match, but it's got to fit somewhere in this sprawling story and album layout, where it just can't quite seem to work in. By that point Steve had had enough, but I'm not sure there was a whole lot of alternative given Genesis' output during the early 70s.

And yet, Steve's right that the band likely never would've done it anyway. Looking forward, *A Trick of the Tail* has a pretty consistent sound of its own, and 'Shadow of the Hierophant' ain't it. *Wind & Wuthering*? Well, that could work, possibly, at the cost of cutting one of Tony's pieces. Yet even *Wind* has a kind of warmth about it that 'Shadow of the Hierophant' is missing. And then, of course, begins the gradual pop turn.

So no, Genesis was never going to record 'Shadow of the Hierophant' and it therefore isn't a Genesis tune, but it *did* begin as one, and it *was* co-written by half of the band at the time of its release and performed by three-quarters of the band on the record (albeit with additional personnel as well). How does that all work out?

> **Steve:** *It was in a way a version of the group, but without having to answer to the committee.* [70]

Well, in order to do proper justice to 'Shadow of the Hierophant', I'm afraid I need to rewind a bit and go back to the embryonic stages of *Voyage of the Acolyte* as a whole. You see, Steve's solo debut is a concept album, and despite 'Hierophant' being (mostly) written back in 1972, it's been situated as the album closer, and so is in a way subordinated to concepts from the other pieces that didn't arise until later, chronologically speaking. So let's take some time to get a grasp on the album's concept here. It all starts, as these things so often do, with a *Lamb*.

> **Steve:** *I had six or seven months of solid touring and to keep myself sane...I would write back at the hotel each night.* [129]

Half a year is a long time, and it's no surprise that Steve came out of this *Lamb* touring period with a wealth of material; nor is it a surprise that he would be on stage with Genesis every night and then retire to a hotel room to write stuff that sounded, at times, quite like Genesis. In any case, Steve happened to have another personal interest developing in parallel with his songwriting: tarot cards.

> **Steve:** *What really turned me onto tarot cards: this particular person at that particular time in my life, when certain things were suggested to me...Things I would never have come to by myself.* [131]

This is delightfully vague, which is pretty much the modus operandi of fortune telling in general, so it works really well in microcosm here. In any case, it was in these quasi-magical cards that Steve was able to find his muse.

> **Steve:** *Writing mostly instrumental music, I found it helped me to write from pictorial form...You can read into a tarot card spread whatever you will, really.* [132]

Well, sounds like he's maybe not such a true believer after all...

> **Steve:** *I'm into it, but I'm not preaching the gospel...I wrote about the cards which came over strongest to me.* [128]

Hey, fair enough! So now we have a strong mental image forming: Steve sitting in a hotel room with a guitar and a deck of tarot cards, staring at the pictures and asking himself, "What does this picture *sound* like?" It's a bit out there to be sure, but all the same there's a simple kind of brilliance about the exercise. And as these different instrumental pieces begin to take shape, they start to form a kind of logical flow and order. In essence, *Voyage of the Acolyte* is **itself** a tarot card reading - of Steve! What fate might it portend for him? Let's take a brisk walk down the track order and try to make sense of this thing, shall we?

'Ace of Wands' represents the card of the same name, which itself carries meanings of "creation".

> **Steve:** *'Ace of Wands' symbolises the beginning of a new venture. [The tarot card suit of] Wands represents fire, initiative, and skill. What better way to begin the album?* [133]

It's a blistering track with a rapid succession of ideas that maybe don't all mesh with one another, but the chaos is pretty well in keeping with the concept of fire. It's also pretty well in keeping with the concept of recording an album in the middle of the night.

> **Steve:** *It comes bursting into life. Furiously fast pace on this one. I remember rehearsing it up with Mike Rutherford and Phil Collins; you wouldn't believe we were recording this at about 3 in the morning. Where does all that energy come from at 3 in the morning?! But it did! This very first track, I wanted to pack it full of so many events. I think I was writing nervously in those days. I thought, "It's got to hold the attention," so I mean, it goes from one mood to another very, very sharply.* [13]

So here we have it, the first card of the reading: "An exciting new venture awaits!" Something like, say, creating a debut solo album, for example.

'Hands of the Priestess, Part I' follows the frenetic opener with a more measured hand. The Priestess card of the tarot tends to represent qualities like intuition, or one's inner voice. It's a gentle, peaceful number, a meditation of sorts. Thus, the second card might be interpreted as "Find your inner voice. Grow in confidence as a writer."

'A Tower Struck Down' refers to the tarot card of The Tower, which is usually depicted as being struck by lightning, complete with hapless victims plummeting to their doom. Fittingly then, the song sounds, well, something like hapless victims plummeting to their doom. The card itself is said to represent upheaval, or perhaps disaster. Thus, the third card may well be interpreted as "IMPENDING DOOM." Or, more immediately to Steve's situation, the card and song can act as a kind of musical stand-in for Steve's own doubts and lack of confidence about this very effort. "This album is probably going to fail."

'Hands of the Priestess, Part II' is a second doling out of The Priestess card and a chance for both listener and fortune-telling recipient (that is, Steve himself) to catch their breath. It may be described as "What in the world just happened?" from a listener point of view, or as coming to terms with a rocky future from a tarot reading standpoint. "Yes, this album might suck. You must look inside yourself and accept this risk if you are to move forward."

'The Hermit' then represents that very acceptance. It's a card that signifies the search for truth, or maybe "inner guidance." That it's the first time we get to hear Steve himself singing lead vocal is both a treat and telling: the only answers that will matter here are those he can find within himself, and he must decide for himself whether to press on.

> **Steve:** *I based a track like 'The Hermit' on a particular card, and it's very introspective. By looking at the cards and pulling out the strongest feelings, it mapped out a way of working.* [129]

The strongest feelings, indeed.

'Star of Sirius' is notable for featuring Phil Collins on vocals as well as drums, but at the moment that's a bit beside the point. The Star is a tarot card that represents hope and healing, depicted as a maiden pouring out water under a shining sky full of stars. This is the "turn" of the album, kicking off its second side with something a bit more positive than the gloom, doom, and meek acceptance of the preceding tracks.

> **Steve:** *'Star of Sirius' is an optimistic looking to the future. After some of the heaviness and introspection of the other tracks, I wanted something lightheaded with a bouncy pop song feel.* [126]

It might as well be on the soundtrack to quirky, ball-rolling video game Katamari Damacy, if I'm being honest. I make no value judgments as to whether that's a good or bad thing. It also marks another appearance of Steve's distinct style of tapping, which wouldn't become popularised - or named - for years to come. In any case, it's Steve making a conscious decision to look at this endeavour in the best light that he can.

'The Lovers' is an interesting case in that it's a song/card that I'm not sure would've been on the album at all initially, but for a chance meeting in New York City.

> **Steve:** *I met somebody roundabout the time we were just starting to perform The Lamb Lies Down on Broadway. A lady who, strangely enough, was also into tarot cards, and had done a lot of paintings that were based on the group's work. And I started speaking to her, and discussing her work, and how much I would like her to do an album cover for me. It was still pretty much a glimmer of an idea at that time. And she said to me, "I know you're going to do this album, and it's going to be very good for you. It's going to broaden you in all sorts of respects." And it was her encouragement which kind of saw me through it. You really need other people to feed off...I feel...stronger spiritually than ever before.* [134]

That "somebody" was a Brazilian artist and Genesis superfan named Kim Poor, who ended up creating a Genesis art book as well as many album covers for Steve. And oh yeah - she married him, too. It's notable that it wasn't anyone in Genesis itself who encouraged him to see this music through, but a woman he just happened to meet and immediately fall in love with. The Lovers as a card, as one might surmise, is all about partnerships and duality. Steve interprets this in a somewhat literal way by playing the second half of the short song backwards. This is his reading saying, essentially, "Love will see you through." Or, maybe, "If you want to *go* it alone, you can't *do* it alone."

'Shadow of the Hierophant' then closes the album with a bang, and it's immediately clear that *this* was the track Genesis had been rehearsing. If you listened to this album without knowing which track was in the band's backlog, you'd pick this one out right away, every time.

> **Steve:** *I had the band's Mellotron at home and I started to write with the string sound... The big, romantic sound at the beginning was written on the Mellotron. I was keen to do an album that would make full use of the world of malevolent Mellotron. Every chord I played on it felt instantly magical and powerful.* [70]

Yet as clear as the influence is, it's also a Genesis song out of time; out of temporal sync with the band's continued development as songwriters. For one thing, the transitions are a bit abrupt. The epic intro into the first acoustic verse works well, very similar in feel and effect to what Genesis did with 'The Chamber of 32 Doors'. But the transitions from the acoustic parts back into the epic sound are a little bit jagged, something that by 1975 the band had outgrown. 1972, though? Well, that makes a little bit more sense. Though of course, the lead vocal line is sung by a woman with an operatic sound, so you know, that's a bit different.

> **Steve:** *I loved the sound of Sally Oldfield's voice in the folk duo The Sallyangie (with her brother Mike), which reminded me of Marianne Faithful - that seductive, fast vibrato I so loved in other female singers too, like Buffy Sainte-Marie and Edith Piaf. I tracked Sally down and ran the idea of 'Shadow of the Hierophant' by her. Her brother Mike was more in the limelight at that time, but it was her voice I was interested in and she luckily seemed happy to be asked. She was later to have much deserved solo success.* [70]

Opting for a female singer was a bit of a bold choice for Steve, but Sally Oldfield's voice works really well with the gentle guitar, the floaty flute, and the lyrics about dreams and water. Those lyrics are rather important, I think, as calls to other tarot cards themselves. The recurring line of the song is "the moon eclipsed the sun," and both The Moon and The Sun are themselves also cards in the tarot deck: The Sun represents joy and positivity, and The Moon represents illusions and unconsciousness. Thus we can interpret that dreams and visions of things to come (perhaps those dark portents from The Tower earlier?) are making it difficult to find happiness. A line about a fountain failing to heal is probably likewise a call-back to The Star, indicating that the clouding doubts can't be cleansed simply by a steely resolve to be upbeat. It takes something a little more.

> **Steve:** *'Shadow of the Hierophant' with its contrasting energies symbolised both shadow and light in the ancient world and its healing mysteries. It had an aspect of Greek tragedy about it as in the Oresteia, with its strange hybrid of ritual, oppression, and triumph with the processional feel of a musical crescendo.* [70]

From the conclusion of the vocal segment the song melts into another tapping section that sounds to me almost like ELO's 'Fire on High' before landing into a more traditional sounding guitar passage for a short while. And that's apt, because The Hierophant card in the tarot deck represents tradition itself, conformity to an ideal. An ideal like, say, the songwriting both of Genesis and of Steve's own style.

> **Steve:** *I tried to do one track on my album in that [virtuoso guitarist] style...it was like ELO meets The Who, with heavy chords, cliches, and a baroque bit in the middle, all at a crazy speed. It was based on The Fool in the tarot cards, and I ended up not using it in the end. I decided it was too stupid. I wanted a basically stupid track, but it came out so hammy, it would have been obnoxious.* [129]

Tasteful restraint is what The Hierophant is all about, baby. But then the music shifts again. It starts with tinkling bells, which give way to a quiet guitar figure on the same dark notes, and it all gets louder and bigger over the next five-plus minutes. That's a long time! It's just this inexorably growing THING that simply won't go away.

> **Steve:** *This is kind of a long crescendo. I was thinking I could add more and more instruments as it goes. I feel in a way there was something about this that's kind of timeless, and it became different things with different bands. When I was playing it live in recent years, we let the drums go more and more manic. I mean, this particular version of the thing was found in my dad's shed! We had this monitor mix that was there and lost for thirty years, and then unearthed like out of an Egyptian tomb! But at the time, it was really a monitor mix to be able to hear the drums, and they were considered to be maybe a little bit too loud. Of course, things have changed since then where drums became king over time, so this reflects the time that we were in when that was going on.* [13]

He's not lying; Phil is going nuts on this by the end. Can you imagine Genesis just sitting there for more than five minutes playing what essentially amounts to the same few bars of a 3/4 pattern over and over? Who would stand for that? Hilariously, later releases of *Voyage of the Acolyte* include a couple bonus tracks, one of which is called 'Shadow of the Hierophant (Extended Playout Version)'. This is exactly what it sounds like it is, adding *another* five minutes to the giant ending crescendo, which extends the song to a length of seventeen minutes total, with a whopping ten being just the outro. It's madness.

> **Steve:** *Not everyone's going to dig it; there's a universal spirit but there isn't a universal music.* [128]

And now we finally come to the crux of the thing. The Hierophant card represents conformity and tradition, yes, but that's not the song's title now is it? No, this is '**Shadow** of the Hierophant'. And in tarot readings, every card actually has a pair of meanings. The primary meaning is what you see when you simply view the card, but there is also a meaning for when you receive the card upside-down. This meaning is the reverse, or perhaps *inverse* of the card's basic meaning. It becomes a mirror, or, if you like, a shadow. The Hierophant is conventional thinking, sure, but The Hierophant's Shadow? That's the precise *opposite:* rebellion, non-conformity. *New methods.*

> *Imaginative guitarist/writer seeks involvement with receptive musicians, determined to strive beyond existing stagnant music forms.* [135]

Such is the wording of the ad Steve placed in Melody Maker which scored him an audition into Genesis. And now, five years later, Steve finds himself trying to strive beyond once again.

> **Steve:** *You're the captain of your own ship. When you're doing a solo album you're running your own show. People are looking to you for all the answers. Once you've successfully negotiated that, going back into a band is like returning to the crew. You realise you've outgrown the need for permission. And I also made the grave error of having a hit with the thing. I suspect from then on I became much less containable within the group.* [1]

'Shadow of the Hierophant' is a song from 1972 written by two blokes from Genesis, but that Genesis never did because it was a little too bold. And realising this, it wasn't long after the song's release that Steve Hackett realised he was stagnating again. So The Tower was struck down, and The Hermit moved on. This song may be among the earliest written on the album, but it's the culmination of all the other pieces, the climax of one journey and the start of another one.

> **Steve:** *The whole record was like a musical journey, ending with an overwhelming sense of empowerment plus a dream achieved.* [70]

After 45+ years and 27 studio albums (and counting!) as a solo artist, I think it's fair to say that this particular fortune-telling ended up being a good one.

Peter Gabriel

1980 - *Peter Gabriel*

'Intruder' and the Gated Reverb Heard 'Round the World

Unlike the previous entries in this section, 'Intruder' is not a case of a member of Genesis sitting down with one or more other members of Genesis and writing a song for a solo project. No, now on his third solo album, Peter Gabriel was quite self-sufficient, and 'Intruder' was all his baby...or was it? Prepare for things to get a little bit murky as we dive into the history behind not only the opening track from *Peter Gabriel 3* aka *Melt*, but also the sound that helped define a decade of popular music.

By now most everyone has probably heard the term "gated drum sound" or something along those lines. We all vaguely understand what it means, or think we do anyway, and even if we have trouble describing it, many of us could probably hear it in a song on the radio and say, "That right there, that's it." If you're a Genesis fan reading this book, you probably also know it's an effect strongly associated with Phil Collins and his producer of the 80s, Hugh Padgham. Perhaps you even have some awareness that Peter Gabriel (and 'Intruder' specifically) has some kind of connection to this phenomenon, or technique, or whatever it is. But if you're like me, you've heard all these things and filed them away in your mental trivia database without actually understanding the whats and hows of the whole affair. Thus, I thought it'd be nice for my own edification as well as that of anyone else who might be interested, to look at the history of this "gated drum sound" and figure out once and for all: what the heck are we really talking about?

Despite the intimate association the term now has with Phil Collins and the 1980s, our story actually starts with Peter Gabriel in 1979. Now two albums into his solo career, Pete had just finished a tour, where he was joined at the end by an old friend smackin' the snares.

> **Phil:** *Considering all the historic interest in supposed tension between Gabriel-era Genesis and Collins-era Genesis, it's not often noticed that I play with Peter a lot at this time. If I may be so bold, I'm the best drummer he knows. He can rely on me. With Peter being a drummer himself, he's pretty picky...Contrary to what people might like to think, there was never any bad blood between us. We were great friends.* [12]

> **Peter:** *He's an amazing drummer. I'd forgotten quite how good he is. It was interesting to see what he came up with for my songs. I think he had a good time just drumming and not having to sing at all.* [136]

From that tour Peter set out to write his third solo album, but after a bit of mutual dissatisfaction with the way the previous album came out under producer Robert Fripp, he felt it was time for a significant change of approach.

> **Peter:** *There was a radical re-think of the process of writing involved...Traditionally I've begun with chords and melodies and sustained my early interest in an idea through movement in those areas. This time I wanted to try the reverse of that and work from the rhythm. I think the rhythm track is always the spine of a piece of music...* [137]

Starting from a place of rhythm meant Gabriel would want a producer sympathetic to that side of the music, but preferably not one so famous and entrenched in any one particular sound that he'd feel pushed in one creative direction or another. Thus, a perfect candidate seemed to be a fellow by the name of Steve Lillywhite, who had just recently scored a hit with Siouxsie and the Banshees' 'Hong Kong Garden' on the strength of the way he recorded the drums; he laid down the snares and bass drum separately from the rest, enabling echo to be added to the drum hits but not the cymbal splashes. This was the exact kind of innovative sensibility Peter Gabriel was looking for; that his surname happened to be a call-back to a blind but wise guide from *The Lamb Lies Down on Broadway* certainly couldn't have hurt either.

With this change in producer came a change in studio as well, to The Townhouse in London, where a young audio engineer named Hugh Padgham had recently signed on. Luckily, he seemed to have the same kinds of ideas about rhythm and sound as both Gabriel and Lillywhite, and so pretty quickly a sense of teamwork and trust developed.

> **Peter:** *It took until the next record to find out what I was as a solo artist, or could be. That was in the framework of feeling more settled with the band, and having the great team of Steve Lillywhite and Hugh Padgham.* [138]

This was all exciting, certainly, but it was also a lot of new blood in the room. Ultimately Pete felt that he needed someone he could really trust to be a steadying influence and ensure that his visions for these rhythm sections were realised. So, recalling the recent good vibes they'd shared from the tour, and the fact that Genesis was on a break to allow Mike and Tony to do their own solo albums, Pete gave Phil a call and asked him to come by and play on a few tracks. Phil, ever the friendly workhorse, agreed. It was only after he'd gotten there that he found out to what, precisely, he had agreed.

> **Peter:** *I'd been thinking about the things I didn't like on rock records, and one of the things was cymbals splashing around all over the place. They take up an incredible amount of space in the higher sound frequencies. And if you take them out you give yourself a whole country to explore. So I said no cymbals. And that meant that the drummers – mainly Jerry Marotta but also Phil Collins and Morris Pert – couldn't do what they normally do. Suddenly they had to think differently. And that affected the spine of the piece, the rhythm. And everything else.* [138]

> **Phil:** *I loved what Peter did. It was great fun…"Nothing metal" was the way he described it. "I don't want any metal on this album, Phil." I was okay with it, but I didn't know what to do with my left hand…* [99]

This is a really bold idea. No cymbals? For a whole album? I love that Phil didn't have a problem with it in principle, but it was a big problem in practice. Apparently he'd instinctively go to hit cymbals on the kit during the sessions and then be thrown off completely when he got empty air, so they had to stick some toms where the cymbals would go in order to keep things rolling. In any case, this gave audio engineer Hugh Padgham a chance to really play around with his new sound mixing console.

> **Hugh Padgham:** *The SSL desk was amazing - it had compressors and noise gates on every channel, which hadn't been heard of before. The whole idea of SSL desks is that they're great to work [with] and you don't have to think of patching something in, you can just punch a button and there it is.* [139]

Aaaaaand with that it's time to back up a bit. Maybe you're well versed in the world of recording equipment and already know what this technobabble means, but for us laymen Hugh might as well be speaking Klingon. So let's start breaking this statement down term by term to make it more digestible. First, "SSL" stands for "Solid State Logic," but don't fret: they're just the company that manufactured Padgham's sound equipment there. You don't need to worry about that aspect anymore. "Desk", meanwhile, is a shorthand way of saying "audio mixing console," since these things are huge and resemble enormous desks full of futuristic switches and lights, like something straight out of 1960s Star Trek. So that's also refreshingly straightforward. But compressors? Noise gates? What on Earth are those?

A **compressor** is a bit of hardware or software that can amplify the sound of quiet noises as well as soften the sound of loud noises. It's called "compression" because doing this ultimately reduces the dynamic range of a piece. "Dynamic range" *also* sounds like technobabble, but here it's strictly a musical term: in music, volume levels and markings are referred to as dynamics, so a song's dynamic range is simply the difference (in decibels, if you like) between its quietest point and its loudest point. If you make the loudest part quieter, or the quietest part louder, you're shrinking that difference, effectively "compressing" the dynamic range of the piece. Sound engineers can set the thresholds at which they want volumes raised or lowered, and thus manipulate the audio output.

A **noise gate**, on the other hand, is like "what if compressor, but also bouncer at a pub?" A compressor reads all the sounds coming through and then adjusts them based on the target thresholds. A noise gate reads the sounds coming through and outright rejects any sound that isn't in that target range. Thus, instead of amplifying a quiet noise, the quiet noise is eliminated entirely. This functionality is used to eliminate things like background noise in the recording studio, or perhaps low hums from live sound equipment, etc. It can also be triggered on a timer, to cut off smaller sounds within a certain time window of a bigger sound, for instance. So now one can imagine Padgham's excitement at having a new system that has this kind of technology available on every sound channel; it was an unprecedented level of control for an audio engineer, a veritable Christmas morning of knobs and buttons.

If we're mostly clear on that, let's go back to the studio, where Phil is sitting in a stone room, very "live" as they call it, in that sound waves are prone to bounce all over the place. This creates a heavy reverb, or echoing effect; sounds linger in a room with these kinds of acoustics. This is the ol' Lillywhite special of getting some natural echo on a drum sound before overlaying the cymbals, except of course that in this case Peter Gabriel has expressly forbidden cymbals, so the echo will do on its own.

Hugh: *One day we were getting a drum sound with Phil Collins...We had these microphones just hanging down in the studio so that we could hear what was going on there, and built into the desk there's this huge sort of compressor that you can't alter or anything. One day I was trying to speak to Phil and he was playing on his drums in the studio, and I and everybody else in the control room stopped in their shoes and said, "Bloody hell that sounds amazing!" So we faded up the microphones and used the desk compressors. While Phil was playing this drum beat I thought I'd put a noise gate in it for a laugh. It ended up being that song 'Intruder' on the Peter Gabriel 3 album where it goes "doo doo cha, doo doo cha," and in the gap at the end of each phrase the noise gate closes up. It sounds like it's sort of going backwards and forwards.* [139]

We've defined these terms, but reading this paragraph still made my eyes glaze over a bit, so let me do us a favour and translate this. Essentially, Phil is doodling on his drum kit in a room with a ton of echo, and the control room guys flip on the ambient microphones in that room so that when they talk to him, they can hear his responses. However, the main recording microphone is still on at this time, and Phil is still actively drumming. So now they're getting this flood of really powerful drumming noise coming through both the main and ambient microphones, picking up the core thrust of the sound in addition to all the echoing reverb of the room. At that point they use the audio compressors to increase the volume on the ambient mics (making the quietest bits louder), which causes even more of the natural reverb from the room to come through. Then Padgham sticks the noise gate on there, programming it to cut off the reverberating sound less than a second after each drum hit, creating an effect of an echo that doesn't *actually* echo. It's inventive, it's eerie, it's the 80s in advance. It's "gated reverb", and hopefully now you, like me, have just learned what it means.

Hugh: *Peter Gabriel thought it was so great that he just told Phil to play it continually for five minutes...* [139]

Peter: *I got quite excited...I remember saying, "This is going to revolutionise drum sounds." I wanted to do a track that was entirely based around that sound.* [138]

Phil: *You know what happened with 'Intruder'? When Peter first heard that sound – we called it the "facehugger" like that thing in Alien – he got off the sofa and went, "What is that?" I said, "What are you going to do with it? That's my baby." He said, "I'm going to use it"...Then Peter rewrote 'Intruder' to fit the drum rhythm. I said, "Can I at least have a credit?" – which he gave me, a little begrudgingly, I think.* [99]

Indeed, if you check the credits of the album and 'Intruder' in particular, you'll see that Peter Gabriel is still listed as the song's sole writer, but Phil Collins has a curious credit for "drum pattern."

Peter: *I'd written ['Intruder'] with another pattern, and we were just getting the drum sound for a song which didn't make the album called 'Margharita', and Phil was just fooling around on the kit, and that's when he first played the particular pattern which was used on 'Intruder', and I thought that sounded great. So I said, "Hold it! Let's switch the tapes and record just this drum track on its own with a rhythm box as a meter guide and then I'll try putting 'Intruder' on top of it afterwards." So that's what happened. Which is why Phil gets the drum pattern credit.* [137]

It's a little funny, and though I think Phil is in good humour about it, he does have a bone to pick. Here's Peter Gabriel saying that rhythm is the backbone of the music and he wants an album where rhythm is the most important thing, so his drummer invents a rhythm, which he uses as the backbone of a song, but he insists that it doesn't merit an actual songwriting credit. A little bit of talking out of both ends of the mouth on that one, Pete.

Nevertheless, 'Intruder' is of course more than just a drum pattern. It's ironic that on an album devoted to the primacy of rhythm, 'Intruder' is a song where the rhythm came last - if only because it initially had a different one. Regardless, Peter, like in Genesis so many times before, was all about setting a mood.

Peter: *I was playing around with a flattened fifth - the devil's harmony, as it's known - and was looking for a sense of menace in the music, and then began to think of some lyrical situation which would apply, and I liked the idea of the intruder and intrusion of different sorts.* [137]

And...yeah. The nails-on-a-chalkboard sort of effect from the sound of a glass cutter, dissonant chords that are themselves running in opposition to *other* dissonant chords, wailing background vocals...this song is creepy as all get out. The vocal delivery is the icing on the cake: quiet and monotone through the verses while making it clear that this isn't an act of desperation but an actual hobby, then nearly psychotic when snipping the telephone wires. And then...is that a xylophone solo, of all things? One interviewer around the time challenged Peter when he claimed that the songs on this album were a bit more personal and introspective. It's like, are you saying you're a sociopathic home invader?

Peter: *The criminals who are portrayed in the popular press as monsters or sub-human are on one fringe of human activity and it's a mistake to think only, "I'm not like that."* [140]

Then that WHISTLE. Heebie-jeebies all over, man. Just casually whistling like Steamboat Willie while cutting into your window.

Peter: *It is nicely creepy...there's a transvestite element, a clothes fetish. There's part of me in that...It's definitely dark but real. I always used to enjoy performing it.* [141]

Well, no surprise there I guess from the guy who tossed on a red dress and a fox's head in order to get his band some press. Geniuses come in all forms, and Pete's a weird dude. And 'Intruder' is a weird song about an even weirder dude. I also like what he did with it live (as heard on his aptly titled *Plays Live* album); without the ability to perfectly replicate the drum sound on stage, something else had to step up, and so Pete ratcheted up his vocal performance to match. It transforms that last, quiet "I am the intruder" in the outro from a quiet menace to something of a triumphant shout-from-the-mountaintops moment, which is suitably impressive for ending a song like this in front of an audience.

At any rate, Lillywhite and Padgham seemingly couldn't wait to use this fancy new gated reverb drum sound anywhere they could, immediately taking it over to recording sessions for the band XTC, notably on their song 'Making Plans for Nigel', evidently recorded after Collins and Padgham "discovered" the sound, but released well in advance of *Peter Gabriel 3*, which struggled to find a label in North America and so didn't come out until the middle of 1980. XTC guitarist Dave Gregory recalls that the signature Padgham technique hadn't properly been developed yet, but the embryonic form of the gated reverb, fresh off the Collins kit, can be heard on that song. It was the start of a long - and lucrative - legacy for all involved.

First the sound was refined...

Hugh: *When you stand next to a drum kit and the bloke's playing, you can't hear because it's so loud and clattering. Drums never sounded like that on records. Steve Lillywhite felt the same way and so between us we were well into getting an outrageous sound, even if it was over the top - we ended up with something more like what we felt real drums sounded like when you go to a gig.* [139]

Then Collins took it for himself...

Phil: *Hugh is a bass player but he loves drums, and we'd developed that ground-breaking sound on Peter's track 'Intruder'. With hindsight, I now know that that day or two we'd spent working on Peter's third album...was life changing...We fool around [in 1980] with 'In the Air Tonight', but at the moment there's no big drum fill, so none of that gated drum sound, just me coming in on the drums for the last choruses...But...we say, "Let's try that sound we had with Pete..."* [12]

Which caught Tony Banks' attention...

Tony: *Although Phil had already been working with Hugh Padgham, one of the main reasons we chose Hugh [in 1981 for Abacab] was on the strength of his work on Peter's third solo album, Number Three - or whatever it was called, because Peter never gave them names, did he? - the one with 'Intruder'...on it. Phil had played on the album and been very impressed with Hugh's engineering. While we were writing Duke, Phil brought along a tape of the drum loop which was being used on 'Intruder', just the drums with no cymbals, and with the compression techniques that had been applied by Hugh, they had created an incredible drum sound. As Pete said at the time, "With a beat like that you don't really need to do anything else. That on its own is the hit."* [1]

And suddenly, 'Intruder' itself becomes an afterthought.

Peter: *It's a minor thing, but when people listen to that song and say, "You took that Phil Collins drum sound," that niggles me.* [138]

Oh well. That's just how it goes sometimes, eh Phil?

Phil: *We were different animals. I was just trying to write the best songs I could, but Peter got all the credibility... and I got the money! Ha. I've never said that before, but that does sum it up.* [99]

Phil Collins

1981 - *Face Value*

Bursting Out from 'Behind the Lines'

It's easy to forget given the Genesis history, but Phil Collins showed an interest in songwriting right from the get-go. In 1968, having just joined a band called Hickory, Phil was riding high.

> **Phil:** *Suitably inspired, I embark on...trying to write a song... I start messing about on the piano in the back room. I hover around D minor - which, as any Spinal Tap fan knows, is the saddest chord of all - and pick through some lyrical ideas... Soon I think I have something... This is 'Lying, Crying, Dying', and it is the first song seventeen-year-old [me] has ever written... I am, temporarily, a songwriter.* [12]

But we know how that story ends: Hickory becomes Flaming Youth, releases a concept album called *Ark 2* which goes nowhere, and Phil quits for the greener pastures of Genesis. What's curious is how Phil, excited to have written a song that he thought was pretty good, evidently lost all songwriting ambition as soon as he joined this other band. Where did it all go?

My contention is that it didn't really ever go anywhere; that it was merely suppressed for a time. Look at the evolution of Phil's role with the band over the course of the 1970s and I think you'll see what I mean. First, as any new band member must, he has to learn the existing catalogue (essentially just *Trespass* tunes and 'The Musical Box' at that point in time). Then, starting with *Nursery Cryme* proper, he can add a little bit of his own voice to the mix. Literally, considering 'For Absent Friends'. 1972 comes and finds him jamming in earnest, writing the Apocalypse in 9/8 section of 'Supper's Ready' with Tony and Mike (and Steve?). They explore that three-piece energy further in 1973's 'The Cinema Show' even as Phil gets another spotlight performance singing 'More Fool Me'.

By *The Lamb Lies Down on Broadway* in 1974, Phil is so highly respected by his Genesis peers that there's no flinching when he encourages them to stretch a little more. His influence is instrumental in getting the band to do more, well, instrumentals.

> **Phil:** *The blowing side of the band, like the area on The Lamb for instance. Like 'Silent Sorrow in Empty Boats' and 'The Waiting Room'. Which we all loved, you know, that's really one of the things the band does best: visible soundtracks, these little pictures...* [142]

Then of course comes the transition to singer for *A Trick of the Tail*. A reluctant frontman, and yet this is the same bloke who recorded 'Silver Song' with Anthony Phillips and felt hopeful that it might just be a hit single with his name on it. But stepping out from the drum stool in Genesis left a kind of void of its own; a desire to really go at it on the drums. Enter Brand X, another extra-Genesis creative outlet. Which adds confidence coming back for *Wind & Wuthering* in convincing Tony Banks to do a song like 'Wot Gorilla?' And then he's cowriting songs in earnest on both that album as well as *And Then There Were Three*. Again, that feels like more growth until we catch what he said about his chorus for 'Blood on the Rooftops': that it was something he'd "had for ages." How does someone with no interest in writing songs have a strong chorus "just sitting around" for years?

So while the common wisdom is that Phil Collins didn't really have any interest in writing songs until he started cobbling together his demos for what would eventually become *Face Value*, I don't think that's the whole picture. I think the key detail is that Phil Collins didn't really have any interest in writing songs *for Genesis* until around the turn of the decade from the 70s to the 80s. And that *because* of Genesis, he didn't really have time to write songs on his own, either. But the desire to put himself out there in musical form? That was always there.

> **Phil:** *In Genesis sometimes I felt like I was playing a part, rather than being me. Even when I was singing my lyrics, I felt that it wasn't really me.* [143]

> **Mike:** *The fact that the first album came out so well makes you realise he always had in his mind an idea of how things should be. And for the first time he could do it exactly how he*

wanted to do it, and it came out great. There was always a very good arranger, I think, in Phil's head. [143]

Face Value must have been such a liberating endeavour for him. Sure, the lack of a wealth of straightforward songwriting experience created a bit of trepidation over whether the material would be any good, but the vision was always there, and it probably had been for years.

Phil: *When I'm in the band there's a group thinking, but outside the group I'm a free man.* [59]

Heck, we're talking about a guy who co-founded a fusion outfit on the side of Genesis, and then ended up quitting that band because at the end of the day it was still a band!

Phil: *That was one of the reasons I stopped playing with Brand X. Too many people thought it was my thing. And I didn't like all of it enough to say "this is my thing."* [33]

"It has to be *my thing.*" That's so important. And with *Face Value*, Phil at last had the opportunity to make something all his own. There's a reason the credits on the back of the album say "Me" as opposed to his name. Genesis and Collins manager Tony Smith clocked the importance of it as well.

Tony Smith: *For the first time, he was making the record that he wanted to make, and nobody else had any influence on it.* [143]

Now, obviously 'In the Air Tonight' was the big hit from this album and is therefore the first thing people think of when *Face Value* comes up. There's also another single there in 'I Missed Again' and a cover of The Beatles' 'Tomorrow Never Knows'. But I don't think any song on the album that better exemplifies the way Phil Collins wanted to break free of the Genesis mould than the song that is, in fact, a Genesis song: 'Behind the Lines'.

I know, I know. That sounds really counterintuitive. Here's a piece written by the trio of Banks, Collins, and Rutherford. The lyrics are all Mike's. It's easy to look at the song and think, "Well, he must have needed another track to pad the runtime, so he just went to the Genesis well as a cross-promotional kind of thing." You know, kind of using the band's clout to sell his own record. But I don't think that's true. I think the exact opposite thing was at play here. 'Behind the Lines' on *Face Value* isn't about Phil making a connection to his Genesis roots. It's about him severing that connection as thoroughly as he can.

Phil: *One day [during the recording of Duke] we'd finished the backing track of 'Behind the Lines' and we wanted to clean some tracks up: stuff we didn't need anymore, so we could do some vocals. And we ran the tape at double speed just to sort of, you know, time is money! And suddenly this other song appeared. You get that with the Beatles records sometimes: you put them on double speed, you hear something else.* [143]

Mike: *We played it back at a higher speed and it sounded very like a sort of Michael Jackson, kind of funky track. We all kind of got off on it. Obviously that stayed in his mind, and he sort of drew from that.* [143]

Tony and Mike hear this double tempo rendition of the song and have themselves a laugh before dismissing it. Phil though? Phil goes, "Well hang on…" See, while saying "That sounds kind of like a funky Michael Jackson track" (*Off the Wall* had just come out a few months before the *Duke* recording sessions) was a fun little curiosity for guys like Tony and Mike, for Phil it was a revelation. An aspiration. Former Atlantic Records boss and *Face Value* evangelist Ahmet Ertegun got to the heart of the matter.

Ahmet Ertegun: *His feeling, his soul…are very much influenced by black American music.* [143]

Listen to 'I Missed Again' and you'll catch that same sort of vibe. This is punchy, poppy, rhythm and blues style stuff. And so as Phil has the feedback from those around him that yes, this album sounds great and it needs to be made, he's suddenly got full creative control over the sound. He's got some ballads, he's got the dark, brooding nature of 'In the Air Tonight' (built, incidentally, around that "saddest" of D-minor chords), but he's also still thinking back to that really funky sounding sped-up version of 'Behind the Lines'. And somewhere along the way comes the decision to do the song, but to blow up essentially everything about it along the way.

> **Phil:** *Basically I wanted to do the track...just for the horns, really.* [143]

Of course we with the benefit of hindsight know that both 'Paperlate' and 'No Reply At All' were soon to follow from Genesis, but only a year prior the thought of Motown-style horns on a Genesis record was borderline blasphemous. Phil wanted to make sure his listeners knew: "Yes, the writing credit includes the names Banks and Rutherford, but this is not their song. This is *my thing.*" It was a musical culture clash that was virtually unheard of at the time. Phil knew he wanted the horn section from Earth, Wind & Fire to play on the track, since they were his favourite and he knew they'd provide the sound he wanted, but there's an innate distrust between the musicians that has to be overcome. "Will these Phenix Horns agree to take specific direction from a bloke who looks like me?" "Does this Collins cat even make music we can get behind?" Phenix Horns leader and arranger Tom Tom Washington explains the gulf that needed to be bridged.

> **Tom Tom Washington:** *We didn't know who Phil Collins was... There was some inference that he played with a group called Genesis - which didn't mean anything to us neither! We didn't know anything about him at that particular time. He wanted a certain sound: he wanted THAT particular sound, and he would get THOSE players. And that's how we evolved around it. And so Phil would always give us some challenging things to do, and he would leave me the ability to write at my own discretion, and there were certain things that he favoured, that he would like to hear. So he has an ear also for what things should do.* [143]

After sending the Phenix Horns management some samples of his tracks to make sure his music "matched brands" with what they were all about, in they came. And now there's a Genesis track on the solo album of a white, balding British man, run up-tempo, jazzy and funky in feel, with prominent horn playing from black American musicians. Nobody knew how to handle it. It's just Phil, Tom Tom Washington, and engineer/producer Hugh Padgham breaking boundaries with the music and seeing what might happen.

> **Hugh Padgham:** *People didn't have black horn sections on their songs in those days. It sounds crazy to say that now, but American radio wouldn't play some of Phil's songs to start with. Because they'd [think], "White guy with a black horn section? That's not right!" You know, "That should be R&B music! Everybody should be black or everybody should be white." It's amazing that [not too long ago] attitudes like that still existed.* [143]

Then, as if to deliver the coup de grâce to the Genesis influence on the record, Phil chopped out the entire grand, bombastic intro for the song that introduced *Duke* with such aplomb. No extended instrumentals here. Genesis has a blowing side. Brand X was in its entirety a blowing side. Phil Collins doesn't need to blow. Oh, maybe he'll vamp a little. Maybe toss some na-na-nas in there to flavour the jazzy outro. But this is succinct. This is direct. This is distinct from Genesis, and if that's still not clear, Phil Collins is going to switch record labels entirely to get it done. Sorry, Charisma, but we can't have any of the preconceived notions your name engenders floating around in the heads of would-be listeners. Phil Collins is a Virgin Records man now. And if Virgin happens to acquire Charisma Records in 1983 and render all this moot, well, the point will still have been made.

Throughout this entire section I've been highlighting the moments in the solo careers of the members of Genesis when they came together in collaboration to produce something that ultimately was released under just one man's name. 'Behind the Lines' fits that bill only on a technicality. It's not the moment Phil decided to work together with his mates for a solo song; it's the moment he decided to break with them completely, using their own group song to do it. This is Phil Collins finally embracing his inner songwriter and emerging once and for all out from "behind the lines" to front and centre where he arguably belonged all along.

That he gave us ten more years of Genesis music afterward anyhow is really something of a blessing, isn't it?

Mike Rutherford

1985 - *Mike + the Mechanics*

Strength in Numbers and 'A Call to Arms'

Now here's something interesting. Each one of these "solo song" focuses has been a little bit different in nature. With Ant, we had a song that Genesis outgrew before he even left the band, co-written by Mike Rutherford. With Steve, we had a song that Genesis was likely to never perform, and so Steve set it free after a little help from Mike Rutherford. Then Peter finds himself begrudgingly giving Phil Collins credit for a song a year before Phil himself dismantles a Genesis song even as he sings lyrics by, you guessed it, Mike Rutherford.

If you're picking up a pattern here, it might be that this Mike Rutherford guy was pretty important to not only what made Genesis into Genesis, but also into helping to ease his bandmates (sans Peter) into their own solo careers. Even Tony's debut solo album *A Curious Feeling* came on the heels of a collaborative effort with Rutherford, though more on that in the next entry.

But my point is that Mike seems to have been the glue holding the various parts of the band together, at least when viewed through this particular lens. Which brings us to the question: who's going to step up for Mike Rutherford on his own solo material?

To get to our answer, we need to flash back to that pivotal year of 1979, when all things Genesis screeched suddenly to a halt. After all, when Phil Collins decided to head to Vancouver to save his marriage, he assumed that was it for his time in the group.

> **Phil:** *I say, "If we can carry on the band while I'm in Vancouver, we've still got a band. But as that's almost 5000 miles, eight time zones, and a ten-hour flight away, I doubt we can do that. So I guess that means I have to leave Genesis."* [12]

To his surprise, Tony and Mike had evidently grown up quite a bit in the five years since their "you're all in or all out" lack of compassion for family matters drove Peter Gabriel to quit the band. Here instead they decided that Phil could certainly take some leave and try to make things work; the other guys would just do some solo albums in the intervening time. At any rate though, despite them temporarily going their separate ways, Tony and Mike seemed to still be operating with a single musical mind. "I'll do a concept album," they each thought.

Tony's *A Curious Feeling* was based on Flowers for Algernon by Daniel Keyes, while Mike's *Smallcreep's Day* was based on, well, Smallcreep's Day by Peter Currell Brown. Both, notably, opted to hire in other singers for the records. Mike in particular wanted a guy by the name of Paul Carrack, but that didn't work out.

> **Mike:** *I realised how inadequate my voice was from hearing Peter and Phil. I knew Paul [Carrack] from his Ace days, but he couldn't make it, so our manager Tony Smith got Noel McAlla, who was amazing.* [144]

Regardless, neither album particularly did anything sales-wise, Phil's marriage was unsalvageable, and so the band got back together for a pair of albums and a trio of tours. Then, having all tasted solo success (Phil's *Face Value* emerging between Genesis' *Duke* and *Abacab*), they scheduled in another Genesis gap year for more solo records.

Seeing the meteoric success of Phil's solo output, it seems Mike and Tony both had the same idea again: "He's getting this success because he's the singer. You know, *we* ought to sing, too."

> **Mike:** *I had no real desire to sing, but people would always ask if I was going to try it, and eventually I decided...I'd give it a shot. But it was one of those times when, even before you start, a little voice inside tells you it isn't a good idea. And you end up doing it anyway.* [14]

1982 brought along Mike's *Acting Very Strange*, joined several months later by Tony's *The Fugitive* in 1983, though the bulk of that album was also recorded in '82 before Genesis reconvened at the Farm to make the album that eventually would be called, simply, *Genesis*.

Again neither album did anything on the sales charts, and moreover now the critics had ample ammunition to dismiss the efforts, saying, and I'm paraphrasing here, "Why on earth would either of these yuk-yuks think they have the talent to sing lead?"

> **Mike:** *I didn't even know I possessed a singing voice three months [before recording Acting Very Strange]. Once I decided I'd give it a shot, I basically had to assimilate the hard vocal edge that most singers take six years of singing on the road, screaming and throwing their voices, and generally abusing themselves to accomplish. Thanks to gallons of brandy and hard work I think it worked, but I'm not sure I could do it again tomorrow. At one point I considered calling the LP Abuse.* [145]

The "gallons of brandy" had a two-fold effect here. First, they would decimate Mike's throat lining, giving him a raw, ragged sound that could potentially work for rock and roll music. Second and more importantly, they'd get him drunk enough that the little voice inside telling him not to sing would be silenced, and he would start to believe that he could actually pull this thing off. In the end, *Acting Very Strange* might as well have been called *Abuse*, because listening to a full album of Mike's lead vocals is a true trial by fire.

Look, I'm not saying this just to pile onto Mike. It's hard to put yourself out there, in Mike's case further than he ever had before, and have your hopes shattered by both critics and the market alike. The silver lining was that Genesis was still wildly successful and growing more so with every album. There was still a strong chemistry there, something to fall back on when times got tough on the solo front. His ego blows softened by the friendly and productive band environment, Genesis soldiered on, creating their self-titled album. Notably, that album would be the only one since Peter Gabriel's departure from the band to not spawn any additional tracks; no non-album singles, no B-sides, no EPs. The nine tracks of *Genesis* - which arguably ought to be just eight when you consolidate the two 'Homes by the Sea' - are all that emerged.

But then, that's not *quite* true, is it? There, amidst the rubble of unused rhythms and discarded riffs, lay an idea. Something more than a simple bit, but still less than a song. Something that Mike found attractive and was particularly keen to develop, but which Phil and Tony surprisingly didn't care for at all.

> **Mike:** *Choosing the right material is so important. That's what Tony and Phil do. They choose the best bits.* [146]

Confidence in his own musical compass at perhaps an all-time low, Mike opted here to trust in his bandmates' wisdom, allowing the work-in-progress song to be taken out behind the old woodshed Genesis kept at The Farm and put out of its misery. Then, a follow-up tour, and then...what? Phil would go off to sneeze out a third consecutive platinum record, and Tony was off to try to break into the Hollywood soundtrack scene, but what would Mike do? Another solo album? What would be the point of that?

> **Mike:** *[I decided I] wasn't going to make any more solo efforts after [Acting Very Strange]. I came to terms with the fact that I wasn't going to have success like Genesis.* [144]

That's a sobering, depressing statement to read. But also very self-aware and likely accurate! Credit to Mike for reading the writing on the wall, I suppose. And yet! No sooner had he decided to phone it in when that phone rang with a very unexpected caller. Eddie Van Halen had heard the doomed single 'Halfway There' from *Acting Very Strange* (!), actually *liked* it (!!), and wanted as a result to collaborate with Mike on something, with Mike singing lead on the project (!!!).

> **Mike:** *When Eddie suggested that we should have a go at doing something together, I don't think he realised...that my vocal ability was pretty well linked to my alcohol consumption.* [14]

Still, how can you say no to that? Grab a big jug of brandy, head out to the studio, get lit, and make some noise! That's what it's all about, right? So off Mike went to explore this crazy idea. What he found, though, was disappointing. The two didn't exactly lack chemistry from a musical standpoint, but from a sleep schedule standpoint they couldn't have been more incompatible. Turns out Eddie van Halen did all his working in the wee hours of the night, and Mike was a man who liked to sleep when the sun was down, thank-you-very-much. It only took a few days of exhaustion for Mike to bail on the project altogether. And yet that few days is all it took for a seed to plant itself in Mr. Rutherford's mind.

> **Mike:** *Even though it hadn't worked with Eddie, the idea of doing something collaboratively still appealed to me.* [14]

While mulling it over in his head, this thought would eventually mature and expand from "I'd like to do something with other writers" to "I *need* other writers if I'm going to stay in this career."

> **Mike:** *I realised that the whole idea of going off and doing a solo album was a mistake for me. Everything I do with Genesis is done in collaboration with Phil and Tony, and I'm good at that; I enjoy it and it's something I get a real buzz from. After trying to write, record, and produce on my own, I now realise that I do need other people to do my best work...It doesn't have to be Phil and Tony, but I do need other input...* [147]

Mike + The Mechanics formed in earnest when Mike, trying to replicate the trio writing feel he had with Genesis, got handed a list of songwriters from his publishing company.

> **Mike:** *At the top...were B.A. Robertson and Chris Neil, so that's where I decided to start...To be honest, the whole thing was an absolute punt - their names just happened to be the first two on the piece of paper I'd been given - which meant that it was wonderful to find that the three of us seemed to have a chemistry straightaway.* [14]

No surprise there. This is a dude who was willing to fly to America to aggressively pour liquor down his throat on the off chance he might strike musical gold at 2:30 in the morning. Of course he's going to just call the first two names on the list and see what happens. It's a marvel that it worked, but I suppose if you take enough chances, one of them is bound to come through sooner or later. Now writing together as Mike's sort of "Genesis 2", as it were, Mike thought back fondly to that black sheep of the *Genesis* recording, and started to trust his own instincts again. "Well I still like it. Might these guys?"

> **Mike:** *It just didn't fit in before, but I knew it would make a good Mechanics track, so Phil and Tony agreed to us appropriating it. There were a couple of other Genesis odds and ends, but nothing you could salvage.* [144]

Robertson and Neil saw beauty in this ugly duckling, and developed the Genesis recording into a finished product. Every song on the *Mike + The Mechanics* debut album is credited to two or three writers. Everything, that is, except the piece that came to be known as 'A Call to Arms', which is credited to five: Mike Rutherford, B.A. Robertson, Christopher Neil, Tony Banks, and Phil Collins.

It's impossible to really definitively know who wrote what in the end. Genesis won't talk about it because they disowned the track, and the Mechanics won't talk about it because they're sensitive to being labelled as a sort of "Genesis 2." Quite rightly, I might add, given that I've already done that mere paragraphs ago. But boot up 'A Call to Arms' and tell me that isn't a romantic, Genesisian blast of sound at the very outset. Then, after that warm initial 30 seconds, a brooding sort of darkness that itself is very typical of the 1983 Genesis sound in particular. 'Mama', 'Home by the Sea', 'It's Gonna Get Better'...they all reside in this same kind of place. The pounding drum sound is quite Padgham-esque, right in that kind of groove that Phil was exploring around the time.

In short, though it was a pair of Mechanics who helped finish it off, this song still *feels* a lot like Genesis. The album's press kit even tries to sell us on this fact, with Rutherford calling the track out specifically as:

> **Mike:** *An old song Genesis never recorded that I've always liked.* [146]

If I could be so bold, I'd like to suggest that if you stuck Phil Collins on the vocals for this track, you'd never know it *wasn't* just a Genesis tune that didn't make it onto the album. But of course, that's the other element that Mike had to figure out. "I've got these songs...now who's going to sing them? How will I release them?"

> **Mike:** *It was strange to write an album under your own name, but not sing on it. But I realised I don't have much singing talent, so I thought I'd present it as a group. [The Mechanics name] came from Tony Smith - we realised that if we were going to tour, we'd need a singer and identity. I insisted that the name was not Mike & The Mechanics featuring Mike Rutherford. Here was my chance to put my music out on its own merits and see whether it would sink or swim.* [144]

While most Mechanics songs ended up using either Paul Carrack - Mike had managed to scoop him up this time after all - or Paul Young on lead, with 'A Call to Arms' Mike thought "Eh, why not?" and dumped the whole bag of vocalists right on in. You've got Gene Stashuk (of Red 7 fame) doing screams and the first half of each verse, Paul Carrack doing the verses' second halves, both of them doubling over the chorus, and

Paul Young just soaring over top with the complementary lines like a freakin' phoenix setting the sky ablaze. No Phil? No problem! We'll just replace him with three other people!

It speaks not only to Collins' sheer vocal talent, but also to Mike's own keen music sense; one he perhaps shouldn't have doubted in the first place. While never a single, one can't help but think that the song's presence on the album helped propel *Mike + The Mechanics* in some small way towards success. Certainly it didn't hurt. In the end, Mike had his vindication.

> **Mike:** *It was not a piece, but an idea that we had always rejected. Now that a Mechanics song has come out of it, Genesis are excited too. I don't really care who a piece was composed for. It is always shaped by the people who import it. The line-up is also the only, but crucial difference between the two bands.* [148]

'A Call to Arms' is the Genesis song that never was, but it's also quite distinctly the Mechanics song that already is. It straddles both worlds, and perhaps is all the better for it. As for Mike's penchant for experimentation and rolling the dice? Well, I think it's fair to say that probably never really left him.

> **Mike:** *I love bands that are full of energy like Nickelback... You've got to love them, 'cos they're just so up for anything, and they're the type of guys you'd like to work with.* [144]

On the one hand, one could take this as a kind of soft confirmation that perhaps a true "third era" of Genesis in the wake of 1997's *Calling All Stations* would've taken a heavier turn to better align with their personnel and the changing musical landscape. On the other hand, I'm not sure I can even imagine what a Nickelback-style Genesis album would sound like. Perhaps I don't want to know.

Tony Banks

1995 - *Strictly Inc.*

'An Island in the Darkness' and the End of an Era

While this section has spotlighted songs that were created by multiple members of Genesis, there's one prominent member of that band who broke the mould by keeping his solo career completely distinct from the band, all the way through the years. In fact, with the exception of 'From the Undertow' on *A Curious Feeling* being a (still solo-written) Genesis castoff bit, there's essentially no tie back to Genesis at all in Tony Banks' discography. Yet to walk through the solo works of the various Genesis band members and leave Tony Banks out entirely would feel deeply wrong, wouldn't it?

So I'd like to break convention a little bit now and look not at the Tony song that best represents the spirit of Genesis in terms of collaborative songwriting efforts, but instead at the one that I believe best represents the spirit of Genesis in terms of ambition and overall mission. Let me preface this by saying that, while generally familiar, I am by no means an expert on the solo career of Tony Banks. At the time of this writing there are still quite a number of songs of his that I've never heard, and many of the ones that I have listened to I haven't come anywhere close to fully digesting. So I am ill qualified to make any kind of comprehensive, sweeping statements about his solo catalogue. OK? We've all accepted that disclaimer and we're willing to continue? Still with me? OK, good.

'An Island in the Darkness' is the best song Tony Banks ever created outside of Genesis, and it's not even particularly close. I daresay it might be the best solo song *any* of the Genesis members have ever produced, and I've probably only heard 10% of their collective solo output (thanks, Steve and Ant). It's the perfect capstone to an underexposed solo career, a perfect representation of Tony as a songwriter, and dang near a perfect song, period.

> **Tony:** *I was writing my solo material in parallel with Genesis and the style changes a little bit over [time], in the same way the Genesis stuff does. I did the solo albums because I had much more material than could ever come out in Genesis, and wanted to have an outlet for them. I'm primarily a writer, though I love recording music as well. So, the albums give me great satisfaction. I was very pleased with them at the time I did them and I'm still pleased with them. I'm not one of those people who tends to rubbish their old material. I think they're still valid and still could be appreciated by the Genesis audience—particularly the older Genesis audience... I don't know that I've changed that much over time. I always tend to ramble a bit. That's part of my musical style, which was also my approach within Genesis. Perhaps I did slightly more concise music when it came to the later solo period—a bit like it was with Genesis. But I still had the big, long rambling moments with 'An Island in the Darkness', which is probably the strongest moment on Strictly Inc.* [18]

Let's take a very brisk walk through Tony's solo career to see how we got to this point, shall we? First things first: just like Mike Rutherford, Tony's no singer.

> **Tony:** *Although I have sung on previous solo albums, I don't regard myself as a singer. I'm not really comfortable in the role of frontman and all that involves.* [149]

For his debut album, 1979's *A Curious Feeling*, he needs a singer. The band String Driven Thing are labelmates of Genesis on Charisma, and toured Europe together during the early part of the 1970s, so there's a familiarity there. Before String Driven Thing disbanded in the mid-70s, their singer was a guy named Kim Beacon. Thus it's only a hop, skip, and jump before Beacon is singing on *A Curious Feeling*. But by the time Tony's solo itch demanded another scratching, it was 1983 and there was a pivot of priorities. Here Tony penned both a soundtrack for a film called The Wicked Lady as well as a new rock LP called *The Fugitive*, on which Tony decided to sing his own vocal lead so he could better score hits. The results were predictably poor.

So it's back to the Hollywood scene, with Tony releasing an underwhelming *Soundtracks* compilation album in 1986. Mostly instrumental but with a few different voices scattered in for end credits appeal, and then Tony went back to the drawing board for his own pop music fame. Seeing the success Mike was having with his Mechanics project, Tony sought to replicate that by forming his own band, releasing a "self-titled" album, and using two different lead singers on it. Thus, 1989's *Bankstatement*. The downside? The singers

Tony selected weren't always well-suited to his songs, and so it was yet another commercial flop. Frustrated, Tony grabbed a bunch of different vocalists for a "true" solo album with *Still* in 1991. Perhaps because it lacked a consistent voice or identity, that album failed as well, sending Tony back to the band concept once more, which meant he was also once more looking for anyone who might fit well with him as a singer. One, more than one, didn't matter anymore. Gotta get that Mechanics money, ya know?

> **Tony:** *I've worked with Fish, Toyah, Nik Kershaw, and Jack Hues from...what the fuck's the name of the group? I'm getting old. Wang Chung! I've always looked for singers I liked, like Peter.* [9]

Ah yes, that one guy from Whatshisface, perfect. This is boding quite well. Everybody's definitely gonna have fun tonight.

> **Tony:** *With this album, I knew I needed a singer who could get into my corner and do a better job than I ever could. Jack was perfect in that his vocal style was similar to mine, only far superior. He was ideally suited to these songs. Jack's voice has a slightly hysterical quality that I like. It's unpredictable and a little eccentric, which fits these songs perfectly.* [149]

I joke about it, but Tony's right on the money here: Jack Hues actually sounds fantastic on this album, beginning to end. Tony probably thought he'd found one of the two or three singers he'd eventually need, but then ran through the whole set of material with Hues, just to see.

> **Tony:** *Jack has an intriguing voice with the edge that's needed on the vocals I write. When we started work, the obviously suitable songs sounded fantastic, but then we went on to the ones that I thought might work less well, and they sounded really good too. It was very exciting.* [150]

Now this is working. Now there's some chemistry here. Jack's allowed "in," so to speak, more than anyone else has really been to this point.

> **Tony:** *It was the first time I've worked all the way through an album with a singer who was involved in more than just the singing. Kim Beacon sang on A Curious Feeling, but didn't write lyrics. Jack Hues was involved in a couple of lyrics. He was also around quite a bit when I was making the album. He played guitar on some of the pieces but didn't want to do some of the lead guitar work. He was happy to do little bits and pieces and that worked well. So, Strictly Inc. was more of a unit with Jack and Nick Davis, who produced it.* [18]

And in a fascinating bit of foreshadowing…

> **Tony:** *All the music is by me, and Jack wrote the lyrics on a couple of songs. That's the stage that Jack came in. If we were to do it again, Jack would be more involved.* [151]

Heck of a shame that he wasn't able to retain that thought a mere two years later when bringing Ray Wilson in late on the *Calling All Stations* sessions for Genesis, isn't it? Regardless, the point remains: Tony was all-in on this band thing again.

> **Tony:** *[Jack] and I have given ourselves the name Strictly Inc as a duo, so this is not a Tony Banks solo album.* [150]

OK, so maybe that sentiment didn't quite stand the test of time either. Perhaps it's best if I just move on. *Strictly Inc.* is pretty much a pop/prog-pop/soft rock album through and through. It's an inoffensive listen with tracks that grow on you. There are even a couple tunes you could envision being radio hits, if the radio ever played songs like these, and also if people's tastes during the mid-90s were entirely different from what they were. Poor Tony had to resort to direct and desperate pleas in interviews to try to get this thing any airplay at all.

> **Tony:** *I just want people to give Strictly Inc. a chance. Some people think that it's just the voice they like about Genesis, but much of it is down to the chord progressions and those sorts of things. I suppose that's me - I've always been one of the major writers of the group, and if you like our songs it's worth giving Strictly Inc. a listen.* [150]

To put it succinctly, *Strictly Inc.* was a clout-chasing, radio-begging, hit-starving Hail Mary of a record from a man who'd spent well over a decade choking on his bandmates' Top 40 dust. And I'm saying that as someone who actually *likes* the album. A typical prog fan picking this up will play the first nine tracks, declare themselves hopelessly bored, and have an angry rant of a comment all queued up on their favourite fan site, just waiting to smash that enter key so they can inflict their sourness upon an unsuspecting world.

But just before they do, something wildly unexpected happens. What is *this* song? And what is it doing *here*, of all places?

> **Tony:** *I never quite know whether I was trying to keep the songs a bit shorter as I hoped. I mean, I always wanted the odd shorter song, because I like short songs, and I thought perhaps I'd got a bit too...some of that early stuff, you sort of feel maybe was too long, I don't know. Looking back, I'm not sure it was, but [I] got that feeling a little bit. Certainly in the late 70s, early 80s, there was a definite move away from those kind of what you might call "very proggy" pieces. And I just thought [by this time], "I just want to do a piece," you know. This is Tony Banks undiluted, really. So I wrote a fifteen minute piece.* [152]

"I just want to do a piece." Amidst the push for radio play and solo success and trying to crack the code of what the everyman really wants to hear, Tony Banks just needs a moment to himself.

> **Tony:** *I can't really say why 'An Island in the Darkness' should come out now. I just had these ideas, and I wanted to let them go to see what would happen. It wasn't my intention to make it any particular length, and when I finished it I didn't realise that it was 18 minutes long. But for some people it will be the track. There's something about it...a sort of excitement.* [150]

This is 25 years of Genesis progressive sensibility bubbling over uncontrollably to the fore, with all the mastery those years bring, now unfettered by anyone telling him to edit himself down. It's a blending of new, old, older, and timeless in one epic package; the second longest song Tony has ever done in any form after 'Supper's Ready'. Longer than any of his soundtrack pieces, longer than any of his classical works. This is it, the biggun, the hoss from the boss.

> **Tony:** *There are a few moments [in my solo career] that are worth talking about, I suppose. A very long song, 'An Island in the Darkness', which lasts for about 15 minutes and perhaps is comparable to the early Genesis days more than any other, I think has the most to it. It's the most "meaty" piece...* [90]

It opens with gentle piano and nothing else. Though it sounds nothing like 'Firth of Fifth', it's got the same kind of effect of drawing you in. There's something really compelling about pure piano sound, and you almost don't even notice when the gentle synth notes sweep in to texture it all.

> **Tony:** *What I did with this one was just record it on the piano all the way through. And then we did all the arrangement to it, if you like.... The piano is absolutely crucial to the whole thing... I've done a lot of pieces like this over the years, whether it be with Genesis like 'One for the Vine' or whatever. You start with piano as a basis. Now you might lose it at times completely from the mix, but it acts as a kind of template for the whole thing to be worked with. And in this particular song, I think most of it survives, actually... In a sense, the sound - it's not exciting in itself, but it kind of forms a sort of backbone to the whole thing, which kind of makes sense of everything else.* [152]

It's an introduction that runs for nearly two minutes. 'From the Undertow' was a piano introduction to 'Undertow' that the other two-thirds of Genesis told him had to go, but Tony didn't have to answer to anyone this time around. You want a two-minute introduction to this piece? Go for it, man.

> **Tony:** *I write what appeals to me and follow that through with no compromises. Basically, I prefer music that has some odd quality to it... I get most excited when something a little weird is going on within a song. It might be a certain lyric or a particular chord change, but I like to put something in that steers the song away from the beaten path and leads it elsewhere - hopefully somewhere a bit more interesting.* [149]

From that 'Firth'/'Undertow' intro sensibility it's into 'Duchess' territory, with a prominent drum machine pattern anchoring the verses and choruses of the song's primary melodies. There's Tony on piano, Tony on synth, Tony on synth that sounds like guitars, Tony just building on this drum pattern any which way he wants to. It all works.

Tony: *It's such an aid to writing - you get a drum loop going, play along, and see what it does for you.* [150]

And here after an album full of pop efforts, and after a successful career as a new wave artist before that, Jack Hues is unleashed as a progressive rock vocalist, and the haunting quality of his voice just nails the atmosphere in this track. It's a bizarre match, but it's somehow an ideal one at the same time.

Tony: *I felt I'd written a lot of strong material for Strictly Inc., but I'm particularly happy with 'An Island in the Darkness', which was a long piece and I thought was the backbone of the album. Jack also sang a little bit the way I would want to sing if I could sing. I thought he sounded great on that track.* [18]

Now, it's a pretty down-tempo song to this point. We're definitively in the "darkness" part of the equation, the foggy gloom of the whole affair. So it feels completely natural when, after two verses and two choruses themselves spanning nearly four unbroken minutes, Tony goes into a very restrained, sombre, melodic keyboard solo. If I can again draw parallel to 'Firth of Fifth', this is like the flute solo in the middle; same feel, same kind of effect. So if we're following that formula, we'd expect the next bit to be an up-tempo bit, maybe reprising the lively piano introduction...except that, as you'll recall, that piano introduction was *also* mostly melancholy and reserved. At this point the song has run for seven and a half minutes and hasn't had a lick of pep whatsoever. It's so good you don't even notice, really, but by now you're aching for something "up," lest you wallow in this mood forever.

And so, the "island" in the darkness. The drum machine pattern vanishes, replaced by tight cymbal work by renowned session drummer John Robinson, who by this point in time had drummed on **thirty-six** Billboard Hot 100 top ten hits, including seventeen number one hits alone. You want solid? Let's get solid.

Tony: *The drummer is John Robinson...he's so quick to learn. 'An Island in the Darkness' is eighteen minutes long and, having heard it just once, John pretty much played it straight through!* [150]

OK, granted we've just established that the first seven plus of those minutes are just drum machine, but still! You may recall Phil Collins won the Genesis audition by hearing how something was supposed to go and then playing it right back, so it must've felt like coming home for Tony to get that with someone else a quarter of a century later.

But impressive as the cymbal playing is, it's not where the attention is drawn here. It's rather to the flaring piano arpeggios, beaming through the haze like rays of brilliant sunlight, and though other synth tones and chords threaten to take over, ultimately they just fall in line so that the arpeggios are THE thing. Then more countermelodies, tight drumming with dramatic cymbal crashes...you wanted up? We're going up, baby. Up and up and up on an arpeggiating journey that doesn't want to end. You can't get off Mr. Banks' Wild Ride. It's two and a half minutes of instrumental consisting of almost nothing but keyboard solos, but to describe it as a keyboard solo would be woefully inaccurate and actually undersell the whole thing.

When it finally comes back to earth, we're back to pure piano again, just as with the song's introduction. Reflective, meditative, still somehow triumphant, like a weary soul resting on the shore, looking out upon the tumultuous sea he/she just emerged from. And then we're off again into arpeggiating glory.

Except this time, Jack Hues is back, and there's a quiet menace in his voice. *"Now the fog surrounds you,"* he says, undermining all that you feel you've just accomplished. You've gotten so accustomed to those arpeggios that you can almost still hear them in this chord structure, but they're not there, and Jack is taunting you about it. *"All you see are phantoms always just out of reach."* Then come the almost hypnotic suggestions: *"You don't want to be here anymore."* The effect is downright eerie, I tell you.

And now he gets that hysteria in his voice that Tony was talking about. And now those arpeggios are back, but they're coming from synth strings this time, sounding out of control, dangerous. *"You cannot choose direction or control the motion."* This was supposed to be my island, man! Why am I back in the darkness again?! *"Tell me are you frightened on your own?"* Yes! Yes I am!

The final sounds you hear from Jack Hues on this track are a deathly wail, like he's falling from some towering precipice to his untimely doom. *"Do you have the will to carry on?"* I say final sound, because even though Jack is a guitar player and played guitars on *Strictly Inc.*, Tony opted to bring in a familiar face for the ending of this song.

Tony: *Most of the guitar on the album is played by Jack, although Daryl Stuermer plays a solo on 'Island' and guitar on one other track.* [150]

Perhaps this is a Genesis collaboration of sorts after all, eh? After more than thirteen minutes of only occasional and subtle background guitar, Daryl comes ripping in with a solo that's far more artistic than technical, though in typical Stuermer fashion he nails both facets with relative ease. A very deliberate kind of underlying rhythm, emphasizing the third beats of each measure just to keep you on your toes, and this solo's gonna keep going even after it sounds like it's about to end. "Pull back a bit, Tony?" Nah, friends. Not this time. Not ever again.

Tony: *The guitar solo's my favourite bit, the emotional high point on the album. It's a cliché, I suppose, but it seems to work.* [150]

Daryl gets two-plus minutes of his own to work his magic here, and it's just breath-taking, especially given everything that came before. That's the ol' 'Supper's Ready' mentality at work here: give 'em a payoff, even if they didn't know they wanted it.

Tony: *Nowadays everything is too concise. Everyone is working at the four minute pop song. I listen to groups that I like...and I yearn for them to take it just a little bit further. Pop music has become too rigid - you have to fit the format all the time, and I don't think that it needs to be that way. In fact, ask the people who don't listen to the radio what they want to hear, and you'll find that they want something more ambitious, that's got atmosphere.* [150]

Tony spends the final minute and change scaling back down. It's piano overlaid with synth oboe, then back to the piano alone, gentle arpeggios caressing once again before it all slows and ends on a chord that hits precisely all the right notes and lasts precisely two seconds too short. It's honestly the only thing wrong with the song, I think. It's Tony's second longest piece of all time and my only complaint is that it wasn't two measly seconds longer. That's a job well done, I think.

Lyrically, it's not quite obvious when listening, but Tony positioned this piece as another vague political message:

Tony: *'An Island in the Darkness' is about political situations: striving for something, getting there, and fighting to hold onto it. You know...Russia was so optimistic, and now it's going through a much more difficult stage. The same thing will happen in South Africa - the euphoria will disappear and then, having reached the goal that seemed so marvellous, things won't quite hold together. Many people will feel that it's worth carrying on, but they'll really have to fight.* [150]

I mentioned this all the way back in the entries for 'Domino' and 'Land of Confusion', but Tony almost fell into the standard trap here. When writing a song about the political upheavals of the early 1990s, there's not going to be much interest beyond that era. Thankfully, the lyrics don't get specific and the song retains its sense of timelessness. Indeed, over the years Tony himself became a bit more pragmatic about it.

Tony: *I had written a long piece, and it was a good 50-60 percent instrumental, and I wanted the lyrics to follow the flow of the song, which starts in a certain place and goes darker and the end is optimistic. So, it's a song about ambition and achieving what you set out to do, and then about sustaining it, and how it goes for you after that, and how you cope with failure and all the rest of it. But a lot of people have different interpretations of the song, and I intentionally kept the song quite ambiguous, so people could put their own ideas into it a little bit. But it is about finding yourself in a place that you perhaps didn't think you would have ever been in - a good place. And then perhaps later on, finding yourself in a bad place, and then how you cope with that.* [90]

Hmm. That sounds almost like Tony's solo career, doesn't it?

Tony: *I was really excited by Strictly Inc. and when we listened to it when it was completed, Jack said "Well, that's fantastic. If this was the new Genesis album, everyone would be very happy." I felt I'd covered all bases on this album. It had some range and quality about it that made it special. Of course, I was trying to quietly shy away from me "being the man." That's why I put it out under the group name Strictly Inc and of course, for that reason, it didn't do* *anything. People didn't even know it was a Tony Banks album. I regret that the most about the project. I would have definitely liked it to have had a much higher profile.* [18]

Strictly Inc. sold about a baker's dozen copies and then, as its title suggested, vanished entirely from whatever small pocket of the public consciousness it had ever laid claim to. For nine out of ten tracks on the album, that doesn't come as a huge surprise. But ohhhh, that tenth. With the utter commercial failure of Strictly, Inc. and the collapse of Genesis as a recording band a couple years later, Tony decided to call it a day. He'd pivot over to the orchestral world, where he seems a natural fit, and his music there is great stuff. But he'd never again record as a proper solo artist, making 'An Island in the Darkness' effectively the swan song of his solo career.

What a way to go out.

Tony: *The important thing though is that people listen to it with an open mind… If they do that, then I think they'll find something that will move them or excite them…* [149]

As for the song's enduring legacy, you'd think that an attention-demanding epic track concluding an album nobody bought from an artist nobody even cared about wouldn't have any legacy at all, right? But you'd be wrong!

See, Quebec is an interesting place, and if there's one non-stereotypical thing French Canadians love, it's Genesis. So it was that an eighth grade teacher in the heart of that province had a radical idea that she could teach English as a second language to her students by playing them music. The concept goes that associating certain sounds and inflections with melodies would help them "stick" better in the kids' memories, and since the children might like hearing these songs for their musical merits anyway, there would be some built-in repetition. This is sound logic, and works pretty well, and also it's totally just lip service because what this lady REALLY wanted to do was get her kids hooked on Genesis.

To that end, she made them listen - *repeatedly*, one would imagine - to 'An Island in the Darkness'. Whether the obsession was their own or just a homework assignment from a fanatic making dubious use of her authority position, the kids ended up making Tony a book based on the song as well as writing him a letter thanking him for, well, being Tony Banks. You've got this whole classroom of kids, none of them native English speakers, holding a promotional poster of Tony's album *The Fugitive*, screaming "WE LOVE YOU TONY BANKS!" in unison, hoping that he'll write a response to their fan mail. It's the most bizarre thing ever, and when the local news managed to get hold of Tony to bring him up to speed on the story and get his reactions, he was clearly a little flabbergasted in how to respond.

Tony: *I thank them for their time, and the fact that they gave it a chance. You know, you give it a listen. I mean, this isn't…it's not an easy piece of music; it's not a piece of music that's been particularly successful, either, you know what I mean? So it's not something that you have to listen to or do anything…But I think it can speak to people because of its lyrical idea. I mean, nobody's gonna suggest… It's quite an open lyric; it lends itself to quite a few interpretations, I think. And obviously they found some of those interpretations within the things they wrote. So I think it's very good. I'm very impressed.* [153]

These literal children write him a BOOK based on a sprawling epic off his least successful album and half his response to them is just the self-pity that the album didn't have better sales. It's hilarious, it's tragic, it's Tony Banks in a nutshell. I love it. And if that's all the legacy this song was destined to have, you know what? It's enough. It's enough.

Index

...And Then There Were Three...	426
...In That Quiet Earth	106
7/8	138
A Call to Arms	461
A Place to Call My Own	16
A Trick of the Tail	159
Album	440
A Winter's Tale	25
Abacab	272
Album	417
After the Ordeal	289
Afterglow	217
Aisle of Plenty	130
Alien Afternoon	100
All in a Mouse's Night	102
Alone Tonight	134
Am I Very Wrong?	30
An Island in the Darkness	465
Another Record	53
Anything Now	203
Anything She Does	39
Anyway	313
Back in N.Y.C.	188
Ballad of Big	23
Banjo Man	215
Behind the Lines	155
Phil Collins version	458
Blood on the Rooftops	302
Broadway Melody of 1974	103
Build Me a Mountain	32
Burning Rope	319
Calling All Stations	241
Album	424
Can-Utility and the Coastliners	123
Congo	117
Counting Out Time	185
Cuckoo Cocoon	176
Cul-de-sac	167
Dance on a Volcano	126
Dancing with the Moonlit Knight	236
Deep in the Motherlode	144
Do the Neurotic	265
Dodo/Lurker	245
Domino	285
Down and Out	136
Dreaming While You Sleep	322
Driving the Last Spike	339
Duchess	353
Duke	442
Duke's End	157
Duke's Travels	335
Dusk	186
Eleventh Earl of Mar	88
Entangled	375
Evidence of Autumn	68
Fading Lights	387
Feeding the Fire	326
Fireside Song	115
Firth of Fifth	408
Fly on a Windshield	206
Follow You Follow Me	232
For Absent Friends	222
Foxtrot	420
From Genesis to Revelation	416
Genesis	422
Get 'Em Out by Friday	42
Going Out to Get You	14
Guide Vocal	122
Hair on the Arms and Legs	34
Hairless Heart	329
Happy the Man	79
Harlequin	135
Harold the Barrel	81
Hearts on Fire	196
Heathaze	372
Here Comes the Supernatural Anaesthetist	91
Hey!	51
Hidden in the World of Dawn	26
Hold on My Heart	99
Home by the Sea	253
Horizons	269
I Can't Dance	128
I Know What I Like (In Your Wardrobe)	97
I'd Rather Be You	133
If That's What You Need	213
Illegal Alien	70
Image Blown Out	35
In Hiding	67
In Limbo	38
In the Beginning	19
In the Cage	260
In the Rapids	47
In the Wilderness	44
In Too Deep	210
Inside and Out	224
Intruder	454
Invisible Touch	104
Album	428
it.	80
It's Gonna Get Better	59
It's Yourself	108
Jesus He Knows Me	220
Just a Job to Do	149
Keep It Dark	151
Land of Confusion	299
Let Us Now Make Love	33
Like It or Not	72
Lilywhite Lilith	95
Living Forever	258
Looking for Someone	251
Los Endos	357
Mad Man Moon	332
Mama	180
Man of Our Times	125
Man on the Corner	161
Many Too Many	248
Match of the Day	141
Me and Sarah Jane	142
Me and Virgil	18
Misunderstanding	243
More Fool Me	178
Naminanu	69

Song	Page
Never a Time	150
No Reply at All	96
No Son of Mine	316
Not About Us	169
Nowhere Else to Turn	90
Nursery Cryme	432
On the Shoreline	109
One Day	46
One Eyed Hound	20
One for the Vine	378
One Man's Fool	84
Open Door	52
Pacidy	82
Papa He Said	31
Paperlate	94
Phret	198
Pigeons	114
Please Don't Ask	65
Ravine	22
Resignation	57
Riding the Scree	158
Ripples	293
Robbery, Assault and Battery	63
Run Out of Time	73
Say It's Alright Joe	45
Scenes from a Night's Dream	110
Sea Bee	62
Second Home by the Sea	346
Selling England by the Pound	438
Seven Stones	296
Shadow of the Hierophant	449
Shepherd	148
Shipwrecked	75
Sign Your Life Away	171
Silent Sorrow in Empty Boats	140
Silent Sun	54
Silver Rainbow	116
Silver Song	445
Since I Lost You	131
Small Talk	77
Snowbound	160
Squonk	183
Stagnation	146
Submarine	194
Supper's Ready	391
Taking It All Too Hard	208
Tell Me Why	61
That's All	281
That's Me	56
The Battle of Epping Forest	36
The Brazilian	350
The Carpet Crawlers	200
The Chamber of 32 Doors	277
The Cinema Show	362
The Colony of Slippermen	92
The Conqueror	41
The Day the Light Went Out	50
The Dividing Line	255
The Fountain of Salmacis	310
The Grand Parade of Lifeless Packaging	120
The Knife	112
The Lady Lies	119
The Lamb Lies Down on Broadway	163
Album	436
The Lamia	382
The Light Dies Down on Broadway	230
The Magic of Time	60
The Musical Box	367
The Mystery of the Flannan Isle Lighthouse	17
The Return of the Giant Hogweed	28
The Serpent	24
The Waiting Room	48
There Must Be Some Other Way	227
Throwing It All Away	165
Time Table	86
Tonight, Tonight, Tonight	307
Trespass	430
Try a Little Sadness	21
Turn It On Again	192
Twilight Alehouse	83
Uncertain Weather	283
Undertow	343
Unquiet Slumbers for the Sleepers	107
Vancouver	27
Visions of Angels	87
Watcher of the Skies	173
Way of the World	305
We Can't Dance	434
Where the Sour Turns to Sweet	49
White Mountain	275
Who Dunnit?	10
Wind & Wuthering	418
Window	74
Wot Gorilla?	76
You Might Recall	121
Your Own Special Way	55

Bibliography

[1] Banks, Collins, Gabriel, Hackett, Phillips, Rutherford (2007). *Genesis: Chapter & Verse*. (P. Dodd, Ed.) New York: Thomas Dunne Books.
[2] Banks, T. (2016, October). Needle Time. (N. McCormick, Interviewer)
[3] Banks, Collins, Gabriel, Hackett, Phillips, Rutherford, Wilson (2007). CD Reissue Interviews.
[4] Smith, R. (1981, December 18). The Big Creep's Way. *Record Mirror*.
[5] Parker, J. (1997, October). Genesis. *Record Collector*, pp. 40-44.
[6] Banks, T. (1994, April 9). The A to Z of Genesis. (P. Morton, J. Dann, A. Hewitt, Interviewers) [Published in *The Waiting Room* fanzine between May 1994 and November 1998.]
[7] Banks, Collins, Rutherford. (1981, September). Hallam Rock Radio.
[8] Phillips, A. (1992, November). (J. Guenther, Translator) *It*.
[9] Jones, T. (2000, December). Turning it on again. *Record Collector*, pp. 56-61.
[10] Young, J. (1982, March). The Genesis Autodiscography. *Trouser Press*, pp. 16-21.
[11] Phillips, A. (1989, April 28). Genesis Revelations. (P. Morton, T. Sayers, A. Hewitt, Interviewers)
[12] Collins, P. (2016). *Not Dead Yet*. London: Century.
[13] Hackett, S. (2020). Retrieved from HackettSongs YouTube Channel: https://www.youtube.com/user/hackettsongs/videos
[14] Rutherford, M. (2014). *The Living Years*. London: Constable.
[15] Welch, C. (1973, July 28). What Genesis did on their "holidays". *Melody Maker*.
[16] Banks, Collins, Rutherford. (1986). Invisible Touch Tour Promotional Interviews. (Various Interviewers)
[17] Fielder, H. (1978, April 1). Genesis Track by Track. *Sounds*, pp. 17-18.
[18] Prasad, A. (2019). Tony Banks - Beyond the Physical. *Innerviews*. Retrieved from https://www.innerviews.org/inner/tony-banks
[19] Phillips, A. (2001, July 9). Private Parts & Pieces. (D. Negrin, Interviewer) Retrieved from http://www.worldofgenesis.com/AnthonyPhillips-Interview2001.htm
[20] Gittins, I. (1992, January). 3 Men and a Baby. *Zounds Das Musikmagazin*.
[21] Banks, T. (2015, June 27). So that's what it does! (S. Barnes, F. Rogers, Interviewers)
[22] Welch, C. (1984, February). Brum Punch. *Kerrang!*, p. 28.
[23] Milano, D. (1984, November). Tony Banks & the Evolution of Genesis. *Keyboard*, pp. 36-48.
[24] Collins, P. (1986). ("Hitmen Magazine", Interviewer) Retrieved from http://www.philcollins.co.uk/hitmen86b.htm
[25] Banks, T. (1997, August 22). An Alien Afternoon with Tony Banks. (A. Hewitt, S. Pound, Interviewers)
[26] Wilson, R. (2006, July 19). Ray Wilson Interview in Heiligenhaus. (C. Gerhardts, Interviewer)
[27] Easlea, D. (2017, April 22). Wind & Wuthering: Genesis look back on their boldest prog statement. *Louder*.
[28] Rutherford, Wilson, Zidkyahu. (1997, September 25). Another Chiddingfold Afternoon. (A. Hewitt, I. Jones, S. Pound, Interviewers)
[29] Hackett, S. (1995, May 28). Genesis Revelations. (A. Hewitt, Interviewer)
[30] Hackett, S. (1997, August 21). Just for the record. (A. Hewitt, Interviewer)
[31] Clarke, S. (1977, January 1). The Genesis Guide to Genesis. *New Musical Express*, pp. 6-7.
[32] Wilson, R. (2000). There must be some other way to do an interview! (A. Hewitt, Interviewer)
[33] Fielder, H. (1981, February 7). Phil Collins: Why I Had to Leave the Nest. *Sounds*, pp. 22-23.
[34] Fielder, H. (1981, September 26). The Great Escape. *Sounds*, pp. 18-20.
[35] Dyson, G. (Director). (1991). Genesis - No Admittance [Documentary].
[36] Welch, C. (1976, December 25). Wuthering heights. *Melody Maker*, p. 14.
[37] Barnett, L. (2014, October 14). Phil Collins and Mike Rutherford: How we made Invisible Touch. *The Guardian*.
[38] Yukich, J. (Director). (2001). *Genesis - The Way We Walk - Live in Concert* [DVD Interviews].
[39] Hackett, S. (2018, July). The Genesis Years. Retrieved from HackettSongs: http://www.hackettsongs.com/blog/steve211.html
[40] Banks, Collins, Rutherford. (1991). Rockline. (M. Quinn, Interviewer) MTV.
[41] Collins, Rutherford. (1978, March). Views from the Three. (N. Horne, Interviewer) BBC Radio One.
[42] Hackett, S. (2009, March 27). Steve Hackett On Stage Interview.
[43] Smeaton, B. (Director). (2001). *The Genesis Songbook* [Documentary].
[44] Greene, A. (2016, February 29). Phil Collins: My Life in 15 Songs. *Rolling Stone*.
[45] Hackett, S. (2020, March 31). Steve Hackett on Genesis - Selling England by the Pound. Facebook Live. Retrieved from https://www.facebook.com/stevehackettofficial/videos/269756404036508/
[46] Phil Collins. (1997, May 3). *Storytellers*, VH1.
[47] Radel, C. (1991, November 10). Together Again. *The Cincinnati Enquirer*.
[48] Banks, Collins, Rutherford. (2020, March 15). Planet Rock. (I. Danter, Interviewer)
[49] Bowler, D. and Dray, B. (1992). *Genesis: A Biography*. London: Sidgwick & Jackson, Ltd.
[50] Clarke, S. (1977, April 16). Oh to be a tax exile, now that April's here... *New Musical Express*, pp. 7-8.
[51] Murphy, L. (2017, March). Steve Hackett - Lured by the siren's cry... *Classic Rock Society*, pp. 26-29.
[52] Orme, S. (Director). (1982). *Genesis - Three Sides Live* [Motion Picture].
[53] Banks, T. (2009, September 30). A Curious Interview. (H. Janisch, Interviewer)
[54] Welch, C. (1980, March 1). Who the hell is Mike Rutherford? *Musicians Only*, pp. 3, 12.
[55] Van Matre, L. (1980, June 27). Genesis - No concept behind Genesis' 'Duke' album. *Ft. Lauderdale News*, p. 21S.
[56] Collins, P. (1994, January). One to One. VH1.
[57] Gabriel, P. (1974, November 16). The Lamb Lies Down on Broadway [story on album sleeve]. Charisma Records.
[58] Rutherford, M. (2007). Genesis - Turning It On Again. (A. Prasad, Interviewer)
[59] Barber, L. (1981, February 7). Facing up to new values. *Melody Maker*, pp. 28-29.
[60] Gilbert, J. (1973, September 1). Genesis Battle Against Forest and Fire. *Sounds*, p. 8.
[61] Genesis (1983). On *Three Into One - An Authorised 3 Hour Special*.
[62] Welch, C. (1976, July 3). Genesis's man for all seasons... *Melody Maker*, p. 12.
[63] Hackett, S. (1974). (S. Rosen, Interviewer)
[64] Blake, M. (2015, October 2). The Story Behind the Song: Turn It On Again by Genesis. *Louder*.
[65] Ferranti, M. (1981, October 18). Magic Word: Abacab. *Ciao 2001*, pp. 10-13.
[66] Banks, Rutherford. (2007). Genesis Interview in Hannover. (C. Gerhardts, Interviewer)
[67] Genesis. (1998, March 4). *The Night Fly*. VH1.
[68] Greenwald, T. (1987, February). Tony Banks. *Keyboard*, pp. 51-57.
[69] Fielder, H. (1984). *The Book of Genesis*. New York City: St. Martin's Press.

[70] Hackett, S. (2020). *A Genesis In My Bed*. Bedford: Wymer Publishing.
[71] Giammetti, M. (2021). *Genesis: 1975-2021 - The Phil Collins Years*. Surrey: Kingmaker Publishing.
[72] Banks, Collins, Rutherford. (1986). Invisible Touch Tour Promotional Interviews.
[73] Banks, Collins. (1986). *The Meldrum Tapes*. (I. Meldrum, Interviewer) ABC.
[74] Collins, P. (2005, November 2). *Room 101*. (P. Merton, Interviewer) BBC Two.
[75] Hackett, S. (2017). The Steve Hackett Interview. (S. Perry, Interviewer)
[76] Lester, P. (2017, July 20). The Stories Behind the Songs. *Louder*.
[77] Mechanical Touch. (1988, December). *Making Music*, pp. 20-21.
[78] Carruthers, B. (Director). (2012). *Genesis - In Their Own Words* [Motion Picture].
[79] Hackett, S. (2014, October 12). 'Selling England by the Pound' remains Genesis' most complete album: 'It fights off its shackles'. (N. Deriso, Interviewer)
[80] Black, B. (1983, September 17). Mothercare. *Sounds*, pp. 16-17.
[81] Banks, Collins, Rutherford. (1991, November). Radio Forth RFM.
[82] Doerschuk, R. L. (1992, February). Genesis. *Keyboard*, pp. 82-94.
[83] Collins, Rutherford. (1989). *In the Studio with Redbeard*. (D. Hill, Interviewer)
[84] Oakes, T. (1983, November). Tony Banks. *Electronics & Music Maker*, pp. 12-14.
[85] Goodyer, T. (1986, July). And Then There Was One... *Electronics & Music Maker*, pp. 46-50.
[86] Welch, C. (1973, October 6). Genesis: Chapter and Verse. *Melody Maker*, p. 13.
[87] Gilbert, J. (1972, March 4). The babes, from the nursery onto the stage. *Sounds*, p. 31.
[88] Nursery Cryme US Press Kit. (1971). The Buddah Group.
[89] Welch, C. (1972, July 20). The Book of Genesis. *Melody Maker*.
[90] Banks, T. (2015, July 28). Tony Banks of Genesis. (G. Prato, Interviewer) Songfacts.
[91] Banks, Collins, Rutherford. (1986). *Whistle Test Special*.
[92] Banks, Collins, Rutherford. (1991). We Can't Dance electronic press kit.
[93] Welch, C. (1975, April 26). Backseat driver. *Melody Maker*.
[94] Gabriel, P. (1975, September 6). Why I quit Genesis. *Melody Maker*, p. 9.
[95] Fielder, H. (1980, May 10). Duke of Hazard. *Sounds*, p. 31.
[96] Fielder, H. (1979, October 27). The return of Getting It Together in the Country. *Sounds*.
[97] Genesis (Performer). (1980, May). The Lyceum Theatre, London, United Kingdom.
[98] Marsden, B. (1991, December). We Can't Dance. *VOX*, pp. 13-19.
[99] Blake, M. (2016, February 26). Phil Collins: from Genesis to resurrection. *Louder*.
[100] Mesaric, R. (2007, May 20). *VH1 Rock Honors 2007 Concert Review*. Retrieved from Sleaze Roxx: https://sleazeroxx.com/concerts/vh1-rock-honors-2007-concert-review/
[101] Gilbert, J. (1973, June 9). Genesis planning Project X. *Sounds*, p. 15.
[102] Selling England by the Pound US press kit. (1973, October 29). Atlantic Records.
[103] Banks, Hackett. (1978). (S. Rosen, Interviewer)
[104] Hackett, S. (2001, January). Interview with Steve Hackett. (D. M. Epstein, Interviewer)
[105] Taylor, S. (1979, November 10). Hard working for a living. *Melody Maker*, pp. 27-28.
[106] Hackett, S. (2012). *Steve Hackett's Genesis Revisited II Tracklist Commentary*. Retrieved from HackettSongs: http://www.hackettsongs.com/news/newsGeneral46.html
[107] Banks, T. (1992, April 27). *Rockline*. (B. Coburn, Interviewer)
[108] We Can't Dance US Press Kit. (1991, November). Atlantic Records.
[109] Welch, C. (1973, March 3). Genesis - Melody Maker Band Breakdown. *Melody Maker*, pp. 28-29.
[110] Gabriel, P. (1972). Foxtrot Tour Concert Program.
[111] Gabriel, P. (1986, June 16). *Rockline*. (B. Coburn, Interviewer)
[112] Wall, M. (2016, November 19). Supper's Ready by Genesis: the story behind the song. *Louder*.
[113] Roberts, C. (2017, March 22). Genesis on Supper's Ready: "This is where we started to become significant". *Louder*.
[114] Gilbert, J. (1972, September 9). Genesis Doing the Foxtrot. *Sounds*.
[115] Tyler, T. (1972, November 18). Genesis - Poised on the Brink. *New Musical Express*, pp. 30-31.
[116] Irvin, J. (2007). *The Mojo Collection* (4th ed.). Edinburgh: Canongate Books Ltd.
[117] Banks, T. (2018, February 20). (C. Wiser, Interviewer) Songfacts.
[118] Smith, B. (2006). Interview with Bill Smith - Album Cover Designer Extraordinaire! (S. Miller, Interviewer)
[119] Whitehead, P. (2001, July 25). (D. Negrin, Interviewer)
[120] Cerio, S. (1998). Interview with Storm Thorgerson. *Seconds*.
[121] Phillips, A. (1992, April). The Geese & The Ghost. (J. Dann, A. Hewitt, Interviewers)
[122] Phillips, A. (2009, December). Genesis Website Interview. Retrieved from http://www.anthonyphillips.co.uk/interviews/gsite.htm
[123] Phillips, A. (2015, January). Interview with Anthony Phillips. (D. M. Epstein, Interviewer)
[124] *FAQ - Frequently Asked Questions*. (n.d.). Retrieved from Anthony Phillips: http://www.anthonyphillips.co.uk/faq.htm
[125] Gilbert, J. (1973, November 3). Phil: Showing Off His Colors. *Sounds*, p. 18.
[126] Harvey, P. (1974, January 19). "Our act was slowly taking us over". *Record Mirror*.
[127] Phillips, A. (1994). Private Parts & Pieces. (J. Dann, A. Hewitt, Interviewers)
[128] Clarke, S. (1975, October 25). Are you ready for a concept LP about the Tarot? *New Musical Express*, p. 32.
[129] Welch, C. (1975, October 18). Steve Hackett of Genesis talks to Chris Welch. *Melody Maker*, p. 34.
[130] Hackett, S. (2014, September). Paul Golder talks to Steve Hackett. (P. Golder, Interviewer) Phoenix FM.
[131] Hackett, S. (1976, April 8). (S. Muni, Interviewer)
[132] Player of the Month - Steve Hackett. (1975, November). *Beat Instrumental*, pp. 16-17.
[133] Charone, B. (1975, October 25). Hackett relieves himself. *Sounds*, p. 37.
[134] Hackett, S. (1976, April 28). *The Import Show*. (A. Amador, Interviewer)
[135] Hackett, S. (1970, December 12). Classified ad. Melody Maker.
[136] Clarke, S. (1979, January 20). The Technology of Being Gabriel. *New Musical Express*, pp. 22-23, 44.
[137] Elder, B. (180, July 5). Gabriel Without Frontiers. *Melody Maker*, pp. 25-27, 41.
[138] Fielder, H. (2020, August 16). Peter Gabriel: my life story. *Louder*.
[139] Angus, J. (1985, January). Hugh Padgham - Producer Extraordinaire. *Home Studio Recording*, pp. 25-29.
[140] Sutcliffe, P. (1980, June 14). Mr. Clean. *Sounds*, pp. 17-18.
[141] Gabriel, P. (2011, September 19). An Invasion of Privacy: Peter Gabriel Interviewed. (J. Doran, Interviewer)
[142] Collins, P. (1981, January 27). *Castle Rock*. (J. Shaw, Interviewer) Radio Trent.
[143] Phil Collins: Face Value. (1999, November 3). *Classic Albums*.
[144] Jones, T. (2004, October). Mechanical music. *Record Collector*.
[145] Griffin, J. (1982, August 28). Genesis in orbit with new image and album topping Top Twenty. *The Montreal Gazette*, p. E-2.
[146] Mike + the Mechanics US Press Kit. (1985, September). Atlantic Records.

[147] Mechanisation. (1989, March). *International Musician and Recording World*, pp. 42-47.
[148] Ranner, T. (1986, June). Mike & the Mechanics. *Musik Scene*, p. 81.
[149] Strictly Inc. UK Press Kit. (1995). Virgin Records.
[150] Reid, G. (1995, October). Bank Holiday. *Keyboard Review*, pp. 36-40.
[151] Kempster, C. (1995, December). From Genesis to Revelation. *The Mix*, pp. 94-98.
[152] Banks, T. (2019, August 7). *In Conversation with Tony Banks: Demonstrating the orchestration behind 'An Island in the Darkness'*. Retrieved from Tony Banks YouTube Channel: https://www.youtube.com/user/tonybanksmusic/videos
[153] Banks, T. (2009, October 2). (D. Tremblay, Interviewer) Ottawa. Retrieved from Banksian Central YouTube channel, https://www.youtube.com/watch?v=WQaE4RzuGoo